HISTORIC BATTLESHIPS & AIRCRAFT CARRIERS IN THE UNITED STATES

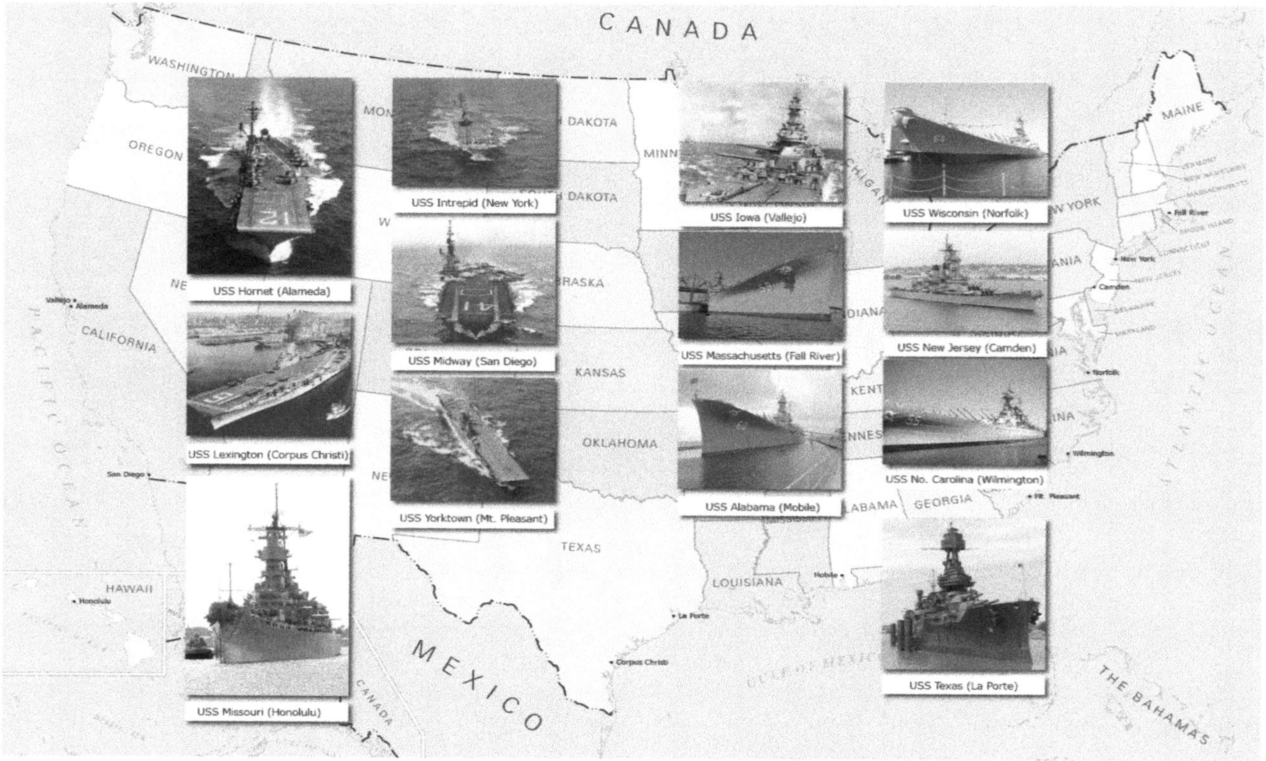

THE FYDDEYE GUIDE TO AMERICA'S MARITIME HISTORY

2,000+ Tall Ships, Lighthouses, Historic Ships, Maritime Museums, & More

edited by JOE FOLLANSBEE
with contributions by writers at Fyddeye.com

Copyright © 2010 Fyddeye Media
All rights reserved.

ISBN: 0615381537
ISBN-13: 9780615381534
Library of Congress Control Number: 2010930870

Cover photo of brig Lady Washington copyright 2010 Michael Berman
www.michaelbermanphotography.com.

CONTENTS

DEDICATION xi

ABOUT THE EDITOR xiii

PREFACE xv

INTRODUCTION. xvii

CHAPTER 1 – SHIPS 1
    Skeptical in Seattle No More: Lady Washington Woos and Wins Writer x
    Ferries 5
    Fireboats 6
    Tall Ships. 7
    Tugboats & Towboats 37
    Other Ships 46
    Steamboats 55
    The Forgotten History of Steamboats on the Okanogan River 57
    Steamers 59
    Submarines 64
    Warships – Pre-20th Century 67
    Warships – World War I 69
    Warships – Post World War II. 69
    Warships – World War II. 73
        Aircraft Carriers. 73
        Battleships. 74
        Coast Guard Vessels. 75
        Cruisers 76
        Destroyers 77
        Destroyer Escorts. 78
        Landing Craft 78
        Liberty & Victory Ships 80
        Minesweepers 81
        PT Boats & Small Craft 81
        Submarines 82
        Tugboats 86

CHAPTER 2 – SHIPWRECKS 87

CHAPTER 3 – MUSEUMS. 89
    Maritime Museums 89
        Alaska 89
        Alabama 90
        Arkansas 90
        California. 90

CONTENTS

Mystic Seaport: A Family Trip Back in Time 92
    Connecticut 94
    District of Columbia 96
    Delaware 96
    Florida 97
    Georgia 99
    Hawaii 99
    Illinois 100
    Indiana 100
    Kentucky 101
    Iowa 101
    Louisiana 102
    Maine 103
    Maryland 104
    Massachusetts 107
    Michigan 111
    Minnesota 114
    Mississippi 114
    Missouri 114
    Nebraska 115
    New Hampshire 115
    New Jersey 117
    New York 117
    North Carolina 123
    Ohio 124
    Oklahoma 125
    Oregon 126
    Pennsylvania 127
    Rhode Island 128
    South Carolina 128
    South Dakota 129
    Tennessee 129
    Texas 129
    Virginia 131
    Vermont 133
    Washington 133
    Wisconsin 136
Other Museums 137
    Alabama 137
    Arkansas 138
    California 138
    Florida 138
    Kentucky 139
    Maine 139
    Maryland 140
    Massachusetts 141
    Michigan 141
    New Jersey 142
    New York 142
    North Carolina 143
    Ohio 143

CONTENTS

    Oregon 143
    South Carolina 144
    Washington 144
    Wisconsin 146

CHAPTER 4 – RESEARCH LIBRARIES 147
Research Libraries 147
Other Libraries 151

CHAPTER 5 – LIGHTHOUSES & LIGHTSHIPS 153
East Coast Lighthouses 154
    Connecticut 154
    New England and Mid-Atlantic Lighthouse Tour Itinerary 155
    Delaware 158
    Florida 159
    Georgia 161
    Maine 162
    Maryland 171
    Massachusetts 175
    New Hampshire 183
    New Jersey 184
    New York 187
    North Carolina 193
    Pennsylvania 195
    Puerto Rico 195
    Rhode Island 198
    South Carolina 201
    Vermont 202
    Virgin Islands 203
    Virginia 203
Great Lakes Lighthouses 205
    Illinois 205
    Indiana 206
    Michigan 207
    Lighthouses of Michigan Tour Itinerary 208
    Minnesota 223
    New York 225
    Ohio 228
    Pennsylvania 231
    Wisconsin 232
Gulf Coast Lighthouses 238
    Alabama 238
    Florida 239
    Louisiana 241
    Mississippi 243
    Texas 244
Best West Coast Lighthouse Books 245
West Coast, Alaska, and Hawaii Lighthouses 249
    Alaska 249
    California 251
    California Coastal Lighthouse Tour Itinerary 252

CONTENTS

      Hawaii 259
      Oregon 260
      Washington 262
   Lightships 265

CHAPTER 6 – LIFE-SAVING STATIONS 269
   East Coast 269
   Great Lakes 273
   Gulf Coast 275
   West Coast 276

CHAPTER 7 – EDUCATION 279
   Higher Education 280
   Schools 280

CHAPTER 8 – DISTRICTS 283
   Alaska 283
   California 284
   Hawaii 284
   Louisiana 284
   Maine 284
   Massachusetts 285
   Ohio 287
   Pennsylvania 288
   Washington 288
   Maritime Festivals Celebrate Culinary and Cultural Heritage 290

CHAPTER 9 – STRUCTURES & SITES 297
   California 297
   Florida 298
   Illinois 298
   Indiana 299
   Maine 300
   Massachusetts 300
   Maryland 302
   Michigan 302
   Minnesota 302
   New Hampshire 303
   New York 303
   Ohio 304
   Oklahoma 304
   Pennsylvania 304
   Rhode Island 305
   South Carolina 305
   Washington 305
   Wisconsin 308

CONTENTS

CHAPTER 10 – MARKERS & MONUMENTS 309
- Arkansas 309
- Hawaii 310
- Iowa 310
- Massachusetts 310
- Michigan 311
- New York 311
- Ohio 312
- South Carolina 312
- Texas 312
- Washington 312
- Wisconsin 314

CHAPTER 11 – ORGANIZATIONS 315
- Alaska 315
- Alabama 316
- Arkansas 317
- California 317
- Connecticut 320
- Delaware 321
- District of Columbia 322
- Florida 323
- Georgia 324
- Hawaii 325
- Idaho 325
- Illinois 325
- Indiana 326
- Louisiana 327
- Maine 327
- Maryland 329
- Massachusetts 331
- Michigan 335
- Minnesota 338
- Mississippi 339
- Nebraska 339
- New Hampshire 339
- New Jersey 340
- New York 341
- North Carolina 345
- Ohio 347
- Oklahoma 348
- Oregon 348
- Pennsylvania 349
- Puerto Rico 350
- Rhode Island 350
- South Carolina 351

CONTENTS

    Tennessee...352
    Texas..352
    Vermont...353
    Virgin Islands..353
    Virginia..353
    Washington...355
    Wisconsin..360
    National...360

CHAPTER 12 – OTHER...361

CITY INDEX..363

PHOTO CREDITS..373

ACKNOWLEDGEMENTS..375

DEDICATION

To my father.

ABOUT THE EDITOR

Joe Follansbee is a Seattle-based journalist, author and researcher who has published four books, including *Shipbuilders, Sea Captains, and Fishermen: The Story of the Schooner* Wawona. He also builds and manages websites, including Fyddeye, www.fyddeye.com. Over his 25-year career, he has written for newspapers, magazines, and produced reports for National Public Radio.

PREFACE

Maritime history has held my interest ever since the day I walked aboard a historic wooden schooner in 1999. The ship's name was *Wawona*, and though she was slowly rotting after nearly a century of soaking from Pacific Northwest rain, I fell in love with her. Seven years later, in 2006, I published a book about her, *Shipbuilders, Sea Captains, and Fishermen: The Story of the Schooner* Wawona. After I finished that project, I sought out more Northwest maritime history.

I immediately ran into a problem. As a confirmed Internet junkie, I unhappily discovered that I had to spend hours online searching for the most basic information about historic ships, maritime museums, lighthouses, and other treasures of the country's maritime past. Few websites offered a comprehensive guide to even parts of America's growth and development as a maritime nation. A few did a pretty good job of pulling some things together, such as lighthouses and tall ships, but they often had gaping holes in their listings. I decided to create an all-in-one resource for all maritime heritage and history sites in the United States.

Using experience gained from a website I managed called "Maritime Heritage Network," which focused on Washington State's heritage, I created Fyddeye. I launched the site in 2009 at www.fyddeye.com, intending to create a virtual gathering place for Americans to find all the basic information about how to discover their local and national maritime history. And as a former news reporter that consumes more news on a daily basis than is really good for me, I also wanted to bring together all the little bits and pieces of news about the preservation and loss of maritime heritage and present them to Fyddeye readers. As of this writing, Fyddeye has more than 2,000 records of lighthouses, maritime museums, historic districts, and other places steeped in maritime history. The Ships category alone contains hundreds of tall ships, warships going back to the 18th century, commercial vessels, tugboats, and many more types of floating history.

But even in our online age, I knew many people, particularly those of a certain age who treasure the tactile pleasure of the page, would prefer a book-style directory. That led to this volume, which is a snapshot of the Fyddeye site, along with a few non-Fyddeye items, such as Natalie Johnson's eye-opening article about the history of steamboats on the Okanogan River in north-central Washington State. (Natalie also happens to be my niece.) The book suffers from the weakness of all printed matter; it's more or less out of date the moment the printer finishes the run. While the website is constantly updated with new information about what's happening today in the country's maritime

PREFACE

heritage community, I'm hoping to publish regular updates of the *Fyddeye Guide to America's Maritime History* so that bookworms and history lovers have an alternate means to access this information.

I have one other motivation for publishing this guide. As I learned more about the *Wawona*, I grew keenly aware of the fragility of our maritime past. Though many thousands of individuals and hundreds of small not-for-profits in our country perform heroic tasks of preservation and honor our heritage every day, America as a whole isn't doing a very good job at keeping our history alive. We'd rather spend time and money on the next new thing than on remembering the last new thing. After seeing *Wawona* towed away for demolition ten years after I first met her, I wanted Fyddeye to be my small attempt to raise awareness of a heritage that is by-and-large slowing decaying. Perhaps if people understand the breadth and scope of our heritage by presenting it in one place, they might recognize that keeping our history is part of what keeps our country whole.

-- *Joe Follansbee, Spring 2010*

INTRODUCTION

Welcome to *The Fyddeye Guide to America's Maritime History*. The *Guide* is the most comprehensive directory of lighthouses, historic ships, tall ship replicas, maritime museums, and maritime history organizations available in print or online. The *Guide* helps maritime history enthusiasts like you discover local maritime heritage and rediscover your national maritime heritage. And its companion website at www.fyddeye.com offers an even richer experience with maps, discussions, articles, and news about the preservation and enjoyment of America's incredible maritime past.

You can use this book in many ways, starting with its more than 2,000 listings, ranging from West Quoddy Lighthouse on the eastern-most point of Maine (and the United States) to the historic aircraft carrier *Midway* in San Diego. The listings are conveniently divided into chapters on specific types of artifacts or institutions, such as maritime museums. Each chapter is introduced by a beautiful photograph of an artifact, such as an historic warship. The chapters are broken down into geographic region, individual states, or type of artifact. For example, you can explore the ships by type, starting with historic ferries, followed by fireboats and tall ships.

In addition, travelers can use the *Guide* as a companion to their exploration of America's historic cities. A large percentage of the listings, especially the maritime museums, are open to the public, and the *Guide* includes hours of operation and admission fees for these listings. As an added convenience, the *Guide* features the latitude and longitude for each listing for users of car and hand-held GPS devices. (Note: Latitude and longitude information is based on street address and published resources. Please check a local map before attempting to find a remote location.) The *Guide* highlights the best attractions with a four-point compass rose ✦. And as an added feature for lighthouse lovers, the *Guide* includes three suggested itineraries for exploring lighthouses in California, Michigan, and the New England / Mid-Atlantic states.

The Fyddeye Guide to America's Maritime History includes articles about fascinating and little known aspects of our history, as well as information on ways to enjoy it. Tall ship sailor Domino Hawks writes about her first journey on the *Lady Washington*, a replica tall ship based in Aberdeen, Wash. Natalie Johnson, a young journalist from eastern Washington State, tells the story of the brief heyday of steamboats on the Okanogan River, a branch of the Columbia River. Writer Steven Wells reviews four of the best books on west coast lighthouses. I wrote two pieces: one about the country's premier maritime museum, Mystic Seaport, and a sample directory of the country's best-known maritime festivals from all regions, where you can sample local maritime culture, music, and delicious seafood.

INTRODUCTION

> How to read a *Guide* listing:

 YORKTOWN

Launched in 1943, the World War II-era aircraft carrier USS Yorktown is the centerpiece of the Patriots Point Naval & Maritime Museum. *Address:* 40 Patriots Point Road *City:* Mount Pleasant *State:* SC *Zip:* 29464 *Phone:* 843-884-2727 *Toll-free:* 866-831-1720 *Web:* www.patriotspoint.org *Visitors welcome?* Yes *Hours:* Contact attraction directly *Admission:* $16 adults, $13 seniors and active military, $8 children six to 11, under six FREE *Operated by:* Patriots Point Naval & Maritime Museum *NR?* Yes *NHL?* Yes *Year established/built:* 1943 *Latitude:* 32.7940 *Latitude:* -79.9051

✦ RECOMMENDED FOR VISITING

Address/City/State/Zip: Street address or approximate location, sometimes nearest city, as in the case of some remote lighthouses.
Phone: Information phone
Toll-free: Toll-free phone
Web: Website
Email: Email address
Visitors welcome? Open for tours or visits? (Yes/No)
Hours: Operating hours, if open for visits
Admission: Admission fee, if open for visits
Operated by: Organization operating the attraction
NR? Is the attraction listed on the National Register of Historic Places?
NHL? Is the attraction listed as a National Historic Landmark?
Year established/built: Year constructed or established.
Latitude/Longitude: Approximate latitude and longitude of the attraction

Notes: The National Register of Historic Places is official list of cultural resources worthy of preservation in the United States. A National Historic Landmark is a similar list, but more prestigious and exclusive with tighter criteria. The latitude and longitude information is based on data, such as addresses, provided by the attraction owner or listed in publicly accessible map resources. *Guide* readers should double-check these before using them in GPS-enabled devices.

The editors and contributors to the *Guide* have created a unique compilation of all the historic maritime places and vessels you can visit and appreciate. But information changes: ships move, museums update their hours, organizations fold. By the same token, new museums open, new replicas of historic ships are built, and new organizations form to take up the banner of preserving maritime heritage. Please let us know if you see any errors or missed updates. Email us at contact@fyddeye.com, or visit our website, register, and post your information in our user forums. We'll update the online directory immediately, and include the new information in the next edition of the *Guide*.

We know you will enjoy the *Fyddeye Guide* as much as we had fun putting it together. Ultimately, we hope it will help you appreciate the incredible breadth and depth of our maritime past and spur you to do your own part to kept the legacy vibrant and alive. The vast majority of preservation and heritage work is done by local organizations in your community. Please seek them out and consider donating time or money so that your children and grand-children will have an equal or better chance of seeing our maritime past through to the future.

CHAPTER 1 – SHIPS
Sailing and powered vessels preserved or operated to illustrate a period of maritime history

Pilgrim (Dana Point, Calif.)

Nothing personifies the concept of maritime history better than the ship, which we define as a moderately large to enormous watercraft designed to travel significant distances, though we don't mind including a large number of exceptions, such as fishing boats and submarines, which the U.S. Navy calls a "boat." For most of human history, the ship was a civilization's high-water mark of technology; until the advent of the steam engine, few man-made creations were as complex or difficult to construct and operate as an ocean-going cargo ship or warship. And for our purposes, a ship doesn't have to be an actual vessel that participated in history. The group can include working replicas of historic ships, especially sailing vessels that take passengers on living history expeditions lasting hours or days. Replicas and

CHAPTER 1 – SHIPS

reconstructions are unsurpassed platforms for bringing the ancients back to life. Everything from small steamers to aircraft carriers is represented in the maritime history tableau, and they're not just on saltwater or freshwater coasts; preserved riverine craft dot the river ports of the Midwest. This chapter includes all vessels preserved and/or operated in the service of maritime history education.

Skeptical in Seattle No More: Lady Washington Woos and Wins Writer
by
Domino Hawks

Editor's Note: The brig Lady Washington *is a replica of a U.S.-flagged vessel that sailed from approximately 1750-1798. The modern ship is best known for its role as* HMS Interceptor *in the 2003 film* Pirates of the Caribbean: The Curse of the Black Pearl.

I first sailed upon the tall ship *Lady Washington* in late August 2004 – it was only a jaunt in the Punch Bowl (what the crew refers to when sailing the nearly-windless conditions of Lake Union in Seattle). At first I was dubious of this brig's ability to charm me. As one of the volunteers battling to protect and restore the 1897 historic wooden schooner *Wawona* – I was of a mindset to scoff at the comparative appeal of a replica ship, being only accustomed to the nobility and silvery patina of a 109-year old.

Lady Washington under sail in Grays Harbor.

Being more used to tortured planking and dry rot, I found myself completely fascinated by the seemingly pristine quality of the *Lady*'s decks. I had never seen flawlessly caulked decking before, and later commented to someone that I based this on application of the 10-second rule -- i.e. would I pick up and eat a cookie

CHAPTER 1 – SHIPS

dropped on this surface if it had lain there for that long? I thought that I would eat that cookie (especially if it was an Oreo), for it was a delightfully pretty deck. However, after being educated by one crewmember on how the deck is maintained, I changed that decision to "perhaps not". It sure does look nice, though.

Even on the still lake, the *Lady*'s ability to thrill was unhampered. The crew, a kind, humorous and memorable lot, still put her through various maneuvers, taking advantage of the conditions to practice a no-touch 360°, a square-rigger's equivalent of spinning donuts. I spent a good deal of time talking with various crewmembers, and was surprised at their friendliness, their openness and enthusiasm. If they suffer from the ribbing similar to what I've heard the costumed characters at Disneyland do, they sure didn't show it. Although I cringed every time I heard someone approach them with an "Arrrghhhhhh!!!" they bore it with remarkable grace and good humor. I believe that one reason for this is that this crew is too busy to let things get to them – every shouted order from the sailing master inspired responsive calls and a stampede to action. I think that these individuals are skilled in ways that inspire most of us, but they can remember a time when they were just beginners, too. So, sure, they will tell you what a "baggywrinkle"[1] is.

We recovered some wind once we reached the ship lane, and we made for the acoustically favorable underside of the Aurora (old Highway 99) Bridge to enhance the already earth-shaking report of the ship's cannons and swivel guns. Any lingering standoffishness I may have felt towards the *Lady* was banished by both hearing and feeling the blast in my solar plexus, followed by the rolling booms echoing from the underside of the bridge, and smelling the black powder smoke. People lining the shore screamed. I imagine that the residents of the surrounding neighborhood of Fremont would be cleaning up after their startled indoor pets – probably after removing them from the ceiling.

As we traveled back to our starting place in the darkness, I became conscious of the sounds of the ship – the flap of the canvas sails and the booming sound they make as they fill, the buzz of rope traveling through wooden blocks, and the creaking of the yards. The skyline of Seattle drew closer and became harder to ignore.

I simply did not want to go back to the dock. When we arrived and tied off, I did not want to disembark. When I did, dragging my feet the whole way, I was so wired and exhilarated that I could not go home, could not go to sleep. I began to have my own ambitions that some might question – to be a "splat"…to wear silly pants (the required historic garb), to earn some calluses…to become a square-rig sailor.

Okay, maybe not the silly pants so much.

And trust me on this…if you confess this secret ambition to friends or family members, be prepared to be looked at as if you had just divulged your desire to become an Elvis impersonator. "Ah, yes…" they say, while edging towards the door. But if they don't do that, they will surely try to make you talk like a pirate.

Since that time, I have sailed on the brig six times, the last three as a sail trainee. The first time, I simply belayed (the act of literally herding line—on a square rigger, an endless pursuit). On each subsequent sail, I learned additional duties such as taking slack off a line while setting sail, and hauling and trimming spanker sails. Although by themselves minute, in the world of the *Lady*, each task is a crucial part of the bigger picture. You truly feel a part of this primitive and thrilling machine. The experience of sailing gives me much respect for those that traversed the globe with their only mode of transportation being a ship like this.

The time spent in learning this obscure skill is a memorable thing. It is exhausting, and exhilarating, and one wakes up so sore, you can barely climb out of bed in the morning. Afterwards, I treasured the heat of my rope-burned hands, a reminder of the last three days. The strangest part was that for two weeks afterwards, I felt the swaying of the ship every time I was trying to sleep or take a shower. Funny, but it took me no time at all to get used to the ship's galloping motion when I was on board, but it was hard to adjust to land afterwards. I was kind of sad when that swaying of terra firma went away….

---

1   A soft covering for lines or cables to prevent chafing.

CHAPTER 1 – SHIPS

Lady Washington Statistics
Length on deck 67 feet
Length on the waterline 72 feet
Overall length 112 feet
Draft 11 feet
Beam 22 feet
Mast height 89 feet
Displacement 210 tons
Gross tonnage 99 tons
Total sail area 4,442 square feet
Rigging approximately six miles
Guns two, three pounders. two swivels, aft.
Crew compliment 12
Passenger capacity 45

Domino Hawks is a landlocked freelance writer with an abiding love for wooden ships. She has traded (for the time being) the moss and mildew of the Pacific Northwest for the Southwest's sagebrush, sand, and red cliffs. This article also appeared at Fyddeye.com.

CHAPTER 1 – SHIPS

FERRIES

ADIRONDACK
Launched in 1913, the Adirondack is an operating car and passenger ferry on Lake Champlain. *Address:* King Street Dock *City:* Burlington *State:* VT *Zip:* 05401 *Phone:* 802-864-9804 *Web:* www.ferries.com *Email:* lct@ferries.com *Visitors welcome?* Yes *Hours:* Contact attraction directly *Admission:* Contact attraction directly *Operated by:* Lake Champlain Maritime Museum *NR?* No *NHL?* No *Year established/built:* 1913 *Latitude:* 44.4745 *Latitude:* -73.2202

 BADGER
Launched in 1952, the car ferry Badger is still in operation on Lake Michigan. *Address:* 701 Maritime Drive *City:* Ludington *State:* MI *Zip:* 49431 *Phone:* 231-843-1509 *Toll-free:* 800-841-4243 *Web:* www.ssbadger.com *Email:* info@ssbadger.com *Visitors welcome?* Yes *Hours:* Contact attraction directly *Admission:* Contact attraction directly *Operated by:* Lake Michigan Car Ferry Service *NR?* Yes *NHL?* No *Year established/built:* 1952 *Latitude:* 43.9494 *Latitude:* -86.4498

BEMUS-STOW FERRY
The Bemus Point-Stow Ferry is one of the last remaining cable-drawn ferries in the nation. *Address:* Stow Ferry Road *City:* Stow *State:* NY *Zip:* 14710 *Phone:* 716-326-6633 *Web:* www.sealionprojectltd.com *Visitors welcome?* Yes *Hours:* Memorial Day to Labor Day: Fridays, 4 p.m. to 9 p.m.; Saturday and Sunday, 1 p.m. to 9 p.m. *Admission:* Donation *Operated by:* Sea Lion Project, Ltd *NR?* No *NHL?* No *Latitude:* 42.1561 *Latitude:* -79.4030

Did you spot an error? Email your correction to contact@fyddeye.com.

BERKELEY
Launched in 1898, the steam ferry Berkeley operated for 60 years on San Francisco Bay and is now on exhibit at the San Diego Maritime Museum. *Address:* 1492 North Harbor Drive *City:* San Diego *State:* CA *Zip:* 92101 *Phone:* 619-234-9153 *Web:* www.sdmaritime.com *Email:* info@sdmaritime.org *Visitors welcome?* Yes *Hours:* Daily, 9 a.m. to 8 p.m. *Operated by:* Maritime Museum Association of San Diego *NR?* Yes *NHL?* Yes *Year established/built:* 1898 *Latitude:* 32.7276 *Latitude:* -117.1800

BINGHAMTON
Launched in 1905, the ferry Binghamton is now a restaurant. *Address:* 725 River Road *City:* Edgewater *State:* NJ *Zip:* 07020 *Phone:* 201-941-2300 *Visitors welcome?* Yes *Hours:* Contact attraction directly *Admission:* Contact attraction directly *Operated by:* Private owner *NR?* Yes *NHL?* No *Year established/built:* 1905 *Latitude:* 40.8196 *Latitude:* -73.9768

CITY OF MILWAUKEE
Launched in 1931, the railroad car ferry City of Milwaukee is now a floating museum. *Address:* 99 Arthur Street *City:* Manistee *State:* MI *Zip:* 49660 *Phone:* 231-723-3587 *Web:* www.carferry.com *Email:* lspencer@carferry.com *Visitors welcome?* Yes *Hours:* Contact attraction directly *Admission:* $8 adults, $5 children six to 17, children under six FREE *Operated by:* S.S. City of Milwaukee - National Historic Landmark *NR?* Yes *NHL?* Yes *Year established/built:* 1931 *Latitude:* 44.2595 *Latitude:* -86.3164

COMMANDER
Launched in 1917, the M/V Commander is an operating passenger ferry. *Address:* 616 Beach Road *City:* West Haverstraw *State:* NY *Zip:* 10993 *Phone:* 845-534-7245 *Web:* www.commanderboat.com *Email:*

CHAPTER 1 – SHIPS

rideaboat@ ol.com *Visitors welcome?* Yes *Hours:* Contact attraction directly *Admission:* Contact attraction directly *Operated by:* Hudson Highlands Cruises *NR?* Yes *NHL?* No *Year established/built:* 1917 *Latitude:* 41.2125 *Latitude:* -73.9689

EUREKA

Launched in 1890, the current configuration of the Eureka is as a passenger and car ferry. It is now a museum ship at the San Francisco Maritime National Historical Park. *Address:* San Francisco Maritime National Historical Park *City:* San Francisco *State:* CA *Zip:* 94123 *Phone:* 415-561-7000 *Web:* www.nps.gov/safr/ *Visitors welcome?* Yes *Hours:* $5.00 *Admission:* Contact attraction directly *Operated by:* San Francisco Maritime National Historical Park *NR?* Yes *NHL?* Yes *Year established/built:* 1890 *Latitude:* 37.8070 *Latitude:* -122.4220

KALAKALA

Launched in 1935, the car ferry Kalakala is undergoing restoration in Tacoma. *Address:* Taylor Way and Lincoln Ave. *City:* Tacoma *State:* WA *Web:* www.kalakala.org *Email:* kalakala.info@comcast.net *Visitors welcome?* Yes *Hours:* Contact attraction directly *Admission:* Access limited *Operated by:* Kalakala Alliance Foundation *NR?* Yes *NHL?* No *Year established/built:* 1935 *Latitude:* 47.2713 *Latitude:* -122.3840

KIRKLAND

Lauched in 1934, the car ferry Kirkland is now an excursion vessel. *Address:* Central Way and Market St. *City:* Kirkland *State:* WA *Visitors welcome?* Yes *Hours:* Contact attraction directly *Operated by:* Argosy Cruises *NR?* Yes *NHL?* No *Year established/built:* 1924 *Latitude:* 47.6765 *Latitude:* -122.2100

PLOVER

Launched in 1944, the foot ferry Plover is now an operating museum vessel. *Address:* 235 Marine Dr. *City:* Blaine *State:* WA *Zip:* 98230 *Visitors welcome?* Yes *Hours:* Memorial Day through Labor Day: Call for sailings *Admission:* Children under 12, FREE; Youth, $1; Adults $2 *Operated by:* Drayton Harbor Maritime *NR?* Yes *NHL?* No *Year established/built:* 1944 *Latitude:* 48.9945 *Latitude:* -122.7590

SKANSONIA

Launched in 1949, the car ferry Skansonia is a now a floating restaurant and site for weddings. *Address:* 205 NE Northlake Way *City:* Seattle *State:* WA *Visitors welcome?* Yes *Hours:* Contact attraction directly *Admission:* Contact attraction directly *Operated by:* Skansonia Waterfront Catering *NR?* No *NHL?* No *Year established/built:* 1949 *Latitude:* 47.6532 *Latitude:* -122.3260

YANKEE

Launched in 1907, the passenger ferry Yankee is now a museum vessel. *Address:* Canal Street Station *City:* New York *State:* NY *Zip:* 10003 *Phone:* 212-267-7236 *Visitors welcome?* Yes *Hours:* Contact attraction directly *Admission:* Contact attraction directly *Operated by:* Jim Gallagher *NR?* Yes *NHL?* No *Year established/built:* 1907 *Latitude:* 40.7219 *Latitude:* -74.0054

FIREBOATS

DUWAMISH

Launched in 1909, the fireboat Duwamish is now a floating museum exhibit and education vessel. *Address:* 860 Terry Ave. N. *City:* Seattle *State:* WA *Zip:* 93777 *Visitors welcome?* Yes *Hours:* Contact attraction directly

Admission: Donation *Operated by:* Puget Sound Fireboat Foundation *NR?* No *NHL?* Yes *Year established/built:* 1909 *Latitude:* 47.6276 *Latitude:* -122.3370

EDWARD M. COTTER
Launched in 1900, the fireboat Edward M. Cotter is a working vessel on Buffalo's waterfront. *Address:* 155 Ohio St. *City:* Buffalo *State:* NY *Zip:* 14203 *Phone:* 716-846-4265 *Web:* www.emcotter.com *Email:* neotechnics@adelphia.net *Visitors welcome?* Yes *Hours:* Contact attraction directly *Admission:* Contact attraction directly *Operated by:* Friends of the Edward M. Cotter *NR?* No *NHL?* Yes *Year established/built:* 1900 *Latitude:* 42.8721 *Latitude:* -78.8721

FIREBOAT NO. 1
Launched in 1929, Fireboat No. 1 is now a dry-berth exhibit at a waterfront park in Tacoma. *Address:* 3300 Ruston Way *City:* Tacoma *State:* WA *Visitors welcome?* Yes *Hours:* Daily *Admission:* FREE *Operated by:* Metro Parks Tacoma *NR?* No *NHL?* Yes *Year established/built:* 1929 *Latitude:* 47.2817 *Latitude:* -122.4800

JOHN J. HARVEY
Launched in 1931, the fireboat John J. Harvey is now a floating museum in New York Harbor. *Address:* Pier 66 *City:* New York *State:* NY *Web:* www.fireboat.org *Visitors welcome?* Yes *Hours:* Contact attraction directly *Admission:* Contact attraction directly *Operated by:* Fireboat John J. Harvey *NR?* No *NHL?* No *Year established/built:* 1931 *Latitude:* 40.9233 *Latitude:* -73.9047

RALPH J. SCOTT
Launched in 1925, the fireboat Ralph J. Scott is berthed on the Los Angeles waterfront. *Address:* Port of Los Angeles, Berth 87 *City:* San Pedro *State:* CA *Phone:* 213-485-6002 *Web:* www.lafd.org *Visitors welcome?* Yes *Hours:* Contact attraction directly *Admission:* Contact attraction directly *Operated by:* City of Los Angeles Fire Department *NR?* Yes *NHL?* Yes *Year established/built:* 1925 *Latitude:* 33.7359 *Latitude:* -118.2920

TALL SHIPS

A.J. MEERWALD
Launched in 1928, the Delaware Bay oyster schooner A.J. Meerwald now serves as an operational museum ship. *Address:* 2800 High Street-Bivalve *City:* Port Norris *State:* NJ *Zip:* 08349 *Phone:* 856-785-2060 *Web:* www.ajmeerwald.org *Email:* info@bayshorediscoveryproject.org *Visitors welcome?* Yes *Hours:* Contact attraction directly *Admission:* Contact attraction directly *Operated by:* Bayshore Discovery Project *NR?* Yes *NHL?* No *Year established/built:* 1928 *Latitude:* 39.2332 *Latitude:* -75.0336

ADA FEARS
Launched in 1968, the skipjack Ada Fears is an operating excursion and education vessel. *Address:* 4864 Piney Neck Road *City:* Rock Hall *State:* MD *Zip:* 21661 *Phone:* 410-639-2174 *Web:* www.skipjackadafears.com *Email:* skipjackadafears@earthlink.net *Visitors welcome?* Yes *Hours:* Contact attraction directly *Admission:* Contact attraction directly *Operated by:* Skipjack Ada Fears *NR?* No *NHL?* No *Year established/built:* 1968 *Latitude:* 39.1086 *Latitude:* -76.1957

ADVENTURE
Built in 1926, Adventure is a 121-foot fishing schooner and a National Historical Landmark. The fishing schooner played a vital role from the earliest days of our nation when Gloucester was its busiest port and we depended on the sea for sustenance and transportation. *Address:* 4 Harbor Loop *City:* Gloucester *State:*

CHAPTER 1 – SHIPS

MA *Zip:* 01930 *Phone:* 978-281-8079 *Web:* www.schooner-adventure.org *Email:* scurry@schooner-adventure.org *Visitors welcome?* Yes *Hours:* Contact attraction directly *Admission:* Contact attraction directly *Operated by:* Schooner Adventure *NR?* No *NHL?* Yes *Year established/built:* 1926 *Latitude:* 42.6118 *Latitude:* -70.6607

ADVENTURE
Adventure is a replica of a 17th century trading vessel. A new ship is expected to be displayed at Charles Towne Landing. *Address:* 1500 Old Towne Road *City:* Charleston *State:* SC *Zip:* 29407 *Phone:* 843-852-4200 *Web:* www.charlestowne.org *Email:* charlestowne@scprt.com *Visitors welcome?* Yes *Hours:* Contact attraction directly *Admission:* Contact attraction directly *Operated by:* Friends of Charles Towne Landing *NR?* No *NHL?* No *Latitude:* 32.8100 *Latitude:* -79.9953

✥ ADVENTURESS
Launched in 1913, the schooner Adventuress is an excursion and environmental education vessel in Puget Sound. *Address:* Water St. and Polk St. *City:* Port Townsend *State:* WA *Zip:* 98368 *Phone:* 360-379-0438 *Web:* www.soundexp.org *Email:* mail@soundexp.org *Visitors welcome?* Yes *Hours:* Contact attraction directly *Admission:* Contact attraction directly *Operated by:* Sound Experience *NR?* No *NHL?* Yes *Year established/built:* 1913 *Latitude:* 48.1136 *Latitude:* -122.7590

ALABAMA (SCHOONER)
Launched in 1926, the schooner Alabama is now an excursion and sail training vessel. *City:* Vineyard Haven *State:* MA *Zip:* 02568 *Phone:* 508-693-1699 *Web:* www.theblackdogtallships.com *Email:* office@theblackdogtallships.com *Visitors welcome?* Yes *Hours:* Contact attraction directly *Admission:* Contact attraction directly *Operated by:* Black Dog Tall Ship Co. *NR?* No *NHL?* No *Year established/built:* 1926 *Latitude:* 41.4543 *Latitude:* -70.6036

ALICE E.
Launched in 1899 and now an excursion vessel, the friendship sloop Alice E. is the oldest working vessel of her type. *Address:* Dysart's Great Harbor Marina *City:* Southwest Harbor *State:* ME *Zip:* 04679 *Phone:* 207-266-5210 *Web:* www.downeastfriendshipsloop.com *Email:* info@downeastfriendshipsloop.com *Visitors welcome?* Yes *Hours:* Contact attraction directly *Admission:* Contact attraction directly *Operated by:* Downeast Friendship Sloop Charters *NR?* No *NHL?* No *Year established/built:* 1899 *Latitude:* 44.2986 *Latitude:* -68.3624

ALLIANCE
Launched in 1995, the schooner Alliance is an excursion and sail training vessel. *Address:* 506 Monroe Ave. *City:* Cape Charles *State:* VA *Zip:* 23310 *Phone:* 757-639-1233 *Web:* www.schooneralliance.com *Email:* info@schooneralliance.com *Visitors welcome?* Yes *Hours:* Contact attraction directly *Admission:* Contact attraction directly *Operated by:* Yorktown Sailing Charters *NR?* No *NHL?* No *Year established/built:* 1995 *Latitude:* 37.2700 *Latitude:* -76.0151

ALMA
Launched in 1891, the scow schooner Alma is an operational museum ship at the San Francisco National Maritime Historical Park. *Address:* San Francisco Maritime National Historical Park *City:* San Francisco *State:* CA *Zip:* 94123 *Phone:* 415-561-7006 *Web:* www.nps.gov/safr/ *Email:* lynn_cullivan@nps.gov *Visitors welcome?* Yes *Hours:* $5.00 *Admission:* Contact attraction directly *Operated by:* San Francisco Maritime National Historical Park *NR?* Yes *NHL?* Yes *Year established/built:* 1891 *Latitude:* 37.8096 *Latitude:* -122.4210

CHAPTER 1 – SHIPS

AMAZING GRACE
The schooner Amazing Grace is an excursion vessel and leadership training facility. *Address:* 9017 North Harborview Drive *City:* Gig Harbor *State:* WA *Zip:* 98332 *Phone:* 253-851-9737 *Web:* www.amazinggracetallship.com *Email:* info@maritimeleadership.org *Visitors welcome?* Yes *Hours:* Contact attraction directly *Admission:* Contact attraction directly *Operated by:* Maritime Leadership *NR?* No *NHL?* No *Latitude:* 47.3400 *Latitude:* -122.5880

AMERICAN
Launched in 1934, the schooner American is now berthed next to a restaurant in Cape May. *Address:* Fisherman's Wharf, Cape May Harbor *City:* Cape May *State:* NJ *Phone:* 609-884-8296 *Web:* www.thelobsterhouse.com *Visitors welcome?* Yes *Hours:* Contact attraction directly *Admission:* Contact attraction directly *Operated by:* Lobster House *NR?* No *NHL?* No *Year established/built:* 1934 *Latitude:* 38.9351 *Latitude:* -74.9060

AMERICAN EAGLE
Launched in 1930, the auxiliary schooner American Eagle began as a fishing vessel and now operates as an excursion ship. *Address:* 5 Achorn Street *City:* Rockland *State:* ME *Zip:* 04841 *Phone:* 207-594-8007 *Toll-free:* 800-648-4544 *Web:* www.schooneramericaneagle.com *Email:* info@schooneramericaneagle.com *Visitors welcome?* Yes *Hours:* Contact attraction directly *Admission:* Contact attraction directly *Operated by:* North End Shipyard Schooners *NR?* Yes *NHL?* Yes *Year established/built:* 1930 *Latitude:* 44.1127 *Latitude:* -69.1049

AMERICAN PRIDE
Launched in 1941, the schooner American Pride is an excursion and sail training vessel. *Address:* Rainbow Harbor, Dock 3 *City:* Long Beach *State:* CA *Phone:* 714-970-8800 *Toll-free:* 714-970-8474 *Web:* www.americanpride.org *Email:* theamericanpride@aol.com *Visitors welcome?* Yes *Hours:* Contact attraction directly *Admission:* Contact attraction directly *Operated by:* Children's Maritime Foundation *NR?* No *NHL?* No *Year established/built:* 1941 *Latitude:* 33.7670 *Latitude:* -118.1890

 AMISTAD
Launched in 2000, the schooner Amistad is a museum ship which conducts living history excursions. *Address:* 746 Chapel St. *City:* New Haven *State:* CT *Zip:* 06510 *Phone:* 203-495-1839 *Toll-free:* 866-264-7823 *Web:* www.amistadamerica.org *Email:* operations@amistadamerica.org *Visitors welcome?* Yes *Hours:* Contact attraction directly *Admission:* Contact attraction directly *Operated by:* Amistad America *NR?* No *NHL?* No *Year established/built:* 2000 *Latitude:* 41.3048 *Latitude:* -72.9232

ANGELIQUE
Launched in 1980, the schooner Angelique is an authentic reproduction of classic 19th-century English Channel and North Sea windjammers. *City:* Camden *State:* ME *Zip:* 04843 *Phone:* 800-282-9989 *Web:* www.sailangelique.com *Email:* windjam@sailangelique.com *Visitors welcome?* Yes *Hours:* Contact attraction directly *Admission:* Contact attraction directly *Operated by:* Yankee Packet Company *NR?* No *NHL?* No *Year established/built:* 1980 *Latitude:* 44.2098 *Latitude:* -69.0648

APPLEDORE II
Launched in 1978, the schooner Appledore II is an excursion and sail training vessel. *City:* Camden *State:* ME *Zip:* 04843 *Phone:* 207-236-8353 *Toll-free:* 800-233-7437 *Web:* www.appledore2.com *Email:* sail@appledore2.com *Visitors welcome?* Yes *Hours:* Contact attraction directly *Admission:* Contact attraction directly *Operated by:* Schooner Exploration Associates *NR?* No *NHL?* No *Year established/built:* 1978 *Latitude:* 44.2098 *Latitude:* -69.0648

CHAPTER 1 – SHIPS

APPLEDORE IV
Launched in 1989, the schooner Appledore IV is an excursion and sail training vessel. *Address:* 107 Fifth Street *City:* Bay City *State:* MI *Zip:* 48708 *Phone:* 989-895-5193 *Web:* www.baysailbaycity.org *Email:* info@baysailbaycity.org *Visitors welcome?* Yes *Hours:* Contact attraction directly *Admission:* Contact attraction directly *Operated by:* BaySail *NR?* No *NHL?* No *Year established/built:* 1989 *Latitude:* 43.5993 *Latitude:* -83.8899

APPLEDORE V
Launched in 1992, the schooner Appledore V is an excursion and sail training vessel. *Address:* 107 Fifth Street *City:* Bay City *State:* MI *Zip:* 48708 *Phone:* 989-895-5193 *Web:* www.baysailbaycity.org *Email:* info@baysailbaycity.org *Visitors welcome?* Yes *Hours:* Contact attraction directly *Admission:* Contact attraction directly *Operated by:* BaySail *NR?* No *NHL?* No *Year established/built:* 1992 *Latitude:* 43.5993 *Latitude:* -83.8899

AQUIDNECK
The schooner Aquidneck operates as an excursion vessel. *Address:* 32 Bowen's Wharf *City:* Newport *State:* RI *Zip:* 02840 *Phone:* 401-849-3333 *Toll-free:* 800-709-7245 *Web:* www.sightsailing.com *Email:* info@sightsailing.com *Visitors welcome?* Yes *Hours:* Contact attraction directly *Admission:* Contact attraction directly *Operated by:* Sightsailing *NR?* No *NHL?* No *Latitude:* 41.4870 *Latitude:* -71.3159

ARABELLA
Launched in 1983, the sailing yacht Arabella is an excursion vessel. *Address:* 1 Christies Landing *City:* Newport *State:* RI *Zip:* 02840 *Phone:* 401-849-3023 *Toll-free:* 800-395-1343 *Web:* www.cruisearabella.com *Email:* reservations@cruisearabella.com *Visitors welcome?* Yes *Hours:* Contact attraction directly *Admission:* Contact attraction directly *Operated by:* Classic Cruises of Newport *NR?* No *NHL?* No *Year established/built:* 1983 *Latitude:* 41.4838 *Latitude:* -71.3147

ARGIA
Launched in 1986, the schooner Argia is a day-sailer out of Mystic. *Address:* 15 Holmes Street *City:* Mystic *State:* CT *Zip:* 06355 *Phone:* 860-536-0416 *Web:* www.voyagermystic.com *Email:* amyblumberg@voyagermystic.com *Visitors welcome?* Yes *Hours:* Contact attraction directly *Admission:* Contact attraction directly *Operated by:* Voyager Cruises *NR?* No *NHL?* No *Year established/built:* 1986 *Latitude:* 41.3562 *Latitude:* -71.9658

ARGUS
Launched in 1905, the topsail ketch Argus is now a sail-training vessel operated by the Boy Scouts. *Address:* 1931 W. Coast Hwy *City:* Newport Beach *State:* CA *Phone:* 714-546-4990 *Web:* www.ocbsa.org/site/c.khKQIWPBIoE/b.3841869/ *Visitors welcome?* Yes *Hours:* Contact attraction directly *Admission:* Contact attraction directly *Operated by:* Orange County BSA -- Newport Sea Base *NR?* No *NHL?* No *Year established/built:* 1904 *Latitude:* 33.6170 *Latitude:* -117.9190

BAGHEERA
Launched in 1924, the schooner Bagheera operates as an excursion and sail training vessel. *Address:* Maine State Pier, 56 Commercial St. *City:* Portland *State:* ME *Zip:* 04101 *Phone:* 207-766-2500 *Toll-free:* 877-246-6637 *Web:* www.portlandschooner.com *Email:* scott@portlandschooner.com *Visitors welcome?* Yes *Hours:* Contact attraction directly *Admission:* Contact attraction directly *Operated by:* Portland Schooner Company *NR?* Yes *NHL?* No *Year established/built:* 1924 *Latitude:* 43.6577 *Latitude:* -70.2500

CHAPTER 1 – SHIPS

 BALCLUTHA
Launched in 1886, the three-masted, square-rigged Balclutha is now a museum at the San Francisco Maritime National Historical Park. *Address:* San Francisco Maritime National Historical Park *City:* San Francisco *State:* CA *Zip:* 94123 *Phone:* 415-561-7000 *Web:* www.nps.gov/safr/ *Visitors welcome?* Yes *Hours:* Contact attraction directly *Admission:* $5.00 *Operated by:* San Francisco Maritime National Historical Park *NR?* Yes *NHL?* Yes *Year established/built:* 1886 *Latitude:* 37.8097 *Latitude:* -122.4220

BEAVER
The brig Beaver is a replica of an 18th century vessel that played a role in the Boston Tea Party, and serves as a floating exhibit at the Boston Tea Party Ships & Museum. *Address:* 304 Congress St. *City:* Boston *State:* MA *Zip:* 02210 *Phone:* 617-338-1773 *Web:* www.bostonteapartyship.com *Email:* teapartyship@historictours.com *Visitors welcome?* Yes *Hours:* Contact attraction directly *Admission:* Contact attraction directly *Operated by:* Historic Tours of America *NR?* No *NHL?* No *Latitude:* 42.3517 *Latitude:* -71.0506

BILL OF RIGHTS
Built in 1971, the Bill of Rights sailed from Norfolk, Virginia, to join LAMI's TopSail Youth Program in March of 1998. *Address:* Berth 84, Foot of 6th St. *City:* San Pedro *State:* CA *Zip:* 90731 *Phone:* 310-548-7618 *Web:* www.lamitopsail.org *Email:* bigben@lamitopsail.org *Visitors welcome?* Yes *Hours:* Contact attraction directly *Admission:* Contact attraction directly *Operated by:* Los Angeles Maritime Institute *NR?* No *NHL?* No *Year established/built:* 1971 *Latitude:* 33.7387 *Latitude:* -118.2790

BONNIE LYNN
Launched in 1997, the schooner Bonnie Lynn is an excursion vessel. *City:* Islesboro *State:* ME *Zip:* 04848 *Phone:* 401-835-3368 *Web:* www.bonnielynn.com *Email:* mack@bonnielynn.com *Visitors welcome?* Yes *Hours:* Contact attraction directly *Admission:* Contact attraction directly *Operated by:* Schooner Bonnie Lynn *NR?* No *NHL?* No *Year established/built:* 1997 *Latitude:* 44.2957 *Latitude:* -68.9124

BOUNTY
Launched in 1960, the full-rigged ship Bounty is a replica of the ship made famous by the Mutiny on the Bounty. *Address:* 2806 Ship Wheel Dr. *City:* North Myrtle Beach *State:* SC *Zip:* 29582 *Phone:* 631-584-7900 *Web:* www.tallshipbounty.org *Email:* mramsey@tallshipbounty.org *Visitors welcome?* Yes *Hours:* Contact attraction directly *Admission:* Contact attraction directly *Operated by:* HMS Bounty Organization LLC *NR?* No *NHL?* No *Year established/built:* 1960 *Latitude:* 33.8546 *Latitude:* -78.6466

BOWDOIN
Launched in 1921, the schooner Bowdoin is a research and education vessel operated by the Maine Maritime Academy. *Address:* Pleasant Street *City:* Castine *State:* ME *Zip:* 04420 *Phone:* 207-326-4311 *Web:* www.mainemaritime.edu *Email:* tleach@mma.edu *Visitors welcome?* Yes *Hours:* Contact attraction directly *Admission:* Contact attraction directly *Operated by:* Maine Maritime Academy *NR?* Yes *NHL?* Yes *Year established/built:* 1921 *Latitude:* 44.3870 *Latitude:* -68.7980

BRANDARIS
Launched in 1938, the sloop Brandaris is now an excursion and sail training vessel. *Address:* 37 Ocean Ave. *City:* North Kingston *State:* RI *Zip:* 02852 *Phone:* 401-294-1481 *Web:* www.yachtbrandaris.com *Email:* doug@yachtbrandaris.com *Visitors welcome?* Yes *Hours:* Contact attraction directly *Admission:* Contact attraction directly *Operated by:* Friends of Brandaris *NR?* No *NHL?* No *Year established/built:* 1938 *Latitude:* 41.5753 *Latitude:* -71.4497

CHAPTER 1 – SHIPS

BRILLIANT

Launched in 1932, the auxiliary gaff schooner Brilliant serves as a sailing training and education vessel at Mystic Seaport Museum. *Address:* 75 Greenmanville Avenue *City:* Mystic *State:* CT *Zip:* 06355 *Phone:* 860-572-5323 *Web:* www.mysticseaport.org *Visitors welcome?* Yes *Hours:* Daily, April to October, 9 a.m. to 5 p.m.; November to March, 10 a.m. to 4 p.m. *Admission:* Adults, $18.50; Seniors, $16.50; Children 6-17, $13; Under six, FREE *Operated by:* Mystic Seaport: The Museum of America and the Sea *NR?* Yes *NHL?* No *Year established/built:* 1932 *Latitude:* 41.3617 *Latitude:* -71.9634

 C.A. THAYER

Launched in 1895, the three-masted lumber schooner is now a museum ship at the San Francisco Maritime National Historical Park. *Address:* San Francisco Maritime National Historical Park *City:* San Francisco *State:* CA *Zip:* 94123 *Phone:* 415-561-7006 *Web:* www.nps.gov/safr/ *Visitors welcome?* Yes *Hours:* $5.00 *Admission:* Contact attraction directly *Operated by:* San Francisco Maritime National Historical Park *NR?* Yes *NHL?* Yes *Year established/built:* 1895 *Latitude:* 37.8070 *Latitude:* -122.4220

CALEB W. JONES

Launched in 1953, the skipjack Caleb W. Jones is undergoing restoration at the Chesapeake Bay Maritime Museum. *Address:* 213 N. Talbot Street *City:* St. Michaels *State:* MD *Zip:* 21663 *Phone:* 410-745-2916 *Web:* www.cbmm.org *Email:* cbland@cbmm.org *Visitors welcome?* Yes *Hours:* Contact attraction directly *Admission:* Contact attraction directly *Operated by:* Private owner *NR?* No *NHL?* No *Year established/built:* 1953 *Latitude:* 38.7876 *Latitude:* -76.2249

✥ CALIFORNIAN

Launched in 1984, the Californian is a replica of the cutter C.W. Lawrence, that patrolled the coast of California enforcing federal law during the California Gold Rush. She is an operating vessel that takes passengers on sailing excursions for the San Diego Maritime Museum. *Address:* 1492 North Harbor Drive *City:* San Diego *State:* CA *Zip:* 92101 *Phone:* 619-234-9153 *Web:* www.sdmaritime.com *Email:* info@sdmaritime.org *Visitors welcome?* Yes *Hours:* Daily, 9 a.m. to 8 p.m. *Admission:* $14 adults; $11 seniors, active military; $8 children 6-17; under six FREE *Operated by:* Maritime Museum Association of San Diego *NR?* No *NHL?* No *Year established/built:* 1984 *Latitude:* 32.7276 *Latitude:* -117.1800

CAPTAIN EDWARD H. ADAMS

Launched in 1982, the gundalow Captain Edward H. Adams is a museum vessel honoring the maritime history of the Piscataqua River. *City:* Portsmouth *State:* NH *Zip:* 03802 *Phone:* 603-433-9505 *Web:* www.gundalow.org *Email:* info@gundalow.org *Visitors welcome?* Yes *Hours:* Contact attraction directly *Admission:* Contact attraction directly *Operated by:* Gundalow Company *NR?* No *NHL?* No *Year established/built:* 1982 *Latitude:* 43.0719 *Latitude:* -70.7632

✥ CHARLES W. MORGAN

Launched in 1841, the barque and whaleship Charles W. Morgan is the premiere floating maritime exhibit at Mystic Seaport. *Address:* 75 Greenmanville Avenue *City:* Mystic *State:* CT *Zip:* 06355 *Phone:* 860-572-5315 *Web:* www.mysticseaport.org *Visitors welcome?* Yes *Hours:* Daily, April to October, 9 a.m. to 5 p.m.; November to March, 10 a.m. to 4 p.m. *Admission:* Adults, $18.50; Seniors, $16.50; Children 6-17, $13; Under six, FREE *Operated by:* Mystic Seaport: The Museum of America and the Sea *NR?* Yes *NHL?* Yes *Year established/built:* 1841 *Latitude:* 41.3617 *Latitude:* -71.9634

CHRISTEEN

Launched in 1883, the oyster sloop Christeen is an excursion and floating classroom operated by the Waterfront Center. *Address:* 1 West End Ave. *City:* Oyster Bay *State:* NY *Zip:* 11771 *Phone:* 516-922-7245 *Web:*

CHAPTER 1 – SHIPS

www.thewaterfrontcenter.org *Email:* info@thewaterfrontcenter.org *Visitors welcome?* Yes *Hours:* Contact attraction directly *Admission:* Contact attraction directly *Operated by:* Waterfront Center *NR?* No *NHL?* Yes *Year established/built:* 1883 *Latitude:* 40.6552 *Latitude:* -73.4775

CITY OF CRISFIELD
Launched in 1949, the skipjack City of Crisfield is privately owned. *City:* Deal Island *State:* MD *Visitors welcome?* No *Operated by:* Private owner *NR?* No *NHL?* No *Year established/built:* 1949 *Latitude:* 38.1590 *Latitude:* -75.9480

CITY OF NORFOLK
Launched in 1900, the skipjack City of Norfolk is owned and operated by the city's parks department. *Address:* 501 Boush St. *City:* Norfolk *State:* VA *Zip:* 23510 *Phone:* 804-441-2149 *Visitors welcome?* Yes *Hours:* Contact attraction directly *Admission:* Contact attraction directly *Operated by:* City of Norfolk Dept. of Recreation, Parks, and Open Space *NR?* No *NHL?* No *Year established/built:* 1900 *Latitude:* 36.8537 *Latitude:* -76.2913

CLARENCE CROCKETT
Launched in 1908, the skipjack Clarence Crockett is privately owned. *City:* Wenona *State:* MD *Visitors welcome?* No *Operated by:* Private owner *NR?* Yes *NHL?* No *Year established/built:* 1908 *Latitude:* 38.1390 *Latitude:* -75.9502

CLAUD W. SOMERS
Launched in 1911, the skipjack Claud W. Somers is an operating museum and excursion vessel. *Address:* 504 Main Street *City:* Reedville *State:* VA *Zip:* 22539 *Phone:* 804-453-6529 *Web:* www.rfmuseum.org *Email:* office@rfmuseum.org *Visitors welcome?* Yes *Hours:* May 1 to October: Daily, 10:30 a.m. to 4:30 p.m. *Admission:* $5 adults, $3 seniors, children under 12 FREE *Operated by:* Reedville Fisherman's Museum *NR?* Yes *NHL?* No *Year established/built:* 1911 *Latitude:* 37.8454 *Latitude:* -76.2742

CLEARWATER
Launched in 1969, the Hudson River sloop Clearwater specializes in environmental education activities. *Address:* 112 Little Market St. *City:* Poughkeepsie *State:* NY *Zip:* 12601 *Phone:* 845-454-7673 *Toll-free:* 800-677-5667 *Web:* www.clearwater.org *Email:* office@clearwater.org *Visitors welcome?* Yes *Hours:* Contact attraction directly *Admission:* Contact attraction directly *Operated by:* Hudson River Sloop Clearwater *NR?* No *NHL?* No *Year established/built:* 1969 *Latitude:* 41.6998 *Latitude:* -73.9316

CORWITH CRAMER
Launched in 1987, the brigantine Corwith Cramer is a sail training and research vessel. *City:* Woods Hole *State:* MA *Zip:* 02543 *Phone:* 508-540-3954 *Toll-free:* 800-552-3633 *Web:* www.sea.edu *Email:* admission@sea.edu *Visitors welcome?* Yes *Hours:* Contact attraction directly *Admission:* Contact attraction directly *Operated by:* Sea Education Association *NR?* No *NHL?* No *Year established/built:* 1987 *Latitude:* 41.5302 *Latitude:* -70.6603

DEE OF ST. MARY'S
Launched in 1979, the skipjack Dee of St. Mary's conducts environmental education and natural history excursions. *Address:* 16129 Piney Point Road *City:* Piney Point *State:* MD *Zip:* 20674 *Phone:* 301-994-2245 *Web:* www.skipjacktours.com *Email:* info@thebaylab.org *Visitors welcome?* Yes *Hours:* Contact attraction directly *Admission:* Contact attraction directly *Operated by:* Skipjack Tours *NR?* No *NHL?* No *Year established/built:* 1979 *Latitude:* 38.1273 *Latitude:* -76.4916

CHAPTER 1 – SHIPS

 DENIS SULLIVAN
Launched in 2000, the schooner Denis Sullivan is a sailing training, goodwill ambassador, and education vessel. *Address:* 500 N. Harbor Dr. *City:* Milwaukee *State:* WI *Zip:* 53202 *Phone:* 414-765-9966 *Web:* www.discoveryworld.org *Email:* info@discoveryworld.org *Visitors welcome?* Yes *Hours:* Contact attraction directly *Admission:* Contact attraction directly *Operated by:* Discovery World *NR?* No *NHL?* No *Year established/built:* 2000 *Latitude:* 43.0331 *Latitude:* -87.8997

DISCOVERY
Launched in 2007, the Discovery is a working replica of a ship that brought the first colonists to the Jamestown settlement. *Address:* 2218 Jamestown Rd. *City:* Williamsburg *State:* VA *Zip:* 23185 *Phone:* 757-253-7308 *Web:* historyisfun.org *Visitors welcome?* Yes *Hours:* Contact attraction directly *Admission:* Contact attraction directly *Operated by:* Jamestown-Yorktown Foundation *NR?* No *NHL?* No *Year established/built:* 2007 *Latitude:* 37.2251 *Latitude:* -76.7862

DREAM CATCHER
Launched in 1996, the schooner Dream Catcher is a sailing training and excursion vessel. *Address:* 28555 Jolly Roger Dr. *City:* Little Torch Key *State:* FL *Zip:* 33042 *Phone:* 305-304-5100 *Web:* www.sailingkeywestflorida.com *Email:* saildreamcatcher@mindspring.com *Visitors welcome?* Yes *Hours:* Contact attraction directly *Admission:* Contact attraction directly *Operated by:* Coastal Sailing Adventures *NR?* No *NHL?* No *Year established/built:* 1996 *Latitude:* 24.6546 *Latitude:* -81.3863

E.C. COLLIER
Launched in 1910, the skipjack E.C. Collier is a dry-berth exhibit at the Chesapeake Bay Maritime Museum. *Address:* 213 N. Talbot Street *City:* St. Michaels *State:* MD *Zip:* 21663 *Phone:* 410-745-2916 *Web:* www.cbmm.org *Email:* cbland@cbmm.org *Visitors welcome?* Yes *Hours:* Daily, hours vary by season *Admission:* $13 adults; $10 seniors over 62; $6 kids 6 to 17; kids under 6 FREE *Operated by:* Chesapeake Bay Maritime Museum *NR?* Yes *NHL?* No *Year established/built:* 1910 *Latitude:* 38.7876 *Latitude:* -76.2249

EAGLE
Launched in 1936, the barque USCG Eagle is the sail-training vessel for the U.S. Coast Guard Academy. *Address:* 31 Mohegan Avenue *City:* New London *State:* CT *Zip:* 06320 *Phone:* 860-444-8444 *Toll-free:* 800-883-8724 *Web:* www.cga.edu *Visitors welcome?* Yes *Hours:* Contact attraction directly *Admission:* Contact attraction directly *Operated by:* U.S. Coast Guard Academy *NR?* No *NHL?* No *Year established/built:* 1936 *Latitude:* 41.3703 *Latitude:* -72.1055

EDNA E. LOCKWOOD
The Edna E. Lockwood is the last sailing log-bottom bugeye. A bugeye's hull is constructed by pinning together a series of logs and hollowing them out as a unit. *Address:* 213 N. Talbot Street *City:* St. Michaels *State:* MD *Zip:* 21663 *Phone:* 410-745-2916 *Web:* www.cbmm.org *Email:* cbland@cbmm.org *Visitors welcome?* Yes *Hours:* Daily, hours vary by season *Admission:* $13 adults; $10 seniors over 62; $6 kids 6 to 17; kids under 6 FREE *Operated by:* Chesapeake Bay Maritime Museum *NR?* No *NHL?* Yes *Latitude:* 38.7876 *Latitude:* -76.2249

ELISSA
Launched in 1877, the iron-hulled barque Elissa is the premier operating exhibit at the Texas Seaport Museum. *Address:* Pier 21, Number 8 *City:* Galveston *State:* TX *Zip:* 77550 *Phone:* 409-763-1877 *Web:* www.tsm-elissa.org *Email:* elissa@galvestonhistory.org *Visitors welcome?* Yes *Hours:* Daily, 10 a.m. to 5 p.m. *Admission:* $8

CHAPTER 1 – SHIPS

adults, $5 students six through 18, children five and under FREE *Operated by:* Galveston Historical Foundation *NR?* Yes *NHL?* Yes *Year established/built:* 1877 *Latitude:* 29.3263 *Latitude:* -94.7951

ELIZABETH II
Launched in 1983, the barque Elizabeth II is a replica of a typical 16th century vessel that sailed between England and America. It is now used as a sail training and living history classroom. *Address:* One Festival Park *City:* Manteo *State:* NC *Zip:* 27954 *Phone:* 252-475-1500 *Web:* www.roanokeisland.com *Email:* scott.stroh@ncmail.com *Visitors welcome?* Yes *Hours:* Contact attraction directly *Admission:* Contact attraction directly *Operated by:* Roanoke Island Festival Park *NR?* No *NHL?* No *Year established/built:* 1983 *Latitude:* 35.9113 *Latitude:* -75.6673

ELSWORTH
Launched in 1901, the skipjack Elsworth is now operated by an outdoor school for youth. *Address:* 13655 Bloomingneck Road *City:* Worton *State:* MD *Zip:* 21678 *Phone:* 410-348-5880 *Web:* www.ehos.org *Email:* john@ehos.org *Visitors welcome?* Yes *Hours:* Contact attraction directly *Admission:* Contact attraction directly *Operated by:* Echo Hill Outdoor School *NR?* No *NHL?* No *Year established/built:* 1901 *Latitude:* 39.3554 *Latitude:* -76.1130

ELVA C
Launched in 1922, the deck boat Elva C is an operating museum and excursion vessel. *Address:* 504 Main Street *City:* Reedville *State:* VA *Zip:* 22539 *Phone:* 804-453-6529 *Web:* www.rfmuseum.org *Email:* office@rfmuseum.org *Visitors welcome?* Yes *Hours:* May 1 to October: Daily, 10:30 a.m. to 4:30 p.m. *Admission:* $5 adults, $3 seniors, children under 12 FREE *Operated by:* Reedville Fisherman's Museum *NR?* Yes *NHL?* No *Year established/built:* 1922 *Latitude:* 37.8454 *Latitude:* -76.2742

EMMA C. BERRY
Launched in 1866, the sloop Emma C. Berry is now part of the Mystic Seaport ship collection. *Address:* 75 Greenmanville Avenue *City:* Mystic *State:* CT *Zip:* 06355 *Phone:* 860-572-5315 *Web:* www.mysticseaport.org *Visitors welcome?* Yes *Hours:* Daily, April to October, 9 a.m. to 5 p.m.; November to March, 10 a.m. to 4 p.m. *Admission:* Adults, $18.50; Seniors, $16.50; Children 6-17, $13; Under six, FREE *Operated by:* Mystic Seaport: The Museum of America and the Sea *NR?* Yes *NHL?* Yes *Year established/built:* 1866 *Latitude:* 41.3617 *Latitude:* -71.9634

EQUATOR
Launched in 1888, the schooner Equator is now a covered dry-berth exhibit at the Port of Everett. *Address:* W. Marine View Dr. and 10th St. *City:* Everett *State:* WA *Visitors welcome?* Yes *Hours:* Daily *Admission:* FREE *NR?* Yes *NHL?* No *Year established/built:* 1888 *Latitude:* 48.0043 *Latitude:* -122.2140

ERNESTINA
Launched in 1894, the fishing schooner Ernestina is now an operational museum vessel. *Address:* New Bedford State Pier *City:* New Bedford *State:* MA *Zip:* 02741 *Phone:* 508-992-4900 *Web:* ernestina.org *Email:* office@ernestina.org *Visitors welcome?* Yes *Hours:* Contact attraction directly *Admission:* Contact attraction directly *Operated by:* Schooner Ernestina Commission *NR?* Yes *NHL?* Yes *Year established/built:* 1894 *Latitude:* 41.6351 *Latitude:* -70.9198

EVELINA M. GOULART
Launched in 1927, the fishing schooner Evelina M. Goulart is undergoing preservation and documentation at the Essex Shipbuilding Museum. *Address:* 66 Main Street *City:* Essex *State:* MA *Zip:* 01929 *Phone:* 978-768-7541 *Web:* www.essexshipbuildingmuseum.org *Email:* info@essexshipbuildingmuseum.org *Visitors welcome?*

Yes *Hours:* June to October, Wednesday to Sunday, 10 a.m. to 5 p.m.; November to May, Saturday and Sunday, 10 a.m. to 5 p.m. *Admission:* $7 adults, $6 seniors, $5 children, under six FREE *Operated by:* Essex Historical Society & Shipbuilding Museum *NR?* No *NHL?* No *Year established/built:* 1927 *Latitude:* 42.6323 *Latitude:* -70.7795

Is your tall ship missing from the Fyddeye Guide? Email info to contact@fyddeye.com.

 EXY JOHNSON
Completed in 2003, the Exy Johnson was purpose-designed to meet the specific needs of LAMI's TopSail Youth Program. One of twin brigantines, this state-of-the-art sail training vessel joins Irving Johnson as the flag ship of the LAMI fleet. *Address:* Berth 84, Foot of 6th St. *City:* San Pedro *State:* CA *Zip:* 90731 *Phone:* 310-548-7618 *Web:* www.lamitopsail.org *Email:* bigben@lamitopsail.org *Visitors welcome?* Yes *Hours:* Contact attraction directly *Admission:* Contact attraction directly *Operated by:* Los Angeles Maritime Institute *NR?* No *NHL?* No *Year established/built:* 2003 *Latitude:* 33.7387 *Latitude:* -118.2790

F.C. LEWIS, JR.
Launched in 1907, the skipjack F.C. Lewis, Jr. is a dry-berth exhibit at the Choptank River Heritage Center. *Address:* 10215 River Landing Rd. *City:* West Denton *State:* MI *Zip:* 21629 *Phone:* 410-479-4150 *Web:* www.riverheritage.org *Email:* info@riverheritage.org *Visitors welcome?* Yes *Hours:* May to September: Friday and Saturday, 11 a.m. to 3 p.m. *Admission:* Contact attraction directly *Operated by:* Choptank River Heritage Center *NR?* Yes *NHL?* No *Year established/built:* 1907 *Latitude:* 38.8881 *Latitude:* -75.8399

FALLS OF CLYDE
Launched in 1878, Falls of Clyde is the only surviving iron-hulled four-masted full rigged ship and the only surviving sail-driven oil tanker in the world. She is currently berthed at Honolulu Harbor. Volunteers and visitors are allowed on board the ship *Address:* Pier 7 *City:* Honolulu *State:* HI *Zip:* 96813 *Phone:* 808-526-1559 *Web:* www.friendsoffallsofclyde.org *Email:* bmcewan@friendsoffallsofclyde.org *Visitors welcome?* Yes *Operated by:* Friends of Falls of Clyde *NR?* Yes *NHL?* Yes *Year established/built:* 1878 *Latitude:* 21.3165 *Latitude:* -157.8890

FAME
The schooner Fame of Salem is a replica of the original Fame, a fast Chebacco fishing schooner that was reborn as a privateer when war broke out in the summer of 1812. *Address:* Derby St. and Congress St. *City:* Salem *State:* MA *Zip:* 01970 *Phone:* 978-729-7600 *Web:* www.schoonerfame.com *Email:* SchoonerFame@aol.com *Visitors welcome?* Yes *Hours:* Daily, Memorial Day through Halloween *Admission:* Contact attraction directly *Operated by:* Pennant Enterprises *NR?* No *NHL?* No *Year established/built:* 2003 *Latitude:* 42.5207 *Latitude:* -70.8901

FANNIE L. DAUGHERTY
Launched in 1904, the skipjack Fannie L. Daugherty was recently restored by the Chesapeake Bay Maritime Museum. *City:* Deal Island *State:* MD *Visitors welcome?* No *Operated by:* Private owner *NR?* No *NHL?* No *Year established/built:* 1904 *Latitude:* 38.1590 *Latitude:* -75.9480

FLORA A. PRICE
The skipjack Flora A. Price is the largest surviving Chesapeake Bay skipjack, and it is used a floating classroom by the Choptank River Heritage Center. *Address:* 10215 River Landing Rd. *City:* West Denton *State:* MI *Zip:* 21629 *Phone:* 410-479-4150 *Web:* www.riverheritage.org *Email:* info@riverheritage.org *Visitors welcome?* Yes *Hours:* May to September: Friday and Saturday, 11 a.m. to 3 p.m. *Admission:* Contact attraction directly *Operated by:* Choptank River Heritage Center *NR?* No *NHL?* No *Latitude:* 38.8881 *Latitude:* -75.8399

CHAPTER 1 – SHIPS

FLORENCE
Launched in 1926, the western-rigged dragger Florence is part of the Mystic Seaport ship collection. *Address:* 75 Greenmanville Avenue *City:* Mystic *State:* CT *Zip:* 06355 *Phone:* 860-572-5315 *Web:* www.mysticseaport.org *Visitors welcome?* Yes *Hours:* Daily, April to October, 9 a.m. to 5 p.m.; November to March, 10 a.m. to 4 p.m. *Admission:* Adults, $18.50; Seniors, $16.50; Children 6-17, $13; Under six, FREE *Operated by:* Mystic Seaport: The Museum of America and the Sea *NR?* No *NHL?* No *Year established/built:* 1926 *Latitude:* 41.3617 *Latitude:* -71.9634

FRIENDS GOOD WILL
Friends Good Will is a reproduction of a sloop that participated in the 1812 Battle of Lake Erie. *Address:* 260 Dyckman Ave. *City:* South Haven *State:* MI *Zip:* 49090 *Phone:* 269-637-8078 *Toll-free:* 800-747-3810 *Web:* michiganmaritimemuseum.org *Email:* info@michiganmaritimemuseum.org *Visitors welcome?* Yes *Hours:* Memorial Day to Labor Day: Monday to Saturday, 10 a.m. to 5 p.m.; Sunday noon to 5 p.m. Labor Day to Memorial Day: Friday, Saturday, Sunday, 10 a.m. to 5 p.m. *Admission:* $5 adults, $4 seniors, $3.50 children *Operated by:* Michigan Maritime Museum *NR?* No *NHL?* No *Year established/built:* 2004 *Latitude:* 42.4070 *Latitude:* -86.2745

FRIENDSHIP
The East Indiaman Friendship is a replica of the original vessel launched in 1797. She made 15 voyages during her career to Batavia, India, China, South America, the Caribbean, England, Germany, the Mediterranean, and Russia. *Address:* 2 New Liberty Street *City:* Salem *State:* MA *Zip:* 01970 *Phone:* 978-740-1650 *Web:* www.nps.gov/sama/ *Email:* colleen_bruce@nps.gov *Visitors welcome?* Yes *Hours:* Daily, 9 a.m. to 5 p.m. *Admission:* $5 adults, $3 children and seniors, children under six FREE *Operated by:* Salem National Maritime Historic Site *NR?* No *NHL?* No *Year established/built:* 1996 *Latitude:* 42.5227 *Latitude:* -70.8920

FRITHA
Launched in 1985, the brigantine Fritha is a sail training and education vessel. *Address:* 32 Washington St. *City:* Fairhaven *State:* MA *Zip:* 02719 *Phone:* 508-992-4025 *Toll-free:* 800-767-4025 *Web:* www.northeastmaritime.com *Email:* registration@northeastmaritime.com *Visitors welcome?* Yes *Hours:* Contact attraction directly *Admission:* Contact attraction directly *Operated by:* Northeast Maritime Institute *NR?* No *NHL?* No *Year established/built:* 1985 *Latitude:* 41.6374 *Latitude:* -70.9034

GAZELA PRIMEIRO
Launched in 1883, the barkentine Gazela Primiero is a fishing vessel converted to a working museum ship. *Address:* Foot of Market Street *City:* Philadelphia *State:* PA *Zip:* 19106 *Phone:* 215-238-0280 *Web:* www.gazela.org *Email:* office@gazela.org *Visitors welcome?* Yes *Hours:* Contact attraction directly *Admission:* Contact attraction directly *Operated by:* Philadelphia Ship Preservation Guild *NR?* No *NHL?* No *Year established/built:* 1883 *Latitude:* 39.9505 *Latitude:* -75.1481

GLENN L. SWETMAN
The Maritime & Seafood Industry Museum in Biloxi, Miss., has recaptured a piece of its history with their two schooners, the Glenn L. Swetman and the Mike Sekul. Available for day sailing or charter, the vessels can accommodate weddings, dockside parties, and other functions. *Address:* 115 First Street *City:* Biloxi *State:* MS *Zip:* 39530 *Phone:* 228-435-6320 *Web:* www.maritimemuseum.org *Email:* info@maritimemuseum.org *Visitors welcome?* Yes *Hours:* Contact attraction directly *Admission:* $25 adults, $10 children under 12 *Operated by:* Maritime & Seafood Industry Museum *NR?* No *NHL?* No *Latitude:* 30.3937 *Latitude:* -88.8591

CHAPTER 1 – SHIPS

GODSPEED
Launched in 2006, the Godspeed is a working replica of a ship that brought the first colonists to the Jamestown settlement. *Address:* 2218 Jamestown Rd. *City:* Williamsburg *State:* VA *Zip:* 23185 *Phone:* 757-253-7308 *Web:* historyisfun.org *Visitors welcome?* Yes *Hours:* Contact attraction directly *Admission:* Contact attraction directly *Operated by:* Jamestown-Yorktown Foundation *NR?* No *NHL?* No *Year established/built:* 2006 *Latitude:* 37.2251 *Latitude:* -76.7862

GOVERNOR STONE
Launched in 1877, the schooner Governor Stone is the last survivor of the Gulf schooner cargo vessel. It is now an operational museum ship. *City:* Fort Walton Beach *State:* FL *Zip:* 32549 *Web:* govstone.com *Email:* govstone@cox.net *Visitors welcome?* Yes *Hours:* Contact attraction directly *Admission:* Contact attraction directly *Operated by:* Friends of the Governor Stone *NR?* No *NHL?* No *Year established/built:* 1877 *Latitude:* 30.4057 *Latitude:* -86.6188

GRACE BAILEY
Launched in 1882, the schooner Grace Bailey is now an excursion vessel. *Address:* Camden Waterfront *City:* Camden *State:* ME *Zip:* 04843 *Phone:* 207-236-2938 *Toll-free:* 800-736-7981 *Web:* www.mainewindjammercruises.com *Email:* sail@mainewindjammercruises.com *Visitors welcome?* Yes *Hours:* Contact attraction directly *Admission:* Contact attraction directly *Operated by:* Maine Windjammer Cruises *NR?* Yes *NHL?* Yes *Year established/built:* 1882 *Latitude:* 44.2098 *Latitude:* -69.0648

H.M. KRENTZ
Launched in 1955, the skipjack H.M. Krentz is an excursion vessel. *City:* St. Michaels *State:* MD *Zip:* 21663 *Phone:* 410-745-6080 *Web:* www.oystercatcher.com *Email:* hmkrentz@bluecrab.org *Visitors welcome?* Yes *Hours:* Contact attraction directly *Admission:* Contact attraction directly *Operated by:* Skipjack H.M. Krentz *NR?* No *NHL?* No *Year established/built:* 1955 *Latitude:* 38.7827 *Latitude:* -76.2363

HAILE & MATTHEW
The new schooner Haile & Matthew sails overnight passengers out of historic downtown Eastport, Maine, (the most easterly city in the U.S.) the beginning of the Maine Coast and nestled among Canadian islands of Campobello, Deer Island and Grand Manan. *City:* Eastport *State:* ME *Phone:* 305-896-8004 *Web:* www.schoonerhaliematthew.com *Email:* sailhaliematthew@gmail.com *Visitors welcome?* Yes *NR?* No *NHL?* No *Year established/built:* 2005 *Latitude:* 44.9062 *Latitude:* -66.9900

HALF MOON
The Half Moon is a reproduction of the ship that Henry Hudson sailed from Holland to the New World in 1609. *Address:* 181 S Riverside Ave. *City:* Croton-on-Hudson *State:* NY *Zip:* 10520 *Phone:* 518-443-1609 *Web:* www.newnetherland.org *Email:* wtr@halfmoon.mus.ny.us *Visitors welcome?* Yes *Hours:* Contact attraction directly *Admission:* Contact attraction directly *Operated by:* New Netherland Museum & Half Moon Visitor's Center *NR?* No *NHL?* No *Latitude:* 41.2024 *Latitude:* -73.8875

HARVEY GAMAGE
Launched in 1973, the schooner Harvey Gamage is a sailing training vessel. *Address:* 29 McKown St. *City:* Boothbay Harbor *State:* ME *Zip:* 04538 *Phone:* 207-633-2750 *Toll-free:* 800-724-7245 *Web:* www.oceanclassroom.org *Email:* mail@oceanclassroom.org *Visitors welcome?* Yes *Hours:* Contact attraction directly *Admission:* Contact attraction directly *Operated by:* Ocean Classroom Foundation *NR?* No *NHL?* No *Year established/built:* 1973 *Latitude:* 43.8404 *Latitude:* -69.6459

CHAPTER 1 – SHIPS

 HAWAIIAN CHIEFTAIN
Launched in 1988, the topsail ketch Hawaiian Chieftain is an excursion and sail training vessel. *Address:* 712 Hagara St. *City:* Aberdeen *State:* WA *Zip:* 98520 *Visitors welcome?* Yes *Hours:* Contact attraction directly *Admission:* Contact attraction directly *Operated by:* Grays Harbor Historical Seaport Authority *NR?* No *NHL?* No *Year established/built:* 1988 *Latitude:* 46.9685 *Latitude:* -123.7730

HELEN VIRGINIA
Launched in 1948, the skipjack Helen Virginia is working vessel on Chesapeake Bay. *Address:* 6903 Main St. *City:* Queenstown *State:* MD *Zip:* 21658 *Phone:* 202-439-0260 *Web:* www.skipjack-maryland.org *Email:* marylandskipjack@gmail.com *Visitors welcome?* Yes *Hours:* Contact attraction directly *Admission:* Contact attraction directly *Operated by:* Skipjack Helen Virginia *NR?* Yes *NHL?* No *Year established/built:* 1948 *Latitude:* 38.9877 *Latitude:* -76.1600

HERITAGE
Launched in 1983, the schooner Heritage was constructed along the traditional lines of the schooners that navigated the waters off the coast of Maine more than a hundred years ago. *Address:* 5 Achorn Street *City:* Rockland *State:* ME *Zip:* 04841 *Phone:* 207-594-8007 *Toll-free:* 800-648-4544 *Web:* www.schoonerheritage.com *Email:* info@schoonerheritage.com *Visitors welcome?* Yes *Hours:* Contact attraction directly *Admission:* Contact attraction directly *Operated by:* North End Shipyard Schooners *NR?* No *NHL?* No *Year established/built:* 1983 *Latitude:* 44.1127 *Latitude:* -69.1049

HERITAGE OF MIAMI II
Launched in 1988, the schooner Heritage of Miami II is a sail training and excursion vessel. *Address:* 3145 Virginia St. *City:* Coconut Grove *State:* FL *Zip:* 33133 *Phone:* 305-442-9697 *Web:* www.heritageschooner.com *Email:* heritage2@mindspring.com *Visitors welcome?* Yes *Hours:* Contact attraction directly *Admission:* Contact attraction directly *Operated by:* Heritage Schooner Cruises *NR?* No *NHL?* No *Year established/built:* 1988 *Latitude:* 25.7328 *Latitude:* -80.2414

HIGHLANDER SEA
Launched in 1924, the schooner Highlander Sea is an excursion and sail training vessel. *Address:* 2336 Military St. *City:* Port Huron *State:* MI *Zip:* 48060 *Phone:* 810-966-3488 *Web:* www.highlandersea.com *Email:* info@highlandersea.com *Visitors welcome?* Yes *Hours:* Contact attraction directly *Admission:* Contact attraction directly *Operated by:* Acheson Ventures *NR?* No *NHL?* No *Year established/built:* 1924 *Latitude:* 42.9591 *Latitude:* -82.4274

HILDA M. WILLING
Launched in 1905, the skipjack Hilda M. Willing is a working vessel on Chesapeake Bay. *City:* Tilghman Island *State:* MD *Visitors welcome?* No *Operated by:* Private owner *NR?* Yes *NHL?* Yes *Year established/built:* 1905 *Latitude:* 38.7037 *Latitude:* -76.3386

HOPE
Launched in 1948, the gaff sloop Hope is an educational vessel for a public aquarium and environmental science facility. *Address:* 10 Water St. *City:* Norwalk *State:* CT *Zip:* 06854 *Phone:* 203-852-0700 *Web:* www.maritimeaquarium.org *Visitors welcome?* Yes *Hours:* Daily, 10 a.m. to 5 p.m. *Admission:* Contact attraction directly *Operated by:* Maritime Center at Norwalk *NR?* No *NHL?* No *Year established/built:* 1948 *Latitude:* 41.1008 *Latitude:* -73.4167

CHAPTER 1 – SHIPS

HOWARD
Launched in 1909, the skipjack Howard is a working vessel on Chesapeake Bay. *City:* Wenona *State:* MD *Visitors welcome?* No *Operated by:* Private owner *NR?* Yes *NHL?* No *Year established/built:* 1909 *Latitude:* 38.1390 *Latitude:* -75.9502

IDA MAY
Launched in 1906, the skipjack Ida May is a working vessel on Chesapeake Bay. *City:* Deal Island *State:* MD *Visitors welcome?* No *Operated by:* Private owner *NR?* Yes *NHL?* No *Year established/built:* 1906 *Latitude:* 38.1590 *Latitude:* -75.9480

INLAND SEAS
Launched in 1994, the schooner Inland Seas is a sailing training and maritime education vessel. *Address:* 100 Dame St. *City:* Suttons Bay *State:* MI *Zip:* 49682 *Phone:* 231-271-3077 *Web:* www.schoolship.org *Email:* isea@schoolship.org *Visitors welcome?* Yes *Hours:* Contact attraction directly *Admission:* Contact attraction directly *Operated by:* Inland Seas Education Association *NR?* No *NHL?* No *Year established/built:* 1994 *Latitude:* 44.9750 *Latitude:* -85.6497

✦ IRVING JOHNSON
Completed in 2003, the Irving Johnson was purpose-designed to meet the specific needs of LAMI's TopSail Youth Program. One of twin brigantines, this state-of-the-art sail training vessel joins Exy Johnson as the flag ship of the LAMI fleet. *Address:* Berth 84, Foot of 6th St. *City:* San Pedro *State:* CA *Zip:* 90731 *Phone:* 310-548-7618 *Web:* www.lamitopsail.org *Email:* bigben@lamitopsail.org *Visitors welcome?* Yes *Hours:* Contact attraction directly *Admission:* Contact attraction directly *Operated by:* Los Angeles Maritime Institute *NR?* No *NHL?* No *Year established/built:* 2003 *Latitude:* 33.7387 *Latitude:* -118.2790

ISAAC H. EVANS
Launched in 1886, the schooner Isaac H. Evans is now an excursion vessel. *City:* Rockland *State:* ME *Zip:* 04841 *Phone:* 877-238-1325 *Web:* www.midcoast.com/~evans/ *Email:* evans@midcoast.com *Visitors welcome?* Yes *Hours:* Contact attraction directly *Admission:* Contact attraction directly *Operated by:* Schooner Isaac H. Evans *NR?* Yes *NHL?* Yes *Year established/built:* 1886 *Latitude:* 44.1037 *Latitude:* -69.1089

J. & E. RIGGIN
Launched in 1927, the schooner J. & E. Riggin is now an excursion and cruise vessel. *Address:* 136 Holmes Street *City:* Rockland *State:* ME *Zip:* 04841 *Phone:* 207-594-1875 *Toll-free:* 800-869-0604 *Web:* www.mainewindjammer.com *Email:* info@MaineWindjammer.com *Visitors welcome?* Yes *Hours:* Contact attraction directly *Admission:* Contact attraction directly *Operated by:* Schooner J. & E. Riggin *NR?* Yes *NHL?* Yes *Year established/built:* 1927 *Latitude:* 44.0966 *Latitude:* -69.1171

JOSEPH CONRAD
Launched in 1882, the ship Joseph Conrad is a floating exhibit and training vessel at Mystic Seaport. *Address:* 75 Greenmanville Avenue *City:* Mystic *State:* CT *Zip:* 06355 *Phone:* 860-572-5315 *Web:* www.mysticseaport.org *Visitors welcome?* Yes *Hours:* Daily, April to October, 9 a.m. to 5 p.m.; November to March, 10 a.m. to 4 p.m. *Admission:* Adults, $18.50; Seniors, $16.50; Children 6-17, $13; Under six, FREE *Operated by:* Mystic Seaport: The Museum of America and the Sea *NR?* Yes *NHL?* No *Year established/built:* 1882 *Latitude:* 41.3617 *Latitude:* -71.9634

JOY PARKS
The 64-foot skipjack Joy Parks is on display at the northern campus of the Piney Point Lighthouse Museum. *Address:* 44720 Lighthouse Road *City:* Piney Point *State:* MD *Zip:* 20674 *Phone:* 301-994-1471 *Web:* www.

co.saint-marys.md.us/recreate/museums/ppl.asp *Visitors welcome?* Yes *Hours:* Mid-April to September, Daily, 10 a.m. to 5 p.m. *Admission:* $3 adults, $1.50 children 6 to 18, children under five FREE *Operated by:* St. Mary's County Museum Division *NR?* No *NHL?* No *Latitude:* 38.1408 *Latitude:* -76.5202

KALMAR NYCKEL
Launched in 1998, the replica Kalmar Nyckel is Delware's goodwill ambassador and a catalyst for social and economic development. *Address:* 1124 E. Seventh St. *City:* Wilmington *State:* DE *Zip:* 19801 *Phone:* 302-429-7447 *Web:* www.kalmarnyckel.org *Email:* info@kalmarnyckel.org *Visitors welcome?* Yes *Hours:* Contact attraction directly *Admission:* Contact attraction directly *Operated by:* Kalmar Nyckel Foundation *NR?* No *NHL?* No *Year established/built:* 1998 *Latitude:* 39.7377 *Latitude:* -75.5367

KATHRYN
The skipjack Kathryn is a privately operated dredge boat on Chesapeake Bay. *Address:* Tilghman Island *City:* Tilghman *State:* MD *Visitors welcome?* No *Operated by:* Private owner *NR?* No *NHL?* Yes *Year established/built:* 1901 *Latitude:* 38.7171 *Latitude:* -76.3344

L.A. DUNTON
Launched in 1921, the schooner L.A. Dunton is a floating exhibit at Mystic Seaport. *Address:* 75 Greenmanville Avenue *City:* Mystic *State:* CT *Zip:* 06355 *Phone:* 860-572-5315 *Web:* www.mysticseaport.org *Visitors welcome?* Yes *Hours:* Daily, April to October, 9 a.m. to 5 p.m.; November to March, 10 a.m. to 4 p.m. *Admission:* Adults, $18.50; Seniors, $16.50; Children 6-17, $13; Under six, FREE *Operated by:* Mystic Seaport: The Museum of America and the Sea *NR?* Yes *NHL?* Yes *Year established/built:* 1921 *Latitude:* 41.3617 *Latitude:* -71.9634

The schooner Adventuress (Port Townsend, Wash.)

LADY KATIE
Launched in 1956, the skipjack Lady Katie is a working vessel on Chesapeake Bay. *City:* Cambridge *State:* MD *Visitors welcome?* No *Operated by:* Private owner *NR?* No *NHL?* No *Year established/built:* 1956 *Latitude:* 38.5632 *Latitude:* -76.0788

CHAPTER 1 – SHIPS

LADY MARYLAND
Launched in 1986, the schooner Lady Maryland is a sail training and excursion vessel. *Address:* 701 East Pratt Street *City:* Baltimore *State:* MD *Zip:* 21231 *Phone:* 410-685-0295 *Web:* www.livingclassrooms.org *Email:* web@livingclassrooms.org *Visitors welcome?* Yes *Hours:* Contact attraction directly *Admission:* Contact attraction directly *Operated by:* Living Classrooms Foundation *NR?* No *NHL?* No *Year established/built:* 1986 *Latitude:* 39.2864 *Latitude:* -76.6056

LADY WASHINGTON
Launched in 1989, the brig Lady Washington is a replica of the first American-flagged ship to sail to the west coast of North America. *Address:* 712 Hagara St. *City:* Aberdeen *State:* WA *Zip:* 98520 *Visitors welcome?* Yes *Hours:* Contact attraction directly *Admission:* Contact attraction directly *Operated by:* Grays Harbor Historical Seaport Authority *NR?* No *NHL?* No *Year established/built:* 1989 *Latitude:* 46.9685 *Latitude:* -123.7730

LAVENGRO
Launched in 1927, the schooner Lavengro is now an excursion and sail training vessel. *Address:* N. Northlake Way and N. Northlake Pl *City:* Seattle *State:* WA *Visitors welcome?* Yes *Hours:* Contact attraction directly *Admission:* Contact attraction directly *Operated by:* Northwest Schooner Society *NR?* No *NHL?* No *Year established/built:* 1927 *Latitude:* 47.6470 *Latitude:* -122.3380

LETTIE G. HOWARD
Launched in 1893, the Lettie G. Howard is a floating exhibit at the South Street Seaport Museum. *Address:* 12 Fulton St. *City:* New York *State:* NY *Zip:* 10038 *Phone:* 212-748-8600 *Web:* www.southstreetseaportmuseum.org *Email:* info@southstseaport.org *Visitors welcome?* Yes *Hours:* November-March: Friday to Sunday, 10 a.m. to 5 p.m.; Monday 10am-5pm: Schermerhorn Row galleries only. Tuesday to Sunday 10 a.m. to 6 p.m: All galleries and ships open *Admission:* $10 adults, $8 students/seniors, $5 children 5-12, under 5 FREE *Operated by:* South Street Seaport Museum *NR?* Yes *NHL?* Yes *Year established/built:* 1893 *Latitude:* 40.7066 *Latitude:* -74.0034

LEWIS R. FRENCH
Launched in 1871, the schooner Lewis R. French is now an excursion vessel. *City:* Camden *State:* ME *Zip:* 04843 *Phone:* 207-594-2241 *Toll-free:* 800-469-4635 *Web:* www.schoonerfrench.com *Email:* captain@schoonerfrench.com *Visitors welcome?* Yes *Hours:* Contact attraction directly *Admission:* Contact attraction directly *Operated by:* Schooner Lewis R. French *NR?* Yes *NHL?* Yes *Year established/built:* 1871 *Latitude:* 44.2098 *Latitude:* -69.0648

LIBERTY CLIPPER
Launched in 1983, the schooner Liberty Clipper is a sail training and excursion vessel. *Address:* 67 Long Wharf *City:* Boston *State:* MA *Zip:* 02110 *Phone:* 617-742-0333 *Web:* www.libertyfleet.com *Email:* liberty@libertyfleet.com *Visitors welcome?* Yes *Hours:* Contact attraction directly *Admission:* Contact attraction directly *Operated by:* Liberty Fleet *NR?* No *NHL?* No *Year established/built:* 1983 *Latitude:* 42.3608 *Latitude:* -71.0501

LIBERTY SCHOONER
Launched in 1993, the schooner Liberty is an excursion and sail training vessel. The schooner winters in Miami Beach, Fla. *Address:* 80 Audrey Zapp Drive *City:* Jersey City *State:* NJ *Zip:* 07305 *Phone:* 973-309-1884 *Web:* www.libertyschooner.com *Email:* liberty.schooner@gmail.com *Visitors welcome?* Yes *Hours:* Contact attraction directly *Admission:* Contact attraction directly *Operated by:* Liberty Schooner *NR?* No *NHL?* No *Year established/built:* 1993 *Latitude:* 40.7094 *Latitude:* -74.0478

CHAPTER 1 – SHIPS

LOIS McCLURE
The schooner Lois McClure is a modern replica of an 1862 sailing canal boat developed for the growing water trade on the region's network of canals. Launched in 2004, the Lois McClure is used to tour the remaining navigable stretches of the canals that cr *Address:* 4472 Basin Harbor Rd. *City:* Vergennes *State:* VT *Zip:* 05491 *Phone:* 802-475-2022 *Web:* www.lcmm.org *Email:* info@lcmm.org *Visitors welcome?* Yes *Hours:* Daily, 10 a.m. to 5 p.m. *Admission:* $10 adults, $9 seniors, $6 students 5-17, under five, FREE *Operated by:* Lake Champlain Maritime Museum *NR?* No *NHL?* No *Year established/built:* 2004 *Latitude:* 44.1973 *Latitude:* -73.3567

LOTUS (SCHOONER)
Launched in 1917, the bald-headed gaff auxiliary schooner Lotus is operated by the Sea Scouts. *City:* Webster *State:* NY *Zip:* 14580 *Phone:* 315-589-6781 *Web:* ithilien.mine.nu/lotus/ *Email:* bellis10@rochester.rr.com *Visitors welcome?* Yes *Hours:* Contact attraction directly *Admission:* Contact attraction directly *Operated by:* SSS Lotus *NR?* Yes *NHL?* No *Year established/built:* 1917 *Latitude:* 43.2123 *Latitude:* -77.4300

 LYNX
Launched in 2001, the schooner Lynx is a sailing training and education vessel. *Address:* 509 29th St. *City:* Newport Beach *State:* CA *Zip:* 92663 *Phone:* 866-446-5969 *Web:* www.privateerlynx.org *Email:* privateerlynx1812@verizon.net *Visitors welcome?* Yes *Hours:* Contact attraction directly *Admission:* Contact attraction directly *Operated by:* Lynx Educational Foundation *NR?* No *NHL?* No *Year established/built:* 2001 *Latitude:* 33.6142 *Latitude:* -117.9280

MADELINE
Launched in 1990, the schooner Madeline is a sail training and living history education vessel. *Address:* 13268 S. West Bayshore Dr *City:* Traverse City *State:* MI *Zip:* 49684 *Phone:* 231-946-2647 *Web:* www.maritimeheritagealliance.org *Email:* mark@maritimeheritagealliance.org *Visitors welcome?* Yes *Hours:* Contact attraction directly *Admission:* Contact attraction directly *Operated by:* Maritime Heritage Alliance *NR?* No *NHL?* No *Year established/built:* 1990 *Latitude:* 45.3593 *Latitude:* -85.0713

MAGGIE LEE
The skipjack Maggie Lee is one of two remaining skipjacks with fore-and-aft planking. It is on exhibit at the Choptank River Heritage Center. *Address:* 10215 River Landing Rd. *City:* West Denton *State:* MI *Zip:* 21629 *Phone:* 410-479-4150 *Web:* www.riverheritage.org *Email:* info@riverheritage.org *Visitors welcome?* Yes *Hours:* May to September: Friday and Saturday, 11 a.m. to 3 p.m. *Admission:* Contact attraction directly *Operated by:* Choptank River Heritage Center *NR?* No *NHL?* No *Latitude:* 38.8881 *Latitude:* -75.8399

MAKANI OLU
Launched in 1998, the schooner Makani Olu (Gracious Wind) is a youth sailing training vessel. *Address:* 45-021 Likeke Pl. *City:* Kaneohe *State:* HI *Zip:* 96744 *Phone:* 808-236-2288 *Web:* www.marimed.org *Email:* info@marimed.org *Visitors welcome?* Yes *Hours:* Contact attraction directly *Admission:* Contact attraction directly *Operated by:* Marimed Foundation *NR?* No *NHL?* No *Year established/built:* 1998 *Latitude:* 21.4116 *Latitude:* -157.7780

MAMIE A. MISTER
Launched in 1911, the skipjack Mamie A. Mister is a working vessel on Chesapeake Bay. *City:* Deal Island *State:* MD *Visitors welcome?* No *Operated by:* Private owner *NR?* No *NHL?* No *Year established/built:* 1911 *Latitude:* 38.1590 *Latitude:* -75.9480

CHAPTER 1 – SHIPS

MANITOU
Launched in 1982, the schooner Manitou is an excursion vessel. *Address:* 13390 S.W. Bay Shore Dr. *City:* Traverse City *State:* MI *Zip:* 49684 *Phone:* 231-941-2000 *Toll-free:* 800-678-0383 *Web:* www.tallshipsailing.com *Email:* info@tallshipsailing.com *Visitors welcome?* Yes *Hours:* Contact attraction directly *Admission:* Contact attraction directly *Operated by:* Traverse Tall Ship Co. *NR?* No *NHL?* No *Year established/built:* 1982 *Latitude:* 44.7840 *Latitude:* -85.6379

MARTHA (SCHOONER)
Launched in 1907, the schooner Martha is now an excursion and sail training vessel. *Address:* 380 Jefferson Street *City:* Port Townsend *State:* WA *Zip:* 98368 *Phone:* 360-385-3628 *Web:* www.schoonermartha.org *Email:* rob@nwmaritime.org *Visitors welcome?* Yes *Hours:* Contact attraction directly *Admission:* Contact attraction directly *Operated by:* Schooner Martha Foundation *NR?* Yes *NHL?* No *Year established/built:* 1907 *Latitude:* 48.1184 *Latitude:* -122.7520

MARTHA (DRAKETAIL)
Known as a Hooper Island draketail because of her unique stern design, Martha was built by Bronza Parks in 1934 and was primarily used for crabbing and oystering, as well as pleasure. *Address:* 213 N. Talbot Street *City:* St. Michaels *State:* MD *Zip:* 21663 *Phone:* 410-745-2916 *Web:* www.cbmm.org *Email:* cbland@cbmm.org *Visitors welcome?* Yes *Hours:* Daily, hours vary by season *Admission:* $13 adults; $10 seniors over 62; $6 kids 6 to 17; kids under 6 FREE *Operated by:* Chesapeake Bay Maritime Museum *NR?* No *NHL?* No *Year established/built:* 1934 *Latitude:* 38.7876 *Latitude:* -76.2249

MARTHA LEWIS
Launched in 1955, the skipjack Martha Lews is now an excursion and environmental education vessel. *Address:* 121 North Union Ave, Suite C *City:* Havre de Grace *State:* MD *Zip:* 21078 *Phone:* 410-939-4078 *Web:* www.skipjackmarthalewis.org *Email:* director@skipjackmarthalewis.org *Visitors welcome?* Yes *Hours:* Contact attraction directly *Admission:* Contact attraction directly *Operated by:* Chesapeake Heritage Conservancy *NR?* No *NHL?* No *Year established/built:* 1955 *Latitude:* 39.5485 *Latitude:* -76.0911

MARY DAY
The schooner Mary Day is an excursion vessel. *City:* Camden *State:* ME *Zip:* 04843 *Phone:* 800-992-2218 *Web:* www.schoonermaryday.com *Email:* captains@schoonermaryday.com *Visitors welcome?* Yes *Hours:* Contact attraction directly *Admission:* Contact attraction directly *Operated by:* Schooner Mary Day *NR?* No *NHL?* No *Latitude:* 44.2098 *Latitude:* -69.0648

MARY E.
Launched in 1906, the schooner Mary E is now an excursion vessel. *Address:* 210 Bellerose Ave. *City:* East Northport *State:* NY *Zip:* 11731 *Phone:* 631-332-0699 *Web:* www.schoonermarye.com *Email:* captericvandy@aol.com *Visitors welcome?* Yes *Hours:* Contact attraction directly *Admission:* Contact attraction directly *Operated by:* Halyard Enterprises *NR?* No *NHL?* No *Year established/built:* 1906 *Latitude:* 40.8812 *Latitude:* -73.3209

MARY W. SOMERS
Launched in1904, the skipjack Mary W. Somers is a working vessel on Chesapeake Bay. *City:* St. Mary's City *State:* MD *Visitors welcome?* No *Operated by:* Private owner *NR?* No *NHL?* No *Year established/built:* 1904 *Latitude:* 38.1871 *Latitude:* -76.4344

MARYLAND DOVE
The Maryland Dove is a re-creation of a 17th-century square-rigged vessel. The vessel is on display at Historic St. Mary's City. *Address:* Historic St. Mary's City *City:* St. Mary's City *State:* MD *Zip:* 20686 *Phone:* 240-895-

CHAPTER 1 – SHIPS

4990 *Toll-free:* 800-762-1634 *Web:* www.stmaryscity.org *Email:* sgwilkinson@smcm.edu *Visitors welcome?* Yes *Hours:* Mid-March to mid-June: Tuesday to Saturday, 10 a.m. to 5 p.m.; mid-June through November: Wednesday to Sunday, 10 a.m. to 5 p.m.; December: museum store open 10 a.m. to 5 p.m. *Admission:* $10 adults, $8 seniors, $6 students w/ ID, $3.50 children six to 12, under six FREE *Operated by:* Historic St. Mary's City *NR?* No *NHL?* No *Latitude:* 38.1724 *Latitude:* -76.4317

 **MAYFLOWER II**
Mayflower II, the jewel of Plymouth Harbor, is a reproduction of the 17th-century ship that brought the English Colonists, (popularly known as Pilgrims) to Plymouth in 1620. Onboard visitors meet contemporary interpreters who speak about the reproduction' *Address:* State Pier, Plymouth Waterfront *City:* Plymouth *State:* MA *Zip:* 02360 *Phone:* 508-746-1622 *Web:* www.plimoth.org *Email:* kcurtin@plimoth.org *Visitors welcome?* Yes *Hours:* April - November: daily, 9 a.m. to 5 p.m., with extended hours in summer months *Admission:* Contact attraction directly *Operated by:* Plimoth Plantation *NR?* No *NHL?* No *Year established/built:* 1959 *Latitude:* 41.9584 *Latitude:* -70.6673

MERCANTILE
Launched in 1916, the schooner Mercantile is now an excursion vessel. *Address:* Camden Waterfront *City:* Camden *State:* ME *Zip:* 04843 *Phone:* 207-236-2938 *Toll-free:* 800-736-7981 *Web:* www.mainewindjammercruises.com *Email:* sail@mainewindjammercruises.com *Visitors welcome?* Yes *Hours:* Contact attraction directly *Admission:* Contact attraction directly *Operated by:* Maine Windjammer Cruises *NR?* Yes *NHL?* Yes *Year established/built:* 1916 *Latitude:* 44.2098 *Latitude:* -69.0648

MERRIE ELLEN
The gaff schooner Merrie Ellen is now an excursion vessel in Puget Sound. *Address:* 235 Salmon St. *City:* Brinnon *State:* WA *Zip:* 98320 *Phone:* 360-796-3172 *Web:* www.schoonermerrieellen.com *Email:* john_holbert55@yahoo.com *Visitors welcome?* Yes *Hours:* Contact attraction directly *Admission:* Contact attraction directly *Operated by:* Schooner Merrie Ellen *NR?* No *NHL?* No *Year established/built:* 1922 *Latitude:* 47.6459 *Latitude:* -122.9430

MIKE SEKUL
The Maritime & Seafood Industry Museum in Biloxi, Miss., has recaptured a piece of its history with their two schooners, the Glenn L. Swetman and the Mike Sekul. Available for day sailing or charter, the vessels can accommodate weddings, dockside partites, and other functions. *Address:* 115 First Street *City:* Biloxi *State:* MS *Zip:* 39530 *Phone:* 228-435-6320 *Web:* www.maritimemuseum.org *Email:* info@maritimemuseum.org *Visitors welcome?* Yes *Hours:* Contact attraction directly *Admission:* $25 adults, $10 children under 12 *Operated by:* Maritime & Seafood Industry Museum *NR?* No *NHL?* No *Latitude:* 30.3937 *Latitude:* -88.8591

MINNIE V
Launched in 1906, the skipjack Minnie V is now used as a floating classroom for at-risk youth programs. *Address:* 701 East Pratt Street *City:* Baltimore *State:* MD *Zip:* 21231 *Phone:* 410-685-0295 *Web:* www.livingclassrooms.org *Email:* web@livingclassrooms.org *Visitors welcome?* Yes *Hours:* Contact attraction directly *Admission:* Contact attraction directly *Operated by:* Living Classrooms Foundation *NR?* Yes *NHL?* No *Year established/built:* 1906 *Latitude:* 39.2864 *Latitude:* -76.6056

MISTRESS
Launched in 1967, the schooner Mistress is now an excursion vessel. *Address:* Camden Waterfront *City:* Camden *State:* ME *Zip:* 04843 *Phone:* 207-236-2938 *Toll-free:* 800-736-7981 *Web:* www.mainewindjammercruises.com *Email:* sail@mainewindjammercruises.com *Visitors welcome?* Yes *Hours:* Contact attraction

CHAPTER 1 – SHIPS

directly *Admission:* Contact attraction directly *Operated by:* Maine Windjammer Cruises *NR?* No *NHL?* No *Year established/built:* 1967 *Latitude:* 44.2098 *Latitude:* -69.0648

MODESTY
Launched in 1923, the sloop Modesty is now an operational museum vessel. *Address:* 86 West Ave. *City:* West Sayville *State:* NY *Zip:* 11796 *Phone:* 631-854-4974 *Web:* www.limaritime.org *Email:* limm@limaritime.org *Visitors welcome?* Yes *Hours:* Monday to Saturday: 10 a.m. to 4 p.m.; Sunday, noon to 4 p.m. *Admission:* $4 adults, $2 senior/child three to 17, under three FREE *Operated by:* Long Island Maritime Museum *NR?* No *NHL?* No *Year established/built:* 1923 *Latitude:* 40.7218 *Latitude:* -73.0938

MOSHULU
Launched in 1904, the barque Moshulu is now a floating restaurant. *Address:* 401 S. Columbus Blvd. *City:* Philadelphia *State:* PA *Zip:* 19106 *Phone:* 215-923-2500 *Web:* www.moshulu.com *Email:* info@moshulu.com *Visitors welcome?* Yes *Hours:* Contact attraction directly *Admission:* Contact attraction directly *Operated by:* Moshulu Restaurant *NR?* No *NHL?* No *Year established/built:* 1904 *Latitude:* 39.9420 *Latitude:* -75.1423

MYSTIC
The barkentine Mystic operates as an excursion and sail training vessel out of Mystic Harbor. *Address:* 15 Holmes Street *City:* Mystic *State:* CT *Zip:* 06355 *Phone:* 860-536-0416 *Web:* www.voyagermystic.com *Email:* amyblumberg@voyagermystic.com *Visitors welcome?* Yes *Hours:* Contact attraction directly *Admission:* Contact attraction directly *Operated by:* Voyager Cruises *NR?* No *NHL?* No *Latitude:* 41.3562 *Latitude:* -71.9658

MYSTIC WHALER
Launched in 1967, the schooner Mystic Whaler is an excursion vessel. *Address:* 35 Water St. *City:* New London *State:* CT *Zip:* 06320 *Phone:* 860-447-1249 *Toll-free:* 800-697-8420 *Web:* www.mysticwhaler.com *Email:* info@mysticwhaler.com *Visitors welcome?* Yes *Hours:* Contact attraction directly *Admission:* Contact attraction directly *Operated by:* Mystic Whaler Cruises *NR?* No *NHL?* No *Year established/built:* 1967 *Latitude:* 41.3569 *Latitude:* -72.0949

NATHAN OF DORCHESTER
Launched in 1992, the skipjack Nathan of Dorchester is an education vessel on Chesapeake Bay. *City:* Cambridge *State:* MD *Zip:* 21613 *Web:* www.skipjack-nathan.org *Email:* info@skipjack-nathan.org *Visitors welcome?* Yes *Hours:* Contact attraction directly *Admission:* Contact attraction directly *Operated by:* Dorchester Skipjack Committee *NR?* No *NHL?* No *Year established/built:* 1992 *Latitude:* 38.5632 *Latitude:* -76.0788

NATHANIEL BOWDITCH
Launched in 1922, the schooner Nathaniel Bowditch is an excursion vessel. *Address:* 256 Old County Road *City:* Rockland *State:* ME *Zip:* 04841 *Phone:* 207-596-0401 *Toll-free:* 800-288-4098 *Web:* www.windjammervacation.com *Email:* info@windjammervacation.com *Visitors welcome?* Yes *Hours:* Contact attraction directly *Admission:* Contact attraction directly *Operated by:* Schooner Nathaniel Bowditch *NR?* No *NHL?* No *Year established/built:* 1922 *Latitude:* 44.1144 *Latitude:* -69.1308

NEITH
Launched in 1907, the cutter Neith is an excursion vessel. *City:* West Mystic *State:* CT *Zip:* 06388 *Phone:* 860-460-5620 *Email:* neith1907@sbcglobal.net *Visitors welcome?* Yes *Hours:* Contact attraction directly *Admission:* Contact attraction directly *Operated by:* Neith, LLC *NR?* No *NHL?* No *Year established/built:* 1907 *Latitude:* 41.3544 *Latitude:* -71.9669

CHAPTER 1 – SHIPS

NELLIE L. BYRD
Launched in 1911, the skipjack Nellie L. Byrd is a working vessel on Chesapeake Bay. *City:* Tilghman Island *State:* MD *Visitors welcome?* No *Operated by:* Private owner *NR?* Yes *NHL?* No *Year established/built:* 1911 *Latitude:* 38.7037 *Latitude:* -76.3386

 NIAGARA
The U.S. Brig Niagara is a reconstruction of the U.S. Navy warship that won the Battle of Lake Erie in the war of 1812. The reconstruction incorporates a small number of timbers recovered from the original Niagara, which was scuttled in Lake Erie shortly after the War of 1812. *Address:* 150 East Front Street *City:* Erie *State:* PA *Zip:* 16507 *Phone:* 814-452-2744 *Web:* www.brigniagara.org *Email:* wrybka@state.pa.us *Visitors welcome?* Yes *Hours:* April to December: Monday to Saturday, 9 a.m. to 5 p.m., Sunday, noon to 5 p.m.; January to March, Tuesday to Saturday, 9 a.m. to 5 p.m. *Admission:* $6 adults, $5 senior, $3 children six to 17, under six FREE *Operated by:* Flagship Niagara League *NR?* No *NHL?* No *Year established/built:* 1998 *Latitude:* 42.1361 *Latitude:* -80.0837

 NINA
Launched in 1992, the replica 15th-century caravel redondo Nina is an operating museum vessel. *City:* St. Thomas *State:* VI *Zip:* 00803 *Phone:* 284-495-4618 *Web:* www.thenina.com *Email:* columfnd@surfbvi.com *Visitors welcome?* Yes *Hours:* Contact attraction directly *Admission:* Contact attraction directly *Operated by:* Columbus Foundation *NR?* No *NHL?* No *Year established/built:* 1992 *Latitude:* 18.3436 *Latitude:* -64.9314

OLAD
Launched in 1927, the schooner Olad is an excursion vessel. *City:* Camden *State:* ME *Zip:* 04843 *Phone:* 207-236-2323 *Web:* www.maineschooners.com *Email:* info@maineschooners.com *Visitors welcome?* Yes *Hours:* Contact attraction directly *Admission:* Contact attraction directly *Operated by:* Fully Found *NR?* No *NHL?* No *Year established/built:* 1927 *Latitude:* 44.2098 *Latitude:* -69.0648

✦ PEACEMAKER
Launched in 1989, the barkentine Peacemaker is a sail-training and excursion vessel. *City:* Brunswick *State:* GA *Phone:* 912-399-6946 *Web:* www.peacemakermarine.com *Email:* lee@peacemakermarine.com *Visitors welcome?* Yes *Hours:* Contact attraction directly *Admission:* Contact attraction directly *Operated by:* Peacemaker Marine *NR?* No *NHL?* No *Year established/built:* 1989 *Latitude:* 31.1500 *Latitude:* -81.4915

PEKING
Launched in 1911, the barque Peking is a floating exhibit at the South Street Seaport Museum. *Address:* 12 Fulton St. *City:* New York *State:* NY *Zip:* 10038 *Phone:* 212-748-8600 *Web:* www.southstreetseaportmuseum.org *Email:* info@southstseaport.org *Visitors welcome?* Yes *Hours:* November-March: Friday to Sunday, 10 a.m. to 5 p.m.; Monday 10am-5pm: Schermerhorn Row galleries only. Tuesday to Sunday 10 a.m. to 6 p.m: All galleries and ships open *Admission:* $10 adults, $8 students/seniors, $5 children 5-12, under 5 FREE *Operated by:* South Street Seaport Museum *NR?* No *NHL?* No *Year established/built:* 1911 *Latitude:* 40.7066 *Latitude:* -74.0034

PHILADELPHIA II
Philadelphia II is a modern replica of a Revolutionary War gunboat built to challenge the British Navy on Lake Champlain. The original Philadelphia sank in a 1776 naval engagement, and the remains were raised in 1935. The replica is used for living histor *Address:* 4472 Basin Harbor Rd. *City:* Vergennes *State:* VT *Zip:* 05491 *Phone:* 802-475-2022 *Web:* www.lcmm.org *Email:* info@lcmm.org *Visitors welcome?* Yes *Hours:* Daily, 10 a.m. to 5 p.m. *Admission:* $10 adults, $9 seniors, $6 students 5-17, under five, FREE *Operated by:* Lake

CHAPTER 1 – SHIPS

Champlain Maritime Museum *NR?* No *NHL?* No *Year established/built:* 1991 *Latitude:* 44.1973 *Latitude:* -73.3567

 PILGRIM
Launched in 1945, the brig Pilgrim is an education vessel. *Address:* 24200 Dana Point Dr. *City:* Dana Point *State:* CA *Zip:* 92629 *Phone:* 949-496-2274 *Toll-free:* 949-496-4296 *Web:* www.ocean-institute.org *Email:* oi@ocean-institute.org. *Visitors welcome?* Yes *Hours:* Contact attraction directly *Admission:* Contact attraction directly *Operated by:* Ocean Institute *NR?* No *NHL?* No *Year established/built:* 1945 *Latitude:* 33.4613 *Latitude:* -117.7070

> The Fyddeye website is constantly updated with new information about the activities of tall ships. Visit the site at www.fyddeye.com.

PIONEER
Launched in 1885, the schooner Pioneer is a floating exhibit at the South Street Seaport Museum. *Address:* 12 Fulton St. *City:* New York *State:* NY *Zip:* 10038 *Phone:* 212-748-8600 *Web:* www.southstreetseaportmuseum.org *Email:* info@southstseaport.org *Visitors welcome?* Yes *Hours:* November-March: Friday to Sunday, 10 a.m. to 5 p.m.; Monday 10am-5pm: Schermerhorn Row galleries only. Tuesday to Sunday 10 a.m. to 6 p.m: All galleries and ships open *Admission:* $10 adults, $8 students/seniors, $5 children 5-12, under 5 FREE *Operated by:* South Street Seaport Museum *NR?* No *NHL?* No *Year established/built:* 1885 *Latitude:* 40.7066 *Latitude:* -74.0034

PIRATE
Launched in 1926, the Pirate is a Seattle-designed racing boat now on display at the Center for Wooden Boats. *Address:* Center For Wooden Boats, 1010 Valley Street *City:* Seattle *State:* WA *Visitors welcome?* Yes *Hours:* Contact attraction directly *Admission:* Contact attraction directly *Operated by:* Center for Wooden Boats *NR?* Yes *NHL?* No *Year established/built:* 1926 *Latitude:* 47.6258 *Latitude:* -122.3370

PRIDE OF BALTIMORE II
Launched in 1988, the square-topsail schooner Pride of Baltimore II is a sail training vessel and goodwill ambassador for the city of Baltimore. *Address:* 401 East Pratt St. *City:* Baltimore *State:* MD *Zip:* 21202 *Phone:* 410-539-1151 *Toll-free:* 888-557-7433 *Web:* www.marylandspride.org *Email:* pride2@pride2.org *Visitors welcome?* Yes *Hours:* Contact attraction directly *Admission:* Contact attraction directly *Operated by:* Pride of Baltimore *NR?* No *NHL?* No *Year established/built:* 1988 *Latitude:* 39.2859 *Latitude:* -76.6097

PRISCILLA
Launched in 1888, the schooner Priscilla is an operational museum vessel. *Address:* 86 West Ave. *City:* West Sayville *State:* NY *Zip:* 11796 *Phone:* 631-854-4974 *Web:* www.limaritime.org *Email:* limm@limaritime.org *Visitors welcome?* Yes *Hours:* Monday to Saturday: 10 a.m. to 4 p.m.; Sunday, noon to 4 p.m. *Admission:* $4 adults, $2 senior/child three to 17, under three FREE *Operated by:* Long Island Maritime Museum *NR?* No *NHL?* No *Year established/built:* 1888 *Latitude:* 40.7218 *Latitude:* -73.0938

PROVIDENCE
Launched in 1976, the sloop Providence is a living history and education vessel. *Address:* 408 Broadway *City:* Providence *State:* RI *Zip:* 02901 *Phone:* 401-274-7447 *Web:* www.sloopprovidenceonline.org *Email:* inf_sloopprovidenceri@cox.net *Visitors welcome?* Yes *Hours:* Contact attraction directly *Admission:* Contact attraction directly *Operated by:* Providence Maritime Heritage Foundation *NR?* No *NHL?* No *Year established/built:* 1976 *Latitude:* 41.8211 *Latitude:* -71.4238

CHAPTER 1 – SHIPS

QUINNIPIACK
Launched in 1984, the schooner Quinnipiack is an environmental education vessel. *Address:* 60 South Water St. *City:* New Haven *State:* CT *Zip:* 06519 *Phone:* 203-865-1737 *Web:* www.schoonerinc.org *Email:* captain@schoonerinc.org *Visitors welcome?* Yes *Hours:* Contact attraction directly *Admission:* Contact attraction directly *Operated by:* Schooner, Inc *NR?* No *NHL?* No *Year established/built:* 1984 *Latitude:* 41.2822 *Latitude:* -72.9285

R.H. LEDBETTER
The full-rigged ship R.H. Ledbetter is the flagship of the Culver Summer Naval School, located on Lake Maxinkuckee in Culver, Indiana. *Address:* 1300 Academy Rd. #138 *City:* Culver *State:* IN *Zip:* 46511 *Phone:* 574-842-8300 *Toll-free:* 800-221-2020 *Web:* www.culver.org/summer *Email:* summer@culver.org *Visitors welcome?* Yes *Hours:* Contact attraction directly *Admission:* Contact attraction directly *Operated by:* Culver Summer Schools & Camps *NR?* No *NHL?* No *Latitude:* 41.2224 *Latitude:* -86.4074

REBECCA T. RUARK
Launched in 1886, the skipjack Rebecca T. Ruark is now a working fishing and excursion vessel. *Address:* 21308 Phillips Road *City:* Tilghman *State:* MD *Zip:* 21671 *Phone:* 410-829-3976 *Web:* www.skipjack.org *Visitors welcome?* Yes *Hours:* Contact attraction directly *Admission:* $30 adults, $15 children under 12, tiny ones" FREE" *Operated by:* Capt. Wade H. Murphy, Jr. *NR?* Yes *NHL?* Yes *Year established/built:* 1886 *Latitude:* 38.7095 *Latitude:* -76.3387

RED WITCH
Launched in 1986, the schooner Red Witch is an excursion and sail training vessel. *Address:* 401 East Illinois St. *City:* Chicago *State:* IL *Zip:* 60611 *Phone:* 312-404-5800 *Web:* www.redwitch.com *Email:* captbruce@lakeshoresail.com *Visitors welcome?* Yes *Hours:* Contact attraction directly *Admission:* Contact attraction directly *Operated by:* Lakeshore Sail Charters *NR?* No *NHL?* No *Year established/built:* 1986 *Latitude:* 41.8910 *Latitude:* -87.6171

REGINA M.
Launched in 1900, the fishing vessel Regina M. is part of the Mystic Seaport vessel collection. *Address:* 75 Greenmanville Avenue *City:* Mystic *State:* CT *Zip:* 06355 *Phone:* 860-572-5315 *Web:* www.mysticseaport.org *Visitors welcome?* Yes *Hours:* Daily, April to October, 9 a.m. to 5 p.m.; November to March, 10 a.m. to 4 p.m. *Admission:* Adults, $18.50; Seniors, $16.50; Children 6-17, $13; Under six, FREE *Operated by:* Mystic Seaport: The Museum of America and the Sea *NR?* No *NHL?* No *Year established/built:* 1900 *Latitude:* 41.3617 *Latitude:* -71.9634

RESOLUTE
Launched in 1939, the yawl Resolute is a sail training and education vessel. *City:* Steilacoom *State:* WA *Zip:* 98388 *Phone:* 253-588-3066 *Web:* www.resolutesailing.org *Email:* resolute@telisphere.com *Visitors welcome?* Yes *Hours:* Contact attraction directly *Admission:* Contact attraction directly *Operated by:* Resolute Sailing Foundation *NR?* No *NHL?* No *Year established/built:* 1939 *Latitude:* 47.1698 *Latitude:* -122.6030

ROBERT C. SEAMANS
The brigantine Robert C. Seamans is a sail training and research vessel. *City:* Woods Hole *State:* MA *Zip:* 02543 *Phone:* 508-540-3954 *Toll-free:* 800-552-3633 *Web:* www.sea.edu *Email:* admission@sea.edu *Visitors welcome?* Yes *Hours:* Contact attraction directly *Admission:* Contact attraction directly *Operated by:* Sea Education Association *NR?* No *NHL?* No *Latitude:* 41.5302 *Latitude:* -70.6603

CHAPTER 1 – SHIPS

ROSEWAY
Launched in 1925, the schooner Roseway is a sail training and education vessel. *City:* Christiansted *State:* VI *Zip:* 00824 *Phone:* 340-626-7877 *Web:* www.worldoceanschool.org *Email:* wos@worldoceanschool.org *Visitors welcome?* Yes *Hours:* Contact attraction directly *Admission:* Contact attraction directly *Operated by:* World Ocean School *NR?* No *NHL?* No *Year established/built:* 1925 *Latitude:* 17.7488 *Latitude:* -64.7039

ROSIE PARKS
Designed specifically for dredging up the vast quantities of oysters found on the Chesapeake Bay's floor, only a handful of skipjacks continue to work the bay. They are the only commercial sailing fleet left in the United States. *Address:* 213 N. Talbot Street *City:* St. Michaels *State:* MD *Zip:* 21663 *Phone:* 410-745-2916 *Web:* www.cbmm.org *Email:* cbland@cbmm.org *Visitors welcome?* Yes *Hours:* Daily, hours vary by season *Admission:* $13 adults; $10 seniors over 62; $6 kids 6 to 17; kids under 6 FREE *Operated by:* Chesapeake Bay Maritime Museum *NR?* No *NHL?* No *Year established/built:* 1955 *Latitude:* 38.7876 *Latitude:* -76.2249

RUBY G. FORD
Launched in 1891, the status of the skipjack Ruby G. Ford is unknown. *Visitors welcome?* No *Operated by:* Private owner *NR?* No *NHL?* No *Year established/built:* 1891

SANTA CLARA
The replica 15th-century caravel redondo Santa Clara is an operating museum ship. *City:* St. Thomas *State:* VI *Zip:* 00803 *Phone:* 284-495-4618 *Web:* www.thenina.com *Email:* columfnd@surfbvi.com *Visitors welcome?* Yes *Hours:* Contact attraction directly *Admission:* Contact attraction directly *Operated by:* Columbus Foundation *NR?* No *NHL?* No *Latitude:* 18.3436 *Latitude:* -64.9314

SEA GULL
Launched in 1924, the skipjack Sea Gull is a working vessel on Chesapeake Bay. *City:* Deal Island *State:* MD *Visitors welcome?* No *Operated by:* Private owner *NR?* Yes *NHL?* No *Year established/built:* 1924 *Latitude:* 38.1590 *Latitude:* -75.9480

SEA LION
The Sea Lion is a reproduction of a sixty-three foot sailing vessel that offers excursions. *Address:* Daniel Reed Pier *City:* Westfield *State:* NY *Zip:* 14787 *Phone:* 716-326-6633 *Web:* sealionprojectltd.com *Visitors welcome?* Yes *Hours:* Contact attraction directly *Admission:* Contact attraction directly *Operated by:* Sea Lion Project, Ltd *NR?* No *NHL?* No *Latitude:* 42.3223 *Latitude:* -79.5781

SEAWARD
Launched in 1988, the schooner Seaward is a sailing training and excursion vessel. *Address:* #278, 3020 Bridgeway *City:* Sausalito *State:* CA *Zip:* 94965 *Phone:* 415-331-3214 *Web:* www.callofthesea.org *Email:* info@callofthesea.org *Visitors welcome?* Yes *Hours:* Contact attraction directly *Admission:* Contact attraction directly *Operated by:* Call of the Sea *NR?* No *NHL?* No *Year established/built:* 1988 *Latitude:* 37.8704 *Latitude:* -122.5020

SEMANA
Launched in 1975, the ketch Semana is a sail training and education vessel. *Address:* 5600 Royal Dane Mall, Suite 12 *City:* St. Thomas *State:* VI *Zip:* 00802 *Phone:* 207-321-9249 *Web:* www.sailingschool.com *Email:* svsamana@sailingschool.com *Visitors welcome?* Yes *Hours:* Contact attraction directly *Admission:* Contact attraction directly *Operated by:* School of Ocean Sailing *NR?* No *NHL?* No *Year established/built:* 1975 *Latitude:* 18.3436 *Latitude:* -64.9322

CHAPTER 1 – SHIPS

SHAMROCK V
Launched in 1928, the racing sloop Shamrock V is in private hands in Newport, Rhode Island. *Address:* 28 Church St. *City:* Newport *State:* RI *Zip:* 02840 *Phone:* 401-849-3060 *Visitors welcome?* Yes *Hours:* Contact attraction directly *Admission:* Contact attraction directly *Operated by:* J-Class Management *NR?* No *NHL?* No *Year established/built:* 1928 *Latitude:* 41.4876 *Latitude:* -71.3142

SHENANDOAH
Launched in 1926, the square topsail schooner Shenandoah is an excursion and sail training vessel. *City:* Vineyard Haven *State:* MA *Zip:* 02568 *Phone:* 508-693-1699 *Web:* www.shenandoahfoundation.org *Email:* morgan@shenandoahfoundation.org *Visitors welcome?* Yes *Hours:* Contact attraction directly *Admission:* Contact attraction directly *Operated by:* Shenandoah Foundation *NR?* No *NHL?* No *Year established/built:* 1964 *Latitude:* 41.4543 *Latitude:* -70.6036

SHERMAN ZWICKER
The Sherman Zwicker is a 142-foot wooden schooner built in 1942 in for the Zwicker and Co., by the Smith and Rhuland Shipyard in Lunenberg, Nova Scotia. The Sherman Zwicker is a transition vessel designed with a classic schooner hull. *Address:* Maine Maritime Museum *City:* Bath *State:* ME *Phone:* 207-633-4727 *Web:* www.schoonermuseum.org *Email:* staff@schoonermuseum.org *Visitors welcome?* Yes *Hours:* Contact attraction directly *Admission:* Contact attraction directly *Operated by:* Grand Banks Schooner Museum Trust *NR?* No *NHL?* No *Year established/built:* 1942 *Latitude:* 43.8937 *Latitude:* -69.8148

SIGSBEE
Launched in 1901, the skipjack Sigsbee is now used as a floating classroom for at-risk youth programs. *Address:* 701 East Pratt Street *City:* Baltimore *State:* MD *Phone:* 410-685-0295 *Web:* www.livingclassrooms.org *Email:* web@livingclassrooms.org *Visitors welcome?* Yes *Hours:* Contact attraction directly *Admission:* Contact attraction directly *Operated by:* Living Classrooms Foundation *NR?* Yes *NHL?* No *Year established/built:* 1901 *Latitude:* 39.2864 *Latitude:* -76.6056

SOMERSET
Launched in 1949, the skipjack Somerset is a working vessel on Chesapeake Bay. *City:* Deal Island *State:* MD *Visitors welcome?* No *Operated by:* Private owner *NR?* No *NHL?* No *Year established/built:* 1949 *Latitude:* 38.1590 *Latitude:* -75.9480

SPIKE AFRICA
Launched in 1977, the schooner Spike Africa is an excursion vessel based in Friday Harbor, Wash. *Address:* 685 Spring Street *City:* Friday Harbor *State:* WA *Zip:* 98250 *Phone:* 360-378-2224 *Web:* www.sanjuan-sailcharter.com *Email:* schoonersnorth@gmail.com *Visitors welcome?* Yes *Hours:* Contact attraction directly *Admission:* Contact attraction directly *Operated by:* Spike Africa *NR?* No *NHL?* No *Year established/built:* 1977 *Latitude:* 48.5313 *Latitude:* -123.0240

SPIRIT OF 1608
Launched in 2006, the barge Spirit of 1608 is a reproduction of a typical 17th-century barge used in the Chesapeake Bay area. It is an operating museum and excursion vessel. *Address:* 504 Main Street *City:* Reedville *State:* VA *Zip:* 22539 *Phone:* 804-453-6529 *Web:* www.rfmuseum.org *Email:* office@rfmuseum.org *Visitors welcome?* Yes *Hours:* May 1 to October: Daily, 10:30 a.m. to 4:30 p.m. *Admission:* $5 adults, $3 seniors, children under 12 FREE *Operated by:* Reedville Fisherman's Museum *NR?* No *NHL?* No *Year established/built:* 2006 *Latitude:* 37.8454 *Latitude:* -76.2742

CHAPTER 1 – SHIPS

SPIRIT OF DANA POINT
Launched in 1983, the schooner Spirit of Dana Point is a sail training and excursion vessel. *Address:* 24200 Dana Point Dr. *City:* Dana Point *State:* CA *Zip:* 92629 *Phone:* 949-496-2274 *Toll-free:* 949-496-4296 *Web:* www.ocean-institute.org *Email:* oi@ocean-institute.org. *Visitors welcome?* Yes *Hours:* Contact attraction directly *Admission:* Contact attraction directly *Operated by:* Ocean Institute *NR?* No *NHL?* No *Year established/built:* 1983 *Latitude:* 33.4613 *Latitude:* -117.7070

SPIRIT OF MASSACHUSETTS
Launched in 1984, the schooner Spirit of Massachusetts is a sail traiing and excursion vessel. *Address:* 29 McKown St. *City:* Boothbay Harbor *State:* ME *Zip:* 04538 *Phone:* 207-633-2750 *Toll-free:* 800-724-7245 *Web:* www.oceanclassroom.org *Email:* mail@oceanclassroom.org *Visitors welcome?* Yes *Hours:* Contact attraction directly *Admission:* Contact attraction directly *Operated by:* Ocean Classroom Foundation *NR?* No *NHL?* No *Year established/built:* 1984 *Latitude:* 43.8404 *Latitude:* -69.6459

SPIRIT OF SOUTH CAROLINA
Launched in 2007, the pilot schooner Spirit of South Carolina is a sail training and education vessel. *City:* Charleston *State:* SC *Phone:* 843-722-1030 *Web:* www.scmaritime.org *Email:* info@scmaritime.org *Visitors welcome?* Yes *Hours:* Contact attraction directly *Admission:* Contact attraction directly *Operated by:* South Carolina Maritime Heritage Foundation *NR?* No *NHL?* No *Year established/built:* 2007 *Latitude:* 32.7766 *Latitude:* -79.9309

ST. CHRISTOPHER
The St. Christopher is a Dutch built, classic design, three masted, steel sailing schooner built in 1932. She measures approximately 115' at the water line and is 140 feet long length overall. The vessel is 19 feet at the beam and draws 6.5 feet. It is currently in a marsh near Pascagoula, Miss., awaiting refloating. *Address:* 9275 Old Highway 43 *City:* Creola *State:* AL *Zip:* 36525 *Phone:* 251-442-3247 *Fax:* 251-665-0350 *Web:* www.stchristopherservices.org *Email:* bryan@stchristopherservices.org *Visitors welcome?* No *Hours:* Closed to the public *Operated by:* St. Christopher Services *NR?* No *NHL?* No *Year established/built:* 1932 *Latitude:* 30.8843 *Latitude:* -88.0385

STANLEY NORMAN
Launched in 1902, the skipjack Stanley Norman is an educational vessel. *City:* Annapolis *State:* MD *Zip:* 21403 *Phone:* 410-268-8816 *Web:* www.cbf.org *Email:* educationcoordinator@cbf.org *Visitors welcome?* Yes *Hours:* Contact attraction directly *Admission:* Contact attraction directly *Operated by:* Chesapeake Bay Foundation *NR?* No *NHL?* No *Year established/built:* 1902 *Latitude:* 38.9784 *Latitude:* -76.4922

STAR OF INDIA
Launched in 1863, the barque Star of India is a museum ship and the world's oldest active ship. She is owned and operated by the San Diego Maritime Museum. *Address:* 1492 North Harbor Drive *City:* San Diego *State:* CA *Zip:* 92101 *Phone:* 619-234-9153 *Web:* www.sdmaritime.com *Email:* info@sdmaritime.org *Visitors welcome?* Yes *Hours:* Daily, 9 a.m. to 8 p.m. *Admission:* $14 adults; $11 seniors, active military; $8 children 6-17; under six FREE *Operated by:* Maritime Museum Association of San Diego *NR?* Yes *NHL?* Yes *Year established/built:* 1863 *Latitude:* 32.7276 *Latitude:* -117.1800

STAR PILOT
Launched in 1924, the schooner Star Pilot is home-ported in San Diego. *Address:* 1220 Roseevans St., Suite 308 *City:* San Diego *State:* CA *Zip:* 92106 *Phone:* 805-686-4484 *Visitors welcome?* Yes *Hours:* Contact attrac-

CHAPTER 1 – SHIPS

tion directly *Admission:* Contact attraction directly *Operated by:* Schooner Pilot Trust *NR?* No *NHL?* No *Year established/built:* 1924 *Latitude:* 32.7228 *Latitude:* -117.2380

STEPHEN TABER
Launched in 1871, the schooner Stephen Taber is now an excursion vessel. *Address:* Windjammer Wharf *City:* Rockland *State:* ME *Zip:* 04841 *Phone:* 207-594-4723 *Toll-free:* 800-999-7352 *Web:* www.stephentaber.com *Email:* info@stephentaber.com *Visitors welcome?* Yes *Hours:* Contact attraction directly *Admission:* Contact attraction directly *Operated by:* Schooner Stephen Taber *NR?* Yes *NHL?* Yes *Year established/built:* 1871 *Latitude:* 44.1037 *Latitude:* -69.1089

 SULTANA
Launched in 2001, the schooner Sultana is a sail training and environmental education vessel. *Address:* 105 South Cross St. *City:* Chestertown *State:* MD *Zip:* 21620 *Phone:* 410-778-5954 *Toll-free:* 410-778-4531 *Web:* www.sultanaprojects.org *Email:* dmcmullen@sultanaprojects.org *Visitors welcome?* Yes *Hours:* Contact attraction directly *Admission:* Contact attraction directly *Operated by:* Sultana Projects *NR?* No *NHL?* No *Year established/built:* 2001 *Latitude:* 39.2090 *Latitude:* -76.0665

SUNDERLAND
Launched in 1885, the schooner Sunderland is now an excursion vessel. *City:* Langley *State:* WA *Zip:* 98260 *Phone:* 206-321-4840 *Visitors welcome?* Yes *Hours:* Contact attraction directly *Admission:* Contact attraction directly *Operated by:* Pacific Northwest Passages *NR?* No *NHL?* No *Year established/built:* 1885 *Latitude:* 48.0401 *Latitude:* -122.4060

SURPRISE (FULL-RIGGED SHIP)
Launched in 1970 as HMS Rose, HMS Surprise is a full rigged ship that appeared in the 2004 movie Master and Commander: The Far Side of the World. The vessel is now an excursion and museum ship for the San Diego Maritime Museum. *Address:* 1492 North Harbor Drive *City:* San Diego *State:* CA *Zip:* 92101 *Phone:* 619-234-9153 *Web:* www.sdmaritime.com *Email:* info@sdmaritime.org *Visitors welcome?* Yes *Hours:* Daily, 9 a.m. to 8 p.m. *Admission:* $14 adults; $11 seniors, active military; $8 children 6-17; under six FREE *Operated by:* Maritime Museum Association of San Diego *NR?* No *NHL?* No *Year established/built:* 1970 *Latitude:* 32.7276 *Latitude:* -117.1800

SURPRISE (SCHOONER)
Launched in 1918, the schooner Surprise is now an excursion vessel. *Address:* Camden Harbor *City:* Camden *State:* ME *Zip:* 04843 *Phone:* 207-236-4687 *Web:* www.camdenmainesailing.com *Email:* surprise@midcoast.com *Visitors welcome?* Yes *Hours:* Contact attraction directly *Admission:* Contact attraction directly *Operated by:* Schooner Surprise *NR?* Yes *NHL?* No *Year established/built:* 1918 *Latitude:* 44.2143 *Latitude:* -69.0580

SUSAN CONSTANT
Launched in 1991, the Susan Constant is a working replica of a ship that brought the first colonists to the Jamestown settlement in 1607. *Address:* 2218 Jamestown Rd. *City:* Williamsburg *State:* VA *Zip:* 23185 *Phone:* 757-253-7308 *Web:* historyisfun.org *Visitors welcome?* Yes *Hours:* Contact attraction directly *Admission:* Contact attraction directly *Operated by:* Jamestown-Yorktown Foundation *NR?* No *NHL?* No *Year established/built:* 1991 *Latitude:* 37.2251 *Latitude:* -76.7862

SUSAN MAY
Launched in 1901, the skipjack Susan May is a working vessel on Chesapeake Bay. *City:* Wenona *State:* MD *Visitors welcome?* No *Operated by:* Private owner *NR?* Yes *NHL?* No *Year established/built:* 1901 *Latitude:* 38.1390 *Latitude:* -75.9502

CHAPTER 1 – SHIPS

SWIFT OF IPSWICH
Built in 1938 as a replica of a 1787 schooner, the Swift of Ipswich was the private yacht of actor James Cagney for a number of years. A fast schooner, the Swift has served southern California youth since joining the LAMI fleet in 1991. *Address:* Berth 84, Foot of 6th St. *City:* San Pedro *State:* CA *Zip:* 90731 *Phone:* 310-548-7618 *Web:* www.lamitopsail.org *Email:* bigben@lamitopsail.org *Visitors welcome?* Yes *Hours:* Contact attraction directly *Admission:* Contact attraction directly *Operated by:* Los Angeles Maritime Institute *NR?* No *NHL?* No *Year established/built:* 1938 *Latitude:* 33.7387 *Latitude:* -118.2790

TABOR BOY
Launched in 1914, the schooner Tabor Bay is now an education vessel at Tabor Academy. *Address:* 66 Spring Street *City:* Marion *State:* MA *Zip:* 2738 *Phone:* 508-748-2000 *Web:* www.taboracademy.org *Email:* communications@taboracademy.org *Visitors welcome?* Yes *Hours:* Contact attraction directly *Admission:* Contact attraction directly *Operated by:* Tabor Academy *NR?* No *NHL?* No *Year established/built:* 1914 *Latitude:* 41.7067 *Latitude:* -70.7682

TALBOT LADY
Launched in 1986, the skipjack Talbot Lady is a working vessel on Chesapeake Bay. *City:* Canton *State:* NJ *Visitors welcome?* No *Operated by:* Private owner *NR?* No *NHL?* No *Year established/built:* 1986 *Latitude:* 39.4709 *Latitude:* -75.4149

THOMAS E. LANNON
The schooner Thomas E. Lannon offers two-hour sails from Seven Seas Wharf at the Gloucester House Restaurant, Rogers Street, Gloucester from mid-May through the end of October. *Address:* 63 Rogers St. *City:* Gloucester *State:* MA *Zip:* 01930 *Phone:* 978-281-6634 *Web:* www.schooner.org *Email:* info@schooner.org *Visitors welcome?* Yes *Hours:* Contact attraction directly *Admission:* Contact attraction directly *Operated by:* Schooner Thomas E. Lannon *NR?* No *NHL?* No *Year established/built:* 1997 *Latitude:* 42.6110 *Latitude:* -70.6633

THOMAS W. CLYDE
Launched in 1911, the skipjack Thomas W. Clyde is a working vessel on Chesapeake Bay. *City:* Tilghman Island *State:* MD *Visitors welcome?* No *Operated by:* Private owner *NR?* Yes *NHL?* No *Year established/built:* 1911 *Latitude:* 38.7037 *Latitude:* -76.3386

TIMBERWIND
Launched in 1931, the gaff schooner Timberwind is now an excursion vessel. *Address:* Rockport Harbor *City:* Rockport *State:* ME *Zip:* 04856 *Phone:* 207-236-0801 *Toll-free:* 800-759-9250 *Web:* www.schoonertimberwind.com *Email:* info@schoonertimberwind.com *Visitors welcome?* Yes *Hours:* Contact attraction directly *Admission:* Contact attraction directly *Operated by:* Schooner Timberwind *NR?* Yes *NHL?* No *Year established/built:* 1931 *Latitude:* 44.1781 *Latitude:* -69.1676

TOLE MOUR
Launched in 1988, the schooner Tole Mour is a sail training and educational excursion vessel. *City:* Long Beach *State:* CA *Zip:* 90802 *Phone:* 310-508-0952 *Web:* www.tolemour.org *Visitors welcome?* Yes *Hours:* Contact attraction directly *Admission:* Contact attraction directly *Operated by:* CIMI Tall Ship Expeditions *NR?* No *NHL?* No *Year established/built:* 1988 *Latitude:* 33.7687 *Latitude:* -118.1880

TREE OF LIFE
Launched in 1991, the schooner Tree of Life is a sail training and excursion vessel. *Address:* 443 Bellevue Ave. *City:* Newport *State:* RI *Zip:* 02840 *Phone:* 401-640-9777 *Web:* www.schoonertreeoflife.com *Email:* johnon-

CHAPTER 1 – SHIPS

tree@aol.com *Visitors welcome?* Yes *Hours:* Contact attraction directly *Admission:* Contact attraction directly *Operated by:* Schooner Tree of Life *NR?* No *NHL?* No *Year established/built:* 1991 *Latitude:* 41.4736 *Latitude:* -71.3086

VENTURA
Launched in 1922, the centerboard cutter Ventura is now an excursion vessel. *Address:* World Financial Center, North Cove Marina *City:* New York *State:* NY *Zip:* 10274 *Phone:* 212-786-1204 *Web:* sailnewyork.com *Email:* ventura@sailnewyork.com *Visitors welcome?* Yes *Hours:* Contact attraction directly *Admission:* Contact attraction directly *Operated by:* Atlantic Sail and Charter *NR?* No *NHL?* No *Year established/built:* 1922 *Latitude:* 40.7131 *Latitude:* -74.0286

VICTORY CHIMES
Launched in 1900, the three-masted ram schooner Victory Chimes is now an excursion vessel. *Address:* Foot of Tillson Avenue *City:* Rockland *State:* ME *Phone:* 800-745-5651 *Web:* www.victorychimes.com *Email:* info@victorychimes.com *Visitors welcome?* Yes *Hours:* Contact attraction directly *Admission:* Contact attraction directly *Operated by:* Victory Chimes *NR?* Yes *NHL?* Yes *Year established/built:* 1900 *Latitude:* 44.1044 *Latitude:* -69.1054

VIRGINIA
Launched in 2004, the schooner Virginia is a recreation of a typical Chesapeake Bay pilot schooner. It operates as a sail training and living history education vessel. *Address:* 500 E. Main Street *City:* Norfolk *State:* VA *Zip:* 23510 *Phone:* 757-627-7400 *Web:* www.schoonervirginia.org *Email:* jon@schoonervirginia.org *Visitors welcome?* Yes *Hours:* Contact attraction directly *Admission:* Contact attraction directly *Operated by:* Virginia Maritime Heritage Foundation *NR?* No *NHL?* No *Year established/built:* 2004 *Latitude:* 36.8458 *Latitude:* -76.2883

VIRGINIA W
Launched in 1904, the skipjack Virginia W is a working vessel on Chesapeake Bay. *City:* Kinsale *State:* VA *Visitors welcome?* No *Operated by:* Private owner *NR?* Yes *NHL?* No *Year established/built:* 1904 *Latitude:* 38.0296 *Latitude:* -76.5808

VIXEN
Launched in 1930, the clamboat Vixen is an operational museum vessel. *Address:* 86 West Ave. *City:* West Sayville *State:* NY *Zip:* 11796 *Phone:* 631-854-4974 *Web:* www.limaritime.org *Email:* limm@limaritime.org *Visitors welcome?* Yes *Hours:* Monday to Saturday: 10 a.m. to 4 p.m.; Sunday, noon to 4 p.m. *Admission:* $4 adults, $2 senior/child three to 17, under three FREE *Operated by:* Long Island Maritime Museum *NR?* No *NHL?* No *Year established/built:* 1930 *Latitude:* 40.7218 *Latitude:* -73.0938

WAVERTREE
Launched in 1885, the ship Wavertree is now a floating exhibit. *Address:* 12 Fulton St. *City:* New York *State:* NY *Zip:* 10038 *Phone:* 212-748-8600 *Web:* www.southstreetseaportmuseum.org *Email:* info@southstseaport.org *Visitors welcome?* Yes *Hours:* November-March: Friday to Sunday, 10 a.m. to 5 p.m.; Monday 10am-5pm: Schermerhorn Row galleries only. Tuesday to Sunday 10 a.m. to 6 p.m: All galleries and ships open *Admission:* $10 adults, $8 students/seniors, $5 children 5-12, under 5 FREE *Operated by:* South Street Seaport Museum *NR?* Yes *NHL?* No *Year established/built:* 1885 *Latitude:* 40.7066 *Latitude:* -74.0034

WELCOME
Launched in 1976 and rebuilt in 2007, the armed sloop replica Welcome is a sailing training and living history education vessel on the Great Lakes. *Address:* 13268 S. West Bayshore Dr *City:* Traverse City *State:* MI *Zip:* 49684 *Phone:* 231-946-2647 *Web:* www.maritimeheritagealliance.org *Email:*

mark@maritimeheritagealliance.org *Visitors welcome?* Yes *Hours:* Contact attraction directly *Admission:* Contact attraction directly *Operated by:* Maritime Heritage Alliance *NR?* No *NHL?* No *Year established/built:* 1976 *Latitude:* 45.3593 *Latitude:* -85.0713

WENDAMEEN
Launched in 1912, the gaff-rigged schooner yacht Wendameen is now an excursion vessel. *Address:* Maine State Pier, 56 Commercial St. *City:* Portland *State:* ME *Zip:* 04101 *Phone:* 207-766-2500 *Toll-free:* 877-246-6637 *Web:* www.portlandschooner.com *Email:* scott@portlandschooner.com *Visitors welcome?* Yes *Hours:* Contact attraction directly *Admission:* Contact attraction directly *Operated by:* Portland Schooner Company *NR?* Yes *NHL?* No *Year established/built:* 1912 *Latitude:* 43.6577 *Latitude:* -70.2500

WESTERN UNION
Launched in 1939, the schooner Western Union is an operational museum vessel. *Address:* Truman Waterfront *City:* Key West *State:* FL *Phone:* 305-292-1766 *Web:* www.schoonerwesternunion.com *Visitors welcome?* Yes *Hours:* Contact attraction directly *Admission:* Contact attraction directly *Operated by:* Schooner Western Union Preservation Society *NR?* No *NHL?* No *Year established/built:* 1939 *Latitude:* 24.5557 *Latitude:* -81.7826

WESTWARD
Launched in 1961, the schooner Westward is a sail traiing and excursion vessel. *Address:* 29 McKown St. *City:* Boothbay Harbor *State:* ME *Zip:* 04538 *Phone:* 207-633-2750 *Toll-free:* 800-724-7245 *Web:* www.oceanclassroom.org *Email:* mail@oceanclassroom.org *Visitors welcome?* Yes *Hours:* Contact attraction directly *Admission:* Contact attraction directly *Operated by:* Ocean Classroom Foundation *NR?* No *NHL?* No *Year established/built:* 1961 *Latitude:* 43.8404 *Latitude:* -69.6459

WILLIAM H. ALBURY
Launched in 1964, the schooner William H. Albury is a sail training and excursion vessel. *Address:* 3145 Virginia St. *City:* Coconut Grove *State:* FL *Zip:* 33133 *Phone:* 305-442-9697 *Web:* www.heritageschooner.com *Email:* heritage2@mindspring.com *Visitors welcome?* Yes *Hours:* Contact attraction directly *Admission:* Contact attraction directly *Operated by:* Heritage Schooner Cruises *NR?* No *NHL?* No *Year established/built:* 1964 *Latitude:* 25.7328 *Latitude:* -80.2414

WILMA LEE
Launched in 1940, the skipjack Wilma Lee is a working vessel on Chesapeake Bay. *City:* Kinsale *State:* VA *Visitors welcome?* No *Operated by:* Private owner *NR?* Yes *NHL?* No *Year established/built:* 1940 *Latitude:* 38.0296 *Latitude:* -76.5808

WINDY
Launched in 1996, the schooner Windy is a sail training and excursion vessel. *Address:* 600 E. Grand Ave., Navy Pier *City:* Chicago *State:* IL *Zip:* 60611 *Phone:* 312-595-5555 *Web:* www.tallshipwindy.com *Email:* tallshipwindy@aol.com *Visitors welcome?* Yes *Hours:* Contact attraction directly *Admission:* Contact attraction directly *Operated by:* Windy of Chicago *NR?* No *NHL?* No *Year established/built:* 1996 *Latitude:* 41.8919 *Latitude:* -87.6041

WM. B. TENNISON
Launched in 1899, the buyboat Wm B. Tennison is now an operational museum vessel. *Address:* State Route 2 *City:* Solomons *State:* MD *Zip:* 20688 *Phone:* 410-326-2042 *Web:* www.calvertmarinemuseum.com *Email:* mccormmj@co.cal.md.us *Visitors welcome?* Yes *Hours:* Daily, 10 a.m to 5 p.m. *Admission:* $7 adults, $6 seniors, $2 children 5 to 12; under five FREE *Operated by:* Calvert Marine Museum *NR?* Yes *NHL?* Yes *Year established/built:* 1899 *Latitude:* 38.3332 *Latitude:* -76.4720

CHAPTER 1 – SHIPS

WOODWIND
Launched in 1993, the schooner Woodwind and her sister Woodwind II are sail training and excursion vessel. *Address:* 80 Compromise St. *City:* Annapolis *State:* MD *Zip:* 21401 *Phone:* 410-263-7837 *Web:* www.schoonerwoodwind.com *Email:* info@schoonerwoodwind.com *Visitors welcome?* Yes *Hours:* Contact attraction directly *Admission:* Contact attraction directly *Operated by:* Running Free *NR?* No *NHL?* No *Year established/built:* 1993 *Latitude:* 38.9756 *Latitude:* -76.4859

WOODWIND II
Launched in 1993, the schooner Woodwind and her sister Woodwind II are sail training and excursion vessel. *Address:* 80 Compromise St. *City:* Annapolis *State:* MD *Zip:* 21401 *Phone:* 410-263-7837 *Web:* www.schoonerwoodwind.com *Email:* info@schoonerwoodwind.com *Visitors welcome?* Yes *Hours:* Contact attraction directly *Admission:* Contact attraction directly *Operated by:* Running Free *NR?* No *NHL?* No *Year established/built:* 1993 *Latitude:* 38.9756 *Latitude:* -76.4859

YANKEE CLIPPER
Launched in 1941, the ketch Yankee Clipper is a sail training vessel that works with the Sea Scouts. *Address:* Fisherman's Terminal *City:* Seattle *State:* WA *Phone:* 206-947-6199 *Web:* www.tallshiptraining.org *Email:* info@tallshiptraining.org *Visitors welcome?* Yes *Hours:* Contact attraction directly *Admission:* Contact attraction directly *Operated by:* Yankee Clipper Foundation *NR?* No *NHL?* No *Year established/built:* 1941 *Latitude:* 47.6062 *Latitude:* -122.3320

 ZODIAC
Launched in 1924, the schooner Zodiac is now an excursion vessel. *Address:* N. Northlake Way and N. Northlake Pl *City:* Seattle *State:* WA *Web:* www.schoonerzodiac.com *Email:* info@schoonerzodiac.com *Visitors welcome?* Yes *Hours:* Contact attraction directly *Admission:* Contact attraction directly *Operated by:* Vessel Zodiac Corporation *NR?* Yes *NHL?* No *Year established/built:* 1924 *Latitude:* 47.6470 *Latitude:* -122.3380

TUGBOATS & TOWBOATS

Sand Man (Olympia, Wash.)

37

CHAPTER 1 – SHIPS

ARTHUR FOSS
Launched in 1889, the tug Arthur Foss is a floating museum and exhibit in Seattle. *Address:* 860 Terry Ave. N. *City:* Seattle *State:* WA *Zip:* 98109 *Phone:* 206-447-9800 *Web:* www.nwseaport.org *Email:* seaport@oz.net *Visitors welcome?* Yes *Hours:* Contact attraction directly *Admission:* Donation *Operated by:* Northwest Seaport Maritime Heritage Ctr *NR?* No *NHL?* Yes *Year established/built:* 1889 *Latitude:* 47.6276 *Latitude:* -122.3370

BALTIMORE
Launched in 1906, the steam tug Baltimore is an operational museum ship. *Address:* 1415 Key Highway *City:* Baltimore *State:* MD *Zip:* 21230 *Phone:* 410-727-4818 *Web:* www.steamtug.org *Email:* Sgheaver@aol.com *Visitors welcome?* Yes *Hours:* Contact attraction directly *Admission:* Contact attraction directly *Operated by:* Baltimore and Chesapeake Steamboat Company *NR?* Yes *NHL?* Yes *Year established/built:* 1906 *Latitude:* 39.2742 *Latitude:* -76.6012

BARBARA H
Launched in 1923, the sternwheeler towboat Barbara H, formerly Donald B., is a floating exhibit and excursion vessel on the Ohio River. To visit, please call for an appointment. *Address:* Ohio River Mile 546 *City:* Lamb *State:* IN *Phone:* 812-427-9480 *Web:* www.hspsi.org *Email:* info@hspsi.org *Visitors welcome?* Yes *Hours:* Contact attraction directly *Admission:* Contact attraction directly *Operated by:* Historic Sternwheeler Preservation Society *NR?* Yes *NHL?* Yes *Year established/built:* 1923 *Latitude:* 38.6920 *Latitude:* -85.1880

BUDDY O.
Launched in 1936, the fishing tug Buddy O. is a dry-berth exhibit at the Rogers Street Fishing Village Museum. *Address:* 2010 Rogers St. *City:* Two Rivers *State:* WI *Zip:* 54241 *Phone:* 920-793-5905 *Web:* www.rogersstreet.com *Email:* szipperer@rogersstreet.com *Visitors welcome?* Yes *Hours:* May to October: Daily, 10 a.m. to 4 p.m. *Admission:* $4 adults, $2 children under 16 *Operated by:* Rogers Street Fishing Village & Great Lakes Coast Guard Museum *NR?* No *NHL?* No *Year established/built:* 1936 *Latitude:* 44.1518 *Latitude:* -87.5626

BUFFALO
Launched in 1923, the steam tug Buffalo is now undergoing restoration. *City:* Waterford *State:* NY *Zip:* 12188 *Web:* www.waterfordmaritime.org *Email:* info@waterfordmaritime.org *Visitors welcome?* Yes *Hours:* Contact attraction directly *Admission:* Contact attraction directly *Operated by:* Waterford Maritime Historical Society *NR?* No *NHL?* No *Year established/built:* 1923 *Latitude:* 42.7926 *Latitude:* -73.6812

Share your favorite tugboat photos on the Fyddeye website at www.fyddeye.com.

C.L. CHURCHILL
The tug C.L. Churchill, built in 1964, assists operations of the Lake Champlain Maritime Museum's schooner Lois McClure. The tug is based in Burlington. *Address:* 4472 Basin Harbor Rd. *City:* Vergennes *State:* VT *Zip:* 05491 *Phone:* 802-475-2022 *Web:* www.lcmm.org *Email:* info@lcmm.org *Visitors welcome?* Yes *Hours:* Contact attraction directly *Admission:* Contact attraction directly *Operated by:* Lake Champlain Maritime Museum *NR?* No *NHL?* No *Year established/built:* 1964 *Latitude:* 44.1973 *Latitude:* -73.3567

CATAWISSA
Launched in 1896, the steam tug Catawissa is undergoing restoration. *Address:* 300 Greenkill Ave. *City:* Kingston *State:* NY *Zip:* 12401 *Phone:* 845-340-0506 *Web:* www.tugmuseum.com *Email:* steve@tugmuseum.com *Visitors welcome?* No *Hours:* Contact attraction directly *Admission:* Contact attraction directly *Operated by:*

North River Tugboat Museum *NR?* No *NHL?* No *Year established/built:* 1896 *Latitude:* 41.9230 *Latitude:* -74.0155

CHALLENGER
Launched in 1944, the tug Challenger is now a "bunk and breakfast." *Address:* 1001 Fairview Ave. N. *City:* Seattle *State:* WA *Zip:* 98109 *Phone:* 206-340-1201 *Visitors welcome?* Yes *Hours:* Contact attraction directly *Admission:* Contact attraction directly *Operated by:* MV Challenger Bunk and Breakfast *NR?* No *NHL?* No *Year established/built:* 1944 *Latitude:* 47.6290 *Latitude:* -122.3320

CHANCELLOR
Launched in 1938, the tug Chancellor is a floating museum under the care of the Waterford Maritime Historical Society. *Address:* 300 Greenkill Ave. *City:* Kingston *State:* NY *Zip:* 12401 *Phone:* 845-340-0506 *Web:* www.waterfordmaritime.org *Email:* info@waterfordmaritime.org *Visitors welcome?* Yes *Hours:* Contact attraction directly *Admission:* Contact attraction directly *Operated by:* Waterford Maritime Historical Society *NR?* Yes *NHL?* No *Year established/built:* 1938 *Latitude:* 41.9230 *Latitude:* -74.0155

CHARLEY BORDER
The towboat Charley Border is a floating exhibit at the Arkansas River Historical Society Museum. *Address:* 5350 Cimarron Road *City:* Catoosa *State:* OK *Zip:* 74015 *Phone:* 918-266-2291 *Web:* www.tulsaweb.com *Email:* museum@tulsaport.com *Visitors welcome?* Yes *Hours:* Monday to Friday, 8:30 a.m. to 4:30 p.m. *Admission:* FREE *Operated by:* Arkansas River Historical Society *NR?* No *NHL?* No *Year established/built:* 1971 *Latitude:* 36.2312 *Latitude:* -95.7417

CHARLOTTE
Launched in 1880, the tug Charlotte is an operational museum vessel. *Address:* 86 West Ave. *City:* West Sayville *State:* NY *Zip:* 11796 *Phone:* 631-854-4974 *Web:* www.limaritime.org *Email:* limm@limaritime.org *Visitors welcome?* Yes *Hours:* Monday to Saturday: 10 a.m. to 4 p.m.; Sunday, noon to 4 p.m. *Admission:* $4 adults, $2 senior/child three to 17, under three FREE *Operated by:* Long Island Maritime Museum *NR?* No *NHL?* No *Year established/built:* 1880 *Latitude:* 40.7218 *Latitude:* -73.0938

CHICKAMAUGA
Address: 1515 Fairview Avenue East *City:* Seattle *State:* WA *Visitors welcome?* Yes *NR?* No *NHL?* No *Year established/built:* 1915 *Latitude:* 47.6330 *Latitude:* -122.3280

CLAIRE E
Launched in 1926, the towboat Claire E is now a residence and a bed & breakfast. *Address:* 127 Ohio St. *City:* Marietta *State:* OH *Zip:* 45750 *Phone:* 614-374-2233 *Visitors welcome?* Yes *Hours:* Contact attraction directly *Admission:* Contact attraction directly *Operated by:* Private owner *NR?* No *NHL?* No *Year established/built:* 1926 *Latitude:* 39.4109 *Latitude:* -81.4505

 COMANCHE
Launched in 1944, the tug Comanche is undergoing restoration near Olympia, Wash. *Address:* 660 West Ewing St. *City:* Seattle *State:* WA *Zip:* 98119 *Visitors welcome?* Yes *Hours:* Contact attraction directly *Admission:* Contact attraction directly *Operated by:* Comanche 202 Foundation *NR?* No *NHL?* No *Year established/built:* 1944 *Latitude:* 47.6528 *Latitude:* -122.3660

DEKAURY
Launched in 1943, the tug DeKaury is an operational museum vessel on San Francisco Bay. *City:* San Francisco *State:* CA *Web:* www.hters.org *Email:* info@hters.org *Visitors welcome?* Yes *Hours:* Contact

CHAPTER 1 – SHIPS

attraction directly *Admission:* Contact attraction directly *Operated by:* Historic Tugboat Restoration and Education Society *NR?* No *NHL?* No *Year established/built:* 1943 *Latitude:* 37.7749 *Latitude:* -122.4190

DELAWARE
The tugboat Delaware is a product of area boatbuilding at the beginning of the 19th century, and apart from the 1900 ram schooner Victory Chimes, may be the only survivor of that yard. *Address:* 213 N. Talbot Street *City:* St. Michaels *State:* MD *Zip:* 21663 *Phone:* 410-745-2916 *Web:* www.cbmm.org *Email:* cbland@cbmm.org *Visitors welcome?* Yes *Hours:* Daily, hours vary by season *Admission:* $13 adults; $10 seniors over 62; $6 kids 6 to 17; kids under 6 FREE *Operated by:* Chesapeake Bay Maritime Museum *NR?* No *NHL?* No *Year established/built:* 1912 *Latitude:* 38.7876 *Latitude:* -76.2249

EDNA G
Launched in 1896, the tug Edna G. is a floating exhibit in Two Harbors, Minn. *Address:* 522 First Ave. *City:* Two Harbors *State:* MN *Zip:* 55616 *Phone:* 218-834-4898 *Visitors welcome?* Yes *Hours:* Contact attraction directly *Admission:* Contact attraction directly *Operated by:* City of Two Harbors *NR?* Yes *NHL?* No *Year established/built:* 1896 *Latitude:* 47.0198 *Latitude:* -91.6696

ELISE ANN CONNORS
Launched in 1881, the tug Elise Ann Connors is privately owned. *Address:* PO Box 1065 *City:* Port Ewen *State:* NY *Zip:* 12466 *Phone:* 914-339-1052 *Visitors welcome?* No *Operated by:* Private owner *NR?* No *NHL?* No *Year established/built:* 1881 *Latitude:* 41.9105 *Latitude:* -73.9845

EPPLETON HALL
Launched in 1914, the paddle tug Eppleton Hall is now a museum ship at the San Francisco Maritime National Historical Park. *Address:* San Francisco Maritime National Historical Park *City:* San Francisco *State:* CA *Zip:* 94123 *Phone:* 415-561-7000 *Web:* www.nps.gov/safr/ *Visitors welcome?* Yes *Hours:* $5.00 *Admission:* Contact attraction directly *Operated by:* San Francisco Maritime National Historical Park *NR?* No *NHL?* No *Year established/built:* 1914 *Latitude:* 37.8070 *Latitude:* -122.4220

F.D. RUSSELL
Launched in 1939, the owners of the tug F. D. Russell also own and operated the Ponce de Leon Inlet Lighthouse. *Address:* 4931 South Peninsula Drive *City:* Ponce Inlet *State:* FL *Zip:* 32127 *Phone:* 386-761-1821 *Web:* www.ponceinlet.org *Visitors welcome?* Yes *Hours:* Contact attraction directly *Admission:* Contact attraction directly *Operated by:* Ponce de Leon Inlet Light Station Preservation Association *NR?* No *NHL?* No *Year established/built:* 1938 *Latitude:* 29.0807 *Latitude:* -80.9281

FRANCES TURACAMO
Launched in 1957, the tug Frances Turacamo is undergoing restoration. *Address:* 300 Greenkill Ave. *City:* Kingston *State:* NY *Zip:* 12401 *Phone:* 845-340-0506 *Web:* www.tugmuseum.com *Email:* steve@tugmuseum.com *Visitors welcome?* No *Hours:* Contact attraction directly *Admission:* Contact attraction directly *Operated by:* North River Tugboat Museum *NR?* No *NHL?* No *Year established/built:* 1957 *Latitude:* 41.9230 *Latitude:* -74.0155

GEORGE M. VERITY
Launched in 1927, the river towboat George M. Verity is a dry-berth exhibit at Victory Park on the Mississippi River. *Address:* 415 Blondeau St. *City:* Keokuk *State:* IA *Zip:* 52632 *Phone:* 319-524-2050 *Web:* www.geomverity.org *Visitors welcome?* Yes *Hours:* Memorial Day to Labor Day, daily, 9 a.m. to 5 p.m. *Admission:* $4 adults, $3 seniors, $2 children eight to 18, under eight FREE *Operated by:* Verity Museum Commission *NR?* Yes *NHL?* Yes *Year established/built:* 1927 *Latitude:* 40.3958 *Latitude:* -91.3815

CHAPTER 1 – SHIPS

HELEN MCALLISTER
Launched in 1900, the tug Helen McAllister is a floating exhibit at the South Street Seaport Museum. *Address:* 12 Fulton St. *City:* New York *State:* NY *Zip:* 10038 *Phone:* 212-748-8600 *Web:* www.southstreetseaportmuseum.org *Email:* info@southstseaport.org *Visitors welcome?* Yes *Hours:* November-March: Friday to Sunday, 10 a.m. to 5 p.m.; Monday 10am-5pm: Schermerhorn Row galleries only. Tuesday to Sunday 10 a.m. to 6 p.m: All galleries and ships open *Admission:* $10 adults, $8 students/seniors, $5 children 5-12, under 5 FREE *Operated by:* South Street Seaport Museum *NR?* No *NHL?* No *Year established/built:* 1900 *Latitude:* 40.7066 *Latitude:* -74.0034

 HERCULES
Launched in 1907, the steam tug Hercules is now a museum ship at the San Francisco Maritime National Historical Park. *Address:* San Francisco Maritime National Historical Park *City:* San Francisco *State:* CA *Zip:* 94123 *Phone:* 415-561-7000 *Web:* www.nps.gov/safr/ *Visitors welcome?* Yes *Hours:* $5.00 *Admission:* Contact attraction directly *Operated by:* San Francisco Maritime National Historical Park *NR?* Yes *NHL?* Yes *Year established/built:* 1907 *Latitude:* 37.8070 *Latitude:* -122.4220

HOGA
Launched in May 1941, the service tug USS Hoga took part in the defense of Pearl Harbor December 7, 1941. *Address:* 120 Riverfront Park Dr. *City:* North Little Rock *State:* AR *Zip:* 72114 *Phone:* 501-371-8320 *Web:* www.aimm.museum *Email:* info@aimm.museum *Visitors welcome?* Yes *Hours:* Friday, 10 a.m. to 6 p.m.; Saturday, 10 a.m. to 6 p.m.; Sunday, 1 p.m. to 6 p.m. *Admission:* Contact attraction directly *Operated by:* Arkansas Inland Maritime Museum *NR?* Yes *NHL?* Yes *Year established/built:* 1941 *Latitude:* 34.7541 *Latitude:* -92.2681

HOPE
The fishing tug Hope was built in 1930 by the Sturgeon Bay Boat Works and operated in Lake Michigan until 1992. Along with the Hope is the remake of a net shed complete with fishing boxes, a net reel, and other traditional fishing supplies. *Address:* 12724 E Wisconsin Bay Rd *City:* Gills Rock *State:* WI *Zip:* 54210 *Phone:* 920-854-1844 *Web:* www.dcmm.org *Email:* info@dcmm.org *Visitors welcome?* Yes *Hours:* Daily, 10 a.m. to 5 p.m. *Admission:* $4.50 adults, $1.50 children *Operated by:* Door County Maritime Museum & Lighthouse Preservation Society *NR?* No *NHL?* No *Year established/built:* 1930 *Latitude:* 45.2905 *Latitude:* -87.0095

HUNTINGTON
Launched in 1933, the tug Huntington visits the Nauticus museum in Norfolk for tours and activities. *Address:* 333 Waterside Dr. *City:* Norfolk *State:* VA *Zip:* 23510 *Phone:* 757-627-4884 *Visitors welcome?* Yes *Hours:* Contact attraction directly *Admission:* Contact attraction directly *Operated by:* Tugboat Museum *NR?* No *NHL?* No *Year established/built:* 1933 *Latitude:* 36.8442 *Latitude:* -76.2878

ISLAY
Launched in 1892, the shipyard tug Islay is undergoing restoration in Milwaukee. *City:* Milwaukee *State:* WI *Web:* www.northeasternmaritime.org *Email:* contact@northeasternmaritime.org *Visitors welcome?* Yes *Hours:* Contact attraction directly *Admission:* Contact attraction directly *Operated by:* Northeastern Maritime Historical Foundation *NR?* No *NHL?* No *Year established/built:* 1892 *Latitude:* 43.0389 *Latitude:* -87.9065

JOHN PURVES
Launched in 1919, the tug John Purves is an historic vessel berthed near the Door County Maritime Museum. *Address:* 120 N. Madison Ave. *City:* Sturgeon Bay *State:* WI *Zip:* 54235 *Phone:* 920-743-5958 *Web:* www.dcmm.org *Email:* info@dcmm.org *Visitors welcome?* Yes *Hours:* Wednesday, Friday, Saturday, Sunday, 11 a.m.

CHAPTER 1 – SHIPS

to 3 p.m. *Admission:* $5 *Operated by:* Door County Maritime Museum & Lighthouse Preservation Society *NR?* No *NHL?* No *Year established/built:* 1919 *Latitude:* 44.8301 *Latitude:* -87.3844

JOSIAH WHITE II
The replica towboat Josiah White II is a passenger excursion vessel that is part of the National Canal Museum. *Address:* 30 Centre Square *City:* Easton *State:* PA *Zip:* 18042 *Phone:* 610-559-6613 *Web:* canals.org *Email:* toms@canals.org *Visitors welcome?* Yes *Hours:* Contact attraction directly *Admission:* Contact attraction directly *Operated by:* National Canal Museum *NR?* No *NHL?* No *Latitude:* 40.6912 *Latitude:* -75.2099

 JUPITER
Launched in 1902, the tug Jupiter is now an operating museum ship. *Address:* Foot of Market Street *City:* Philadelphia *State:* PA *Zip:* 19106 *Phone:* 215-238-0280 *Web:* www.gazela.org *Email:* office@gazela.org *Visitors welcome?* Yes *Hours:* Contact attraction directly *Admission:* Contact attraction directly *Operated by:* Philadelphia Ship Preservation Guild *NR?* No *NHL?* No *Year established/built:* 1902 *Latitude:* 39.9505 *Latitude:* -75.1481

K WHITTELSEY
Launched in 1930, the tug K Whittelsey is undergoing restoration. *Address:* 300 Greenkill Ave. *City:* Kingston *State:* NY *Zip:* 12401 *Phone:* 845-340-0506 *Web:* www.tugmuseum.com *Email:* steve@tugmuseum.com *Visitors welcome?* No *Hours:* Contact attraction directly *Admission:* Contact attraction directly *Operated by:* North River Tugboat Museum *NR?* No *NHL?* No *Year established/built:* 1930 *Latitude:* 41.9230 *Latitude:* -74.0155

KINGSTON II
The harbor tug Kingston II is thought to be one of the earliest all-welded vessels. *Address:* 75 Greenmanville Avenue *City:* Mystic *State:* CT *Zip:* 06355 *Phone:* 860-572-5315 *Web:* www.mysticseaport.org *Visitors welcome?* Yes *Hours:* Daily, April to October, 9 a.m. to 5 p.m.; November to March, 10 a.m. to 4 p.m. *Admission:* Adults, $18.50; Seniors, $16.50; Children 6-17, $13; Under six, FREE *Operated by:* Mystic Seaport *NR?* No *NHL?* No *Year established/built:* 1930 *Latitude:* 41.362992 *Latitude:* -71.963389

LOGSDON
Launched in 1941, the towboat Logsdon is a dry-berth exhibit at the Mississippi River Museum. The Logsdon, formerly owned by Ray Logsdon of the Logsdon River Construction Co., saw most of its service on the Illinois River pushing pile-driving equipment. The vessel was acquired by the museum in 1989. *Address:* 350 East Third St. *City:* Dubuque *State:* IA *Zip:* 52001 *Phone:* 563-557-9545 *Toll-free:* 800-226-3369 *Web:* www.mississippirivermuseum.com *Visitors welcome?* Yes *Hours:* Memorial Day weekend through October: Daily, 9 a.m. to 5 p.m.; November through Memorial Day weekend: Daily, 10 a.m. to 5 p.m. *Admission:* $10.50 adults, $9.50 seniors, $8 youth seven to 17, $4.50 children three to six, under three FREE *Operated by:* Dubuque County Historical Society *NR?* No *NHL?* No *Year established/built:* 1941 *Latitude:* 42.4963 *Latitude:* -90.6591

LONE STAR
Launched in 1868, the towboat Lone Star is a dry-berth exhibit at the Buffalo Bill Museum in Le Claire. *Address:* 199 N. Front St. *City:* Le Claire *State:* IA *Zip:* 52753 *Phone:* 563-289-5580 *Web:* www.buffalobillmuseumleclaire.com *Email:* museum@buffalobillmuseumleclaire.com *Visitors welcome?* Yes *Hours:* Monday to Saturday, 9 a.m. to 5 p.m.; Sunday, noon to 5 p.m. *Admission:* $5 adults, $1 children *Operated by:* Buffalo Bill Museum *NR?* Yes *NHL?* Yes *Year established/built:* 1868 *Latitude:* 41.5976 *Latitude:* -90.3432

CHAPTER 1 – SHIPS

LORETTA HOWARD
Launched in 1929, the sternwheel towboat Loretta Howard is undergoing restoration. To visit, please call ahead for an appointment. *Address:* Ohio River Mile 546 *City:* Lamb *State:* IN *Phone:* 812-427-9480 *Web:* www.hspsi.org *Email:* info@hspsi.org *Visitors welcome?* Yes *Hours:* Contact attraction directly *Admission:* Contact attraction directly *Operated by:* Historic Sternwheeler Preservation Society *NR?* No *NHL?* No *Year established/built:* 1929 *Latitude:* 38.6920 *Latitude:* -85.1880

LUDINGTON
Launched in 1944, the tug Ludington is a floating exhibit in Kewaunee Harbor. *Address:* Port of Kewaunee *City:* Kewaunee *State:* WI *Zip:* 54216 *Phone:* 920-388-5000 *Web:* www.cityofkewaunee.org/content/recreation/tug/tugludington.shtml *Email:* info@cityofkewaunee.org *Visitors welcome?* Yes *Hours:* Contact attraction directly *Admission:* Contact attraction directly *Operated by:* City of Kewaunee *NR?* No *NHL?* No *Year established/built:* 1944 *Latitude:* 44.4583 *Latitude:* -87.5031

LUNA
Launched in 1930, the tugboat Luna is a museum ship undergoing restoration in the Boston area. *Address:* Commonwealth Pier *City:* Boston *State:* MA *Zip:* 02446 *Phone:* 617-282-1941 *Web:* www.tugboatluna.org *Email:* info@tugboatluna.org *Visitors welcome?* Yes *Hours:* Contact attraction directly *Admission:* Contact attraction directly *Operated by:* Luna Preservation Society *NR?* No *NHL?* Yes *Year established/built:* 1930 *Latitude:* 42.3422 *Latitude:* -71.1241

MATHILDA
Launched in 1899, the tug Mathilda is a dry-berth exhibit at the Hudson River Maritime Museum. *Address:* 50 Rondout Landing *City:* Kingston *State:* NY *Zip:* 12401 *Phone:* 845-338-0071 *Web:* www.hrmm.org *Email:* hrmm@hvc.rr.com *Visitors welcome?* Yes *Hours:* May to October: Thursday, Friday, Saturday, Sunday, and Monday: 11 a.m. to 5 p.m.; Call for winter hours *Admission:* $5 adults; $4 seniors, children 6 to 12; 5 under, FREE *Operated by:* Hudson River Maritime Museum *NR?* No *NHL?* No *Year established/built:* 1899 *Latitude:* 41.9235 *Latitude:* -73.9836

MAUD
The 40-foot diesel towboat Maud is part of the collection of the Mississippi River Museum. It once operated on the Illinois River and is an example of 20th century commercial river craft. *Address:* 350 East Third St. *City:* Dubuque *State:* IA *Zip:* 52001 *Phone:* 563-557-9545 *Toll-free:* 800-226-3369 *Web:* www.mississippirivermuseum.com *Visitors welcome?* Yes *Hours:* Memorial Day weekend through October: Daily, 9 a.m. to 5 p.m.; November through Memorial Day weekend: Daily, 10 a.m. to 5 p.m. *Admission:* $10.50 adults, $9.50 seniors, $8 youth seven to 17, $4.50 children three to six, under three FREE *Operated by:* Dubuque County Historical Society *NR?* No *NHL?* No *Latitude:* 42.4963 *Latitude:* -90.6591

MAZAPETA
Mazapeta is a former U.S. Navy tug/fire boat built in 1943. She is used to educate people about World War II and the importance of tugboats. *Address:* Alameda Naval Air Station *City:* Alameda *State:* CA *Phone:* 650-483-1963 *Web:* www.navsource.org/archives/14/08181.htm *Visitors welcome?* Yes *Hours:* Contact attraction directly *Admission:* Contact attraction directly *NR?* No *NHL?* No *Year established/built:* 1943 *Latitude:* 37.7906 *Latitude:* -122.3260

MIKE FINK
Launched in 1936, the towboat Mike Fink is now a floating restaurant on the Covington riverfront. *Address:* 212 Greenup St. *City:* Covington *State:* KY *Zip:* 41011 *Phone:* 606-261-4212 *Visitors welcome?* Yes *Hours:*

CHAPTER 1 – SHIPS

Contact attraction directly *Admission:* Contact attraction directly *Operated by:* Bensons, Inc. *NR?* Yes *NHL?* No *Year established/built:* 1936 *Latitude:* 39.0893 *Latitude:* -84.5082

MOUNT MCKAY
Launched in 1908, the iron tug Mount McKay is undergoing restoration. *City:* Duluth *State:* MN *Web:* www.northeasternmaritime.org *Email:* contact@northeasternmaritime.org *Visitors welcome?* Yes *Hours:* Contact attraction directly *Admission:* Contact attraction directly *Operated by:* Northeastern Maritime Historical Foundation *NR?* No *NHL?* No *Year established/built:* 1908 *Latitude:* 46.7833 *Latitude:* -92.1066

N.Y. CENTRAL NO. 13
Launched in 1887, the tug N.Y. Central No. 83 is undergoing restoration. *Address:* Garpo Marine Trailer *City:* Staten Island *State:* NY *Zip:* 10307 *Phone:* 347-983-4190? *Visitors welcome?* No *Operated by:* Private owner *NR?* No *NHL?* No *Year established/built:* 1887 *Latitude:* 40.5071 *Latitude:* -74.2443

NOKOMIS
Launched in 1939, the tug Nokomis is an operational museum vessel on San Francisco Bay. *City:* San Francisco *State:* CA *Web:* www.hters.org *Email:* info@hters.org *Visitors welcome?* Yes *Hours:* Contact attraction directly *Admission:* Contact attraction directly *Operated by:* Historic Tugboat Restoration and Education Society *NR?* No *NHL?* No *Year established/built:* 1939 *Latitude:* 37.7749 *Latitude:* -122.4190

PAUL BUNYAN
Launched in 1926, the towboat Paul Bunyan is a dry-berth exhibit. *Address:* 36094 Memory Lane *City:* Polson *State:* MT *Zip:* 59860 *Phone:* 406-883-6804 *Web:* www.miracleofamericamuseum.org *Email:* info@MiracleOfAmericaMuseum.org *Visitors welcome?* Yes *Hours:* Summer: Daily, 8 a.m. to 5 p.m.; Rest of the year: Monday to Saturday, 8 a.m. to 5 p.m.; Sunday, 1:30 p.m. to 5 p.m. *Admission:* $5 adults, $4.50 seniors, $2 children three to 12, under three FREE *Operated by:* Miracle of America Museum and Pioneer Village *NR?* No *NHL?* No *Year established/built:* 1926 *Latitude:* 47.6791 *Latitude:* -114.1070

PEGASUS
Launched in 1907, the tug Pegasus is undergoing restoration on New York Harbor. *Address:* 83 Murray Street, No. 4 *City:* New York *State:* NY *Zip:* 10007 *Web:* www.tugpegasus.org *Email:* info@tugpegasus.org *Visitors welcome?* Yes *Hours:* Contact attraction directly *Admission:* Contact attraction directly *Operated by:* Tug Pegasus Preservation Project *NR?* No *NHL?* No *Year established/built:* 1907 *Latitude:* 40.7148 *Latitude:* -74.0110

PORTLAND
Launched in 1947, the ship assist towboat Portland is a floating exhibit. *Address:* 115 SW Ash St. Suite 400C *City:* Portland *State:* OR *Zip:* 97204 *Phone:* 503-224-7724 *Web:* www.oregonmaritimemuseum.org *Email:* info@oregonmaritimemuseum.org *Visitors welcome?* Yes *Hours:* Contact attraction directly *Admission:* Contact attraction directly *Operated by:* Oregon Maritime Center & Museum *NR?* Yes *NHL?* No *Year established/built:* 1947 *Latitude:* 45.5218 *Latitude:* -122.6720

Q.A. GILLMORE
Launched in 1913, the steam tug Q.A. Gillmore is a floating exhibit at the Keewatin Maritime Museum. *Address:* Blue Star Highway and Union St. *City:* Saugatuck *State:* MI *Zip:* 49453 *Phone:* 269-857-2464 *Web:* www.keewatinmaritimemuseum.com *Email:* contact@northeasternmaritime.org *Visitors welcome?* Yes *Hours:* Memorial Day to Labor Day, 10:30 a.m. to 4 p.m. *Admission:* Contact attraction directly *Operated by:* Northeastern Maritime Historical Foundation *NR?* No *NHL?* No *Year established/built:* 1913 *Latitude:* 42.6466 *Latitude:* -86.2025

CHAPTER 1 – SHIPS

REISS
Launched in 1913, the tug Reiss is part of the Keewatin Marine Museum collection. *Address:* Blue Star Highway and Union St. *City:* Saugatuck *State:* MI *Zip:* 49453 *Phone:* 269-857-2464 *Web:* www.keewatinmaritimemuseum.com *Visitors welcome?* Yes *Hours:* Memorial Day to Labor Day, 10:30 a.m. to 4 p.m. *Admission:* Contact attraction directly *Operated by:* Keewatin Maritime Museum *NR?* No *NHL?* No *Year established/built:* 1913 *Latitude:* 42.6466 *Latitude:* -86.2025

 SAND MAN
Launched in 1910, the tug Sand Man is now an operational museum. *Address:* Eastbay Dr NE and Olympia Ave NE *City:* Olympia *State:* WA *Phone:* 360-786-9474 *Web:* www.tugsandman.org *Email:* pderanleau@msn.com *Visitors welcome?* Yes *Hours:* Saturday, Sunday, some holidays; 10 a.m. to 3 p.m. *Admission:* FREE *Operated by:* Sand Man Foundation *NR?* Yes *NHL?* No *Year established/built:* 1910 *Latitude:* 47.0465 *Latitude:* -122.9030

SERGEANT FLOYD
Launched in 1932, the towboat Sergeant Floyd is a dry-berth exhibit and welcome center. *Address:* 1000 Larsen Park Road *City:* Sioux City *State:* IA *Zip:* 51103 *Phone:* 712-279-0198 *Web:* www.siouxcitymuseum.org/sgt_floyd.asp *Email:* scpm@sioux-city.org *Visitors welcome?* Yes *Hours:* Daily, 9 a.m. to 5 p.m. *Admission:* FREE *Operated by:* Sergeant Floyd River Museum & Welcome Center *NR?* Yes *NHL?* Yes *Year established/built:* 1932 *Latitude:* 42.4879 *Latitude:* -96.4004

SNOHOMISH
Launched in 1943, the Coast Guard tug Snohomish is undergoing restoration. *City:* Charleston *State:* SC *Web:* www.northeasternmaritime.org *Email:* contact@northeasternmaritime.org *Visitors welcome?* Yes *Hours:* Contact attraction directly *Admission:* Contact attraction directly *Operated by:* Northeastern Maritime Historical Foundation *NR?* No *NHL?* No *Year established/built:* 1943 *Latitude:* 32.7766 *Latitude:* -79.9309

SPIRIT OF ALGOMA
Launched in 1916, the steam tug Spirit of Algoma is in the collection of the Northeastern Maritime Historical Foundation. *City:* Duluth *State:* MN *Web:* www.northeasternmaritime.org *Email:* contact@northeasternmaritime.org *Visitors welcome?* Yes *Hours:* Contact attraction directly *Admission:* Contact attraction directly *Operated by:* Northeastern Maritime Historical Foundation *NR?* No *NHL?* No *Year established/built:* 1916 *Latitude:* 46.7833 *Latitude:* -92.1066

ST. HELENA III
The towboat St. Helena III is a replica of a freighter that operated on the Ohio & Erie Canal more than a century ago. *Address:* 125 Tuscarawas St. W. *City:* Canal Fulton *State:* OH *Zip:* 44614 *Phone:* 330-854-6835 *Toll-free:* 888-281-6650 *Web:* www.discovercanalfulton.com/canalway_center.html *Email:* canalway@cityofcanalfulton-oh.gov *Visitors welcome?* Yes *Hours:* April and October: Saturday and Sunday, 10 a.m. to 4 p.m.; May to September: Daily, 10 a.m. to 6 p.m. *Admission:* Contact attraction directly *Operated by:* Canal Fulton Heritage Society *NR?* No *NHL?* No *Latitude:* 40.8892 *Latitude:* -81.5985

SUSAN ELIZABETH
Launched in 1886, the tug Susan Elizabeth is undergoing restoration. *Address:* 300 Greenkill Ave. *City:* Kingston *State:* NY *Zip:* 12401 *Phone:* 845-340-0506 *Web:* www.tugmuseum.com *Email:* steve@tugmuseum.com *Visitors welcome?* No *Hours:* Contact attraction directly *Admission:* Contact attraction directly *Operated by:* North River Tugboat Museum *NR?* No *NHL?* No *Year established/built:* 1886 *Latitude:* 41.9230 *Latitude:* -74.0155

TAVERN

The 42-foot Tavern is a towboat/dredger tender that accompanies the steamboat William M. Black. *Address:* 350 East Third St. *City:* Dubuque *State:* IA *Zip:* 52001 *Phone:* 563-557-9545 *Toll-free:* 800-226-3369 *Web:* www.mississippirivermuseum.com *Visitors welcome?* Yes *Hours:* Memorial Day weekend through October: Daily, 9 a.m. to 5 p.m.; November through Memorial Day weekend: Daily, 10 a.m. to 5 p.m. *Admission:* $10.50 adults, $9.50 seniors, $8 youth seven to 17, $4.50 children three to six, under three FREE *Operated by:* Dubuque County Historical Society *NR?* No *NHL?* No *Latitude:* 42.4963 *Latitude:* -90.6591

URGER

Launched in 1901, the tug Urger is now an educational vessel on the New York Canal System. *Address:* 200 Southern Blvd *City:* Albany *State:* NY *Zip:* 12209 *Phone:* 518-436-2799 *Web:* www.nyscanals.gov/cculture/tugboat.html *Visitors welcome?* Yes *Hours:* Contact attraction directly *Admission:* Contact attraction directly *Operated by:* New York State Canals *NR?* No *NHL?* No *Year established/built:* 1901 *Latitude:* 42.6298 *Latitude:* -73.7765

W. O. DECKER

Launched in 1930, the tug W.O. Decker is an operational museum vessel. *Address:* 12 Fulton St. *City:* New York *State:* NY *Zip:* 10038 *Phone:* 212-748-8600 *Web:* www.southstreetseaportmuseum.org *Email:* info@southstseaport.org *Visitors welcome?* Yes *Hours:* November-March: Friday to Sunday, 10 a.m. to 5 p.m.; Monday 10am-5pm: Schermerhorn Row galleries only. Tuesday to Sunday 10 a.m. to 6 p.m: All galleries and ships open *Admission:* $10 adults, $8 students/seniors, $5 children 5-12, under 5 FREE *Operated by:* South Street Seaport Museum *NR?* Yes *NHL?* No *Year established/built:* 1930 *Latitude:* 40.7066 *Latitude:* -74.0034

W.P. SNYDER, JR.

Launched in 1918, the towboat W.P. Snyder, Jr. is the last steam-powered, stern-wheeled towboat in the United States. It is now a floating exhibit on the Muskingum River near the Ohio River Museum. *Address:* 601 Front Street *City:* Marietta *State:* OH *Zip:* 45750 *Phone:* 740-373-3750 *Toll-free:* 800-860-0145 *Web:* www.campusmartiusmuseum.org *Email:* info@campusmartiusmuseum.org *Visitors welcome?* Yes *Hours:* Memorial Day to Sept. 1: Saturday, 9:30 a.m. to 5 p.m.; Sunday, noon to 5 p.m.; Memorial Day & Labor Day: Noon to 5 p.m. *Admission:* $7 adults, $3 youth six to 12, under five FREE *Operated by:* Friends of the Museums *NR?* Yes *NHL?* Yes *Year established/built:* 1918 *Latitude:* 39.4210 *Latitude:* -81.4640

⚓ WENONAH

Launched in 1941, the tug Wenonah is an operational museum vessel on San Francisco Bay. *City:* San Francisco *State:* CA *Web:* www.hters.org *Email:* info@hters.org *Visitors welcome?* Yes *Hours:* Contact attraction directly *Admission:* Contact attraction directly *Operated by:* Historic Tugboat Restoration and Education Society *NR?* No *NHL?* No *Year established/built:* 1941 *Latitude:* 37.7749 *Latitude:* -122.4190

For more tugboat listings, see the sub-section "Tugboats" under "Warships – World War II."

OTHER SHIPS

ACACIA

Launched in 1944, the buoy tender USCGC Acacia is now an educational vessel in Manistee, Mich. *Address:* 99 Arthur Street *City:* Manistee *State:* MI *Zip:* 49660 *Web:* www.aai-acacia.org *Email:* overnights@uscgcacacia.org *Visitors welcome?* Yes *Hours:* Contact attraction directly *Admission:* Contact attraction directly *Operated by:* American Academy of Industry *NR?* No *NHL?* No *Year established/built:* 1944 *Latitude:* 44.2595 *Latitude:* -86.3164

CHAPTER 1 – SHIPS

ADMIRAL
Launched in 1907, the passenger vessel Admiral is now a casino on the St. Louis Riverfront. *Address:* 1000 N. Leonor K. Sullivan Blvd. *City:* St. Louis *State:* MO *Zip:* 63102 *Phone:* 314-621-4040 *Toll-free:* 800-772-3647 *Web:* www.presidentcasino.com *Visitors welcome?* Yes *Hours:* Contact attraction directly *Admission:* Contact attraction directly *Operated by:* President Casinos *NR?* No *NHL?* No *Year established/built:* 1907 *Latitude:* 38.6245 *Latitude:* -90.1839

ALOHA
Launched in 1937, the fishing boat American is now a dry-berth exhibit at the Sleeping Bear Dunes National Lakeshore visitor's center. *Address:* 9922 Front St. *City:* Empire *State:* MI *Zip:* 49630 *Phone:* 616-326-5134 *Web:* www.nps.gov/SLBE/ *Visitors welcome?* Yes *Hours:* Daily *Admission:* FREE *Operated by:* Sleeping Bear Dunes National Lakeshore *NR?* No *NHL?* No *Year established/built:* 1937 *Latitude:* 44.8111 *Latitude:* -86.0506

ARCTIC SCOUT
Launched in 1965, the USCG Arctic survey boat Arctic Scout is an education and excursion vessel. *Address:* 63 Pilots Point Dr. *City:* Westbrook *State:* CT *Zip:* 06498 *Phone:* 203-375-6638 *Toll-free:* 866-423-7529 *Web:* www.glaciersociety.org *Email:* glockett@glaciersociety.org *Visitors welcome?* Yes *Hours:* Contact attraction directly *Admission:* Contact attraction directly *Operated by:* Glacier Society *NR?* No *NHL?* No *Year established/built:* 1965 *Latitude:* 41.2716 *Latitude:* -72.4682

BAY ARK
Launched approximately 1896, the houseboat Bay Ark, also called the Lewis Ark, is now a dry-berthed museum vessel at the San Francisco Maritime National Historical Park. *Address:* San Francisco Maritime National Historical Park *City:* San Francisco *State:* CA *Zip:* 94123 *Phone:* 415-561-7006 *Web:* www.nps.gov/safr/ *Visitors welcome?* Yes *Hours:* 5 *Admission:* Contact attraction directly *Operated by:* San Francisco Maritime National Historical Park *NR?* No *NHL?* No *Year established/built:* 1896 *Latitude:* 37.8070 *Latitude:* -122.4220

BETTY
The auxiliary cutter Betty is undergoing restoration in Brookings, Ore. *Address:* 16060 Lower Harbor Road *City:* Harbor *State:* OR *Zip:* 97415 *Phone:* 541-469-3970 *Web:* www.savethebetty.org *Email:* elloboarts@charter.net *Visitors welcome?* Yes *Hours:* Contact attraction directly *Admission:* Contact attraction directly *Operated by:* Save the Betty Charitable Foundation *NR?* No *NHL?* No *Year established/built:* 1909 *Latitude:* 42.0446 *Latitude:* -124.2640

CANTON
The 32-foot U.S. Army Corps of Engineers workboat Canton is part of the collection of the Mississippi River Museum. *Address:* 350 East Third St. *City:* Dubuque *State:* IA *Zip:* 52001 *Phone:* 563-557-9545 *Toll-free:* 800-226-3369 *Web:* www.mississippirivermuseum.com *Visitors welcome?* Yes *Hours:* Memorial Day weekend through October: Daily, 9 a.m. to 5 p.m.; November through Memorial Day weekend: Daily, 10 a.m. to 5 p.m. *Admission:* $10.50 adults, $9.50 seniors, $8 youth seven to 17, $4.50 children three to six, under three FREE *Operated by:* Dubuque County Historical Society *NR?* No *NHL?* No *Latitude:* 42.4963 *Latitude:* -90.6591

CAPTAIN MERIWETHER LEWIS
Launched in 1932, the self-propelled dustpan dredge Captain Meriweather Lewis is now a dry-berth exhibit and a museum. *Address:* Nebraska Ave & E Allen St. *City:* Brownville *State:* NE *Zip:* 68321 *Phone:* 402-825-4131 *Web:* www.meriwetherlewisfoundation.org *Visitors welcome?* Yes *Hours:* Contact attraction directly

CHAPTER 1 – SHIPS

Admission: Contact attraction directly *Operated by:* Captain Meriwether Lewis Foundation *NR?* Yes *NHL?* Yes *Year established/built:* 1932 *Latitude:* 40.3933 *Latitude:* -95.6548

CARLISLE II
Carlisle II is an historic mosquito fleet vessel, one of hundreds of small passenger vessels that ferried passengers to dozens of small towns and cities before the advent of good roads and car ferries. *Address:* 10 Washington Avenue *City:* Bremerton *State:* WA *Visitors welcome?* Yes *Hours:* Daily *Admission:* Contact attraction directly *Operated by:* Kitsap Transit *NR?* No *NHL?* No *Year established/built:* 1917 *Latitude:* 47.5673 *Latitude:* -122.6240

CG 36500
Launched in 1946, the Coast Guard motor lifeboat CG 36500 is now a working exhibit owned by the Orleans Historical Society. *Address:* 3 River Road *City:* Orleans *State:* MA *Zip:* 02653 *Phone:* 508-240-1329 *Web:* www.cg36500.org *Email:* orleanshs@verizon.net *Visitors welcome?* Yes *Hours:* July and August, Thursday to Saturday, 10 a.m. to 1 p.m. *Admission:* Contact attraction directly *Operated by:* Orleans Historical Society *NR?* Yes *NHL?* No *Year established/built:* 1946 *Latitude:* 41.7832 *Latitude:* -69.9774

CG 52302D
Launched in 1944, the buoy boat CG 52302D is a dry-berth exhibit at the Lake Champlain Maritime Museum. *Address:* 4472 Basin Harbor Rd *City:* Vergennes *State:* VT *Zip:* 05491 *Phone:* 802-475-2022 *Web:* www.lcmm.org *Email:* info@lcmm.org *Visitors welcome?* Yes *Hours:* Daily, 10 a.m. to 5 p.m. *Admission:* $10 adults, $9 seniors, $6 students 5-17, under five, FREE *Operated by:* Lake Champlain Maritime Museum *NR?* No *NHL?* No *Year established/built:* 1944 *Latitude:* 44.1973 *Latitude:* -73.3567

CHUGACH
Launched in 1925, the ranger boat Chugach is a working vessel owned by the U.S. Forest Service. *City:* Petersburg *State:* AK *Phone:* 907-225-3101 *Web:* www.fs.fed.us/r10/tongass/ *Visitors welcome?* Yes *Hours:* Contact attraction directly *Admission:* Contact attraction directly *Operated by:* Tongass National Forest *NR?* Yes *NHL?* No *Year established/built:* 1925 *Latitude:* 56.8125 *Latitude:* -132.9560

DERRICK BARGE NO. 8
Launched in 1925, Derrick Barge No. 8 is in the collection of the H. Lee White Marine Museum. *Address:* West 1st Street Pier *City:* Oswego *State:* NY *Zip:* 13126 *Phone:* 315-342-0480 *Web:* www.hleewhitemarinemuseum.com *Email:* info@hleewhitemarinemuseum.com *Visitors welcome?* Yes *Hours:* September to June, daily, 1 p.m. to 5 p.m.; July and August, daily 10 a.m. to 5 p.m. *Admission:* $5 adults; $3 youth 5 to 12; under 5 FREE *Operated by:* H. Lee White Marine Museum *NR?* No *NHL?* No *Year established/built:* 1925 *Latitude:* 43.4553 *Latitude:* -76.5105

Is your community's historic ship missing from the Fyddeye Guide? Submit information and a photo via our website at www.fyddeye.com.

DOROTHY A. PARSONS
The 84-foot Dorothy A. Parsons is on display at the northern campus of the Piney Point Lighthouse Museum. *Address:* 44720 Lighthouse Road *City:* Piney Point *State:* MD *Zip:* 20674 *Phone:* 301-994-1471 *Web:* www.co.saint-marys.md.us/recreate/museums/ppl.asp *Visitors welcome?* Yes *Hours:* Mid-April to September, Daily, 10 a.m. to 5 p.m. *Admission:* $3 adults, $1.50 children 6 to 18, children under five FREE *Operated by:* St. Mary's County Museum Division *NR?* No *NHL?* No *Latitude:* 38.1408 *Latitude:* -76.5202

CHAPTER 1 – SHIPS

EVELYN S
Launched in 1939, the fish tug Evelyn S is a dry-berth exhibit at the Michigan Maritime Museum. *Address:* 260 Dyckman Ave. *City:* South Haven *State:* MI *Zip:* 49090 *Phone:* 269-637-8078 *Toll-free:* 800-747-3810 *Web:* michiganmaritimemuseum.org *Email:* info@michiganmaritimemuseum.org *Visitors welcome?* Yes *Hours:* Memorial Day to Labor Day: Monday to Saturday, 10 a.m. to 5 p.m.; Sunday noon to 5 p.m. Labor Day to Memorial Day: Friday, Saturday, Sunday, 10 a.m. to 5 p.m. *Admission:* $5 adults, $4 seniors, $3.50 children *Operated by:* Michigan Maritime Museum *NR?* No *NHL?* No *Year established/built:* 1939 *Latitude:* 42.4070 *Latitude:* -86.2745

FOGGY RIVER
Launched in 1962, the chunk-stern deadrise Foggy River is undergoing restoration at the Reedville Fisherman's Museum. *Address:* 504 Main Street *City:* Reedville *State:* VA *Zip:* 22539 *Phone:* 804-453-6529 *Web:* www.rfmuseum.org *Email:* office@rfmuseum.org *Visitors welcome?* Yes *Hours:* May 1 to October: Daily, 10:30 a.m. to 4:30 p.m. *Admission:* $5 adults, $3 seniors, children under 12 FREE *Operated by:* Reedville Fisherman's Museum *NR?* No *NHL?* No *Year established/built:* 1962 *Latitude:* 37.8454 *Latitude:* -76.2742

GEN. FRANK M. COXE
Launched in 1921, the military transport Gen. Frank M. Coxe is now a floating restaurant, renamed the Sherman. *Address:* 410 Airport Blvd *City:* Burlingame *State:* CA *Zip:* 94010 *Phone:* 650-344-7447 *Web:* theshermanrestaurant.com *Email:* gm@theshermanrestaurant.com *Visitors welcome?* Yes *Hours:* Daily *Admission:* Contact attraction directly *Operated by:* The Sherman Restaurant *NR?* No *NHL?* No *Year established/built:* 1921 *Latitude:* 37.5910 *Latitude:* -122.3380

 GENERAL HARRISON
The passenger vessel General Harrison is a mule-drawn replica of canal boats used on the Miami & Erie Canal. The vessel is a working exhibit at the Piqua Historical Area. More information on current activities is at the Ohio Historical Society blog. *Address:* 9845 North Hardin Road *City:* Piqua *State:* OH *Zip:* 45356 *Phone:* 937-773-2522 *Toll-free:* 800-752-2619 *Web:* ohsweb.ohiohistory.org/places/nw13/index.shtml *Email:* ahite@ohiohistory.org *Visitors welcome?* Yes *Hours:* April, May, September, & October: Monday-Friday 9 a.m. - 2 p.m. ; June, July, and August: Thursday & Friday 10 a.m. - 5 p.m., Saturday & Sunday Noon - 5 p.m. ; Groups by appointment *Operated by:* Piqua Historical Area *NR?* No *NHL?* No *Latitude:* 40.1810 *Latitude:* -84.2559

GLACIER
Launched in 1954, the USS/USCG icebreaker Glacier is in the process of being acquired by the Glacier Society for use an education and museum ship. *Address:* 63 Pilots Point Dr. *City:* Westbrook *State:* CT *Zip:* 06498 *Phone:* 203-375-6638 *Toll-free:* 866-423-7529 *Web:* www.glaciersociety.org *Email:* glockett@glaciersociety.org *Visitors welcome?* No *Hours:* Contact attraction directly *Admission:* Contact attraction directly *Operated by:* Glacier Society *NR?* No *NHL?* No *Year established/built:* 1954 *Latitude:* 41.2716 *Latitude:* -72.4682

GOLDSTREAM DREDGE NO. 8
Launched in 1928, the Goldstream Dredge No. 8 is a gold mining dredge that is at the center of a National Historic District. *Address:* 1755 Old Steese Hwy N. *City:* Fairbanks *State:* AK *Zip:* 99712 *Phone:* 907-457-6058 *Web:* www.golddredgeno8.com *Email:* info@golddredgeno8.com *Visitors welcome?* Yes *Hours:* Daily *Admission:* Contact attraction directly *Operated by:* Gold Dredge No. 8 *NR?* Yes *NHL?* No *Year established/built:* 1928 *Latitude:* 64.9417 *Latitude:* -147.6560

CHAPTER 1 – SHIPS

GRACIE L.
Launched in 1982, the Mackinaw boat Gracie L is a sailing training and education vessel. *Address:* 322 Sixth St. *City:* Traverse City *State:* MI *Zip:* 49684 *Phone:* 231-946-2647 *Web:* www.maritimeheritagealliance.org *Email:* kelly@maritimeheritagealliance.org *Visitors welcome?* Yes *Hours:* Contact attraction directly *Admission:* Contact attraction directly *Operated by:* Maritime Heritage Alliance *NR?* No *NHL?* No *Year established/built:* 1982 *Latitude:* 44.7617 *Latitude:* -85.6266

GYRFALCON
Launched in 1981, the Viking faering boat Gyrfalcon is a replica of a traditional Viking four-oared vessel. It is used as a living history exhibit. *City:* Oakley *State:* MD *Phone:* 301-390-4089 *Web:* www.longshipco.org *Email:* longshipco@hotmail.com *Visitors welcome?* Yes *Hours:* Contact attraction directly *Admission:* Contact attraction directly *Operated by:* Longship Company *NR?* No *NHL?* No *Year established/built:* 1981 *Latitude:* 38.2729 *Latitude:* -76.7397

HALF SHELL
Launched in 1928, the buyboat Half Shell is now an environmental education training vessel operated by the Mathew Henson Earth Conservation Center of the Earth Conservation Corps. *Address:* 2000 Half Street SW *City:* Washington *State:* DC *Zip:* 20024 *Phone:* 202-554-1960 *Web:* www.ecc1.org *Visitors welcome?* Yes *Hours:* Contact attraction directly *Admission:* Contact attraction directly *Operated by:* Earth Conservation Corps *NR?* No *NHL?* No *Year established/built:* 1928 *Latitude:* 38.8661 *Latitude:* -77.0107

HJEMKOMST
Launched in 1980, the replica Viking ship Hjemkomst was built and sailed by a local high school teacher. The ship is now part of the Hjemkomst Center. *Address:* 202 First Avenue N. *City:* Moorhead *State:* MN *Zip:* 56560 *Phone:* 218-299-5511 *Web:* www.hjemkomst-center.com *Email:* maureen.jonason@ci.moorhead.mn.us *Visitors welcome?* Yes *Hours:* Monday to Saturday, 9 a.m. to 5 p.m.; Sunday, noon to 5 p.m. *Admission:* $7 adults, $6 seniors/students, $5 children five to 17, children under four FREE *Operated by:* Historical and Cultural Society of Clay County *NR?* No *NHL?* No *Year established/built:* 1980 *Latitude:* 46.8771 *Latitude:* -96.7773

JACOB PIKE
The 83-foot Jacob Pike is a 1949 sardine carrier that was based in Rockland, Maine. Designed by Ray Wallace, the vessel worked until 1997, when she was sold. The boat eventually came into the hands of the Penobscot Marine Museum, which plans to make it a *Address:* 5 Church Street *City:* Searsport *State:* ME *Zip:* 04974 *Phone:* 207-548-2529 *Web:* www.penobscotmarinemuseum.org *Email:* newmember@penobscotmarinemuseum.org *Visitors welcome?* Yes *Hours:* Contact attraction directly *Admission:* Contact attraction directly *Operated by:* Penobscot Marine Museum *NR?* No *NHL?* No *Year established/built:* 1949 *Latitude:* 44.4209 *Latitude:* -69.0006

JANE
Launched in 1929, the fish tug Jane is in the collection of the Northeastern Maritime Historical Foundation. *City:* Duluth *State:* MN *Web:* www.northeasternmaritime.org *Email:* contact@northeasternmaritime.org *Visitors welcome?* Yes *Hours:* Contact attraction directly *Admission:* Contact attraction directly *Operated by:* Northeastern Maritime Historical Foundation *NR?* No *NHL?* No *Year established/built:* 1929 *Latitude:* 46.7833 *Latitude:* -92.1066

JOHN N. COBB
Launched in 1950, the John N. Cobb is a former research vessel that is now used in maritime education. *Address:* Lake Union *City:* Seattle *State:* WA *Phone:* 206-587-3800 *Web:* seattlecentral.edu *Visitors welcome?*

CHAPTER 1 – SHIPS

Yes *Hours:* Contact attraction directly *Admission:* Contact attraction directly *Operated by:* Seattle Maritime Academy *NR?* Yes *NHL?* No *Year established/built:* 1950 *Latitude:* 47.6531 *Latitude:* -122.3380

LA DUCHESSE
Launched in 1903, the houseboat La Duchesse is a floating exhibit and excursion vessel in Clayton, New York. *Address:* 750 Mary St. *City:* Clayton *State:* NY *Zip:* 13624 *Phone:* 315-686-4104 *Web:* www.abm.org *Email:* john@abm.org *Visitors welcome?* Yes *Hours:* Mid-May to mid-October: Daily, 9 a.m. to 5 p.m. *Admission:* $12 adults, $11 seniors, $6 students/children 7-12/active military, six and under FREE *Operated by:* Antique Boat Museum *NR?* No *NHL?* No *Year established/built:* 1903 *Latitude:* 44.2383 *Latitude:* -76.0893

LANCE KNAPP
Launched in 1925, the floating derrick Lance Knapp, also known as Derrick Boat No. 8, is a dry-berth exhibit on the Oswego waterfront. *Address:* West 1st Street Pier *City:* Oswego *State:* NY *Zip:* 13126 *Phone:* 315-342-0480 *Web:* www.hleewhitemarinemuseum.com *Email:* info@hleewhitemarinemuseum.com *Visitors welcome?* Yes *Hours:* September to June, daily, 1 p.m. to 5 p.m.; July and August, daily 10 a.m. to 5 p.m. *Admission:* $5 adults; $3 youth 5 to 12; under 5 FREE *Operated by:* H. Lee White Marine Museum *NR?* No *NHL?* No *Year established/built:* 1925 *Latitude:* 43.4553 *Latitude:* -76.5105

LEHIGH VALLEY RAILROAD BARGE NO. 79
Launched in 1914, the Lehigh Valley Railroad Barge No. 79 is a floating exhibit for the Waterfront Museum and Showboat Barge. *Address:* 290 Conover St. at Pier 44 *City:* Brooklyn *State:* NY *Zip:* 11231 *Phone:* 718-624-4719 *Web:* www.waterfrontmuseum.org *Email:* dsharps@waterfrontmuseum.org *Visitors welcome?* Yes *Hours:* Thursdays, 4 p.m. to 8 p.m.; Saturdays, 1 p.m. to 5 p.m. *Admission:* By donation *Operated by:* Hudson Waterfront Museum *NR?* Yes *NHL?* No *Year established/built:* 1914 *Latitude:* 40.6754 *Latitude:* -74.0174

LOTUS (HOUSEBOAT CRUISER)
Launched in 1909, the houseboat cruiser Lotus is now a private home also operated as an excursion vessel. *Address:* Lower Hadlock Rd and N. Water St. *City:* Port Townsend *State:* WA *Visitors welcome?* Yes *Hours:* Contact attraction directly *Admission:* Contact attraction directly *Operated by:* MV Lotus Heritage Foundation *NR?* Yes *NHL?* No *Year established/built:* 1909 *Latitude:* 48.1126 *Latitude:* -122.7610

MAJESTIC
Launched in 1923, the showboat Majestic is still in use as an entertainment venue. *Address:* 435 E Mehring Way *City:* Cincinnati *State:* OH *Zip:* 45202 *Phone:* 513-241-6550 *Web:* www.cincinnatilandmarkproductions.com *Visitors welcome?* Yes *Hours:* Shows Wednesday, Thursday, Friday, Saturday, 8 p.m.; Sunday, 2 p.m. *Operated by:* Cincinnati Landmark Productions *NR?* Yes *NHL?* Yes *Year established/built:* 1923 *Latitude:* 39.0949 *Latitude:* -84.5105

MINNEHAHA
Launched in 1905, the streetcar boat Minnehaha is now a floating exhibit and excursion vessel. *City:* Excelsior *State:* MN *Zip:* 55331 *Phone:* 952-474-2115 *Web:* www.steamboatminnehaha.org *Visitors welcome?* Yes *Hours:* Contact attraction directly *Admission:* Contact attraction directly *Operated by:* Museum of Lake Minnetonka *NR?* No *NHL?* No *Year established/built:* 1905 *Latitude:* 44.9033 *Latitude:* -93.5663

MONTGOMERY
Launched in 1926, the snagboat Montgomery is now a floating exhibit. *Address:* 1382 Lock and Dam Road *City:* Carrollton *State:* AL *Zip:* 35447 *Phone:* 205-373-8705 *Web:* montgomery.sam.usace.army.mil *Visitors welcome?* Yes *Hours:* Summer: Tuesday to Saturday, 9 a.m. to 5 p.m.; Winter: Monday through Friday, 8

CHAPTER 1 – SHIPS

a.m. to 4 p.m. *Admission:* FREE *Operated by:* Tom Bevill Visitor Center (USACE) *NR?* Yes *NHL?* Yes *Year established/built:* 1926 *Latitude:* 33.2184 *Latitude:* -88.2709

MR. CHARLIE
Launched in 1953, the offshore drilling rig Mr. Charlie is now a museum. *Address:* 111 First St. *City:* Morgan City *State:* LA *Zip:* 70381 *Phone:* 985-384-3744 *Web:* www.rigmuseum.com *Email:* rigmuseum@petronet.net *Visitors welcome?* Yes *Hours:* Monday to Saturday, 10 a.m. to 2 p.m. *Admission:* $5 adults, $4 seniors, $3.50 children under 12, under five FREE *Operated by:* International Petroleum Museum & Exposition *NR?* No *NHL?* No *Year established/built:* 1953 *Latitude:* 29.6919 *Latitude:* -91.2083

MUSTANG
Launched in 1907, the oyster dredger Mustang is undergoing restoration at the Chesapeake Bay Maritime Museum. *Address:* 213 N. Talbot Street *City:* St. Michaels *State:* MD *Zip:* 21663 *Phone:* 410-745-2916 *Web:* www.cbmm.org *Email:* cbland@cbmm.org *Visitors welcome?* Yes *Hours:* Daily, hours vary by season *Admission:* $13 adults; $10 seniors over 62; $6 kids 6 to 17; kids under 6 FREE *Operated by:* Chesapeake Bay Maritime Museum *NR?* No *NHL?* No *Year established/built:* 1907 *Latitude:* 38.7876 *Latitude:* -76.2249

NORDIC SPIRIT
The Nordic Spirit is a replica of a Norwegian fishing boat constructed around the turn of the 20th century. Donated to the Nordic Heritage Museum in the 1980s, it sat unused until 2008, when museum supporters set out to refurbish it for the 100th anniversary of the 1909 Alaska-Yukon-Pacific Exposition. *Address:* 3014 NW 67th Street *City:* Seattle *State:* WA *Zip:* 98117 *Phone:* 206-789-5707 *Web:* www.nordicmuseum.org *Email:* nordic@nordicmuseum.org *Visitors welcome?* Yes *Hours:* Tuesday to Saturday, 10 a.m. to 4 p.m. *Admission:* $6 adults, $5 students, seniors, $4 children 5 to 12, under five FREE *Operated by:* Nordic Heritage Museum *NR?* No *NHL?* No *Latitude:* 47.6777 *Latitude:* -122.3970

NORSEMAN
Launched in 1992, the longship Norseman is a living history education vessel. *City:* Swarthmore *State:* PA *Zip:* 19081 *Phone:* 410-275-8516 *Web:* www.vikingship.org *Email:* info@vikingship.org *Visitors welcome?* Yes *Hours:* Contact attraction directly *Admission:* Contact attraction directly *Operated by:* Leif Ericson Viking Ship *NR?* No *NHL?* No *Year established/built:* 1992 *Latitude:* 39.9021 *Latitude:* -75.3499

OCEAN STAR
Launched in 1969, the offshore drilling rig Ocean Star is now a museum on Galveston Island. *Address:* Harborside Drive at 20th Street *City:* Galveston *State:* TX *Zip:* 77550 *Phone:* 409-766-7287 *Web:* www.oceanstaroec.com *Email:* osmuseum@aol.com *Visitors welcome?* Yes *Hours:* Contact attraction directly *Admission:* Contact attraction directly *Operated by:* Offshore Energy Center *NR?* No *NHL?* No *Year established/built:* 1969 *Latitude:* 29.3090 *Latitude:* -94.7912

OLD POINT
Old Point is an example of a crabbing dredge boat that harvested Chesapeake Bay crabs in the winter, fish in the summer, and oysters in the fall. *Address:* 213 N. Talbot Street *City:* St. Michaels *State:* MD *Zip:* 21663 *Phone:* 410-745-2916 *Web:* www.cbmm.org *Email:* cbland@cbmm.org *Visitors welcome?* Yes *Hours:* Daily, hours vary by season *Admission:* $13 adults; $10 seniors over 62; $6 kids 6 to 17; kids under 6 FREE *Operated by:* Chesapeake Bay Maritime Museum *NR?* No *NHL?* No *Latitude:* 38.7876 *Latitude:* -76.2249

PENGUIN
Launched in 1935, the deadrise workboat Penguin is a dry-berth exhibit at the Calvert Marine Museum. *Address:* State Route 2 *City:* Solomons *State:* MD *Zip:* 20688 *Phone:* 410-326-2042 *Web:* www.calvertmarine-

museum.com *Email:* mccormmj@co.cal.md.us *Visitors welcome?* Yes *Hours:* Daily, 10 a.m to 5 p.m. *Admission:* $7 adults, $6 seniors, $2 children 5 to 12; under five FREE *Operated by:* Calvert Marine Museum *NR?* No *NHL?* No *Year established/built:* 1935 *Latitude:* 38.3332 *Latitude:* -76.4720

PERSERVERANCE
The Perserverance is a replica of a colonial era bateau used for military and commercial purposes. *Address:* 4472 Basin Harbor Rd. *City:* Vergennes *State:* VT *Zip:* 05491 *Phone:* 802-475-2022 *Web:* www.lcmm.org *Email:* info@lcmm.org *Visitors welcome?* Yes *Hours:* Daily, 10 a.m. to 5 p.m. *Admission:* $10 adults, $9 seniors, $6 students 5-17, under five, FREE *Operated by:* Lake Champlain Maritime Museum *NR?* No *NHL?* No *Year established/built:* 1986 *Latitude:* 44.1973 *Latitude:* -73.3567

SAE HRAFN
Launched in 2004, the Viking longship Sae Hrafn is a replica of a traditional Viking longship. It is used as a living history exhibit. *City:* Oakley *State:* MD *Phone:* 301-390-4089 *Web:* www.longshipco.org *Email:* longshipco@hotmail.com *Visitors welcome?* Yes *Hours:* Contact attraction directly *Admission:* Contact attraction directly *Operated by:* Longship Company *NR?* No *NHL?* No *Year established/built:* 2004 *Latitude:* 38.2729 *Latitude:* -76.7397

SANTA MARIA
Launched in 1937, the restored shrimp boat Santa Maria is part of the Texas Seaport Museum collection. *Address:* Pier 21, Number 8 *City:* Galveston *State:* TX *Zip:* 77550 *Phone:* 409-763-1877 *Web:* www.tsm-elissa.org *Email:* elissa@galvestonhistory.org *Visitors welcome?* Yes *Hours:* Daily, 10 a.m. to 5 p.m. *Admission:* $8 adults, $6 students six to 18, children five and under FREE *Operated by:* Galveston Historical Foundation *NR?* No *NHL?* No *Year established/built:* 1937 *Latitude:* 29.3263 *Latitude:* -94.7951

SCRANTON
The shrimpboat Scranton is now a floating museum in the city of Pascagoula. *Address:* Pascagoula River Park *City:* Pascagoula *State:* MS *Zip:* 39567 *Phone:* 228-938-6612 *Web:* www.cityofpascagoula.com/recreation.htm *Email:* jturner@cityofpascagoula.com *Visitors welcome?* Yes *Hours:* Contact attraction directly *Admission:* Contact attraction directly *Operated by:* City of Pascagoula *NR?* No *NHL?* No *Latitude:* 30.3743 *Latitude:* -88.5647

SHARK
Launched in 1940, the fish tug Shark is now a dry-berth exhibit at the Gitche Gumee Agate and History Museum. *Address:* E21739 Brazel Street *City:* Grand Marais *State:* MI *Zip:* 49839 *Phone:* 906-494-2590 *Web:* www.agatelady.com *Email:* karen@agatelady.com *Visitors welcome?* Yes *Hours:* Mid-May to June: Sunday to Friday 2 p.m. to 5 p.m; Saturday noon to 5 p.m; July to August: Monday to Saturday noon to 7p.m. (lecture nightly at 7 p.m.); September: Sunday to Friday 2 p.m. to 5 p.m; Saturday noon to 5 p.m. *Admission:* Contact attraction directly *Operated by:* Gitchee Gumee Agate and History Museum *NR?* No *NHL?* No *Year established/built:* 1940 *Latitude:* 46.6473 *Latitude:* -85.9501

SHENANDOAH (FISHING VESSEL)
Launched in 1925, the purse-seiner Shenandoah is the last vessel of her type built at the Skansie Ship Building Company at Gig Harbor, Wash. It is now a dry-berth exhibit. *Address:* 4218 Harborview Dr. *City:* Gig Harbor *State:* WA *Visitors welcome?* Yes *Hours:* Tuesday to Saturday, 10 a.m. to 4 p.m. *Admission:* Children 12 and under, FREE; Seniors and students (13-18), $1; Adults, $2 *Operated by:* Gig Harbor Peninsula Historical Society *NR?* No *NHL?* No *Year established/built:* 1925 *Latitude:* 47.3374 *Latitude:* -122.5970

CHAPTER 1 – SHIPS

SOUTH TWIN
Launched in 1938, the fish tug South Twin is now a dry-berth exhibit. *City:* Red Cliff *State:* MN *Visitors welcome?* Yes *Hours:* Daily *Admission:* FREE *Operated by:* Cecil Peterson's Grocery *NR?* No *NHL?* No *Year established/built:* 1938 *Latitude:* 47.7782 *Latitude:* -90.1908

SUMPTER VALLEY
Constructed in 1935, the gold dredge Sumpter Valley is within a state park and is a museum. *Address:* 575 SW Dredge Loop Rd. *City:* Sumpter *State:* OR *Zip:* 97877 *Phone:* 541-894-2472 *Web:* www.friendsofthedredge.com *Email:* info@friendsofthedredge.com *Visitors welcome?* Yes *Hours:* Daily, 8:30 a.m. to 5 p.m. *Admission:* Contact attraction directly *Operated by:* Friends of Sumpter Valley Dredge *NR?* Yes *NHL?* No *Year established/built:* 1935 *Latitude:* 44.7883 *Latitude:* -118.2140

SUNDEW
Launched in 1944, the buoy tender USCG Sundew is now a floating exhibit. *Address:* 301 Harbor Drive *City:* Duluth *State:* MN *Zip:* 55802 *Phone:* 218-727-0722 *Web:* www.decc.org/attractions/irvin/ *Visitors welcome?* Yes *Hours:* Memorial Day to Labor Day: Daily, 10 a.m. to 5 p.m. *Admission:* $5 adults, $3 children 13 and under *Operated by:* Duluth Entertainment Convention Center *NR?* No *NHL?* No *Year established/built:* 1944 *Latitude:* 46.7837 *Latitude:* -92.0983

SYLVINA W. BEAL
Launched in 1911, the Sylvina W. Beal is now an excursion vessel. *Address:* 104 Water Street *City:* Eastport *State:* ME *Zip:* 04631 *Phone:* 207-853-2500 *Web:* www.eastportwindjammers.com *Visitors welcome?* Yes *Hours:* Contact attraction directly *Admission:* Contact attraction directly *Operated by:* Eastport Windjammers *NR?* No *NHL?* No *Year established/built:* 1911 *Latitude:* 44.9065 *Latitude:* -66.9852

TWILIGHT
Launched in 1933, the salmon troller Twilight is now a floating exhibit at Lake Union Park in Seattle. *Address:* 860 Terry Ave. N. *City:* Seattle *State:* WA *Visitors welcome?* Yes *Hours:* Contact attraction directly *Admission:* Donation *Operated by:* Northwest Seaport Maritime Heritage Ctr *NR?* No *NHL?* No *Year established/built:* 1933 *Latitude:* 47.6276 *Latitude:* -122.3370

TWILITE
The fish tug Twilite is a dry-berth exhibit at the Little Sand Bay Visitors Center in the Apostle Islands National Lakeshore. *Address:* Little Sand Bay Road *City:* Bayfield *State:* WI *Phone:* 715-779-7007 *Web:* www.nps.gov/apis/ *Visitors welcome?* Yes *Hours:* Contact attraction directly *Admission:* FREE *Operated by:* Apostle Islands National Lakeshore *NR?* No *NHL?* No *Latitude:* 46.9329 *Latitude:* -90.8730

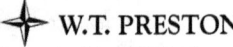 W.T. PRESTON
Launched in 1939, the snagboat W.T. Preston is now a dry-berth exhibit. *Address:* 713 R Ave. *City:* Anacortes *State:* WA *Phone:* 360-293-1915 *Web:* museum.cityofanacortes.org *Email:* coa.museum@cityofanacortes.org *Visitors welcome?* Yes *Hours:* Daily 11 a.m. to 5 p.m. June, July, August; Weekends only April to October *Admission:* Children under 8 FREE; Children 8 to 16 and seniors 65 and over, $1; Adults $2 *Operated by:* Anacortes History Museum *NR?* Yes *NHL?* Yes *Year established/built:* 1939 *Latitude:* 48.5158 *Latitude:* -122.6090

WAKE ROBIN
Launched in 1926, the lighthouse tender Wake Robin is a recreational vessel. *Address:* 212 Greenup St. *City:* Covington *State:* KY *Zip:* 41011 *Phone:* 606-261-4212 *Visitors welcome?* Yes *Hours:* Contact attraction directly *Admission:* Contact attraction directly *Operated by:* Bensons, Inc. *NR?* No *NHL?* No *Year established/built:* 1926 *Latitude:* 39.0893 *Latitude:* -84.5082

CHAPTER 1 – SHIPS

WILLIAM M. BLACK
Launched in 1934, the hydralic pipeline dredge William M. Black was one of the last great steam-powered side-wheelers used for dredging operations on the Mississippi River. *Address:* 350 East Third St. *City:* Dubuque *State:* IA *Zip:* 52001 *Phone:* 563-557-9545 *Toll-free:* 800-226-3369 *Web:* www.mississippirivermuseum.com *Visitors welcome?* Yes *Hours:* Memorial Day weekend through October: Daily, 9 a.m. to 5 p.m.; November through Memorial Day weekend: Daily, 10 a.m. to 5 p.m. *Admission:* $10.50 adults, $9.50 seniors, $8 youth seven to 17, $4.50 children three to six, under three FREE *Operated by:* Dubuque County Historical Society *NR?* Yes *NHL?* Yes *Year established/built:* 1934 *Latitude:* 42.4963 *Latitude:* -90.6591

YANKEE FORK
Launched in 1940, the gold dredge Yankee Fork is now a museum near Sunbeam, Idaho. *Address:* Yankee Fork Road *City:* Sunbeam *State:* ID *Phone:* 208-838-2529 *Visitors welcome?* Yes *Hours:* Memorial Day to Labor Day, 10 a.m. to 5 p.m. *Admission:* $3 adults, $1 children *Operated by:* Yankee Fork Gold Dredge Association *NR?* No *NHL?* No *Year established/built:* 1940 *Latitude:* 44.2876 *Latitude:* -114.7260

STEAMBOATS

BELLE OF LOUISVILLE
Launched in 1914, the steamboat Belle of Louisville is now a museum ship and river excursion vessel. *Address:* 401 W. River Road *City:* Louisville *State:* KY *Zip:* 40202 *Phone:* 502-574-2992 *Web:* belleoflouisville.org *Visitors welcome?* Yes *Hours:* Contact attraction directly *Operated by:* Belle of Louisville & Spirit of Jefferson Cruises *NR?* Yes *NHL?* Yes *Year established/built:* 1914 *Latitude:* 38.2589 *Latitude:* -85.7523

CHAUTAUQUA BELLE
The sternwheeler Chautauqua Belle is a private excursion vessel offering steamboat rides. *Address:* 78 Water St. *City:* Mayville *State:* NY *Zip:* 14757 *Phone:* 716-269-2355 *Web:* www.269belle.com *Email:* questions@269belle.com *Visitors welcome?* Yes *Hours:* Contact attraction directly *Operated by:* U.S. Steam Lines, Ltd *NR?* No *NHL?* No *Latitude:* 42.2433 *Latitude:* -79.4966

CITY OF CLINTON
Launched in 1935, the showboat City of Clinton is now dry-berthed and used as a theatre. *Address:* 6th Ave. N. and Riverview Dr. *City:* Clinton *State:* IA *Zip:* 52733 *Phone:* 563-242-6760 *Web:* summer-stock.org *Email:* boxoffice@clintonshowboat.org *Visitors welcome?* Yes *Hours:* Contact attraction directly *Operated by:* Clinton Area Showboat Theatre *NR?* No *NHL?* No *Year established/built:* 1935 *Latitude:* 41.8493 *Latitude:* -90.1830

COLUMBIA GORGE
The reproduction sternwheeler Columbia Gorge is an excursion vessel. *Address:* 1 NW Portage Rd *City:* Cascade Locks *State:* OR *Zip:* 97014 *Phone:* 503-224-3900 *Toll-free:* 800-224-3901 *Web:* www.sternwheeler.com *Email:* sales@portlandspirit.com *Visitors welcome?* Yes *Hours:* Contact attraction directly *Operated by:* Portland Spirit *NR?* No *NHL?* No *Latitude:* 45.6711 *Latitude:* -121.8890

DELTA KING
Launched in 1926, the river steamboat Delta King is a floating hotel in Old Sacramento. *Address:* 1000 Front Street *City:* Sacramento *State:* CA *Zip:* 95814 *Phone:* 916-444-5464 *Toll-free:* 800-825-5464 *Web:* www.deltaking.com *Email:* tcaufield@deltaking.com *Visitors welcome?* Yes *Hours:* Contact attraction

CHAPTER 1 – SHIPS

directly *Operated by:* The Delta King Hotel *NR?* Yes *NHL?* No *Year established/built:* 1926 *Latitude:* 38.5834 *Latitude:* -121.5060

 DELTA QUEEN

Launched in 1926, the river steamboat Delta Queen is operated as an excursion vessel on the Mississippi River. *Address:* 30 Robin Street Wharf *City:* New Orleans *State:* LA *Zip:* 70130 *Phone:* 504-586-0631 *Web:* www.majesticamericaline.com *Visitors welcome?* Yes *Hours:* Contact attraction directly *Operated by:* Majestic America Line *NR?* Yes *NHL?* Yes *Year established/built:* 1926 *Latitude:* 29.9336 *Latitude:* -90.0700

GATEWAY

Launched in 1923, the riverboat Gateway is now an excursion boat. *City:* Lycoming *State:* NY *Zip:* 13093 *Phone:* 315-598-2628 *Visitors welcome?* Yes *Hours:* Contact attraction directly *Operated by:* Gateway Boat Rides *NR?* No *NHL?* No *Year established/built:* 1923 *Latitude:* 43.4989 *Latitude:* -76.3861

GOLDENROD

Launched in 1910, the showboat Goldenrod closed in 2001 due to finanical problems. *Address:* 1000 Riverside Dr. *City:* St. Charles *State:* MO *Zip:* 63301 *Phone:* 314-946-2020 *Visitors welcome?* Yes *Hours:* Contact attraction directly *Operated by:* Showboat Goldenrod *NR?* Yes *NHL?* Yes *Year established/built:* 1910 *Latitude:* 38.7741 *Latitude:* -90.4841

MARY E. WOODS 2

Launched in 1931, the sternwheeler Mary E. Woods 2 is a floating museum at Jacksonport State Park. *Address:* 205 Avenue St. *City:* Newport *State:* AR *Zip:* 72112 *Phone:* 870-523-2143 *Web:* www.arkansasstateparks.com/jacksonport/ *Email:* jacksonport@arkansas.com *Visitors welcome?* Yes *Hours:* Contact attraction directly *Operated by:* Jacksonport State Park *NR?* No *NHL?* No *Year established/built:* 1931 *Latitude:* 35.6407 *Latitude:* -91.3071

NENANA

Launched in 1933, the river steamboat Nenana is now a dry-berth exhibit at Alaskaland Park. *Address:* Alaskaland Park *City:* Fairbanks *State:* AK *Zip:* 99707 *Phone:* 907-456-8848 *Visitors welcome?* Yes *Hours:* Contact attraction directly *Operated by:* Fairbanks Historical Preservation Foundation *NR?* Yes *NHL?* Yes *Year established/built:* 1933 *Latitude:* 64.8390 *Latitude:* -147.7680

PRESIDENT

Launched in 1924, the river steamboat President is now a casino on the St. Louis Riverfront. *Address:* 1000 N. Leonor K. Sullivan Blvd. *City:* St. Louis *State:* MO *Zip:* 63102 *Phone:* 314-621-4040 *Toll-free:* 800-772-3647 *Web:* www.presidentcasino.com *Visitors welcome?* Yes *Hours:* Contact attraction directly *Operated by:* President Casinos *NR?* Yes *NHL?* Yes *Year established/built:* 1824 *Latitude:* 38.6245 *Latitude:* -90.1839

SPIRIT OF JEFFERSON

Launched in 1963 as the Mark Twain, the riverboat Spirit of Jefferson is an excursion vessel. *Address:* 401 W. River Road *City:* Louisville *State:* KY *Zip:* 40202 *Phone:* 502-574-2992 *Web:* belleoflouisville.org *Visitors welcome?* Yes *Hours:* Contact attraction directly *Operated by:* Belle of Louisville & Spirit of Jefferson Cruises *NR?* No *NHL?* No *Year established/built:* 1963 *Latitude:* 38.2589 *Latitude:* -85.7523

CHAPTER 1 – SHIPS

The Forgotten History of Steamboats on the Okanogan River

By Natalie Johnson

The rich history of steamboats on the Mississippi River often overshadows the dynamic history of steamboating on another major American river: the Columbia. Just as steamboats pushed the boundaries of the Midwest into the Mississippi's tributaries, aggressive captains took sternwheelers carrying settlers, freight and supplies up the Okanogan River, a major branch of the Columbia draining the eastern foothills of the Cascade Mountains, to expand one of the last frontiers in the United States, the Okanogan Valley.

The steamer Okanogan, photographed by pioneer photographer Frank Matsura, passes under a steel bridge at Okanogan in 1914.

Boats like the *City of Ellensburg* and the *Enterprise* carried pioneers into a landscape marked by bone-dry coulees and populated with rattlesnakes, quail and a few hardy residents. On one side of the Okanogan River was the Colville Indian Reservation, one of the largest reservations in the country, and on the other, growing pioneer towns like Monse, Okanogan and Riverside. Settlers sought cheap farmland, logging jobs, or even the Mother Lode in one of the area's mining towns, some of which were already declining by the time sternwheelers navigated the Okanogan. The boats at times reached as far north as Oroville, barely five miles south of the Canadian border. Today, the only traces of this brief maritime history remain in the museums, ghost towns, and hidden remnants of steamboating ingenuity.

The journey wasn't easy for the early settlers. From the 1880s to the 1910's, they could take a train as far as Wenatchee, located almost dead center in Washington State beside the Columbia. But travelers needed another way to venture deep into the frontier towns of the Okanogan Valley further north. Some took a stage-coach, others walked, but most relied on riverboats, primarily steam-powered sternwheelers, that transported people, mail, and goods from one frontier town to the next.

The first sternwheeler to service the Okanogan Valley was the *City of Ellensburg*, which until 1893 was the only steamboat in Okanogan County. It made its first journey in July 1888 from Pasco to the Columbia River, finishing on the Okanogan River near Monse, a town that once boomed in the area between

CHAPTER 1 – SHIPS

present-day Brewster, now a small town surrounded by fruit orchards near the Columbia's confluence with the Okanogan river, and the city of Okanogan.

Most of the sternwheelers braving the rapids of the Columbia and Okanogan rivers were managed by the Columbia and Okanogan (C&O) Steamboat Company. Throughout most of the year, the company's sternwheelers were lucky to make it as far as Brewster, and were often delayed in Wenatchee due to low water or bad weather. But during the spring thaw, for six to eight weeks when snowmelt from the Cascades swelled the river, riverboats could make it past Brewster to make stops in Okanogan, Omak, Riverside, and very rarely, past McLoughlin Falls to Oroville.

At first glance, the sternwheelers of the Okanogan look much like their more famous cousins on the Mississippi. But the Okanogan craft had several key differences which helped make them functional in the river's shallow waters. One of the largest sternwheelers was the *Okanogan*. At 137 feet long, the craft was less than half the size of the second largest Mississippi riverboat, the *Mississippi Queen*. The Columbia and Okanogan sternwheelers also had a much shallower draft than the larger boats on the Mississippi, only requiring two feet of water.

Over time, boat builders adapted classic designs to the demands of the Okanogan and rapids at Entiat and Pateros on the Columbia. One small sternwheeler, the *Enterprise*, built in 1905, had only a seven-inch draft.

While the sternwheelers' steam engines, fueled by wood cut from surrounding forest land, could propel them through calm water easily, crews developed creative ways to haul the riverboats over the rapids at Entiat and Pateros, which was called Ives Landing until 1900. To get past these natural barriers, crews scrambled ashore and attached tow cables to hooks fastened to rocks. Crews engaged a forward deck winch to tighten the cables and pull the boat up and over the rapids. There are also accounts of crew members standing on the shore and using ropes to re-orient a sternwheeler stuck on a rock. Though the Pateros Rapids have been long covered by overflow from the Wells Hydroelectric Dam, built in 1967, some of the cable hooks can still be viewed near the former site of the rapids.

As on other major rivers in the United States, sternwheelers encouraged the growth of the Okanogan Valley; four separate towns were founded for the express purpose of creating more steamboat landings near the mouth of the Okanogan River. Three of these settlements, Port Columbia, Swansea, and Virginia City, don't exist today. Brewster, founded on a pioneer's homestead, is now a hub of apple orchards and fruit packing plants. The riverboat traffic also shaped the built landscape. In Okanogan, engineers erected high bridges over the river for pedestrians. The Okanogan high bridge is immortalized on a downtown building in modern Okanogan. in a mural based on a famous photograph by one of the Okanogan Valley's most famous settlers, Frank Matsura. The photographer also took many images of the visiting steamboats.

Though the Mississippi River's steamboats lasted more than a century as major modes of transportation, the sternwheelers of the upper Columbia River and Okanogan River barely lasted a generation. In 1914, the Great Northern Railroad reached Oroville from Wenatchee, making the Okanogan sternwheelers obsolete with reliable and efficient rail service twice daily.

Over the next few years, most of the sternwheelers were allowed to disintegrate, sink, or burn. Some of the towns they helped populate fared no better. Monse is little more than a ghost town today, with only a few homes, and the empty shells of its schoolhouse, general store and post office. Riverside, a once booming steamboat stop on the Okanogan, now only has a small general store and a few hundred residents.

The cities of Pateros, Brewster, Okanogan, Omak, Tonasket, and Oroville still have populations in the thousands, supported by the region's agriculture economy, but most traces of the sternwheeler's legacy have been lost. The Okanogan County Historical Society has done extensive research on the history of sternwheelers in Okanogan County, and has a large collection of historical photos and documents.

However, most physical evidence of the brief life of Okanogan and upper Columbia River steamboats, and the part they played in bringing thousands of settlers into the Okanogan Valley, is gone. But if you visit towns like Pateros, Okanogan or Oroville, and experience the rolling rivers and majestically barren landscape, untouched even in the industrial world we live in, you may be able to imagine why pioneers made the arduous journey into the frontier on the sternwheelers of the Okanogan Valley.

CHAPTER 1 – SHIPS

A "u-bolt" used to haul steamboats over Okanogan River rapids is one of the few physical reminders of the river's steamboat history.

Natalie Johnson was born in Seattle, but grew up in Okanogan, Wash. She returned to Seattle to attend the University of Washington, graduating in 2010 with a degree in sociology and comparative literature. While at the UW, she wrote for the student newspaper, The Daily. *She has contributed to Fyddeye.com, and worked as a reporter at the Shelton/Mason County Journal in 2010.*

Interested in writing for the next edition of the Fyddeye Guide? Pitch your article by sending an email to contact@fyddeye.com.

STEAMERS

CATALYST
Launched in 1932, the fantail motor yacht Catalyst operates as an excursion vessel in Washington, British Columbia, and Alaska. *City:* Friday Harbor *State:* WA *Zip:* 98250 *Phone:* 360-378-7123 *Toll-free:* 800-378-1708 *Web:* www.pacificcatalyst.com *Email:* shannon@pacificcatalyst.com *Visitors welcome?* Yes *Hours:* Contact attraction directly *Operated by:* Pacific Catalyst II, Inc. *NR?* No *NHL?* No *Year established/built:* 1932 *Latitude:* 48.5343 *Latitude:* -123.0170

COLUMBIA
Launched in 1920, the passenger steamer Columbia is undergoing restoration outside Detroit. *City:* Detroit *State:* MI *Phone:* 212-228-3128 *Web:* www.sscolumbia.org *Email:* contact@sscolumbia.org *Visitors welcome?* No *Hours:* Contact attraction directly *Operated by:* S.S. Columbia Project *NR?* No *NHL?* No *Year established/built:* 1902 *Latitude:* 42.3314 *Latitude:* -83.0458

CHAPTER 1 – SHIPS

DAY PECKINPAUGH
Launched in 1921, the motor ship Day Peckinpaugh is a traveling exhibit and classroom managed by the New York State Museum. *Address:* 222 Madison Ave. *City:* Albany *State:* NY *Zip:* 12230 *Phone:* 518-474-5877 *Web:* www.nysm.nysed.gov *Visitors welcome?* Yes *Hours:* Contact attraction directly for reservations *Operated by:* New York State Museum *NR?* No *NHL?* No *Year established/built:* 1921 *Latitude:* 42.6481 *Latitude:* -73.7600

ELEANOR D
Launched in 1948, the fishboat Eleanor D is undergoing restoration at the H. Lee White Marine Museum. *Address:* West 1st Street Pier *City:* Oswego *State:* NY *Zip:* 13126 *Phone:* 315-342-0480 *Web:* www.hleewhitemarinemuseum.com *Email:* info@hleewhitemarinemuseum.com *Visitors welcome?* Yes *Hours:* Contact attraction directly *Operated by:* H. Lee White Marine Museum *NR?* No *NHL?* No *Year established/built:* 1948 *Latitude:* 43.4553 *Latitude:* -76.5105

ENA
Launched in 1904, the launch Ena is now a dry-berth exhibit. *Address:* 313 E. Robert Bush Dr. *City:* South Bend *State:* WA *Visitors welcome?* Yes *Hours:* Contact attraction directly *Operated by:* Willapa Maritime Museum *NR?* No *NHL?* No *Year established/built:* 1904 *Latitude:* 46.6635 *Latitude:* -123.8030

HELENE
Launched in 1927, the yacht Helene is now an excursion vessel. *Address:* 14441 Harbor Island *City:* Detroit *State:* MI *Zip:* 48215 *Phone:* 313-822-0225 *Visitors welcome?* Yes *Hours:* Contact attraction directly *Operated by:* Shamrock Chartering *NR?* No *NHL?* No *Year established/built:* 1927 *Latitude:* 42.3598 *Latitude:* -82.9358

IDA M.
Launched in 1926, the yacht Ida M. is now an excursion vessel. *City:* San Rafael *State:* CA *Phone:* 415-459-6933 *Visitors welcome?* Yes *Hours:* Contact attraction directly *Operated by:* Historic Charters *NR?* No *NHL?* No *Year established/built:* 1926 *Latitude:* 37.9735 *Latitude:* -122.5310

J-3795
Launched in 1954, the passenger launch J-3795 is now a dry-berth exhibit at the U.S. Army Transportation Museum. *Address:* 300 Washington Blvd., Besson Hall *City:* Fort Eustis *State:* VA *Zip:* 23604 *Phone:* 757-878-1115 *Web:* www.transchool.eustis.army.mil/museum/museum.html *Visitors welcome?* Yes *Hours:* Contact attraction directly *Operated by:* U.S. Army Transportation Museum *NR?* No *NHL?* No *Year established/built:* 1954 *Latitude:* 37.1585 *Latitude:* -76.5844

KATAHDIN
Launched in 1914, the steam passenger vessel Katahdin now operates as an excursion vessel on Moosehead Lake. *City:* Greenville *State:* ME *Zip:* 04441 *Phone:* 207-695-2716 *Web:* www.katahdincruises.com *Email:* info@katahdincruises.com *Visitors welcome?* Yes *Hours:* Contact attraction directly *Operated by:* Moosehead Marine Museum *NR?* Yes *NHL?* No *Year established/built:* 1914 *Latitude:* 45.4595 *Latitude:* -69.5906

KEEWATIN
Launched in 1907, the passenger steamer Keewatin is now a floating exhibit. *Address:* Blue Star Highway and Union St. *City:* Saugatuck *State:* MI *Zip:* 49453 *Phone:* 269-857-2464 *Web:* www.keewatinmaritimemuseum.com *Visitors welcome?* Yes *Hours:* Memorial Day to Labor Day, 10:30 a.m. to 4 p.m. *Operated by:* Keewatin Maritime Museum *NR?* No *NHL?* No *Year established/built:* 1907 *Latitude:* 42.6466 *Latitude:* -86.2025

CHAPTER 1 – SHIPS

MADAKET
Launched in 1910, the launch Madaket is operated as an excursion vessel by the Humboldt Bay Maritime Museum. *Address:* Foot of F Street *City:* Eureka *State:* CA *Zip:* 95501 *Phone:* 707-444-9440 *Web:* www.humboldtbaymaritimemuseum.com *Email:* joshhbmm@suddenlinkmail.com *Visitors welcome?* Yes *Hours:* Contact attraction directly *Operated by:* Humboldt Bay Maritime Museum *NR?* No *NHL?* No *Year established/built:* 1910 *Latitude:* 40.7933 *Latitude:* -124.1640

MARION M
Launched in 1932, the chandlery lighter Marion M is a floating exhibit at the South Street Seaport Museum. *Address:* 12 Fulton St. *City:* New York *State:* NY *Zip:* 10038 *Phone:* 212-748-8600 *Web:* www.southstreetseaportmuseum.org *Email:* info@southstseaport.org *Visitors welcome?* Yes *Hours:* November-March: Friday to Sunday, 10 a.m. to 5 p.m.; Monday 10am-5pm: Schermerhorn Row galleries only. Tuesday to Sunday 10 a.m. to 6 p.m: All galleries and ships open *Operated by:* South Street Seaport Museum *NR?* No *NHL?* No *Year established/built:* 1932 *Latitude:* 40.7066 *Latitude:* -74.0034

MARY WHALEN
Launched in 1938, the tanker Mary Whalen is a floating museum in Brooklyn, New York. *Address:* Pier 98 *City:* Brooklyn *State:* NY *Phone:* 718-852-0821 *Web:* www.portsidenewyork.org *Email:* portsidenewyork@gmail.com *Visitors welcome?* Yes *Hours:* Contact attraction directly *Operated by:* Portside New York *NR?* No *NHL?* No *Year established/built:* 1938 *Latitude:* 40.7729 *Latitude:* -73.9954

MEDEA
Launched in 1904, the steam yacht Medea is now used as an excursion vessel by the Maritime Museum of San Diego. *Address:* 1492 North Harbor Drive *City:* San Diego *State:* CA *Zip:* 92101 *Phone:* 619-234-9153 *Web:* www.sdmaritime.com *Email:* info@sdmaritime.org *Visitors welcome?* Yes *Hours:* Daily, 9 a.m. to 8 p.m. *Operated by:* Maritime Museum Association of San Diego *NR?* No *NHL?* No *Year established/built:* 1904 *Latitude:* 32.7276 *Latitude:* -117.1800

METEOR
Launched in 1896, the whaleback Meteor is a floating exhibit on the Superior waterfront. *Address:* 300 Marina Dr. *City:* Superior *State:* WI *Zip:* 54880 *Phone:* 715-394-5712 *Web:* www.superiorpublicmuseums.org *Email:* info@superiorpublicmuseums.org *Visitors welcome?* Yes *Hours:* Mid-May to August 31: Monday to Saturday, 9 a.m. to 5 p.m.; Sunday, 11 a.m. to 5 p.m. September to mid-October: Thursday to Saturday, 9 a.m. to 5 p.m.; Sunday, 11 a.m. to 5 p.m. *Operated by:* Superior Public Museums *NR?* Yes *NHL?* No *Year established/built:* 1896 *Latitude:* 46.7213 *Latitude:* -92.0653

MILWAUKEE CLIPPER
Launched in 1905, the passenger steamer Milwaukee Clipper is now a floating museum. *City:* Muskegon *State:* MI *Zip:* 49443 *Phone:* 231-722-3533 *Web:* www.milwaukeeclipper.com *Email:* RES035d8@gte.net *Visitors welcome?* Yes *Hours:* Memorial Day through Labor Day, 1 p.m. to 5 p.m. *Operated by:* S.S. Milwaukee Clipper Preservation *NR?* No *NHL?* No *Year established/built:* 1905 *Latitude:* 43.2345 *Latitude:* -86.2484

MISS ANN
Launched in 1926, the motor yacht Miss Ann is a pleasure cruiser operated by a luxury resort. *Address:* 480 King Carter Dr. *City:* Irvington *State:* VA *Zip:* 22480 *Phone:* 804-438-5000 *Web:* www.tidesinn.com *Email:* concierge@tidesinn.com *Visitors welcome?* Yes *Hours:* Contact attraction directly *Operated by:* Tides Inn *NR?* Yes *NHL?* No *Year established/built:* 1926 *Latitude:* 37.6629 *Latitude:* -76.4283

CHAPTER 1 – SHIPS

OCEAN WAIF
Launched in 1927, the yacht Ocean Waif is in the collection of the Los Angeles Maritime Museum. *Address:* Berth 84, Foot of 6th St. *City:* San Pedro *State:* CA *Zip:* 90731 *Phone:* 310-548-7618 *Web:* www.lamaritimemuseum.org *Visitors welcome?* Yes *Hours:* Tuesday to Saturday, 10 a.m. to 5 p.m.; Sunday, noon to 5 p.m. *Operated by:* Los Angeles Maritime Museum *NR?* No *NHL?* No *Year established/built:* 1927 *Latitude:* 33.7387 *Latitude:* -118.2790

OSPREY
Built in 1881, the steam launch Osprey is a dry-berth exhibit at the Adirondack Museum. *Address:* Route 28N/30 *City:* Blue Mountain Lake *State:* NY *Zip:* 12812 *Phone:* 518-352-7311 *Web:* www.adkmuseum.org *Email:* cwelsh@adkmuseum.org *Visitors welcome?* Yes *Hours:* Mid-May to mid-October: Daily, 10 a.m. to 5 p.m. *Operated by:* Adirondack Museum *NR?* No *NHL?* No *Year established/built:* 1881 *Latitude:* 43.8728 *Latitude:* -74.4509

PILOT
Launched in 1914, Pilot served as San Diego Bay *Address:* 1492 North Harbor Drive *City:* San Diego Bay's pilot transfer vessel for many years. *State:* CA *Zip:* 92101 *Phone:* 619-234-9153 *Web:* www.sdmaritime.com *Email:* info@sdmaritime.org *Visitors welcome?* Yes *Hours:* Daily, 9 a.m. to 8 p.m. *Operated by:* Maritime Museum Association of San Diego *NR?* No *NHL?* No *Year established/built:* 1914 *Latitude:* 32.7276 *Latitude:* -117.1800

POTOMAC
Launched in 1934, the presidential yacht USS Potomac is now an excursion and museum vessel also used for educational programs. *Address:* Jack London Square *City:* Oakland *State:* CA *Zip:* 94607 *Phone:* 510-627-1215 *Web:* www.usspotomac.org *Email:* membership@usspotomac.org *Visitors welcome?* Yes *Hours:* Contact attraction directly *Operated by:* USS Potomac Association *NR?* Yes *NHL?* Yes *Year established/built:* 1934 *Latitude:* 37.7942 *Latitude:* -122.2760

PROPELLER
The SSS Propeller is a Sea Scout ship based in the Seattle area. *Address:* N Northlake Way and 36th St *City:* Seattle *State:* WA *Zip:* 98103 *Phone:* 206-335-2033 *Web:* www.sss-propeller.org *Email:* info@sss-propeller.org *Visitors welcome?* Yes *Hours:* Contact owner *Admission:* Contact owner *Operated by:* Sea Scout Ship Propeller *NR?* No *NHL?* No *Latitude:* 47.6509 *Latitude:* -122.3300

QUEEN MARY
Launched in 1936, the luxury passenger liner Queen Mary is now a floating exhibit in Long Beach, Calif. *Address:* 1126 Queen's Highway *City:* Long Beach *State:* CA *Zip:* 90802 *Phone:* 800-437-2934 *Toll-free:* 800-437-2934 *Web:* www.queenmary.com *Visitors welcome?* Yes *Hours:* Contact attraction directly *Operated by:* Queen Mary *NR?* Yes *NHL?* No *Year established/built:* 1936 *Latitude:* 33.7526 *Latitude:* -118.1900

✦ SABINO
Launched in 1908, the passenger vessel Sabino is an operational part of the Mystic Seaport museum program. *Address:* 75 Greenmanville Avenue *City:* Mystic *State:* CT *Zip:* 06355 *Phone:* 860-572-5315 *Web:* www.mysticseaport.org *Visitors welcome?* Yes *Hours:* Daily, April to October, 9 a.m. to 5 p.m.; November to March, 10 a.m. to 4 p.m. *Operated by:* Mystic Seaport: The Museum of America and the Sea *NR?* Yes *NHL?* Yes *Year established/built:* 1908 *Latitude:* 41.3617 *Latitude:* -71.9634

STE. CLAIRE
Launched in 1910, the passenger steamer Ste. Claire is undergoing restoration near Detroit. *City:* River Rouge *State:* MI *Web:* bobloboat.com *Email:* mrlee@bobloboat.com *Visitors welcome?* Yes *Hours:* Contact

attraction directly *Operated by:* Bob-Lo Boat *NR?* No *NHL?* Yes *Year established/built:* 1910 *Latitude:* 42.2734 *Latitude:* -83.1344

SUWANEE
Launched in 1928, the sternwheel passenger steamer Suwanee is now an excursion vessel at The Henry Ford: Greenfield Village. *Address:* 20900 Oakwood Blvd. *City:* Dearborn *State:* MI *Zip:* 48124 *Phone:* 313-982-6001 *Web:* www.thehenryford.org *Visitors welcome?* Yes *Hours:* Contact attraction directly *Operated by:* Henry Ford Museum: Greenfield Village *NR?* No *NHL?* No *Year established/built:* 1928 *Latitude:* 42.3001 *Latitude:* -83.2329

TICONDEROGA
Launched in 1906, the passenger steamer Ticonderoga is a dry-berth exhibit at the Shelburne Museum. *Address:* 5555 Shelburne Rd. *City:* Shelburne *State:* VT *Zip:* 05482 *Phone:* 802-985-3346 *Web:* www.shelburnemuseum.org *Email:* info@shelburnemuseum.org *Visitors welcome?* Yes *Hours:* Contact attraction directly *Operated by:* Shelburne Museum *NR?* Yes *NHL?* Yes *Year established/built:* 1906 *Latitude:* 44.3768 *Latitude:* -73.2285

TRADEWINDS KINGFISHER
Launched in 1941, the motor cruiser Tradewinds Kingfisher is now a charter fishing vessel. *Address:* Highway 101 *City:* Depoe Bay *State:* OR *Zip:* 97341 *Phone:* 541-765-2345 *Toll-free:* 800-445-8730 *Web:* www.tradewindscharters.com *Email:* tradewinds@centurytel.net *Visitors welcome?* Yes *Hours:* Contact attraction directly *Operated by:* Tradewinds Charters *NR?* Yes *NHL?* No *Year established/built:* 1941 *Latitude:* 44.8047 *Latitude:* -124.0610

UNITED STATES
Launched in 1952, the SS United States was the last and greatest of the large American-built ocean liners built in the years before commercial airplanes became the main mode of transatlantic and transpacific travel. *Address:* Pier 82 *City:* Philadelphia *State:* PA *Web:* www.ssunitedstatesconservancy.org *Email:* info@ssunitedstatesconservancy.org *Visitors welcome?* No *Operated by:* SS United States Conservancy *NR?* No *NHL?* No *Year established/built:* 1952 *Latitude:* 39.9180 *Latitude:* -75.1369

VALLEY CAMP
Launched in 1917, the Great Lake freighter Valley Camp is now a museum ship. *Address:* 501 East Water Street *City:* Sault Ste. Marie *State:* MI *Zip:* 49783 *Phone:* 906-632-3658 *Toll-free:* 888-744-7867 *Web:* www.thevalleycamp.com *Visitors welcome?* Yes *Hours:* Mid-May to June: Daily, 10 a.m. to 5 p.m.; July to August: Daily, 9 a.m. to 6 p.m.; September: Daily, 9 a.m. to 5 p.m.; October 1 to mid-October: Daily, 10 a.m. to 5 p.m. *Operated by:* Sault Historic Sites *NR?* Yes *NHL?* No *Year established/built:* 1917 *Latitude:* 46.4987 *Latitude:* -84.3374

 VIRGINIA V
Launched in 1922, the passenger steamer Virginia V is now a museum ship and excursion vessel. *Address:* 860 Terry Ave. N. *City:* Seattle *State:* WA *Zip:* 98109 *Phone:* 206-624-9119 *Web:* www.virginiav.org *Email:* info@virginiav.org *Visitors welcome?* Yes *Hours:* Contact attraction directly *Operated by:* Steamer Virginia V Foundation *NR?* Yes *NHL?* Yes *Year established/built:* 1922 *Latitude:* 47.6276 *Latitude:* -122.3370

WELCOME
Launched in 1919, the milk boat Welcome is undergoing restoration. *Address:* 1220 Sherman Ave. *City:* North Bend *State:* OR *Zip:* 97459 *Phone:* 541-756-6320 *Web:* www.cooshistory.org *Email:* info@cooshistory.org *Visitors welcome?* Yes *Hours:* Tuesday to Saturday, 10 a.m. to 4 p.m.; Sundays (July 1 to Labor Day), noon to 4 p.m. *Operated by:* Coos County Historical Society *NR?* No *NHL?* No *Year established/built:* 1919 *Latitude:* 43.3966 *Latitude:* -124.2240

CHAPTER 1 – SHIPS

WILLIAM A. IRVIN
Launched in 1938, the Great Lakes freighter William A. Irvin is now a floating exhibit. *Address:* 301 Harbor Drive *City:* Duluth *State:* MN *Zip:* 55802 *Phone:* 218-722-7876 *Web:* www.decc.org/attractions/irvin/ *Visitors welcome?* Yes *Hours:* May 1 to Memorial Day: Daily, 10 a.m. to 4 p.m.; Memorial Day to Labor Day: Daily, 9 a.m. to 6 p.m.; Labor Day to Sept. 27: Daily, 10 a.m. to 4 p.m. *Operated by:* Duluth Entertainment Convention Center *NR?* Yes *NHL?* No *Year established/built:* 1938 *Latitude:* 46.7837 *Latitude:* -92.0983

WILLIAM G. MATHER
Launched in 1925, the Great Lakes freighter William G. Mather is now a museum ship. *Address:* 305 Mather Way *City:* Cleveland *State:* OH *Zip:* 44114 *Phone:* 216-574-6262 *Web:* wgmather.nhlink.net *Visitors welcome?* Yes *Hours:* May: Friday, Saturday, Sunday, 10 a.m. to 5 p.m.; June, July, August: Daily, 10 a.m. to 5 p.m.; September, October: Friday, Saturday, Sunday, 10 a.m. to 5 p.m. *Operated by:* Great Lakes Science Center *NR?* No *NHL?* No *Year established/built:* 1925 *Latitude:* 41.5594 *Latitude:* -81.5989

WILLIS B. BOYER
Launched in 1911, the Great Lake freighter Willis B. Boyer is now a museum ship. *Address:* One Maritime Plaza *City:* Toledo *State:* OH *Zip:* 43604 *Phone:* 419-936-3070 *Web:* willisbboyer.org *Email:* willisbboyer.org@hotmail.com *Visitors welcome?* Yes *Hours:* May 1 to Oct. 31: Monday to Saturday, 10 a.m. to 5 p.m.; Sunday, noon to 5 p.m. *Operated by:* S.S. Willis B. Boyer *NR?* No *NHL?* No *Year established/built:* 1911 *Latitude:* 41.6539 *Latitude:* -83.5282

SUBMARINES

USS Blueback (Portland, Ore.)

CHAPTER 1 – SHIPS

ALBACORE
Launched in 1953, the USS Albacore pioneered modern submarine technologies. The vessel is now dry-berthed as a museum. *Address:* Albacore Park, 600 Market Street *City:* Portsmouth *State:* NH *Zip:* 03801 *Phone:* 603-436-3680 *Web:* www.ussalbacore.org *Email:* info@ussalbacore.org *Visitors welcome?* Yes *Hours:* Daily *Admission:* FREE *Operated by:* Port of Portsmouth Maritime Museum *NR?* Yes *NHL?* Yes *Year established/built:* 1953 *Latitude:* 43.0718 *Latitude:* -70.7626

ALUMINAUT
Launched in 1964, the deep submergence vessel Aluminaut is now on display at the Science Museum of Virginia. *Address:* 2500 West Broad St. *City:* Richmond *State:* VA *Zip:* 23220 *Phone:* 804-864-1400 *Toll-free:* 800-659-1727 *Web:* www.smv.org *Email:* info@smv.org *Visitors welcome?* Yes *Hours:* Tuesday to Saturday, 9:30 a.m. to 5 p.m.; Sunday, 11:30 a.m. to 5 p.m. *Admission:* $10 adults, $9 youth *Operated by:* Science Museum of Virginia *NR?* No *NHL?* No *Year established/built:* 1964 *Latitude:* 37.5616 *Latitude:* -77.4660

B-39
Launched in the early 1970s, the Soviet Attack Submarine B-39 is a Cold War exhibit on display at the San Diego Maritime Museum. *Address:* 1492 North Harbor Drive *City:* San Diego *State:* CA *Zip:* 92101 *Phone:* 619-234-9153 *Web:* www.sdmaritime.com *Email:* info@sdmaritime.org *Visitors welcome?* Yes *Hours:* Daily, 9 a.m. to 8 p.m. *Admission:* $14 adults; $11 seniors, active military; $8 children 6-17; under six FREE *Operated by:* Maritime Museum Association of San Diego *NR?* No *NHL?* No *Year established/built:* 1970 *Latitude:* 32.7276 *Latitude:* -117.1800

BLUEBACK
Launched in 1959, the submarine USS Blueback is on exhibit at the Oregon Museum of Science & Industry. *Address:* 1945 SE Water Avenue *City:* Portland *State:* OR *Zip:* 97214 *Phone:* 503-797-4624 *Web:* www.omsi.edu *Visitors welcome?* Yes *Hours:* Tuesday to Sunday, 9:30 a.m. to 5:30 p.m. *Admission:* $5.50 *Operated by:* Oregon Museum of Science & Industry *NR?* No *NHL?* No *Year established/built:* 1959 *Latitude:* 45.5085 *Latitude:* -122.6660

DEEP QUEST
The research submersible RV Deep Quest is a dry-berth display at the Naval Undersea Museum near Keyport, Wash. *Address:* 1103 Hunley Road *City:* Silverdale *State:* WA *Zip:* 98315 *Phone:* 360-396-4148 *Web:* www.history.navy.mil/museums/keyport/index1.htm *Visitors welcome?* Yes *Hours:* Summer (June to September): Daily, 10 a.m. to 4 p.m; Winter (October to May): Wednesday to Monday, 10 a.m. to 4 p.m. *Admission:* FREE *Operated by:* Naval History & Heritage Command *NR?* No *NHL?* No *Latitude:* 47.6980 *Latitude:* -122.6970

 FENIAN RAM
Launched in 1881, the experimental submarine Fenian Ram is on exhibit at the Paterson Museum. *Address:* 2 Market Street *City:* Paterson *State:* NJ *Zip:* 07501 *Phone:* 973-321-1260 *Web:* www.thepatersonmuseum.com *Email:* patersonmuseum@hotmail.com *Visitors welcome?* Yes *Hours:* Contact attraction directly *Admission:* Contact attraction directly *Operated by:* Paterson Museum *NR?* No *NHL?* No *Year established/built:* 1881 *Latitude:* 40.9137 *Latitude:* -74.1792

GROWLER
Launched in 1954, the Cold War-era submarine USS Growler is a floating exhibit at the Intrepid Sea, Air & Space Museum in New York. *Address:* Pier 86, W. 46th St. and 12th Ave. *City:* New York *State:* NY *Zip:* 10036 *Phone:* 212-245-0072 *Toll-free:* 877-957-7447 *Web:* www.intrepidmuseum.org *Visitors welcome?* Yes *Hours:* Daily *Admission:* $19.50 adults; $15.50 students, seniors, veterans; $14.50 youth six to 17; children

CHAPTER 1 – SHIPS

two to five, $7.50; under two FREE *Operated by:* Intrepid Sea-Air-Space Museum *NR?* No *NHL?* No *Year established/built:* 1954 *Latitude:* 40.7631 *Latitude:* -73.9996

✤ H.L. HUNLEY

Wrecked on Feb. 17, 1864, the Civil War-era submarine H.L. Hunley is undergoing conservation at the Warren Lasch Conservation Center in the former Charleston Navy Yard. *Address:* 1250 Supply St. *City:* North Charleston *State:* SC *Zip:* 29405 *Phone:* 843-743-4865 *Web:* www.hunley.org *Email:* info@hunley.org *Visitors welcome?* Yes *Hours:* Saturday, 10 a.m. to 5 p.m.; Sunday noon to 5 p.m. *Admission:* $12 adults, under five FREE *Operated by:* Friends of the Hunley *NR?* No *NHL?* No *Year established/built:* 1863 *Latitude:* 32.8563 *Latitude:* -79.9583

✤ HOLLAND BOAT NO. 1

Launched in 1878, the experimental submarine Holland Boat No. 1 is on exhibit at the Paterson Museum. *Address:* 2 Market Street *City:* Paterson *State:* NJ *Zip:* 07501 *Phone:* 973-321-1260 *Web:* www.thepatersonmuseum.com *Email:* patersonmuseum@hotmail.com *Visitors welcome?* Yes *Hours:* Contact attraction directly *Admission:* Contact attraction directly *Operated by:* Paterson Museum *NR?* No *NHL?* No *Year established/built:* 1878 *Latitude:* 40.9137 *Latitude:* -74.1792

INTELLIGENT WHALE

Launched in 1865, the Civil War submarine Intelligent Whale is a dry-berth exhibit at the Sea Girt campus of the National Guard Militia Museum of New Jersey. *Address:* Sea Girt Avenue and Camp Drive *City:* Sea Girt *State:* NJ *Zip:* 08750 *Phone:* 732-974-5966 *Web:* www.state.nj.us/military/museum *Visitors welcome?* Yes *Hours:* Monday to Friday, 10 a.m. to 3 p.m. *Admission:* Contact attraction directly *Operated by:* National Guard Militia Museum of New Jersey *NR?* No *NHL?* No *Year established/built:* 1865 *Latitude:* 40.1298 *Latitude:* -74.0423

JULIETT 484

Launched in 1965, Cold War-era Soviet submarine Juliett 484 is undergoing evaluation for possible scrapping or restoration. *Address:* 434 Allens Ave. *City:* Providence *State:* RI *Phone:* 401-521-3600 *Web:* www.saratogamuseum.org *Email:* saratogamuseum@aol.com *Visitors welcome?* No *Hours:* Contact attraction directly *Admission:* Contact attraction directly *Operated by:* USS Saratoga Museum Foundation *NR?* No *NHL?* No *Year established/built:* 1965 *Latitude:* 41.8016 *Latitude:* -71.4005

MARLIN

Launched in 1953, the submarine Marlin is a dry-berth exhibit at Freedom Park in Omaha. *Address:* Freedom Park *City:* Omaha *State:* NE *Phone:* 402-444-7000 *Visitors welcome?* Yes *Hours:* Daily *Admission:* FREE *Operated by:* City of Omaha *NR?* Yes *NHL?* No *Year established/built:* 1953 *Latitude:* 41.2716 *Latitude:* -95.9210

Photographers! Showcase your photos on the Fyddeye website! We'll link to your site in return. Go to www.fyddeye.com.

NAUTILUS

Aboard Nautilus, experience first-hand the thrill of being a submariner as you walk the decks that made naval history: the world's first nuclear powered vessel, first ship to go to the North Pole, and first submarine to journey 20,000 leagues under the sea. The submarine is on exhibit at the Submarine Force Museum. *Address:* Naval Submarine Base New London *City:* Groton *State:* CT *Zip:* 06349 *Phone:* 860-694-3174 *Web:* www.ussnautilus.org *Email:* gregory.caskey@navy.mil *Visitors welcome?* Yes *Hours:* May 1 to Oct. 1: Daily, 9 a.m. to 4:45 p.m.; Winter: Nov. 1 to April 30, daily, 9 a.m. to 3:45 p.m. *Admission:* FREE *Operated by:* Naval History & Heritage Command *NR?* No *NHL?* No *Latitude:* 41.3499 *Latitude:* -72.0759

CHAPTER 1 – SHIPS

RUSSIAN SUBMARINE SCORPION
Launched in 1971, the Soviet Foxtrot-class submarine is a floating museum berthed next to the Queen Mary in Long Beach. *Address:* 1126 Queens Highway *City:* Long Beach *State:* CA *Zip:* 90802 *Phone:* 562-432-0424 *Email:* russianscorpionb427@verizon.net *Visitors welcome?* Yes *Hours:* Daily, 10 a.m. to 6 p.m. *Admission:* $10.95 adults, $9.95 seniors, children, active military *Operated by:* Russian Submarine Scorpion *NR?* No *NHL?* No *Year established/built:* 1971 *Latitude:* 33.7526 *Latitude:* -118.1900

TRIESTE
Launched in 1953, the deep submergence vessel Trieste is now a dry-berth exhibit at the Washington Navy Yard. *Address:* 805 Kidder Breese SE, Washington Navy Yard *City:* Washington *State:* DC *Zip:* 20374 *Phone:* 202-433-6897 *Web:* www.history.navy.mil/branches/nhcorg8.htm *Visitors welcome?* Yes *Hours:* Monday to Friday, 9 a.m. to 5 p.m.; Weekends and holidays, 10 a.m . To 5 p.m. *Admission:* Contact attraction directly *Operated by:* Naval History & Heritage Command *NR?* No *NHL?* No *Year established/built:* 1953 *Latitude:* 38.8755 *Latitude:* -76.9935

TRIESTE II
Launched in 1953, the deep submergence vessel Trieste II is now a dry-berth exhibit at the Washington Navy Yard. *Address:* 805 Kidder Breese SE, Washington Navy Yard *City:* Washington *State:* DC *Zip:* 20374 *Phone:* 202-433-6897 *Web:* www.history.navy.mil/branches/nhcorg8.htm *Visitors welcome?* Yes *Hours:* Monday to Friday, 9 a.m. to 5 p.m.; Weekends and holidays, 10 a.m . To 5 p.m. *Admission:* Contact attraction directly *Operated by:* Naval History & Heritage Command *NR?* No *NHL?* No *Year established/built:* 1953 *Latitude:* 38.8755 *Latitude:* -76.9935

X-1
Launched in 1955, the midget submarine X-1 is now a dry-berth exhibit at the Submarine Force Museum. *Address:* Naval Submarine Base New London *City:* Groton *State:* CT *Zip:* 06349 *Phone:* 860-694-3174 *Web:* www.ussnautilus.org *Email:* gregory.caskey@navy.mil *Visitors welcome?* Yes *Hours:* May 1 to Oct. 1: Daily, 9 a.m. to 5 p.m.; Winter: Nov. 1 to April 30, daily, 9 a.m. to 4 p.m. *Admission:* FREE *Operated by:* Naval History & Heritage Command *NR?* No *NHL?* No *Year established/built:* 1955 *Latitude:* 41.3499 *Latitude:* -72.0759
For more submarine listings, see the sub-section "Submarines" under "Warships – World War II."

WARSHIPS – PRE-20TH CENTURY

CAIRO
Launched in 1862, the remains of the ironclad USS Cairo were raised in 1964. They are now part of the Vicksburg National Military Park. The engines and boilers have been designated National Historic Mechanical Engineering Landmarks by the American Society of Mechanical Engineers. *Address:* Vicksburg National Military Park *City:* Vicksburg *State:* MS *Zip:* 39183-3495 *Phone:* 601-636-0583 *Web:* www.nps.gov/vick/ *Visitors welcome?* Yes *Hours:* Daily, 8 a.m. to 5 p.m. *Admission:* FREE admission; $8 vehicle charge *Operated by:* Vicksburg National Military Park *NR?* No *NHL?* No *Year established/built:* 1862 *Latitude:* 32.3731 *Latitude:* -90.8508

CHATTAHOOCHEE
Launched in 1862, the remains of the Civil War gunboat CSS Chattahoochee are on display at the National Civil War Naval Museum. *Address:* 1002 Victory Drive *City:* Columbus *State:* GA *Zip:* 31901 *Phone:* 706-327-9798 *Web:* www.portcolumbus.org *Email:* director@portcolumbus.org *Visitors welcome?* Yes *Hours:* Daily,

CHAPTER 1 – SHIPS

9 a.m. to 5 p.m. *Admission:* $6.50 adults, $5.50 seniors/active military, $5 students *Operated by:* National Civil War Naval Museum *NR?* Yes *NHL?* No *Year established/built:* 1862 *Latitude:* 32.4475 *Latitude:* -84.9792

 CONSTELLATION

Built in 1854, USS Constellation is the last all-sail ship built by the U.S. Navy that is still afloat. In 1859, Constellation became the flagship of the U.S. African Squadron, charged with intercepting ships engaged in the illegal Transatlantic Slave Trade. During the Civil War, Constellation protected U.S. shipping in the Mediterranean and served on the West Gulf Blockade. During World War II, Constellation served as the flagship of the Atlantic Fleet. Constellation also served as a training vessel for the U.S. Naval Academy. *Address:* Pier 1, Baltimore Inner Harbor (301 E. Pratt St.) *City:* Baltimore *State:* MD *Zip:* 21202 *Phone:* 410-539-1797 *Web:* www.historicships.org *Email:* administration@historicships.org *Visitors welcome?* Yes *Hours:* Contact attraction directly *Admission:* Contact attraction directly *Operated by:* Historic Ships in Baltimore *NR?* Yes *NHL?* Yes *Year established/built:* 1854 *Latitude:* 39.2866 *Latitude:* -76.6087

CONSTITUTION

Nicknamed Old Ironsides during the War of 1812, the USS Constitution is the oldest commissioned warship in the U.S. Navy and a premier example of the nation's maritime heritage. *Address:* Constitution Road *City:* Boston *State:* MA *Zip:* 02129 *Phone:* 617-242-7511 *Web:* www.ussconstitution.navy.mil *Visitors welcome?* Yes *Hours:* Contact attraction directly *Admission:* FREE *Operated by:* Naval History & Heritage Command *NR?* No *NHL?* No *Year established/built:* 1797 *Latitude:* 42.3720 *Latitude:* -71.0595

JACKSON

Launched in 1864, the remains of the ironclad ram CSS Jackson are on display at the National Civil War Naval Museum. *Address:* 1002 Victory Drive *City:* Columbus *State:* GA *Zip:* 31901 *Phone:* 706-327-9798 *Web:* www.portcolumbus.org *Email:* director@portcolumbus.org *Visitors welcome?* Yes *Hours:* Daily, 9 a.m. to 5 p.m. *Admission:* $6.50 adults, $5.50 seniors/active military, $5 students *Operated by:* National Civil War Naval Museum *NR?* No *NHL?* No *Year established/built:* 1864 *Latitude:* 32.4475 *Latitude:* -84.9792

MONITOR

Launched in 1862, the Civil War-era USS Monitor was the first ironclad ship to be commissioned in the U.S. Navy. The remains are now in the USS Monitor Center at the Mariners Museum in Norfolk, Virginia. *Address:* 100 Museum Drive *City:* Newport News *State:* VA *Zip:* 23606 *Phone:* 757-596-2222 *Web:* www.mariner.org *Email:* marketing@mariner.org *Visitors welcome?* Yes *Hours:* Monday to Saturday, 10 a.m. to 5 p.m.; Sunday, noon to 5 p.m. *Admission:* $12.50 general, $11.50 AAA/military/seniors, $7.25 children six to 17, children under six FREE *Operated by:* Mariners Museum *NR?* No *NHL?* No *Year established/built:* 1862 *Latitude:* 37.0420 *Latitude:* -76.4882

OLYMPIA

Launched in 1892, the cruiser Olympia is the oldest steel-hulled afloat in the world. Decommissioned in 1922, the Olympia is now an exhibit at the Independence Seaport Museum. *Address:* 211 South Columbus Blvd. *City:* Philadelphia *State:* PA *Zip:* 19106 *Phone:* 215-413-8655 *Web:* www.phillyseaport.org *Email:* mdigirolamo@phillyseaport.org *Visitors welcome?* Yes *Hours:* Daily, 10 a.m. to 5 p.m. *Admission:* $12 adults; $10 seniors; $7 children, seniors, military; under two FREE *Operated by:* Independence Seaport Museum *NR?* Yes *NHL?* Yes *Year established/built:* 1892 *Latitude:* 39.9457 *Latitude:* -75.1419

PHILADELPHIA

Launched in 1776, the gunboat Philadelphia is a dry-berth exhibit in the Smithsonian's National Museum of American History. *Address:* 12th and Constitution Ave. NW *City:* Washington *State:* DC *Zip:* 20560 *Phone:* 202-357-1300 *Web:* americanhistory.si.edu *Visitors welcome?* Yes *Hours:* Daily, 10 a.m. to 5 p.m. *Admission:*

CHAPTER 1 – SHIPS

Contact attraction directly *Operated by:* Smithsonian Institution *NR?* Yes *NHL?* Yes *Year established/built:* 1776 *Latitude:* 38.8921 *Latitude:* -77.0280

WARSHIPS – WORLD WAR I

 TEXAS
Launched in 1914, the World War I and II-era battleship Texas is now a floating museum at San Jacinto Battleground State Park. *Address:* 3527 Battleground Rd. *City:* La Porte *State:* TX *Zip:* 77571 *Phone:* 281-479-2431 *Web:* www.battleshiptexas.org *Email:* bb35foundation@sbcglobal.net *Visitors welcome?* Yes *Hours:* Contact attraction directly *Admission:* Contact attraction directly *Operated by:* Battleship Texas Foundation *NR?* Yes *NHL?* Yes *Year established/built:* 1914 *Latitude:* 29.7311 *Latitude:* -95.0838

WARSHIPS – POST WORLD WAR II

ARIES
Launched in 1982, the guided missile hydrofoil gunboat Aries is a now a museum ship. *Address:* Grand River Waterfront *City:* Brunswick *State:* MO *Phone:* 660-269-9200 *Web:* www.ussaries.org *Email:* eliot@custom-composites.com *Visitors welcome?* Yes *Hours:* Contact attraction directly *Admission:* Contact attraction directly *Operated by:* USS Aries Hydrofoil Memorial *NR?* No *NHL?* No *Year established/built:* 1982 *Latitude:* 39.4234 *Latitude:* -93.1305

BARC 3-X
Launched in 1952, BARC (Barge, Amphibious Resupply, Cargo) 3-X is a dry berth exhibit at the U.S. Army Transportation Museum in Fort Eustis. The BARC, and a later version, LARC (Lighter, Amphibious Resupply, Cargo), were welded, steel-hulled amphibious cargo vehicles. *Address:* 300 Washington Blvd., Besson Hall *City:* Fort Eustis *State:* VA *Zip:* 23604-5260 *Phone:* 757-878-1115 *Web:* www.transchool.eustis.army.mil/museum/museum.html *Visitors welcome?* Yes *Hours:* Contact attraction directly *Admission:* Contact attraction directly *Operated by:* U.S. Army Transportation Museum *NR?* No *NHL?* No *Year established/built:* 1952 *Latitude:* 37.1585 *Latitude:* -76.5844

BARRY
Launched in 1955, the USS Barry is a Sherman-class destroyer berthed at the Washington Navy Yard's Pier 2. It serves as an historical exhibit. *Address:* 91 M. Street SW *City:* Washington *State:* DC *Zip:* 20374 *Phone:* 202-433-3377 *Web:* www.history.navy.mil/visit/visit5.htm *Visitors welcome?* Yes *Hours:* Contact attraction directly *Admission:* Contact attraction directly *Operated by:* Naval History & Heritage Command *NR?* No *NHL?* No *Year established/built:* 1955 *Latitude:* 38.8764 *Latitude:* -77.0106

BRAMBLE
The U.S. Coast Guard Cutter Bramble was commissioned in 1944 at a cost of just over $925,000. *Address:* Port Huron Seaway Terminal *City:* Port Huron *State:* MI *Zip:* 48060 *Phone:* 810-982-0891 *Email:* bramble@phmuseum.org *Visitors welcome?* Yes *Hours:* Daily, Memorial Day to Labor Day, 11 a.m. to 5 p.m.; Sept. to Dec., Thursday to Monday; April to May, Thursday to Monday; Jan. to March, closed *Admission:* Contact attraction directly *Operated by:* Port Huron Museum *NR?* No *NHL?* No *Year established/built:* 1944 *Latitude:* 42.9709 *Latitude:* -82.4249

CHAPTER 1 – SHIPS

EDSON
Launched in 1958, the destroyer USS Edson is a floating exhibit on the Bay City waterfront. *Address:* Philadelphia Navy Yard *City:* Bay City *State:* MI *Zip:* 48706 *Phone:* 989-684-3946 *Web:* www.ussedson.org *Email:* kegley@chartermi.net *Visitors welcome?* Yes *Hours:* Contact attraction directly *Admission:* Contact attraction directly *Operated by:* Saginaw Valley Naval Ship Museum *NR?* Yes *NHL?* Yes *Year established/built:* 1958 *Latitude:* 43.5945 *Latitude:* -83.8889

HIDDENSEE
Launched in 1985, the Russian-built missile corvette Hiddensee is a floating exhibit at Battleship Cove. *Address:* Five Water Street *City:* Fall River *State:* MA *Zip:* 02722-0111 *Phone:* 508-678-1100 *Toll-free:* 800-533-3194 *Web:* www.battleshipcove.org *Visitors welcome?* Yes *Hours:* Summer: daily, 9 a.m. to 4:30 p.m.; Winter: daily, 9 a.m. to 5:30 p.m. *Admission:* Contact attraction directly *Operated by:* Battleship Cove *NR?* No *NHL?* No *Year established/built:* 1985 *Latitude:* 41.7040 *Latitude:* -71.1597

LT-1967
Launched in 1951, USAT LT-1967 is moored at Naval Base San Diego and is not open to the public. *Address:* 1551 Shelter Island Drive *City:* San Diego *State:* CA *Zip:* 92106 *Phone:* 619-200-7417 *Web:* www.sdmaritimeinformationcenter.org *Email:* rbentley@sandiegoboating.com *Visitors welcome?* No *Hours:* Contact attraction directly *Admission:* Contact attraction directly *Operated by:* Coordinated Maritime Services *NR?* No *NHL?* No *Year established/built:* 1951 *Latitude:* 32.7099 *Latitude:* -117.2310

LUCID
Launched in 1953, the minesweeper USS Lucid is now a museum ship on Bradford Island, Calif. *City:* Bradford Island *State:* CA *Phone:* 877-285-8243 *Web:* www.usslucid.org *Email:* usslucid@usslucid.org *Visitors welcome?* Yes *Hours:* Contact attraction directly *Admission:* Contact attraction directly *Operated by:* Lucid MSO-458 Foundation *NR?* No *NHL?* No *Year established/built:* 1953 *Latitude:* 75.5401 *Latitude:* -101.3790

MSB-5
Launched in 1952, the minesweeper MSB-5, also called the Vosseller, is now a dry-berth exhibit at the Pate Museum of Transportation. *Address:* 18501 Hwy 377 S. *City:* Fort Worth *State:* TX *Zip:* 76101 *Phone:* 817-396-4305 *Visitors welcome?* Yes *Hours:* Tuesday to Saturday, 10 a.m. to 5 p.m.; Sundays, noon to 5 p.m. *Admission:* FREE *Operated by:* Pate Museum of Transportation *NR?* No *NHL?* No *Year established/built:* 1952 *Latitude:* 32.6144 *Latitude:* -97.5404

✈ PACV-4
Launched in 1965, the hovercraft PACV-4 is a dry-berth exhibit at the Bellingham International Maritime Museum. *Address:* 800 Cornwall Ave. *City:* Bellingham *State:* WA *Zip:* 98225 *Phone:* 360-592-4112 *Web:* www.bimm.us *Email:* mikeg@bimm.us *Visitors welcome?* Yes *Hours:* Contact attraction directly *Admission:* Contact attraction directly *Operated by:* Bellingham International Maritime Museum *NR?* No *NHL?* No *Year established/built:* 1965 *Latitude:* 48.7487 *Latitude:* -122.4810

PATROL BOAT, FAST
The Buffalo and Erie County Naval and Military Park collection include a Vietnam-era Patrol Boat, Fast boat. *Address:* One Naval Park Cove *City:* Buffalo *State:* NY *Zip:* 14202 *Phone:* 716-847-1773 *Web:* www.buffalonavalpark.org *Email:* info@buffalonavalpark.org *Visitors welcome?* Yes *Hours:* April to October, daily, 10 a.m. to 5 p.m.; November, Saturday, Sunday, Friday after Thanksgiving, 10 a.m. to 4 p.m. *Admission:* $9 adults, $6 seniors, children six to 16, under six FREE *Operated by:* Buffalo and Erie County Naval & Military Park *NR?* No *NHL?* No *Latitude:* 42.8994 *Latitude:* -78.8759

CHAPTER 1 – SHIPS

PBR (EVERETT, WA)
The PBR (Patrol Boat, River) was a riverine patrol craft first deployed in the early years of the Vietnam War and served throughout the conflict. Two versions, the Mark I and Mark II, were constructed in Bellingham, Wash. *City:* Everett *State:* WA *Visitors welcome?* Yes *Hours:* Contact attraction directly *Admission:* FREE *Operated by:* Gamewardens Northwest Chapter *NR?* No *NHL?* No *Year established/built:* 1973 *Latitude:* 47.9790 *Latitude:* -122.2020

✦ PBR 722 (BELLINGHAM, WA)
The Vietnam-era PBR (Patrol Boat, River) 722 is on display at the Bellingham International Maritime Museum. *Address:* 800 Cornwall Ave. *City:* Bellingham *State:* WA *Zip:* 98225 *Phone:* 360-592-4112 *Web:* www.bimm.us *Email:* mikeg@bimm.us *Visitors welcome?* Yes *Hours:* Contact attraction directly *Admission:* Contact attraction directly *Operated by:* Bellingham International Maritime Museum *NR?* No *NHL?* No *Latitude:* 48.7487 *Latitude:* -122.4810

PBR MARK I (MOUNT PLEASANT, SC)
The Mark I River Patrol Boat (PBR) is a Vietnam-era river craft that supported ground operations. The craft is part of an exhibit that replicates a typical naval support base in South Vietnam. *Address:* 40 Patriots Point Road *City:* Mount Pleasant *State:* SC *Zip:* 29464 *Phone:* 843-884-2727 *Toll-free:* 866-831-1720 *Web:* www.patriotspoint.org *Visitors welcome?* Yes *Hours:* Contact attraction directly *Admission:* $16 adults, $13 seniors and active military, $8 children six to 11, under six FREE *Operated by:* Patriots Point Naval & Maritime Museum *NR?* No *NHL?* No *Latitude:* 32.7940 *Latitude:* -79.9051

PBR MARK II (BELLINGHAM, WA)
The Vietnam-era PBR (Patrol Boat, River) Mark II is on display at the Bellingham International Maritime Museum. *Address:* 800 Cornwall Ave. *City:* Bellingham *State:* WA *Zip:* 98225 *Phone:* 360-592-4112 *Web:* www.bimm.us *Email:* mikeg@bimm.us *Visitors welcome?* Yes *Hours:* Contact attraction directly *Admission:* Contact attraction directly *Operated by:* Bellingham International Maritime Museum *NR?* No *NHL?* No *Latitude:* 48.7487 *Latitude:* -122.4810

PBR MARK II (HACKENSACK, NJ)
The PBR (Patrol Boat, River) Mark II is a dry-berth display at the New Jersey Naval Museum. *Address:* 78 River St. *City:* Hackensack *State:* NJ *Zip:* 07601 *Phone:* 201-342-3268 *Web:* www.njnm.com *Email:* njnavalmuseum@yahoo.com *Visitors welcome?* Yes *Hours:* Saturday and Sunday, 10 a.m. to 4 p.m. *Admission:* $9 adults, $4 children 12 and under *Operated by:* Submarine Memorial Association *NR?* Yes *NHL?* No *Year established/built:* 1943 *Latitude:* 40.8805 *Latitude:* -74.0415

PBR MARK II (MOBILE, AL)
The PBR Mark II was a river patrol boat developed for use in Vietnam. *Address:* Battleship Memorial Park *City:* Mobile *State:* AL *Zip:* 36601-0065 *Phone:* 251-433-2703 *Web:* www.ussalabama.com *Email:* btunnell@ussalabama.com *Visitors welcome?* Yes *Hours:* October to March, daily, 8 a.m. to 4 p.m.; April to Sept., daily, 8 a.m. to 6 p.m. *Admission:* $12 adults, $6 children six to 11, under six FREE *Operated by:* USS Alabama *NR?* Yes *NHL?* No *Latitude:* 30.6818 *Latitude:* -88.0148

PBR MARK II (ORLANDO, FL)
The Vietnam-era PBR (Patrol Boat, River) Mark II is a dry-berth display. *Address:* 3400 North Tanner Road *City:* Orlando *State:* FL *Zip:* 32826-3433 *Phone:* 407-273-0201 *Web:* www.nvwm.com *Email:* nvwm@bellsouth.net *Visitors welcome?* Yes *Hours:* Contact attraction directly *Admission:* Contact attraction directly *Operated by:* National Vietnam War Museum *NR?* No *NHL?* No *Latitude:* 28.5904 *Latitude:* -81.1718

CHAPTER 1 – SHIPS

PBR MARK II (VALLEJO, CA)
The Vietnam-ear PBR (Patrol Boat, River) Mark II is a dry-berth display at the Mare Island Historic Park museum in Vallejo. *Address:* Building 46, Mare Island Historic Park *City:* Vallejo *State:* CA *Zip:* 94592 *Phone:* 707-557-1538 *Web:* www.mareislandhpf.org *Visitors welcome?* Yes *Hours:* Weekdays, 10 a.m. to 2 p.m.; 1st and 3rd weekends, 10 a.m. to 4 p.m. *Admission:* Contact attraction directly *Operated by:* Mare Island Historic Park Foundation *NR?* No *NHL?* No *Latitude:* 38.0888 *Latitude:* -122.2710

PCF-1
Launched in 1965, PCF-1, also known as a Swift Boat, was a river patrol craft. It is now a dry-berth exhibit at the Washington Navy Yard. *Address:* 805 Kidder Breese SE, Washington Navy Yard *City:* Washington *State:* DC *Zip:* 20374-5060 *Phone:* 202-433-6897 *Visitors welcome?* Yes *Hours:* Monday to Friday, 9 a.m. to 5 p.m.; Weekends and holidays, 10 a.m . To 5 p.m. *Admission:* Contact attraction directly *Operated by:* Naval History & Heritage Command *NR?* No *NHL?* No *Year established/built:* 1965 *Latitude:* 38.8755 *Latitude:* -76.9935

PT-658
Launched in 1945, the fast patrol boat PT-658 is undergoing restoration at the Naval and Marine Corps Reserve Center, Swan Island. *Address:* 6735 N Basin Ave. *City:* Portland *State:* OR *Zip:* 97217 *Phone:* 503-285-4566 *Web:* www.savetheptboatinc.com *Email:* wboerger@wildwoodgrp.com *Visitors welcome?* Yes *Hours:* Contact attraction directly *Admission:* Contact attraction directly *Operated by:* Save The PT Boat, Inc. *NR?* No *NHL?* No *Year established/built:* 1945 *Latitude:* 45.5711 *Latitude:* -122.7200

PTF-3
Launched in 1963, the fast patrol boat PTF-3 is undergoing restoration by Boy Scout Troop 544. *Address:* Deland Naval Air Station Museum, 910 Biscayne Blvd. *City:* Deland *State:* FL *Zip:* 32724 *Phone:* 386-738-4149 *Web:* www.ptf3restoration.org *Email:* info@Scout544ptf.com *Visitors welcome?* Yes *Hours:* Contact attraction directly *Admission:* Contact attraction directly *Operated by:* PTF 3 Restoration Project *NR?* No *NHL?* No *Year established/built:* 1963 *Latitude:* 29.0576 *Latitude:* -81.2876

PTF-17
Launched in 1968, the Trumpy class, fast patrol boat PTF-17 is a dry-berth exhibit. *Address:* One Naval Park Cove *City:* Buffalo *State:* NY *Zip:* 14202 *Phone:* 716-847-1773 *Web:* www.buffalonavalpark.org *Email:* info@buffalonavalpark.org *Visitors welcome?* Yes *Hours:* April to October, daily, 10 a.m. to 5 p.m.; November, Saturday, Sunday, Friday after Thanksgiving, 10 a.m. to 4 p.m. *Admission:* $9 adults, $6 seniors, children six to 16, under six FREE *Operated by:* Buffalo and Erie County Naval & Military Park *NR?* No *NHL?* No *Year established/built:* 1968 *Latitude:* 42.8994 *Latitude:* -78.8759

PTF-26
Launched in 1968, PTF 26, called Liberty, is the last of the Fast Patrol Boats constructed. The vessel saw service in Vietnam. *Address:* 1601 Garden Highway *City:* Sacramento *State:* CA *Zip:* 95833 *Phone:* 916-393-2221 *Toll-free:* 916-393-2223 *Web:* libertymaritime.com *Email:* liberty-maritime@msn.com *Visitors welcome?* Yes *Hours:* Contact attraction directly *Admission:* Contact attraction directly *Operated by:* Liberty Maritime Museum *NR?* No *NHL?* No *Year established/built:* 1968 *Latitude:* 38.6051 *Latitude:* -121.5240

SALEM
Launched in 1947, the heavy cruiser USS Salem is now a floating exhibit. *Address:* 739 Washington Street *City:* Quincy *State:* MA *Zip:* 02169 *Phone:* 617-479-7900 *Web:* www.uss-salem.org *Email:* adventure@uss-salem.org *Visitors welcome?* Yes *Hours:* Contact attraction directly *Admission:* $5 adults, children under three FREE *Operated by:* United States Naval Shipbuilding Museum *NR?* No *NHL?* No *Year established/built:* 1947 *Latitude:* 42.2452 *Latitude:* -70.9700

CHAPTER 1 – SHIPS

TURNER JOY
Launched in 1957, the destroyer USS Turner Joy is now a floating museum on Puget Sound. *Address:* 300 Washington Ave. *City:* Bremerton *State:* WA *Visitors welcome?* Yes *Hours:* May 1 to Sept. 30: Daily 10 a.m. to 5 p.m; Oct. 1 to April 30: Friday to Sunday, 10 a.m. to 4 p.m. *Admission:* Children under 5 FREE; Children 5 to 12, $6; Seniors, $7; Adults, $8 *Operated by:* Bremerton Historic Ships Association *NR?* No *NHL?* No *Year established/built:* 1957 *Latitude:* 47.5673 *Latitude:* -122.6240

WARSHIPS – WORLD WAR II

AIRCRAFT CARRIERS

HORNET
Launched in 1943, the World War II-era aircraft carrier USS Hornet also played a role in the Apollo space program in the 1960s. It is now a museum ship. *Address:* 707 W Hornet Ave. *City:* Alameda *State:* CA *Zip:* 94501 *Phone:* 510-521-8448 *Web:* www.uss-hornet.org *Email:* info@uss-hornet.org *Visitors welcome?* Yes *Hours:* Daily, 10 a.m. to 5 p.m. *Admission:* $14 adults; $12 seniors, students, military; $6 youth five to 17; under five FREE *Operated by:* Aircraft Carrier Hornet Foundation *NR?* Yes *NHL?* Yes *Year established/built:* 1943 *Latitude:* 37.7721 *Latitude:* -122.2960

 INTREPID
Launched in 1943, the World War II-era aircraft carrier USS Intrepid is the premier exhibit of the Intrepid Sea, Air & Space Museum. *Address:* Pier 86, W. 46th St. and 12th Ave. *City:* New York *State:* NY *Zip:* 05933 *Phone:* 212-245-0072 *Toll-free:* 877-957-7447 *Web:* www.intrepidmuseum.org *Visitors welcome?* Yes *Hours:* Daily *Admission:* $19.50 adults; $15.50 students, seniors, veterans; $14.50 youth six to 17; children two to five, $7.50; under two FREE *Operated by:* Intrepid Sea-Air-Space Museum *NR?* Yes *NHL?* Yes *Year established/built:* 1943 *Latitude:* 40.7631 *Latitude:* -73.9996

LEXINGTON
Launched in 1942, the World War II-era aircraft carrier USS Lexington is now a floating exhibit and museum ship. *Address:* 2914 N. Shoreline Blvd. *City:* Corpus Christi *State:* TX *Zip:* 23076 *Phone:* 361-888-4873 *Toll-free:* 800-523-9539 *Web:* www.usslexington.com *Email:* rocco@usslexington.com *Visitors welcome?* Yes *Hours:* Labor Day to Memorial Day, 9 a.m. to 5 p.m.; Memorial Day to Labor Day, 9 a.m. to 6 p.m. *Admission:* $12.95 adults, $10.95 senior, active military, retired military; $7.95 children four to 12; under four FREE *Operated by:* USS Lexington Museum on the Bay *NR?* No *NHL?* Yes *Year established/built:* 1942 *Latitude:* 27.8165 *Latitude:* -97.3907

MIDWAY
Launched in 1945 just as World War II ended, the aircraft carrier USS Midway is the centerpiece of the USS Midway Museum. *Address:* 910 N. Harbor Dr. *City:* San Diego *State:* CA *Zip:* 92101 *Phone:* 619-544-9600 *Web:* www.midway.org *Visitors welcome?* Yes *Hours:* Contact attraction directly *Admission:* $17 adults, $13 seniors/students, $10 retired military, $9 youth *Operated by:* USS Midway Museum *NR?* No *NHL?* No *Year established/built:* 1945 *Latitude:* 32.7147 *Latitude:* -117.1740

CHAPTER 1 – SHIPS

 YORKTOWN
Launched in 1943, the World War II-era aircraft carrier USS Yorktown is the centerpiece of the Patriots Point Naval & Maritime Museum. *Address:* 40 Patriots Point Road *City:* Mount Pleasant *State:* SC *Zip:* 29464 *Phone:* 843-884-2727 *Toll-free:* 866-831-1720 *Web:* www.patriotspoint.org *Visitors welcome?* Yes *Hours:* Contact attraction directly *Admission:* $16 adults, $13 seniors and active military, $8 children six to 11, under six FREE *Operated by:* Patriots Point Naval & Maritime Museum *NR?* Yes *NHL?* Yes *Year established/built:* 1943 *Latitude:* 32.7940 *Latitude:* -79.9051

BATTLESHIPS

ALABAMA
Launched in 1942, the battleship USS Alabama is now a floating exhibit and museum ship. *Address:* Battleship Memorial Park *City:* Mobile *State:* AL *Zip:* 36601 *Phone:* 251-433-2703 *Web:* www.ussalabama.com *Email:* btunnell@ussalabama.com *Visitors welcome?* Yes *Hours:* October to March, daily, 8 a.m. to 4 p.m.; April to Sept., daily, 8 a.m. to 6 p.m. *Admission:* $12 adults, $6 children six to 11, under six FREE *Operated by:* USS Alabama *NR?* Yes *NHL?* Yes *Year established/built:* 1942 *Latitude:* 30.6818 *Latitude:* -88.0148

IOWA
Launched in 1943, the World War II-era battleship USS Iowa is awaiting disposition as a museum ship. *Address:* Mare Island Historic Park *City:* Vallejo *State:* CA *Zip:* 94590 *Phone:* 415-905-5700 *Web:* www.battleshipiowa.org *Visitors welcome?* Yes *Hours:* Contact attraction directly *Admission:* Contact attraction directly *Operated by:* Historic Ships Memorial at Pacific Square *NR?* No *NHL?* No *Year established/built:* 1943 *Latitude:* 38.1052 *Latitude:* -122.2480

MASSACHUSETTS
Launched in 1942, the World War II-era battleship USS Massachusetts is a floating exhibit and memorial at Battleship Cove. *Address:* 5 Water St. *City:* Fall River *State:* MA *Zip:* 02722 *Phone:* 508-678-1100 *Toll-free:* 800-533-3194 *Web:* www.battleshipcove.org *Visitors welcome?* Yes *Hours:* Summer: daily, 9 a.m. to 4:30 p.m.; Winter: daily, 9 a.m. to 5:30 p.m. *Admission:* Contact attraction directly *Operated by:* Battleship Cove *NR?* Yes *NHL?* Yes *Year established/built:* 1942 *Latitude:* 41.7040 *Latitude:* -71.1597

 MISSOURI
Launched in 1944, the battleship USS Missouri was the site where the Imperial Japanese surrendered at the end of World War II. The ship is now a floating exhibit and war memorial. *Address:* 1 Arizona Memorial Road *City:* Honolulu *State:* HI *Zip:* 96818 *Phone:* 808-455-1600 *Toll-free:* 877-644-4896 *Web:* www.ussmissouri.com *Email:* MightyMo@ussmissouri.org *Visitors welcome?* Yes *Hours:* Daily, 9 a.m. to 5 p.m. *Admission:* $16 adults, $8 children *Operated by:* USS Missouri Memorial Association *NR?* Yes *NHL?* No *Year established/built:* 1944 *Latitude:* 21.3643 *Latitude:* -157.9370

NEW JERSEY
Launched in 1943, the World War II-era battleship New Jersey is a now a floating museum. *Address:* 62 Battleship Pl. *City:* Camden *State:* NJ *Zip:* 08103 *Phone:* 856-966-1652 *Toll-free:* 866-877-6262 *Web:* www.battleshipnewjersey.org *Visitors welcome?* Yes *Hours:* Contact attraction directly *Admission:* $18.50 adults, $14 seniors/veterans, $14 children six to 11, under six, BB62 vets and active military, FREE *Operated by:* Battle-

CHAPTER 1 – SHIPS

ship New Jersey Museum and Memorial *NR?* No *NHL?* No *Year established/built:* 1943 *Latitude:* 39.9347 *Latitude:* -75.1108

NORTH CAROLINA
Launched in 1941, the World War II-era battleship North Carolina is now a museum and war memorial. *Address:* One Battleship Road *City:* Wilmington *State:* NC *Zip:* 28402 *Phone:* 910-251-5797 *Web:* www.battleshipnc.com *Email:* ncbb55@battleshipnc.com *Visitors welcome?* Yes *Hours:* Memorial Day to Labor Day: 8 a.m. to 8 p.m.; Labor Day to Memorial Day: 8 a.m. to 5 p.m. *Admission:* Contact attraction directly *Operated by:* Battleship North Carolina *NR?* Yes *NHL?* Yes *Year established/built:* 1941 *Latitude:* 34.2349 *Latitude:* -77.9533

WISCONSIN
The USS Wisconsin is an Iowa-class battleship that served in World War II, the Korean War, and the First Gulf War after a period of deactivation. She is now a museum ship at Nauticus in Norfolk, Virginia. *Address:* One Waterside Drive *City:* Norfolk *State:* VA *Zip:* 23510 *Phone:* 757-322-2987 *Web:* www.hrnm.navy.mil *Email:* gordon.b.calhoun@navy.mil *Visitors welcome?* Yes *Hours:* Contact attraction directly *Admission:* FREE *Operated by:* Naval History & Heritage Command *NR?* No *NHL?* No *Year established/built:* 1943 *Latitude:* 36.8442 *Latitude:* -76.2878

COAST GUARD VESSELS

CG-83527
Launched in 1944, the World War II-era CG-83527 is now used as a living history and marine safety education vessel. *Address:* Swansonville Rd. and Oak Bay Rd. *City:* Port Ludlow *State:* WA *Visitors welcome?* Yes *Hours:* Contact attraction directly *Admission:* Contact attraction directly *Operated by:* Combatant Craft of America *NR?* No *NHL?* No *Year established/built:* 1944 *Latitude:* 47.9294 *Latitude:* -122.6850

 INGHAM
Launched in 1936, the U.S. Coast Guard cutter Ingham is now a floating exhibit alongside USS Mohawk. *Address:* Truman Waterfront *City:* Key West *State:* FL *Zip:* 33041 *Phone:* 305-292-5072 *Web:* www.ussmohawk.org *Email:* info@ussmohawk.org *Visitors welcome?* Yes *Hours:* Contact attraction directly *Admission:* Contact attraction directly *Operated by:* USS Mohawk CGC Memorial Museum *NR?* Yes *NHL?* Yes *Year established/built:* 1936 *Latitude:* 24.5554 *Latitude:* -81.7828

MACKINAW
Launched in 1944 and decommissioned in 2006, the World War II-era icebreaker USCGC Mackinaw is now a museum ship. *Address:* 131 S. Huron Ave. *City:* Mackinaw City *State:* MI *Zip:* 49701 *Phone:* 231-436-9825 *Web:* www.themackinaw.org *Email:* contact@TheMackinaw.org *Visitors welcome?* Yes *Hours:* May and June, 11 a.m. to 7 p.m.; July to Sept., 10 a.m. to 8 p.m.; Sept. to October, 10 a.m. to 6 p.m. *Admission:* $10 adults, $6 youth six to 17, under five FREE *Operated by:* Icebreaker Mackinaw Maritime Museum *NR?* No *NHL?* No *Year established/built:* 1944 *Latitude:* 45.7821 *Latitude:* -84.7248

MCLANE
Launched in 1927, the Coast Guard cutter McLane is a floating exhibit at the Great Lakes Naval Memorial & Museum. *Address:* 1346 Bluff Street *City:* Muskegon *State:* MI *Zip:* 49441 *Phone:* 231-755-1230 *Web:* www.glnmm.org *Email:* contactus@glnmm.org *Visitors welcome?* Yes *Hours:* January to April: Monday to Friday,

10 a.m. to 4 p.m.; May to October: Daily, 10 a.m. to 5:30 p.m.; November to December: Monday to Friday, 10 a.m. to 4:30 p.m., Saturday, 10 a.m. to 5:30 p.m. *Admission:* $10 adults; $8 students/seniors; $7 children; WWII vets, active military, and children FREE *Operated by:* Great Lakes Naval Memorial & Museum *NR?* No *NHL?* No *Year established/built:* 1927 *Latitude:* 43.2273 *Latitude:* -86.3368

MOHAWK
Launched in 1935, the World War II-era icebreaker and escort USS Mohawk CGC is a museum ship. *Address:* Truman Waterfront *City:* Key West *State:* FL *Zip:* 33041 *Phone:* 305-292-5072 *Web:* www.ussmohawk.org *Email:* info@ussmohawk.org *Visitors welcome?* Yes *Hours:* Monday to Saturday, 10 a.m. to 4 p.m. *Admission:* $5 adults, $2.50 children ten to 18; under ten FREE *Operated by:* USS Mohawk CGC Memorial Museum *NR?* No *NHL?* No *Year established/built:* 1935 *Latitude:* 24.5554 *Latitude:* -81.7828

TANEY
The U.S. Coast Guard Cutter Taney is the only warship still afloat that saw action during the December 7, 1941 attack on Pearl Harbor. Commissioned in 1936, this 327-foot High Endurance Cutter is one of seven Secretary class ships built. Beside World War II, Taney also saw service in Korea and Vietnam. In addition to her wartime duties, Taney carried out search and rescues; fishery, ocean weather, and drug interdiction patrols; and summer training cruises for the Coast Guard Academy. *Address:* Pier 5, Baltimore Inner Harbor (301 E. Pratt St.) *City:* Baltimore *State:* MD *Zip:* 21202 *Phone:* 410-539-1797 *Web:* www.historicships.org *Email:* administration@historicships.org *Visitors welcome?* Yes *Hours:* Contact attraction directly *Admission:* Contact attraction directly *Operated by:* Historic Ships in Baltimore *NR?* Yes *NHL?* Yes *Year established/built:* 1936 *Latitude:* 39.2866 *Latitude:* -76.6087

ZUNI
Launched in 1943, the World War II-era fleet tug Zuni, later the USCGC Tamaroa, is a museum ship. *City:* Richmond *State:* VA *Zip:* 23228 *Phone:* 804-273-0247 *Web:* zunitamaroa.org *Email:* snafu.manor@verizon.net *Visitors welcome?* Yes *Hours:* Contact attraction directly *Admission:* Contact attraction directly *Operated by:* Zuni Maritime Foundation *NR?* No *NHL?* No *Year established/built:* 1943 *Latitude:* 37.6164 *Latitude:* -77.4817

CRUISERS

FALL RIVER
Launched in 1944, the World War II and Korean War-era cruiser USS Fall River is now a floating exhibit at Battleship Cove. *Address:* 5 Water St. *City:* Fall River *State:* MA *Zip:* 02722 *Phone:* 508-678-1100 *Toll-free:* 800-533-3194 *Web:* www.battleshipcove.org *Visitors welcome?* Yes *Hours:* Summer: daily, 9 a.m. to 4:30 p.m.; Winter: daily, 9 a.m. to 5:30 p.m. *Admission:* Contact attraction directly *Operated by:* Battleship Cove *NR?* No *NHL?* No *Year established/built:* 1944 *Latitude:* 41.7040 *Latitude:* -71.1597

LITTLE ROCK
Launched in 1945, the cruiser USS Little Rock, first a World War II-era cruise and later refitted with guided missiles, is a floating exhibit on the Buffalo waterfront. *Address:* One Naval Park Cove *City:* Buffalo *State:* NY *Zip:* 14202 *Phone:* 716-847-1773 *Web:* www.buffalonavalpark.org *Email:* info@buffalonavalpark.org *Visitors welcome?* Yes *Hours:* April to October, daily, 10 a.m. to 5 p.m.; November, Saturday, Sunday, Friday after Thanksgiving, 10 a.m. to 4 p.m. *Admission:* $9 adults, $6 seniors, children six to 16, under six FREE *Operated*

CHAPTER 1 – SHIPS

by: Buffalo and Erie County Naval & Military Park *NR?* No *NHL?* No *Year established/built:* 1945 *Latitude:* 42.8994 *Latitude:* -78.8759

DESTROYERS

CASSIN YOUNG
USS Cassin Young was built by Bethlehem Steel Corporation at San Pedro, California and commissioned on December 31, 1943. Assigned to the Central Pacific, Cassin Young first experienced combat in April 1944, attacking Japanese strongholds in the Caroline Islands. *Address:* Boston National Historic Park, Charlestown Navy Yard *City:* Boston *State:* MA *Zip:* 02129 *Phone:* 617-242-5601 *Web:* www.nps.gov/bost/historyculture/usscassinyoung.htm *Visitors welcome?* Yes *Hours:* Daily, 9 a.m. to 5 p.m. *Admission:* FREE *Operated by:* National Park Service *NR?* No *NHL?* No *Year established/built:* 1943 *Latitude:* 42.3722 *Latitude:* -71.0546

JOSEPH P. KENNEDY
Launched in 1945, the World War II-era destroyer USS Joseph P. Kennedy, Jr. is a floating exhibit at Battleship Cove. *Address:* 5 Water St. *City:* Fall River *State:* MA *Zip:* 02722 *Phone:* 508-678-1100 *Toll-free:* 800-533-3194 *Web:* www.battleshipcove.org *Visitors welcome?* Yes *Hours:* Summer: daily, 9 a.m. to 4:30 p.m.; Winter: daily, 9 a.m. to 5:30 p.m. *Admission:* Contact attraction directly *Operated by:* Battleship Cove *NR?* Yes *NHL?* Yes *Year established/built:* 1945 *Latitude:* 41.7040 *Latitude:* -71.1597

KIDD
Launched in 1943, the World War II-era destroyer USS Kidd is now a floating exhibit and veterans memorial. *Address:* 305 South River Road *City:* Baton Rouge *State:* LA *Zip:* 70802 *Phone:* 225-342-1942 *Web:* www.usskidd.com *Email:* info@usskidd.com *Visitors welcome?* Yes *Hours:* Daily, 9 a.m. to 5 p.m. *Admission:* $7 adults, $6 seniors, $5 active military, $4 children five to 12, under five FREE *Operated by:* Louisiana Naval War Memorial Commission *NR?* Yes *NHL?* Yes *Year established/built:* 1943 *Latitude:* 30.4444 *Latitude:* -91.1899

 LAFFEY
Launched in 1944, the World War II-era destroyer USS Laffey is now a floating exhibit at the Patriots Point Naval & Maritime Museum. *Address:* 40 Patriots Point Road *City:* Mount Pleasant *State:* SC *Zip:* 29464 *Phone:* 843-884-2727 *Toll-free:* 866-831-1720 *Web:* www.patriotspoint.org *Visitors welcome?* Yes *Hours:* Contact attraction directly *Admission:* $16 adults, $13 seniors and active military, $8 children six to 11, under six FREE *Operated by:* Patriots Point Naval & Maritime Museum *NR?* Yes *NHL?* Yes *Year established/built:* 1944 *Latitude:* 32.7940 *Latitude:* -79.9051

ORLECK
Launched in 1945, the World War II-era destroyer USS Orleck is a floating museum. *City:* Lake Charles *State:* LA *Phone:* 409-882-9191 *Web:* www.ussorleck.org *Email:* info@ussorleck.org *Visitors welcome?* Yes *Hours:* Contact attraction directly *Admission:* Contact attraction directly *Operated by:* Southeast Texas War Memorial and Heritage Foundation *NR?* No *NHL?* No *Year established/built:* 1945

THE SULLIVANS
Launched in 1943, the World War II-era destroyer USS The Sullivans is a floating exhibit on the Buffalo waterfront. *Address:* One Naval Park Cove *City:* Buffalo *State:* NY *Zip:* 14202 *Phone:* 716-847-1773 *Web:* www.buffalonavalpark.org *Email:* info@buffalonavalpark.org *Visitors welcome?* Yes *Hours:* April to October, daily, 10 a.m. to 5 p.m.; November, Saturday, Sunday, Friday after Thanksgiving, 10 a.m. to 4 p.m. *Admission:*

$9 adults, $6 seniors, children six to 16, under six FREE *Operated by:* Buffalo and Erie County Naval & Military Park *NR?* Yes *NHL?* Yes *Year established/built:* 1943 *Latitude:* 42.8994 *Latitude:* -78.8759

DESTROYER ESCORTS

SLATER
Launched in 1944, the World War II-era destroyer escort USS Slater is now a floating museum in Albany, New York. *Address:* 141 Broadway *City:* Albany *State:* NY *Zip:* 12202 *Phone:* 518-431-1943 *Web:* www.ussslater.org *Email:* info@ussslater.org *Visitors welcome?* Yes *Hours:* April to November: Wednesday to Sunday, 10 a.m. to 4 p.m. *Admission:* $7 adults, $6 seniors, $5 children six to 14, under six FREE *Operated by:* Destroyer Escort Historical Foundation *NR?* Yes *NHL?* No *Year established/built:* 1944 *Latitude:* 42.6420 *Latitude:* -73.7510

STEWART
Launched in 1942, the Edsall-class destroyer escort Stewart is a museum vessel at Seawolf Park. *Address:* Seawolf Park, Pelican Island *City:* Galveston *State:* TX *Zip:* 77550 *Phone:* 409-797-5114 *Web:* www.galveston.com/seawolfpark/ *Email:* macm@galvestonparkboard.org *Visitors welcome?* Yes *Hours:* Daily, 8 a.m. to dusk *Admission:* FREE *Operated by:* Seawolf Park *NR?* No *NHL?* No *Year established/built:* 1942 *Latitude:* 29.3316 *Latitude:* -94.8021

LANDING CRAFT

LCI(L)-713
Launched in 1944, the landing craft infantry (large) LCI(L)-713 is a floating museum on the Columbia River. *Address:* 8070 E. Mill Plain Boulevard *City:* Vancouver *State:* WA *Zip:* 98664 *Phone:* 503-266-9173 *Web:* www.amphibiousforces.org *Email:* kripochef@aol.com *Visitors welcome?* Yes *Hours:* Contact attraction directly *Admission:* Contact attraction directly *Operated by:* Amphibious Forces Memorial Museum *NR?* No *NHL?* No *Year established/built:* 1944 *Latitude:* 45.6254 *Latitude:* -122.5910

LCI(L)-1019
The Humboldt Naval Sea/Air Museum is restoring a World War II-era landing-craft, infantry (large) as a floating museum. *City:* Eureka *State:* CA *Phone:* 707-442-8050 *Visitors welcome?* No *Operated by:* Humboldt Bay Naval Sea/Air Museum *NR?* No *NHL?* No *Latitude:* 40.8021 *Latitude:* -124.1640

LCM-56
Battleship Cove's artifact collection includes the dry-berthed amphibious LCM 56, one of thousands of short-range craft that delivered men and materiel to invasion beaches, such as Normandy. *Address:* 5 Water St. *City:* Fall River *State:* MA *Zip:* 02722 *Phone:* 508-678-1100 *Toll-free:* 800-533-3194 *Web:* www.battleshipcove.org *Visitors welcome?* Yes *Hours:* Summer: daily, 9 a.m. to 4:30 p.m.; Winter: daily, 9 a.m. to 5:30 p.m. *Admission:* Contact attraction directly *Operated by:* Battleship Cove *NR?* No *NHL?* No *Latitude:* 41.7040 *Latitude:* -71.1597

CHAPTER 1 – SHIPS

LCS-102
The World War II-era landing craft support ship LCS-102 is now undergoing restoration at Mare Island. *Address:* Mare Island Historic Park *City:* Vallejo *State:* CA *Zip:* 94592 *Phone:* 707-557-1538 *Web:* www.mare-islandhpf.org *Visitors welcome?* Yes *Hours:* Contact attraction directly *Admission:* Contact attraction directly *Operated by:* Mare Island Historic Park Foundation *NR?* No *NHL?* No *Latitude:* 38.0888 *Latitude:* -122.2710

LCT-203
Launched in 1942, the World War II-era landing craft, tank LCT-203, also called Outer Island, is an operating museum vessel. *City:* Bayfield *State:* WI *Phone:* 615-865-0579 *Web:* ww2lct.org *Email:* bud.farmer@ww2lct.org *Visitors welcome?* Yes *Hours:* Contact attraction directly *Admission:* Contact attraction directly *Operated by:* Outer Island *NR?* No *NHL?* No *Year established/built:* 1942 *Latitude:* 46.8108 *Latitude:* -90.8182

LSM
Launched in 1944, a landing ship, mechanical will be part of an exhibit at the planned Museum of the Marine in Jacksonville, North Carolina. *Address:* Museum of the Marine *City:* Jacksonville *State:* NC *Zip:* 28541 *Phone:* 910-937-0033 *Web:* www.museumofthemarine.org *Visitors welcome?* No *Operated by:* Museum of the Marine *NR?* No *NHL?* No *Year established/built:* 1944 *Latitude:* 34.7538 *Latitude:* -77.4309

LSM-45
Launched in 1944, the medium landing ship LSM-45 is a dry-berth exhibit at Freedom Park in Omaha. *Address:* Freedom Park *City:* Omaha *State:* NE *Phone:* 402-444-7000 *Visitors welcome?* Yes *Hours:* Daily *Admission:* FREE *Operated by:* City of Omaha *NR?* Yes *NHL?* Yes *Year established/built:* 1944 *Latitude:* 41.2716 *Latitude:* -95.9210

LST-325
Launched in 1943, the landing ship tank LST-325 is now a museum ship. *Address:* 840 LST Drive *City:* Evansville *State:* IN *Zip:* 47713 *Phone:* 812-435-8678 *Web:* www.lstmemorial.com *Email:* webskipper@LST-Memorial.Org *Visitors welcome?* Yes *Hours:* Tuesday to Saturday, 10 a.m. to 4 p.m.; Sunday, noon to 4 p.m. *Admission:* $10 adults, $5 children five to 18; under five FREE *Operated by:* USS LST Ship Memorial *NR?* No *NHL?* No *Year established/built:* 1943 *Latitude:* 37.9518 *Latitude:* -87.5760

LST-393
Launched in 1942, the landing ship tank LST 393 is now a floating museum. *Address:* 560 Mart St. *City:* Muskegon *State:* MI *Zip:* 49440 *Phone:* 231-730-1477 *Web:* www.lst393.org *Visitors welcome?* Yes *Hours:* Daily, May to September, 10 a.m. to 4 p.m. *Admission:* $5 adults, $3 students, under six FREE *Operated by:* USS LST 393 *NR?* No *NHL?* No *Year established/built:* 1942 *Latitude:* 43.2334 *Latitude:* -86.2573

LVCP
The World War II-era Landing Craft Personnel Vehicles (LVCP) is a dry-berth exhibit at the Washington Navy Yard. *Address:* 805 Kidder Breese SE, Washington Navy Yard *City:* Washington *State:* DC *Zip:* 20374 *Phone:* 202-433-6897 *Web:* www.history.navy.mil/ *Visitors welcome?* Yes *Hours:* Monday to Friday, 9 a.m. to 5 p.m.; Weekends and holidays, 10 a.m . To 5 p.m. *Admission:* Contact attraction directly *Operated by:* Naval History & Heritage Command *NR?* No *NHL?* No *Latitude:* 38.8755 *Latitude:* -76.9935

CHAPTER 1 – SHIPS

LIBERTY & VICTORY SHIPS

Lane Victory (San Pedro, Calif.)

AMERICAN VICTORY
Launched in 1945, the World War II-era cargo ship American Victory is now a museum vessel. *Address:* 705 Channelside Drive *City:* Tampa *State:* FL *Zip:* 33602 *Phone:* 813-228-8766 *Web:* www.americanvictory.org *Visitors welcome?* Yes *Hours:* Tuesday to Saturday, 10 a.m. to 4 p.m.; Sunday, noon to 4 p.m. *Admission:* $10 adults, $3 children, under three FREE *Operated by:* American Victory Museum & Ship *NR?* No *NHL?* No *Year established/built:* 1945 *Latitude:* 27.9440 *Latitude:* -82.4464

✦ JEREMIAH O'BRIEN
Launched in 1943, the World War II-era Liberty Ship Jeremiah O'Brien is now a museum ship and excursion vessel. *Address:* Pier 45, Fisherman's Wharf *City:* San Francisco *State:* CA *Phone:* 415-544-0100 *Web:* www.ssjeremiahobrien.org *Email:* liberty@ssjeremiahobrien.org *Visitors welcome?* Yes *Hours:* Daily, 9 a.m. to 4 p.m. *Admission:* $8 adults, $5 seniors, $4 youth six to 14, children under six FREE *Operated by:* National Liberty Ship Memorial, SS Jeremiah O'Brien *NR?* Yes *NHL?* Yes *Year established/built:* 1943 *Latitude:* 37.8102 *Latitude:* -122.4180

✦ JOHN W. BROWN
Launched in 1942, the World War II-era Liberty Ship John W. Brown is now a museum ship and excursion vessel. *Address:* 2000 S. Clinton St. *City:* Baltimore *State:* MD *Zip:* 21224 *Phone:* 410-558-0646 *Web:* www.liberty-ship.com *Email:* john.w.brown@usa.net *Visitors welcome?* Yes *Hours:* Wednesdays and Saturdays, 9 a.m. to 2 p.m. *Admission:* Contact attraction directly *Operated by:* Project Liberty Ship *NR?* Yes *NHL?* No *Year established/built:* 1942 *Latitude:* 39.2684 *Latitude:* -76.5688

✦ LANE VICTORY
Launched in 1945, the World War II-era Victory Ship Lane Victory is now an operational excursion vessel in the Los Angeles area. *Address:* Berth 94 *City:* San Pedro *State:* CA *Zip:* 90733 *Phone:* 310-519-9545

CHAPTER 1 – SHIPS

Web: www.lanevictory.org *Email:* info@lanevictory.org *Visitors welcome?* Yes *Hours:* Contact attraction directly *Admission:* Contact attraction directly *Operated by:* SS Lane Victory *NR?* Yes *NHL?* Yes *Year established/built:* 1945 *Latitude:* 33.7595 *Latitude:* -118.2620

RED OAK VICTORY
Launched in 1944, the Victory Ship Red Oak Victory is a floating exhibit on the Richmond, Calif. waterfront. *Address:* 1337 Canal Blvd., Berth 6A *City:* Richmond *State:* CA *Zip:* 94804 *Phone:* 510-237-2933 *Web:* www.ssredoakvictory.com *Visitors welcome?* Yes *Hours:* Saturday, Sunday, Tuesday, Thursday: 10 a.m. to 3 p.m. *Admission:* $5 adults, $4 seniors, $2 children under five *Operated by:* Point Richmond History Association *NR?* Yes *NHL?* No *Year established/built:* 1944 *Latitude:* 37.9219 *Latitude:* -122.3500

MINESWEEPERS

HAZARD
Launched in 1944, the World War II-era minesweeper USS Hazard is a dry-berth exhibit at Freedom Park on the Omaha riverfront. *Address:* Freedom Park *City:* Omaha *State:* NE *Phone:* 402-444-7000 *Visitors welcome?* Yes *Hours:* Daily *Admission:* FREE *Operated by:* City of Omaha *NR?* Yes *NHL?* Yes *Year established/built:* 1944 *Latitude:* 41.2716 *Latitude:* -95.9210

PT BOATS & SMALL CRAFT

JAPANESE SUICIDE DEMOLITION BOAT
Battleship Cove's artifact collection includes a Japanese suicide attack boat from World War II. Discovered in a cave and donated to the museum in 1973, the boat has not been positively identified. *Address:* 5 Water St. *City:* Fall River *State:* MA *Zip:* 02722 *Phone:* 508-678-1100 *Toll-free:* 800-533-3194 *Web:* www.battleshipcove.org *Visitors welcome?* Yes *Hours:* Summer: daily, 9 a.m. to 4:30 p.m.; Winter: daily, 9 a.m. to 5:30 p.m. *Admission:* Contact attraction directly *Operated by:* Battleship Cove *NR?* No *NHL?* No *Latitude:* 41.7040 *Latitude:* -71.1597

PT BOATS (PT 617, PT 796)
Battleship Cove's artifact collection includes two PT Boats, small, fast attack boat used primarily in the Pacific Theatre of World War II. *Address:* 5 Water St. *City:* Fall River *State:* MA *Zip:* 02722 *Phone:* 508-678-1100 *Toll-free:* 800-533-3194 *Web:* www.battleshipcove.org *Visitors welcome?* Yes *Hours:* Summer: daily, 9 a.m. to 4:30 p.m.; Winter: daily, 9 a.m. to 5:30 p.m. *Admission:* Contact attraction directly *Operated by:* Battleship Cove *NR?* No *NHL?* No *Latitude:* 41.7040 *Latitude:* -71.1597

Are you restoring a small historic craft? Send your story to contact@fyddeye.com.

PT-309
Launched in 1944, the World War II-era motor torpedo boat PT-309 is a dry-berth exhibit at the National Museum of the Pacific War. *Address:* 340 East Main St. *City:* Fredericksburg *State:* TX *Zip:* 78624 *Phone:* 830-997-4379 *Web:* www.nimitz-museum.org *Email:* info@nimitzfoundation.org *Visitors welcome?* Yes *Hours:* Daily, 9 a.m. to 5 p.m. *Admission:* $7 adults, $6 senior/active military, $4 students, under six FREE

CHAPTER 1 – SHIPS

Operated by: Admiral Nimitz Foundation *NR?* No *NHL?* No *Year established/built:* 1944 *Latitude:* 30.2722 *Latitude:* -98.8682

TORPEDO BOAT
The Defenders of America Naval Museum is restoring a World War II-era torpedo boat launched in 1943. *Address:* Defenders of America Museum *City:* Kemah *State:* TX *Phone:* 281-476-0394 *Visitors welcome?* Yes *Hours:* Contact attraction directly *Admission:* Contact attraction directly *Operated by:* Defenders Of America Naval Museum *NR?* No *NHL?* No *Year established/built:* 1943 *Latitude:* 29.5427 *Latitude:* -95.0205

SUBMARINES

BATFISH
Launched in 1943, the World War II-ear submarine USS Batfish is a dry-berth exhibit at the USS Batfish War Memorial and Museum. *Address:* Muskogee War Memorial Park *City:* Muskogee *State:* OK *Zip:* 74402 *Phone:* 918-682-6294 *Web:* www.ussbatfish.com *Email:* ussbatfish@sbcglobal.net *Visitors welcome?* Yes *Hours:* Summer: Wednesday to Sunday, 10 a.m. to 6 p.m.; Sunday, 1 p.m. to 6 p.m. Winter: Thursday to Saturday, 10 a.m. to 5 p.m.; Sunday, 1 p.m. to 5 p.m. *Admission:* $6 adults, $3 children seven to 13, $4 seniors, children under six FREE *Operated by:* USS Batfish War Memorial Museum and Park *NR?* No *NHL?* No *Year established/built:* 1943 *Latitude:* 35.7938 *Latitude:* -95.3106

BECUNA
Launched in 1944, the World War II-era Balao-class submarine Becuna was decommissioned in 1969 and added to the collection of the Independence Seaport Museum. *Address:* 211 South Columbus Blvd. *City:* Philadelphia *State:* PA *Zip:* 19106 *Phone:* 215-413-8655 *Web:* www.phillyseaport.org *Email:* mdigirolamo@phillyseaport.org *Visitors welcome?* Yes *Hours:* Daily, 10 a.m. to 5 p.m. *Admission:* $12 adults; $10 seniors; $7 children, seniors, military; under two FREE *Operated by:* Independence Seaport Museum *NR?* Yes *NHL?* Yes *Year established/built:* 1944 *Latitude:* 39.9457 *Latitude:* -75.1419

✦ BOWFIN
Launched in 1942, the World War II-era submarine USS Bowfin is a floating exhibit with an accompanying museum. *Address:* 11 Arizona Memorial Drive *City:* Honolulu *State:* HI *Zip:* 96818 *Phone:* 808-423-1341 *Web:* www.bowfin.org *Email:* info@bowfin.org *Visitors welcome?* Yes *Hours:* Daily, 8 a.m. to 5 p.m. *Admission:* $10 adults, $7 seniors, active military, $4 children four to 12, under four permitted in museum but not submarine *Operated by:* Pacific Fleet Submarine Memorial Association *NR?* Yes *NHL?* Yes *Year established/built:* 1942 *Latitude:* 21.3643 *Latitude:* -157.9380

CAVALLA
Launched in 1944, the World War II-era submarine Cavalla is a dry-berth display at Seawolf Park on Pelican Island near Galveston. *Address:* Seawolf Park, Pelican Island *City:* Galveston *State:* TX *Zip:* 77550 *Phone:* 409-744-7854 *Web:* www.cavalla.org *Email:* macm@airmail.net *Visitors welcome?* Yes *Hours:* Daily, 8 a.m. to dusk *Admission:* FREE *Operated by:* Cavalla Historical Foundation *NR?* No *NHL?* No *Year established/built:* 1944 *Latitude:* 29.3316 *Latitude:* -94.8021

CLAMAGORE
Launched in 1945, the World War II-era submarine USS Clamagore is now a floating exhibit at the Patriots Point Naval & Maritime Museum. *Address:* 40 Patriots Point Road *City:* Mount Pleasant *State:* SC *Zip:* 29464

Phone: 843-884-2727 *Toll-free:* 866-831-1720 *Web:* www.patriotspoint.org *Email:* htant@patriotspoint.org *Visitors welcome?* Yes *Hours:* Contact attraction directly *Admission:* $16 adults, $13 seniors and active military, $8 children six to 11, under six FREE *Operated by:* Patriots Point Naval & Maritime Museum *NR?* Yes *NHL?* Yes *Year established/built:* 1945 *Latitude:* 32.7940 *Latitude:* -79.9051

COBIA

Moored along the Manitowoc River, adjacent to the Wisconsin Maritime Museum, is the World War II fleet submarine USS Cobia (SS-245). Cobia has local and national significance as an icon of Wisconsin's shipbuilding heritage. *Address:* 75 Maritime Drive *City:* Manitowoc *State:* WI *Zip:* 54220 *Phone:* 920-684-0218 *Toll-free:* 866-724-2356 *Web:* www.wisconsinmaritime.org *Email:* museum@wisconsinmaritime.org *Visitors welcome?* Yes *Hours:* Summer: daily, 9 a.m. to 6 p.m. Winter: daily, 9 a.m. to 5 p.m. *Admission:* $12 adults, $10 children six to 15, five and under FREE *Operated by:* Wisconsin Maritime Museum *NR?* No *NHL?* No *Year established/built:* 1943 *Latitude:* 44.0931 *Latitude:* -87.6570

COD

Launched in 1943, the World War II-era submarine USS Cod is now a floating exhibit in Cleveland. *Address:* 1089 E. 9th St. *City:* Cleveland *State:* OH *Zip:* 44114 *Phone:* 440-566-8770 *Web:* www.usscod.org *Email:* usscod@en.com *Visitors welcome?* Yes *Hours:* Daily, May 1 to Sept. 30, 10 a.m. to 5 p.m. *Admission:* $6 adults, $5 seniors, $3 students and active military, under six and military in uniform FREE *Operated by:* USS Cod Submarine Memorial *NR?* Yes *NHL?* Yes *Year established/built:* 1943 *Latitude:* 41.5092 *Latitude:* -81.6948

CROAKER

Launched in 1942, the World War II-era submarine USS Croaker is a floating exhibit on the Buffalo waterfront. *Address:* One Naval Park Cove *City:* Buffalo *State:* NY *Zip:* 14202 *Phone:* 716-847-1773 *Web:* www.buffalonavalpark.org *Email:* info@buffalonavalpark.org *Visitors welcome?* Yes *Hours:* April to October, daily, 10 a.m. to 5 p.m.; November, Saturday, Sunday, Friday after Thanksgiving, 10 a.m. to 4 p.m. *Admission:* $9 adults, $6 seniors, children six to 16, under six FREE *Operated by:* Buffalo and Erie County Naval & Military Park *NR?* No *NHL?* No *Year established/built:* 1942 *Latitude:* 42.8994 *Latitude:* -78.8759

DRUM

Launched in 1941, the World War II-era submarine USS Drum is now a land-based exhibit at Battleship Memorial Park. *Address:* Battleship Memorial Park *City:* Mobile *State:* AL *Zip:* 36601 *Phone:* 251-433-2703 *Web:* www.ussalabama.com *Email:* btunnell@ussalabama.com *Visitors welcome?* Yes *Hours:* Contact attraction directly *Admission:* Contact attraction directly *Operated by:* USS Alabama Battleship Commisison *NR?* Yes *NHL?* Yes *Year established/built:* 1941 *Latitude:* 30.6818 *Latitude:* -88.0148

HA-8

Launched in 1938, the World War II-era Japanese midget submarine HA-8 is a dry-berth exhibit at the Submarine Force Museum at Naval Base Groton. *Address:* Naval Submarine Base New London *City:* Groton *State:* CT *Zip:* 06349 *Phone:* 860-694-3174 *Web:* www.ussnautilus.org *Email:* gregory.caskey@navy.mil *Visitors welcome?* Yes *Hours:* May 1 to Oct. 1: Daily, 9 a.m. to 5 p.m.; Winter: Nov. 1 to April 30, daily, 9 a.m. to 4 p.m. *Admission:* FREE *Operated by:* Naval History & Heritage Command *NR?* No *NHL?* No *Year established/built:* 1938 *Latitude:* 41.3499 *Latitude:* -72.0759

HA-19

Launched in 1938, the Imperial Japanese midget submarine HA-19 is a dry-berth exhibit at the National Museum of the Pacific War. *Address:* 340 East Main St. *City:* Fredericksburg *State:* TX *Zip:* 78624 *Phone:* 830-997-4379 *Web:* www.nimitz-museum.org *Email:* info@nimitzfoundation.org *Visitors welcome?* Yes *Hours:* Daily, 9 a.m. to 5 p.m. *Admission:* $7 adults, $6 senior/active military, $4 students, under six FREE *Operated by:* Admiral Nimitz Foundation *NR?* No *NHL?* No *Year established/built:* 1938 *Latitude:* 30.2722 *Latitude:* -98.8682

KAITEN (HACKENSACK, NJ)
The Japanese Kaiten suicide torpedo is on display as a dry-berth exhibit at the New Jersey Naval Museum. *Address:* 78 River St. *City:* Hackensack *State:* NJ *Zip:* 07601 *Phone:* 201-342-3268 *Web:* www.njnm.com *Email:* njnavalmuseum@yahoo.com *Visitors welcome?* Yes *Hours:* Saturday and Sunday, 10 a.m. to 4 p.m. *Admission:* $9 adults, $4 children 12 and under *Operated by:* Submarine Memorial Association *NR?* Yes *NHL?* No *Latitude:* 40.8805 *Latitude:* -74.0415

KAITEN (HONOLULU, HI)
The Imperial Japanese Navy one-man submarine Kaiten is a dry-berth exhibit at the USS Bowfin memorial display. *Address:* 11 Arizona Memorial Drive *City:* Honolulu *State:* HI *Zip:* 96818 *Phone:* 808-423-1341 *Web:* www.bowfin.org *Email:* info@bowfin.org *Visitors welcome?* Yes *Hours:* Daily, 8 a.m. to 5 p.m. *Admission:* $10 adults, $7 seniors, active military, $4 children four to 12, under four permitted in museum but not submarine *Operated by:* Pacific Fleet Submarine Memorial Association *NR?* No *NHL?* No *Latitude:* 21.3643 *Latitude:* -157.9380

LING
Launched in 1943, the World War II-era submarine USS Ling is now a floating exhibit at the New Jersey Naval Museum. *Address:* 78 River St. *City:* Hackensack *State:* NJ *Zip:* 07601 *Phone:* 201-342-3268 *Web:* www.njnm.com *Email:* njnavalmuseum@yahoo.com *Visitors welcome?* Yes *Hours:* Saturday and Sunday, 10 a.m. to 4 p.m. *Admission:* $9 adults, $4 children 12 and under *Operated by:* Submarine Memorial Association *NR?* Yes *NHL?* No *Year established/built:* 1943 *Latitude:* 40.8805 *Latitude:* -74.0415

LIONFISH
Launched in 1944, the World War II-era submarine USS Lionfish is a floating exhibit at Battleship Cove. *Address:* 5 Water St. *City:* Fall River *State:* MA *Zip:* 02722 *Phone:* 508-678-1100 *Toll-free:* 800-533-3194 *Web:* www.battleshipcove.org *Visitors welcome?* Yes *Hours:* Summer: daily, 9 a.m. to 4:30 p.m.; Winter: daily, 9 a.m. to 5:30 p.m. *Admission:* Contact attraction directly *Operated by:* Battleship Cove *NR?* Yes *NHL?* Yes *Year established/built:* 1944 *Latitude:* 41.7040 *Latitude:* -71.1597

PAMPANITO
Launched in 1943, the World War II-era submarine USS Pampanito is now a museum ship on the San Francisco waterfront. *Address:* Fisherman's Wharf *City:* San Francisco *State:* CA *Zip:* 94133 *Phone:* 415-775-1943 *Web:* www.maritime.org *Visitors welcome?* Yes *Hours:* Daily, 9 a.m. to 5 p.m. *Admission:* $9 adults, $6 children six to 12, under six FREE *Operated by:* San Francisco Maritime National Park Association *NR?* Yes *NHL?* Yes *Year established/built:* 1943 *Latitude:* 37.8067 *Latitude:* -122.4110

RAZORBACK
Launched in 1944, the World War II-era submarine USS Razorback is a floating museum. *Address:* 120 Riverfront Park Dr. *City:* North Little Rock *State:* AR *Zip:* 72114 *Phone:* 501-371-8320 *Web:* www.aimm.museum *Email:* info@aimm.museum *Visitors welcome?* Yes *Hours:* Friday, 10 a.m. to 6 p.m.; Saturday, 10 a.m. to 6 p.m.; Sunday, 1 p.m. to 6 p.m. *Admission:* Contact attraction directly *Operated by:* Arkansas Inland Maritime Museum *NR?* No *NHL?* No *Year established/built:* 1944 *Latitude:* 34.7541 *Latitude:* -92.2681

REQUIN
Launched in 1945, the World War II-era submarine USS Requin is a floating exhibit on the Pittsburgh riverfront. *Address:* One Allegheny Ave. *City:* Pittsburgh *State:* PA *Zip:* 15212 *Phone:* 412-237-1550 *Web:* www.

CHAPTER 1 – SHIPS

carnegiesciencecenter.org *Visitors welcome?* Yes *Hours:* Sunday through Friday, 10 a.m. to 4:30 p.m.; Saturday, 10 a.m. to 6:30 p.m. *Admission:* Contact attraction directly *Operated by:* Carnegie Science Center *NR?* No *NHL?* No *Year established/built:* 1945 *Latitude:* 40.4518 *Latitude:* -80.0059

SEEHUND (HACKENSACK, NJ)

The World War II-era German Navy Seehund midget submarine is a dry-berth display at the New Jersey Naval Museum. *Address:* 78 River St. *City:* Hackensack *State:* NJ *Zip:* 07601 *Phone:* 201-342-3268 *Web:* www.njnm.com *Email:* njnavalmuseum@yahoo.com *Visitors welcome?* Yes *Hours:* Saturday and Sunday, 10 a.m. to 4 p.m. *Admission:* $9 adults, $4 children 12 and under *Operated by:* Submarine Memorial Association *NR?* No *NHL?* No *Latitude:* 40.8805 *Latitude:* -74.0415

SEEHUND (QUINCY, MA)

The Seehund is an example of World War II-era German Navy midget submarine. *Address:* 739 Washington Street *City:* Quincy *State:* MA *Zip:* 02169 *Phone:* 617-479-7900 *Web:* www.uss-salem.org *Email:* adventure@uss-salem.org *Visitors welcome?* Yes *Hours:* Contact attraction directly *Admission:* $5 adults, children under three FREE *Operated by:* United States Naval Shipbuilding Museum *NR?* No *NHL?* No *Latitude:* 42.2452 *Latitude:* -70.9700

SILURO SAN BARTOLOMEO

The World War II-era submersible Siluro San Bartolomeo is an Italian craft designed for commando operations. It is now a dry-berth exhibit at the Submarine Force Museum. *Address:* Naval Submarine Base New London *City:* Groton *State:* CT *Zip:* 06349 *Phone:* 860-694-3174 *Web:* www.ussnautilus.org *Email:* gregory.caskey@navy.mil *Visitors welcome?* Yes *Hours:* May 1 to Oct. 1: Daily, 9 a.m. to 4:45 p.m.; Winter: Nov. 1 to April 30, daily, 9 a.m. to 3:45 p.m. *Admission:* FREE *Operated by:* Naval History & Heritage Command *NR?* No *NHL?* No *Latitude:* 41.3499 *Latitude:* -72.0759

SILVERSIDES

Launched in 1941, the World War II-era submarine USS Silversides is a floating exhibit at the Great Lakes Naval Memorial & Museum. *Address:* 1346 Bluff Street *City:* Muskegon *State:* MI *Zip:* 49441 *Phone:* 231-755-1230 *Web:* www.glnmm.org *Email:* contactus@glnmm.org *Visitors welcome?* Yes *Hours:* January to April: Monday to Friday, 10 a.m. to 4 p.m.; May to October: Daily, 10 a.m. to 5:30 p.m.; November to December: Monday to Friday, 10 a.m. to 4:30 p.m., Saturday, 10 a.m. to 5:30 p.m. *Admission:* $10 adults; $8 students/seniors; $7 children; WWII vets, active military, and children FREE *Operated by:* Great Lakes Naval Memorial & Museum *NR?* Yes *NHL?* Yes *Year established/built:* 1941 *Latitude:* 43.2273 *Latitude:* -86.3368

TORSK

USS Torsk was launched in late 1944 and represented the state-of-the-art U.S. submarine technology in World War II. The submarine carried out two wartime patrols in the Pacific, and on August 14, 1945, sank two Japanese costal defense frigates, the last enemy ships sunk during the war. Torsk also has an amazing service record of 11,884 dives, among the highest total of any submarine in U.S. history. *Address:* Pier 3, Baltimore Inner Harbor (301 E. Pratt St.) *City:* Baltimore *State:* MD *Zip:* 21202 *Phone:* 410-539-1797 *Web:* www.historicships.org *Email:* administration@historicships.org *Visitors welcome?* Yes *Hours:* Contact attraction directly *Admission:* Contact attraction directly *Operated by:* Historic Ships in Baltimore *NR?* Yes *NHL?* Yes *Year established/built:* 1944 *Latitude:* 39.2866 *Latitude:* -76.6087

U-505

Launched in 1941, the World War II-era submarine U-505 is now a dry-berth exhibit at the Chicago Museum of Science and Industry. *Address:* 57th Street and Lake Shore Drive *City:* Chicago *State:* IL *Zip:* 60637 *Phone:* 773-684-1414 *Web:* www.msichicago.org *Email:* contact@msichicago.org *Visitors welcome?* Yes

CHAPTER 1 – SHIPS

Hours: Monday to Saturday, 9:30 a.m. to 4:30 p.m.; Sunday, 11 a.m. to 4 p.m. *Admission:* Contact attraction directly *Operated by:* Museum of Science and Industry *NR?* Yes *NHL?* Yes *Year established/built:* 1941 *Latitude:* 41.7925 *Latitude:* -87.5802.

For non-World War II-era submarine listings, see the section "Submarines" in this chapter.

TUGBOATS

ANGELS GATE
Launched in 1944, the World War II-era tugboat Angels Gate is an operational display at the Los Angeles Maritime Museum. *Address:* Berth 84, Foot of 6th St. *City:* San Pedro *State:* CA *Zip:* 90731 *Phone:* 310-548-7618 *Web:* www.lamaritimemuseum.org *Visitors welcome?* Yes *Hours:* Tuesday to Saturday, 10 a.m. to 5 p.m.; Sunday, noon to 5 p.m. *Admission:* $3 adults, $1 seniors/youths, children FREE *Operated by:* Los Angeles Maritime Museum *NR?* No *NHL?* No *Year established/built:* 1944 *Latitude:* 33.7387 *Latitude:* -118.2790

BOLSTER
Launched in 1945, the World War II-era rescue tug Bolster is now undergoing restoration near Sacramento. *City:* San Rafael *State:* CA *Phone:* 707-645-1377 *Web:* www.americanfleettugmuseum.org *Email:* fleettugmuseum@sbcglobal.net *Visitors welcome?* Yes *Hours:* Contact attraction directly *Admission:* Contact attraction directly *Operated by:* American Fleet Tug Museum *NR?* No *NHL?* No *Year established/built:* 1945 *Latitude:* 37.9735 *Latitude:* -122.5310

JOHN T. NASH
Launched in 1943, the World War II-era tug John T. Nash, also known as LT-5, is a floating exhibit at the H. Lee White Marine Museum. *Address:* West 1st Street Pier *City:* Oswego *State:* NY *Zip:* 13126 *Phone:* 315-342-0480 *Web:* www.hleewhitemarinemuseum.com *Email:* info@hleewhitemarinemuseum.com *Visitors welcome?* Yes *Hours:* September to June, daily, 1 p.m. to 5 p.m.; July and August, daily 10 a.m. to 5 p.m. *Admission:* $5 adults; $3 youth 5 to 12; under 5 FREE *Operated by:* H. Lee White Marine Museum *NR?* Yes *NHL?* Yes *Year established/built:* 1943 *Latitude:* 43.4553 *Latitude:* -76.5105

For more tugboats, see the section "Tugboats & Towboats" in this chapter.

CHAPTER 2 – SHIPWRECKS
WRECKS OF VESSELS EXPLORED BY MARINE ARCHAEOLOGISTS AND TREASURE HUNTERS

H.L. Hunley (North Charleston, S.C.)

Maritime history is often the story of great adventure, which sometimes end in death. Shipwrecks capture our imaginations because they are simultaneously graveyards and living reminders of a time and an era. Unlike sites on land, they are uniquely inaccessible; special equipment and excavation techniques are required even for wrecks a few feet below the surface. And the vessels themselves, if they have survived, are the tombs of their former inhabitants, and ought to be treated as such. Still, without the efforts of archaeologists and treasure hunters to bring pieces of wrecks to the surface, ordinary people would miss the chance to learn something about the lives of those who sailed to their doom. This chapter lists shipwrecks and exhibits of shipwreck artifacts.

ARABIA STEAMBOAT MUSEUM
Wrecked in 1856, the steamboat Arabia was excavated and the artifacts are now displayed in a museum. *Address:* 400 Grand Blvd. *City:* Kansas City *State:* MO *Zip:* 64106 *Phone:* 816-471-4030 *Web:* www.1856.com *Visitors welcome?* Yes *Hours:* Daily, 10:30 a.m. to 5:30 p.m. *Admission:* $12.50 adults, $11.50 seniors, $4.75 children four to 12, under four FREE *Operated by:* Arabia Steamboat Museum *NR?* No *NHL?* No *Year established/built:* 1856 *Latitude:* 39.1089 *Latitude:* -94.5814

CHAPTER 2 – SHIPWRECKS

BELLE
The wreck of the explorer La Salle's vessel Belle in Matagorda Bay was excavated in 1996-97. *Address:* Matagorda Bay *State:* TX *Visitors welcome?* Yes *Operated by:* Texas Historical Commission *NR?* No *NHL?* No *Latitude:* 28.5505 *Latitude:* -96.3013

BERTRAND
Wrecked in 1865, the steamboat Bertrand was excavated in 1969. Artifacts are now on display at the DeSoto National Wildlife Refuge visitor center. *Address:* 1434 316th Lane *City:* Missouri Valley *State:* IA *Zip:* 51555 *Phone:* 712-642-4121 *Web:* www.fws.gov/midwest/desoto/bertrand.htm *Email:* larry_klimek@fws.gov *Visitors welcome?* Yes *Hours:* Daily, 9:30 a.m. to 4 p.m. *Admission:* FREE *Operated by:* DeSoto National Wildlife Refuge *NR?* No *NHL?* No *Year established/built:* 1865 *Latitude:* 41.5506 *Latitude:* -96.0240

BLACK PANTHER HISTORIC SHIPWRECK PRESERVE
The Black Panther Historic Shipwreck Preserve is the final resting place of U-1105, a Germany Navy U-boat that was sunk off the Maryland coast in the waning days of World War II. It is now a recreational dive site. *Address:* Off Piney Point *City:* Colton's Point *State:* MD *Zip:* 20626 *Phone:* 301-769-2222 *Web:* www.co.saintmarys.md.us/recreate/museums/u1105.asp *Email:* christina.barbour@stmarysmd.com *Visitors welcome?* Yes *Hours:* Contact attraction directly *Admission:* Contact attraction directly *Operated by:* St. Mary's County Museum Division *NR?* No *NHL?* No *Year established/built:* 1945 *Latitude:* 38.2330 *Latitude:* -76.7654

DENBIGH
The Denbigh Project is an effort by the Institute of Nautical Archaeology at Texas A&M University to identify, document and preserve the wreck of Denbigh (41GV143), one of the most successful blockade runners of the American Civil War. *Address:* Bolivar Roads *Web:* nautarch.tamu.edu/PROJECTS/denbigh/denbigh.html *Email:* barnold@tamu.edu *Visitors welcome?* No *Operated by:* Denbigh Project *NR?* No *NHL?* No *Latitude:* 29.3505 *Latitude:* -94.7527

JOFFRE
Launched in 1918, the trawler Joffre sank in August 1947. It is now part of the Stellwagen Bank National Marine Sanctuary. *Address:* Stellwagen Bank National Marine Sanctuary *City:* Scituate *State:* MA *Zip:* 02066 *Phone:* 781-545-8026 *Web:* stellwagen.noaa.gov *Email:* craig.macdonald@noaa.gov *Visitors welcome?* Yes *Hours:* Contact attraction directly *Admission:* Contact attraction directly *Operated by:* Stellwagen Bank National Marine Sanctuary *NR?* Yes *NHL?* No *Year established/built:* 1918 *Latitude:* 42.1959 *Latitude:* -70.7259

SPARROW-HAWK
The remains of the 17th-century vessel Sparrow-Hawk, which carried settlers to New England, is preserved in the Pilgrim Hall Museum. *Address:* 75 Court St. *City:* Plymouth *State:* MA *Zip:* 02360 *Phone:* 508-746-1620 *Web:* www.pilgrimhall.org *Email:* pegbaker@pilgrimhall.org *Visitors welcome?* Yes *Hours:* Daily (except January): 9:30 a.m. to 4:30 p.m. *Admission:* $7 adults, $6 seniors, $4 children five to 17, under five FREE *Operated by:* Pilgrim Hall Museum *NR?* No *NHL?* No *Year established/built:* 1626 *Latitude:* 41.9588 *Latitude:* -70.6681

CHAPTER 3 – MUSEUMS
INSTITUTIONS THAT SPECIALIZE IN PRESERVING, STUDYING, AND INTERPRETING MARITIME CULTURE

Nauticus with USS Wisconsin (Norfolk, Va.)

Few institutions serve a more important purpose in preserving memory than the history museum. Of these, a few specialize by preserving the stories and artifacts of a specific maritime region or industry. They present their research to the public with exhibits and other educational activities. Their collections ranged from shipbuilders tools and logbooks to full-sized, operating vessels. A few, such as the famed Mystic Seaport in Mystic, Conn., attempt to present an earlier time with actors in a faithfully recreated waterfront atmosphere. In addition, some history museums with a broad mandate to preserve the story of a geographic region feature a set of exhibits or a wing dedicated to the maritime story. This chapter lists maritime museums and other institutions with a strong maritime collection available to the public.

MARITIME MUSEUMS

ALASKA

KODIAK MARITIME MUSEUM
Kodiak Maritime Museum is the only organization in the U.S. solely dedicated to preserving Alaska's illustrious maritime heritage. *Address:* Eagan Way and Mill Bay Road *City:* Kodiak *State:* AK *Zip:* 99615 *Phone:*

907-486-0384 *Web:* www.kodiakmaritimemuseum.org *Email:* info@kodiakmaritimemuseum.org *Visitors welcome?* Yes *Hours:* Contact attraction directly *Admission:* Contact attraction directly *Operated by:* Kodiak Maritime Museum *NR?* No *NHL?* No *Year established/built:* 1996 *Latitude:* 57.8016 *Latitude:* -152.3810

ALABAMA

GULFQUEST - NATIONAL MARITIME MUSEUM OF THE GULF OF MEXICO
Projected to open in the Spring of 2011, GulfQuest will be the first museum dedicated to the Gulf Coast's rich maritime traditions – and only the third interactive maritime museum in the world. *Address:* 250 N. Water Street, Suite 13 *City:* Mobile *State:* AL *Zip:* 36602 *Phone:* 251-436-8901 *Fax:* 251-436-8903 *Web:* www.nationalmaritime.us *Email:* tzodrow@gulfquest.org *Visitors welcome?* Yes *Hours:* Contact owner *Admission:* Contact owner *Operated by:* City of Mobile *NR?* No *NHL?* No *Year established/built:* 2011 *Latitude:* 30.6972 *Latitude:* -88.0408

ARKANSAS

ARKANSAS INLAND MARITIME MUSEUM
The mission of the Arkansas Inland Maritime Museum is to commemorate America's rich naval and maritime heritage through the preservation and exhibition of historic naval vessels with an emphasis on the era of World War II through the present. *Address:* 120 Riverfront Park Dr. *City:* North Little Rock *State:* AR *Zip:* 72114 *Phone:* 501-371-8320 *Web:* www.aimm.museum *Email:* info@aimm.museum *Visitors welcome?* Yes *Hours:* Friday, 10 a.m. to 6 p.m.; Saturday, 10 a.m. to 6 p.m.; Sunday, 1 p.m. to 6 p.m. *Admission:* Contact attraction directly *Operated by:* Arkansas Inland Maritime Museum *NR?* No *NHL?* No *Latitude:* 34.7541 *Latitude:* -92.2681

CALIFORNIA

HUMBOLDT BAY MARITIME MUSEUM
The Humboldt Bay Maritime Museum invites you to explore the vast maritime history of California's north coast. From shipwrecks to shipbuilding, the museum holds what was left behind to share with the future. *Address:* Samoa Court *City:* Samoa *State:* CA *Zip:* 95564 *Phone:* 707-444-9440 *Web:* www.humboldtbaymaritimemuseum.com *Email:* joshhbmm@suddenlinkmail.com *Visitors welcome?* Yes *Hours:* Summer: Wednesday to Sunday, 11 a.m. to 4 p.m. *Admission:* Contact attraction directly *Operated by:* Humboldt Bay Maritime Museum *NR?* No *NHL?* No *Year established/built:* 1977 *Latitude:* 40.8190 *Latitude:* -124.1870

LOS ANGELES MARITIME MUSEUM
The Los Angeles Maritime Museum creates an awareness and appreciation of the maritime history of coastal California, with an emphasis on the people and institutions of the port city of Los Angeles. *Address:* Berth 84, Foot of 6th St. *City:* San Pedro *State:* CA *Zip:* 90731 *Phone:* 310-548-7618 *Web:* www.lamaritimemuseum.org *Visitors welcome?* Yes *Hours:* Tuesday to Saturday, 10 a.m. to 5 p.m.; Sunday, noon to 5 p.m. *Admission:* $3

adults, $1 seniors/youths, children FREE *Operated by:* Los Angeles Maritime Museum *NR?* No *NHL?* No *Year established/built:* 1980 *Latitude:* 33.7387 *Latitude:* -118.2790

MARITIME MUSEM OF SAN DIEGO

The Maritime Museum of San Diego enjoys a worldwide reputation for excellence in restoring, maintaining and operating historic vessels. The museum has one of the world's finest collections of historic ships, including the world's oldest active ship, Star of India. *Address:* 1492 North Harbor Drive *City:* San Diego *State:* CA *Zip:* 92101 *Phone:* 619-234-9153 *Web:* www.sdmaritime.com *Email:* info@sdmaritime.org *Visitors welcome?* Yes *Hours:* Daily, 9 a.m. to 8 p.m. *Admission:* $14 adults; $11 seniors, active military; $8 children 6-17; under six FREE *Operated by:* Maritime Museum Association of San Diego *NR?* No *NHL?* No *Latitude:* 32.7276 *Latitude:* -117.1800

MONTEREY MARITIME MUSEUM

The Monterey Maritime Museum preserves the early maritime history of one of the oldest settlements in California. *Address:* 5 Custom House Plaza *City:* Monterey *State:* CA *Zip:* 93940 *Phone:* 831-372-2608 *Web:* www.montereyhistory.org *Email:* AlexDVance@MontereyHistory.org *Visitors welcome?* Yes *Hours:* Tuesday to Saturday, 10 a.m. to 5 p.m. *Admission:* FREE *Operated by:* Monterey History & Art Association *NR?* No *NHL?* No *Year established/built:* 1971 *Latitude:* 36.6014 *Latitude:* -121.8940

NEWPORT HARBOR NAUTICAL MUSEUM

The Newport Harbor Nautical Museum is dedicated to preserving and promoting the nautical heritage of Newport Harbor, southern California and the eastern Pacific through stimulating exhibitions and inspiring education programs pertaining to nautical arts. *Address:* 600 East Bay Ave. *City:* Newport Beach *State:* CA *Zip:* 92661 *Phone:* 949-673-7863 *Web:* www.nhnm.org *Email:* nhnm@nhnm.org *Visitors welcome?* Yes *Hours:* Contact attraction directly *Admission:* $5 donation adults, children under 12 FREE *Operated by:* Newport Harbor Nautical Museum *NR?* No *NHL?* No *Latitude:* 33.6031 *Latitude:* -117.9000

SANTA BARBARA MARITIME MUSEUM

Opened in 2000, the Santa Barbara Maritime Museum offers a wide variety of traveling exhibitions on 8,000 square feet of museum space. The museum also offers educational programs, including docent tours, summer camps and overnight tall ship stays. *Address:* 113 Harbor Way *City:* Santa Barbara *State:* CA *Zip:* 93109 *Phone:* 805-962-8404 *Web:* www.sbmm.org *Email:* museum@sbmm.org *Visitors welcome?* Yes *Hours:* Daily (except Wednesday), 10 a.m. to 5 p.m. *Admission:* $7 adults, $4 seniors/students/active military, $2 children one to five, infants FREE *Operated by:* Santa Barbara Maritime Museum *NR?* No *NHL?* No *Year established/built:* 2000 *Latitude:* 34.4040 *Latitude:* -119.6950

TAHOE MARITIME MUSEUM

Located on the West Shore of Lake Tahoe, the Tahoe Maritime Museum's mission is to stimulate an interest in and an understanding of Lake Tahoe's rich maritime history through the highest standards of historic preservation, innovative interpretation, and public education. *Address:* 5205 West Lake Blvd. *City:* Homewood *State:* CA *Zip:* 96141 *Phone:* 530-525-9253 *Web:* www.tahoemaritimemuseum.org *Email:* info@tahoemaritime.org *Visitors welcome?* Yes *Hours:* Summer: Daily (except Wednesday), 10 a.m. to 5 p.m.; Winter: Friday, Saturday, Sunday, 10 a.m. to 5 p.m. *Admission:* $5 adults, children under 12 FREE *Operated by:* Tahoe Maritime Museum *NR?* No *NHL?* No *Latitude:* 39.0846 *Latitude:* -120.1600

U.S. NAVAL MUSEUM OF ARMAMENT AND TECHNOLOGY

The U.S. Naval Museum of Armament and Technology is supported by the China Lake Museum Foundation. *Address:* 1 Pearl Harbor Way *City:* China Lake *State:* CA *Zip:* 93555 *Phone:* 760-939-2916 *Web:* www.history.navy.mil/museums/china_lake/china_lake.htm *Visitors welcome?* Yes *Hours:* Monday to Thursday, 6 a.m to 4 p.m.; non-flex Fridays, 6 a.m. to 3 p.m. *Admission:* FREE *Operated by:* Naval History & Heritage Command *NR?* No *NHL?* No *Latitude:* 35.6508 *Latitude:* -117.6620

U.S. NAVY SEABEE MUSEUM
The mission of the U.S. Navy Seabee Museum is to stand the watch over the legacy of the 'Can do!' spirit for the U.S. Navy Seabees and the Civil Engineer Corps of the Navy, veterans, and the public. *Address:* Naval Base Ventura County *City:* Ventura *State:* CA *Zip:* 93043 *Phone:* 805-982-5167 *Web:* www.seabeehf.org/museum/ *Email:* info@seabeehf.org *Visitors welcome?* Yes *Hours:* Tuesday to Friday, 8 a.m. to 4 p.m.; Sunday, 10 a.m. to 3 p.m. *Admission:* FREE *Operated by:* Naval History & Heritage Command *NR?* No *NHL?* No *Latitude:* 34.1571 *Latitude:* -119.1990

USS MIDWAY MUSEUM
The USS Midway Museum's centerpiece is the World War II-era aircraft carrier USS Midway. *Address:* 910 N. Harbor Dr. *City:* San Diego *State:* CA *Zip:* 92101 *Phone:* 619-544-9600 *Web:* www.midway.org *Visitors welcome?* Yes *Hours:* Contact attraction directly *Admission:* $17 adults, $13 seniors/students, $10 retired military, $9 youth *Operated by:* USS Midway Museum *NR?* No *NHL?* No *Latitude:* 32.7147 *Latitude:* -117.1740

VALLEJO NAVAL AND HISTORICAL MUSEUM
The Vallejo Naval and Historical Museum collects and shares with its visitors the fascinating history of the City of Vallejo and the U.S. Navy at Mare Island. *Address:* 734 Marin St. *City:* Vallejo *State:* CA *Zip:* 94590 *Phone:* 707-643-0077 *Web:* www.vallejomuseum.org *Email:* valmuse@pacbell.net *Visitors welcome?* Yes *Hours:* Wednesday to Sunday, noon to 4 p.m. *Admission:* $5 adults, $3 seniors/students, children under 12 FREE *Operated by:* Vallejo Naval and Historical Museum *NR?* Yes *NHL?* No *Latitude:* 38.1026 *Latitude:* -122.2570

VENTURA COUNTY MARITIME MUSEUM
The mission of the Venture County Maritime Museum is to provide a rewarding museum experience based on the age of sail and to enhance the understanding of our rich maritime heritage through world-class maritime art, unique ship models and dynamic exhibits. *Address:* 2731 Victoria Ave. *City:* Ventura *State:* CA *Zip:* 93035 *Phone:* 805-984-6260 *Web:* vcmm.org *Email:* vcmminfo@aol.com *Visitors welcome?* Yes *Hours:* Daily, 11 a.m. to 5 p.m. *Admission:* Contact attraction directly *Operated by:* Ventura County Maritime Museum *NR?* No *NHL?* No *Year established/built:* 1991 *Latitude:* 34.1755 *Latitude:* -119.2220

WHALERS CABIN AND WHALERS STATE MUSEUM
The Whalers Cabin Museum and Whalers Station Museum are located within Point Lobos State Reserve on Highway 1 near Carmel. *Address:* Point Lobos State Reserve *City:* Carmel *State:* CA *Zip:* 93923 *Phone:* 831-624-4909 *Web:* pt-lobos.parks.state.ca.us *Email:* pointlobos@parks.ca.gov *Visitors welcome?* Yes *Hours:* Contact attraction directly *Admission:* Contact attraction directly *Operated by:* Point Lobos Association *NR?* No *NHL?* No *Latitude:* 36.5202 *Latitude:* -121.9470

Mystic Seaport: A Family Trip Back in Time
by Joe Follansbee

I'll never forget the day I argued with a man about the candidacy of Abraham Lincoln for president. The gentleman was decked out in a dusty top hat and a frayed top coat, and we met under a tree in the 19th-century village at Mystic Seaport. He ignored my typical summer tourist outfit: t-shirt, shorts, and sandals. I was just another visitor wandering the grounds of the country's premier maritime museum with his wife and two young daughters. The gentleman, one of the museum's "living history" actors, tried to persuade me that

Mr. Lincoln was not the best man for the job in a time when the country was in such turmoil over slavery and states' rights, and that his rival Stephen Douglas was the better choice.

Crew scrambles on the foretopsail of the whaleship Charles W. Morgan at Mystic Seaport.

I was completely captivated by this conversation. I knew he was an actor, but he was an expert at his role, and it was great fun to become a walk-on on this open-air stage surrounded by restored waterfront buildings and real tall ships on the banks of the Mystic River in Connecticut. I don't remember who won our little debate; I recall that we parted agreeing to disagree. But the experience sold me 100 percent on the power of re-created history to bring the past to life in the present, with Mystic Seaport the archetype showing the way. Of all America's 260 or so maritime museums, Mystic Seaport tops the list as the country's must-visit maritime history institution.

The museum—official name Mystic Seaport: The Museum of America and the Sea—was founded in 1929 with one goal: to tell the story of America's relationship with the ocean, primarily as a platform for commercial activity. The centerpiece of the 37-acre site is the whaleship *Charles W. Morgan*, the museum's first major vessel acquisition in 1941. Launched exactly 100 years earlier, the 113-foot, two-masted bark returned home from its maiden voyage with 600 barrels of sperm oil, 800 barrels of whale oil and 10,000 lbs of whalebone. When I visited it in 2004, museum guides showed visitors that it was a real ship by having groups walk from the port side to the starboard across the 27-foot, six-inch beam. The deck tipped slightly with the shifting weight. Today, Mystic Seaport is in the midst of a three-year, $5 million restoration of the *Morgan*'s hull, so access may be limited for a while.

If you can't board the *Morgan*, you may be able to watch some of the work at the museum's Preservation Shipyard, where volunteers and professional shipwrights maintain the museum's collection of 16 historic boats and ships with traditional tools and techniques. (The workers aren't above using power tools though; I saw one using an electric sander.) The cavernous main building is constructed with a visitor's gallery, which allows you to look down on the work from a distance safe from small hands, but close enough to satisfy wood-working geeks. If you're very lucky, you might catch the yard on a major project; in 2001, Mystic Seaport launched the schooner *Amistad*, a replica of the vessel made famous by an 1839 rebellion of African captives heading for slavery in the New World.

Most of the museum's vessel collection, such as the sloop *Emma C. Berry* and the schooner *L.A. Dunton*, are made of wood, which require constant care. The museum's largest vessel, the 1882 *Joseph Conrad*, is an iron-hulled three-master. But even metal hulls need maintenance; the ship was recently hauled out for restoration work at the Preservation Shipyard. The museum also has one steamer, the *Sabino*, which takes passengers on brief tours of the waterfront and nearby sights. You can take your time visiting all the vessels on a recreated 19th-century waterfront, including self-guided tours of the boats themselves. I came away with a sense of the tight spaces and almost complete lack of privacy for the seafarers who worked for months, sometimes years at a time on one of these boats.

Virtually all of Mystic Seaport's grounds are kid-friendly with plenty of places for young ones to run around in the open air and explore fabulous spaces. My daughters, just 10 and seven at the time of my visit, loved climbing on a beached whaleboat. They also enjoyed the Mystic Seaport exhibits and galleries, which often have hands-on interactive exhibits suited to young minds. At this writing, the museum had just opened an exhibit titled "Building America's Canals," which focuses on the nation's historic canal system. The exhibit featured model cranes for loading and unloading imaginary cargo. Kids can also build toy boats or create maritime art at the museum.

Once you and your crew have exhausted themselves clambering about on boats and in historic buildings, the museum offers several restaurant options. The museum recently opened Latitude 41°, formerly the Seamen's Inne Restaurant & Pub. I remember the old restaurant as looking a bit careworn, so it was nice to hear about the upgrade. The museum also features the family-oriented Gallery Restaurant, a tavern open during the summer, and a small café with baked goods. There's another great option for eating out: the nearby historic village of Mystic. My family enjoyed a pizza in one of the town's small downtown restaurants near the picturesque drawbridge.

Mystic Seaport is pricier than most museums; adults pay $18.50 for a ticket, but kids under six get in free. However, you get a lot for your money, and you could easily spend a couple of days exploring the grounds. The museum also has a definite and understandable east coast bias, something noticeable to a west coast native such as myself. But it's a minor point. The experience of talking with maritime history experts and "roleplayers," as the museum calls them, make a visit much more valuable than a visit to any conventional history museum on either coast. You might even find yourself in an entertaining discussion with a gentleman in a top hat who might just persuade you that Stephen Douglas was a better choice in 1860.

Mystic Seaport: The Museum of America and the Sea. 75 Greenmanville Avenue, Mystic, Conn., 06355. 860-572-5315; www.mysticseaport.org. Open daily, April to October, 9 a.m. to 5 p.m.; November to March, 10 a.m. to 4 p.m. Adults $18.50; Seniors, $16.50; Children 6-17, $13; under six, FREE.

Joe Follansbee is the editor of the Fyddeye Guide and Fyddeye.com.

Email your family's maritime heritage story to contact@fyddeye.com.

CONNECTICUT

CAPTAIN PALMER HOUSE
Captain Palmer House is a 16-room Victorian mansion built in 1852 by two brothers, Captains Nathaniel Brown Palmer and Alexander Smith Palmer. *Address:* 40 Palmer Street *City:* Stonington *State:* CT *Zip:* 06378 *Phone:* 860-535-8445 *Web:* www.stoningtonhistory.org *Email:* palmerhouse@stoningtonhistory.org *Visitors welcome?* Yes *Hours:* Wednesday to Sunday, 1 p.m. to 5 p.m. *Admission:* Contact attraction directly *Operated by:* Stonington Historical Society *NR?* No *NHL?* No *Year established/built:* 1852 *Latitude:* 41.3428 *Latitude:* -71.9051

COAST GUARD MUSEUM AT THE U.S. COAST GUARD ACADEMY
Tucked away on the grounds of the picturesque U. S. Coast Guard Academy, the Coast Guard Museum contains artifacts that span the two hundred year history of America's premier maritime service. *Address:* 15

Mohegan Avenue *City:* New London *State:* CT *Zip:* 06320 *Phone:* 860-444-8511 *Web:* www.uscg.mil/hq/cg092/museum/ *Visitors welcome?* Yes *Hours:* Contact attraction directly *Admission:* Contact attraction directly *Operated by:* U.S. Coast Guard (District 1) *NR?* No *NHL?* No *Latitude:* 41.3702 *Latitude:* -72.1060

CONNECTICUT RIVER MUSEUM
Located on the waterfront in historic Essex, the Connecticut River Museum is the perfect place to explore the heritage and experience the wonders of New England. *Address:* 67 Main St. *City:* Essex *State:* CT *Zip:* 06426 *Phone:* 860-767-8269 *Web:* www.ctrivermuseum.org *Email:* jroberts@ctrivermuseum.org *Visitors welcome?* Yes *Hours:* Tuesday to Sunday, 10 a.m. to 5 p.m. *Admission:* $8 adults, $7 seniors, $5 children six to 12, under six FREE *Operated by:* Connecticut River Museum *NR?* No *NHL?* No *Latitude:* 41.3514 *Latitude:* -72.3864

CUSTOM HOUSE MARITIME MUSEUM
The mission of the Custom House Maritime Museum is to preserve New London's U.S. Custom House and to promote and interpret the maritime history of the port of New London and the surrounding region through museum exhibitions and educational programs. *Address:* 150 Bank St. *City:* New London *State:* CT *Zip:* 06320 *Phone:* 860-447-2501 *Web:* www.nlmaritimesociety.org *Email:* nlmaritimedirector@gmail.com *Visitors welcome?* Yes *Hours:* April to December, Tuesday to Saturday, 1 p.m. to 5 p.m. *Admission:* FREE *Operated by:* New London Maritime Society *NR?* No *NHL?* No *Year established/built:* 1833 *Latitude:* 41.3524 *Latitude:* -72.0956

MYSTIC SEAPORT: THE MUSEUM OF AMERICA AND THE SEA
Mystic Seaport: The Museum of America and the Sea is the nation's leading maritime museum. *Address:* 75 Greenmanville Avenue *City:* Mystic *State:* CT *Zip:* 06355 *Phone:* 860-572-5315 *Web:* www.mysticseaport.org *Visitors welcome?* Yes *Hours:* Daily, April to October, 9 a.m. to 5 p.m.; November to March, 10 a.m. to 4 p.m. *Admission:* Adults, $18.50; Seniors, $16.50; Children 6-17, $13; Under six, FREE *Operated by:* Mystic Seaport: The Museum of America and the Sea *NR?* No *NHL?* No *Year established/built:* 1929 *Latitude:* 41.3617 *Latitude:* -71.9634

NATIONAL COAST GUARD MUSEUM
The Coast Guard Foundation / National Coast Guard Museum Association has recently won approval to build a stunning, 60,000 square-foot facility on the Thames River in New London, Conn. The site combines historical significance with aesthetic beauty. It *Address:* Thames River *City:* New London *State:* CT *Visitors welcome?* Yes *Hours:* Contact attraction directly *Admission:* Contact attraction directly *Operated by:* Coast Guard Foundation/National Coast Guard Museum Association *NR?* No *NHL?* No *Latitude:* 41.3023 *Latitude:* -72.0795

OLD LIGHTHOUSE MUSEUM
Established in 1823, the Old Lighthouse Museum, once the Stonington Harbor Lighthouse was constructed in 1840 and deactivated in 1889. *Address:* 7 Water Street *City:* Stonington *State:* CT *Zip:* 06378 *Phone:* 860-535-1440 *Web:* www.stoningtonhistory.org *Email:* lighthouse@stoningtonhistory.org *Visitors welcome?* Yes *Hours:* Daily, May to October, 10 a.m to 5 p.m. *Admission:* Contact attraction directly *Operated by:* Stonington Historical Society *NR?* Yes *NHL?* No *Year established/built:* 1823 *Latitude:* 41.3286 *Latitude:* -71.9059

SUBMARINE FORCE MUSEUM
Visit the Submarine Force Museum and peer into the lives of the men who sail the ocean depths in their "sharks of steel." Exhibits include the Nautilus, the world's first nuclear-powered submarine. *Address:* Naval Submarine Base New London *City:* Groton *State:* CT *Zip:* 06349 *Phone:* 860-694-3174 *Web:* www.ussnautilus.org *Email:* gregory.caskey@navy.mil *Visitors welcome?* Yes *Hours:* May 1 to Oct. 1: Daily, 9 a.m. to 5 p.m.; Winter: Nov. 1 to April 30, daily, 9 a.m. to 4 p.m. *Admission:* FREE *Operated by:* Naval History & Heritage Command *NR?* No *NHL?* No *Latitude:* 41.3499 *Latitude:* -72.0759

CHAPTER 3 – MUSEUMS

DISTRICT OF COLUMBIA

DECATUR HOUSE
Decatur House is the home built for War of 1812 naval hero Stephen Decatur and his wife, Susan. *Address:* 1610 H Street NW *City:* Washington *State:* DC *Zip:* 20006 *Phone:* 242-842-0920 *Web:* www.decaturhouse. org *Email:* decatur_house@nthp.org *Visitors welcome?* Yes *Hours:* Call for guided tour schedule *Admission:* $5 per person *Operated by:* Decatur House *NR?* No *NHL?* No *Year established/built:* 1818 *Latitude:* 38.8999 *Latitude:* -77.0385

DELAWARE

BOWERS BEACH MARITIME MUSEUM
Bowers Beach Maritime Museum is located on the site of a Colonial period fishing village. *Address:* 3357 Main St. *City:* Frederica *State:* DE *Zip:* 19946 *Phone:* 302-335-1400 *Visitors welcome?* Yes *Hours:* Contact attraction directly *Admission:* Contact attraction directly *Operated by:* Bowers Beach Maritime Museum *NR?* No *NHL?* No *Year established/built:* 1976 *Latitude:* 39.0593 *Latitude:* -75.4023

CANNONBALL HOUSE MARITIME MUSEUM
The Cannonball House is the home of the Lewes Historical Society's maritime museum. *Address:* 110 Shipcarpenter St. *City:* Lewes *State:* DE *Zip:* 19958 *Phone:* 302-645-7670 *Web:* www.historiclewes.org/museums/cbh. html *Email:* tours@historiclewes.org *Visitors welcome?* Yes *Hours:* May through mid-June: Saturday, 11 a.m. to 4 p.m.; mid-June to mid-September: Monday to Saturday, 11 a.m. to 4 p.m.; mid-September to early October: Saturday, 11 a.m. to 4 p.m. *Admission:* $2 adults, under 12 FREE *Operated by:* Lewes Historical Society *NR?* No *NHL?* No *Year established/built:* 1765 *Latitude:* 38.7771 *Latitude:* -75.1421

DISCOVERSEA SHIPWRECK MUSEUM
DiscoverSea Shipwreck Museum was founded with the goal of recovering and preserving our maritime heritage. *Address:* 708 Coastal Highway *City:* Fenwick Island *State:* DE *Zip:* 19944 *Phone:* 302-539-9366 *Tollfree:* 888-743-5524 *Web:* www.discoversea.com *Email:* dsmuseum@aol.com *Visitors welcome?* Yes *Hours:* June, July, and August: Daily, 11 a.m. to 8 p.m.; September through May: Saturday and Sunday, 11 a.m. to 4 p.m. *Admission:* Contact attraction directly *Operated by:* DiscoverSea Shipwreck Museum *NR?* No *NHL?* No *Year established/built:* 1995 *Latitude:* 38.4600 *Latitude:* -75.0521

KALMAR NYCKEL SHIPYARD AND MUSEUM
When the Kalmar Nyckel is not visiting other ports, she resides at the Kalmar Nyckel Shipyard on the Christina River in her home port of Wilmington. *Address:* 1124 E. Seventh St. *City:* Wilmington *State:* DE *Zip:* 19801 *Phone:* 302-429-7447 *Web:* www.kalmarnyckel.org *Email:* info@kalmarnyckel.org *Visitors welcome?* Yes *Hours:* Contact attraction directly *Admission:* Contact attraction directly *Operated by:* Kalmar Nyckel Foundation *NR?* No *NHL?* No *Latitude:* 39.7377 *Latitude:* -75.5367

PORT PENN INTERPRETIVE CENTER
The Port Penn Interpretive Center offers displays and programs which explain the folk life of the historic wetland communities along the shores of the Delaware River. *Address:* Fort DuPont State Park *City:* Delaware City *State:* DE *Zip:* 19706 *Phone:* 302-834-7941 *Web:* www.destateparks.com/attractions/port-penn/ *Email:* nicole. jenkins@state.de.us *Visitors welcome?* Yes *Hours:* Contact attraction directly *Admission:* Contact attraction directly *Operated by:* Delaware State Parks *NR?* No *NHL?* No *Latitude:* 39.5634 *Latitude:* -75.5873

CHAPTER 3 – MUSEUMS

TREASURES OF THE SEA
The Treasures of the Sea exhibit features items recovered from the 17th-century wreck Nuestra Senora de Atocha. *Address:* Seashore Highway *City:* Georgetown *State:* DE *Zip:* 19947 *Phone:* 302-856-5700 *Web:* www.treasuresofthesea.org *Visitors welcome?* Yes *Hours:* Monday and Tuesday, 10 a.m. to 4 p.m.; Friday, noon to 4 p.m.; Saturday, 9 a.m. to 1 p.m. *Admission:* $3 adults, $2.50 seniors, $1 students/children, under four FREE *Operated by:* Delaware Technical and Community College *NR?* No *NHL?* No *Latitude:* 38.7134 *Latitude:* -75.3187

FLORIDA

APALACHICOLA MARITIME MUSEUM
The Apalachicola Maritime Museum celebrates the maritime history of Apalachicola in the form of a maritime museum, active sailing and boat building and restoration programs, educational programs and stewardship of ecosystems in the Apalachicola Chattahoochee basin. *Address:* 103 Water St. *City:* Apalachicola *State:* FL *Zip:* 32328 *Phone:* 850-653-2500 *Web:* www.ammfl.org *Email:* admin@apalachicolamaritimemuseum.org *Visitors welcome?* Yes *Hours:* Monday to Saturday, 10 a.m. to 4 p.m.; Saturday, noon to 4 p.m. *Admission:* Contact attraction directly *Operated by:* Apalachicola Maritime Museum *NR?* No *NHL?* No *Year established/built:* 1987 *Latitude:* 29.7256 *Latitude:* -84.9815

JACKSONVILLE MARITIME MUSEUM
The mission of the Jacksonville Maritime Museum Society is to preserve and interpret the maritime history of Jacksonville and the First Coast in order to foster among all residents and visitors a deeper appreciation of our maritime heritage. *Address:* 1015 Museum Circle *City:* Jacksonville *State:* FL *Zip:* 32207 *Phone:* 904-398-9011 *Web:* www.jaxmaritimemuseum.org *Email:* jaxmarmus@bellsouth.net *Visitors welcome?* Yes *Hours:* Monday to Friday, 10:30 a.m. to 3 p.m.; Saturday and Sunday, 1 p.m. to 5 p.m. *Admission:* Contact attraction directly *Operated by:* Jacksonville Maritime Museum Society *NR?* No *NHL?* No *Latitude:* 30.3206 *Latitude:* -81.6590

KEY WEST SHIPWRECK HISTOREUM MUSEUM
Address: 1 Whitehead Street *City:* Key West *State:* FL *Zip:* 33040 *Phone:* 305-292-8990 *Web:* www.shipwreckhistoreum.com *Email:* shipwreck@historictours.com *Visitors welcome?* Yes *Hours:* Monday to Sunday, 9:40 a.m. to 5 p.m. *Admission:* $12 adults, $5 children, three and under FREE *Operated by:* Key West Shipwreck HISTOREUM® Museum *NR?* No *NHL?* No *Latitude:* 24.5593 *Latitude:* -81.8073

MAN IN THE SEA MUSEUM
The Man in the Sea Museum showcases the progress of underwater technology, from the earliest days of diving to the most modern underwater habitats. *Address:* 17314 Panama City Beach Parkway *City:* Panama City Beach *State:* FL *Zip:* 32413 *Phone:* 850-235-4101 *Web:* www.maninthesea.org *Email:* info@maninthesea.org *Visitors welcome?* Yes *Hours:* Daily, 10 a.m. to 4 p.m. *Admission:* $5 adults, $4.50 seniors, children under seven FREE *Operated by:* Man in the Sea Museum *NR?* No *NHL?* No *Latitude:* 30.2325 *Latitude:* -85.8934

MARITIME & CLASSIC BOAT MUSEUM
The Maritime & Classic Boat Museum preserves the rich history of recreational boating in Florida. *Address:* 1707 NE Indian River Drive *City:* Jensen Beach *State:* FL *Zip:* 34957 *Phone:* 772-692-1234 *Web:* www.mcbmfl.org *Email:* info@mcbmfl.org *Visitors welcome?* Yes *Hours:* Monday to Friday, 11 a.m. to 4 p.m. *Admission:* FREE *Operated by:* Maritime & Classic Boat Museum *NR?* No *NHL?* No *Year established/built:* 1993 *Latitude:* 27.2278 *Latitude:* -80.2138

MARITIME MUSEUM OF THE FLORIDA KEYS
Located inside a reproduction castle, the Maritime Museum of the Florida Keys features artifacts from Spanish shipwrecks from the 16th through 18th centuries. *Address:* 102670 U.S. Highway 1 *City:* Key Largo *State:* FL *Zip:* 33037 *Phone:* 305-451-6444 *Visitors welcome?* Yes *Hours:* Daily, 9:30 a.m. to 5 p.m. *Admission:* $5 adults, $4.50 seniors, $3 children five to 12, under five FREE *Operated by:* Maritime Museum of the Florida Keys *NR?* No *NHL?* No *Latitude:* 25.1281 *Latitude:* -80.4105

Did you spot an error? Email your correction to contact@fyddeye.com.

MEL FISHER MARITIME MUSEUM
The Mel Fisher Maritime Museum features a research library and laboratory for the conservation of Key West and Gulf Coast maritime history. *Address:* 200 Greene Street *City:* Key West *State:* FL *Zip:* 33040 *Phone:* 305-294-2633 *Web:* www.melfisher.org *Email:* office@melfisher.org *Visitors welcome?* Yes *Hours:* Monday to Friday, 8:30 a.m. to 5 p.m.; Saturday and Sunday, 9:30 a.m. to 5 p.m. *Admission:* $12 adults, $10.50 students, $6 children *Operated by:* Mel Fisher Maritime Heritage Society *NR?* No *NHL?* No *Latitude:* 24.5582 *Latitude:* -81.8064

NATIONAL NAVY UDT-SEAL MUSEUM
The National Navy UDT-SEAL Museum is the only museum dedicated solely to preserving the history of the Navy SEALs and their predecessors, including the Underwater Demolition Teams, Naval Combat Demolition Units, Office of Strategic Services Maritime Units *Address:* 3300 North A1A, North Hutchinson Island *City:* Fort Pierce *State:* FL *Zip:* 34949 *Phone:* 772-595-5845 *Web:* www.navysealmuseum.com *Visitors welcome?* Yes *Hours:* Tuesday to Saturday, 10 a.m. to 4 p.m.; Sunday, noon to 4 p.m.; Monday (January to April) 10 a.m. to 4 p.m. *Admission:* $6 adults, $3 children six to 12; five and under FREE *Operated by:* National Navy UDT-SEAL Museum *NR?* No *NHL?* No *Latitude:* 27.8126 *Latitude:* -80.4250

PALM BEACH MARITIME MUSEUM
The Palm Beach Maritime Museum focuses on the maritime history of the Intra-coastal Waterway. *Address:* 2400 N. Flagler Dr. *City:* Palm Beach *State:* FL *Phone:* 561-540-5147 *Web:* www.pbmm.org *Email:* museum@pbmm.org *Visitors welcome?* Yes *Hours:* Wednesday to Saturday, 10:30 a.m. to 3:30 p.m. *Admission:* Contact attraction directly *Operated by:* Palm Beach Maritime Museum *NR?* No *NHL?* No *Year established/built:* 1999 *Latitude:* 26.7334 *Latitude:* -80.0498

USS MOHAWK CGC MEMORIAL MUSEUM
The USS Mohawk (WPG-78) CGC Memorial Museum preserves the icebreaker USCGC Mohawk. *Address:* Truman Waterfront *City:* Key West *State:* FL *Zip:* 33041 *Phone:* 305-292-5072 *Web:* www.ussmohawk.org *Email:* info@ussmohawk.org *Visitors welcome?* Yes *Hours:* Monday to Saturday, 10 a.m. to 4 p.m. *Admission:* $5 adults, $2.50 children ten to 18; under ten FREE *Operated by:* USS Mohawk CGC Memorial Museum *NR?* No *NHL?* No *Latitude:* 24.5554 *Latitude:* -81.7828

VICE ADMIRAL JOHN H. FETTERMAN STATE OF FLORIDA MARITIME MUSEUM AND RESEARCH CENTER
City: Pensacola *State:* FL *Web:* uwf.edu/maritime *Email:* dvangalen@uwf.edu *Visitors welcome?* Yes *Hours:* Contact attraction directly *Admission:* Contact attraction directly *Operated by:* Friends of the Vince Whibbs Sr. Community Maritime Park *NR?* No *NHL?* No *Latitude:* 30.4213 *Latitude:* -87.2169

WRECKERS MUSEUM
The Wreckers Museum, located in the Oldest House in South Florida, documents the activities of legal wreckers, which saved crews and benefited from salvaged cargo. *Address:* 322 Duval St. *City:* Key West *State:* FL *Zip:* 33040 *Phone:* 305-294-9501 *Web:* www.oirf.org *Email:* OldIsland@bellsouth.net *Visitors welcome?* Yes *Hours:* Daily, 10 a.m. to 4 p.m. *Admission:* FREE *Operated by:* Old Island Restoration Foundation *NR?* No *NHL?* No *Year established/built:* 1829 *Latitude:* 24.5572 *Latitude:* -81.8043

GEORGIA

MARITIME CENTER AT HISTORIC COAST GUARD STATION
Built in 1810 to mark the entrance to St. Simons Sound, the original lighthouse was destroyed by Confederate troops in the Civil War to prevent its use by Union forces. A replacement tower was built in 1872. *Address:* 4201 First Street, East Beach *City:* St. Simons Island *State:* GA *Zip:* 31522 *Phone:* 912-638-4666 *Web:* www.saintsimonslighthouse.org *Email:* ssi1872@comcast.net *Visitors welcome?* Yes *Hours:* Monday to Saturday 10 a.m. to 5 p.m.; Sunday, 1:30 p.m. to 5 p.m. *Admission:* $6 adults; $3 children; under six FREE *Operated by:* Coastal Georgia Historical Society *NR?* No *NHL?* No *Year established/built:* 1872 *Latitude:* 31.2358 *Latitude:* -81.3729

✧ NATIONAL CIVIL WAR NAVAL MUSEUM
The National Civil War Naval Museum at Port Columbus preserves the history of the Sea Services during the Civil War. *Address:* 1002 Victory Drive *City:* Columbus *State:* GA *Zip:* 31901 *Phone:* 706-327-9798 *Web:* www.portcolumbus.org *Email:* director@portcolumbus.org *Visitors welcome?* Yes *Hours:* Daily, 9 a.m. to 5 p.m. *Admission:* $6.50 adults, $5.50 seniors/active military, $5 students *Operated by:* National Civil War Naval Museum *NR?* No *NHL?* No *Latitude:* 32.4475 *Latitude:* -84.9792

SHIPS OF THE SEA MARITIME MUSEUM
Located in the William Scarbrough House, Ships of the Sea Maritime Museum exhibits ship models, paintings and maritime antiques, principally from the great era of Atlantic trade and travel between England and America during the 18th and 19th centuries. Exhibits include models of the Titanic, the SS Savannah, and the schooner Wanderer. *Address:* 41 M.L. King Boulevard *City:* Savannah *State:* GA *Zip:* 31401 *Phone:* 912-232-1511 *Web:* shipsofthesea.org *Email:* contact@shipsofthesea.org *Visitors welcome?* Yes *Hours:* Tuesday to Sunday, 10 a.m. to 5 p.m. *Admission:* Contact attraction directly *Operated by:* Ships of the Sea Maritime Museum *NR?* Yes *NHL?* No *Year established/built:* 1966 *Latitude:* 32.0811 *Latitude:* -81.0971

ST. MARYS SUBMARINE MUSEUM
Located in historic downtown St Marys, Ga., the museum is a great place to learn about the Silent Service. *Address:* 102 St. Marys Street West *City:* St. Marys *State:* GA *Zip:* 31558 *Phone:* 912-882-7282 *Web:* www.stmaryssubmuseum.com *Email:* submus@tds.net *Visitors welcome?* Yes *Hours:* Tuesday to Saturday, 10 a.m. to 4 p.m.; Sunday, 1 p.m. to 5 p.m. *Admission:* $4 adults, $3 seniors/active military, $2 children six to 18, under six FREE *Operated by:* St. Marys Submarine Museum *NR?* No *NHL?* No *Latitude:* 30.7208 *Latitude:* -81.5500

U.S. NAVY SUPPLY CORPS MUSEUM
The U.S. Navy Supply Corps Museum traces the Supply Corps' growth and development, explain its many and varied functions in supplying today's Navy, and commemorate noteworthy individuals associated with the corps. *Address:* 1425 Prince Ave. *City:* Athens *State:* GA *Zip:* 30606 *Phone:* 706-354-7349 *Web:* www.history.navy.mil/branches/org8-9.htm#supply *Visitors welcome?* Yes *Hours:* Contact attraction directly *Admission:* FREE *Operated by:* Naval History & Heritage Command *NR?* No *NHL?* No *Latitude:* 33.9640 *Latitude:* -83.4020

HAWAII

WHALERS VILLAGE MUSEUM
The Whalers Village Museum is part of the Whalers Village retail district on Maui. *Address:* 2435 Ka'anapali Pkwy *City:* Lahaina *State:* HI *Zip:* 96761 *Phone:* 808-661-5992 *Web:* www.whalersvillage.com/museum.htm *Email:* info@whalersvillage.com *Visitors welcome?* Yes *Hours:* Daily, 9 a.m. to 10 p.m. *Admission:* FREE *Operated by:* Whalers Village *NR?* No *NHL?* No *Latitude:* 20.9213 *Latitude:* -156.6950

CHAPTER 3 – MUSEUMS

ILLINOIS

CAIRO CUSTOMS HOUSE
Constructed in 1872, the Cairo Customs House was one of the most important ports of entry in the nation for river traffic after it passed through the Port of New Orleans. The building is now a museum. *Address:* 1400 Washington Ave. *City:* Cairo *State:* IL *Zip:* 62914 *Phone:* 618-734-9632 *Web:* www.southernmostillinoishistory.net/customhouse.htm *Visitors welcome?* Yes *Hours:* Monday and Friday, 10 a.m. to noon, 1 p.m. to 3 p.m. *Admission:* FREE *Operated by:* Cairo Customs House *NR?* No *NHL?* No *Year established/built:* 1872 *Latitude:* 37.0024 *Latitude:* -89.1718

GREAT LAKES NAVAL MUSEUM
The Naval Training Center Great Lakes Museum Exhibit is a government-owned and operated museum dedicated to telling the story 'boot camp' training in the United States Navy, and in particular, the Naval Training Station/Center Great Lakes, Illinois. *Address:* Naval Station Great Lakes, Building 158, Camp Barry *City:* North Chicago *State:* IL *Phone:* 847-688-3500 *Web:* www.nsgreatlakes.navy.mil/museum/ *Email:* therese.gonzalez@navy.mil *Visitors welcome?* Yes *Hours:* Friday, 1 p.m. to 4 p.m.; Saturday and Sunday, 7 a.m. to 3 p.m. *Admission:* FREE *Operated by:* Naval History & Heritage Command *NR?* No *NHL?* No *Latitude:* 42.3256 *Latitude:* -87.8412

ILLINOIS & MICHIGAN CANAL MUSEUM
The Illinois & Michigan Canal Museum is located in an original 1837 home of a canal commissioner. *Address:* 803 South State St. *City:* Lockport *State:* IL *Zip:* 60441 *Phone:* 815-838-5080 *Web:* www.willcountyhistory.org *Email:* info@willcountyhistory.org *Visitors welcome?* Yes *Hours:* Tuesday to Saturday, noon to 4 p.m. *Admission:* Contact attraction directly *Operated by:* Will County Historical Society *NR?* No *NHL?* No *Year established/built:* 1969 *Latitude:* 41.5902 *Latitude:* -88.0575

⚓ NATIONAL MUSEUM OF SHIP MODELS AND SEA HISTORY
The museum is dedicated to the critical role that ships have played in the course of history and the development of the modern world. The museum is home to dozens of maritime exhibits and more that 250 intricately crafted models from all periods of history. *Address:* 201 S. Market St. *City:* Sadorus *State:* IL *Zip:* 61872 *Phone:* 217-352-1672 *Web:* www.lincolnshireprop.com/museum/ *Email:* info@lincolnshireprop.com *Visitors welcome?* Yes *Hours:* May 1 to Nov. 30: Saturdays, 11 a.m. to 4:30 p.m. *Admission:* $5 *Operated by:* National Museum of Ship Models and Sea History *NR?* No *NHL?* No *Year established/built:* 2001

INDIANA

HOWARD STEAMBOAT MUSEUM
Housed in an 1894 mansion, the Howard Steamboat Museum is located in a former home of famed steamboat builders, the Howard family of Jeffersonville. *Address:* 1101 E. Market St. *City:* Jeffersonville *State:* IN *Zip:* 47130 *Phone:* 812-283-3728 *Toll-free:* 888-472-0606 *Web:* www.steamboatmuseum.org *Email:* hsmsteam@aol.com *Visitors welcome?* Yes *Hours:* Tuesday to Saturday, 10 a.m. to 4 p.m.; Sunday, 1 p.m. to 4 p.m. *Admission:* Contact attraction directly *Operated by:* Howard Steamboat Museum *NR?* No *NHL?* No *Year established/built:* 1894 *Latitude:* 38.2777 *Latitude:* -85.7256

OLD LIGHTHOUSE MUSEUM

The Old Lighthouse Museum features three beautiful ship models, an exhibit on Miss Harriet Colfax, the keeper from 1861 until 1904, a new display of running lights from the ship, Showboat, and more historical curiosities from the history of Michigan City, Indiana. *Address:* Franklin Street and Water Street *City:* Michigan City *State:* IN *Zip:* 46361 *Phone:* 219-872-6133 *Web:* www.michigancity.com/MCHistorical/ *Visitors welcome?* Yes *Hours:* Daily, 1 p.m. to 4 p.m. *Admission:* Contact attraction directly *Operated by:* Michigan City Historical Society *NR?* No *NHL?* No *Latitude:* 41.7219 *Latitude:* -86.9042

KENTUCKY

RIVER HERITAGE MUSEUM

The River Heritage Museum is located within the oldest surviving antebellum building in Paducah's historic downtown. *Address:* 117 S. Water St. *City:* Paducah *State:* KY *Zip:* 42001 *Phone:* 270-575-9958 *Web:* www.riverdiscoverycenter.org *Email:* ej@riverheritagemuseum.org *Visitors welcome?* Yes *Hours:* Monday to Saturday, 9:30 a.m. to 5 p.m.; Sunday (April to November), 1 p.m. to 5 p.m. *Admission:* $5 adults, $3 children under 12 *Operated by:* River Heritage Museum *NR?* No *NHL?* No *Latitude:* 37.0878 *Latitude:* -88.5948

IOWA

 FRED W. WOODWARD RIVERBOAT MUSEUM

Opened July 15, 1982, the Fred W. Woodward Riverboat Museum was originally a freight house built in 1901 by Dubuque Ice Harbor railroad companies. Later the building was purchased by Captains Robert and Ruth Kehl, who donated the freight house to the Dubuque County Historical Society in 1978 to develop a museum, which is now a part of the National Mississippi River Museum & Aquarium campus on the Dubuque riverfront. *Address:* 350 East Third St. *City:* Dubuque *State:* IA *Zip:* 52001 *Phone:* 563-557-9545 *Toll-free:* 800-226-3369 *Web:* www.rivermuseum.com *Email:* info@rivermuseum.com *Visitors welcome?* Yes *Hours:* Memorial Day weekend thru Labor Day: Daily, 9 a.m. – 6 p.m.; Labor Day thru October 31st: Daily, 9 a.m. – 5 p.m.; November through Memorial Day Weekend: Daily, 10 a.m. – 5 p.m.; Holiday Hours: Closed Thanksgiving and Christmas Day. Open Christmas Eve, 10 *Admission:* $10.50 adults, $9.50 seniors, $8 youth seven to 17, $4.50 children three to six, under three FREE *Operated by:* Dubuque County Historical Society *NR?* Yes *NHL?* No *Year established/built:* 1982 *Latitude:* 42.4963 *Latitude:* -90.6591

GEORGE M. VERITY RIVERBOAT MUSEUM

The George M. Verity Riverboat Museum features a dry-berth exhibit of the steamboat George M. Verity. *Address:* 415 Blondeau St. *City:* Keokuk *State:* IA *Zip:* 52632 *Phone:* 319-524-2050 *Web:* www.geomverity.org *Visitors welcome?* Yes *Hours:* Memorial Day to Labor Day, daily, 9 a.m. to 5 p.m. *Admission:* $4 adults, $3 seniors, $2 children eight to 18, under eight FREE *Operated by:* Verity Museum Commission *NR?* No *NHL?* No *Latitude:* 40.3958 *Latitude:* -91.3815

IOWA GREAT LAKES MARITIME MUSEUM

View rare artifacts and immerse yourself in the lore of the Iowa Great Lakes. *Address:* 243 West Broadway St. *City:* Arnolds Park *State:* IA *Zip:* 51360 *Phone:* 712-332-5264 *Web:* www.arnoldspark.com/maritimeMuseum.php

Visitors welcome? Yes *Hours:* Mid-May to mid-September *Admission:* Contact attraction directly *Operated by:* Arnolds Park *NR?* No *NHL?* No *Latitude:* 43.3678 *Latitude:* -95.1282

✦ NATIONAL MISSISSIPPI RIVER MUSEUM & AQUARIUM
The National Mississippi River Museum & Aquarium campus includes the William Woodward Discovery Center, the National Rivers Hall of Fame, the Fred W. Woodward Riverboat Museum, the Pfohl Boatyard, a wetland, the Carver Wet Lab, and a refurbished train dep *Address:* 350 East Third St. *City:* Dubuque *State:* IA *Zip:* 52001 *Phone:* 563-557-9545 *Toll-free:* 800-226-3369 *Web:* www.mississippirivermuseum.com *Email:* info@rivermuseum.com *Visitors welcome?* Yes *Hours:* Memorial Day weekend through Labor Day: Daily, 9 a.m. – 6 p.m.; Labor Day through October 31st: Daily, 9 a.m. – 5 p.m.; November through Memorial Day Weekend: Daily, 10 a.m. – 5 p.m.; Holiday Hours: Closed Thanksgiving and Christmas Day. Open Christmas E *Admission:* $10.50 adults, $9.50 seniors, $8 youth seven to 17, $4.50 children three to six, under three FREE *Operated by:* Dubuque County Historical Society *NR?* No *NHL?* No *Latitude:* 42.4963 *Latitude:* -90.6591

SERGEANT FLOYD RIVER MUSEUM & WELCOME CENTER
The Sergeant Floyd River Museum and Welcome Center in Sioux City, Iowa serves the tri-state areas of Iowa, Nebraska and South Dakota as an information center. *Address:* 1000 Larsen Park Road *City:* Sioux City *State:* IA *Zip:* 51103 *Phone:* 712-279-0198 *Web:* www.siouxcitymuseum.org/sgt_floyd.asp *Email:* scpm@sioux-city.org *Visitors welcome?* Yes *Hours:* Daily, 9 a.m. to 5 p.m. *Admission:* FREE *Operated by:* Sergeant Floyd River Museum & Welcome Center *NR?* No *NHL?* No *Latitude:* 42.4879 *Latitude:* -96.4004

The riverboat Sergeant Floyd at the Sergeant Floyd River Museum and Welcome Center in Sioux City, Iowa.

LOUISIANA

✦ LAKE PONTCHARTRAIN BASIN MARITIME MUSEUM
The Lake Pontchartrain Basin Maritime Museum sits on the banks of the Tchefuncte River in Madisonville, Louisiana about three miles before this historic stream flows into Lake Pontchartrain. *Address:* 133 Mabel Dr.

City: Madisonville *State:* LA *Zip:* 70447 *Phone:* 985-845-9200 *Web:* www.lpbmaritimemuseum.org *Visitors welcome?* Yes *Hours:* Tuesday to Saturday, 10 a.m. to 4 p.m.; Sunday, noon to 4 p.m. *Admission:* Contact attraction directly *Operated by:* Lake Pontchartrain Basin Maritime Museum *NR?* No *NHL?* No *Latitude:* 30.3993 *Latitude:* -90.1559

MAINE

DOWNEAST MARITIME MUSEUM
The Downeast Maritime Museum is operated by the Border Historical Society, which preserves the local history of Passamaquoddy Bay on the Canadian/U.S. border. *Address:* 74 Washington St. *City:* Eastport *State:* ME *Zip:* 04631 *Phone:* 207-853-0644 *Web:* www.borderhistoricalsociety.com *Email:* borderhistoricalsociety@yahoo.com *Visitors welcome?* Yes *Hours:* Contact attraction directly *Admission:* Contact attraction directly *Operated by:* Border Historical Society *NR?* No *NHL?* No *Latitude:* 44.9062 *Latitude:* -66.9923

GREAT HARBOR MARITIME MUSEUM
City: Northeast Harbor *State:* ME *Zip:* 04662 *Phone:* 207-276-5262 *Visitors welcome?* Yes *Hours:* Contact attraction directly *Admission:* Contact attraction directly *Operated by:* Great Harbor Maritime Museum *NR?* No *NHL?* No *Latitude:* 44.2960 *Latitude:* -68.2893

KENNEBUNKPORT MARITIME MUSEUM & GALLERY
Housed in an historic boathouse, the Kennebunkport Maritime Museum & Gallery houses artifacts from the shipwreck of the Ragina. *Address:* Ocean Avenue *City:* Kennebunkport *State:* ME *Zip:* 04046 *Phone:* 207-967-4195 *Visitors welcome?* Yes *Hours:* Contact attraction directly *Admission:* Contact attraction directly *Operated by:* Kennebunkport Maritime Museum & Gallery *NR?* No *NHL?* No *Latitude:* 43.3476 *Latitude:* -70.4583

KITTERY HISTORICAL & NAVAL MUSEUM
The Kittery Historical & Naval Museum preserves the local history, including maritime history, of the oldest incorporated town in Maine. *Address:* 200 Rogers Road Extension *City:* Kittery *State:* ME *Zip:* 03904 *Phone:* 207-439-3080 *Web:* www.kitterymuseum.com *Email:* kitterymuseum@netzero.net *Visitors welcome?* Yes *Hours:* June to October: Daily, 10 a.m. to 4 p.m. *Admission:* Contact attraction directly *Operated by:* Kittery Historical & Naval Society *NR?* No *NHL?* No *Latitude:* 43.0881 *Latitude:* -70.7362

MAINE LIGHTHOUSE MUSEUM
The mission of the Maine Lighthouse Museum is to educate the public regarding the longstanding traditions, heroism and progress of America's lighthouses. *Address:* One Park Drive *City:* Rockland *State:* ME *Zip:* 04841 *Phone:* 207-594-3301 *Web:* www.mainelighthousemuseum.com *Email:* info@mainelighthousemuseum.org *Visitors welcome?* Yes *Hours:* Memorial Day to Columbus Day: Monday to Friday, 9 a.m. to 5 p.m.; Saturday and Sunday, 10 a.m. to 4 p.m.; Columbus Day to Memorial Day: Wednesday to Friday, 10 a.m. to 4 p.m.; Saturday, 10 a.m. to 4 p *Admission:* $5 adults, $4 seniors, children under 12, FREE *Operated by:* Maine Lighthouse Museum *NR?* No *NHL?* No *Latitude:* 44.1024 *Latitude:* -69.1075

MAINE MARITIME MUSEUM
Maine Maritime Museum offers a myriad of opportunities to explore Maine's maritime heritage and culture and to experience the mystique of Maine. *Address:* 243 Washington Street *City:* Bath *State:* ME *Zip:* 04530 *Phone:* 207-443-1316 *Web:* www.mainemaritimemuseum.org *Email:* curator@maritimeme.org *Visitors welcome?* Yes *Hours:* Daily, 9:30 a.m. to 5 p.m. *Admission:* $10 adults; $9 seniors; $7 children 6-17; under six

FREE *Operated by:* Maine Maritime Museum *NR?* No *NHL?* No *Year established/built:* 1962 *Latitude:* 43.8939 *Latitude:* -69.8171

MAINE WATERCRAFT MUSEUM
The Maine Watercraft Museum displays small watercraft tracing the local boatbuilding industry. *Address:* 4 Knox St. *City:* Thomaston *State:* ME *Zip:* 04861 *Phone:* 207-354-0444 *Visitors welcome?* Yes *Hours:* Contact attraction directly *Admission:* Contact attraction directly *Operated by:* Maine Watercraft Museum *NR?* No *NHL?* No *Year established/built:* 1986 *Latitude:* 44.0786 *Latitude:* -69.1826

MOOSEHEAD MARINE MUSEUM
The Moosehead Marine Museum partners with the passenger vessel Katahdin for cruises of Moosehead Lake. *Address:* Main Street *City:* Greenville *State:* ME *Zip:* 04441 *Phone:* 207-695-2716 *Web:* www.katahdincruises.com *Email:* info@katahdincruises.com *Visitors welcome?* Yes *Hours:* Contact attraction directly *Admission:* Contact attraction directly *Operated by:* Moosehead Marine Museum *NR?* No *NHL?* No *Latitude:* 45.6249 *Latitude:* -69.4815

PENOBSCOT MARINE MUSEUM
The Penobscot Marine Museum, Maine's oldest maritime museum, was founded in 1936 by descendants of Searsport sea captain families. The original building was Old Town Hall, built in 1845 and given to the museum by the town of Searsport. *Address:* 5 Church Street *City:* Searsport *State:* ME *Zip:* 04974 *Phone:* 207-548-2529 *Web:* www.penobscotmarinemuseum.org *Email:* museumoffices@pmm-maine.org *Visitors welcome?* Yes *Hours:* Monday to Saturday, 10 a.m. to 5 p.m.; Sunday, Noon to 5 p.m. (May to October) *Admission:* $8 adults; $3 children seven to 12; children six and under, FREE *Operated by:* Penobscot Marine Museum *NR?* No *NHL?* No *Year established/built:* 1936 *Latitude:* 44.4209 *Latitude:* -69.0006

SAILOR'S MEMORIAL MUSEUM
The Sailor's Memorial Museum is located in the keeper's dwelling of the Grindle Point Lighthouse. *Address:* Grindle Point Lighthouse Keeper's Dwelling *City:* Islesboro *State:* ME *Zip:* 04848 *Phone:* 207-734-2253 *Visitors welcome?* Yes *Hours:* Summer, Saturday and Sunday, 9 a.m. to 4:30 p.m. *Admission:* Contact attraction directly *Operated by:* Town of Islesboro *NR?* No *NHL?* No *Year established/built:* 1874 *Latitude:* 44.2957 *Latitude:* -68.9124

SARDINE MUSEUM
The Sardine Museum is in a reconstructed sardine cannery with period artifacts. *Address:* Route 189 *City:* Lubec *State:* ME *Zip:* 04652 *Phone:* 207-733-2822 *Visitors welcome?* Yes *Hours:* Contact attraction directly *Admission:* Contact attraction directly *Operated by:* Sardine Museum *NR?* No *NHL?* No *Latitude:* 44.8159 *Latitude:* -67.0667

MARYLAND

ANNAPOLIS MARITIME MUSEUM
The Annapolis Maritime Museum seeks to connect the richness of the maritime heritage of the Annapolis area with our local youth and adults. The museum operates from a waterside campus on the shores of Back Creek, with unequaled views of Annapolis Harbor a *Address:* 723 Second Street *City:* Annapolis *State:* MD *Zip:* 21403 *Phone:* 410-295-0104 *Web:* www.amaritime.org *Email:* office@amaritime.org *Visitors welcome?* Yes *Hours:* Contact attraction directly *Admission:* Contact attraction directly *Operated by:* Annapolis Maritime Museum *NR?* No *NHL?* No *Latitude:* 38.9689 *Latitude:* -76.4763

CHAPTER 3 – MUSEUMS

BRANNOCK MARITIME MUSEUM
The Brannock Maritime Museum features early navigational instruments, ship models, Chesapeake Bay, a library, and local maritime memorabilia. *Address:* 210 Talbot Ave. *City:* Cambridge *State:* MD *Zip:* 21613 *Phone:* 410-228-1245 *Visitors welcome?* Yes *Hours:* Friday and Saturday: 10 a.m. to 4 p.m.; Sunday, 1 p.m. to 4 p.m. *Admission:* Contact attraction directly *Operated by:* Brannock Maritime Museum *NR?* No *NHL?* No *Latitude:* 38.5798 *Latitude:* -76.0835

CALVERT MARINE MUSEUM
The Calvert Marine Museum is a public, non-profit, educational, regionally oriented museum dedicated to the collection, preservation, research, and interpretation of the culture and natural history of Southern Maryland. *Address:* State Route 2 *City:* Solomons *State:* MD *Zip:* 20688 *Phone:* 410-326-2042 *Web:* www.calvertmarinemuseum.com *Email:* mccormmj@co.cal.md.us *Visitors welcome?* Yes *Hours:* Daily, 10 a.m to 5 p.m. *Admission:* $7 adults, $6 seniors, $2 children 5 to 12; under five FREE *Operated by:* Calvert Marine Museum *NR?* No *NHL?* No *Year established/built:* 1970 *Latitude:* 38.3332 *Latitude:* -76.4720

CHESAPEAKE & DELAWARE CANAL MUSEUM
The C & D Canal Museum at Chesapeake City provides visitors with a glimpse of the canal's early days. The waterwheel and pumping engines remain in the original pumphouse (now the museum). These steam engines are the oldest of their type in America still in operation. *Address:* 815 Bethel Rd *City:* Chesapeake City *State:* MD *Phone:* 215-656-6515 *Web:* www.nap.usace.army.mil/sb/c&d.htm *Email:* edward.c.voigt@usace.army.mil *Visitors welcome?* Yes *Hours:* Monday to Friday, 8 a.m. to 4 p.m. *Admission:* FREE *Operated by:* U.S. Army Corps of Engineers (Philadelphia District) *NR?* No *NHL?* No *Latitude:* 39.5210 *Latitude:* -75.7936

CHESAPEAKE BAY MARITIME MUSEUM
The Chesapeake Bay Maritime Museum is dedicated to furthering an interest in, understanding of, and appreciation for the culture and maritime heritage of the Chesapeake Bay and its environs. *Address:* 213 N. Talbot Street *City:* St. Michaels *State:* MD *Zip:* 21663 *Phone:* 410-745-2916 *Web:* www.cbmm.org *Email:* cbland@cbmm.org *Visitors welcome?* Yes *Hours:* Daily, hours vary by season *Admission:* $13 adults; $10 seniors over 62; $6 kids 6 to 17; kids under 6 FREE *Operated by:* Chesapeake Bay Maritime Museum *NR?* No *NHL?* No *Year established/built:* 1965 *Latitude:* 38.7876 *Latitude:* -76.2249

CHOPTANK RIVER HERITAGE CENTER & JOPPA WHARF MUSEUM
The Choptank River Heritage Center is located in a historic schooner and steamboat warehouse at the restored Joppa Steamboat Wharf on the upper Choptank River in West Denton, Maryland. *Address:* 10215 River Landing Rd. *City:* West Denton *State:* MD *Zip:* 21629 *Phone:* 410-479-4150 *Web:* www.riverheritage.org *Email:* info@riverheritage.org *Visitors welcome?* Yes *Hours:* May to September: Friday and Saturday, 11 a.m. to 3 p.m. *Admission:* Contact attraction directly *Operated by:* Choptank River Heritage Center *NR?* No *NHL?* No

HAVRE DE GRACE MARITIME MUSEUM
Discover, relive & treasure the Maritime Heritage of the Upper Bay at the Havre de Grace Maritime Museum. *Address:* 100 Lafayette St. *City:* Havre de Grace *State:* MD *Zip:* 21078 *Phone:* 410-939-4800 *Web:* www.hdgmaritimemuseum.org *Visitors welcome?* Yes *Hours:* September to May: Monday, Wednesday, Friday, Saturday, Sunday: 11 a.m. to 5 p.m.; Tuesday, 6 p.m. to 9:30 p.m.; June to August: Daily, 11 a.m. to 5 p.m. *Admission:* $3 adults, $2 seniors/students, children under eight FREE *Operated by:* Havre de Grace Maritime Museum *NR?* No *NHL?* No *Year established/built:* 1989 *Latitude:* 39.5407 *Latitude:* -76.0854

HISTORIC SHIPS IN BALTIMORE
The mission of Historic Ships in Baltimore is to preserve, exhibit and interpret the four National Historic Landmarks and associated artifacts for the purpose of public enrichment, education, historic preservation and

historic research. *Address:* 301 E. Pratt St. *City:* Baltimore *State:* MD *Zip:* 21202 *Phone:* 410-539-1797 *Web:* www.historicships.org *Email:* administration@constellation.org *Visitors welcome?* Yes *Hours:* Daily, March to October, 10 a.m. to 5:30 p.m,; Daily, November to February, 10 a.m. to 4:30 p.m. *Admission:* Contact attraction directly *Operated by:* Historic Ships in Baltimore *NR?* No *NHL?* No *Latitude:* 39.2866 *Latitude:* -76.6117

PATUXENT RIVER NAVAL AIR MUSEUM

The Patuxent River Naval Air Museum is supported by the Patuxent Naval Air Museum Foundation. *Address:* 22156 Three Notch Road *City:* Lexington Park *State:* MD *Zip:* 20653 *Phone:* 301-863-7418 *Web:* www.paxmuseum.com *Email:* director@paxmuseum.com *Visitors welcome?* Yes *Hours:* Tuesday to Sunday, 10 a.m. to 5 p.m. *Admission:* FREE *Operated by:* Naval History & Heritage Command *NR?* No *NHL?* No *Latitude:* 38.2758 *Latitude:* -76.4638

RICHARDSON MARITIME MUSEUM

The Richardson Maritime Museum in Cambridge features a large collection of ship models, shipwright's tools, and information on the new Richardson Maritime Heritage Center. The museum is one of three attractions operated by the James B. Richardson Foundation; ; the other two are Ruark Boatworks and the Brannock Center, scheduled to open soon to the public. *Address:* 401 High Street *City:* Cambridge *State:* MD *Zip:* 21613 *Web:* www.richardsonmuseum.org *Email:* info@richardsonmuseum.org *Visitors welcome?* Yes *Hours:* Wednesday and Saturdays, 1 p.m. to 4 p.m.; Saturdays, 10 a.m. to 4 p.m. *Admission:* $3 suggested donation *Operated by:* James B. Richardson Foundation *NR?* No *NHL?* No *Latitude:* 38.5711 *Latitude:* -76.0776

RUARK BOATWORKS

The Ruark Boatworks preserves traditional methods of wooden shipbuilding as it was practiced on Chesapeake Bay. The shop is located in an historic structure once part of a basket factory. The shop is one of three facilities operated by the James B. Richardson Foundation in Cambridge, Md. The other two are the Richardson Maritime Museum and the Brannock Center. *Address:* 103 Hayward St. *City:* Cambridge *State:* MD *Zip:* 21613 *Phone:* 410-221-8844 *Web:* www.richardsonmuseum.org *Email:* info@richardsonmuseum.org *Visitors welcome?* Yes *Hours:* Monday, Wednesday, Friday 9 a.m. to 3 p.m. *Admission:* FREE *Operated by:* James B. Richardson Foundation *NR?* No *NHL?* No *Latitude:* 38.5708 *Latitude:* -76.0704

SUSQUEHANNA MUSEUM AT THE LOCK HOUSE

The Susquehanna Museum at the Lock House focuses on the history of the Susquehanna and Tidewater Canal. *Address:* 817 Conesteo St. *City:* Havre de Grace *State:* MD *Zip:* 21078 *Phone:* 410-939-5780 *Web:* www.lockhousemuseum.org *Email:* director@lockhousemuseum.org *Visitors welcome?* Yes *Hours:* Saturday and Sunday, 1 p.m. to 5 p.m. *Admission:* Donation *Operated by:* Susquehanna Museum *NR?* No *NHL?* No *Latitude:* 39.5553 *Latitude:* -76.0941

U.S. NAVAL ACADEMY MUSEUM

The U. S. Naval Academy Museum serves as an educational and inspirational resource for the Brigade of Midshipmen at the U. S. Naval Academy, other students of American naval history, and thousands of visitors each year. *Address:* 118 Maryland Avenue *City:* Annapolis *State:* MD *Zip:* 21402 *Phone:* 410-293-2108 *Web:* www.nadn.navy.mil/Museum/ *Email:* jsharmon@usna.edu *Visitors welcome?* Yes *Hours:* Monday to Saturday, 9 a.m. to 5 p.m.; Sunday, 11 a.m. to 5 p.m. *Admission:* FREE *Operated by:* Naval History & Heritage Command *NR?* No *NHL?* No *Latitude:* 38.9820 *Latitude:* -76.4875

MASSACHUSETTS

BATTLESHIP COVE
Battleship Cove features several floating exhibits, including the battleship USS Massachusetts. *Address:* Five Water Street *City:* Fall River *State:* MA *Zip:* 02722 *Phone:* 508-678-1100 *Toll-free:* 800-533-3194 *Web:* www.battleshipcove.org *Visitors welcome?* Yes *Hours:* Summer: daily, 9 a.m. to 4:30 p.m.; Winter: daily, 9 a.m. to 5:30 p.m. *Admission:* Contact attraction directly *Operated by:* Battleship Cove *NR?* No *NHL?* No *Latitude:* 41.7040 *Latitude:* -71.1597

BOSTON TEA PARTY SHIP & MUSEUM
Boston Tea Party Ships(sm) & Museum preserves and displays artifacts related to the Boston Tea Party. *Address:* 304 Congress St. *City:* Boston *State:* MA *Zip:* 02210 *Phone:* 617-338-1773 *Web:* www.bostonteapartyship.com *Email:* teapartyship@historictours.com *Visitors welcome?* Yes *Hours:* Contact attraction directly *Admission:* Contact attraction directly *Operated by:* Historic Tours of America *NR?* No *NHL?* No *Latitude:* 42.3517 *Latitude:* -71.0506

CAPE COD MARITIME MUSEUM
The Cape Cod Maritime Museum preserves the maritime history of one of the most storied waterfronts in America. *Address:* 135 South Street *City:* Hyannis *State:* MA *Zip:* 02601 *Phone:* 508-775-1723 *Web:* www.capecodmaritimemuseum.org *Email:* info@capecodmaritimemuseum.org *Visitors welcome?* Yes *Hours:* Tuesday to Saturday, 10 a.m. to 4 p.m.; Sunday, noon to 4 p.m. *Admission:* $5 adults, $4 students/seniors, six and under FREE *Operated by:* Cape Cod Maritime Museum *NR?* No *NHL?* No *Latitude:* 41.6513 *Latitude:* -70.2800

CAPTAIN JOHN KENDRICK MARITIME MUSEUM
The Captain John Kendrick Maritime Museum is located in a house purchased by Kendrick in 1778. Kendrick lead an expedition to China in 1787 aboard the brig Lady Washington and opened up the lucrative China Trade for tea, silks and ceramics. He was also the first American to attempt trade with Japan. The museum contains furnishings from the 18th and 19th century, textiles, costumes, maritime paintings, and a model of the schooner Ernestina, which served as a packet ship for many years sailing between the U.S. and the Cape Verde islands. *Address:* 124 Main St. *City:* Wareham *State:* MA *Zip:* 02571 *Phone:* 508-291-2274 *Visitors welcome?* Yes *NR?* No *NHL?* No *Latitude:* 41.7571 *Latitude:* -70.7141

COAST GUARD HERITAGE MUSEUM
The Coast Guard Heritage Museum is housed in the 1855 Customs House in downtown Barnstable. *Address:* 3353 Main St. *City:* Barnstable *State:* MA *Zip:* 02630 *Phone:* 508-362-8521 *Web:* www.coastguardheritagemuseum.org *Email:* cgheritage@comcast.net *Visitors welcome?* Yes *Hours:* May to October: Tuesday to Saturday, 10 a.m. to 3 p.m. *Admission:* Contact attraction directly *Operated by:* Trayser Museum Group *NR?* No *NHL?* No *Year established/built:* 1855 *Latitude:* 41.7002 *Latitude:* -70.2989

COHASSET MARITIME MUSEUM
Built in 1760, the Cohasset Maritime Museum was originally a ship's chandlery and now houses a museum with ship models and artifacts from local maritime history. *Address:* 4 Elm St. *City:* Cohasset *State:* MA *Zip:* 02025 *Phone:* 781-383-1434 *Web:* www.cohassethistoricalsociety.org *Email:* cohassethistory@yahoo.com *Visitors welcome?* Yes *Hours:* Open summers. Contact attraction for details. *Admission:* By donation *Operated by:* Cohasset Historical Society *NR?* Yes *NHL?* No *Year established/built:* 1760 *Latitude:* 42.2408 *Latitude:* -70.8016

CHAPTER 3 – MUSEUMS

CUSTOM HOUSE MARITIME MUSEUM
Discover the abundant and interesting maritime heritage of Newburyport, MA at the Custom House Maritime Museum. *Address:* 25 Water St. *City:* Newburyport *State:* MA *Zip:* 01950 *Phone:* 978-462-8681 *Web:* www.customhousemaritimemuseum.org *Email:* info@thechmm.org *Visitors welcome?* Yes *Hours:* Thursday to Saturday, 11 a.m. to 4 p.m.; Sunday, Noon to 4 p.m. *Admission:* $7 adults, $5 seniors and students, active military and children under 12 FREE *Operated by:* Custom House Maritime Museum *NR?* No *NHL?* No *Year established/built:* 1835 *Latitude:* 42.8081 *Latitude:* -70.8602

> Have you seen a new maritime heritage exhibit? Review it at www.fyddeye.com.

EGAN MARITIME INSTITUTE
Located at the historic Coffin School, an impressive 1854 Greek Revival-style building in the heart of Nantucket Town, the Egan Maritime Institute is the island's maritime museum. *Address:* 4 Winter St. *City:* Nantucket *State:* MA *Zip:* 02554 *Phone:* 508-228-2505 *Web:* www.eganmaritime.org *Email:* egan@eganmaritime.org *Visitors welcome?* Yes *Hours:* Late May to mid-October: Daily, 10 a.m. to 4 p.m. *Admission:* Contact attraction directly *Operated by:* Egan Maritime Institute *NR?* No *NHL?* No *Latitude:* 41.2825 *Latitude:* -70.1022

ESSEX SHIPBUILDING MUSEUM
The Essex Shipbuilding Museum tells the extraordinary story of a small New England village that built more two-masted wooden fishing schooners than any other place in the world. *Address:* 66 Main Street *City:* Essex *State:* MA *Zip:* 01929 *Phone:* 978-768-7541 *Web:* www.essexshipbuildingmuseum.org *Email:* info@essexshipbuildingmuseum.org *Visitors welcome?* Yes *Hours:* June to October, Wednesday to Sunday, 10 a.m. to 5 p.m.; November to May, Saturday and Sunday, 10 a.m. to 5 p.m. *Admission:* $7 adults, $6 seniors, $5 children, under six FREE *Operated by:* Essex Historical Society & Shipbuilding Museum *NR?* No *NHL?* No *Year established/built:* 1976 *Latitude:* 42.6323 *Latitude:* -70.7795

GLOUCESTER MARITIME HERITAGE CENTER
The Gloucester Maritime Heritage Center is the only working historic waterfront in the Northeast that combines a historic working marine railway, where wooden vessels are hauled and repaired, with a Gulf of Maine aquarium, and vessels tracing the fishing history of the area. *Address:* 23 Harbor Loop *City:* Gloucester *State:* MA *Zip:* 01930 *Phone:* 978-281-0470 *Web:* www.gloucestermaritimecenter.org *Email:* hwebster@gloucestermaritimecenter.org *Visitors welcome?* Yes *Hours:* Memorial Day to Labor Day: Daily 10 a.m. to 5 p.m. *Admission:* Contact attraction directly *Operated by:* Gloucester Maritime Heritage Center *NR?* No *NHL?* No *Latitude:* 42.6114 *Latitude:* -70.6590

HART NAUTICAL GALLERY
The Hart Nautical Gallery features 40 full-hull ship models. *Address:* 55 Massachusetts Ave., Building 5 *City:* Cambridge *State:* MA *Zip:* 02135 *Phone:* 617-253-5942 *Web:* web.mit.edu/museum/exhibitions/hart.html *Email:* kurt@mit.edu *Visitors welcome?* Yes *Hours:* Daily, 10 a.m. to 5 p.m. *Admission:* FREE *Operated by:* MIT Museum *NR?* No *NHL?* No *Latitude:* 42.3587 *Latitude:* -71.0934

✦ HULL LIFESAVING MUSEUM
The Hull Lifesaving Museum, the museum of Boston Harbor heritage, preserves the region's lifesaving tradition and maritime culure through collections, exhibits, experiential and interpretive education, research and service to others. *Address:* 1117 Nantasket Ave. *City:* Hull *State:* MA *Zip:* 02045 *Phone:* 781-925-5433 *Web:* www.lifesavingmuseum.org *Email:* lifesavingmuseum@comcast.net *Visitors welcome?* Yes *Hours:* Daily *Admission:* $5 adults, $3 seniors, children under 18 FREE *Operated by:* Hull Lifesaving Museum *NR?* No *NHL?* No *Latitude:* 42.3055 *Latitude:* -70.8974

LOWELL'S BOAT SHOP
Established in 1793, Lowell's Boat Shop is the oldest continuously operating boat shop in the United States and is cited as the birthplace of the legendary fishing dory. *Address:* 459 Main Street *City:* Amesbury *State:* MA *Zip:* 01913 *Phone:* 978-834-0050 *Web:* www.lowellsboatshop.com *Email:* info@lowellsboatshop.com *Visitors welcome?* Yes *Hours:* Monday to Friday, 10 a.m. to 3 p.m. *Admission:* Contact attraction directly *Operated by:* Lowell's Maritime Foundation *NR?* No *NHL?* Yes *Year established/built:* 1793 *Latitude:* 42.8425 *Latitude:* -70.9140

MARINE MUSEUM AT FALL RIVER
The Marine Museum At Fall River houses a diverse collection of marine artifacts and memorabilia including what the museum claims is one of the largest Titanic exhibitions in the world. *Address:* 70 Water St. *City:* Fall River *State:* MA *Zip:* 02721 *Phone:* 508-674-3533 *Visitors welcome?* Yes *Hours:* Monday to Friday, 9 a.m. to 5 p.m.; Saturday, noon to 5 p.m.; Sunday, noon to 4 p.m. *Admission:* Contact attraction directly *Operated by:* Marine Museum at Fall River *NR?* No *NHL?* No *Latitude:* 41.7043 *Latitude:* -71.1611

MARITIME AND IRISH MOSSING MUSEUM
Located in a 1739 home, the Maritime and Irish Mossing Museum focuses on local Massachusetts maritime history. *Address:* 301 Driftway *City:* Scituate *State:* MA *Zip:* 02066 *Phone:* 781-545-1083 *Web:* www.scituatehistoricalsociety.org *Email:* director@scituatehistoricalsociety.org *Visitors welcome?* Yes *Hours:* September to June: Sundays, 1 p.m. to 4 p.m.; July and August: Saturday and Sunday, 1 p.m. to 4 p.m. *Admission:* $4 adults, $3 seniors, under 18 FREE *Operated by:* Scituate Historical Society *NR?* No *NHL?* No *Year established/built:* 1739 *Latitude:* 42.1777 *Latitude:* -70.7426

MIDDLESEX CANAL MUSEUM & VISITORS CENTER
The Middlesex Canal Museum & Visitors Center was created to preserve and illuminate the history of the Middlesex Canal. *Address:* 71 Faulkner St. *City:* North Billerica *State:* MA *Zip:* 01862 *Phone:* 978-670-2740 *Web:* www.middlesexcanal.org *Email:* middlesexcanalcomm.jreardon@juno.com *Visitors welcome?* Yes *Hours:* Mid-April to mid-June, early Sept. to late Nov.: Saturday and Sunday, noon to 4 p.m. *Admission:* Contact attraction directly *Operated by:* Middlesex Canal Association *NR?* No *NHL?* No *Latitude:* 42.5922 *Latitude:* -71.2841

NANTUCKET WHALING MUSEUM
Housed in a historic candle factory, the Nantucket Whaling Museum tells the story of Nantucket whalers from their beginnings in the 17th century to the present day. *Address:* 15 Broad Street *City:* Nantucket *State:* MA *Zip:* 02554 *Phone:* 508-228-1894 *Web:* www.nha.org *Visitors welcome?* Yes *Hours:* Contact attraction directly *Admission:* $15 adults, $12 seniors, $8 youth, under six FREE *Operated by:* Nantucket Historical Association *NR?* No *NHL?* No *Year established/built:* 1930 *Latitude:* 41.2855 *Latitude:* -70.0989

NEW ENGLAND PIRATE MUSEUM
The New England Pirate Museum includes the little-known history of pirates off the New England coast. *Address:* 274 Derby St. *City:* Salem *State:* MA *Zip:* 01970 *Phone:* 978-741-2800 *Web:* www.piratemuseum.com *Email:* SalemWitchPirate@aol.com *Visitors welcome?* Yes *Hours:* May to October: Daily, 10 a.m. to 5 p.m.; April and November: Saturday and Sunday, 10 a.m. to 5 p.m. *Admission:* $8 adults, $7 seniors, $6 children four to 13, under four FREE *Operated by:* New England Pirate Museum *NR?* No *NHL?* No *Latitude:* 42.5208 *Latitude:* -70.8908

OSTERVILLE HISTORICAL MUSEUM
Osterville Historical Museum is dedicated to preserving the history of the village of Osterville. *Address:* 155 West Bay Road *City:* Osterville *State:* MA *Zip:* 02655 *Phone:* 508-428-5861 *Web:* www.ostervillemuseum.

org *Email:* OHS@OstervilleMuseum.org *Visitors welcome?* Yes *Hours:* Wednesday: 5:30 p.m. to 6:30 p.m.; Thursday to Sunday: 1:30 p.m. to 4:30 p.m. *Admission:* Contact attraction directly *Operated by:* Osterville Historical Society *NR?* No *NHL?* No *Latitude:* 41.6247 *Latitude:* -70.3874

PEABODY ESSEX MUSEUM MARITIME ART COLLECTION
The Peabody Essex Museum's maritime art and history collection, begun in 1803, is the finest in America. It is internationally renowned for holdings of approximately 30,000 paintings, drawings, and prints. The collection also encompasses 20,000 maritime objects. *Address:* East India Square, 161 Essex St. *City:* Salem *State:* MA *Zip:* 01970 *Phone:* 978-745-9500 *Web:* pem.org *Visitors welcome?* Yes *Hours:* Contact attraction directly *Admission:* Contact attraction directly *Operated by:* Peabody Essex Museum *NR?* No *NHL?* No *Latitude:* 42.5218 *Latitude:* -70.8928

PT BOAT MUSEUM AND LIBRARY
The PT Boat Museum and Library at Battleship Cove features more than 4,000 square feet devoted to 43 commissioned squadrons, some 80 bases and 19 tender ships, including two completely restored PT boats. *Address:* Battleship Cove, Five Water Street *City:* Fall River *State:* MA *Zip:* 02722 *Phone:* 508-678-1100 *Toll-free:* 800-533-3194 *Web:* www.battleshipcove.org *Visitors welcome?* Yes *Hours:* Summer: daily, 9 a.m. to 4:30 p.m.; Winter: daily, 9 a.m. to 5:30 p.m. *Admission:* Contact attraction directly *Operated by:* PT Boats, Inc. *NR?* No *NHL?* No *Latitude:* 41.7027 *Latitude:* -71.1641

UNITED STATES NAVAL SHIPBUILDING MUSEUM
The United States Naval Shipbuilding Museum operates and maintains one of the world's only preserved heavy cruisers, USS Salem. The USNSM's primary goal is to preserve our nation's history for all generations. *Address:* 739 Washington Street *City:* Quincy *State:* MA *Zip:* 02169 *Phone:* 617-479-7900 *Web:* www.uss-salem.org *Email:* adventure@uss-salem.org *Visitors welcome?* Yes *Hours:* Contact attraction directly *Admission:* $5 adults, children under three FREE *Operated by:* United States Naval Shipbuilding Museum *NR?* No *NHL?* No *Latitude:* 42.2452 *Latitude:* -70.9700

✦ USS CONSTITUTION MUSEUM
Only yards away from Old Ironsides, the museum is a must-see for everyone visiting Boston, where interactive galleries take adults, families and children of all ages on a 200-year voyage. *Address:* Charlestown Navy Yard *City:* Boston *State:* MA *Zip:* 02129 *Phone:* 617-426-1812 *Web:* www.ussconstitutionmuseum.org *Email:* MuseumAdmin@ussconstitutionmuseum.org *Visitors welcome?* Yes *Hours:* April 15 to Oct. 31, daily, 9 a.m. to 6 p.m.; Nov. 1 to April 14: daily, 10 a.m. to 5 p.m. *Admission:* FREE *Operated by:* USS Constitution Museum *NR?* No *NHL?* No *Latitude:* 42.3722 *Latitude:* -71.0546

✦ WHYDAH MUSEUM
The Whydah Museum displays artifacts raised from the 1717 wreck of the pirate vessel Whydah. *Address:* 16 Macmillan Wharf *City:* Provincetown *State:* MA *Zip:* 02657 *Phone:* 508-487-8899 *Web:* www.whydah.com *Email:* whydahmuseum@yahoo.com *Visitors welcome?* Yes *Hours:* May to October: Daily, 10 a.m. to 5 p.m. *Admission:* $10 adults, $8 children six to 12, under six FREE *Operated by:* Expedition Whydah Sea-Lab & Learning Center *NR?* No *NHL?* No *Latitude:* 42.0496 *Latitude:* -70.1831

WOODS HOLE HISTORICAL MUSEUM
The Woods Hole Historical Museum is a lively small museum with several buildings and changing exhibits and diverse programs appealing to people with wide interests. *Address:* 573 Woods Hole Rd. *City:* Woods Hole *State:* MA *Zip:* 02543 *Phone:* 508-548-7270 *Web:* www.woodsholemuseum.org *Email:* woods_hole_historical@hotmail.com *Visitors welcome?* Yes *Hours:* Mid-June to mid-October: Tuesday to Saturday, 10 a.m. to

4 p.m. *Admission:* Contact attraction directly *Operated by:* Woods Hole Historical Museum *NR?* No *NHL?* No *Year established/built:* 1973 *Latitude:* 41.5236 *Latitude:* -70.6673

MICHIGAN

BEAVER ISLAND MARINE MUSEUM
Located in a historic 1906 net shed, the Beaver Island Marine Museum houses a growing collection of local maritime memorabilia. *Address:* 38105 Michigan Ave. *City:* Beaver Island *State:* MI *Zip:* 49782 *Phone:* 231-448-2479 *Visitors welcome?* Yes *Hours:* Contact attraction directly *Admission:* Contact attraction directly *Operated by:* Beaver Island Historical Society *NR?* No *NHL?* No *Year established/built:* 1906 *Latitude:* 45.7498 *Latitude:* -85.5101

CANNERY BOATHOUSE MUSEUM
The cannery was first built as a warehouse and converted to a state-of-the-art cannery for cherries in the early 1920s. In recent years, the Cannery has housed a museum of historic boats used around Glen Haven and the Manitou Islands. *Address:* Sleeping Bear Dunes National Lakeshore *City:* Leland *State:* MI *Phone:* 231-326-5134 *Visitors welcome?* Yes *Hours:* Daily, May to Labor Day, 11 a.m. to 4 p.m. *Admission:* FREE *Operated by:* Sleeping Bear Dunes National Lakeshore *NR?* No *NHL?* No *Latitude:* 45.0347 *Latitude:* -85.7913

DE TOUR PASSAGE HISTORICAL MUSEUM
The DeTour Passage Historical Museum features displays of the region's early maritime history. *Address:* 104 Elizabeth St. *City:* De Tour Village *State:* MI *Zip:* 49725 *Phone:* 906-297-3404 *Visitors welcome?* Yes *Hours:* Contact attraction directly *Admission:* Contact attraction directly *Operated by:* DeTour Reef Light Preservation Society *NR?* No *NHL?* No *Latitude:* 45.9924 *Latitude:* -83.9023

✢ DOSSIN GREAT LAKES MUSEUM
The Great Lakes Maritime Institute promotes interest in the Great Lakes; preserves items related to their history; encourages building of scale models of lake ships, small craft and racing boats and furthers programs of the Dossin Great Lakes Museum. *Address:* 100 Strand Dr. *City:* Detroit *State:* MI *Zip:* 48207 *Phone:* 313-852-4051 *Web:* www.glmi.org *Email:* web@glmi.org *Visitors welcome?* Yes *Hours:* Contact attraction directly *Admission:* Contact attraction directly *Operated by:* Great Lakes Maritime Institute *NR?* No *NHL?* No *Year established/built:* 1952 *Latitude:* 42.3346 *Latitude:* -82.9868

GREAT LAKES LORE MARITIME MUSEUM
The Great Lakes Lore Maritime Museum is a maritime museum that specializes in memories not just artifacts. It is located in Rogers City, in Michigan's lower peninsula. In the heart of the inland seas known as the Great Lakes, you'll find a place where the *Address:* 367 North 3rd Street *City:* Rogers City *State:* MI *Zip:* 49779 *Phone:* 989-734-0706 *Fax:* 989-734-0706 *Web:* www.gllmm.com *Email:* lor@i2k.net *Visitors welcome?* Yes *Hours:* Daily, 10 a.m. to 4 p.m. *Admission:* $3 adults; children K-12 free *Operated by:* Great Lakes Lore Maritime Museum *NR?* No *NHL?* No *Latitude:* 45.4227 *Latitude:* -83.8195

GREAT LAKES MARITIME CENTER – VANTAGE POINT
The Great Lakes Maritime Center offers a variety of opportunities to learn about the history and current events of the Great Lakes. A variety of video formats, displays, and speaker programs present a wide variety of information. *Address:* 51 Water St. *City:* Port Huron *State:* MI *Zip:* 48060 *Phone:* 810-985-4817 *Visitors*

CHAPTER 3 – MUSEUMS

welcome? Yes *Hours:* Contact attraction directly *Admission:* Contact attraction directly *Operated by:* Acheson Ventures *NR?* No *NHL?* No *Latitude:* 42.9835 *Latitude:* -82.4397

GREAT LAKES MARITIME HERITAGE CENTER
The Great Lakes Maritime Heritage Center features thousands of artifacts from shipwrecks in the Thunder Bay region. *Address:* 500 W Fletcher St. *City:* Alpena *State:* MI *Zip:* 49707 *Phone:* 989-356-8805 *Web:* www.thunderbay.noaa.gov *Email:* thunderbay@noaa.gov *Visitors welcome?* Yes *Hours:* Monday to Saturday, 10 a.m. to 4 p.m. *Admission:* FREE *Operated by:* Thunder Bay National Marine Sanctuary *NR?* No *NHL?* No *Latitude:* 45.0673 *Latitude:* -83.4330

GREAT LAKES NAVAL MEMORIAL & MUSEUM
Great Lakes Naval Memorial and Museum, in Muskegon, MI, invites you to step back into time aboard two historic vessels as well as the new state-of-the-art museum facility. *Address:* 1346 Bluff Street *City:* Muskegon *State:* MI *Zip:* 49441 *Phone:* 231-755-1230 *Web:* www.glnmm.org *Email:* contactus@glnmm.org *Visitors welcome?* Yes *Hours:* January to April: Monday to Friday, 10 a.m. to 4 p.m.; May to October: Daily, 10 a.m. to 5:30 p.m.; November to December: Monday to Friday, 10 a.m. to 4:30 p.m., Saturday, 10 a.m. to 5:30 p.m. *Admission:* $10 adults; $8 students/seniors; $7 children; WWII vets, active military, and children FREE *Operated by:* Great Lakes Naval Memorial & Museum *NR?* No *NHL?* No *Latitude:* 43.2273 *Latitude:* -86.3368

✥ GREAT LAKES SHIPWRECK MUSEUM
The Great Lakes Shipwreck Museum is the only one of its kind dedicated to the perils of maritime transport on the Great Lakes. It is located at Whitefish Point, Michigan, site of the oldest active lighthouse on Lake Superior. *Address:* 18335 N. Whitefish Point Road *City:* Paradise *State:* MI *Zip:* 49768 *Phone:* 888-492-3747 *Web:* www.shipwreckmuseum.com *Visitors welcome?* Yes *Hours:* Daily, May 1 to Oct. 1, 10 a.m. to 6 p.m. *Admission:* $12 adults, $8 children five to 17, under five FREE *Operated by:* Great Lakes Shipwreck Historical Society *NR?* No *NHL?* No *Latitude:* 46.7703 *Latitude:* -84.9577

ICEBREAKER MACKINAW MARITIME MUSEUM
The icebreaker Mackinaw was decommissioned in 2006 and docked at the old railroad dock in Mackinaw City. She is open for tours. *Address:* 131 S. Huron Ave. *City:* Mackinaw City *State:* MI *Zip:* 49701 *Phone:* 231-436-9825 *Web:* www.themackinaw.org *Email:* contact@TheMackinaw.org *Visitors welcome?* Yes *Hours:* May and June, 11 a.m. to 7 p.m.; July to Sept., 10 a.m. to 8 p.m.; Sept. to October, 10 a.m. to 6 p.m. *Admission:* $10 adults, $6 youth six to 17, under five FREE *Operated by:* Icebreaker Mackinaw Maritime Museum *NR?* No *NHL?* No *Latitude:* 45.7821 *Latitude:* -84.7248

KEEWATIN MARITIME MUSEUM
The Keewatin Maritime Museum preserves the passenger steamer Keewatin as a floating exhibit. *Address:* Blue Star Highway and Union St. *City:* Saugatuck *State:* MI *Zip:* 49453 *Phone:* 269-857-2464 *Web:* www.keewatinmaritimemuseum.com *Visitors welcome?* Yes *Hours:* Memorial Day to Labor Day, 10:30 a.m. to 4 p.m. *Admission:* Contact attraction directly *Operated by:* Keewatin Maritime Museum *NR?* No *NHL?* No *Latitude:* 42.6466 *Latitude:* -86.2025

LES CHENEAUX MARITIME MUSEUM
The O.M. Reif Boathouse at the Les Cheneaux Maritime Museum is home to displays of vintage boats, marine artifacts, antique outboard motors, historic photos of area boating, a boat building workshop, and a gift shop. *Address:* 105 S. Meridian St. *City:* Cedarville *State:* MI *Zip:* 49719 *Phone:* 906-484-3354 *Web:* www.lchistorical.org/marimus.html *Email:* lcha@lchistorical.org *Visitors welcome?* Yes *Hours:* Mid-May to mid-September: Tuesday to Saturday, 10 a.m. to 4 p.m.; Sunday, 1 p.m. to 4 p.m. *Admission:* Contact attraction directly *Operated by:* Les Cheneaux Historical Association *NR?* No *NHL?* No *Latitude:* 45.9979 *Latitude:* -84.3629

CHAPTER 3 – MUSEUMS

LIGHTHOUSE KEEPERS HOME AND MUSEUM
The former keepers house for the Grand Marais Lighthouse is operated as a museum by the Grand Marais Historical Society. *Address:* Coast Guard Point *City:* Grand Marais *State:* MI *Zip:* 49839 *Phone:* 906-494-2404 *Web:* historicalsociety.grandmaraismichigan.com *Visitors welcome?* Yes *Hours:* Daily, July and August, 1 p.m. to 4 p.m.; Weekends, June and September, 1 p.m. to 4 p.m. *Admission:* Contact attraction directly *Operated by:* Grand Marais Historical Society *NR?* No *NHL?* No *Latitude:* 46.6473 *Latitude:* -85.9501

MARQUETTE MARITIME MUSEUM
Began in 1980 as the Marquette Maritime Museum Association, the museum was opened in the old City Waterworks building in 1982. *Address:* 300 Lakeshore Blvd. *City:* Marquette *State:* MI *Zip:* 49855 *Phone:* 906-226-2006 *Web:* mqtmaritimemuseum.com *Email:* mqtmaritimemuseum@yahoo.com *Visitors welcome?* Yes *Hours:* Memorial Day to Mid-October, Monday - Sunday 10 a.m. to 5 p.m. *Admission:* $4 adults, $3 children under 12 *Operated by:* Marquette Maritime Museum *NR?* No *NHL?* No *Year established/built:* 1982 *Latitude:* 46.5453 *Latitude:* -87.3800

MICHIGAN MARITIME MUSEUM
The Michigan Maritime Museum works to preserve the maritime history of South Haven and the State of Michigan. *Address:* 260 Dyckman Ave. *City:* South Haven *State:* MI *Zip:* 49090 *Phone:* 269-637-8078 *Toll-free:* 800-747-3810 *Web:* michiganmaritimemuseum.org *Email:* info@michiganmaritimemuseum.org *Visitors welcome?* Yes *Hours:* Memorial Day to Labor Day: Monday to Saturday, 10 a.m. to 5 p.m.; Sunday noon to 5 p.m. Labor Day to Memorial Day: Friday, Saturday, Sunday, 10 a.m. to 5 p.m. *Admission:* $5 adults, $4 seniors, $3.50 children *Operated by:* Michigan Maritime Museum *NR?* No *NHL?* No *Latitude:* 42.4070 *Latitude:* -86.2745

PORT HURON MUSEUM
The Port Huron Museum boasts five different museum sites for you and your family to explore: Port Huron Museum, the Huron Lightship, the Cutter Bramble, the Fort Gratiot Lighthouse, and the Edison Depot. *Address:* 1115 6th Street *City:* Port Huron *State:* MI *Zip:* 48060 *Phone:* 810-982-0891 *Web:* www.phmuseum.org *Visitors welcome?* Yes *Hours:* Daily, 11 a.m. to 5 p.m. *Admission:* $20 families, $7 adults, $5 seniors and students, five and under FREE *Operated by:* Port Huron Museum *NR?* No *NHL?* No *Year established/built:* 1967 *Latitude:* 42.9724 *Latitude:* -82.4261

SAGINAW VALLEY NAVAL SHIP MUSEUM
The Saginaw Valley Naval Ship Museum is working to acquire the retired destroyer USS Edson for its riverfront site. *Address:* Bay City Riverfront *City:* Bay City *State:* MI *Zip:* 48706 *Phone:* 989-684-3946 *Web:* www.ussedson.org *Email:* kegley@chartermi.net *Visitors welcome?* Yes *Hours:* Contact attraction directly *Admission:* Contact attraction directly *Operated by:* Saginaw Valley Naval Ship Museum *NR?* No *NHL?* No *Latitude:* 43.5945 *Latitude:* -83.8889

SLEEPING BEAR POINT COAST GUARD STATION MARITIME MUSEUM
Exhibits cover the U.S. Life-Saving Service, the U.S. Coast Guard, and Great Lakes shipping history. A room on the second floor is outfitted as a Steamer Wheelhouse with a panoramic view of the Manitou Passage shipping channel. *Address:* West of Glen Haven, Sleeping Bear Dunes National Lakeshore *City:* Glen Haven *State:* MI *Phone:* 231-326-5134 *Web:* www.nps.gov/slbe/planyourvisit/maritimemusem.htm *Visitors welcome?* Yes *Hours:* Daily, hours vary by season *Admission:* FREE *Operated by:* Sleeping Bear Dunes National Lakeshore *NR?* No *NHL?* No *Year established/built:* 1871 *Latitude:* 44.9019 *Latitude:* -86.0276

CHAPTER 3 – MUSEUMS

MINNESOTA

CORPS OF ENGINEERS' LAKE SUPERIOR MARITIME VISITORS CENTER
The Lake Superior Maritime Visitors Center features exhibits and programs on the maritime history of Lake Superior and Duluth Harbor, as well as information on current operations. *Address:* 600 S. Lake Ave. *City:* Duluth *State:* MN *Zip:* 55802 *Phone:* 218-720-5260, ext.1 then ext.2 *Email:* Thomas.R.Holden@LRE02.usace.army.mil *Visitors welcome?* Yes *Hours:* Contact attraction directly *Admission:* FREE *Operated by:* U.S. Army Corps of Engineers *NR?* No *NHL?* No *Latitude:* 46.7790 *Latitude:* -92.0929

✦ MINNESOTA LAKES MARITIME MUSEUM
The Minnesota Lakes Maritime Museum is a nonprofit organization dedicated to the preservation of antique and classic watercraft, resort memorabilia and sporting equipment used on the Minnesota lakes. *Address:* 205 3rd Ave. W. *City:* Alexandria *State:* MN *Zip:* 56308 *Phone:* 320-759-1114 *Web:* www.mnlakesmaritime.org *Email:* bruce@mnlakesmaritime.org *Visitors welcome?* Yes *Hours:* May 15 to October 15: Tuesday to Friday, 10 a.m. to 5 p.m.; Saturday, 10 a.m. to 4 p.m.; Sunday, noon to 4 p.m. *Admission:* $6 adults, $5 seniors, $3 students five to 17, under five FREE *Operated by:* Minnesota Lakes Maritime Museum *NR?* No *NHL?* No *Latitude:* 45.8895 *Latitude:* -95.3789

MINNESOTA MARINE ART MUSEUM
The Minnesota Marine Art Museum collects and shows marine art of all genres and media. *Address:* 800 Riverview Drive *City:* Winona *State:* MN *Zip:* 55987 *Phone:* 507-474-6626 *Toll-free:* 866-940-6626 *Web:* www.minnesotamarineart.org *Email:* bmidthun@minnesotamarineart.org *Visitors welcome?* Yes *Hours:* Tuesday to Saturdays, 10 a.m. to 5 p.m.; Sunday, 11 a.m. to 5 p.m. *Admission:* $6 adults, $3 students, under five FREE *Operated by:* Minnesota Marine Art Museum *NR?* No *NHL?* No *Year established/built:* 2006 *Latitude:* 44.0588 *Latitude:* -91.6632

MISSISSIPPI

MARITIME & SEAFOOD INDUSTRY MUSEUM
The Maritime & Seafood Industry Museum was established in 1986 to preserve and interpret the maritime history and heritage of Biloxi and the Mississippi Gulf Coast. *Address:* 115 First Street *City:* Biloxi *State:* MS *Zip:* 39530 *Phone:* 228-435-6320 *Web:* www.maritimemuseum.org *Email:* info@maritimemuseum.org *Visitors welcome?* Yes *Hours:* Monday to Friday, 10 a.m. to 4 p.m. *Admission:* Contact attraction directly *Operated by:* Maritime & Seafood Industry Museum *NR?* No *NHL?* No *Year established/built:* 1986 *Latitude:* 30.3937 *Latitude:* -88.8591

MISSOURI

GOLDEN EAGLE RIVER MUSEUM
Located in the Nims Mansion, the Golden Eagle River Museum features local maritime history. *Address:* 2701 Finestown Rd. *City:* St. Louis *State:* MO *Zip:* 63129 *Phone:* 314-846-9073 *Visitors welcome?* Yes *Hours:* May 1 to October 31: Wednesday to Sunday, 1 p.m. to 5 p.m. *Admission:* FREE *Operated by:* Golden Eagle River Museum *NR?* No *NHL?* No *Latitude:* 38.4082 *Latitude:* -90.3278

NEBRASKA

MUSEUM OF MISSOURI RIVER HISTORY
The Museum of Missouri River History features the dredge Captain Meriweather Lewis as the primary exhibit. *Address:* Nebraska Ave & E Allen St. *City:* Brownville *State:* NE *Zip:* 68321 *Phone:* 402-825-4131 *Web:* www.meriwetherlewisfoundation.org *Email:* jm62006@navix.net *Visitors welcome?* Yes *Hours:* Contact attraction directly *Admission:* Contact attraction directly *Operated by:* Captain Meriwether Lewis Foundation *NR?* No *NHL?* No *Latitude:* 40.3933 *Latitude:* -95.6548

NEW HAMPSHIRE

STRAWBERY BANKE MUSEUM
Visitors to Strawbery Banke have the opportunity to experience and imagine how people lived and worked in a typical American coastal village, which includes the gundalow Captain Edward H. Adams and a boatwright's shop. *Address:* 420 Court St. *City:* Portsmouth *State:* NH *Zip:* 03801 *Phone:* 603-433-1100 *Web:* www.strawberybanke.org *Email:* info@strawberybanke.org *Visitors welcome?* Yes *Hours:* May 1 to October 31: Daily, 10 a.m. to 5 p.m.; November: Saturday and Sunday, 10 a.m. to 2 p.m.; December: Monday to Friday, 10 a.m. to 2 p.m. *Admission:* $15 adults, $10 youths five to 17, four and under FREE *Operated by:* Strawbery Banke Museum *NR?* No *NHL?* No *Latitude:* 43.0769 *Latitude:* -70.7535

NEW JERSEY

ATLANTIC HERITAGE CENTER
The Atlantic Heritage Center's collection includes household items and decorative arts, fine arts, weaponry, maritime artifacts, and toys. *Address:* 907 Shore Road *City:* Somers Point *State:* NJ *Zip:* 08244 *Phone:* 609-927-5218 *Web:* www.atlanticheritagecenternj.org *Email:* AHCinfo@comcast.net *Visitors welcome?* Yes *Hours:* Wednesday to Saturday, 10 a.m. to 3:30 p.m. *Admission:* FREE *Operated by:* Atlantic Heritage Center *NR?* No *NHL?* No *Latitude:* 39.3105 *Latitude:* -74.5976

BARNEGAT LIGHT MUSEUM
The museum is in the building that was the one-room school for Barnegat Light from 1903 to 1954. The museum is on the National Register of Historical Places. The museum features artifacts, replicas and photographs depicting the history of Barnegat Light. *Address:* 5th St *City:* Barnegat Light *State:* NJ *Zip:* 08006 *Phone:* 609-494-8578 *Web:* www.bl-hs.org *Visitors welcome?* Yes *Hours:* Saturday and Sunday, June and September, 11 a.m. to 4 p.m.; Daily, July and August, 11 a.m. to 5 p.m. *Admission:* Contact attraction directly *Operated by:* Barnegat Light Historical Society *NR?* Yes *NHL?* No *Year established/built:* 1903 *Latitude:* 39.7601 *Latitude:* -74.1049

BATTLESHIP NEW JERSEY MUSEUM AND MEMORIAL
The Battleship New Jersey Museum and Memorial features the World War II-era battleship New Jersey. *Address:* 62 Battleship Pl. *City:* Camden *State:* NJ *Zip:* 08103 *Phone:* 856-966-1652 *Toll-free:* 866-877-6262 *Web:* www.battleshipnewjersey.org *Visitors welcome?* Yes *Hours:* Contact attraction directly *Admission:* $18.50

adults, $14 seniors/veterans, $14 children six to 11, under six, BB62 vets and active military, FREE *Operated by:* Battleship New Jersey Museum and Memorial *NR?* No *NHL?* No *Latitude:* 39.9347 *Latitude:* -75.1108

CANAL SOCIETY OF NEW JERSEY MUSEUM
The Canal Society of New Jersey Museum is located in Waterloo Village. *Address:* 525 Waterloo Rd. *City:* Stanhope *State:* NJ *Zip:* 07874 *Phone:* 973-347-0900 *Web:* www.canalsocietynj.org/csnjwaterloo.html *Email:* nj-cnal@googlegroups.com *Visitors welcome?* Yes *Hours:* Contact attraction directly *Admission:* Contact attraction directly *Operated by:* Canal Society of New Jersey *NR?* No *NHL?* No *Year established/built:* 1969 *Latitude:* 40.9206 *Latitude:* -74.7413

DELAWARE BAY MUSEUM & FOLKLIFE CENTER
The Delaware Bay Museum & Folklife Center is a project of the Bayshore Discovery Project, which owns and operates the schooner A.J. Meerwald. The museum facilities are currently undergoing restoration. *Address:* Maurice River *City:* Bivalve *State:* NJ *Zip:* 08349 *Phone:* 856-785-2060 *Web:* www.ajmeerwald.org *Email:* info@bayshorediscoveryproject.org *Visitors welcome?* Yes *Hours:* Contact attraction directly *Admission:* Contact attraction directly *Operated by:* Bayshore Discovery Project *NR?* No *NHL?* No *Latitude:* 39.2414 *Latitude:* -75.0845

JAMES KIRK MARITIME MUSEUM
The James Kirk Maritime Museum features ship models and shipbuilding tools. The museum is located in the Linwood Library. *Address:* 301 Davis Ave. *City:* Linwood *State:* NJ *Zip:* 08221 *Phone:* 609-927-2023 *Web:* www.linwoodnj.org/Museums/maritime1.html *Email:* admin@linwoodnj.org *Visitors welcome?* Yes *Hours:* Contact attraction directly *Admission:* FREE *Operated by:* James Kirk Maritime Museum *NR?* No *NHL?* No *Latitude:* 39.3546 *Latitude:* -74.5705

JOHN DUBOIS MARITIME MUSEUM
The John Dubois Maritime Museum houses a large collection of southern New Jersey maritime-related items from the 19th and early 20th centuries. *Address:* 960 Ye Greate Street *City:* Greenwich *State:* NJ *Zip:* 08323 *Phone:* 856-455-4055 *Web:* www.cchistsoc.org *Visitors welcome?* Yes *Hours:* By appointment *Admission:* Contact attraction directly *Operated by:* Cumberland County Historical Society *NR?* No *NHL?* No *Latitude:* 39.3927 *Latitude:* -75.3410

KEYPORT HISTORICAL SOCIETY STEAMBOAT DOCK MUSEUM
The Keyport Historical Society Steamboat Dock Museum's exhibits of Keyport's history cover the plantation century, the docks and shipping, steamboat building, the oyster industry, the Aeromarine Plane & Motor Company, and a printing exhibit. *Address:* American Legion Dr *City:* Keyport *State:* NJ *Zip:* 07735 *Phone:* 732-739-6390 *Web:* www.keyportonline.com/content/274/255/default.aspx *Visitors welcome?* Yes *Hours:* May 15 to Sept. 25: Sundays, noon to 4 p.m.; Mondays, 10 a.m. to noon *Admission:* Contact attraction directly *Operated by:* City of Keyport *NR?* No *NHL?* No *Year established/built:* 1976 *Latitude:* 40.4391 *Latitude:* -74.2025

MUSEUM OF NEW JERSEY MARITIME HISTORY
The Museum of New Jersey Maritime History features exhibits on local maritime history, including the 1934 wreck of the Morro Castle. *Address:* Dock Road and West Avenue *City:* Beach Haven *State:* NJ *Zip:* 08008 *Phone:* 609-492-0202 *Web:* www.museumofnjmh.com *Email:* Curator@MuseumofNJMH.org *Visitors welcome?* Yes *Hours:* June: 10 a.m. to 4 p.m.; July and August: 10 a.m. to 6 p.m.; September to May: Friday, Saturday, Sunday, 10 a.m. to 4 p.m. *Admission:* Contact attraction directly *Operated by:* Museum of New Jersey Maritime History *NR?* No *NHL?* No *Year established/built:* 2005 *Latitude:* 39.5662 *Latitude:* -74.2444

NEW JERSEY NAVAL MUSEUM
The New Jersey Naval Museum features the World War II-ear submarine USS Ling. *Address:* 78 River St. *City:* Hackensack *State:* NJ *Zip:* 07601 *Phone:* 201-342-3268 *Web:* www.njnm.com *Email:* njnavalmuseum@yahoo.com *Visitors welcome?* Yes *Hours:* Saturday and Sunday, 10 a.m. to 4 p.m. *Admission:* $9 adults, $4 children 12 and under *Operated by:* Submarine Memorial Association *NR?* No *NHL?* No *Latitude:* 40.8805 *Latitude:* -74.0415

TOMS RIVER SEAPORT SOCIETY & MARITIME MUSEUM
The Barnegat Bay area and the intracostal waters of New Jersey have produced a number of significant boat types indigenous to the shallow estuaries and bays that provide haven for the feisty blue crab, the flat faces flounder, and other marine species. *Address:* Hooper Ave and Water Street *City:* Toms River *State:* NJ *Zip:* 08754 *Phone:* 732-349-9209 *Web:* www.tomsriverseaport.org *Email:* tomsriverssmm@yahoo.com *Visitors welcome?* Yes *Hours:* Tuesday, Thursday, Saturday, 10 a.m. to 2 p.m. *Admission:* Contact attraction directly *Operated by:* Toms River Seaport Society *NR?* No *NHL?* No *Latitude:* 39.9507 *Latitude:* -74.1941

TUCKERTON SEAPORT
Tuckerton Seaport is a multifaceted site for entertainment, education, and maritime experience. *Address:* 120 W. Main *City:* Tuckerton *State:* NJ *Zip:* 08087 *Phone:* 609-296-8868 *Web:* www.tuckertonseaport.org *Visitors welcome?* Yes *Hours:* Daily, 10 a.m. to 5 p.m. *Admission:* $8 adults, $6 seniors, $3 children 6-12, five and under FREE *Operated by:* Tuckerton Seaport *NR?* No *NHL?* No *Latitude:* 39.6013 *Latitude:* -74.3447

NEW YORK

AMERICAN MERCHANT MARINE MUSEUM
The American Merchant Marine Museum's mission is to educate and inform visitors about the American merchant marine in a learning center for the regiment and public at large, to promote public interest in and understanding of our nation's merchant marine. *Address:* 300 Steamboat Road *City:* Kings Point *State:* NY *Zip:* 11024 *Phone:* 516-773-5515 *Web:* www.usmma.edu/about/Museum *Visitors welcome?* Yes *Hours:* Tuesday to Friday, 10 a.m. to 3 p.m.; Saturday and Sunday, 1 p.m. to 4:30 p.m. *Admission:* Contact attraction directly *Operated by:* U.S. Merchant Marine Academy *NR?* No *NHL?* No *Latitude:* 40.8131 *Latitude:* -73.7610

ANTIQUE BOAT MUSEUM
From humble beginnings as a riverside gathering of antique boat enthusiasts, the Antique Boat Museum has evolved into a national institution which makes substantial economic and cultural contributions to Clayton and the North Country region. *Address:* 750 Mary St. *City:* Clayton *State:* NY *Zip:* 13624 *Phone:* 315-686-4104 *Web:* www.abm.org *Email:* john@abm.org *Visitors welcome?* Yes *Hours:* Mid-May to mid-October: Daily, 9 a.m. to 5 p.m. *Admission:* $12 adults, $11 seniors, $6 students/children 7-12/active military, six and under FREE *Operated by:* Antique Boat Museum *NR?* No *NHL?* No *Year established/built:* 1964 *Latitude:* 44.2383 *Latitude:* -76.0893

BUFFALO AND ERIE COUNTY NAVAL AND MILITARY PARK
The Buffalo and Erie County Naval & Military Park includes the submarine USS Croaker, the cruiser USS Little Rock, and the destroyer USS The Sullivans. *Address:* One Naval Park Cove *City:* Buffalo *State:* NY *Zip:* 14202 *Phone:* 716-847-1773 *Web:* www.buffalonavalpark.org *Email:* info@buffalonavalpark.org *Visitors welcome?* Yes *Hours:* April to October, daily, 10 a.m. to 5 p.m.; November, Saturday, Sunday, Friday after Thanksgiving, 10 a.m. to 4 p.m. *Admission:* $9 adults, $6 seniors, children six to 16, under six FREE *Oper-*

CHAPTER 3 – MUSEUMS

ated by: Buffalo and Erie County Naval and Military Park *NR?* No *NHL?* No *Latitude:* 42.8994 *Latitude:* -78.8759

BUFFALO MARITIME CENTER
Located on the Lake Erie shore, the Buffalo Maritime Center includes the Historic Boat Museum, featuring more than 100 small craft, and the Boat-Building Center, a hands-on learning environment. *Address:* 901 Fuhrmann Blvd. *City:* Buffalo *State:* NY *Zip:* 14203 *Phone:* 716-878-6532 *Web:* www.buffalomaritimecenter.org *Email:* info@buffalomaritimecenter.org *Visitors welcome?* Yes *Hours:* Tuesdays: 10:30 a.m. to 8 p.m.; Thursdays: 10:30 a.m. to 8 p.m.; Fridays: 10:30 a.m. to 6 p.m.; Saturdays: 8 a.m. to noon *Admission:* Contact attraction directly *Operated by:* Buffalo Maritime Center *Year established/built:* 1988 *Latitude:* 42.8568 *Latitude:* -78.8722

CANASTOTA CANAL TOWN MUSEUM
Located beside a remnant of the original Old Erie Canal, the Canastoga Canal Town Museum is filled with authentic memorabilia, art, and other exhibits explaining Canastota maritime history. *Address:* 122 Canal St. *City:* Canastota *State:* NY *Zip:* 13032 *Phone:* 315-697-5002 *Web:* www.canastota.com/organization.asp?key=43 *Visitors welcome?* Yes *Hours:* May and June: Noon to 3 p.m.; July and August: 11 a.m. to 3 p.m.; September and October: Noon to 3 p.m. *Admission:* $3 adults, 12 and under FREE *Operated by:* Canastota Canal Town Museum *NR?* No *NHL?* No *Latitude:* 43.0797 *Latitude:* -75.7520

CAPT. ALBERT ROGERS MANSION
The Greek revival-style mansion was built for whaling Captain Albert Rogers in 1843. *Address:* 17 Meeting House Lane *City:* Southampton *State:* NY *Zip:* 11969 *Phone:* 631-283-2494 *Web:* www.southamptonhistoricalmuseum.org *Email:* info@southamptonhistoricalmuseum.org *Visitors welcome?* Yes *Hours:* Tuesday to Saturday, 11 a.m. to 4 p.m. *Admission:* $4 adults, children under 17 FREE *Operated by:* Southampton Historical Museums and Research Center *NR?* No *NHL?* No *Year established/built:* 1843 *Latitude:* 40.8842 *Latitude:* -72.3893

CENTER FOR HISTORIC MARINE TECHNOLOGY
Though not yet open to the public, the North River Tugboat Museum and the Center for Historic Marine Technology cares for important historic tugs, which it operates as traveling exhibits. *Address:* 300 Greenkill Ave. *City:* Kingston *State:* NY *Zip:* 12401 *Phone:* 845-340-0506 *Web:* www.tugmuseum.com *Email:* steve@tugmuseum.com *Visitors welcome?* No *Hours:* Contact attraction directly *Admission:* Contact attraction directly *Operated by:* North River Tugboat Museum *NR?* No *NHL?* No *Latitude:* 41.9230 *Latitude:* -74.0155

CHITTENANGO LANDING CANAL BOAT MUSEUM
The Chittenango Landing Canal Boat Museum is located within the Old Erie Canal State Historic Park in Central New York State. During the 19th and 20th centuries, 96-foot long cargo boats were built and repaired on this site. *Address:* 7010 Lakeport Rd. *City:* Chittenango *State:* NY *Zip:* 13037 *Phone:* 315-687-3801 *Web:* www.chittenangolandingcanalboatmuseum.com *Email:* CLCBM@centralny.twcbc.com *Visitors welcome?* Yes *Hours:* May to June: Saturday and Sunday: 1 p.m. to 4 p.m.; July and August: Daily, 10 a.m. to 4 p.m.; September to October: Saturday and Sunday: 1 p.m. to 4 p.m. *Admission:* $4 adults, 12 and under FREE *Operated by:* Chittenango Landing Canal Boat Museum *NR?* No *NHL?* No *Latitude:* 43.0612 *Latitude:* -75.8714

CITY ISLAND NAUTICAL MUSEUM
City Island is a small community at the edge of New York City located just beyond Pelham Bay Park in the Bronx and surrounded by the waters of western Long Island Sound and Eastchester Bay. *Address:* 190 Fordham St. *City:* City Island *State:* NY *Zip:* 10464 *Phone:* 718-885-0008 *Web:* www.cityislandmuseum.org *Email:*

CHAPTER 3 – MUSEUMS

CIHS@cityislandmuseum.org *Visitors welcome?* Yes *Hours:* Saturday and Sunday, 1 p.m. to 5 p.m. *Admission:* Donation *Operated by:* City Island Historical Society and Nautical Museum *NR?* No *NHL?* No *Year established/built:* 1976 *Latitude:* 40.8471 *Latitude:* -73.7843

COLD SPRING HARBOR WHALING MUSEUM
The Cold Spring Harbor Whaling Museum collects, preserves, and exhibits objects and documents pertinent to whaling, especially the regional whaling history of Long Island, whale conservation, and the history of Cold Spring Harbor as a maritime port. *Address:* Main Street *City:* Cold Spring Harbor *State:* NY *Zip:* 11724 *Phone:* 631-367-3418 *Web:* www.cshwhalingmuseum.org *Visitors welcome?* Yes *Hours:* Tuesday to Sunday, 11 a.m. to 5 p.m. *Admission:* $6 adults, $5 seniors/students five to 18, under five FREE *Operated by:* Cold Spring Harbor Whaling Museum *NR?* No *NHL?* No *Year established/built:* 1942 *Latitude:* 40.8719 *Latitude:* -73.4544

 D & H CANAL MUSEUM
The purpose of the D & H Canal Historical Society is to preserve, protect and perpetuate the unique history of the Delaware and Hudson Canal, particularly in Ulster County. *Address:* 23 Mohonk Rd. *City:* High Falls *State:* NY *Zip:* 12440 *Phone:* 845-687-9311 *Web:* www.canalmuseum.org *Email:* info@canalmuseum.org *Visitors welcome?* Yes *Hours:* Contact attraction directly *Admission:* $4 adults, $2 children *Operated by:* D & H Canal Historical Society *NR?* No *NHL?* No *Latitude:* 41.8255 *Latitude:* -74.1260

Register at www.fyddeye.com and get a 20% discount on the next edition of the Fyddeye Guide.

DESTROYER ESCORT HISTORICAL MUSEUM
During World War II, 563 Destroyer Escorts battled Nazi U-Boats on the North Atlantic protecting convoys of men and material. In the Pacific they stood in line to defend naval task forces from Japanese submarines and Kamikaze air attacks. Today, only one escort remains afloat in the United States, the USS Slater. *Address:* 141 Broadway *City:* Albany *State:* NY *Zip:* 12202 *Phone:* 518-431-1943 *Web:* www.ussslater.org *Email:* info@ussslater.org *Visitors welcome?* Yes *Hours:* April to November: Wednesday to Sunday, 10 a.m. to 4 p.m. *Admission:* $7 adults, $6 seniors, $5 children six to 14, under six FREE *Operated by:* Destroyer Escort Historical Foundation *NR?* No *NHL?* No *Latitude:* 42.6420 *Latitude:* -73.7510

EAST END SEAPORT AND MARITIME MUSEUM
The East End Seaport and Museum boasts an array of exhibits on the maritime heritage of the area, including displays on the Greenport menhaden fishing industry, the oyster industry, lighthouse lenses, a model ship of the USS Ohio, and more. *Address:* 3 South St. *City:* Greenport *State:* NY *Zip:* 11944 *Phone:* 631-477-2100 *Email:* eseaport@verizon.net *Visitors welcome?* Yes *Hours:* Mid-May to June: Weekends, 11 a.m. to 5 p.m.; July and August, Mon, Wed, Thurs, & Fri. 11 a.m. to 5 p.m., Sat & Sun, 9:30 a.m. to 5 p.m.; September, Weekends, 11 a.m. to 5 p.m. *Admission:* $2 general admission *Operated by:* East End Seaport Museum & Marine Foundation *NR?* No *NHL?* No *Year established/built:* 1992 *Latitude:* 41.1029 *Latitude:* -72.3634

EAST HAMPTON TOWN MARINE MUSEUM
The East Hampton Town Marine Museum is dedicated to documenting and preserving East Hampton maritime history and to showing how our marine environment has impacted upon the economic, social and recreational life of its citizens. *Address:* 301 Bluff Road *City:* Amagansett *State:* NY *Zip:* 11937 *Phone:* 631-324-6850 *Web:* easthamptonhistory.org *Email:* info@easthamptonhistory.org *Visitors welcome?* Yes *Hours:* Saturday, 10 a.m. to 5 p.m.; Sunday, noon to 5 p.m. *Admission:* $4 adults, $3 seniors, $2 students *Operated by:* East Hampton Historical Society *NR?* No *NHL?* No *Latitude:* 40.9709 *Latitude:* -72.1294

CHAPTER 3 – MUSEUMS

ERIE CANAL MUSEUM
The primary mission of the Erie Canal Museum is to keep Erie Canal history alive by educating the public about this rich heritage we all share. *Address:* 318 Erie Blvd. E. *City:* Syracuse *State:* NY *Zip:* 13202 *Phone:* 315-471-0593 *Web:* www.eriecanalmuseum.org *Visitors welcome?* Yes *Hours:* Monday to Saturday, 10 a.m. to 5 p.m.; Sunday, 10 a.m. to 3 p.m. *Admission:* Donation *Operated by:* Erie Canal Museum *NR?* No *NHL?* No *Year established/built:* 1962 *Latitude:* 43.0509 *Latitude:* -76.1563

ERIE CANAL VILLAGE
Erie Canal Village is an outdoor living history museum. It is a reconstructed 19th century settlement on the site where, on July 4, 1817, the first shovelful of earth was turned for the construction of the original Erie Canal. *Address:* 5789 Rome New London Road *City:* Rome *State:* NY *Zip:* 13440 *Phone:* 315-337-3999 *Web:* www.eriecanalvillage.net *Email:* mandm2000@twcny.rr.com *Visitors welcome?* Yes *Hours:* Memorial Day weekend through Labor Day: Wednesday to Saturday, 10 a.m. to noon; Sunday: noon to 5 p.m. *Admission:* $15 adults, $12 seniors, $10 children five to 17; under five FREE *Operated by:* Erie Canal Village *NR?* No *NHL?* No *Latitude:* 43.2260 *Latitude:* -75.5096

✦ H. LEE WHITE MARINE MUSEUM
The H. Lee White Marine Museum is housed in the former administration building for a huge, then state-of the-art 1920's grain elevator complex on the Oswego Harbor's west side pier. *Address:* West 1st Street Pier *City:* Oswego *State:* NY *Zip:* 13126 *Phone:* 315-342-0480 *Web:* www.hleewhitemarinemuseum.com *Email:* info@hleewhitemarinemuseum.com *Visitors welcome?* Yes *Hours:* September to June, daily, 1 p.m. to 5 p.m.; July and August, daily 10 a.m. to 5 p.m. *Admission:* $5 adults; $3 youth 5 to 12; under 5 FREE *Operated by:* H. Lee White Marine Museum *NR?* No *NHL?* No *Year established/built:* 1982 *Latitude:* 43.4553 *Latitude:* -76.5105

HUDSON RIVER MARITIME MUSEUM
The Hudson River Maritime Museum is the only museum in New York State exclusively preserving the maritime history of the Hudson River, its tributaries, and the industries dependent on the river. *Address:* 50 Rondout Landing *City:* Kingston *State:* NY *Zip:* 12401 *Phone:* 845-338-0071 *Web:* www.hrmm.org *Email:* hrmm@hvc.rr.com *Visitors welcome?* Yes *Hours:* May to October: Thursday, Friday, Saturday, Sunday, and Monday: 11 a.m. to 5 p.m.; Call for winter hours *Admission:* $5 adults; $4 seniors, children 6 to 12; 5 under, FREE *Operated by:* Hudson River Maritime Museum *NR?* No *NHL?* No *Year established/built:* 1980 *Latitude:* 41.9235 *Latitude:* -73.9836

✦ INTREPID SEA-AIR-SPACE MUSEUM
The Intrepid Sea, Air & Space Museum is one of America's leading museums of its type. *Address:* Pier 86, W. 46th St. and 12th Ave. *City:* New York *State:* NY *Zip:* 10036 *Phone:* 212-245-0072 *Toll-free:* 877-957-7447 *Web:* www.intrepidmuseum.org *Visitors welcome?* Yes *Hours:* Daily *Admission:* $19.50 adults; $15.50 students, seniors, veterans; $14.50 youth six to 17; children two to five, $7.50; under two FREE *Operated by:* Intrepid Sea-Air-Space Museum *NR?* No *NHL?* No *Year established/built:* 1982 *Latitude:* 40.7631 *Latitude:* -73.9996

LOCKPORT CANAL MUSEUM
The Lockport Canal Museum preserves the history of the local portion of the Erie Canal. *Address:* 80 Richmond Ave. *City:* Lockport *State:* NY *Zip:* 14094 *Phone:* 716-434-3140 *Web:* www.lockport-ny.com/Tourism/canal.htm *Visitors welcome?* Yes *Hours:* Daily *Admission:* FREE *Operated by:* Lockport Canal Museum *NR?* No *NHL?* No *Latitude:* 43.1709 *Latitude:* -78.6935

CHAPTER 3 – MUSEUMS

LONG ISLAND MARITIME MUSEUM
The Long Island Maritime Museum preserves the history and maritime culture of Long Island, New York. *Address:* 86 West Ave. *City:* West Sayville *State:* NY *Zip:* 11796 *Phone:* 631-854-4974 *Web:* www.limaritime.org *Email:* limm@limaritime.org *Visitors welcome?* Yes *Hours:* Monday to Saturday: 10 a.m. to 4 p.m.; Sunday, noon to 4 p.m. *Admission:* $4 adults, $2 senior/child three to 17, under three FREE *Operated by:* Long Island Maritime Museum *NR?* No *NHL?* No *Latitude:* 40.7218 *Latitude:* -73.0938

MARITIME INDUSTRY MUSEUM AT FORT SCHUYLER
The Maritime Industry Museum at Fort Schuyler was established in 1986 when Capt. Jeffrey Monroe, a former Associate Professor of Transportation at the Maritime College, with the help of Jack Hayes, a 1947 engineer graduate of the college. *Address:* 6 Pennyfield Ave. *City:* Bronx *State:* NY *Zip:* 10465 *Phone:* 718-409-7218 *Web:* www.sunymaritime.edu *Email:* maritimeindustry@sunymaritime.edu *Visitors welcome?* Yes *Hours:* Monday to Saturday, 9 a.m. to 4 p.m. *Admission:* FREE *Operated by:* State University of New York Maritime College *NR?* No *NHL?* No *Latitude:* 40.8093 *Latitude:* -73.8019

MATHER HOUSE MUSEUM
The Mather House Museum features a collection of ship models, half-hull models, maritime art, shipwright's tools, and other maritime objects and documents. *Address:* 115 Prospect St. *City:* Port Jefferson *State:* NY *Zip:* 11777 *Phone:* 631-473-2665 *Web:* www.portjeffhistorical.org *Email:* info@portjeffhistorical.org *Visitors welcome?* Yes *Hours:* July and August: Tuesday, Wednesday, Saturday, and Sunday: 1 p.m. to 4 p.m. *Admission:* Contact attraction directly *Operated by:* Historical Society of Greater Port Jefferson *NR?* No *NHL?* No *Latitude:* 40.9458 *Latitude:* -73.0655

NATIONAL LIGHTHOUSE MUSEUM
The National Lighthouse Museum board of directors voted to disband in November, 2009. *Address:* 30 Bay St. *City:* Staten Island *State:* NY *Zip:* 10301 *Phone:* 646-644-3134 *Web:* www.nationallighthousemuseum.org *Email:* ronmeisels@gmail.com *Visitors welcome?* No *Hours:* Closed *Admission:* Closed *NR?* No *NHL?* No *Latitude:* 40.6409 *Latitude:* -74.0758

NEW NETHERLAND MUSEUM & HALF MOON VISITOR'S CENTER
The New Netherland Museum operates the Half Moon, a reproduction of the ship that Henry Hudson sailed from Holland to the New World in 1609. *Address:* 181 S Riverside Ave. *City:* Croton-on-Hudson *State:* NY *Zip:* 10520 *Phone:* 518-443-1609 *Web:* www.newnetherland.org *Email:* info@newnetherland.org *Visitors welcome?* Yes *Hours:* Contact attraction directly *Admission:* Contact attraction directly *Operated by:* New Netherland Museum & Half Moon Visitor's Center *NR?* No *NHL?* No *Latitude:* 41.2024 *Latitude:* -73.8875

NOBLE MARITIME COLLECTION
The mission of the Noble Maritime Collection is to preserve and interpret the art, writings, and historical maritime artifacts of the distinguished marine artist, John A. Noble; to continue Noble's legacy of celebrating the people and traditions of the working waterfront of New York Harbor; to preserve and interpret the history of Sailors' Snug Harbor in its collections, exhibitions and programs; and to operate a maritime study center inspired by John A. Noble and the mariners of Sailors' Snug Harbor. *Address:* 1000 Richmond Terrace, Building D *City:* Staten Island *State:* NY *Zip:* 10301 *Phone:* 718-447-6490 *Web:* www.noblemaritime.org *Email:* ErinUrban@noblemaritime.org *Visitors welcome?* Yes *Hours:* Thursday to Sunday, 1 p.m. to 5 p.m. *Admission:* $5 adults, $3 seniors/students/educators, children under 10 FREE *Operated by:* Noble Maritime Collection *NR?* No *NHL?* No *Latitude:* 40.6453 *Latitude:* -74.1046

CHAPTER 3 – MUSEUMS

NORTH RIVER TUGBOAT MUSEUM
Though not yet open to the public, the North River Tugboat Museum and the Center for Historic Marine Technology cares for important historic tugs, which it operates as traveling exhibits. *Address:* 300 Greenkill Ave. *City:* Kingston *State:* NY *Zip:* 12401 *Phone:* 845-340-0506 *Web:* www.tugmuseum.com *Email:* steve@tugmuseum.com *Visitors welcome?* No *Hours:* Contact attraction directly *Admission:* Contact attraction directly *Operated by:* North River Tugboat Museum *NR?* No *NHL?* No *Latitude:* 41.9230 *Latitude:* -74.0155

NORTHPORT HISTORICAL MUSEUM
The Northport Historical Museum preserves the maritime history of the Northport, NY area. *Address:* 215 Main St. *City:* Northport *State:* NY *Zip:* 11768 *Phone:* 631-757-9859 *Web:* www.northporthistorical.org *Email:* info@northporthistorical.org *Visitors welcome?* Yes *Hours:* Tuesday to Sunday, 1 p.m. to 4:30 p.m. *Admission:* Contact attraction directly *Operated by:* Northport Historical Society *NR?* No *NHL?* No *Latitude:* 40.9011 *Latitude:* -73.3477

SAG HARBOR WHALING & HISTORICAL MUSEUM
The Sag Harbor Whaling & Historical Museum focuses on the history of Sag Harbor as a whaling center in the 19th century. *Address:* 200 Main St. *City:* Sag Harbor *State:* NY *Zip:* 11963 *Phone:* 631-725-0770 *Web:* www.sagharborwhalingmuseum.org *Email:* info@sagharborwhalingmuseum.org *Visitors welcome?* Yes *Hours:* Mid-May through October: Monday to Saturday, 10 a.m. to 5 p.m.; Sunday, 1 p.m. to 5 p.m. *Admission:* Contact attraction directly *Operated by:* Sag Harbor Whaling & Historical Museum *NR?* No *NHL?* No *Latitude:* 40.9977 *Latitude:* -72.2974

SOUTH STREET SEAPORT MUSEUM
The South Street Seaport Museum preserves and interprets the history of New York City as a world port, a place where goods, labor and cultures are exchanged through work, commerce, and the interaction of diverse communities. *Address:* 12 Fulton St. *City:* New York *State:* NY *Zip:* 10038 *Phone:* 212-748-8600 *Web:* www.southstreetseaportmuseum.org *Email:* info@southstseaport.org *Visitors welcome?* Yes *Hours:* November-March: Friday to Sunday, 10 a.m. to 5 p.m.; Monday 10am-5pm: Schermerhorn Row galleries only. Tuesday to Sunday 10 a.m. to 6 p.m: All galleries and ships open *Admission:* $10 adults, $8 students/seniors, $5 children 5-12, under 5 FREE *Operated by:* South Street Seaport Museum *NR?* No *NHL?* No *Year established/built:* 1967 *Latitude:* 40.7066 *Latitude:* -74.0034

WATERFRONT CENTER
The mission of the Waterfront Center is to educate people of all ages, abilities and backgrounds so they can become active stewards of the marine environment, and to promote community sailing and other environmentally friendly ways to enjoy the waters of Oyster Bay. *Address:* 1 West End Ave. *City:* Oyster Bay *State:* NY *Zip:* 11771 *Phone:* 516-922-7245 *Web:* www.thewaterfrontcenter.org *Email:* info@thewaterfrontcenter.org *Visitors welcome?* Yes *Hours:* Contact attraction directly *Admission:* Contact attraction directly *Operated by:* Waterfront Center *NR?* No *NHL?* No *Latitude:* 40.6552 *Latitude:* -73.4775

WATERFRONT MUSEUM AND SHOWBOAT BARGE
Our mission is to provide waterfront access, and promote historic preservation. We foster an understanding of the NY Harbor as a waterway carrying commerce and commuters as well as a means for culture and recreation. *Address:* 290 Conover St. at Pier 44 *City:* Brooklyn *State:* NY *Zip:* 11231 *Phone:* 718-624-4719 *Web:* www.waterfrontmuseum.org *Email:* dsharps@waterfrontmuseum.org *Visitors welcome?* Yes *Hours:* Thursdays, 4 p.m. to 8 p.m.; Saturdays, 1 p.m. to 5 p.m. *Admission:* By donation *Operated by:* Waterfront Museum *NR?* Yes *NHL?* No *Latitude:* 40.6754 *Latitude:* -74.0174

NORTH CAROLINA

CAPE FEAR MUSEUM MARITIME PAVILION
The Maritime Pavilion at the Cape Fear Museum of History and Science traces the developmen of the region's watercraft and maritime industries. *Address:* 814 Market St. *City:* Wilmington *State:* NC *Zip:* 28401 *Phone:* 910-798-4350 *Web:* www.capefearmuseum.com *Visitors welcome?* Yes *Hours:* Memorial Day to Labor Day: Monday to Saturday, 9 a.m. to 5 p.m.; Sunday, 1 p.m. to 5 p.m. Labor Day to Memorial Day: Tuesday to Saturday, 10 a.m. to 5 p.m.; Sunday, 1 p.m. to 5 p.m. *Admission:* $6 adults, $5 seniors/students/military, $3 youth three to 17, under three FREE *Operated by:* Cape Fear Museum of History and Science *NR?* No *NHL?* No *Latitude:* 34.2360 *Latitude:* -77.9389

CSS NEUSE STATE HISTORIC SITE
The CSS Nuese State Historic Site preserves the history of the Confederacy's attempt to regain control of the lower Neuse River and retake the city of New Bern during the Civil War. *Address:* 2612 W. Vernon Ave. *City:* Kinston *State:* NC *Zip:* 28502 *Phone:* 252-522-2091 *Web:* www.nchistoricsites.org *Email:* cssneuse@ncmail.net *Visitors welcome?* Yes *Hours:* Tuesday to Saturday, 9 a.m. to 5 p.m. *Admission:* FREE *Operated by:* North Carolina Department of Cultural Resources *NR?* Yes *NHL?* No *Latitude:* 35.2701 *Latitude:* -77.5951

GRAVEYARD OF THE ATLANTIC MUSEUM
The maritime heritage and shipwrecks of the North Carolina Outer Banks are vital resources for understanding local, regional, and national history. Long ignored, this legacy is in danger of being lost forever. *Address:* 59200 Museum Drive *City:* Hatteras *State:* NC *Zip:* 27943 *Phone:* 252-986-2995 *Web:* www.graveyardoftheatlantic.com *Email:* museum@graveyardoftheatlantic.com *Visitors welcome?* Yes *Hours:* Monday to Friday, 10 a.m. to 4 p.m. *Admission:* FREE *Operated by:* Graveyard of the Atlantic Museum *NR?* No *NHL?* No *Latitude:* 35.2060 *Latitude:* -75.7040

NORTH CAROLINA MARITIME MUSEUM
The North Carolina Maritime Museum documents, collects, preserves, and researches the maritime history of the region. *Address:* 315 Front St. *City:* Beaufort *State:* NC *Zip:* 28516 *Phone:* 252-728-7317 *Web:* www.ncmaritime.org *Email:* maritime@ncmail.net *Visitors welcome?* Yes *Hours:* Monday to Friday, 9 a.m. to 5 p.m.; Saturday, 10 a.m. to 5 p.m.; Sunday, 1 p.m. to 5 p.m. *Admission:* FREE *Operated by:* North Carolina Maritime Museum *NR?* No *NHL?* No *Latitude:* 34.7164 *Latitude:* -76.6646

NORTH CAROLINA MARITIME MUSEUM AT SOUTHPORT
The North Carolina Maritime Museum's Southport branch houses a collection of memorabilia pertaining to the vast nautical history of the Lower Cape Fear area of southeastern North Carolina. *Address:* 116 North Howe St. *City:* Southport *State:* NC *Zip:* 28461 *Phone:* 910-457-0003 *Toll-free:* 910-457-0003 *Web:* www.ncmaritime.org/branches/southport_default.htm *Email:* mary.strickland@ncmail.net *Visitors welcome?* Yes *Hours:* Tuesday to Saturday, 9 a.m. to 5 p.m. *Admission:* FREE *Operated by:* North Carolina Maritime Museum *NR?* No *NHL?* No *Latitude:* 33.9188 *Latitude:* -78.0191

NORTH CAROLINA MARITIME MUSEUM ON ROANOKE ISLAND
The museum offers a variety of educational programs and interpretive exhibits throughout the year. Interpretive exhibits include examples of traditional small watercraft built and sailed on the Outer Banks of North Carolina. Featured at the museum is a *Address:* 104 Fernando Street *City:* Manteo *State:* NC *Zip:* 27954 *Phone:* 252-475-1750 *Web:* www.obxmaritime.org *Email:* obxmaritime@embarqmail.com *Visitors welcome?* Yes *Hours:* Contact attraction directly *Admission:* FREE *Operated by:* North Carolina Maritime Museum on Roanoke Island *NR?* No *NHL?* No *Latitude:* 35.9085 *Latitude:* -75.6700

CHAPTER 3 – MUSEUMS

ROANOKE CANAL MUSEUM AND TRAIL
The Roanoke Canal Museum utilizes traditional and interactive exhibits to explain how the original canal served the region. *Address:* 15 Jackson St. *City:* Roanoke Rapids *State:* NC *Zip:* 27870 *Phone:* 252-537-2769 *Web:* www.roanokecanal.com *Email:* canalmuseum@roanokerapidsnc.com *Visitors welcome?* Yes *Hours:* Tuesday to Saturday, 9 a.m. to 4 p.m. *Admission:* FREE *Operated by:* Roanoke Canal Museum and Trail *NR?* No *NHL?* No *Latitude:* 36.4723 *Latitude:* -77.6504

ROANOKE RIVER LIGHTHOUSE & MARITIME MUSEUM
The Roanoke River Lighthouse and Maritime Museum at the west end of Water Street in Plymouth along with the Rail Switch Nature Trail at the east end are projects of the Washington County Waterways Commission. The lighthouse is a replica of the second Roanoke Lighthouse on the river. *Address:* West Water Street *City:* Plymouth *State:* NC *Zip:* 27962 *Phone:* 252-217-2204 *Web:* www.roanokeriverlighthouse.org *Email:* info@roanokeriverlighthouse.org *Visitors welcome?* Yes *Hours:* Tuesday through Saturday, 11 a.m. to 3 p.m. *Admission:* Contact attraction directly *Operated by:* Washington County Waterways Commission *NR?* No *NHL?* No *Latitude:* 35.8660 *Latitude:* -76.7538

OHIO

FAIRPORT HARBOR MARINE MUSEUM
The museum was founded in 1945 by the Fairport Harbor Historical Society, which is devoted to preserving and perpetuating the historic tradition of Fairport Harbor and the Great Lakes area. *Address:* 129 Second Street *City:* Painsville *State:* OH *Zip:* 44077 *Phone:* 440-354-4825 *Web:* www.ncweb.com/org/fhlh/ *Email:* fhhs@ncweb.com *Visitors welcome?* Yes *Hours:* Memorial Day through September: Wednesdays, Saturdays, Sundays: 1 p.m. to 6 p.m. *Admission:* $3 adults, $2 seniors, $1 ages 6-12, under six FREE *Operated by:* Fairport Harbor Marine Museum *NR?* No *NHL?* No *Latitude:* 41.7571 *Latitude:* -81.2777

GREAT LAKES MARINE AND COAST GUARD MEMORIAL MUSEUM
Housed in the former residence of the Lighthouse Keepers and the Coast Guard Chief, built in 1871/1898, the museum contains models, paintings, marine artifacts, and photos of early Ashtabula Harbor and ore boats and tugs. *Address:* 1071 Walnut Blvd *City:* Ashtabula *State:* OH *Zip:* 44004 *Phone:* 440-964-6847 *Web:* www.ashtabulamarinemuseum.org *Visitors welcome?* Yes *Hours:* Fridays, Saturdays, Sundays: Memorial Day weekend through August: Noon-5 p.m.; September: Noon - 5 p.m. Saturday and Sunday only *Admission:* $4 adults, $3 ages 6-16, under six FREE *Operated by:* Ashtabula Marine Museum *NR?* No *NHL?* No *Latitude:* 41.9018 *Latitude:* -80.7999

INLAND SEAS MUSEUM
In May 1944, a group of individuals dedicated to Great Lakes history decided to organize a Society to preserve and make known this rich history. *Address:* 480 Main Street *City:* Vermilion *State:* OH *Zip:* 44089 *Phone:* 440-967-3467 *Email:* glhs1@inlandseas.org *Visitors welcome?* Yes *Hours:* Summer: Daily, 10 a.m to 5 p.m.; Fall: Monday to Friday, 11 a.m. to 5 p.m., Saturday and Sunday, 10 a.m to 5 p.m.; Winter: Monday to Friday, 11 a.m. to 4 p.m., Saturday and Sunday, 11 a.m. to 5 p.m. *Admission:* $6 adults, $5 seniors, $5 children, $14 families (two adults, up to four children) *Operated by:* Great Lakes Historical Society *NR?* No *NHL?* No *Year established/built:* 1944 *Latitude:* 41.4249 *Latitude:* -82.3668

CHAPTER 3 – MUSEUMS

LAKE ERIE ISLANDS HISTORICAL SOCIETY
The mission of the Lake Erie Islands Historical Society is to preserve, interpret and educate our community and our visitors on the rich history of the Lake Erie Islands. *Address:* 25 Town Hall Place *City:* Put-in-Bay *State:* OH *Zip:* 43456 *Phone:* 419-285-2804 *Web:* www.leihs.org *Email:* director@leihs.org *Visitors welcome?* Yes *Hours:* Mid-May, June and September: Daily, 11 a.m. to 5 p.m.; July and August: Daily, 10 a.m. to 6 p.m.; October: Saturday and Sunday, 11 a.m. to 5 p.m. *Admission:* $2 adults, $1 children 12/older, 12/under FREE *Operated by:* Lake Erie Islands Historical Society *NR?* No *NHL?* No *Year established/built:* 1975 *Latitude:* 41.6347 *Latitude:* -82.8391

MARITIME MUSEUM OF SANDUSKY
The Sandusky Maritime Museum explores the maritime history of the Sandusky region. *Address:* 125 Meigs St. *City:* Sandusky *State:* OH *Zip:* 44870 *Phone:* 419-624-0274 *Web:* www.sanduskymaritime.org *Email:* smmuseum@accsandusky.com *Visitors welcome?* Yes *Hours:* June to August: Tuesday to Saturday, 10 a.m. to 4 p.m.; Sunday, noon to 4 p.m. September to May: Friday and Saturday, 10 a.m. to 4 p.m., Sunday, noon to 4 p.m. *Admission:* $4 adults, $3 seniors/children under 12 *Operated by:* Maritime Museum of Sandusky *NR?* No *NHL?* No *Latitude:* 41.4601 *Latitude:* -82.7027

OHIO RIVER MUSEUM
The Ohio River Museum consists of three exhibit buildings, the first of which houses displays depicting the origins and natural history of the Ohio River. *Address:* 601 Front Street *City:* Marietta *State:* OH *Zip:* 45750 *Phone:* 740-373-3750 *Toll-free:* 800-860-0145 *Web:* www.campusmartiusmuseum.org *Email:* info@campusmartiusmuseum.org *Visitors welcome?* Yes *Hours:* Memorial Day to Sept. 1: Saturday, 9:30 a.m. to 5 p.m.; Sunday, noon to 5 p.m.; Memorial Day & Labor Day: Noon to 5 p.m. *Admission:* $7 adults, $3 youth six to 12, under five FREE *Operated by:* Friends of the Museums *NR?* No *NHL?* No *Latitude:* 39.4210 *Latitude:* -81.4640

USS RADFORD NAVAL MEMORIAL MUSEUM
The USS Radford National Naval Museum preserves artifacts and memories of the World War II-era destroyer USS Radford. *Address:* 238 West Canal St. *City:* Newcomerstown *State:* OH *Zip:* 43832 *Phone:* 740-498-4446 *Web:* www.ussradford446.org *Email:* vanescott@sbcglobal.net *Visitors welcome?* Yes *Hours:* Contact attraction directly *Admission:* Contact attraction directly *Operated by:* USS Radford Association *NR?* No *NHL?* No *Latitude:* 40.2750 *Latitude:* -81.6085

OKLAHOMA

ARKANSAS RIVER HISTORICAL SOCIETY MUSEUM
The Arkansas River Historical Society Museum focuses on the history of the Arkansas River and McClellan-Kerr Arkansas River Navigation System, regional benefits of the waterway, steamboat lore, cargo shipped on the waterway, and archeology. Of note is the *Address:* 5350 Cimarron Road *City:* Catoosa *State:* OK *Zip:* 74015 *Phone:* 918-266-2291 *Web:* www.tulsaweb.com *Email:* museum@tulsaport.com *Visitors welcome?* Yes *Hours:* Monday to Friday, 8:30 a.m. to 4:30 p.m. *Admission:* FREE *Operated by:* Arkansas River Historical Society *NR?* No *NHL?* No *Latitude:* 36.2312 *Latitude:* -95.7417

CHAPTER 3 – MUSEUMS

OREGON

CASCADE LOCKS HISTORICAL MUSEUM
The Cascade Locks Historical Museum, located on the south bank of the Columbia River in Marine Park, focuses on local transportation history. *Address:* 1 NW Portage Rd *City:* Cascade Locks *State:* OR *Zip:* 97014 *Phone:* 541-374-8535 *Web:* www.cascadelocks.net *Visitors welcome?* Yes *Hours:* May to October: Daily, noon to 5 p.m. *Admission:* Contact attraction directly *Operated by:* Port of Cascade Locks *NR?* No *NHL?* No *Latitude:* 45.6711 *Latitude:* -121.8890

✦ COLUMBIA RIVER MARITIME MUSEUM
The Columbia River Maritime Museum was founded in 1962 when Rolf Klep, a native of Astoria, returned to his birthplace after retiring from a successful career as graphic artist on the east coast. It is now a major visitor attraction in Astoria, Wash., which features the lightship Columbia and major exhibits. *Address:* 1792 Marine Dr. *City:* Astoria *State:* OR *Visitors welcome?* Yes *Hours:* Daily, 9:30 a.m. to 5:00 p.m *Admission:* Children under 6, FREE; Children 6-17, $4; Seniors, $7; Adults, $8; Families, $24 *Operated by:* Columbia River Maritime Museum *NR?* No *NHL?* No *Latitude:* 46.1893 *Latitude:* -123.8230

COOS HISTORICAL AND MARITIME MUSEUM
Established in 1948, the Coos Historical and Maritime Museum is in the process of building a new facility on the Coos Bay waterfront. *Address:* 1220 Sherman Ave. *City:* North Bend *State:* OR *Zip:* 97459 *Phone:* 541-756-6320 *Web:* www.cooshistory.org *Email:* info@cooshistory.org *Visitors welcome?* Yes *Hours:* Tuesday to Saturday, 10 a.m. to 4 p.m.; Sundays (July 1 to Labor Day), noon to 4 p.m. *Admission:* $4 adults, children under 12 FREE *Operated by:* Coos County Historical Society *NR?* No *NHL?* No *Year established/built:* 1948 *Latitude:* 43.3966 *Latitude:* -124.2240

✦ GARIBALDI MUSEUM
The Garibaldi Museum is chartered to preserve the maritime heritage of the Pacific Northwest by collecting information concerning Captain Robert Gray and Captain Robert Gray's historical vessels, the Lady Washington and the Columbia Rediviva. *Address:* 112 Garibaldi Ave. *City:* Garibaldi *State:* OR *Zip:* 97118 *Phone:* 503-322-8411 *Web:* www.garibaldimuseum.com *Hours:* May to October, Thursday to Monday, 10 a.m. to 4 p.m.; other months by appointment *Admission:* $3 adults; $2.50 seniors, children five to 18; children under five FREE *Operated by:* Garibaldi Museum *NR?* No *NHL?* No *Latitude:* 45.5598 *Latitude:* -123.9080

OREGON MARITIME MUSEUM
The Oregon Maritime Museum is a not-for-profit organization whose mission is to provide, operate, and maintain facilities dedicated to the collection, preservation, and public display of maritime objects; to collect and preserve maritime records for scholarly public use; to provide public meeting opportunities for maritime interpretation and education; to serve as a memorial to merchant mariners; and to encourage interest in the past, present, and future maritime heritage of Oregon and the Columbia River Basin. Located adjacent to Tom McCall Waterfront Park on the Willamette River in Downtown Portland at base of Pine St. on the west side. The museums offers guided tours of our museum (the historic 1947 steam sternwheel towboat Portland) as well as scholarly access to a world class maritime photo database, including the Larry Barber photographic collection. *Address:* 115 SW Ash St. Suite 400C *City:* Portland *State:* OR *Zip:* 97204 *Phone:* 503-224-7724 *Web:* www.oregonmaritimemuseum.org *Email:* info@oregonmaritimemuseum.org *Visitors welcome?* Yes *Hours:* Contact attraction directly *Admission:* Contact attraction directly *Operated by:* Oregon Maritime Center & Museum *NR?* No *NHL?* No *Latitude:* 45.5218 *Latitude:* -122.6720

PENNSYLVANIA

C. HOWARD HIESTER CANAL CENTER
The C. Howard Hiester Canal Center presents a coherent story of canal transportation. It displays this country's early growth and specifically the important contribution the canal system made to the history of Berks County. *Address:* 2201 Tulpehocken Road *City:* Wyomissing *State:* PA *Zip:* 19610 *Phone:* 610-374-8839 *Web:* www.co.berks.pa.us/parks/cwp/view.asp?a=1229&q=447562 *Visitors welcome?* Yes *Hours:* Contact attraction directly *Admission:* Contact attraction directly *Operated by:* Berks County Heritage Center *NR?* No *NHL?* No *Latitude:* 40.3586 *Latitude:* -75.9682

✦ ERIE MARITIME MUSEUM
As home port of the U.S. Brig Niagara, the Erie Maritime Museum presents the story of Niagara as the reconstructed flagship of Pennsylvania and the warship that won the Battle of Lake Erie in the War of 1812. *Address:* 150 East Front Street *City:* Erie *State:* PA *Zip:* 16507 *Phone:* 814-452-2744 *Web:* www.brigniagara.org *Email:* wrybka@state.pa.us *Visitors welcome?* Yes *Hours:* April to December: Monday to Saturday, 9 a.m. to 5 p.m., Sunday, noon to 5 p.m.; January to March, Tuesday to Saturday, 9 a.m. to 5 p.m. *Admission:* $6 adults, $5 senior, $3 children six to 17, under six FREE; price reduced when Niagara not in port *Operated by:* Flagship Niagara League *NR?* No *NHL?* No *Year established/built:* 1998 *Latitude:* 42.1361 *Latitude:* -80.0837

GREENVILLE CANAL MUSEUM
Greenville's Canal Museum preserves some of the history of the Erie Extension Canal. Address: 60 Alan Ave. City: Greenville State: PA Zip: 16125 Phone: 724-588-7540 *Web:* www.greenvillecanalmuseum.org *Visitors welcome?* Yes *Hours:* Memorial Day to August 31: Saturday and Sunday, contract attraction for hours *Admission:* Contact attraction directly *Operated by:* Greenville Historical Society *NR?* No *NHL?* No *Latitude:* 41.4101 *Latitude:* -80.3898

INDEPENDENCE SEAPORT MUSEUM
Founded in 1960, the Independence Seaport Museum preserves the maritime history of Philadelphia and the surrounding area. *Address:* 211 South Columbus Blvd. *City:* Philadelphia *State:* PA *Zip:* 19106 *Phone:* 215-413-8655 *Web:* www.phillyseaport.org *Email:* mdigirolamo@phillyseaport.org *Visitors welcome?* Yes *Hours:* Daily, 10 a.m. to 5 p.m. *Admission:* $12 adults; $10 seniors; $7 children, seniors, military; under two FREE *Operated by:* Independence Seaport Museum *NR?* No *NHL?* No *Year established/built:* 1960 *Latitude:* 39.9457 *Latitude:* -75.1419

NATIONAL CANAL MUSEUM
The National Canal Museum is the only museum in the country dedicated to telling the story of America's canal system. *Address:* 30 Centre Square *City:* Easton *State:* PA *Zip:* 18042 *Phone:* 610-559-6613 *Web:* canals.org *Email:* toms@canals.org *Visitors welcome?* Yes *Hours:* Tuesday to Friday, 9:30 a.m. to 3:30 p.m.; Saturday, 9:30 a.m. to 5 p.m.; Sunday, noon to 5 p.m. (Hours extended during summer) *Admission:* $9.50 adults and children, $9 seniors, children two and under FREE *Operated by:* National Canal Museum *NR?* No *NHL?* No *Latitude:* 40.6912 *Latitude:* -75.2099

CHAPTER 3 – MUSEUMS

RHODE ISLAND

AMERICA'S CUP HALL OF FAME
The Herreshoff Marine Museum and America's Cup Hall of Fame is dedicated to the education and inspiration of the public through presentations of the history and innovative work of the Herreshoff Manufacturing Company and the America's Cup competition. *Address:* One Burnside Street *City:* Bristol *State:* RI *Zip:* 02809 *Phone:* 401-253-5000 *Web:* www.herreshoff.org *Email:* l.fisher@herreshoff.org *Visitors welcome?* Yes *Hours:* Daily, 10 a.m. to 4 p.m. *Admission:* $8 adults, $7 seniors, $4 students, under 12 FREE *Operated by:* Herreschoff Marine Museum *NR?* No *NHL?* No *Latitude:* 41.6636 *Latitude:* -71.2729

✢ HERRESCHOFF MARINE MUSEUM
The Herreshoff Marine Museum and America's Cup Hall of Fame is dedicated to the education and inspiration of the public through presentations of the history and innovative work of the Herreshoff Manufacturing Company and the America's Cup competition. *Address:* One Burnside Street *City:* Bristol *State:* RI *Zip:* 02809 *Phone:* 401-253-5000 *Web:* www.herreshoff.org *Email:* l.fisher@herreshoff.org *Visitors welcome?* Yes *Hours:* Daily, 10 a.m. to 4 p.m. *Admission:* $8 adults, $7 seniors, $4 students, under 12 FREE *Operated by:* Herreschoff Marine Museum *NR?* No *NHL?* No *Latitude:* 41.6636 *Latitude:* -71.2729

MUSEUM OF YACHTING
The Museum of Yachting has worked to preserve the culture and heritage of yachting. *City:* Newport *State:* RI *Phone:* 401-847-1018 *Web:* moy.org *Email:* tnathan@iyrs.org *Visitors welcome?* Yes *Hours:* Mid-May to mid-October: Daily, 10 a.m. to 6 p.m. *Admission:* $5 adults, students and children under 18 FREE *Operated by:* International Yacht Restoration School *NR?* No *NHL?* No *Latitude:* 41.4901 *Latitude:* -71.3128

NAVAL WAR COLLEGE MUSEUM
The Naval War College, housed in a former poorhouse, is a National Historic Landmark. The Museum's themes are the history of naval warfare, particularly as studied at the College, and the naval heritage of Narragansett Bay. *Address:* 686 Cushing Road *City:* Newport *State:* RI *Zip:* 02841 *Phone:* 401-841-4052 *Web:* www.nwc.navy.mil *Email:* museum@nwc.navy.mil *Visitors welcome?* Yes *Hours:* Monday to Friday, 10 a.m. to 4 p.m.; Weekends, June to September, noon to 4:30 p.m. *Admission:* FREE *Operated by:* Naval History & Heritage Command *NR?* No *NHL?* Yes *Latitude:* 41.5077 *Latitude:* -71.3295

SINGLE-HANDED SAILORS HALL OF FAME
The Single-Handed Sailors Hall of Fame is located within the Museum of Yachting. *City:* Newport *State:* RI *Phone:* 401-847-1018 *Web:* moy.org *Email:* tnathan@iyrs.org *Visitors welcome?* Yes *Hours:* Mid-May to mid-October: Daily, 10 a.m. to 6 p.m. *Admission:* $5 adults, students and children under 18 FREE *Operated by:* International Yacht Restoration School *NR?* No *NHL?* No *Latitude:* 41.4901 *Latitude:* -71.3128

SOUTH CAROLINA

✢ PATRIOTS POINT NAVAL & MARITIME MUSEUM
The Patriots Point Naval & Maritime Museum houses an extensive collection of naval and maritime artifacts, including the carrier USS Yorktown. *Address:* 40 Patriots Point Road *City:* Mount Pleasant *State:* SC *Zip:* 29464 *Phone:* 843-884-2727 *Toll-free:* 866-831-1720 *Web:* www.patriotspoint.org *Visitors welcome?* Yes

Hours: Contact attraction directly *Admission:* $16 adults, $13 seniors and active military, $8 children six to 11, under six FREE *Operated by:* Patriots Point Naval & Maritime Museum *NR?* No *NHL?* No *Latitude:* 32.7940 *Latitude:* -79.9051

SOUTH DAKOTA

BATTLESHIP SOUTH DAKOTA MUSEUM
The Battleship South Dakota Museum features memorabilia of the battleship South Dakota, including a scale model of the vessel. *Address:* 600 E. 7th St. *City:* Sioux Falls *State:* SD *Zip:* 57103 *Phone:* 605-367-7060 *Visitors welcome?* Yes *Hours:* Daily, 9 a.m. to 5 p.m. *Admission:* FREE *Operated by:* City of Sioux Falls *NR?* No *NHL?* No *Year established/built:* 1968 *Latitude:* 43.5500 *Latitude:* -96.7199

TENNESSEE

MISSISSIPPI RIVER MUSEUM
The mission of the Mississippi River Museum at Mud River State Park is to preserve and promote the natural and cultural history of the Lower Mississippi River Valley through excellence in education, interpretation and exhibits. *Address:* 125 North Front St. *City:* Memphis *State:* TN *Zip:* 38103 *Phone:* 901-576-7241 *Toll-free:* 800-507-6507 *Web:* www.mudisland.com/museum.asp *Visitors welcome?* Yes *Hours:* Mid-April to mid-May: Daily, 10 a.m. to 5 p.m.; Mid-May to mid-September: Daily, 10 a.m. to 6 p.m.; September to Oct. 31: Daily, 10 a.m. to 5 p.m. *Admission:* $8 adults, $5 youths five to 11, children four and under FREE *Operated by:* Mud Island River Park *NR?* No *NHL?* No *Latitude:* 35.1489 *Latitude:* -90.0528

TEXAS

HOUSTON MARITIME MUSEUM
The Houston Maritime Musem features more than 150 ship models, over 100 types of navigational instruments, and numerous maritime artifacts provide new and exciting learning experiences for visitors of all ages. *Address:* 2204 Dorrington *City:* Houston *State:* TX *Zip:* 77030 *Phone:* 713-666-1910 *Web:* www.houstonmaritimemuseum.org *Email:* houstonmaritimemus@sbcglobal.net *Visitors welcome?* Yes *Hours:* Tuesday to Saturday, 9 a.m. to 4:30 p.m. *Admission:* $5 adults, $3 children 11 and under *Operated by:* Houston Maritime Museum *NR?* No *NHL?* No *Latitude:* 29.7056 *Latitude:* -95.4098

NATIONAL MUSEUM OF THE PACIFIC WAR
The National Museum of the Pacific War is the only institution in the continental United States dedicated exclusively to telling the story of the Pacific Theater battles of World War II. *Address:* 340 East Main St. *City:* Fredericksburg *State:* TX *Zip:* 78624 *Phone:* 830-997-4379 *Web:* www.nimitz-museum.org *Email:* info@nimitzfoundation.org *Visitors welcome?* Yes *Hours:* Daily, 9 a.m. to 5 p.m. *Admission:* $7 adults, $6 senior/active military, $4 students, under six FREE *Operated by:* Admiral Nimitz Foundation *NR?* No *NHL?* No *Latitude:* 30.2722 *Latitude:* -98.8682

CHAPTER 3 – MUSEUMS

 OCEAN STAR OFFSHORE DRILLING RIG & MUSEUM
Launched in 1969, the offshore drilling rig Ocean Star is now a museum on Galveston Island. *Address:* Pier 19 (Harborside Drive at 20th Street) *City:* Galveston *State:* TX *Zip:* 77550 *Phone:* 409-766-7287 *Web:* www.oceanstaroec.com *Email:* osmuseum@aol.com *Visitors welcome?* Yes *Hours:* Contact attraction directly *Admission:* Contact attraction directly *Operated by:* Offshore Energy Center *NR?* No *NHL?* No *Year established/built:* 1969 *Latitude:* 29.3011 *Latitude:* -94.7886

PORT ISABEL HISTORIC MUSEUM
The Port Isabel Historic Museum is part of a complex that includes the Treasures of the Gulf Museum and the Port Isabel Lighthouse. *Address:* 317 E. Railroad Ave. *City:* Port Isabel *State:* TX *Zip:* 78578 *Phone:* 956-943-7602 *Web:* www.portisabelmuseums.com *Email:* director@portisabelmuseums.com *Visitors welcome?* Yes *Hours:* Tuesday to Saturday, 10 a.m. to 4 p.m. *Admission:* Contact attraction directly *Operated by:* Museums of Port Isabel *NR?* No *NHL?* No *Latitude:* 26.0759 *Latitude:* -97.2077

TEXAS MARITIME MUSEUM
The Texas Maritime Museum is the offical maritime museum of Texas. *Address:* 1202 Navigation Circle *City:* Rockport *State:* TX *Zip:* 78382 *Phone:* 361-729-1271 *Web:* www.texasmaritimemuseum.org *Email:* ceo@texasmaritimemuseum.org *Visitors welcome?* Yes *Hours:* Tuesday to Saturday, 10 a.m. to 4 p.m.; Sunday, 1 p.m. to 4 p.m. *Admission:* $6 adults, $4 seniors, $2 children six to 12, under six FREE *Operated by:* Texas Maritime Museum *NR?* No *NHL?* No *Latitude:* 28.0255 *Latitude:* -97.0495

 TEXAS SEAPORT MUSEUM
Located in the historic port of Galveston, the Texas Seaport Museum tells the story of a rich legacy of seaborne commerce and immigration. *Address:* Pier 21, Number 8 *City:* Galveston *State:* TX *Zip:* 77550 *Phone:* 409-763-1877 *Web:* www.tsm-elissa.org *Email:* elissa@galvestonhistory.org *Visitors welcome?* Yes *Hours:* Daily, 10 a.m. to 5 p.m. *Admission:* $8 adults, $5 students six through 18, children five and under FREE *Operated by:* Galveston Historical Foundation *NR?* No *NHL?* No *Latitude:* 29.3263 *Latitude:* -94.7951

TREASURES OF THE GULF MUSEUM
Treasures of the Gulf Museum spotlights three 1554 Spanish shipwrecks. *Address:* 317 E. Railroad Ave. *City:* Port Isabel *State:* TX *Zip:* 78578 *Phone:* 956-943-7602 *Web:* www.portisabelmuseums.com *Email:* director@portisabelmuseums.com *Visitors welcome?* Yes *Hours:* Tuesday to Saturday, 10 a.m. to 4 p.m. *Admission:* Contact attraction directly *Operated by:* Museums of Port Isabel *NR?* No *NHL?* No *Latitude:* 26.0759 *Latitude:* -97.2077

 USS LEXINGTON MUSEUM ON THE BAY
Arriving almost exactly 50 years after her launch in 1942, USS Lexington became a permanent floating museum on the Corpus Christi waterfront. *Address:* 2914 N. Shoreline Blvd. *City:* Corpus Christi *State:* TX *Zip:* 23076 *Phone:* 361-888-4873 *Toll-free:* 800-523-9539 *Web:* www.usslexington.com *Email:* rocco@usslexington.com *Visitors welcome?* Yes *Hours:* Labor Day to Memorial Day, 9 a.m. to 5 p.m.; Memorial Day to Labor Day, 9 a.m. to 6 p.m. *Admission:* $12.95 adults, $10.95 senior, active military, retired military; $7.95 children four to 12; under four FREE *Operated by:* USS Lexington Museum on the Bay *NR?* No *NHL?* No *Year established/built:* 1992 *Latitude:* 27.8165 *Latitude:* -97.3907

USS ORLECK DD886 NAVAL DESTROYER MUSEUM
The premiere exhibit of the USS Orleck DD886 Naval Destroyer Museum is the World War II-era destroyer USS Orleck. *Address:* 4th St. & W. Front St. *City:* Orange *State:* TX *Zip:* 77630 *Phone:* 409-882-9191 *Web:* www.ussorleck.org *Email:* info@ussorleck.org *Visitors welcome?* Yes *Hours:* Contact attraction directly

Admission: Contact attraction directly *Operated by:* Southeast Texas War Memorial and Heritage Foundation *NR?* No *NHL?* No *Latitude:* 30.0912 *Latitude:* -93.7332

VIRGINIA

ALEXANDRIA SEAPORT FOUNDATION
Through the building and use of wooden boats, the Alexandria Seaport Foundation helps young people turn their lives around and provides families, community groups, and schools with meaningful educational, social, and recreational experiences. *Address:* 1 Cameron St. *City:* Alexandria *State:* VA *Zip:* 22313 *Phone:* 703-549-7078 *Web:* www.alexandriaseaport.org *Email:* ASFOffice@alexandriaseaport.org *Visitors welcome?* Yes *Hours:* Contact attraction directly *Admission:* Contact attraction directly *Operated by:* Alexandria Seaport Foundation *NR?* No *NHL?* No *Latitude:* 38.8053 *Latitude:* -77.0394

ALEXANDRIA WATERFRONT MUSEUM
The Alexandria Waterfront Museum celebrates the history of the Alexandria waterfront and the area's canal system. *Address:* 44 Canal Center Plaza *City:* Alexandria *State:* VA *Zip:* 22314 *Phone:* 703-838-4288 *Visitors welcome?* Yes *Hours:* Contact attraction directly *Admission:* Contact attraction directly *Operated by:* Alexandria Waterfront Museum *NR?* No *NHL?* No *Year established/built:* 1988 *Latitude:* 38.8142 *Latitude:* -77.0388

Fyddeye wants to know about endangered maritime heritage in your community. Visit www.fyddeye.com and tell us your story. We may post it on the site!

CHINCOTEAGUE OYSTER & MARITIME MUSEUM
The Oyster & Maritime Museum, a non-profit educational institution, is located on Maddox Boulevard just before the entrance to the Chincoteague National Wildlife Refuge. *Address:* 7125 Maddox Blvd. *City:* Chincoteague *State:* VA *Zip:* 23336 *Phone:* 757-336-6117 *Web:* www.chincoteaguechamber.com/oyster/ *Email:* oystermuseum@intercom.net *Visitors welcome?* Yes *Hours:* Daily during the summer, weekends in the spring and fall *Admission:* Contact attraction directly *Operated by:* Chincoteague Oyster & Maritime Museum *NR?* No *NHL?* No *Year established/built:* 1965 *Latitude:* 37.9325 *Latitude:* -75.3627

HAMPTON ROADS NAVAL MUSEUM
The Hampton Roads Naval Museum is owned and operated by the United States Navy and we introduce visitors to over 234 years of naval activity in Hampton Roads, Virginia. *Address:* One Waterside Drive *City:* Norfolk *State:* VA *Zip:* 23510 *Phone:* 757-322-2987 *Web:* www.hrnm.navy.mil *Email:* gordon.b.calhoun@navy.mil *Visitors welcome?* Yes *Hours:* Tuesday through Saturday 10 a.m. to 5 p.m. Closed Mondays from September through May. Extended summer hours. Open holidays except Thanksgiving, Christmas Eve, and Christmas Day. *Admission:* FREE *Operated by:* Naval History & Heritage Command *NR?* No *NHL?* No *Latitude:* 36.8442 *Latitude:* -76.2878

 MARINERS MUSEUM
For more than seventy years, the history of the ocean and its relationship with humankind has been told and displayed in one of the largest maritime museums in the world. *Address:* 100 Museum Drive *City:* Newport News *State:* VA *Zip:* 23606 *Phone:* 757-596-2222 *Web:* www.mariner.org *Email:* marketing@mariner.org *Visitors welcome?* Yes *Hours:* Monday to Saturday, 10 a.m. to 5 p.m.; Sunday, noon to 5 p.m. *Admission:* $12.50 adults, $7.50 children six to 17, under six FREE *Operated by:* Mariners Museum *NR?* No *NHL?* No *Year established/built:* 1930 *Latitude:* 37.0420 *Latitude:* -76.4882

CHAPTER 3 – MUSEUMS

NATIONAL MUSEUM OF THE MARINE CORPS
Opened to the public on 13 November 2006, the National Museum of the Marine Corps is a lasting tribute to the U.S. Marines. *Address:* 18900 Jefferson Davis Highway *City:* Triangle *State:* VA *Zip:* 22172 *Phone:* 877-635-1775 *Web:* www.usmcmuseum.com *Email:* info@usmcmuseum.org *Visitors welcome?* Yes *Hours:* Daily, 9 a.m. to 5 p.m. *Admission:* FREE *Operated by:* National Museum of the Marine Corps *NR?* No *NHL?* No *Year established/built:* 2006 *Latitude:* 38.5431 *Latitude:* -77.3384

 NAUTICUS
Nauticus inspires and educates with engaging and interactive experiences that celebrate our connections with today's maritime world. *Address:* One Waterside Drive *City:* Norfolk *State:* VA *Zip:* 23510 *Phone:* 757-664-1000 *Web:* www.nauticus.org *Visitors welcome?* Yes *Hours:* Memorial Day to Labor Day: daily, 10 a.m. to 5 p.m.; Labor Day to Memorial Day: Tuesday to Saturday, 10 a.m. to 5 p.m., Sunday, noon to 5 p.m. *Admission:* $10.95 adults, $9.95 AAA/military/seniors, $8.50 children 4 to 12 *Operated by:* Nauticus *NR?* No *NHL?* No *Latitude:* 36.8442 *Latitude:* -76.2878

PORTSMOUTH NAVAL SHIPYARD MUSEUM
The Portsmouth Naval Shipyard Museum offers a unique perspective on U.S. history, from Colonial to Civil War times and beyond. *Address:* 2 High Street *City:* Portsmouth *State:* VA *Zip:* 23704 *Phone:* 757-393-8591 *Web:* www.portsnavalmuseums.com *Email:* navalmuseums@portsmouthva.gov *Visitors welcome?* Yes *Hours:* Memorial Day to Labor Day: Monday to Saturday, 10 a.m. to 5 p.m., Sunday, 1 p.m. to 5 p.m.; September to May: Tuesday to Saturday, 10 a.m. to 5 p.m., Sunday, 1 p.m. to 5 p.m. *Admission:* Memorial Day to Labor Day: $3; September to May: $1.50 adults, $.50 students two to 17, under two FREE *Operated by:* Portsmouth Naval Shipyard Museum *NR?* No *NHL?* No *Latitude:* 36.8355 *Latitude:* -76.2969

REEDVILLE FISHERMAN'S MUSEUM
The Reedville Fisherman's Museum is dedicated to preserving the heritage of the maritime history of the lower Chesapeake Bay area and the watermen who have plied their trade here for hundreds of years, and the menhaden industry that has existed in Reedville. *Address:* 504 Main Street *City:* Reedville *State:* VA *Zip:* 22539 *Phone:* 804-453-6529 *Web:* www.rfmuseum.org *Email:* office@rfmuseum.org *Visitors welcome?* Yes *Hours:* May 1 to October: Daily, 10:30 a.m. to 4:30 p.m. *Admission:* $5 adults, $3 seniors, children under 12 FREE *Operated by:* Reedville Fisherman's Museum *NR?* No *NHL?* No *Year established/built:* 1988 *Latitude:* 37.8454 *Latitude:* -76.2742

USS MONITOR CENTER
On March 9, 2007, the much-anticipated USS Monitor Center opened its doors, allowing visitors from all over the nation to see for themselves why it is truly one of America's wonders. *Address:* 100 Museum Drive *City:* Newport News *State:* VA *Zip:* 23606 *Phone:* 757-596-2222 *Web:* www.mariner.org *Email:* marketing@mariner.org *Visitors welcome?* Yes *Hours:* Monday to Saturday, 10 a.m. to 5 p.m.; Sunday, noon to 5 p.m. *Admission:* $12.50 general, $11.50 AAA/military/seniors, $7.25 children six to 17, children under six FREE *Operated by:* Mariners Museum *NR?* No *NHL?* No *Year established/built:* 2007 *Latitude:* 37.0420 *Latitude:* -76.4882

WATERMEN'S MUSEUM
The Watermen's Museum is a private non-profit museum located on the York River in historic Yorktown, VA. It was founded in 1981 as a part of the 200th anniversary celebration of the Battle of Yorktown. *Address:* 309 Water St. *City:* Yorktown *State:* VA *Zip:* 23690 *Phone:* 757-887-2641 *Web:* www.watermens.org *Email:* admin@watermens.hrcoxmail.com *Visitors welcome?* Yes *Hours:* April 1 through Thanksgiving: Tuesday to Saturday, 10a .m. to 5 p.m., Sunday, 1 p.m. to 5 p.m.; Thanksgiving to March 31: Saturday, 10 a.m. to 5 p.m., Sunday, 1 p.m. to 5 p.m. *Admission:* $4 adults, $1 K-12 students *Operated by:* Watermen's Museum *NR?* No *NHL?* No *Year established/built:* 1981 *Latitude:* 37.2391 *Latitude:* -76.5107

CHAPTER 3 – MUSEUMS

YORKTOWN BATTLEFIELD VISITORS CENTER
The Yorktown Visitors Center at the Yorktown Battlefield site features exhibits on the Battle of the Capes, the naval engagement that preceded the Battle of Yorktown. *Address:* Yorktown Battlefield *City:* Yorktown *State:* VA *Zip:* 23690 *Phone:* 757-898-2410 *Web:* www.nps.gov/york/ *Visitors welcome?* Yes *Hours:* Daily, 9 a.m. to 5 p.m. *Admission:* FREE *Operated by:* Colonial National Historical Park *NR?* No *NHL?* No *Latitude:* 37.2388 *Latitude:* -76.5097

YORKTOWN VICTORY CENTER
The Yorktown Victory Center at Jamestown Settlement feature artifacts from the Betsy, a British merchant ship scuttled during the Battle of Yorktown. *Address:* 2218 Jamestown Rd. *City:* Williamsburg *State:* VA *Zip:* 23185 *Phone:* 757-253-7308 *Web:* historyisfun.org *Visitors welcome?* Yes *Hours:* Contact attraction directly *Admission:* Contact attraction directly *Operated by:* Jamestown-Yorktown Foundation *NR?* No *NHL?* No *Year established/built:* 1991 *Latitude:* 37.2251 *Latitude:* -76.7862

VERMONT

LAKE CHAMPLAIN MARITIME MUSEUM
Through nautical exploration, hands-on exhibits and learning adventures for all ages, Lake Champlain Maritime Museum brings to life the stories of Lake Champlain and its people. *Address:* 4472 Basin Harbor Rd. *City:* Vergennes *State:* VT *Zip:* 05491 *Phone:* 802-475-2022 *Web:* www.lcmm.org *Email:* info@lcmm.org *Visitors welcome?* Yes *Hours:* Daily, 10 a.m. to 5 p.m. *Admission:* $10 adults, $9 seniors, $6 students 5-17, under five, FREE *Operated by:* Lake Champlain Maritime Museum *NR?* No *NHL?* No *Year established/built:* 1985 *Latitude:* 44.1973 *Latitude:* -73.3567

WASHINGTON

BELLINGHAM INTERNATIONAL MARITIME MUSEUM
The Bellingham International Maritime Museum honors, celebrates, records and preserves the rich maritime history of Bellingham, Whatcom County, and Puget Sound, with a special emphasis on the Pacific Northwest regional trans-border nautical heritage shared with Canada. *Address:* 800 Cornwall Ave. *City:* Bellingham *State:* WA *Zip:* 98225 *Phone:* 360-592-4112 *Web:* www.bimm.us *Email:* mikeg@bimm.us *Visitors welcome?* Yes *Hours:* Contact attraction directly *Admission:* Contact attraction directly *Operated by:* Bellingham International Maritime Museum *NR?* No *NHL?* No *Latitude:* 48.7487 *Latitude:* -122.4810

CENTER FOR WOODEN BOATS
The Center for Wooden Boats is a hands-on, experiential living history museum that focuses on skills and tradtions related to small craft, with a special emphasis on the Pacific Northwest. *Address:* 1010 Valley St. *City:* Seattle *State:* WA *Web:* www.cwb.org *Email:* cwb@cwb.org *Visitors welcome?* Yes *Hours:* Oct. to May: 11 a.m. to 6 p.m; June to Sept: 11 a.m. to 8 p.m. *Admission:* FREE *Operated by:* Center for Wooden Boats *NR?* No *NHL?* No *Latitude:* 47.6258 *Latitude:* -122.3370

COAST GUARD MUSEUM NORTHWEST
Coast Guard Museum Northwest at Pier 36 in Seattle features thousands of historical items recalling the Coast Guard's local history. *Address:* 1519 Alaskan Way S. *City:* Seattle *State:* WA *Visitors welcome?* Yes *Hours:* Monday, Wednesday, Friday: 9 a.m. to 3 p.m; Saturday: 1 p.m. to 5 p.m. *Admission:* FREE *Operated by:* Coast Guard Museum Northwest *NR?* No *NHL?* No *Latitude:* 47.5893 *Latitude:* -122.3380

CHAPTER 3 – MUSEUMS

COLUMBIA PACIFIC HERITAGE MUSEUM
Address: 115 SE Lake St. *City:* Ilwaco *State:* WA *Zip:* 98624 *Phone:* 360-642-3446 *Web:* ilwaco-heritagemuseum.org *Email:* cphm@willapabay.org *Visitors welcome?* Yes *Hours:* Monday to Saturday, 10 a.m. to 4 p.m; Sunday, Noon to 4 p.m. *Admission:* Children, 6 and under, FREE; Children 12-17, $2.50; Seniors, $4; Adults, $5 *Operated by:* Columbia Pacific Heritage Museum *NR?* No *NHL?* No *Latitude:* 46.3081 *Latitude:* -124.0440

FOSS WATERWAY SEAPORT
The Foss Waterway Seaport is a not-for-profit organization that provides a dynamic waterfront space for public education, recreation and community events. The Seaport's interactive museum exhibits showcase the sights, sounds and smells that bring the vitality of Tacoma's early bustling waterfront history to life and connect visitors to today's Puget Sound waterways. Discover the history of the century-old Balfour Dock building; view classic recreational boats; learn about marine life above and below the water; watch maritime woodworkers restore and reproduce heritage boats; explore marine science through on-the-water educational excursions, and stroll the waterfront esplanade. Located at the north end of the Thea Foss Waterway in Tacoma's downtown core, the Seaport provides a great venue for families, field trips and tour groups. A collection of waterfront spaces provide unique venues for business events, community festivals and private gatherings. Deep-water docks and moorage attract heritage sailing vessels and waterfront recreation that enlivens and unites our community. *Address:* 705 Dock St. *City:* Tacoma *State:* WA *Zip:* 98407 *Phone:* 253-272-2750 *Web:* www.wwfrontmuseum.org *Email:* m.hosford@fosswaterwayseaport.org *Visitors welcome?* Yes *Hours:* Monday to Friday, 9 a.m. to 5 p.m; Saturday and Sunday, 12 noon to 5 p.m. (Summer); 12 noon to 4 p.m. (Winter) *Admission:* Children, 2 and under, FREE; Children 3 to 12, seniors 55 and over, $2; adults, $3 *Operated by:* Foss Waterway Seaport *NR?* No *NHL?* No *Latitude:* 47.2579 *Latitude:* -122.4370

GIG HARBOR BOATSHOP
The Gig Harbor BoatShop, located in the former Eddon Boatyard, is perpetuating Gig Harbor's working waterfront by providing boat building and marine skills public programming. *Address:* 3805 Harborview Dr. *City:* Gig Harbor *State:* WA *Zip:* 98335 *Phone:* 253-857-9344 *Web:* www.gigharborboatshop.org *Email:* johnhmcmillan@earthlink.net *Visitors welcome?* Yes *Hours:* Saturday 10 a.m. to 4 p.m. *Admission:* FREE *Operated by:* Gig Harbor BoatShop *NR?* No *NHL?* No *Latitude:* 47.3341 *Latitude:* -122.5890

HARBOR HISTORY MUSEUM
The Harbor History Museum is devoted to the history of Gig Harbor, a small maritime community located in southern Puget Sound just north of Tacoma. *Address:* 4218 Harborview Dr. *City:* Gig Harbor *State:* WA *Zip:* 98335 *Phone:* 253-858-6722 *Visitors welcome?* Yes *Hours:* Tuesday to Saturday, 10 a.m. to 4 p.m. *Admission:* Children 12 and under, FREE; Seniors and students (13-18), $1; Adults, $2 *Operated by:* Gig Harbor Peninsula Historical Society *NR?* No *NHL?* No *Latitude:* 47.3374 *Latitude:* -122.5970

HYDROPLANE & RACEBOAT MUSEUM
The Hydroplane & Raceboat Museum is the nation's only public museum dedicated solely to powerboat racing. *Address:* 5917 South 196th St. *City:* Kent *State:* WA *Visitors welcome?* Yes *Hours:* Tuesday: 10 a.m. to 5 p.m; Thursday: 10 a.m. to 10 p.m; Saturday: 10 am to 4 p.m. *Admission:* $5 adults, $3 children *Operated by:* Hydroplane & Raceboat Museum *NR?* No *NHL?* No *Year established/built:* 1983 *Latitude:* 47.4267 *Latitude:* -122.2590

KITSAP COUNTY MUSEUM
Recent programs at the Kitsap County Museum have included the history of the fishing fleet at Poulsbo, a small community south of Bremerton. *Address:* 280 Fourth St. *City:* Bremerton *State:* WA *Visitors welcome?* Yes *Hours:* Tuesday to Saturday, 10 a.m. to 5 p.m; First Friday until 8 p.m. *Admission:* Children under 7: FREE; Children 7 to 17: $1.00; Adults: $2.00; Family: $5.00 *Operated by:* Kitsap County Historical Society *NR?* No *NHL?* No *Year established/built:* 1949 *Latitude:* 47.5660 *Latitude:* -122.6260

NAVAL MEMORIAL MUSEUM OF THE PACIFIC
The Naval Memorial Museum of the Pacific first opened its door to the public in 1954 as the Shipyard Naval Museum located in the Craven Center on Burwell Avenue. It later relocated to the Washington State Ferry Building on Bremerton's waterfront. *Address:* 251 1st St. *City:* Bremerton *State:* WA *Zip:* 98337 *Phone:* 360-479-7447 *Email:* bremnavmuseum@aol.com *Visitors welcome?* Yes *Hours:* Contact attraction directly *Admission:* FREE *Operated by:* Naval Memorial Museum of the Pacific *NR?* No *NHL?* No *Year established/built:* 1954 *Latitude:* 47.5630 *Latitude:* -122.6270

NAVAL UNDERSEA MUSEUM
A new facility with 20,000 square feet of exhibits, the Naval Undersea Museum in Keyport in Kitsap County preserves, collects, and interprets the history of the U.S. Navy under the ocean for the benefit of the Navy and the people of the United States. *Address:* 1103 Hunley Road *City:* Silverdale *State:* WA *Zip:* 98315 *Phone:* 360-396-4148 *Web:* www.history.navy.mil/museums/keyport/index1.htm *Visitors welcome?* Yes *Hours:* Summer (June to September): Daily, 10 a.m. to 4 p.m; Winter (October to May): Wednesday to Monday, 10 a.m. to 4 p.m. *Admission:* FREE *Operated by:* Naval History & Heritage Command *NR?* No *NHL?* No *Latitude:* 47.6980 *Latitude:* -122.6970

NORTHWEST COAST CANOE CENTER
The Norwest Coast Canoe Center is a planned facility for Lake Union Park just north of downtown Seattle. *Address:* 860 Terry Ave. N. *City:* Seattle *State:* WA *Visitors welcome?* Yes *Hours:* Contact attraction directly *Admission:* Contact attraction directly *Operated by:* United Indians of All Tribes Foundation *NR?* No *NHL?* No *Latitude:* 47.6276 *Latitude:* -122.3370

NORTHWEST MARITIME CENTER
The mission of the Northwest Maritime Center is to engage and educate people of all generations in traditional and contemporary maritime life, in a spirit of adventure and discovery. *Address:* 431 Water St. *City:* Port Townsend *State:* WA *Web:* www.nwmaritime.org *Email:* info@nwmaritime.org *Visitors welcome?* Yes *Hours:* Contact attraction directly *Admission:* Contact attraction directly *Operated by:* Northwest Maritime Center *NR?* No *NHL?* No *Latitude:* 48.1164 *Latitude:* -122.7520

PUGET SOUND MARITIME HISTORICAL SOCIETY MUSEUM
Located in a quiet marina at Chandler's Cove, the Puget Sound Maritime Historical Society Museum features artifacts from local maritime history. *Address:* 901 Fairview Ave. N. *City:* Seattle *State:* WA *Phone:* 206-624-3028 *Web:* www.pugetmaritime.org *Email:* president@pugetmaritime.org *Visitors welcome?* Yes *Hours:* Daily, Noon to 5 p.m. *Admission:* Donation *Operated by:* Puget Sound Maritime Historical Society *NR?* No *NHL?* No *Year established/built:* 1948 *Latitude:* 47.6278 *Latitude:* -122.3340

PUGET SOUND NAVAL SHIPYARD MUSEUM
The Puget Sound Navy Museum is dedicated to collecting, preserving, and interpreting the naval heritage of the Pacific Northwest for the benefit of the U.S. Navy and general public. *Address:* 251 1st Street *City:* Bremerton *State:* WA *Zip:* 98337 *Phone:* 360-479-7447 *Email:* william.galvani@navy.mil *Visitors welcome?* Yes *Hours:* Monday to Saturday, 10 a.m. to 4 p.m.; Sunday, 1 p.m. to 4 p.m. *Admission:* FREE *Operated by:* Naval History & Heritage Command *NR?* No *NHL?* No *Latitude:* 47.5630 *Latitude:* -122.6270

SAN JUAN ISLAND NATIONAL HISTORICAL PARK
San Juan Island National Historical Park was created in 1966 to celebrate the resolution of international problems with non-violent means. *Address:* West Valley Road and Yacht Haven Road *City:* Friday Harbor *State:* WA

Visitors welcome? Yes *Hours:* Contact attraction directly *Admission:* FREE *Operated by:* San Juan National Historical Park *NR?* No *NHL?* No *Year established/built:* 1966 *Latitude:* 48.5343 *Latitude:* -123.0170

SEMIAHMOO PARK MARITIME MUSEUM
Semiahmoo Park Maritime Museum features a restored Bristol Bay sailboat and exhibits that illustrates the history of Semiahmoo's fish cannery days dating back to 1894. *Address:* 9261 Semiahmoo Parkway *City:* Blaine *State:* WA *Zip:* 98230 *Phone:* 360-332-4544 *Web:* www.draytonharbormaritime.org *Email:* rcs3-dhm@comcast.net *Visitors welcome?* Yes *Hours:* Memorial Day to Labor Day: Saturdays & Sundays: 12:30 p.m. to 4:00 p.m. *Admission:* FREE *Operated by:* Drayton Harbor Maritime *NR?* No *NHL?* No *Latitude:* 48.9866 *Latitude:* -122.7860

WESTPORT MARITIME MUSEUM
The historic museum building was built in 1939 to serve as the Coast Guard's Lifeboat Station, Grays Harbor. The Colonial Revival structure served in that role until 1972 when a new station was built several blocks to the South. The old structure was converted to a local maritime museum. *Address:* 2201 Westhaven Dr. *City:* Westport *State:* WA *Zip:* 98595 *Phone:* 360-268-0078 *Web:* www.westportwa.com/museum/ *Email:* westport.maritime@comcast.net *Visitors welcome?* Yes *Hours:* Daily, April to Sept., 10 a.m. to 4 p.m.; Oct. to March, Friday to Monday, 12 p.m. to 4 p.m. *Admission:* Contact attraction directly *Operated by:* Westport South Beach Historical Society *NR?* No *NHL?* No *Year established/built:* 1939 *Latitude:* 46.9077 *Latitude:* -124.1120

WILLAPA BAY INTERPRETIVE CENTER
The Willapa Bay Interpretive Center traces the history of oystering in Willapa Bay, starting in the 1850s through the present day. *Address:* 273rd St and Peninsula Highway *City:* Nahcotta *State:* WA *Visitors welcome?* Yes *Hours:* Memorial Day to Labor Day, Fridays, Saturdays, and Sundays, 10 a.m. to 3 p.m. *Admission:* Contact attraction directly *Operated by:* Port of Peninsula *NR?* No *NHL?* No *Year established/built:* 1993 *Latitude:* 46.4996 *Latitude:* -124.0330

WILLAPA SEAPORT MUSEUM
The Willapa Seaport Museum captures the breadth and depth of the seafaring with exhibits covering military and commercial life. The museum puts emphasis on the communities of Raymond, South Bend, and other towns around Willapa Bay in the southwest corner of Washington State. *Address:* 310 Alder St. *City:* Raymond *State:* WA *Zip:* 98577 *Phone:* 360-942-4149 *Email:* angus35@willapabay.org *Visitors welcome?* Yes *Hours:* Summer: Wednesday to Sunday, 12 noon to 4 p.m; Winter: Wednesday to Saturday, 12 noon to 4 p.m. *Admission:* Donation *Operated by:* Willapa Seaport Museum *NR?* No *NHL?* No *Year established/built:* 1995 *Latitude:* 46.6839 *Latitude:* -123.7330

WOODEN BOAT FOUNDATION
Address: 380 Jefferson St. *City:* Port Townsend *State:* WA *Visitors welcome?* Yes *Hours:* Monday to Friday, 10 a.m. to 4 p.m; Saturday, 10 a.m. to 4 p.m. *Admission:* FREE *Operated by:* Wooden Boat Foundation *NR?* No *NHL?* No *Latitude:* 48.1184 *Latitude:* -122.7520

WISCONSIN

DOOR COUNTY MUSEUM (GILLS ROCK)
The Door County Maritime Museum at Gills Rock is a newly remodeled facility featuring the fishing tug Hope built in 1930 by Sturgeon Bay Boat Works (currently Great Lakes Yacht Works). *Address:* 12724 E Wisconsin Bay Rd *City:* Gills Rock *State:* WI *Zip:* 54210 *Phone:* 920-854-1844 *Web:* www.dcmm.org *Email:*

info@dcmm.org *Visitors welcome?* Yes *Hours:* Daily, 10 a.m. to 5 p.m. *Admission:* $4.50 adults, $1.50 children *Operated by:* Door County Maritime Museum & Lighthouse Preservation Society *NR?* No *NHL?* No *Latitude:* 45.2905 *Latitude:* -87.0095

ROGERS STREET FISHING VILLAGE & GREAT LAKES COAST GUARD MUSEUM
Rogers Street Fishing Village and Great Lakes Coast Guard Museum exhibits an 1886 historic lighthouse, shipwreck displays and artifacts, and commercial fishing exhibits. *Address:* 2010 Rogers St. *City:* Two Rivers *State:* WI *Zip:* 54241 *Phone:* 920-793-5905 *Web:* www.rogersstreet.com *Email:* szipperer@rogersstreet.com *Visitors welcome?* Yes *Hours:* May to October: Daily, 10 a.m. to 4 p.m. *Admission:* $4 adults, $2 children under 16 *Operated by:* Rogers Street Fishing Village & Great Lakes Coast Guard Museum *NR?* No *NHL?* No *Latitude:* 44.1518 *Latitude:* -87.5626

SHIP'S WHEEL GALLERY AND NAUTICAL MUSEUM
The Ship's Wheel Gallery and Nautical Museum is a private marine art gallery and museum featuring local maritime history. *Address:* 224 Ellis St. *City:* Kewaunee *State:* WI *Zip:* 54216 *Phone:* 920-388-0777 *Web:* trotter.infopages.net/shipwhel.htm *Email:* trotter@infopages.net *Visitors welcome?* Yes *Hours:* June to mid-October *Admission:* FREE *Operated by:* Ship's Wheel Gallery and Nautical Museum *NR?* No *NHL?* No *Latitude:* 44.4583 *Latitude:* -87.5019

SOUTHPORT LIGHT STATION MUSEUM
The Southport Light Station Museum is Kenosha's newest museum space, featuring a lighthouse and maritime museum that documents Kenosha's lighthouse keepers, shipping and fishing history. *Address:* 220 51st Place *City:* Kenosha *State:* WI *Zip:* 53140 *Phone:* 262-654-5770 *Web:* www.kenoshahistorycenter.org *Email:* kchs@kenoshahistorycenter.org *Visitors welcome?* Yes *Hours:* Tuesday to Friday, 10 a.m. to 4:30 p.m.; Saturday, 10 a.m. to 4 p.m.; Sunday, noon to 4 p.m. *Admission:* $10 adults, $5 children *Operated by:* Kenosha History Center *NR?* No *NHL?* No *Latitude:* 42.5882 *Latitude:* -87.8137

WISCONSIN MARITIME MUSEUM
Founded in 1970 as the Manitowoc Submarine Memorial Association, the Wisconsin Maritime Museum has grown into one of the largest maritime museums in the Midwest. *Address:* 75 Maritime Drive *City:* Manitowoc *State:* WI *Zip:* 54220 *Phone:* 920-684-0218 *Toll-free:* 866-724-2356 *Web:* www.wisconsinmaritime.org *Email:* museum@wisconsinmaritime.org *Visitors welcome?* Yes *Hours:* Summer: daily, 9 a.m. to 6 p.m. Winter: daily, 9 a.m. to 5 p.m. *Admission:* $12 adults, $10 children six to 15, five and under FREE *Operated by:* Wisconsin Maritime Museum *NR?* No *NHL?* No *Year established/built:* 1970 *Latitude:* 44.0931 *Latitude:* -87.6570

OTHER MUSEUMS

ALABAMA

EL CAZADOR MUSEUM
The El Cazador Museum displays artifacts recovered from the 1784 wreck of the Spanish vessel El Cazador in the Gulf of Mexico. *Address:* 10329 Freeland Ave. *City:* Grand Bay *State:* AL *Zip:* 36541 *Phone:* 251-865-0128 *Web:* www.elcazador.com *Visitors welcome?* Yes *Hours:* Contact attraction directly *Admission:* Contact attraction directly *Operated by:* El Cazador Museum *NR?* No *NHL?* No *Latitude:* 30.4761 *Latitude:* -88.3423

ARKANSAS

JACKSONPORT STATE PARK
Jacksonport State Park celebrates the region's history as a river port. *Address:* 205 Avenue St. *City:* Newport *State:* AR *Zip:* 72112 *Phone:* 870-523-2143 *Web:* www.arkansasstateparks.com/jacksonport/ *Email:* jacksonport@arkansas.com *Visitors welcome?* Yes *Hours:* Contact attraction directly *Admission:* $3.25 adults, $1.75 children six to 12, under six FREE *Operated by:* Jacksonport State Park *NR?* No *NHL?* No *Latitude:* 35.6407 *Latitude:* -91.3071

CALIFORNIA

BANNING RESIDENCE MUSEUM
The Banning Residence Museum preserves the story of General Phineas Banning, who played a vital role in the development of Los Angeles Harbor. *Address:* 401 East M St. *City:* Wilmington *State:* CA *Zip:* 90744 *Phone:* 310-548-7777 *Web:* www.banningmuseum.org *Email:* visit@banningmuseum.org *Visitors welcome?* Yes *Hours:* Contact attraction directly *Admission:* $5 donation requested, $1 children *Operated by:* Friends of Banning Museum *NR?* No *NHL?* No *Latitude:* 33.7891 *Latitude:* -118.2590

CATALINA ISLAND MUSEUM
The Catalina Island Museum was founded in 1953 as an independent nonprofit organization by volunteers concerned that the community *City:* Avalon *State:* CA *Zip:* 90704 *Phone:* 310-510-2414 *Web:* www.catalinamuseum.org *Email:* catalinaislmuseum@catalinaisp.com *Visitors welcome?* Yes *Hours:* April to December: Daily, 10 a.m. to 4 p.m.; January to March: Friday to Wednesday, 10 a.m. to 4 p.m. *Admission:* $5 adults, $4 seniors, $2 children, under five FREE *Operated by:* Catalina Island Museum *NR?* No *NHL?* No *Year established/built:* 1953 *Latitude:* 33.3419 *Latitude:* -118.3260

RICHMOND MUSEUM OF HISTORY
The Richmond Museum of History features a collection of nautical objects, and the museum is owner of the World War II-era Victory Ship Red Oak Victory. *Address:* 400 Nevin Avenue *City:* Richmond *State:* CA *Zip:* 94802 *Phone:* 510-235-7387 *Web:* www.richmondmuseumofhistory.org *Visitors welcome?* Yes *Hours:* Wednesday to Sunday, 1 p.m. to 4 p.m. *Admission:* Contact attraction directly *Operated by:* Point Richmond History Association *NR?* No *NHL?* No *Latitude:* 37.9368 *Latitude:* -122.3660

FLORIDA

FORT EAST MARTELLO MUSEUM AND GARDENS
The Fort East Martello Museum and Gardens features extensive exhibits on the maritime history of Key West from Native American cultures to the 20th century. *Address:* 3501 S. Roosevelt Blvd. *City:* Key West *State:* FL *Zip:* 33040 *Phone:* 305-296-3913 *Web:* www.kwahs.com/martello.htm *Visitors welcome?* Yes *Hours:* Daily, 9:30 a.m. to 4:30 p.m. *Admission:* $6 adults, $5 seniors, $3 children, under six FREE *Operated by:* Key West Art & Historical Society *NR?* No *NHL?* No *Latitude:* 24.5529 *Latitude:* -81.7549

MUSEUM OF FLORIDA HISTORY
The Museum of Florida History collects, preserves, exhibits, and interprets evidence of past and present cultures in Florida, and promotes knowledge and appreciation of this heritage. *Address:* 500 S. Bronough St. *City:* Tallahasee *State:* FL *Zip:* 32399 *Phone:* 850-245-6400 *Web:* www.museumoffloridahistory.com *Visitors welcome?* Yes *Hours:* Monday to Friday, 9 a.m. to 4:30 p.m.; Saturday, 10 a.m. to 4:30 p.m., Sunday, noon to 4:30 p.m. *Admission:* FREE *Operated by:* Museum of Florida History *NR?* No *NHL?* No *Year established/built:* 1977 *Latitude:* 30.4380 *Latitude:* -84.2850

NATIONAL NAVAL AVIATION MUSEUM
The National Naval Aviation Museum is the largest Naval Aviation museum in the world and one of the most visited museums in the state of Florida. Share the excitement of Naval Aviation's rich history and see more than 150 beautifully restored aircraft. *Address:* 1750 Radford Blvd., Suite C, Naval Air Station Pensacola *City:* Pensacola *State:* FL *Zip:* 32508 *Phone:* 850-452-3604 *Web:* www.navalaviationmuseum.org *Email:* museuminfo.navalaviation@mchsi.com *Visitors welcome?* Yes *Hours:* Daily, 9 a.m. to 5 p.m. *Admission:* FREE *Operated by:* Naval History & Heritage Command *NR?* No *NHL?* No *Latitude:* 30.3491 *Latitude:* -87.3165

KENTUCKY

PORTLAND MUSEUM
Housed in an 1852 Italianate mansion, the Portland Museum tells the story of the community of Portland, once an independent port town on the Ohio River. *Address:* 2308 Portland Ave. *City:* Louisville *State:* KY *Zip:* 40212 *Phone:* 502-776-7678 *Web:* www.goportland.org *Email:* turnerm@iglou.com *Visitors welcome?* Yes *Hours:* Tuesday to Friday, 10 a.m. to 4:30 p.m. *Admission:* $5 adults, $4 seniors, children six to 18, five and under FREE *Operated by:* Portland Museum *NR?* No *NHL?* No *Year established/built:* 1852 *Latitude:* 38.2696 *Latitude:* -85.7859

MAINE

19TH CENTURY WILLOWBROOK VILLAGE
19th Century Willowbrook Village is a living history museum depicting a typical Maine community of the 1800s. *Address:* 70 Elm St. *City:* Newfield *State:* ME *Zip:* 04056 *Phone:* 207-793-2784 *Web:* www.willowbrookmuseum.org *Email:* director@willowbrookmuseum.org *Visitors welcome?* Yes *Hours:* Saturday of Memorial Day weekend to October 31: Thursday to Monday, 10 a.m. to 5 p.m. *Admission:* $9 adults, $7.50 seniors, $4 students, under six FREE *Operated by:* 19th Century Willowbrook Village *NR?* No *NHL?* No *Latitude:* 43.6579 *Latitude:* -70.8371

BOOTHBAY REGION HISTORICAL SOCIETY MUSEUM
The Boothbay Region Historical Society Museum preserves the local history of the region, including an extension collection of maritime history artifacts and documents. *Address:* 72 Oak St. *City:* Boothbay Harbor *State:* ME *Zip:* 04538 *Phone:* 207-633-0820 *Web:* www.boothbayhistorical.org *Email:* brhs@gwi.net *Visitors welcome?* Yes *Hours:* Wednesday to Saturday, 10 a.m. to 2 p.m. *Admission:* Contact attraction directly *Operated by:* Boothbay Region Historical Society *NR?* No *NHL?* No *Latitude:* 43.8567 *Latitude:* -69.6250

CHAPTER 3 – MUSEUMS

BRICK STORE MUSEUM
The Brick Store Museum preserves the local history of the Kennebunkports, including maritime history. *Address:* 117 Main St. *City:* Kennebunkport *State:* ME *Zip:* 04043 *Phone:* 207-985-4802 *Web:* www.brickstoremuseum.org *Email:* info@brickstoremuseum.org *Visitors welcome?* Yes *Hours:* Tuesdays to Fridays, 10 a.m. to 4:30 p.m.; Saturday, 10 a.m. to 1 p.m. *Admission:* By donation, $5 suggested per person *Operated by:* Brick Store Museum *NR?* No *NHL?* No *Latitude:* 43.3713 *Latitude:* -70.4455

COUNTING HOUSE MUSEUM
The Counting House Museum in South Berwick features a large collection of shipbuilders tools, navigational instruments, and documents related to local maritime history. *Address:* Maine Street and Liberty Street *City:* South Berwick *State:* ME *Phone:* 207-384-0000 *Web:* www.obhs.net *Email:* info@obhs.net *Visitors welcome?* Yes *Hours:* June to October: Saturdays and Sundays, 1 p.m. to 4 p.m. *Admission:* Donation *Operated by:* Old Berwick Historical Society *NR?* No *NHL?* No *Latitude:* 43.2265 *Latitude:* -70.8070

ISLESFORD HISTORICAL MUSEUM
Explore the Cranberry Isles and the lives of their hardy inhabitants in the Islesford Historical Museum on Little Cranberry Island. *Address:* Little Cranberry Island, Acadia National Park *City:* Little Cranberry Island *State:* ME *Zip:* 04646 *Phone:* 207-288-3338 *Web:* www.nps.gov/acad/planyourvisit/islesfordhistoricalmuseum.htm *Visitors welcome?* Yes *Hours:* Mid-June through September: Daily, 9 a.m. to noon, 12:30 p.m. to 3:30 p.m. *Admission:* FREE *Operated by:* Acadia National Park *NR?* No *NHL?* No *Latitude:* 44.2581 *Latitude:* -68.2295

MUSEUM OF YARMOUTH HISTORY
The Museum of Yarmouth History in the Yarmouth Library features exhibits on local maritime history. *Address:* 215 Main St. *City:* Yarmouth *State:* ME *Zip:* 04096 *Phone:* 207-846-6259 *Email:* yarmouth-history@inetmail.att.net *Visitors welcome?* Yes *Hours:* Contact attraction directly *Admission:* Contact attraction directly *Operated by:* Museum of Yarmouth History *NR?* No *NHL?* No *Latitude:* 43.8013 *Latitude:* -70.1872

MARYLAND

J. MILLARD TAWES HISTORICAL MUSEUM
The J. Millard Tawes Historical Museum, on the waterfront at the Somers Cove Marina, traces the history of the Lower Shore. *Address:* 3 Ninth St. *City:* Crisfield *State:* MD *Zip:* 21817 *Phone:* 410-968-2501 *Web:* www.crisfieldheritagefoundation.org *Email:* contactus@crisfieldheritagefoundation.org *Visitors welcome?* Yes *Hours:* Daily *Admission:* $3 adults, $1 children six to 12, under six FREE *Operated by:* Crisfield Heritage Foundation *NR?* No *NHL?* No *Latitude:* 37.9793 *Latitude:* -75.8605

ST. CLEMENT'S ISLAND MUSEUM
St. Clement's Island Museum focuses on the voyage of The Ark and The Dove departing from the Isle of Wight in England on the feast day of St. Clement, the patron saint of mariners. *Address:* 38370 Point Breeze Rd. *City:* Colton's Point *State:* MD *Zip:* 20626 *Phone:* 301-769-2222 *Web:* www.co.saint-marys.md.us/recreate/museums/stclementsisland.asp *Email:* christina.barbour@stmarysmd.com *Visitors welcome?* Yes *Hours:* Memorial Day to September: Daily, 10 a.m. to 5 p.m.; Oct. 1 to March: Wednesday to Sunday, noon to 4 p.m. *Admission:* Contact attraction directly *Operated by:* St. Mary's County Museum Division *NR?* No *NHL?* No *Latitude:* 38.2257 *Latitude:* -76.7491

CHAPTER 3 – MUSEUMS

UPPER BAY MUSEUM
The Upper Bay Museum focuses on the historical of commercial and recreational waterfowl harvesting, including the art of decoy carving. *Address:* Walnut Street *City:* North East *State:* MD *Zip:* 21901 *Phone:* 410-287-2675 *Visitors welcome?* Yes *Hours:* Contact attraction directly *Admission:* Contact attraction directly *Operated by:* Upper Bay Museum *NR?* No *NHL?* No *Latitude:* 39.5939 *Latitude:* -75.9449

MASSACHUSETTS

FORBES HOUSE MUSEUM
The Forbes House Museum preserves the legacy of Captain Robert Bennet Forbes (1804 - 1889), who was a member of the network of prominent families who helped shape maritime and trading history during the golden era of sailing ships. *Address:* 215 Adams St. *City:* Milton *State:* MA *Zip:* 02186 *Phone:* 617-696-1815 *Web:* www.forbeshousemuseum.org *Email:* info@forbeshousemuseum.org *Visitors welcome?* Yes *Hours:* Sunday tours: 1 p.m., 2 p.m., 3 p.m.; Thursday tours: noon, 1 p.m., 2 p.m. *Admission:* $8 adults, $5 students/seniors, children under 12 FREE *Operated by:* Forbes House Charitable Trust *NR?* No *NHL?* No *Latitude:* 42.2650 *Latitude:* -71.0645

SALT POND VISITOR CENTER
The Salt Pond Visitor Center is the main visitors center for Cape Cod National Seashore. The center features local maritime history exhibits and films. *Address:* 50 Doane Rd. *City:* Eastham *State:* MA *Zip:* 02642 *Phone:* 508-255-3421 *Web:* www.nps.gov/caco/ *Visitors welcome?* Yes *Hours:* Daily, 9:30 a.m. to 4:30 p.m. *Admission:* FREE *Operated by:* Cape Cod National Seashore *NR?* No *NHL?* No *Latitude:* 41.8405 *Latitude:* -69.9629

MICHIGAN

BAY COUNTY HISTORICAL MUSEUM
The Bay County Historical Society has been preserving the unique and rich history of Bay County, Michigan since 1919. *Address:* 321 Washington Ave. *City:* Bay City *State:* MI *Zip:* 48708 *Phone:* 989-893-5733 *Web:* www.bchsmuseum.org *Visitors welcome?* Yes *Hours:* Monday to Friday, 10 a.m. to 5 p.m., Saturday, noon to 4 p.m. *Admission:* Contact attraction directly *Operated by:* Bay County Historical Society *NR?* No *NHL?* No *Latitude:* 43.5933 *Latitude:* -83.8887

MANISTEE COUNTY HISTORICAL MUSEUM
The Manistee County Historical Museum includes artifacts and information about local maritime history for this busy lake port. *Address:* 425 River St. *City:* Manistee *State:* MI *Zip:* 49660 *Phone:* 231-723-5531 *Visitors welcome?* Yes *Hours:* Tuesday to Saturday, 10 a.m. to 5 p.m. *Admission:* Contact attraction directly *Operated by:* Manistee County Historical Museum *NR?* No *NHL?* No *Latitude:* 44.2475 *Latitude:* -86.3251

MICHIGAN LIBRARY AND HISTORICAL CENTER
The Michigan Historical Museum includes extensive collections on Michigan maritime history. *Address:* 702 W. Kalamazoo Street *City:* Lansing *State:* MI *Zip:* 48915 *Phone:* 517-373-3559 *Web:* www.michigan.gov/museum *Visitors welcome?* Yes *Hours:* Monday to Friday, 9:30 a.m. to 4:30 p.m.; Saturday, 10 a.m. to 4 p.m.; Sunday, 1 p.m. to 5 p.m. *Admission:* FREE *Operated by:* Michigan Historical Museum System *NR?* No *NHL?* No *Latitude:* 42.7300 *Latitude:* -84.5617

Fyddeye publishes news releases submitted by maritime heritage organizations. Please put contact@fyddeye.com on your media distribution list. The extra publicity is free!

VALLEY CAMP
The Great Lakes freighter Valley Camp is a floating museum ship with more than 100 exhibits, including artifacts from the famed wreck Edmund Fitzgerald. *Address:* 501 East Water Street *City:* Sault Ste. Marie *State:* MI *Zip:* 49783 *Phone:* 906-632-3658 *Toll-free:* 888-744-7867 *Web:* www.thevalleycamp.com *Visitors welcome?* Yes *Hours:* Mid-May to June: Daily, 10 a.m. to 5 p.m.; July to August: Daily, 9 a.m. to 6 p.m.; September: Daily, 9 a.m. to 5 p.m.; October 1 to mid-October: Daily, 10 a.m. to 5 p.m. *Admission:* $11 adults, $5.50 children *Operated by:* Sault Historic Sites *NR?* Yes *NHL?* No *Year established/built:* 1917 *Latitude:* 46.4987 *Latitude:* -84.3374

NEW JERSEY

PATERSON MUSEUM
The collection of the Paterson Museum includes artifacts, manuscripts, photographs, and papers of John Phillip Holland, who invented the modern submarine. *Address:* 2 Market Street *City:* Paterson *State:* NJ *Zip:* 07501 *Phone:* 973-321-1260 *Web:* www.thepatersonmuseum.com *Email:* patersonmuseum@hotmail.com *Visitors welcome?* Yes *Hours:* Tuesday to Friday, 10 a.m. to 4 p.m.; Saturday and Sunday, 12:30 p.m. to 4:30 p.m. *Admission:* $2 adults, children under 18 FREE *Operated by:* Paterson Museum *NR?* No *NHL?* No *Latitude:* 40.9137 *Latitude:* -74.1792

NEW YORK

ADIRONDACK MUSEUM
The Adirondack Museum expands public understanding of Adirondack history and the relationship between people and the Adirondack wilderness, fostering informed choices for the future. The museum includes a large collection of small craft and powered vessels. *Address:* Route 28N/30 *City:* Blue Mountain Lake *State:* NY *Zip:* 12812 *Phone:* 518-352-7311 *Web:* www.adkmuseum.org *Email:* cwelsh@adkmuseum.org *Visitors welcome?* Yes *Hours:* Mid-May to mid-October: Daily, 10 a.m. to 5 p.m. *Admission:* $16 adults; $15 students/seniors/military; $8 children six to 12; under six FREE *Operated by:* Adirondack Museum *NR?* No *NHL?* No *Year established/built:* 1881 *Latitude:* 43.8728 *Latitude:* -74.4509

NEVERSINK VALLEY AREA MUSEUM AT D AND H CANAL PARK
Located next to a remnant of the Delaware and Hudson Canal, the Neversink Area Valley Museum features historical items related to canal history. *Address:* 26 Hoag Road *City:* Cuddebackville *State:* NY *Zip:* 12729 *Phone:* 845-754-8870 *Web:* www.neversinkmuseum.org *Email:* nvam@frontiernet.net *Visitors welcome?* Yes *Hours:* Contact attraction directly *Admission:* $3 adults, $1.50 children *Operated by:* Neversink Valley Area Museum *NR?* No *NHL?* No *Latitude:* 41.4611 *Latitude:* -74.5982

SKENESBOROUGH MUSEUM
Located in a converted Erie Canal terminal building, the Skenesborough museum tells the story of Whitehall during the Revolutionary War. Whitehall is recognized by the New York State legislature as the birthplace of the U.S. Navy. *Address:* Skenesborough Drive *City:* Whitehall *State:* NY *Zip:* 12887 *Phone:*

518-499-1155 *Email:* cbgbird@yahoo.com *Visitors welcome?* Yes *Hours:* Contact attraction directly *Admission:* $2 adults, $1 students/seniors *Operated by:* Skenesborough Museum *NR?* No *NHL?* No *Year established/built:* 1959 *Latitude:* 43.5509 *Latitude:* -73.4032

NORTH CAROLINA

MUSEUM OF THE ALBEMARLE
The Museum of the Albemarle contains extensive exhibits of the maritime history of the Albemarle area of North Carolina. *Address:* 501 S. Water St. *City:* Elizabeth City *State:* NC *Zip:* 27909 *Phone:* 252-335-1453 *Web:* www.museumofthealbemarle.com *Email:* moa@ncdcr.gov *Visitors welcome?* Yes *Hours:* Tuesday to Saturday, 9 a.m. to 5 p.m.; Sundays, 2 p.m. to 5 p.m. *Admission:* Contact attraction directly *Operated by:* Museum of the Albemarle *NR?* No *NHL?* No *Latitude:* 36.2973 *Latitude:* -76.2191

SMITH ISLAND MUSEUM
The Smith Island Museum houses artifacts related to the maritime history of the Cape Fear area, and it's a companion to the Bald Head Lighthouse next door. *City:* Bald Island *State:* NC *Zip:* 28461 *Phone:* 910-457-7481 *Web:* www.oldbaldy.org *Email:* info@oldbaldy.org *Visitors welcome?* Yes *Hours:* Summer: Tuesday through Saturday, 10 a.m. to 4 p.m.; Winter (Dec. 1 to March 15): Friday to Saturday, 10 a.m. to 4 p.m.; Sunday, 11 a.m. to 4 p.m. *Admission:* $3 person, under three FREE *Operated by:* Old Baldy Foundation *NR?* No *NHL?* No *Latitude:* 33.9900 *Latitude:* -78.0424

OHIO

PIQUA HISTORICAL AREA
The Piqua Historical Area State Memorial celebrates two thousand years of Ohio's rich history from prehistoric Indians to Ohio's canal era. The patio portion of the museum building allows visitors the opportunity to view a restored mile-long section of the canal. *Address:* 9845 North Hardin Road *City:* Piqua *State:* OH *Zip:* 45356 *Phone:* 937-773-2522 *Toll-free:* 800-752-2619 *Web:* ohsweb.ohiohistory.org/places/nw13/index.shtml *Email:* ahite@ohiohistory.org *Visitors welcome?* Yes *Hours:* June to Labor Day: Thursday to Friday, 10 a.m. to 5 p.m.; Saturdays and Sundays, 12 p.m. to 5 p.m. *Admission:* $8 adults, $4 children six to 12, five and under FREE *Operated by:* Piqua Historical Area *NR?* No *NHL?* No *Year established/built:* 1829 *Latitude:* 40.1810 *Latitude:* -84.2559

OREGON

 OREGON COAST HISTORY CENTER
The Oregon Coast History Center includes the Burrows House Museum and the Log Cabin Museum. Plans call for a new maritime museum near Newport's waterfront. *Address:* 545 SW Ninth St. *City:* Newport *State:* OR *Zip:* 97365 *Phone:* 541-265-7509 *Web:* www.oregoncoast.history.museum *Email:* coasthistory@newport-net.com *Visitors welcome?* Yes *Hours:* Contact attraction directly *Admission:* Contact attraction directly *Operated by:* Lincoln County Historical Society *NR?* No *NHL?* No *Latitude:* 44.6315 *Latitude:* -124.0580

UMPQUA DISCOVERY CENTER

Located in Reedsport on the central Oregon coast, the Umpqua Discovery Center is an educational and cultural resource for all ages making active, innovative contributions to preserving the Oregon tidewater community. *Address:* 409 Riverfront Way *City:* Reedsport *State:* OR *Zip:* 97467 *Phone:* 541-271-4816 *Web:* www.umpquadiscoverycenter.com *Email:* umpquadiscoverycenter@charterinternet.com *Visitors welcome?* Yes *Hours:* June 1 to Sept. 30: Daily, 9 a.m. to 5 p.m.; Oct. 1 to May 31, daily, 10 a.m. to 4 p.m. *Admission:* $8 adults, $7 seniors, $4 children six to 15, under six FREE *Operated by:* Umpqua Discovery Center *NR?* No *NHL?* No *Latitude:* 43.7023 *Latitude:* -124.0970

SOUTH CAROLINA

CHARLES TOWNE LANDING

Charles Towne Landing is a living history museum focusing on the 17th century English colonists to South Carolina. *Address:* 1500 Old Towne Road *City:* Charleston *State:* SC *Zip:* 29407 *Phone:* 843-852-4200 *Web:* www.charlestowne.org *Email:* charlestowne@scprt.com *Visitors welcome?* Yes *Hours:* Contact attraction directly *Admission:* Contact attraction directly *Operated by:* Friends of Charles Towne Landing *NR?* No *NHL?* No *Latitude:* 32.8100 *Latitude:* -79.9953

WASHINGTON

ABERDEEN MUSEUM OF HISTORY

The Aberdeen Museum of History focuses on the history of the Grays Harbor County, including local maritime history. *Address:* 111 E. Third St. *City:* Aberdeen *State:* WA *Visitors welcome?* Yes *Hours:* Tuesday to Saturday, 10 a.m. to 5 p.m; Sunday, 11 a.m. to 5 p.m. *Admission:* Donation *Operated by:* Aberdeen Museum of History *NR?* No *NHL?* No *Latitude:* 46.9777 *Latitude:* -123.8210

BAINBRIDGE ISLAND MUSEUM

Housed in a 1908 schoolhouse, the Bainbridge Island Museum features several collections of maritime history artifacts related to the development of the Bainbridge Island community, located in Puget Sound west of Seattle. *Address:* 215 Ericksen Avenue NE *City:* Bainbridge Island *State:* WA *Visitors welcome?* Yes *Hours:* Wednesday to Sunday, 1 p.m. to 4 p.m; Saturday, 10 a.m. to 4 p.m; Sunday, 1 p.m. to 4 p.m. *Admission:* Family, $5.00; adult, $2.50; student/senior, $1.50; under 5: FREE *Operated by:* Bainbridge Island Historical Society *NR?* No *NHL?* No *Latitude:* 47.6256 *Latitude:* -122.5170

BURKE MUSEUM OF NATURAL HISTORY AND CULTURE

The Burke Museum of Natural History and Culture on the University of Washington campus features an extensive collection of artifacts related to Northwest Coast native peoples and their seafaring traditions. *Address:* 17th Avenue NE and NE 45th Street *City:* Seattle *State:* WA *Zip:* 98195 *Phone:* 206-543-5590 *Web:* www.washington.edu/burkemuseum *Email:* theburke@u.washington.edu *Visitors welcome?* Yes *Hours:* Daily, 10 a.m. to 5 p.m. *Admission:* FREE *Operated by:* Burke Museum of Natural History and Culture *NR?* No *NHL?* No *Latitude:* 47.6613 *Latitude:* -122.3100

CHAPTER 3 – MUSEUMS

ISLAND COUNTY HISTORICAL MUSEUM
The Island County Historical Museum in Coupeville on Whidbey Island preserves island history going back to the Spanish in the 17th century. *Address:* 908 NW Alexander St. *City:* Coupeville *State:* WA *Visitors welcome?* Yes *Hours:* Oct. to April: Friday to Monday, 10 a.m. to 4 p.m; May to Sept: daily (except Tuesday) 10 a.m. to 5 p.m. *Admission:* Children under 5, FREE; Senior/Student/Military, $2.50; Adult, $3; Family, $6 *Operated by:* Island County Historical Society *NR?* No *NHL?* No *Latitude:* 48.2212 *Latitude:* -122.6880

JEFFERSON COUNTY HISTORICAL MUSEUM
The Jefferson Count Historical Museum preserves the history of Port Townsend, one of Washington State's oldest communities and the first U.S. port-of-entry on Puget Sound. *Address:* Water St. and Polk St. *City:* Port Townsend *State:* WA *Visitors welcome?* Yes *Hours:* Monday to Saturday, 11 a.m. to 4 p.m; Sunday, 1 p.m. to 4 p.m. *Admission:* Children under 12, $1; Adults, $3 *Operated by:* Jefferson County Historical Society *NR?* No *NHL?* No *Latitude:* 48.1136 *Latitude:* -122.7590

KLONDIKE GOLD RUSH NAT'L HIST. PARK
The Klondike Gold Rush National Historical Park documents the gold rushes of the late 19th and early 20th centuries, including the fleets of private vessels that ferries miners from Seattle to Skagway and other Alaska ports. *Address:* 319 2nd Avenue S. *City:* Seattle *State:* WA *Visitors welcome?* Yes *Hours:* Daily, 9 a.m. to 5 p.m. *Admission:* FREE *Operated by:* Klondike Gold Rush NHP *NR?* No *NHL?* No *Latitude:* 47.5994 *Latitude:* -122.3320

 MAKAH MUSEUM
The Makah Museum in Neah Bay, recognized as the nation's finest tribal museum, welcomes visitors to experience the life of pre-contact Makah people. *City:* Neah Bay *State:* WA *Zip:* 98357 *Phone:* 360-645-2711 *Web:* www.makah.com/mcrchome.htm *Email:* makahmuseum@centurytel.net *Visitors welcome?* Yes *Hours:* Daily *Admission:* $5 adults, $4 seniors/students, under five FREE *Operated by:* Makah Cultural and Research Center *NR?* No *NHL?* No *Latitude:* 48.3681 *Latitude:* -124.6250

MUSEUM AT THE CARNEGIE
The Museum at the Carnegie in Port Angeles offers a glimpse of life from Clallam County's past. *Address:* 207 S. Lincoln St., Port Angeles *City:* Port Angeles *State:* WA *Visitors welcome?* Yes *Hours:* Wednesday to Saturday, 1 p.m. to 4 p.m. *Admission:* Contact attraction directly *Operated by:* Clallam County Historical Society *NR?* No *NHL?* No *Year established/built:* 1919 *Latitude:* 48.1174 *Latitude:* -123.4330

MUSEUM OF HISTORY & INDUSTRY
The Museum of History & Industry features a special permanent exhibit of maritime heritage artifacts collected by Horace W. McCurdy, an early champion of the museum and a major figure in local maritime industry. *Address:* 2700 24th Ave E. *City:* Seattle *State:* WA *Zip:* 98112 *Phone:* 206-324-1126 *Web:* www.seattlehistory.org *Email:* information@seattlehistory.org *Visitors welcome?* Yes *Hours:* Daily, 10 a.m. to 5 p.m; First Thursdays 10 a.m. to 8 p.m. *Admission:* First Thursdays FREE; Pre-School (ages 0-4) FREE; Youth (ages 5-17) $5; Adult (ages 18-61) $7; Senior (ages 62+) $5. *Operated by:* Museum of History & Industry *NR?* No *NHL?* No *Year established/built:* 1952 *Latitude:* 47.6442 *Latitude:* -122.3020

NORDIC HERITAGE MUSEUM
The experience of Scandinavian immigrants enriched the maritime history of Puget Sound from the beginning. The Nordic Heritage Museum honors this experience with a permanent exhibit that tells the story of contribu-

tions by people from Finland, Norway, Denmark, and Sweden. *Address:* 3014 NW 67th St. *City:* Seattle *State:* WA *Zip:* 98117 *Phone:* 206-789-5707 *Web:* www.nordicmuseum.org *Email:* nordic@nordicmuseum.org *Visitors welcome?* Yes *Hours:* Tuesday to Saturday, 10 p.m. to 4 p.m; Sunday, Noon to 4 p.m. *Admission:* Children (5 and under) FREE; Students (K to 12), $4; Seniors, $5; Adults, $6 *Operated by:* Nordic Heritage Museum *NR?* No *NHL?* No *Latitude:* 47.6777 *Latitude:* -122.3970

PACIFIC COUNTY MUSEUM
The maritime way of life drives much of the economy and culture of Pacific County, located in coastal southwestern Washington State. *Address:* 1008 Robert Bush Dr. *City:* South Bend *State:* WA *Visitors welcome?* Yes *Hours:* Daily, 11 a.m. to 4 p.m. *Admission:* Contact attraction directly *Operated by:* Pacific County Historical Society *NR?* No *NHL?* No *Latitude:* 46.6646 *Latitude:* -123.8080

SUQUAMISH MUSEUM/OLD MAN HOUSE PARK
Address: 15838 Sandy Hook Road NE *City:* Suquamish *State:* WA *Visitors welcome?* Yes *Hours:* Winter (October to April): Friday, Saturday, 10 a.m. to 4 p.m; Summer (May to September), daily, 10 a.m. to 5 p.m. *Admission:* Children (12 and under), $2; Seniors (55 and over), $3; Adults, $4 *Operated by:* Suquamish Museum *NR?* No *NHL?* No *Latitude:* 47.7074 *Latitude:* -122.5820

U.S. AND U.K. CAMPS, SAN JUAN ISLAND
Address: West Valley Road and Yacht Haven Road *City:* Friday Harbor *State:* WA *Visitors welcome?* Yes *Admission:* FREE *NR?* No *NHL?* Yes *Latitude:* 48.5343 *Latitude:* -123.0170

WHATCOM MUSEUM OF HISTORY & ART
The Whatcom Museum of History & Art features a collection of ship and boat blueprints, half-hull models, and other documents related to the local shipbuilding industry. *Address:* 121 Prospect St. *City:* Bellingham *State:* WA *Zip:* 98225 *Phone:* 360-676-6981 *Web:* www.whatcommuseum.org *Email:* museuminfo@cob.org *Visitors welcome?* Yes *Hours:* Contact attraction directly *Admission:* Contact attraction directly *Operated by:* Whatcom Museum of History & Art *NR?* No *NHL?* No *Latitude:* 48.7523 *Latitude:* -122.4810

WISCONSIN

DOOR COUNTY MUSEUM (STURGEON BAY)
The Door County Maritime Museum preserves the maritime history of Door County, Wisconsin. *Address:* 120 N. Madison Ave. *City:* Sturgeon Bay *State:* WI *Zip:* 54235 *Phone:* 920-743-5958 *Web:* www.dcmm.org *Email:* info@dcmm.org *Visitors welcome?* Yes *Hours:* Daily, 10 a.m. to 5 p.m. *Admission:* $7 adults, $4 children five to 17, under five FREE *Operated by:* Door County Maritime Museum & Lighthouse Preservation Society *NR?* No *NHL?* No *Latitude:* 44.8301 *Latitude:* -87.3844

CHAPTER 4 – RESEARCH LIBRARIES

LIBRARIES AND ARCHIVES SPECIALIZING IN DOCUMENTS RELATED TO MARITIME HISTORY

Submarine Force Museum (Groton, Conn.)

Most maritime museums and many general history museums have collections of documents related to maritime history, such as logbooks. But a few collections, including some in universities and colleges, enjoy special status as a research library or maritime history archive. They cater to researchers, genealogists, and sometimes an ordinary person who wants to look up something about a favorite boat design or historical event. Documents can ranged from business records, to diaries, to folk art and fine paintings. This chapter lists the libraries that have identified themselves as maritime specialists.

RESEARCH LIBRARIES

BOSTON MARINE SOCIETY COLLECTION AND LIBRARY
The Boston Marine Society collection of artifacts, books, and papers go back to the founding of the society in 1754. *Address:* 32 Shipway Pl. *City:* Boston *State:* MA *Zip:* 02129 *Phone:* 617-242-0522 *Web:* www.bostonmarinesociety.org *Email:* info@bostonmarinesociety.org *Visitors welcome?* Yes *Hours:* Contact attraction directly *Admission:* Contact attraction directly *Operated by:* Boston Marine Society *NR?* No *NHL?* No *Year established/built:* 1754 *Latitude:* 42.3787 *Latitude:* -71.0524

CAPTAIN WILLIAM BOWELL RIVER LIBRARY
The Captain William Bowell River Library, housed in the archives department at the National Mississippi River Museum & Aquarium, has over 20,000 items for river research. *Address:* 350 East Third St. *City:* Dubuque *State:* IA *Zip:* 52001 *Phone:* 563-557-9545 *Toll-free:* 800-226-3369 *Web:* www.mississippirivermuseum.com

Visitors welcome? Yes *Hours:* Memorial Day weekend through October: Daily, 9 a.m. to 5 p.m.; November through Memorial Day weekend: Daily, 10 a.m. to 5 p.m. *Admission:* Contact attraction directly *Operated by:* Dubuque County Historical Society *NR?* No *NHL?* No *Latitude:* 42.4963 *Latitude:* -90.6591

CHICAGO MARITIME SOCIETY
Founded in 1982, the Chicago Maritime Society maintains a research collection on the sixth floor of the Helix Building in Chicago. *Address:* 310 S. Racine Ave. *City:* Chicago *State:* IL *Zip:* 60607 *Phone:* 312-421-9096 *Web:* www.chicagomaritimesociety.org *Email:* geraldhthomas@cs.com *Visitors welcome?* Yes *Hours:* Contact attraction directly *Admission:* Contact attraction directly *Operated by:* Chicago Maritime Society *NR?* No *NHL?* No *Year established/built:* 1982 *Latitude:* 41.8776 *Latitude:* -87.6573

CLARENCE S. METCALF RESEARCH LIBRARY
The Clarence S. Metcalf Great Lakes Maritime Research Library of The Great Lakes Historical Society is a premier research facility dedicated to preserving and making known the history of the Great Lakes. *Address:* 480 Main Street *City:* Vermilion *State:* OH *Zip:* 44089 *Phone:* 440-967-3467 *Email:* glhs1@inlandseas.org *Visitors welcome?* Yes *Hours:* Contact attraction directly *Admission:* Contact attraction directly *Operated by:* Great Lakes Historical Society *NR?* No *NHL?* No *Year established/built:* 1944 *Latitude:* 41.4249 *Latitude:* -82.3668

EMIL BUEHLER NAVAL AVIATION MUSEUM LIBRARY
The Emil Buehler Naval Aviation Museum Library is located within the National Naval Aviation Museum in Pensacola, Fla. *Address:* 1750 Radford Blvd., Suite C, Naval Air Station Pensacola *City:* Pensacola *State:* FL *Zip:* 32508 *Phone:* 850-452-8451 *Web:* www.navalaviationmuseum.org *Email:* ebuehler.navalaviation@mchsi.com *Visitors welcome?* Yes *Hours:* Contact attraction directly *Admission:* Contact attraction directly *Operated by:* Naval History & Heritage Command *NR?* No *NHL?* No *Latitude:* 30.3491 *Latitude:* -87.3165

GREAT LAKES MARINE COLLECTION
The Great Lakes Marine Collection at the Milwaukee Public Library, in affiliation with the Wisconsin Marine Historical Society, includes ship files, log books, vessel plans, and wreck reports. *Address:* 814 W. Wisconsin Ave. *City:* Milwaukee *State:* WI *Zip:* 53233 *Phone:* 414-286-3000 *Web:* www.mpl.org *Visitors welcome?* Yes *Hours:* Contact attraction directly *Admission:* FREE *Operated by:* Milwaukee Public Library *NR?* No *NHL?* No *Latitude:* 43.0395 *Latitude:* -87.9224

HART NAUTICAL COLLECTION
The collections consist of artifacts, books, plans, photographic materials, models, marine art, and technical records. *Address:* 55 Massachusetts Ave., Building 5 *City:* Cambridge *State:* MA *Zip:* 02135 *Phone:* 617-253-5942 *Web:* web.mit.edu/museum/exhibitions/hart.html *Email:* kurt@mit.edu *Visitors welcome?* Yes *Hours:* By appointment *Admission:* Contact attraction directly *Operated by:* MIT Museum *NR?* No *NHL?* No *Latitude:* 42.3587 *Latitude:* -71.0934

HERMAN T. POTT NATIONAL INLAND WATERWAYS LIBRARY
The Herman T. Pott National Inland Waterways Library is a special library within the St. Louis Mercantile Library, at the University of Missouri-St. Louis, which is one of America's great historical research libraries, serving St. Louis and the nation. *Address:* Thomas Jefferson Library Building, 1 University Blvd. *City:* St. Louis *State:* MO *Zip:* 63121 *Phone:* 314-516-7245 *Web:* www.umsl.edu/pott/ *Email:* cribbsd@umsl.edu *Visitors welcome?* Yes *Hours:* Contact attraction directly *Admission:* Contact attraction directly *Operated by:* Herman T. Pott National Inland Waterways Library *NR?* No *NHL?* No *Year established/built:* 1846 *Latitude:* 38.6451 *Latitude:* -90.3106

CHAPTER 4 – RESEARCH LIBRARIES

INLAND RIVERS LIBRARY
The Inland Rivers Library at the Cincinnati Public Library features materials pertaining to the commercial use of the Ohio and Mississippi Rivers and their navigable tributaries. *Address:* 800 Vine St. *City:* Cincinnati *State:* OH *Zip:* 45202 *Phone:* 513-369-6957 *Web:* www.cincinnatilibrary.org *Visitors welcome?* Yes *Hours:* Contact attraction directly *Admission:* FREE *Operated by:* Cincinnati Public Library *NR?* No *NHL?* No *Latitude:* 39.1058 *Latitude:* -84.5133

LIBRARY AT THE MARINERS MUSEUM
The Library at the Mariners Museum holds the largest maritime history collection in the Western Hemisphere. The library's collection includes 1.75 million items, including books, rare books, manuscripts, magazines, maps and charts, vessel plans, and more. *Address:* 100 Museum Drive *City:* Newport News *State:* VA *Zip:* 23606 *Phone:* 757-591-7782 *Web:* www.mariner.org *Email:* library@mariner.org *Visitors welcome?* Yes *Hours:* Monday to Friday, 10 a.m. to 5 p.m. *Admission:* Contact attraction directly *Operated by:* Mariners Museum *NR?* No *NHL?* No *Year established/built:* 1933 *Latitude:* 37.0420 *Latitude:* -76.4882

MARIALYCE CANONIE GREAT LAKES RESEARCH LIBRARY
The Marialyce Canonie Great Lakes Research Library is part of the Michigan Maritime Museum. *Address:* 260 Dyckman Ave. *City:* South Haven *State:* MI *Zip:* 49090 *Phone:* 269-637-9156 *Web:* michiganmaritimemuseum.org *Email:* library@michiganmaritimemuseum.org *Visitors welcome?* Yes *Hours:* By appointment and Thursdays, 10 a.m. to 5 p.m. *Admission:* $5 adults, $4 seniors, $3.50 children *Operated by:* Michigan Maritime Museum *NR?* No *NHL?* No *Latitude:* 42.4070 *Latitude:* -86.2745

MARITIME HERITAGE PROJECT
The Maritime Heritage Project is a web-only research site. Hundreds of thousands of people around the world have found family members through the Project. All of the information on the site is provided free of charge. *City:* Sausalito *State:* CA *Zip:* 94966 *Web:* www.maritimeheritage.org *Email:* DALevy@maritimeheritage.org *Visitors welcome?* Yes *Hours:* Contact attraction directly *Admission:* Contact attraction directly *Operated by:* Maritime Heritage Project *NR?* No *NHL?* No *Year established/built:* 1998 *Latitude:* 37.8592 *Latitude:* -122.4840

MYSTIC SEAPORT: COLLECTIONS RESEARCH CENTER
Mystic Seaport: The Museum of America and the Sea is the nation's leading maritime museum. *Address:* 75 Greenmanville Avenue *City:* Mystic *State:* CT *Zip:* 06355 *Phone:* 860-572-5315 *Web:* www.mysticseaport.org *Visitors welcome?* Yes *Hours:* Contact attraction directly *Admission:* Contact attraction directly *Operated by:* Mystic Seaport: The Museum of America and the Sea *NR?* No *NHL?* No *Year established/built:* 1929 *Latitude:* 41.3617 *Latitude:* -71.9634

NICHOLSON WHALING COLLECTION
The Nicholson Whaling Collection at Providence Public Library is now the second largest whaling logbook collection in America. The library also has a large collection of ship models. *Address:* 150 Empire St. *City:* Providence *State:* RI *Zip:* 02903 *Phone:* 401-455-8000 *Web:* www.provlib.org *Email:* schausse@provlib.org *Visitors welcome?* Yes *Hours:* Contact attraction directly *Admission:* FREE *Operated by:* Providence Public Library *NR?* No *NHL?* No *Latitude:* 41.8219 *Latitude:* -71.4165

PEACHMAN LAKE ERIE SHIPWRECK RESEARCH CENTER
The Peachman Lake Erie Shipwreck Research Center provides the most comprehensive database collection of information available on Lake Erie shipwrecks in the country. It is located in the Inland Seas Museum. *Address:* 480 Main Street *City:* Vermilion *State:* OH *Zip:* 44089 *Phone:* 440-967-3467 *Email:* glhs1@inlandseas.org *Visitors welcome?* Yes *Hours:* Contact attraction directly *Admission:* Contact attraction directly *Operated

by: Great Lakes Historical Society *NR?* No *NHL?* No *Year established/built:* 2000 *Latitude:* 41.4249 *Latitude:* -82.3668

PITCAIRN ISLANDS STUDY CENTER
The Pitcairn Islands Study Center at Pacific Union College preserves records and artifacts related to the 18th century mutiny on HMS Bounty. *Address:* 1 Angwin Avenue *City:* Angwin *State:* CA *Zip:* 94508 *Phone:* 707-965-6625 *Web:* library.puc.edu/pitcairn/studycenter/index.shtml *Email:* hford@puc.edu *Visitors welcome?* Yes *Hours:* Monday to Thursday, 9 a.m. to 5 p.m.; Friday, 9 a.m. to noon *Admission:* FREE *Operated by:* Pitcairn Islands Study Center *NR?* No *NHL?* No *Latitude:* 38.5708 *Latitude:* -122.4430

PORTSMOUTH ATHENAEUM
The Portsmouth Athenæum is a non-profit membership library and museum, incorporated in 1817 and located in the heart of historic Portsmouth, New Hampshire. *Address:* 9 Market Square *City:* Portsmouth *State:* NH *Zip:* 03801 *Phone:* 603-431-2538 *Web:* www.portsmouthathenaeum.org *Email:* info@portsmouthathenaeum.org *Visitors welcome?* Yes *Hours:* Contact attraction directly *Admission:* FREE *Operated by:* Portsmouth Athenaeum *NR?* No *NHL?* No *Year established/built:* 1817 *Latitude:* 43.0771 *Latitude:* -70.7574

PT BOAT MUSEUM AND LIBRARY
The PT Boat Museum and Library at Battleship Cove features more than 4,000 square feet devoted to 43 commissioned squadrons, some 80 bases and 19 tender ships, including two completely restored PT boats. *Address:* Battleship Cove, Five Water Street *City:* Fall River *State:* MA *Zip:* 02722 *Phone:* 508-678-1100 *Toll-free:* 800-533-3194 *Web:* www.battleshipcove.org *Visitors welcome?* Yes *Hours:* Summer: daily, 9 a.m. to 4:30 p.m.; Winter: daily, 9 a.m. to 5:30 p.m. *Admission:* Contact attraction directly *Operated by:* PT Boats, Inc. *NR?* No *NHL?* No *Latitude:* 41.7027 *Latitude:* -71.1641

STEPHEN PHILLIPS MEMORIAL LIBRARY
Research library for the Penobscot Marine Museum *Address:* 5 Church Street *City:* Searsport *State:* ME *Zip:* 04974 *Phone:* 207-548-2529 *Web:* www.penobscotmarinemuseum.org *Email:* library@penobscotmarinemuseum.org *Visitors welcome?* Yes *Hours:* Contact attraction directly *Admission:* Contact attraction directly *Operated by:* Penobscot Marine Museum *NR?* No *NHL?* No *Latitude:* 44.4209 *Latitude:* -69.0006

SUBMARINE FORCE LIBRARY & MUSEUM
The Submarine Force Museum & Library's current collection ranges from submarine pioneer John Holland's notes and calculations for the Navy's first submarine to the many one-of-a-kind artifacts from World War I and World War II. *Address:* One Chrystal Lake Road *City:* Groton *State:* CT *Zip:* 06340 *Phone:* 860-694-3174 *Toll-free:* 800-343-0079 *Web:* www.submarinemuseum.org *Email:* gregory.caskey@navy.mil *Visitors welcome?* Yes *Hours:* May through October: Daily, 9 a.m. to 5 p.m.; November through April: Daily, 9 a.m. to 4 p.m. *Admission:* FREE *Operated by:* Submarine Force Library & Museum Association *NR?* No *NHL?* No *Year established/built:* 1955 *Latitude:* 41.3851 *Latitude:* -72.0868

VALLEJO NAVAL AND HISTORICAL MUSEUM
The research library at the Vallejo Naval and Historical Museum features more than 35,000 photographs of Vallejo and Mare Island. *Address:* 734 Marin St. *City:* Vallejo *State:* CA *Zip:* 94590 *Phone:* 707-643-0077 *Web:* www.vallejomuseum.org *Email:* valmuse@pacbell.net *Visitors welcome?* Yes *Hours:* By appointment *Admission:* $5 adults, $3 seniors/students, children under 12 FREE *Operated by:* Vallejo Naval and Historical Museum *NR?* No *NHL?* No *Latitude:* 38.1026 *Latitude:* -122.2570

WOODS HOLE HISTORICAL COLLECTION ARCHIVES
The Woods Hole Historical Collection includes ship's logs, numerous pieces of personal and business correspondence, including items related to shipping and whaling, diaries, bibles, business records, newspaper articles, postcards and sketchbooks. *Address:* 573 Woods Hole Rd. *City:* Woods Hole *State:* MA *Zip:* 02543 *Phone:* 508-548-7270 *Web:* www.woodsholemuseum.org *Email:* woods_hole_historical@hotmail.com *Visitors welcome?* Yes *Hours:* By appointment *Admission:* Contact attraction directly *Operated by:* Woods Hole Historical Museum *NR?* No *NHL?* No *Year established/built:* 1973 *Latitude:* 41.5236 *Latitude:* -70.6673

OTHER LIBRARIES

BUTTERFIELD RESEARCH LIBRARY
The Butterfield Research Library is operated by the Bay County Historical Society and features extensive archives and artifacts dating back to the Pioneer Society organized in the 1870s. *Address:* 321 Washington Ave. *City:* Bay City *State:* MI *Zip:* 48708 *Phone:* 989-893-5733 *Web:* www.bchsmuseum.org *Visitors welcome?* Yes *Hours:* Tuesday to Thursday, 1 p.m. to 5 p.m. *Admission:* Contact attraction directly *Operated by:* Bay County Historical Society *NR?* No *NHL?* No *Latitude:* 43.5933 *Latitude:* -83.8887

HISTORICAL COLLECTIONS OF THE GREAT LAKES
The Historical Collections of the Great Lakes (HCGL) is part of the Center for Archival Collections at Bowling Green State University. Its purpose is to collect, preserve, and make available to scholars, students, and the public, historical materials, documents, and archives. *Address:* 6th Floor - Jerome Library, Bowling Green State University *City:* Bowling Green *State:* OH *Zip:* 43403 *Phone:* 419-372-9613 *Web:* www.bgsu.edu/colleges/library/cac/page39984.html *Email:* rgraham@bgsu.edu *Visitors welcome?* Yes *Hours:* Daily, 8 a.m. to 5 p.m. *Admission:* FREE *Operated by:* Historical Collections of the Great Lakes *NR?* No *NHL?* No *Latitude:* 41.3781 *Latitude:* -83.6375

LOS ANGELES MUSEUM RESEARCH LIBRARY
The Los Angeles Museum Research Library is a special collection of the Los Angeles Maritime Museum. Books and archival materials donated to the Library were once owned by mariners, port pilots, sailors, ship modelers, authors and avid collectors of history. *Address:* Berth 84, Foot of 6th St. *City:* San Pedro *State:* CA *Zip:* 90731 *Phone:* 310-548-7618 *Web:* www.lamaritimemuseum.org *Visitors welcome?* Yes *Hours:* Tuesday to Saturday, 10 a.m. to 5 p.m.; Sunday, noon to 5 p.m. *Admission:* $3 adults, $1 seniors/youths, children FREE *Operated by:* Los Angeles Maritime Museum *NR?* No *NHL?* No *Year established/built:* 1980 *Latitude:* 33.7387 *Latitude:* -118.2790

OREGON COAST HISTORY CENTER RESEARCH LIBRARY
The Burrows House Museum at the Oregon Coast History Center features a research library focused on the history of the central Oregon coast. *Address:* 545 SW Ninth St. *City:* Newport *State:* OR *Zip:* 97365 *Phone:* 541-265-7509 *Web:* www.oregoncoast.history.museum *Email:* coasthistory@newportnet.com *Visitors welcome?* Yes *Hours:* Contact attraction directly *Admission:* Contact attraction directly *Operated by:* Lincoln County Historical Society *NR?* No *NHL?* No *Latitude:* 44.6315 *Latitude:* -124.0580

PARMELY LIBRARY
Located in the Nims Mansion, the Parmely Library is part of the Golden Eagle River Museum. *Address:* 2701 Finestown Rd. *City:* St. Louis *State:* MO *Zip:* 63129 *Phone:* 314-846-9073 *Visitors welcome?* Yes *Hours:* May

CHAPTER 4 – RESEARCH LIBRARIES

1 to October 31: Wednesday to Sunday, 1 p.m. to 5 p.m. *Admission:* FREE *Operated by:* Golden Eagle River Museum *NR?* No *NHL?* No *Latitude:* 38.4082 *Latitude:* -90.3278

R.W. WOOLWORTH LIBRARY
The Richard W. Woolworth Library is a modern archival facility, with a large reading room with tables for researchers, computers, copiers and a microfilm reader printer. The library is focused on the history of the Stonington area. *Address:* 40 Palmer Street *City:* Stonington *State:* CT *Zip:* 06378 *Phone:* 860-535-1131 *Web:* www.stoningtonhistory.org *Email:* library@stoningtonhistory.org *Visitors welcome?* Yes *Hours:* Mondays, Wednesday, 10 a.m. to 5 p.m.; Saturdays, 10 a.m. to 1 p.m.; Fridays, May to October, 1 p.m. to 5 p.m. *Admission:* Contact attraction directly *Operated by:* Stonington Historical Society *NR?* No *NHL?* No *Year established/built:* 1998 *Latitude:* 41.3428 *Latitude:* -71.9051

CHAPTER 5 – LIGHTHOUSES & LIGHTSHIPS

WORKING AND PRESERVED LIGHTHOUSES AND THEIR FLOATING COUNTERPARTS: LIGHTSHIPS

Cove Point Lighthouse (Cove Point, Md.)

Few man-made structures carry as much emotional meaning as the lighthouse. Since ancient times, the vision of the lonely sentinel patiently waiting and guiding the tired seaman home has inspired poets and artists, and not a few modern historic preservationists. Lighthouses come in all shapes and sizes, not just the high tower capped with the revolving light. Some of the oldest lighthouses still serve their original function as harbor guides. Though all are unmanned today, a few preserve echoes of the lives of solitary lighthouse keepers and their families. Some of those keepers literally went insane with loneliness. A less-known but equally important facet of these traditions is the lightship, essentially a floating lighthouse that marked river entrances or shallows off the coast. This chapter lists all operating and non-operating lighthouses and lightships on U.S. coastlines. And the chapter offers three suggested itineraries for travelers interested in exploring lighthouse history of New England, Michigan, and California.

EAST COAST LIGHTHOUSES

CONNECTICUT

AVERY POINT LIGHTHOUSE
Formerly the site of the U.S. Coast Guard Training Center, Avery Point is now the site of a University of Connecticut campus. The lighthouse operated for just 23 years, from 1944 to 1967. *Address:* Avery Point Light *State:* CT *Visitors welcome?* Yes *Hours:* Daily *Admission:* FREE *Operated by:* Avery Point Lighthouse Society *NR?* No *NHL?* No *Year established/built:* 1944 *Latitude:* 41.3152 *Latitude:* -72.0635

BLACK ROCK HARBOR LIGHTHOUSE
Established in 1808, the current Black Rock Harbor Lighthouse, also called the Fayerweather Island Lighthouse, was constructed in 1817 and deactivated in 1932. The rehabilitated structure is now part of a district on the National Register of Historic Places. *Address:* Black Rock Harbor Light *City:* Bridgeport *State:* CT *Visitors welcome?* Yes *Hours:* Access to grounds only *Admission:* Access to grounds only *Operated by:* City of Bridgeport *NR?* Yes *NHL?* No *Year established/built:* 1808 *Latitude:* 41.1424 *Latitude:* -73.2167

FALKNERS ISLAND LIGHTHOUSE
Established and built in 1802, the Faulkners Island Lighthouse was automated in 1978 and is still an active aid to navigation. The lighthouse is now part of a wildlife refuge and it is maintained by a volunteer group. *Address:* Falkner Island Light *State:* CT *Visitors welcome?* No *Operated by:* Faulkner's Light Brigade *NR?* Yes *NHL?* No *Year established/built:* 1802 *Latitude:* 41.2119 *Latitude:* -72.6536

FILE MILE POINT LIGHTHOUSE
Established in 1805, the current Five Mile Point Lighthouse, also called the Old New Haven Lighthouse, was constructed in 1845. The light was deactivated in 1877, and it was rehabilitated in 1986. *Address:* Lighthouse Point Park *City:* New Haven *State:* CT *Visitors welcome?* Yes *Hours:* Daily *Admission:* FREE *Operated by:* City of New Haven *NR?* Yes *NHL?* No *Year established/built:* 1805 *Latitude:* 41.2484 *Latitude:* -72.9036

GREAT CAPTAIN ISLAND LIGHTHOUSE
Established in 1830, the current Great Captain Island Lighthouse was constructed in 1868 and deactivated in 1970. *Address:* Great Captain Island Light *City:* Greenwich *State:* CT *Visitors welcome?* No *Operated by:* Town of Greenwich *NR?* Yes *NHL?* No *Year established/built:* 1830 *Latitude:* 40.9825 *Latitude:* -73.6235

GREENS LEDGE LIGHTHOUSE
Established and built in 1902, the Greens Ledge Lighthouse was automated in 1972 and is still an active aid to navigation. *Address:* Greens Ledge Light *City:* Scott Cove *State:* CT *Visitors welcome?* No *Operated by:* U.S. Coast Guard (District 1) *NR?* Yes *NHL?* No *Year established/built:* 1902 *Latitude:* 41.0417 *Latitude:* -73.4439

LYNDE POINT LIGHTHOUSE
Established in 1803, the current Lynde Point Lighthouse, also called the Saybrook Lighthouse, was constructed in 1839. Automated in 1975, the light is still an active aid to navigation. *Address:* Lynde Point Light

CHAPTER 5 – LIGHTHOUSES & LIGHTSHIPS

City: Fenwick *State:* CT *Visitors welcome?* No *Operated by:* U.S. Coast Guard (District 1) *NR?* Yes *NHL?* No *Year established/built:* 1803 *Latitude:* 41.2714 *Latitude:* -72.3433

Did you spot an error? Email your correction to contact@fyddeye.com.

MORGAN POINT LIGHTHOUSE
Established in 1831, the current Morgan Point Lighthouse was constructed in 1868 and deactivated in 1919. Renovated in 1993, it is now part of the Noank Historic District. *Address:* Morgan Point *City:* Noank *State:* CT *Visitors welcome?* No *Operated by:* Private owner *NR?* Yes *NHL?* No *Year established/built:* 1831 *Latitude:* 41.3189 *Latitude:* -71.9902

New England and Mid-Atlantic Lighthouse Tour Itinerary

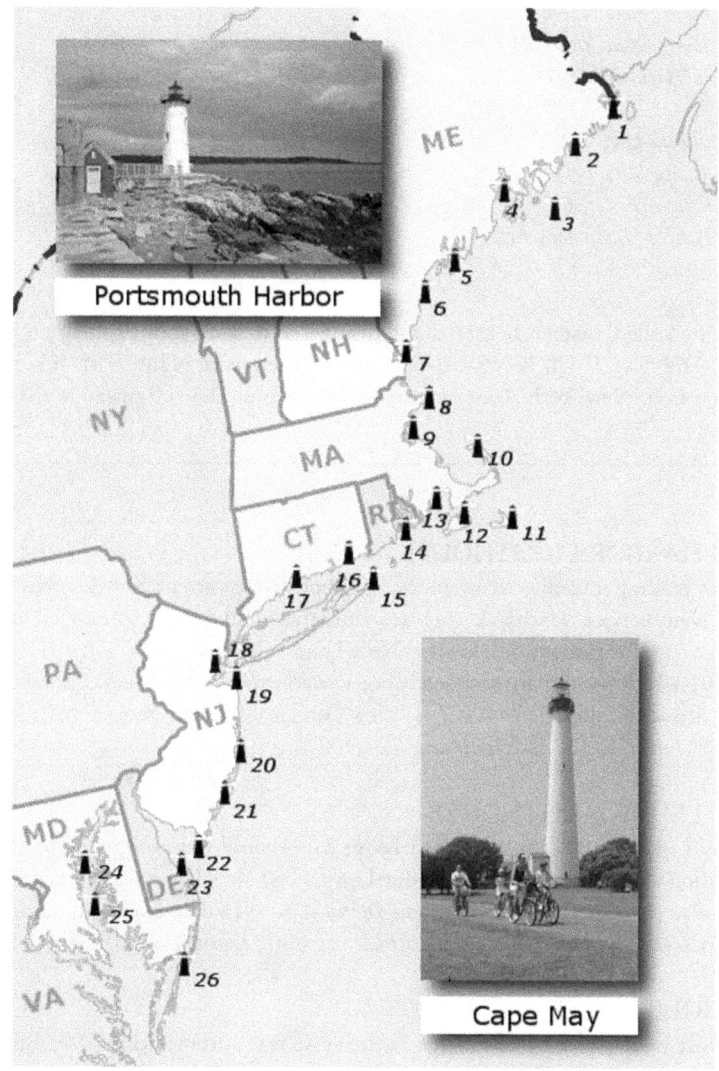

1. *West Quoddy Head (Lubec, ME)*
2. *Moose Peak (Jonesport, ME)*
3. *Mount Desert Rock*

155

CHAPTER 5 – LIGHTHOUSES & LIGHTSHIPS

4. *Goose Rocks (North Haven, ME)*
5. *Seguin Island*
6. *Portland Head (Portland, ME)*
7. *Portsmouth Harbor (Portsmouth, NH)*
8. *Thacher Island (Rockport, ME)*
9. *Boston Harbor (Boston, MA)*
10. *Long Point (Provincetown, MA)*
11. *Sankaty Head (Siasconset, MA)*
12. *Edgartown Harbor (Edgartown, MA)*
13. *Butler Flats (New Bedford, MA)*
14. *Beavertail (Jamestown, RI)*
15. *Montauk (Long Island, NY)*
16. *New London Harbor (New London, CT)*
17. *Five-Mile Point (New Haven, CT)*
18. *Statue of Liberty (New York, NY)*
19. *Sandy Hook (Highlands, NJ)*
20. *Barnegat*
21. *Absecon (Atlantic City, NJ)*
22. *Cape May (Cape May, NJ)*
23. *Harbor of Refuge (Lewes, DE)*
24. *Baltimore Harbor (Baltimore, MD)*
25. *Bloody Bar*
26. *Assateague*

West Quoddy Head on the Canadian border is a perfect place to start your exploration of America's lighthouse history. U.S. Highway 1 will be your main route and reference point, with side routes such as U.S. Highway 6 to Cape Cod, New York Route 27 to Montauk, and U.S. Highway 9 along the New Jersey coastline.

NEW LONDON HARBOR LIGHTHOUSE

Established in 1760, making it Connecticut's oldest lighthouse, the current New London Harbor Lighthouse (or more properly New London Harbor Light) was constructed in 1801. Automated in 1912, the lighthouse is still an active aid to navigation. *Address:* New London Harbor Light *City:* New London *State:* CT *Phone:* 860-447-2501 *Web:* www.nlmaritimesociety.org *Visitors welcome?* Yes *Hours:* Contact attraction directly *Admission:* Contact attraction directly *Operated by:* New London Maritime Society *NR?* Yes *NHL?* No *Year established/built:* 1760 *Latitude:* 41.3167 *Latitude:* -72.0900

NEW LONDON LEDGE LIGHTHOUSE

Established and built in 1909, the New London Ledge Lighthouse was automated in 1909 and is still an active aid to navigation. *Address:* New London Ledge Light *City:* New London *State:* CT *Visitors welcome?* Yes *Hours:* By appointment *Admission:* By appointment *Operated by:* New London Ledge Lighthouse Foundation *NR?* Yes *NHL?* No *Year established/built:* 1909 *Latitude:* 41.3061 *Latitude:* -72.0773

PECK LEDGE LIGHTHOUSE

Established and built in 1906, the Peck Ledge Lighthouse was automated in 1993 and is still an active aid to navigation. *Address:* Norwalk Harbor *City:* Norwalk *State:* CT *Visitors welcome?* No *Operated by:* U.S. Coast Guard (District 1) *NR?* Yes *NHL?* No *Year established/built:* 1906 *Latitude:* 41.0757 *Latitude:* -73.3694

PENFIELD REEF LIGHTHOUSE
Established and built in 1874, the Penfield Reef Lighthouse was automated in 1971 and is still an active aid to navigation. *Address:* Penfield Reef Light *City:* Fairfield *State:* CT *Visitors welcome?* Yes *Hours:* Contact attraction directly *Admission:* Contact attraction directly *Operated by:* Beacon Preservation *NR?* Yes *NHL?* No *Year established/built:* 1874 *Latitude:* 41.1163 *Latitude:* -73.2218

SAYBROOK BREAKWATER LIGHTHOUSE
Established and built in 1886, the Saybrook Breakwater Lighthouse was automated in 1959 and is still an active aid to navigation. *Address:* Saybrook Breakwater Light *City:* Fenwick *State:* CT *Visitors welcome?* Yes *Hours:* No public access to tower *Admission:* No public access to tower *Operated by:* U.S. Coast Guard (District 1) *NR?* Yes *NHL?* No *Year established/built:* 1886 *Latitude:* 41.2632 *Latitude:* -72.3428

SHEFFIELD ISLAND LIGHTHOUSE
Established in 1828, the current Sheffield Island Lighthouse, also called the Norwalk Lighthouse, was constructed in 1868 and deactivated in 1902. *Address:* Sheffield Island Light *City:* South Norwalk *State:* CT *Phone:* 203-838-9444 *Web:* www.seaport.org *Email:* info@seaport.org *Visitors welcome?* Yes *Hours:* Contact attraction directly *Admission:* Contact attraction directly *Operated by:* Norwalk Seaport Association *NR?* Yes *NHL?* No *Year established/built:* 1828 *Latitude:* 41.0488 *Latitude:* -73.4191

SOUTHWEST LEDGE LIGHTHOUSE
Established and built in 1877, the Southwest Ledge Lighthouse, also called the New Haven Breakwater Lighthouse, was automated in 1973 and is still an active aid to navigation. *Address:* Southwest Ledge Light *City:* West Haven *State:* CT *Visitors welcome?* No *Operated by:* U.S. Coast Guard (District 1) *NR?* Yes *NHL?* No *Year established/built:* 1877 *Latitude:* 41.2350 *Latitude:* -72.9116

STAMFORD HARBOR LIGHTHOUSE
Established and built in 1882, the Stamford Harbor Lighthouse, also called the Chatham Rocks Lighthouse, was deactivated in 1953. It is now in private hands. *Address:* Samford Harbor *City:* Stamford *State:* CT *Visitors welcome?* No *Operated by:* Private owner *NR?* Yes *NHL?* No *Year established/built:* 1882 *Latitude:* 41.0534 *Latitude:* -73.5387

STONINGTON HARBOR LIGHTHOUSE
Established in 1823, the current Stonington Harbor Lighthouse was constructed in 1840 and deactivated in 1889. It is now a local history museum. *Address:* 7 Water Street *City:* Stonington *State:* CT *Zip:* 06378 *Phone:* 860-535-1440 *Web:* www.stoningtonhistory.org *Email:* lighthouse@stoningtonhistory.org *Visitors welcome?* Yes *Hours:* Daily, May to October, 10 a.m to 5 p.m. *Admission:* Contact attraction directly *Operated by:* Stonington Historical Society *NR?* Yes *NHL?* No *Year established/built:* 1823 *Latitude:* 41.3286 *Latitude:* -71.9059

STRATFORD POINT LIGHTHOUSE
Established in 1822, the current Stratford Point Lighthouse was constructed in 1881. Automated in 1970, the lighthouse is still an active aid to navigation. *Address:* Stratford Point Light *City:* Bridgeport *State:* CT *Visitors welcome?* No *Operated by:* U.S. Coast Guard (District 1) *NR?* Yes *NHL?* No *Year established/built:* 1822 *Latitude:* 41.1515 *Latitude:* -73.1044

TONGUE POINT LIGHTHOUSE
Established and built in 1895, the Tongue Point Lighthouse--called locally The Bug--is still an active aid to navigation. *Address:* Tongue Point Light *City:* Bridgeport *State:* CT *Visitors welcome?* No *Operated by:* U.S. Coast Guard (District 1) *NR?* No *NHL?* No *Year established/built:* 1895 *Latitude:* 41.1667 *Latitude:* -73.1775

DELAWARE

BAKER SHOAL RANGE REAR LIGHTHOUSE
Established and built in 1904 as one of three range lights, the Baker Shoal Range Rear Lighthouse was automated in 1924 and later abandoned. *Address:* Baker Shoal Range Rear Light *City:* Port Penn *State:* DE *Visitors welcome?* No *Operated by:* U.S. Coast Guard (District 1) *NR?* No *NHL?* No *Year established/built:* 1904 *Latitude:* 39.5416 *Latitude:* -75.5701

BELLEVUE REAR RANGE LIGHTHOUSE
Established in 1834, the current Bellevue Rear Range Lighthouse was constructed in 1909. It is now deactivated. *Address:* Bellevue Rear Range Light *City:* Wilmington *State:* DE *Visitors welcome?* No *Operated by:* U.S. Coast Guard (District 1) *NR?* Yes *NHL?* No *Year established/built:* 1834 *Latitude:* 39.7201 *Latitude:* -75.5181

CHERRY ISLAND RANGE LIGHTHOUSE
Established and built in 1880, the Cherry Island Range Lighthouse was demolished in 1970, leaving a skeletal tower. *Address:* Cherry Island *City:* Edgemoor *State:* DE *Visitors welcome?* No *Operated by:* U.S. Coast Guard (District 1) *NR?* No *NHL?* No *Year established/built:* 1880 *Latitude:* 39.7296 *Latitude:* -75.5166

DELAWARE BREAKWATER LIGHTHOUSE
Established and built in 1885, the Delaware Breakwater Lighthouse was deactivated in 1996. It is now managed by a local not-for-profit organization. *Address:* Delaware Breakwater Light *City:* Lewes *State:* DE *Visitors welcome?* Yes *Hours:* By appointment *Admission:* By appointment *Operated by:* Delaware River & Bay Lighthouse Foundation *NR?* Yes *NHL?* No *Year established/built:* 1885 *Latitude:* 38.7971 *Latitude:* -75.0999

FENWICK ISLAND LIGHTHOUSE
Established and built in 1859, the Fenwick Island Lighthouse was inactive from 1978-1982, when it was relighted. It is now an active aid to navigation and a museum. *Address:* 146th Street and Lighthouse Avenue *City:* Fenwick Island *State:* DE *Phone:* 302-436-8100 *Web:* fenwickislandlighthouse.org *Email:* wlewis@fenwickislandlighthouse.org *Visitors welcome?* Yes *Hours:* Daily, weather permitting *Admission:* Donation *Operated by:* New Friends of Fenwick Island Lighthouse *NR?* Yes *NHL?* No *Year established/built:* 1859 *Latitude:* 38.4512 *Latitude:* -75.0548

FOURTEEN FOOT BANK LIGHTHOUSE
Established in 1876, the Fourteen Foot Bank Lighthouse became operational in 1888 as the country's first caisson lighthouse structure. Automated in 1972, the lighthouse is still an active aid to navigation. *Address:* Fourteen Foot Bank Light *City:* Bowers Beach *State:* DE *Visitors welcome?* No *Operated by:* Private owner *NR?* Yes *NHL?* No *Year established/built:* 1876 *Latitude:* 39.0482 *Latitude:* -75.1836

HARBOR OF REFUGE LIGHTHOUSE
Established in 1896, the current Harbor of Refuge Breakwater Lighthouse, also called the South Breakwater Lighthouse, was constructed in 1926. Automated in 1973, the lighthouse is still an active aid to navigation managed by a local not-for-profit organization. *Address:* Harbor of Refuge Light *City:* Lewes *State:* DE *Visitors welcome?* Yes *Hours:* By appointment *Admission:* By appointment *Operated by:* Delaware River & Bay Lighthouse Foundation *NR?* Yes *NHL?* No *Year established/built:* 1896 *Latitude:* 38.8146 *Latitude:* -75.0924

LISTON FRONT RANGE LIGHTHOUSE
Built in 1904 to replace older range lights, the Liston Front Range Light marks the mouth of the Delaware River. The lighthouse was sold to a private party in 1954. *Address:* Liston Range Front Light *City:* Port Penn

State: DE *Visitors welcome?* No *Operated by:* Private owner *NR?* No *NHL?* No *Year established/built:* 1904 *Latitude:* 39.4829 *Latitude:* -75.5920

LISTON REAR RANGE LIGHTHOUSE
Built in 1877, the Liston Rear Range Lighthouse once served as the Port Penn Rear Range Light and it is still an active aid to navigation. *Address:* Liston Range Rear Light *City:* Biddle's Corner *State:* DE *Visitors welcome?* No *Operated by:* Private owner *NR?* Yes *NHL?* No *Year established/built:* 1877 *Latitude:* 39.5239 *Latitude:* -75.6390

MARCUS HOOK RANGE LIGHTHOUSES
Established and built in 1918, the Marcus Hook Range Lighthouses are still active aids to navigation. The range rear light is 1.5 miles southwest of the front range light. *Address:* Marcus Hook Range Rear Light *City:* Edgemoor *State:* DE *Visitors welcome?* No *Operated by:* U.S. Coast Guard (District 1) *NR?* Yes *NHL?* No *Year established/built:* 1918 *Latitude:* 39.7621 *Latitude:* -75.5031

MISPILLION RIVER LIGHTHOUSE
Established in 1831, the current Mispillion River Lighthouse was constructed in 1873 and deactivated in 1929. *Address:* Mispillion Light *State:* DE *Visitors welcome?* No *Operated by:* Delaware Dept. of Natural Resources & Environmental Control *NR?* Yes *NHL?* No *Year established/built:* 1831 *Latitude:* 38.9473 *Latitude:* -75.3149

NEW CASTLE RANGE LIGHTHOUSE
Built to mark Bulkhead Shoal on the Delaware River, New Castle Range Lighthouse was built around 1876 as a pair of range lights. The lights were automated around 1925, and the property sold in 1953. The original wooden tower was replaced by a steel tower. *Address:* Bulkhead Shoal *City:* New Castle *State:* DE *Visitors welcome?* No *Operated by:* Private owner *NR?* No *NHL?* No *Year established/built:* 1876 *Latitude:* 39.6168 *Latitude:* -75.5969

REEDY ISLAND RANGE REAR LIGHTHOUSE
Established in 1839, the current Reedy Island Rear Range Lighthouse was built in 1910 and is still an active aid to navigation. *Address:* Reedy Island Range Rear Light *City:* Taylor's Bridge *State:* DE *Visitors welcome?* No *Operated by:* U.S. Coast Guard (District 1) *NR?* Yes *NHL?* No *Year established/built:* 1839 *Latitude:* 39.4064 *Latitude:* -75.5898

FLORIDA

AMELIA ISLAND LIGHTHOUSE
Established in 1839, the Amelia Island Lighthouse originally stood on Cumberland Island in Georgia and was moved to its current location in 1820. The lighthouse was automated in 1956 and is still an active aid to navigation. *Address:* Amelia Island Light *City:* Fernandina Beach *State:* FL *Phone:* 904-277-7305 *Visitors welcome?* Yes *Hours:* By appointment *Admission:* Contact attraction directly *Operated by:* City of Fernandina Beach *NR?* Yes *NHL?* No *Year established/built:* 1839 *Latitude:* 30.6732 *Latitude:* -81.4424

CAPE CANAVERAL LIGHTHOUSE
The Cape Canaveral Lighthouse has witnessed more than maritime history; it has seen the launch of the space age, starting with the first rocket tests in 1950. *Address:* Cape Canaveral Light *City:* Cape Canaveral *State:* FL

CHAPTER 5 – LIGHTHOUSES & LIGHTSHIPS

Visitors welcome? No *Operated by:* Cape Canaveral Lighthouse Foundation *NR?* No *NHL?* No *Year established/built:* 1848 *Latitude:* 28.4580 *Latitude:* -80.5445

CAPE FLORIDA LIGHTHOUSE
Established in 1825, the current Cape Florida Lighthouse was constructed in 1846 and automated in 1978. It still functions as a private aid to navigation. *Address:* Cape Florida Light *City:* Key Biscayne *State:* FL *Phone:* 305-361-5811 *Visitors welcome?* Yes *Hours:* Contact attraction directly *Admission:* Contact attraction directly *Operated by:* Florida Division of Recreation and Parks *NR?* Yes *NHL?* No *Year established/built:* 1825 *Latitude:* 25.6666 *Latitude:* -80.1560

CARYSFORT REEF LIGHTHOUSE
Established in 1825, the current Carysfort Reef Lighthouse was the first screwpile lighthouse built in on the Florida Keys in 1852. Automated in 1960, the light is still an active aid to navigation. *Address:* Carysfort Reef Light *City:* Key Largo *State:* FL *Visitors welcome?* No *Operated by:* U.S. Coast Guard (District 7) *NR?* Yes *NHL?* No *Year established/built:* 1825 *Latitude:* 25.2217 *Latitude:* -80.2117

DRY TORTUGAS LIGHTHOUSE
Established and built in 1858, the Dry Tortugas Lighthouse, also known as Loggerhead Key Lighthouse, is part of the Dry Tortugas National Park. It is still an active aid to navigation. *Address:* Dry Tortugas Light *City:* Key West *State:* FL *Phone:* 305-242-7700 *Visitors welcome?* Yes *Hours:* By permit *Admission:* By permit *Operated by:* Dry Tortugas National Park *NR?* No *NHL?* No *Year established/built:* 1858 *Latitude:* 24.6333 *Latitude:* -82.9200

FOWEY ROCKS LIGHTHOUSE
Established and built in 1878, the Fowey Rocks Lighthouse was automated in 1974 and is still an active aid to navigation. *Address:* Fowey Rocks Light *City:* Key Biscayne *State:* FL *Visitors welcome?* No *Operated by:* U.S. Coast Guard (District 7) *NR?* No *NHL?* No *Year established/built:* 1878 *Latitude:* 25.5900 *Latitude:* -80.0967

HILLSBORO INLET LIGHTHOUSE
Established and built in 1907, the Hillsboro Inlet Lighthouse was automated in 1974 and is still an active aid to navigation. *Address:* Hillsboro Inlet *City:* Pompano Beach *State:* FL *Phone:* 954-942-2102 *Web:* www.hillsborolighthouse.org *Email:* info@hillsborolighthouse.org *Visitors welcome?* Yes *Hours:* By appointment *Admission:* Contact attraction directly *Operated by:* Hillsboro Lighthouse Preservation Society *NR?* Yes *NHL?* No *Year established/built:* 1907 *Latitude:* 26.2598 *Latitude:* -80.0826

JUPITER INLET LIGHTHOUSE
Established and built in 1860, the Jupiter Inlet Lighthouse was automated in 1987 and is still an active aid to navigation. A museum is in the historic oil house. *Address:* 500 Captain Armour's Way *City:* Jupiter *State:* FL *Zip:* 33469 *Phone:* 561-747-8380 *Email:* visit@lrhs.org *Visitors welcome?* Yes *Hours:* Tuesday to Sunday, 10 a.m. to 5 p.m. *Admission:* $7 adults; $5 children age 6-18; FREE 5 and under *Operated by:* Loxahatchee River Historical Society *NR?* Yes *NHL?* No *Year established/built:* 1860 *Latitude:* 26.9501 *Latitude:* -80.0818

✤ PONCE DE LEON INLET LIGHTHOUSE
Established in 1835, the Ponce de Leon Inlet Lighthouse, also called the Mosquito Inlet Lighthouse, was constructed in 1887. Automated in 1953, the light is still an active aid to navigation. *Address:* 4931 South Peninsula Drive *City:* Ponce Inlet *State:* FL *Zip:* 32127 *Phone:* 386-761-1821 *Web:* www.ponceinlet.org *Email:* lighthouse@ponceinlet.org *Visitors welcome?* Yes *Hours:* Daily, 10 a.m. to 6 p.m. *Admission:* $5 adults, $1.50

children 11 and under *Operated by:* Ponce de Leon Inlet Light Station Preservation Association *NR?* Yes *NHL?* Yes *Year established/built:* 1835 *Latitude:* 29.0807 *Latitude:* -80.9281

ST. AUGUSTINE LIGHTHOUSE

Established in 1823, the current St. Augustine Lighthouse was constructed in 1874 and automated in 1955. Still an active aid to navigation, the lighthouse is now part of a major museum. *Address:* 81 Lighthouse Avenue *City:* St. Augustine *State:* FL *Zip:* 32080 *Phone:* 904-829-0745 *Web:* www.staugustinelighthouse.com *Email:* info@staugustinelighthouse.com *Visitors welcome?* Yes *Hours:* Daily, 9 a.m. to 7 p.m. *Admission:* $9 adults; $8 seniors; $7 children 6 to 11; under six FREE *Operated by:* St. Augustine Lighthouse *NR?* Yes *NHL?* No *Year established/built:* 1823 *Latitude:* 29.8856 *Latitude:* -81.2886

ST. JOHNS LIGHTHOUSE

Replacing a lightship in 1954, St. Johns Lighthouse first housed its light inside a Plexiglas dome. Later, the lamp was modernized and the dome removed. The light was automated in 1967. *Address:* St. Johns Light *City:* East Mayport *State:* FL *Phone:* 904-270-5226 *Visitors welcome?* Yes *Hours:* Contact attraction directly *Admission:* FREE *Operated by:* U.S. Coast Guard (District 7) *NR?* No *NHL?* No *Year established/built:* 1954 *Latitude:* 30.3861 *Latitude:* -81.3981

ST. JOHNS RIVER LIGHTHOUSE

Established in 1830, the current St. Johns River Lighthouse, also known as the Mayport Lighthouse, is no longer operational. *Address:* St. Johns River Light *City:* Mayport *State:* FL *Phone:* 904-270-5226 *Visitors welcome?* Yes *Hours:* Contact attraction directly *Admission:* Contact attraction directly *Operated by:* U.S. Coast Guard (District 7) *NR?* Yes *NHL?* No *Year established/built:* 1830 *Latitude:* 30.3935 *Latitude:* -81.4260

ST. JOSEPH POINT REAR RANGE LIGHTHOUSE

Established and built in 1902, the St. Joseph Point Rear Range Lighthouse was deactivated in 1960 and is now a private residence. *Address:* 2071 County Road 30 *City:* Simmons Bayou *State:* FL *Visitors welcome?* No *Operated by:* Private owner *NR?* No *NHL?* No *Year established/built:* 1902 *Latitude:* 27.6648 *Latitude:* -81.5158

GEORGIA

COCKSPUR ISLAND LIGHTHOUSE

Established in 1772, the current Cockspur Island Lighthouse in 1857 and deactivated in 1909. It is now part of the Fort Pulaski National Monument. *Address:* Cockspur Island Light *City:* Savannah *State:* GA *Visitors welcome?* Yes *Hours:* Daily, 8:30 a.m. to 5 p.m. (Grounds only) *Admission:* FREE *Operated by:* Fort Pulaski National Monument *NR?* Yes *NHL?* No *Year established/built:* 1772 *Latitude:* 32.0227 *Latitude:* -80.8799

LITTLE CUMBERLAND ISLAND LIGHTHOUSE

Established and built in 1838, the Little Cumberland Island Lighthouse is now privately owned. It was renovated by the owners in 1998. *Address:* Little Cumberland Island Light *City:* Cumberland Island *State:* GA *Visitors welcome?* No *Operated by:* Private owner *NR?* Yes *NHL?* No *Year established/built:* 1838 *Latitude:* 30.9740 *Latitude:* -81.4168

SAPELO ISLAND FRONT RANGE LIGHTHOUSE

In 1868, a wooden frame beacon was constructed about 600 feet east of the Sapelo Lighthouse to serve as a front range light at Doboy Sound. A cast-iron tower replaced it in 1878. It is now owned by the State of

CHAPTER 5 – LIGHTHOUSES & LIGHTSHIPS

George Parks Department. *Address:* Sapelo Island *State:* GA *Phone:* 912-437-3224 *Visitors welcome?* Yes *Hours:* Tuesday to Friday 7:30 a.m. to 5:30 p.m.; Saturday 8 a.m. to 5:30 p.m.; Sunday 1:30 to 5 p.m. *Admission:* Contact attraction directly *Operated by:* Georgia State Parks and Historic Sites *NR?* No *NHL?* No *Year established/built:* 1868 *Latitude:* 31.3974 *Latitude:* -81.2787

SAPELO ISLAND LIGHTHOUSE
Established and built in 1820, the Sapelo Island Lighthouse was deactivated from 1899 to 1998. It is now an active aid to navigation. *Address:* Sapelo Island Light *City:* Sapelo Island *State:* GA *Phone:* 912-437-3224 *Visitors welcome?* Yes *Hours:* Tuesday to Friday 7:30 a.m. to 5:30 p.m.; Saturday 8 a.m. to 5:30 p.m.; Sunday 1:30 to 5 p.m. *Admission:* Contact attraction directly *Operated by:* Georgia State Parks and Historic Sites *NR?* Yes *NHL?* No *Year established/built:* 1820 *Latitude:* 31.3920 *Latitude:* -81.2852

SAVANNAH HARBOR LIGHT
The Savannah Harbor Light, also called the Old Harbor Light, is a cast-iron lamp was installed in 1858 to guide ships into Savannah Harbor. The light was restored in 2001. *Address:* Emmet Park *City:* Savannah *State:* GA *Visitors welcome?* Yes *Hours:* Daily *Admission:* FREE *Operated by:* City of Savannah *NR?* No *NHL?* No *Year established/built:* 1858 *Latitude:* 32.0796 *Latitude:* -81.0853

✛ ST. SIMONS LSLAND LIGHTHOUSE
Established in 1811, the current St. Simons Island Lighthouse was constructed in 1872. Automated in 1954, the lighthouse is still an active aid to navigation. It is now operated as a museum by a Georgia not-for-profit group. *Address:* St. Simons Island Light *City:* St. Simons Island *State:* GA *Zip:* 31522 *Phone:* 912-638-4666 *Web:* www.saintsimonslighthouse.org *Email:* ssi1872@comcast.net *Visitors welcome?* Yes *Hours:* Monday to Saturday 10 a.m. to 5 p.m.; Sunday, 1:30 p.m. to 5 p.m. *Admission:* $6 adults; $3 children; under six FREE *Operated by:* Coastal Georgia Historical Society *NR?* Yes *NHL?* No *Year established/built:* 1811 *Latitude:* 31.1334 *Latitude:* -81.3933

TYBEE ISLAND LIGHTHOUSE
Established in 1736, the current Tybee Island Lighthouse was constructed in 1867. Automated in 1972, the lighthouse is still an active aid to navigation. It is now part of the Fort Screven National Historic District. *Address:* 30 Meddin Drive *City:* Tybee Island *State:* GA *Zip:* 31328 *Phone:* 912-786-5801 *Web:* www.tybeelighthouse.org *Visitors welcome?* Yes *Hours:* Daily, except Tuesday, from 9 a.m. to 5:30 p.m. *Admission:* $6 adults; $5 seniors, children, active military; children under five, FREE *Operated by:* Tybee Island Light Station *NR?* Yes *NHL?* No *Year established/built:* 1736 *Latitude:* 32.0225 *Latitude:* -80.8448

MAINE

BAKER ISLAND LIGHTHOUSE
Established in 1828, the original tower was replaced by the current tower in 1855. The light was automated in 1957. *Address:* Baker Island *City:* Seal Harbor *State:* ME *Visitors welcome?* Yes *Hours:* Grounds only *Admission:* FREE *Operated by:* U.S. Coast Guard (District 1) *NR?* Yes *NHL?* No *Year established/built:* 1828 *Latitude:* 44.2413 *Latitude:* -68.2018

BASS HARBOR HEAD LIGHTHOUSE
Built to guide ships into Blue Hill Bay, Bass Harbor Lighthouse was first lit in 1858. The light was automated in 1974 and was incorporated in Acadia National Park. *Address:* Bass Harbor Head Light *City:* Bass

Harbor *State:* ME *Visitors welcome?* Yes *Hours:* Grounds only *Admission:* FREE *Operated by:* U.S. Coast Guard (District 1) *NR?* Yes *NHL?* No *Year established/built:* 1858 *Latitude:* 44.2219 *Latitude:* -68.3372

BEAR ISLAND LIGHTHOUSE
The Bear Island Lighthouse was established in 1839. The present structure was built in 1889. The light was discontinued in 1989 and transferred to the National Park Service, which leases the light station property to a private individual. *Address:* Bear Island *City:* Northeast Harbor *State:* ME *Visitors welcome?* No *Operated by:* Private owner *NR?* Yes *NHL?* No *Year established/built:* 1839 *Latitude:* 44.2842 *Latitude:* -68.2678

BLUE HILL BAY LIGHTHOUSE
Originally established in 1856, Blue Hill Bay Lighthouse on Green Island was once known as Eggemogin Lighthouse for nearby Eggemogin Reach. Deactivated in 1933, the structure was replaced by an automated beacon on a steel tower, which is still in use. *Address:* Green Island *State:* ME *Visitors welcome?* No *Operated by:* Private owner *NR?* No *NHL?* No *Year established/built:* 1856 *Latitude:* 44.5623 *Latitude:* -67.4439

BOON ISLAND LIGHTHOUSE
The light station was established in 1799 with a daymark, and the first lighthouse was built in 1811. The present structure was constructed in 1855. The lighthouse was automated in 1978 and is now maintained by the American Lighthouse Foundation. *Address:* Boon Island Light *City:* York *State:* ME *Visitors welcome?* No *Operated by:* American Lighthouse Foundation *NR?* Yes *NHL?* No *Year established/built:* 1799 *Latitude:* 43.1217 *Latitude:* -70.4767

BROWNS HEAD LIGHTHOUSE
Located on Vinalhaven Island, the Browns Head Lighthouse was established in 1832, with the present structure built in 1857. The light was discontinued and the keeper's dwelling is now occupied by the Vinalhaven town manager. *Address:* Browns Head *City:* Vinalhaven *State:* ME *Visitors welcome?* No *Operated by:* Town of Vinalhaven *NR?* Yes *NHL?* No *Year established/built:* 1832 *Latitude:* 44.1117 *Latitude:* -68.9106

BURNT COAT HARBOR LIGHTHOUSE
The lighthouse, built in 1872 at Hockamock Head, marks the entrance to Burnt Coat Harbor, one of the best protected harbors on the Maine coast. Originally two range lights, the front range light was shut down in 1884. The light was automated in 1974. *Address:* Burnt Coat Harbor Light *City:* Swan's Island *State:* ME *Zip:* 04685 *Visitors welcome?* Yes *Hours:* Grounds only *Admission:* FREE *Operated by:* Swan's Island Lighthouse Committee *NR?* Yes *NHL?* No *Year established/built:* 1872 *Latitude:* 44.1341 *Latitude:* -68.4472

BURNT ISLAND LIGHTHOUSE
Built in 1821, the lighthouse is still an active aid to navigation, though it is now owned by the Maine Department of Marine Resources. The historic buildings at this lighthouse station have been carefully restored and transformed. *Address:* Burnt Island Light *City:* Boothbay Harbor *State:* ME *Phone:* 207-633-9559 *Web:* www.maine.gov/dmr/burntisland/ *Visitors welcome?* Yes *Hours:* Contact attraction directly *Admission:* Contact attraction directly *Operated by:* Maine Department of Marine Resources *NR?* Yes *NHL?* No *Year established/built:* 1821 *Latitude:* 43.8252 *Latitude:* -69.6402

CAPE ELIZABETH LIGHTHOUSE
The Cape Elizabeth Lighthouse enjoys the distinction of having two towers, first constructed in 1828. In 1873, the rubblestone structures were replaced with cast-iron towers. The west tower was decommissioned in 1924, and the east tower still shows a light. *Address:* Cape Elizabeth Lights *City:* Cape Elizabeth *State:* ME *Visitors welcome?* No *Operated by:* American Lighthouse Foundation *NR?* No *NHL?* No *Year established/built:* 1828 *Latitude:* 43.5661 *Latitude:* -70.2001

CHAPTER 5 – LIGHTHOUSES & LIGHTSHIPS

CAPE NEDDICK LIGHTHOUSE

Lit in 1879 on a tiny island off the mainland called the Nubble Cape Neddick Lighthouse is now part of a park owned by the Town of York. The light still serves as an active aid to navigation. *Address:* Cape Neddick Light *City:* York *State:* ME *Zip:* 03909 *Phone:* 207-363-1000 *Visitors welcome?* Yes *Hours:* Daily, early May to Columbus Day *Admission:* Contact attraction directly *Operated by:* Friends of Nubble Light *NR?* Yes *NHL?* No *Year established/built:* 1879 *Latitude:* 43.1653 *Latitude:* -70.5911

CUCKOLDS ISLAND LIGHTHOUSE

The Cuckolds Island Light Station was established in 1892, though the lighthouse itself was built in 1907. Automated in 1974, the station is now undergoing restoration. *Address:* Southport Island *City:* Boothbay Harbor *State:* ME *Visitors welcome?* No *Operated by:* Cuckolds Island Fog Signal and Light Station Council *NR?* Yes *NHL?* No *Year established/built:* 1892 *Latitude:* 43.8212 *Latitude:* -69.6645

CURTIS ISLAND LIGHTHOUSE

The Curtis Island Lighthouse was established in 1835, and the present structure was constructed in 1896. The station was automated in 1972 and the grounds are now a public park. *Address:* Curtis Island Light *City:* Camden *State:* ME *Zip:* 04843 *Phone:* 207-236-3353 *Visitors welcome?* Yes *Hours:* Grounds only *Admission:* FREE *Operated by:* Town of Camden *NR?* Yes *NHL?* No *Year established/built:* 1835 *Latitude:* 44.2014 *Latitude:* -69.0489

DEER ISLAND THOROFARE LIGHTHOUSE

The Deer Island Thorofare Lighthouse was established in 1858 and the present structure was constructed the same year. The station was automated in 1958 and is now privately owned. *Address:* Mark Island *City:* Stonington *State:* ME *Visitors welcome?* Yes *Hours:* Grounds only *Admission:* FREE *Operated by:* Island Heritage Trust *NR?* No *NHL?* No *Year established/built:* 1858 *Latitude:* 44.1337 *Latitude:* -68.7022

DICE HEAD LIGHTHOUSE

Constructed in 1829 at the mouth of the Penobscot River, the lighthouse stands near places that changed hands between the French and British numerous times in the 17th century. Now inactive, the lighthouse is undergoing restoration. *Address:* Dice Head Light *City:* Castine *State:* ME *Visitors welcome?* Yes *Hours:* Grounds only *Admission:* FREE *Operated by:* Town of Castine *NR?* No *NHL?* No *Year established/built:* 1829 *Latitude:* 44.3827 *Latitude:* -68.8188

DOUBLING POINT LIGHTHOUSE

Doubling Point Lighthouse was built in 1898 on Arrowsic Island on the Kennebec River in Maine. It was one of four lighthouses built that year to provide navigational aid for ships on their way to Bath. The lighthouse is now owned by a not-for-profit group. *Address:* Doubling Point Light *City:* Arrowsic *State:* ME *Zip:* 04530 *Web:* www.doublingpoint.org *Email:* mspencer@student.uchc.edu *Visitors welcome?* Yes *Hours:* Contact attraction directly *Admission:* Contact attraction directly *Operated by:* Friends of the Doubling Point Light *NR?* Yes *NHL?* No *Year established/built:* 1898 *Latitude:* 43.8825 *Latitude:* -69.8068

EAGLE ISLAND LIGHTHOUSE

The Eagle Island Lighthouse is located on one of several islands along the Maine coast named after the majestic birds. This Eagle Island is at East Penobscot Bay. The lighthouse was established in 1839 and the current tower was built the same year. *Address:* Eagle Island Light *City:* Eagle Island *State:* ME *Visitors welcome?* Yes *Hours:* Grounds only *Admission:* FREE *Operated by:* Eagle Light Caretakers *NR?* No *NHL?* No *Year established/built:* 1839 *Latitude:* 44.5040 *Latitude:* -67.7553

EGG ROCK LIGHTHOUSE
Egg Rock Lighthouse was constructed in 1875. It was automated in 1976 and is an active aid to navigation. *Address:* Frenchman's Bay *City:* Bar Harbor *State:* ME *Visitors welcome?* No *Operated by:* Maine Coastal Islands National Wildlife Refuge *NR?* Yes *NHL?* No *Year established/built:* 1875 *Latitude:* 44.3876 *Latitude:* -68.2039

FORT POINT LIGHTHOUSE
The Fort Point Lighthouse was established in 1836 and the current structure built in 1857. The lighthouse was automated in 1988 and is now within a state park. *Address:* Fort Point State Park *City:* Stockton Springs *State:* ME *Phone:* 207-567-3356 *Visitors welcome?* Yes *Hours:* Grounds only *Admission:* FREE *Operated by:* Maine Bureau of Parks and Lands *NR?* Yes *NHL?* No *Year established/built:* 1836 *Latitude:* 44.4668 *Latitude:* -68.8253

FRANKLIN ISLAND LIGHTHOUSE
The Franklin Island Lighthouse was established in 1807 and the current structure was built in 1855. The light was automated in 1933, and the facility is maintained by a local not-for-profit. *Address:* Franklin Island *State:* ME *Visitors welcome?* Yes *Hours:* Grounds only *Admission:* FREE *Operated by:* Franklin Light Preservation Inc. *NR?* No *NHL?* No *Year established/built:* 1807 *Latitude:* 43.8918 *Latitude:* -69.3737

GOAT ISLAND LIGHTHOUSE
The Goat Island Lighthouse was established in 1833 and the present structure built in 1859. It was automated in 1990 and is an active aid to navigation. *Address:* Goat Island Light *City:* Cape Porpoise *State:* ME *Visitors welcome?* Yes *Hours:* Grounds only *Admission:* FREE *Operated by:* Kennebunkport Conservation Trust *NR?* Yes *NHL?* No *Year established/built:* 1833 *Latitude:* 43.3578 *Latitude:* -70.4250

GOOSE ROCKS LIGHTHOUSE
The cast-iron Goose Rocks Lighthouse was established and built in 1890. The U.S. Coast Guard automated it in 1964. *Address:* Goose Rocks Light *City:* North Haven *State:* ME *Phone:* 203-736-9300 *Web:* www.beaconpreservation.org *Email:* info@beaconpreservation.org *Visitors welcome?* Yes *Hours:* By appointment *Admission:* Contact attraction directly *Operated by:* Beacon Preservation *NR?* Yes *NHL?* No *Year established/built:* 1890 *Latitude:* 44.1354 *Latitude:* -68.8307

Are you volunteering at a not-for-profit organization raising money for a lighthouse restoration project? Email your plans to contact@fyddeye.com.

GREAT DUCK ISLAND LIGHTHOUSE
The Great Duck Island Lighthouse was established and built in 1890. The U.S. Coast Guard automated it in 1986. *Address:* Great Duck Island Light *City:* Frenchboro *State:* ME *Visitors welcome?* No *Operated by:* College of the Atlantic *NR?* Yes *NHL?* No *Year established/built:* 1890 *Latitude:* 44.1420 *Latitude:* -68.2458

GRINDLE POINT LIGHTHOUSE
The Gringle Point Lighthouse was established in 1851 and the current structure built in 1874. The station was closed in 1934 and relit by the Town of Islesboro in 1987. *Address:* Grindle Point Light *City:* Islesboro *State:* ME *Zip:* 04848 *Phone:* 207-734-2253 *Visitors welcome?* Yes *Hours:* Summer, Saturday and Sunday, 9 a.m. to 4:30 p.m. *Admission:* Contact attraction directly *Operated by:* Town of Islesboro *NR?* Yes *NHL?* No *Year established/built:* 1851 *Latitude:* 44.2814 *Latitude:* -68.9431

CHAPTER 5 – LIGHTHOUSES & LIGHTSHIPS

HALFWAY ROCK LIGHTHOUSE
Halfway Rock is located near the midpoint between Cape Elizabeth and Cape Small in Casco Bay, and it received its lighthouse in 1871 after a series of disastrous shipwrecks. The light was automated in 1975 and the tower was leased to the American Lighthouse Foundation. *Address:* Casco Bay *City:* Portland *State:* ME *Visitors welcome?* No *Operated by:* American Lighthouse Foundation *NR?* Yes *NHL?* No *Year established/built:* 1871 *Latitude:* 43.6555 *Latitude:* -70.0375

HENDRICKS HEAD LIGHTHOUSE
The Hendricks Head Lighthouse was established in 1829, and the current structure was built in 1875. The light was decommissioned in 1933, but after electrical cables were strung to the island in 1951, the U.S. Coast Guard relit the light. *Address:* Hendricks Head *City:* Hendricks Harbor *State:* ME *Visitors welcome?* No *Operated by:* Private owner *NR?* Yes *NHL?* No *Year established/built:* 1829 *Latitude:* 43.8229 *Latitude:* -69.6912

HERON NECK LIGHTHOUSE
Address: Heron Neck Light *City:* Vinalhaven *State:* ME *Visitors welcome?* Yes *Hours:* Grounds only *Admission:* FREE *Operated by:* Island Institute *NR?* Yes *NHL?* No *Year established/built:* 1854 *Latitude:* 44.0251 *Latitude:* -68.8622

INDIAN ISLAND LIGHTHOUSE
The Indian Island Lighthouse was established in 1850 and the current structure put up in 1875. The light was deactivated in 1934 and the property has remained in private hands since. *Address:* Rockport Harbor *City:* Rockport *State:* ME *Visitors welcome?* No *Operated by:* Private owner *NR?* Yes *NHL?* No *Year established/built:* 1850 *Latitude:* 44.1748 *Latitude:* -69.0689

ISLE AU HAUT LIGHTHOUSE
Built of granite the same year it was established, 1907, the Isle au Haut Lighthouse was automated in 1934. It is currently operated as part of a bed and breakfast. *Address:* The Keepers House *City:* Isle au Haut *State:* ME *Phone:* 207-460-0257 *Visitors welcome?* Yes *Hours:* Contact attraction directly *Admission:* Contact attraction directly *Operated by:* Keeper's House Inn *NR?* Yes *NHL?* No *Year established/built:* 1907 *Latitude:* 44.0754 *Latitude:* -68.6334

KENNEBEC RIVER RANGE LIGHTHOUSE
Also known as the Doubling Point Range Lights, the Kennebec River Range Lights guide mariners along a long stretch of the Kennebec River with two sharp turns. Constructed in 1898, the lights were transferred to a not-for-profit group exactly 100 years later. *Address:* Doubling Point Range Lights *City:* Arrowsic *State:* ME *Visitors welcome?* Yes *Hours:* Grounds only *Admission:* FREE *Operated by:* Range Light Keepers *NR?* Yes *NHL?* No *Year established/built:* 1898 *Latitude:* 43.8848 *Latitude:* -69.7957

LADIES DELIGHT LIGHTHOUSE
Located on an island in the northern end of Lake Cobbosseecontee, the Ladies Delight Lighthouse was established and built in 1908. *Address:* Lake Cobbosseecontee *City:* Manchester *State:* ME *Visitors welcome?* No *Operated by:* Cobbosseecontee Yacht Club *NR?* No *NHL?* No *Year established/built:* 1908 *Latitude:* 44.3140 *Latitude:* -69.8916

LIBBY ISLAND LIGHTHOUSE
The Libby Island Lighthouse was established in 1823, with the current struction at the site built the following year. The station was automated in 1974, and it is now part of a national wildlife refuge. *Address:* Machias Bay *City:* Machiasport *State:* ME *Visitors welcome?* Yes *Hours:* Grounds only *Admission:* FREE *Operated by:* Maine

Coastal Islands National Wildlife Refuge *NR?* Yes *NHL?* No *Year established/built:* 1823 *Latitude:* 44.6492 *Latitude:* -67.3410

LITTLE RIVER ISLAND LIGHTHOUSE
The Little River Lighthouse was established in 1847 and the present structure was built in 1876. The light was moved to a steel tower in 1975, but the lighthouse was relit in 2001. *Address:* Little River Island *City:* East Machias *State:* ME *Visitors welcome?* Yes *Hours:* Grounds only after July 15 *Admission:* FREE *Operated by:* Friends of Little River Lighthouse *NR?* Yes *NHL?* No *Year established/built:* 1847 *Latitude:* 44.6509 *Latitude:* -67.1933

LUBEC CHANNEL LIGHTHOUSE
The Lubec Channel Lighthouse is a cast-iron structure of the coffee pot type built in 1890. The station was automated in 1939. *Address:* Lubec Channel Light *City:* Lubec *State:* ME *Visitors welcome?* No *Operated by:* U.S. Coast Guard (District 1) *NR?* Yes *NHL?* No *Year established/built:* 1890 *Latitude:* 44.8421 *Latitude:* -66.9766

MARSHALL POINT LIGHTHOUSE
The first lighthouse at Marshall Point, made of rubblestone, was built in 1832. In 1858 a new tower was built at its present site, at water's edge. The lighthouse was automated in 1971. A not-for-profit now operates a museum and gift shop on the property. *Address:* Marshall Point Road *City:* Port Clyde *State:* ME *Web:* www.marshallpoint.org *Visitors welcome?* Yes *Hours:* May, Saturday and Sunday, 1 p.m. to 5 p.m.; Memorial Day to Columbus Day, Sunday to Friday, 1 p.m. to 5 p.m., Saturday, 10 a.m. to 5 p.m. *Admission:* Contact attraction directly *Operated by:* Marshall Point Lighthouse Museum *NR?* Yes *NHL?* No *Year established/built:* 1832 *Latitude:* 43.9213 *Latitude:* -69.2550

MATINICUS ROCK LIGHTHOUSE
The two-lighthouse Matinicus Rock Light Station was established in 1827, and both current lighthouses were built in 1857. The north light was shut down in 1924, and the south light was automated in 1983. The station is now part of a wildlife refuge. *Address:* Matinicus Rock Light *City:* Matinicus Island *State:* ME *Visitors welcome?* Yes *Hours:* Grounds only *Admission:* FREE *Operated by:* Maine Coastal Islands National Wildlife Refuge *NR?* Yes *NHL?* No *Year established/built:* 1827 *Latitude:* 43.7835 *Latitude:* -68.8550

MONHEGAN ISLAND LIGHTHOUSE
The legendary Monhegan Island Lighthouse holds a prominent place in maritime history; it may have been visited by Phoenicians and Vikings. Local Penobscot Indians also used the island. The lighthouse was established in 1824. *Address:* 1 Lighthouse *City:* Monhegan Island *State:* ME *Email:* museum@monheganmuseum.org *Visitors welcome?* Yes *Hours:* Daily, July 1 to August 31, 11:30 a.m. to 3:30 p.m.; Sept. 1 to Sept. 30, 1:30 p.m. to 3:30 p.m. *Admission:* Contact attraction directly *Operated by:* Monhegan Historical and Cultural Museum Association *NR?* Yes *NHL?* No *Year established/built:* 1824 *Latitude:* 43.7660 *Latitude:* -69.3116

MOOSE PEAK LIGHTHOUSE
Established in 1826 on Mistake Island, the current tower was constructed in 1851. It was automated in 1972. *Address:* Mistake Island *City:* Jonesport *State:* ME *Visitors welcome?* No *Operated by:* U.S. Coast Guard (District 1) *NR?* No *NHL?* No *Year established/built:* 1826 *Latitude:* 44.4748 *Latitude:* -67.5350

MOUNT DESERT LIGHTHOUSE
Mount Desert Rock is a tiny, rock strewn island 26 miles off Bar Harbor, making it one of the desolate lighthouses on the Atlantic shoreline. First built in 1829, the lighthouse had a reputation for making lighthouse keepers mad. *Address:* Mount Desert Light *City:* Yarmouth *State:* ME *Visitors welcome?* No *Operated by:* College of the Atlantic *NR?* Yes *NHL?* No *Year established/built:* 1829 *Latitude:* 43.9686 *Latitude:* -68.1283

CHAPTER 5 – LIGHTHOUSES & LIGHTSHIPS

NARRAGUAGUS ISLAND LIGHTHOUSE
Also known as Pond Island Lighthouse, the Narraguagus Lighthouse was established in 1853, and the current structure was built the same year. The light was discontinued in 1934, though a buoy marks the entrance to Narraguagus Bay formerly marked by the light. *Address:* Pond Island Light *City:* Milbridge *State:* ME *Visitors welcome?* No *Operated by:* Private owner *NR?* Yes *NHL?* No *Year established/built:* 1853 *Latitude:* 43.7400 *Latitude:* -69.7703

NASH ISLAND LIGHTHOUSE
The Nash Island Light Station was established in 1838, and the present structure was built in 1874. The station is now part of the Petit Manan National Wildlife Refuge. *Address:* Nash Island *City:* Addison *State:* ME *Visitors welcome?* Yes *Hours:* Grounds only, September to March *Admission:* FREE *Operated by:* Friends of Nash Island Light *NR?* No *NHL?* No *Year established/built:* 1838 *Latitude:* 44.4640 *Latitude:* -67.7458

OWLS HEAD LIGHTHOUSE
The Owls Head Lighthouse was established and built in 1825. It was automated in 1989. *Address:* Owls Head State Park *City:* Owls Head *State:* ME *Zip:* 04854 *Phone:* 207-941-4014 *Visitors welcome?* Yes *Hours:* Grounds only *Admission:* FREE *Operated by:* American Lighthouse Foundation *NR?* Yes *NHL?* No *Year established/built:* 1825 *Latitude:* 44.0920 *Latitude:* -69.0456

PERKINS ISLAND LIGHTHOUSE
The Perkins Island Lighthouse was established and built in 1898. The station was automated in 1959. *Address:* Perkins Island *City:* Georgetown *State:* ME *Email:* perkinslight@hotmail.com *Visitors welcome?* Yes *Hours:* Grounds only *Admission:* FREE *Operated by:* Friends of Perkins Island Lighthouse *NR?* Yes *NHL?* No *Year established/built:* 1898 *Latitude:* 43.7868 *Latitude:* -69.7837

PERMAQUID POINT LIGHTHOUSE
Constructed in 1827, the original structure was replaced in 1835. In 1934, the light was the first in the U.S. to be automated. *Address:* Pemaquid Point Light *City:* Permaquid *State:* ME *Visitors welcome?* Yes *Hours:* By appointment *Admission:* Contact attraction directly *Operated by:* Friends of Permaquid Point Lighthouse *NR?* Yes *NHL?* No *Year established/built:* 1827 *Latitude:* 43.8370 *Latitude:* -69.5061

PETIT MANAN LIGHTHOUSE
The Petit Manan Lighthouse was established in 1817 and the current tower was built in 1855. The station was automated in 1972 and the island is part of a national wildlife refuge. *Address:* Petit Manan Island *City:* Steuben *State:* ME *Visitors welcome?* Yes *Hours:* Grounds only *Admission:* FREE *Operated by:* Maine Coastal Islands National Wildlife Refuge *NR?* No *NHL?* No *Year established/built:* 1817 *Latitude:* 44.3673 *Latitude:* -67.8653

POND ISLAND LIGHTHOUSE
The Pond Island Lighthouse was established in 1821, and the current structure was built in 1855. The light was automated in 1960, and the grounds are now part of the Pond Island National Wildlife Refuge. *Address:* Pond Island Light *City:* Phippsburg *State:* ME *Visitors welcome?* Yes *Hours:* Grounds only *Admission:* FREE *Operated by:* Pond Island National Wildlife Refuge *NR?* No *NHL?* No *Year established/built:* 1820 *Latitude:* 43.7400 *Latitude:* -69.7703

PORTLAND BREAKWATER LIGHTHOUSE
The Portland Breakwater Lighthouse was constructed in 1854 to mark the end of a breakwater constructed eighteen years before. The brick lighthouse was replaced in 1875 with a cast-iron structure said to mimic a fourth-century B.C. Greek temple. *Address:* Portland Breakwater Light *City:* South Portland *State:* ME *Phone:* 207-767-3201 *Email:* COSP@southportland.org *Visitors welcome?* Yes *Hours:* Grounds only *Admission:* FREE *Operated by:* City of South Portland *NR?* Yes *NHL?* No *Year established/built:* 1854 *Latitude:* 43.6556 *Latitude:* -70.2347

PORTLAND HEAD LIGHTHOUSE

Originally established in 1791, Portland Head Lighthouse tower has stood for more than two hundred years guarding the entrance to Portland Harbor. The property is now leased to the town of Cape Elizabeth, which operates the facility as a museum and public park. *Address:* Portland Head Light *City:* Cape Elizabeth *State:* ME *Zip:* 04107 *Phone:* 207-799-2661 *Web:* www.portlandheadlight.com *Email:* cephl@aol.com *Visitors welcome?* Yes *Hours:* Daily, Memorial Day to the Friday following Columbus Day, 10 a.m. to 4 p.m. *Admission:* $2 adults; $1 children 6-18 *Operated by:* Portland Head Light *NR?* Yes *NHL?* No *Year established/built:* 1791 *Latitude:* 43.6231 *Latitude:* -70.2078

PROSPECT HARBOR LIGHTHOUSE

Established in 1850, the Prospect Harbor Lighthouse dwelling now standing was built in 1891. The light was automated in 1951, and the grounds are owned by the U.S. Navy. *Address:* Prospect Harbor Light *City:* Prospect Harbor *State:* ME *Visitors welcome?* No *Operated by:* American Lighthouse Foundation *NR?* No *NHL?* No *Year established/built:* 1850 *Latitude:* 44.4034 *Latitude:* -68.0130

PUMPKIN ISLAND LIGHTHOUSE

The Pumpkin Island Lighthouse was established in 1855, although the keeper's house was built the year before. The station was decommissioned by the U.S. Coast Guard in 1933. *Address:* Little Deer Isle *City:* Little Deer Isle *State:* ME *Visitors welcome?* No *Operated by:* Private owner *NR?* No *NHL?* No *Year established/built:* 1855 *Latitude:* 44.2906 *Latitude:* -68.7161

RAM ISLAND LEDGE LIGHTHOUSE

An underwater ledge runs from Ram Island at the entrance to Portland Harbor, and the Ram Island Ledge Lighthouse was built in 1905 to mark the hazard. Several ships have been lost on this rocky outcropping. *Address:* Ram Island Ledge Light *City:* Portland *State:* ME *Visitors welcome?* No *Operated by:* American Lighthouse Foundation *NR?* Yes *NHL?* No *Year established/built:* 1905 *Latitude:* 43.6317 *Latitude:* -70.1867

RAM ISLAND LIGHTHOUSE

The Ram Island Lighthouse was established in 1883 and the current structures were built the same year. The station was automated in 1965, and the facility is owned by the Grand Banks Maritime Museum Trust, which also owns the F/V Sherman Zwicker. *Address:* Ram Island Light *City:* Boothbay *State:* ME *Phone:* 207-882-9721 *Web:* www.schoonermuseum.org *Email:* staff@schoonermuseum.org *Visitors welcome?* Yes *Hours:* Grounds only *Admission:* Contact attraction directly *Operated by:* Grand Banks Schooner Museum Trust *NR?* Yes *NHL?* No *Year established/built:* 1883 *Latitude:* 43.8037 *Latitude:* -69.5992

ROCKLAND BREAKWATER LIGHTHOUSE

The Rockland Breakwater Lighthouse was built in 1902 and automated in 1965. It is now maintained by a community not-for-profit. *Address:* Rockland Breakwater Light *City:* Rockland *State:* ME *Zip:* 04841 *Phone:* 207-785-4609 *Web:* www.rocklandlighthouse.com *Email:* brkwater@midcoast.com *Visitors welcome?* Yes *Hours:* Saturdays, Sundays, and holidays, Memorial Day weekend to Columbus Day *Admission:* Contact attraction directly *Operated by:* Friends of the Rockland Breakwater Lighthouse *NR?* No *NHL?* No *Year established/built:* 1902 *Latitude:* 44.1042 *Latitude:* -69.0775

ROCKLAND HARBOR SOUTHWEST LIGHTHOUSE

The Rockland Harbor Southwest Lighthouse was built by a private party in 1987. *Address:* Rockland Harbor *City:* Owls Head *State:* ME *Visitors welcome?* No *Operated by:* Private owner *NR?* No *NHL?* No *Year established/built:* 1987 *Latitude:* 44.1004 *Latitude:* -69.0906

CHAPTER 5 – LIGHTHOUSES & LIGHTSHIPS

SADDLEBACK LEDGE LIGHTHOUSE

Constructed in 1839 on a bare, windswept island, Saddleback Ledge Lighthouse is considered one of the most isolated light stations in New England. The light was automated in 1954. *Address:* Saddleback Ledge Light *City:* Vinalhaven *State:* ME *Visitors welcome?* No *Operated by:* U.S. Coast Guard (District 1) *NR?* Yes *NHL?* No *Year established/built:* 1839 *Latitude:* 44.0144 *Latitude:* -68.7264

✦ SEGUIN ISLAND LIGHTHOUSE

Commissioned by George Washington in 1795, the Sequin Island Lighthouse was established the next year. The current granite lighthouse was built in 1857 and automated in 1985. Tours are conducted by a not-for-profit organization based in Bath. *Address:* Seguin Island Light *City:* Seguin Island *State:* ME *Phone:* 207-443-4808 *Web:* www.seguinisland.org *Email:* keeper@seguinisland.org *Visitors welcome?* Yes *Hours:* By appointment *Admission:* Contact attraction directly *Operated by:* Friends Of Seguin Island Lighthouse *NR?* Yes *NHL?* No *Year established/built:* 1796 *Latitude:* 44.5176 *Latitude:* -67.5325

SPRING POINT LEDGE LIGHTHOUSE

Spring Point Ledge Lighthouse was constructed in 1897 to mark a dangerous ledge which is now covered by the breakwater. It was automated in the 1980s and is now owned by a not-for-profit organization. *Address:* Spring Point Ledge Light *City:* Portland *State:* ME *Phone:* 207-699-2676 *Web:* www.springpointlight.org *Email:* info@springpointlight.org *Visitors welcome?* Yes *Hours:* Selected days, contact attraction *Admission:* Contact attraction directly *Operated by:* Spring Point Ledge Light Trust *NR?* Yes *NHL?* No *Year established/built:* 1897 *Latitude:* 43.6522 *Latitude:* -70.2236

SQUIRREL POINT LIGHTHOUSE

The Kennebec River has been an important maritime thoroughfare since the 17th century. Arrowsic Island was one of the first areas settled, and ships moved goods up and down the river. The Squirrel Point Lighthouse was built in 1898. *Address:* Squirrel Point Light *City:* Arrowsic *State:* ME *Visitors welcome?* No *Operated by:* Chewonki Foundation *NR?* Yes *NHL?* No *Year established/built:* 1898 *Latitude:* 43.8165 *Latitude:* -69.8024

TENANTS HARBOR LIGHTHOUSE

The Tenants Harbor Lighthouse was established in 1858 and discontinued in 1933. At that time, it was purchased by the Andrew Wyeth family, and the artist's son, Jamie Wyeth, now lives there. *City:* Tenants Harbor *State:* ME *Visitors welcome?* No *Operated by:* Private owner *NR?* Yes *NHL?* No *Year established/built:* 1858 *Latitude:* 43.9673 *Latitude:* -69.2081

TWO BUSH ISLAND LIGHTHOUSE

The Two Bush Island Lighthouse was established and built in 1897. It was automated in 1964 and is now part of a wildlife refuge. *Address:* Two Bush Island *State:* ME *Visitors welcome?* Yes *Hours:* Grounds only *Admission:* FREE *Operated by:* Maine Coastal Islands National Wildlife Refuge *NR?* No *NHL?* No *Year established/built:* 1897 *Latitude:* 43.7529 *Latitude:* -69.9359

WEST QUODDY HEAD LIGHTHOUSE

Built in 1808, West Quoddy Lighthouse marks the Lubec Channel at the easternmost point of the United States. It also has a unique red and white bands, one of only two lighthouse with these marks. *Address:* West Quoddy Head Light *City:* Lubec *State:* ME *Visitors welcome?* Yes *Hours:* Daily, mid-May to mid-October *Admission:* FREE *Operated by:* West Quoddy Head Light Keepers Association *NR?* Yes *NHL?* No *Year established/built:* 1808 *Latitude:* 44.8150 *Latitude:* -66.9506

WHALEBACK LEDGE LIGHTHOUSE
Established in 1830 at the mouth of Piscataqua River just east of the Maine / New Hampshire border, a second structure replaced the original in 1872. The station was automated in 1963. The station is owned by the American Lighthouse Foundation, and managed by its chapter, Friends of Portsmouth Lighthouse. *Address:* Whaleback Light *City:* Kittery *State:* ME *Email:* info@portsmouthharborlighthouse.com *Visitors welcome?* No *Operated by:* Friends of Portsmouth Harbor Lighthouse *NR?* Yes *NHL?* No *Year established/built:* 1830 *Latitude:* 43.0588 *Latitude:* -70.6963

WHITEHEAD ISLAND LIGHTHOUSE
Commissioned by President Thomas Jefferson in1803, the light marks the entrance to Penobscot Bay. The lighthouse is now owned by Pine Island Camp as a recreational and educational facility, although the light itself is still an active aid to navigation. *Address:* Whitehead Island Light *State:* ME *Zip:* 04011 *Phone:* 207-729-7714 *Web:* www.whiteheadlightstation.org *Email:* info@whiteheadlightstation.org *Visitors welcome?* Yes *Hours:* Contact attraction directly *Admission:* Contact attraction directly *Operated by:* Whitehead Light Station *NR?* Yes *NHL?* No *Year established/built:* 1803 *Latitude:* 43.9787 *Latitude:* -69.1243

WHITLOCKS MILL LIGHTHOUSE
In 1892, the U.S. Coast Guard asked a mill operator named Whitlock to place a red lighted lantern on a post at this dog leg in the St. Croix River because of the heavy traffic. In 1909 the last lighthouse to be built in Maine was erected here. *Address:* Whitlocks Mill Light *City:* Whitlocks Mill *State:* ME *Web:* www.stcroixhistorical.org/whitlock/ *Email:* schs@stcroixhistorical.org *Visitors welcome?* Yes *Hours:* Contact attraction directly *Admission:* Contact attraction directly *Operated by:* St. Croix Historical Society *NR?* Yes *NHL?* No *Year established/built:* 1909 *Latitude:* 45.1628 *Latitude:* -67.2273

WINTER HARBOR LIGHTHOUSE
The Winter Harbor lighthouse was established and built in 1857. Shut down by the U.S. Coast Guard in 1933, the property was sold to a private owner. *Address:* Mark Island *City:* Winter Harbor *State:* ME *Visitors welcome?* No *Operated by:* Private owner *NR?* Yes *NHL?* No *Year established/built:* 1857 *Latitude:* 44.3620 *Latitude:* -68.0867

WOOD ISLAND LIGHTHOUSE
Established in 1808, the current Wood Island Lighthouse was buit in 1858. The station was automated by the U.S. Coast Guard in 1986. *Address:* Wood Island Light *City:* Biddeford Pool *State:* ME *Zip:* 04006 *Web:* www.woodislandlighthouse.org *Email:* Brad@woodislandlighthouse.org *Visitors welcome?* Yes *Hours:* Contact attraction directly *Admission:* Contact attraction directly *Operated by:* Friends of Wood Island Light Station *NR?* Yes *NHL?* No *Year established/built:* 1808 *Latitude:* 43.4567 *Latitude:* -70.3283

MARYLAND

BALTIMORE HARBOR LIGHTHOUSE
Established and built in 1908, the Baltimore Harbor Lighthouse was automated in 1964 and is still an active aid to navigation. *Address:* Baltimore Harbor Light *State:* MD *Web:* www.baltimorelight.org *Email:* keeper@baltimorelight.org *Visitors welcome?* Yes *Hours:* By appointment *Admission:* Contact attraction directly *Operated by:* Baltimore Harbor Light *NR?* Yes *NHL?* No *Year established/built:* 1908 *Latitude:* 39.0592 *Latitude:* -76.3990

CHAPTER 5 – LIGHTHOUSES & LIGHTSHIPS

BETHEL BRIDGE LIGHTHOUSE
The Bethel Bridge Lighthouse is a replica of a small number of wooden lighthouses meant to guide rivercraft on the Chesapeake & Delaware Canal. *Address:* 815 Bethel Rd *City:* Chesapeake City *State:* MD *Phone:* 215-656-6515 *Web:* www.nap.usace.army.mil/sb/c&d.htm *Email:* edward.c.voigt@usace.army.mil *Visitors welcome?* Yes *Hours:* Monday to Friday, 8 a.m. to 4 p.m. *Admission:* FREE *Operated by:* U.S. Army Corps of Engineers (Philadelphia District) *NR?* No *NHL?* No *Latitude:* 39.5210 *Latitude:* -75.7936

BLOODY POINT BAR LIGHTHOUSE
Established and built in 1882, the spark plug-style Bloody Bar Lighthouse was automated in 1960 and is still an active aid to navigation. *Address:* Kent Island *City:* Romancoke *State:* MD *Visitors welcome?* No *Operated by:* Private owner *NR?* No *NHL?* No *Year established/built:* 1882 *Latitude:* 38.8812 *Latitude:* -76.3363

CONCORD POINT LIGHTHOUSE
Established in 1827, the current Concord Point Lighthouse, also known as the Havre de Grace Lighthouse, was constructed in 1875. Deactivated in 1975, the lighthouse is the second oldest on Chesapeake Bay. *Address:* Concord and Lafayette Streets *City:* Havre de Grace *State:* MD *Zip:* 21078 *Phone:* 410-939-3213 *Email:* directorcpt@verizon.net *Visitors welcome?* Yes *Hours:* April to October, Saturdays and Sundays, 1 p.m. to 5 p.m. *Admission:* Contact attraction directly *Operated by:* Friends of Concord Point Lighthouse *NR?* Yes *NHL?* No *Year established/built:* 1827 *Latitude:* 39.5407 *Latitude:* -76.0854

COVE POINT LIGHTHOUSE
Established and built in 1828, the Cove Point Lighthouse was automated in 1986 and is still an active aid to navigation. *Address:* Cove Point Light *City:* Cove Point *State:* MD *Phone:* 410-326-2042 *Web:* www.calvertmarinemuseum.com/cove_point.htm *Visitors welcome?* Yes *Hours:* Daily, June to August, 1 p.m. to 4 p.m.; May and September, Saturday and Sunday, 1 p.m. to 4 p.m. *Admission:* Contact attraction directly *Operated by:* Calvert Marine Museum *NR?* Yes *NHL?* No *Year established/built:* 1828 *Latitude:* 38.3863 *Latitude:* -76.3817

CRAIGHILL CHANNEL LOWER FRONT RANGE LIGHTHOUSE
Range lights working in pairs allowed mariners to know their position in channels relative to their destination. The Craighill Channel Lower Front Range Lighthouse marks the channel from Chesapeake Bay to the Patapsco River and Baltimore Harbor. *Address:* Craighill Channel Lower Range Front Light *City:* Fort Howard *State:* MD *Phone:* 703-967-8118 *Web:* www.craighillrange.org *Visitors welcome?* Yes *Hours:* By appointment *Admission:* Contact attraction directly *Operated by:* Historical Place Preservation *NR?* Yes *NHL?* No *Year established/built:* 1873 *Latitude:* 39.2073 *Latitude:* -76.4450

CRAIGHILL CHANNEL LOWER REAR RANGE LIGHTHOUSE
Range lights working in pairs allowed mariners to know their position in channels relative to their destination. The Craighill Channel Lower Rear Range Lighthouse marks the channel from Chesapeake Bay to the Patapsco River and Baltimore Harbor. *Address:* Craighill Channel Lower Rear Range Light *City:* Ramona Beach *State:* MD *Phone:* 703-967-8118 *Web:* www.craighillrange.org *Visitors welcome?* Yes *Hours:* By appointment *Admission:* Contact attraction directly *Operated by:* Historical Place Preservation *NR?* Yes *NHL?* No *Year established/built:* 1873 *Latitude:* 39.2291 *Latitude:* -76.3942

CRAIGHILL CHANNEL UPPER FRONT RANGE LIGHTHOUSE
Range lights working in pairs allowed mariners to know their position in channels relative to their destination. The Craighill Channel Upper Front Range Lighthouse marks the channel from Chesapeake Bay to the Patapsco River and Baltimore Harbor. *Address:* Craighill Channel Upper Front Range Light *City:* Fort Howard *State:* MD *Visitors welcome?* No *Operated by:* U.S. Coast Guard (District 5) *NR?* Yes *NHL?* No *Year established/built:* 1886 *Latitude:* 39.1971 *Latitude:* -76.4482

CRAIGHILL CHANNEL UPPER REAR RANGE LIGHTHOUSE
Range lights working in pairs allowed mariners to know their position in channels relative to their destination. The Craighill Channel Upper Rear Range Lighthouse marks the channel from Chesapeake Bay to the Patapsco River and Baltimore Harbor. *Address:* Craighill Channel Upper Rear Range Light *City:* Sparrows Point *State:* MD *Visitors welcome?* No *Operated by:* U.S. Coast Guard (District 5) *NR?* Yes *NHL?* No *Year established/built:* 1886 *Latitude:* 39.2162 *Latitude:* -76.4627

DRUM POINT LIGHTHOUSE
Established and built in 1883, the Drum Point Lighthouse was moved from its original location on the Patuxent River to Solomons, Maryland, where it is used as a museum. *Address:* Calvert Marine Museum *City:* Solomons *State:* MD *Zip:* 20688 *Phone:* 410-326-2042 *Web:* www.calvertmarinemuseum.com *Email:* mccormmj@co.cal.md.us *Visitors welcome?* Yes *Hours:* Daily, 10 a.m to 5 p.m. *Admission:* $7 adults, $6 seniors, $2 children 5 to 12; under five FREE *Operated by:* Calvert Marine Museum *NR?* Yes *NHL?* No *Year established/built:* 1883 *Latitude:* 38.3433 *Latitude:* -76.4650

FISHING BATTERY LIGHTHOUSE
Built on an artificial island at the mouth of the Susquehanna River, Fishing Battery Island Lighthouse was built in 1853. The island was intended to aid local fishermen as a point to anchor nets and site a fish hatchery. The island is now part of a wildlife refuge. *Address:* Fishing Battery Light *City:* Oakington *State:* MD *Visitors welcome?* Yes *Hours:* Grounds only *Admission:* FREE *Operated by:* U.S. Fish and Wildlife Service *NR?* No *NHL?* No *Year established/built:* 1853 *Latitude:* 39.4950 *Latitude:* -76.0830

FORT CARROLL LIGHTHOUSE
Built in 1854 on Fort Carroll, the Fort Carroll Lighthouse, the original light was replaced by a wooden tower in 1898. The lighthouse was automated in 1920 and the fort abandoned by the Army, except for the years of World War II. The property is now privately owned. *Address:* Fort Carroll Light *State:* MD *Visitors welcome?* No *Operated by:* Struever Bros., Eccles & Rouse *NR?* No *NHL?* No *Year established/built:* 1854 *Latitude:* 39.2147 *Latitude:* -76.5199

FORT WASHINGTON LIGHTHOUSE
Built at Fort Washington, which guards the mouth of the Potomac River, the Fort Washington Lighthouse is now within the grounds of Fort Washington Park. *Address:* Fort Washington Light *City:* Fort Washington *State:* MD *Zip:* 20744 *Phone:* 301-763-4600 *Web:* www.nps.gov/fowa/ *Visitors welcome?* Yes *Hours:* Daily, 8 a.m. to sunset *Admission:* $5 vehicle, $3 individual *Operated by:* Fort Washington Park *NR?* No *NHL?* No *Year established/built:* 1857 *Latitude:* 38.7120 *Latitude:* -77.0370

HOOPER ISLAND LIGHTHOUSE
Established and built in 1902, the spark-plug style Hooper Island Lighthouse was automated in 1961 and is still an active aid to navigation. *Address:* Hooper Island Light *City:* Hoopersville *State:* MD *Visitors welcome?* No *Operated by:* U.S. Coast Guard (District 5) *NR?* Yes *NHL?* No *Year established/built:* 1902 *Latitude:* 38.2560 *Latitude:* -76.2500

HOOPER STRAIT LIGHTHOUSE
Established and built in 1879, the Hooper Strait Lighthouse was deactivated in 1966 and moved to its current location in Talbot for use as a museum. *Address:* 213 N. Talbot Street *City:* St. Michaels *State:* MD *Zip:* 21663 *Phone:* 410-745-2916 *Web:* www.cbmm.org *Email:* cbland@cbmm.org *Visitors welcome?* Yes *Hours:* Daily, hours vary by season *Admission:* $13 adults; $10 seniors over 62; $6 kids 6 to 17; kids under 6 FREE *Operated by:* Chesapeake Bay Maritime Museum *NR?* Yes *NHL?* No *Year established/built:* 1879 *Latitude:* 38.7876 *Latitude:* -76.2249

CHAPTER 5 – LIGHTHOUSES & LIGHTSHIPS

LAZARETTO POINT LIGHTHOUSE

The Lazaretto Lighthouse is a replica of an 1863 structure that was torn down in 1954. The replica, built by the owner of a Baltimore port services company, is on private property. *Address:* Lazaretto Point Light *City:* Baltimore *State:* MD *Zip:* 21224-0163 *Visitors welcome?* No *Operated by:* Rukert Terminals Corp. *NR?* No *NHL?* No *Year established/built:* 1831 *Latitude:* 39.2622 *Latitude:* -76.5715

POINT LOOKOUT LIGHTHOUSE

Established in 1830, the original Point Lookout Lighthouse was near the site of a notorious prisoner of war camp for Confederate soldiers. The lighthouse received a major upgrade in 1927, and it was transferred to the U.S. Navy in the 1960s. *Address:* Point Lookout Light *City:* St. Leonard *State:* MD *Web:* www.ptlookoutlighthouse.com *Email:* admin@ptlookoutlighthouse.com *Visitors welcome?* Yes *Hours:* By appointment *Admission:* Contact attraction directly *Operated by:* Point Lookout Lighthouse Preservation Society *NR?* No *NHL?* No *Year established/built:* 1830 *Latitude:* 38.0387 *Latitude:* -76.3221

POINT NO POINT (MARYLAND) LIGHTHOUSE

Established and built in 1905, the Point No Point (Maryland) Lighthouse was automated in 1962 and is still an active aid to navigation. *Address:* Point No Point Light *City:* Airdele *State:* MD *Visitors welcome?* No *Operated by:* U.S. Coast Guard (District 5) *NR?* No *NHL?* No *Year established/built:* 1905 *Latitude:* 38.1280 *Latitude:* -76.2900

POOLES ISLAND LIGHTHOUSE

The Pooles Island Lighthouse was established in 1824 to mark the entrance to the Bush and Gunpowder rivers. The lighthouse and the island was handed over to the U.S. Army in 1917, and it became part of the Aberdeen Proving Ground. *Address:* Pooles Island Light *City:* Aberdeen *State:* MD *Phone:* 410-278-5201 *Visitors welcome?* No *Operated by:* Aberdeen Proving Ground *NR?* Yes *NHL?* No *Year established/built:* 1824 *Latitude:* 39.2790 *Latitude:* -76.2700

SANDY POINT SHOAL LIGHTHOUSE

Established and built in 1882, the Sandy Point Shoal Lighthouse was automated in 1963 and is now in the hands of a private owner. *Address:* Sandy Point Shoal Light *City:* Cape St. Clair *State:* MD *Visitors welcome?* No *Operated by:* Private owner *NR?* Yes *NHL?* No *Year established/built:* 1882 *Latitude:* 39.0160 *Latitude:* -76.3850

SEVEN FOOT KNOLL LIGHTHOUSE

Built in 1856, Seven Foot Knoll Lighthouse is the oldest screw-pile lighthouse in Maryland. The lighthouse marked the mouth of Baltimore's Harbor for 133 years before being moved to the Inner Harbor for restoration. The lighthouse was built at the mouth of the Patapsco River, marking the shoal known as Seven Foot Knoll. It was built on cast iron pilings with corkscrew-like bases that were screwed into the mud on the bottom of the Bay, eliminating the need for a masonry foundation. *Address:* Pier 5, Baltimore Inner Harbor (301 E. Pratt St.) *City:* Baltimore *State:* MD *Zip:* 21202 *Phone:* 410-539-1797 *Web:* www.historicships.org *Email:* administration@historicships.org *Visitors welcome?* Yes *Hours:* Contact attraction directly *Admission:* Contact attraction directly *Operated by:* Historic Ships in Baltimore *NR?* Yes *NHL?* No *Year established/built:* 1856 *Latitude:* 39.2866 *Latitude:* -76.6087

SHARPS ISLAND LIGHTHOUSE

The Sharps Island Lighthouse marks shoals off Poplar Island and Black Island Point in Chesapeake Bay. The current 1881 caisson structure replaced a screw-pile lighthouse damaged by moving ice fields. *Address:* Sharps Island Light *City:* Fairbank *State:* MD *Visitors welcome?* No *Operated by:* Private owner *NR?* Yes *NHL?* No *Year established/built:* 1865 *Latitude:* 38.6391 *Latitude:* -76.3757

SOLOMONS LUMP LIGHTHOUSE
Solomons Lump Lighthouse marks a shoal extending from Smith Island in Chesapeake Bay. Replacing a light at Fog Point, the 1875 screwpile lighthouse was destroyed by ice and replaced in 1895 caisson-style structure. *Address:* Solomons Lump Light *City:* Smith Island *State:* MD *Visitors welcome?* No *Operated by:* U.S. Coast Guard (District 5) *NR?* Yes *NHL?* No *Year established/built:* 1875 *Latitude:* 38.0480 *Latitude:* -76.0150

THOMAS POINT SHOAL LIGHTHOUSE
First located on land in 1825, the lighthouse was moved offshore onto pilings in 1875. The lighthouse was the last manned station in Chesapeake Bay before it was automated in 1986. It is now owned and operated by a consortium of local governments and not-for-profit organizations. *Address:* Thomas Point Shoal Light *City:* Highland Beach *State:* MD *Web:* www.thomaspointlighthouse.org *Visitors welcome?* Yes *Hours:* Contact attraction directly *Admission:* Contact attraction directly *Operated by:* Thomas Point Shoal Lighthouse *NR?* Yes *NHL?* Yes *Year established/built:* 1825 *Latitude:* 38.8990 *Latitude:* -76.4360

TURKEY POINT LIGHTHOUSE
Established and built in 1833, the Turkey Point Lighthouse sits on a bluff overlooking Chesapeake Bay. It marks the course for ship masters into the Chesapeake & Delaware Canal. In 2008, the lighthouse was decommissioned. *Address:* Turkey Point Light *State:* MD *Phone:* 410-287-8170 *Web:* www.tpls.org *Visitors welcome?* Yes *Hours:* Saturday and Sunday, 11 a.m. to 4 p.m. *Admission:* Contact attraction directly *Operated by:* Turkey Point Light Station *NR?* Yes *NHL?* No *Year established/built:* 1833 *Latitude:* 39.4500 *Latitude:* -76.0090

MASSACHUSETTS

ANNISQUAM LIGHTHOUSE
Established in 1801, the current Annisquam Lighthouse was constructed in 1897 and automated in 1974. The dwelling is now used by the U.S. Coast Guard as housing. *Address:* Annisquam Harbor Light *City:* Annisquam *State:* MA *Visitors welcome?* No *Operated by:* U.S. Coast Guard (District 1) *NR?* Yes *NHL?* No *Year established/built:* 1801 *Latitude:* 42.6619 *Latitude:* -70.6815

BAKER'S ISLAND LIGHTHOUSE
Established in 1791, the current Baker's Island Lighthouse tower was built in 1821. The light was automated in 1971. It is owned by the Essex National Heritage Commission. *Address:* Baker's Island Light *State:* MA *Visitors welcome?* No *Operated by:* Essex National Heritage Commission *NR?* Yes *NHL?* No *Year established/built:* 1791 *Latitude:* 42.5364 *Latitude:* -70.7859

BASS RIVER LIGHTHOUSE
Established and built in 1855, the Bass River Lighthouse is now a prominent hotel and restaurant on Cape Cod. *Address:* 1 Lighthouse Inn Road *City:* West Dennis *State:* MA *Zip:* 02670 *Phone:* 508-398-2244 *Web:* www.lighthouseinn.com *Email:* inquire@lighthouseinn.com *Visitors welcome?* Yes *Hours:* Contact attraction directly *Admission:* Contact attraction directly *Operated by:* Lighthouse Inn *NR?* No *NHL?* No *Year established/built:* 1855 *Latitude:* 41.6520 *Latitude:* -70.1692

BIRD ISLAND LIGHTHOUSE
Bird Island Lighthouse was established and built by the government in 1819, and the orginal tower still stands. The station was inactive from 1933 to 1997, when the light was re-lit by the Town of Marion as a civic landmark. *Address:* Bird Island Light *City:* Marion *State:* MA *Phone:* 508-748-3500 *Visitors welcome?* Yes

Hours: Grounds only *Admission:* FREE *Operated by:* Town of Marion *NR?* Yes *NHL?* No *Year established/built:* 1819 *Latitude:* 41.6694 *Latitude:* -70.7173

BISHOP AND CLERKS LIGHTHOUSE
The Bishop and Clerks Lighthouse was established in 1858 and discontinued in 1928. The tower was demolished in 1952 and replaced by a daymark and light. *Address:* Point Gammon *City:* Yarmouth *State:* MA *Visitors welcome?* No *Operated by:* U.S. Coast Guard (District 1) *NR?* No *NHL?* No *Year established/built:* 1858 *Latitude:* 41.6098 *Latitude:* -70.2661

> Which East Coast lighthouse is your favorite to visit? Best for families? Spookiest? Tell Fyddeye by going to our website at www.fyddeye.com.

BORDEN FLATS LIGHTHOUSE
The Borden Flats Lighthouse, established and built in 1881, warns mariners of submerged hazards at the mouth of the Taunton River. The light was automated in 1963 and is privately owned. *City:* Fall River *State:* MA *Visitors welcome?* No *Operated by:* Private owner *NR?* Yes *NHL?* No *Year established/built:* 1881 *Latitude:* 41.7015 *Latitude:* -71.1550

BOSTON HARBOR LIGHTHOUSE
Considered an iconic American lighthouse, Boston Harbor Lighthouse was established in 1716, and the 1783 tower still stands. The light is an active aid to navigation, though it was automated in 1998. It marks the entrance to Boston Harbor. *Address:* Little Brewster Island *City:* Boston *State:* MA *Visitors welcome?* Yes *Hours:* Grounds only *Admission:* FREE *Operated by:* U.S. Coast Guard (District 1) *NR?* Yes *NHL?* Yes *Year established/built:* 1716 *Latitude:* 42.3279 *Latitude:* -70.8903

BRANT POINT LIGHTHOUSE
The Brant Point Lighthouse was established in 1746. The current wooden tower was constructed in 1901 and automated in 1965. *Address:* Brant Point Light *City:* Nantucket *State:* MA *Visitors welcome?* Yes *Hours:* Grounds only *Admission:* FREE *Operated by:* U.S. Coast Guard (District 1) *NR?* Yes *NHL?* No *Year established/built:* 1746 *Latitude:* 41.2900 *Latitude:* -70.0903

BUTLER FLATS LIGHTHOUSE
Established in 1804, the current cast-iron, caisson-style Butler Flats Lighthouse was established and built in 1898 at the entrance to New Bedford Harbor and automated in 1978. *Address:* Butler Flats Light *City:* New Bedford *State:* MA *Visitors welcome?* No *Operated by:* City of New Bedford *NR?* Yes *NHL?* No *Year established/built:* 1804 *Latitude:* 41.6036 *Latitude:* -70.8944

 ## CAPE ANN LIGHTHOUSE
Established in 1771, two lighthouse were built together on Thacher Island, also known as Cape Ann. Two new towers were constructed of granite in 1961. The light on the northeast tower was shut down in 1932. The lighthouse is now owned by the City of Rockport. *Address:* Cape Ann Light *City:* Rockport *State:* MA *Zip:* 01966 *Phone:* 617-599-2590 *Web:* www.thacherisland.org *Email:* info@thacherisland.org *Visitors welcome?* Yes *Hours:* Contact attraction directly *Admission:* Contact attraction directly *Operated by:* Thacher Island Association *NR?* Yes *NHL?* Yes *Year established/built:* 1771 *Latitude:* 42.6368 *Latitude:* -70.5749

CAPE COD LIGHTHOUSE
Established in 1797, the current Cape Cod Lighthouse, also called the Highland Lighthouse, was constructed in 1857. In 1996, it was moved further from the beach due to erosion concerns. *Address:* Cape Cod Light *City:* Truro *State:* MA *Zip:* 02666 *Phone:* 608-487-1121 *Web:* www.capecodlight.org *Visitors welcome?* Yes

Hours: Mid-May to mid-October, 10 a.m. to 5:30 p.m. *Admission:* $4, children must be 48 inches tall *Operated by:* Truro Historical Society *NR?* Yes *NHL?* No *Year established/built:* 1797 *Latitude:* 42.0395 *Latitude:* -70.0609

CAPE POGE LIGHTHOUSE
Established in 1801, the Cape Poge (also spelled Pogue) Lighthouse's current tower was constructed in 1893 and automated in 1943. *Address:* Cape Poge Light *City:* Martha's Vineyard *State:* MA *Phone:* 508-627-7689 *Email:* islands@ttor.org *Visitors welcome?* Yes *Hours:* By appointment *Admission:* Contact attraction directly *Operated by:* Trustees of Reservations *NR?* Yes *NHL?* No *Year established/built:* 1801 *Latitude:* 41.4188 *Latitude:* -70.4518

CHATHAM LIGHTHOUSE
Established in 1808, the current Chatham Lighthouse tower was built in 1877 and automated in 1982. The local U.S. Coast Guard Auxiliary offers tours during the summer months. *Address:* Main Street and Water Street *City:* Chatham *State:* MA *Phone:* 508-430-0628 *Visitors welcome?* Yes *Hours:* Contact attraction directly *Admission:* Contact attraction directly *Operated by:* U.S. Coast Guard (District 1) *NR?* Yes *NHL?* No *Year established/built:* 1808 *Latitude:* 41.6714 *Latitude:* -69.9503

CLARK'S POINT LIGHTHOUSE
The Clark's Point Lighthouse was established in 1797 on the ground of Fort Taber, now a city park. The current lighthouse tower was constructed in 1869 and deactivated in 1898. The light was relit in 2001. *Address:* Fort Taber Park *City:* New Bedford *State:* MA *Visitors welcome?* Yes *Hours:* Grounds only *Admission:* FREE *Operated by:* City of New Bedford *NR?* Yes *NHL?* No *Year established/built:* 1797 *Latitude:* 41.6362 *Latitude:* -70.9342

CLEVELAND LEDGE LIGHTHOUSE
Established and built in 1943, the Cleveland Ledge Lighthouse is a relative latecomer to the nation's lighthouse inventory. Built in the Art Moderne style, the lighthouse was automated in 1978. *City:* Buzzards Bay *State:* MA *Visitors welcome?* No *Operated by:* U.S. Coast Guard (District 1) *NR?* Yes *NHL?* No *Year established/built:* 1943 *Latitude:* 41.6226 *Latitude:* -70.6956

CUTTYHUNK LIGHTHOUSE
The Cuttyhunk Lighthouse was established in 1803 and deactivated in 1947. A steel skeletal tower now stands at the site. *Address:* Cuttyhunk Island *City:* Cuttyhunk Island *State:* MA *Visitors welcome?* Yes *Hours:* Grounds only *Admission:* FREE *Operated by:* U.S. Coast Guard (District 1) *NR?* No *NHL?* No *Year established/built:* 1823 *Latitude:* 41.4168 *Latitude:* -70.9356

DEER ISLAND LIGHTHOUSE
Established in 1890, the original cast-iron tower of the Deer Island Lighthouse was replaced in 1982 with a fiberglass tower. *Address:* Deer Island Light *City:* Boston *State:* MA *Visitors welcome?* No *Operated by:* U.S. Coast Guard (District 1) *NR?* No *NHL?* No *Year established/built:* 1890 *Latitude:* 42.3399 *Latitude:* -70.9545

DERBY WHARF LIGHTHOUSE
The Derby Wharf Lighthouse was established in 1871 and built the same year. It was deactivated in 1977, but reactivated in 1983. The lighthouse is now part of the Salem National Maritime Historic Site. *Address:* Derby Wharf Light *City:* Salem *State:* MA *Zip:* 01970 *Phone:* 978-740-1650 *Fax:* 978-740-1655 *Web:* www.nps.gov/sama/ *Visitors welcome?* Yes *Hours:* Grounds only, daily, 9 a.m. to 5 p.m. *Admission:* Contact attraction directly *Operated by:* Salem National Maritime Historic Site *NR?* Yes *NHL?* No *Year established/built:* 1871 *Latitude:* 42.5166 *Latitude:* -70.8836

CHAPTER 5 – LIGHTHOUSES & LIGHTSHIPS

DOG BAR BREAKWATER LIGHTHOUSE
The Dog Bar Breakwater Lighthouse is an auxiliary light to the Eastern Point Lighthouse in Gloucester, Mass. *Address:* Eastern Point Light *City:* Gloucester *State:* MA *Visitors welcome?* Yes *Hours:* Grounds only *Admission:* FREE *Operated by:* U.S. Coast Guard (District 1) *NR?* No *NHL?* No *Latitude:* 42.5802 *Latitude:* -70.6644

DUXBURY PIER LIGHTHOUSE
Duxbury Pier Lighthouse was built in 1871 in the main channel in Plymouth Harbor to mark a shoal off Saquish Head. Known locally as The Bug, the lighthouse was constructed in the distinctive coffee pot style. *Address:* Duxbury Pier Light *City:* Duxbury *State:* MA *Zip:* 02331 *Web:* www.buglight.org *Email:* info@buglight.org *Visitors welcome?* No *Operated by:* Project Gurnet & Bug Lights *NR?* No *NHL?* No *Year established/built:* 1871 *Latitude:* 41.9874 *Latitude:* -70.6485

EAST CHOP LIGHTHOUSE
The East Chop Lighthouse, also known as the Telegraph Hill Lighthouse, on Martha's Vineyard was established in 1869 and built in 1878. The station was automated in 1933 and is now cared for by the Martha's Vineyard Historical Society. *Address:* East Chop Light *City:* Martha's Vineyard *State:* MA *Zip:* 02539 *Phone:* 508-627-4441 *Visitors welcome?* Yes *Hours:* Contact attraction directly *Admission:* Contact attraction directly *Operated by:* Martha's Vineyard Historical Society *NR?* Yes *NHL?* No *Year established/built:* 1869 *Latitude:* 41.4702 *Latitude:* -70.5674

EASTERN POINT LIGHTHOUSE
Established in 1832, the current Eastern Point Lighthouse was built in 1890. The station was automated in 1985. *Address:* Eastern Point Light *City:* Gloucester *State:* MA *Visitors welcome?* Yes *Hours:* Grounds only *Admission:* FREE *Operated by:* U.S. Coast Guard (District 1) *NR?* Yes *NHL?* No *Year established/built:* 1832 *Latitude:* 42.5802 *Latitude:* -70.6644

EDGARTOWN HARBOR LIGHTHOUSE
Established in 1828, the current cast-iron tower was built in 1881. The lighthouse was automated in 1939 and is now operated by the Martha's Vineyard Historical Society. *Address:* Edgartown Harbor Light *City:* Martha's Vineyard *State:* MA *Phone:* 508-627-4441 *Email:* KGorman@mvmuseum.org *Visitors welcome?* Yes *Hours:* Grounds only *Admission:* FREE *Operated by:* Martha's Vineyard Historical Society *NR?* Yes *NHL?* No *Year established/built:* 1828 *Latitude:* 41.3909 *Latitude:* -70.5031

FORT PICKERING LIGHTHOUSE
The Fort Pickering Lighthouse, also known as the Winter Island Lighthouse, was established and built in 1871. Now part of a public park, the light was deactivated in 1983. *Address:* 50 Winter Island Road *City:* Salem *State:* MA *Zip:* 01970 *Phone:* 978-745-9595 *Visitors welcome?* Yes *Hours:* Grounds only *Admission:* FREE *Operated by:* City of Salem *NR?* Yes *NHL?* No *Year established/built:* 1871 *Latitude:* 42.5310 *Latitude:* -70.8689

GAY HEAD LIGHTHOUSE
The Gay Head Lighthouse was established in 1799, with the current tower built in 1856. The lighthouse was automated in 1960. *Address:* Gay Head Light *City:* Martha's Vineyard *State:* MA *Phone:* 508-627-4441 *Visitors welcome?* Yes *Hours:* By appointment *Admission:* Contact attraction directly *Operated by:* Martha's Vineyard Historical Society *NR?* Yes *NHL?* No *Year established/built:* 1799 *Latitude:* 41.3484 *Latitude:* -70.8350

GRAVES LIGHTHOUSE
The Graves Lighthouse, named for the underwater ledges it marks, was built in 1905 and is still an operational, though automated, navigation aid. *Address:* The Graves *City:* Boston *State:* MA *Visitors welcome?* No

Operated by: U.S. Coast Guard (District 1) *NR?* Yes *NHL?* No *Year established/built:* 1905 *Latitude:* 42.3654 *Latitude:* -70.8689

GREAT POINT LIGHTHOUSE
The Great Point Lighthouse was established on the northeast tip of Nantucket Island in 1784. The current structure is a replica of the 1818 tower, which was destroyed in a storm in 1984. The structure is now part of a wildlife refuge. *Address:* Great Point Light *City:* Nantucket *State:* MA *Phone:* 508-228-5646 *Email:* islands@ttor.org *Visitors welcome?* Yes *Hours:* Contact attraction directly *Admission:* Contact attraction directly *Operated by:* Trustees of Reservations *NR?* No *NHL?* No *Year established/built:* 1784 *Latitude:* 41.3887 *Latitude:* -70.0481

HOSPITAL POINT RANGE FRONT LIGHTHOUSE
The Hospital Point Front Range Lighthouse was established and constructed in 1872. It was automated in 1947. *Address:* Hospital Point Light *City:* Beverly *State:* MA *Visitors welcome?* No *Operated by:* U.S. Coast Guard (District 1) *NR?* Yes *NHL?* No *Year established/built:* 1872 *Latitude:* 42.5465 *Latitude:* -70.8560

HOSPITAL POINT RANGE REAR LIGHTHOUSE
The Hospital Point Rear Range Lighthouse is located in the steeple of the First Baptist Church in Beverly, Mass. *Address:* 221 Cabot Street *City:* Beverly *State:* MA *Visitors welcome?* No *Operated by:* Private owner *NR?* No *NHL?* No *Year established/built:* 1872 *Latitude:* 42.5487 *Latitude:* -70.8785

HYANNIS REAR RANGE LIGHTHOUSE
Established and built in 1849, the Hyannis Rear Range Lighthouse was deactivated in 1929 and is now part of a private residence. *Address:* Hyannis Harbor *City:* Hyannis *State:* MA *Visitors welcome?* No *Operated by:* Private owner *NR?* No *NHL?* No *Year established/built:* 1849 *Latitude:* 41.6315 *Latitude:* -70.2870

LONG ISLAND HEAD LIGHTHOUSE
Established in 1819, the Long Island Head Lighthouse on Long Island in Boston Harbor was reconstructed in 1901. Deactivated in 1982, it was relit with an automated mechanism in 1985. *Address:* Long Island Head Light *City:* Boston *State:* MA *Visitors welcome?* No *Operated by:* U.S. Coast Guard (District 1) *NR?* Yes *NHL?* No *Year established/built:* 1819 *Latitude:* 42.3303 *Latitude:* -70.9578

LONG POINT LIGHTHOUSE
Established in 1827, the current Long Point Lighthouse was constructed in 1875 and automated in 1952. It is now located within the Cape Cod National Seashore. *Address:* Long Point Light *City:* Provincetown *State:* MA *Visitors welcome?* Yes *Hours:* Grounds only *Admission:* FREE *Operated by:* Cape Cod Chapter, ALF *NR?* Yes *NHL?* No *Year established/built:* 1827 *Latitude:* 42.0331 *Latitude:* -70.1687

MARBLEHEAD LIGHTHOUSE
Established in 1835, the current Marblehead Lighthouse tower was constructed of cast-iron in 1896 and automated in 1960. *City:* Marblehead *State:* MA *Visitors welcome?* Yes *Hours:* Grounds only *Admission:* FREE *Operated by:* U.S. Coast Guard (District 1) *NR?* Yes *NHL?* No *Year established/built:* 1835 *Latitude:* 42.5054 *Latitude:* -70.8388

MAYO'S BEACH LIGHTHOUSE
Established in 1838, the Mayo's Beach Lighthouse was discontinued in 1922 and the cast-iron tower moved to serve as the Point Montaro light in California. The keeper's dwelling remained in Wellfleet. *Address:* Kendrick Avenue *City:* Wellfleet *State:* MA *Visitors welcome?* No *Operated by:* Private owner *NR?* No *NHL?* No *Year established/built:* 1838 *Latitude:* 41.9307 *Latitude:* -70.0372

CHAPTER 5 – LIGHTHOUSES & LIGHTSHIPS

MINOT'S LEDGE LIGHTHOUSE
Established in 1850, the current Minot's Ledge Lighthouse tower was constructed in 1860 and automated in 1947. An original iron tower constructed in 1851 collapsed, killing two keepers. Remnants of the tower were discovered in 2007 by divers at the site. *Address:* Minot's Ledge Light *State:* MA *Visitors welcome?* No *Operated by:* U.S. Coast Guard (District 1) *NR?* Yes *NHL?* No *Year established/built:* 1850 *Latitude:* 42.2698 *Latitude:* -70.7593

MONOMOY POINT LIGHTHOUSE
Established in 1823, Monomoy Point Lighthouse is located off Chatham on Cape Cod. The current tower was built in 1849 and deactivated in 1923. The island is now a wildlife refuge. *Address:* Monomoy Point Light *State:* MA *Phone:* 508-945-0594 *Visitors welcome?* Yes *Hours:* Grounds only *Admission:* FREE *Operated by:* Monomoy National Wildlife Refuge *NR?* Yes *NHL?* No *Year established/built:* 1823 *Latitude:* 41.5592 *Latitude:* -69.9942

NANTUCKET CLIFF RANGE LIGHTHOUSE
The Nantucket Cliff Range Lighthouse is a range light designed to work in conjunction with the Brant Point Lighthouse. *City:* Nantucket *State:* MA *Visitors welcome?* No *Operated by:* Private owner *NR?* No *NHL?* No *Latitude:* 41.2835 *Latitude:* -70.0995

NAUSET BEACH LIGHTHOUSE
Established in 1838, the current Nauset Lighthouse was constructed in 1877, although it was moved 300 feet away from the shore in 1996 to save it from erosion. It is now a private aid to navigation. *Address:* Nauset Beach Light, Cape Cod National Seashore *City:* Eastham *State:* MA *Zip:* 02642 *Phone:* 508-240-2612 *Email:* nausetlight@capecod.net *Visitors welcome?* Yes *Hours:* Open May to October; check lighthouse website for details *Admission:* Donation *Operated by:* Nauset Light Preservation Society *NR?* Yes *NHL?* No *Year established/built:* 1838 *Latitude:* 41.8600 *Latitude:* -69.9533

NED POINT LIGHTHOUSE
Ned's Point Lighthouse was built in 1838 with the lamps first lit in March of that year. The station was automated in 1923 and deactivated in 1952. The light was reactivated in 1961 and continues to be an active aid to navigation. The light is a 6-second osophase light; three seconds on, three seconds off. Contact: Bert Theriault, Aids to Navigation Officer, CGAux Flotilla 63 at nedspointlight@comcast.net. Please note that the tower is not opened for weddings or pre-wedding photography. *Address:* Ned Point Light *City:* Mattapoisett *State:* MA *Email:* nedspointlight@comcast.net *Visitors welcome?* Yes *Hours:* Grounds open daily; Tower: July 10 a.m to noon; August 4 p.m. to 6 p.m. *Admission:* FREE *Operated by:* U.S. Coast Guard; Open to public by the Coast Guard Auxiliary Flotilla 63 *NR?* Yes *NHL?* No *Year established/built:* 1838 *Latitude:* 41.6509 *Latitude:* -70.7956

NEWBURYPORT HARBOR LIGHTHOUSE
The Newburyport Harbor Lighthouse, sometimes called the Plum Island Lighthouse, was established in 1788. The current tower was built in 1898 and automated in 1951. *Address:* Newburyport Harbor Light *City:* Newburyport *State:* MA *Visitors welcome?* Yes *Hours:* Grounds only *Admission:* FREE *Operated by:* Friends of Plum Island Light *NR?* Yes *NHL?* No *Year established/built:* 1788 *Latitude:* 42.8152 *Latitude:* -70.8189

NEWBURYPORT HARBOR RANGE FRONT LIGHTHOUSE
The Newburyport Range Lighthouses were established in 1873 and deactivated in 1961. The front range light is under the care of the New Hampshire-based Lighthouse Preservation Society. *Address:* Newburyport Harbor Front Range Light *City:* Newburyport *State:* MA *Visitors welcome?* Yes *Hours:* Grounds only *Admission:* FREE *Operated by:* Lighthouse Preservation Society *NR?* Yes *NHL?* No *Year established/built:* 1873 *Latitude:* 42.8115 *Latitude:* -70.8649

NEWBURYPORT HARBOR RANGE REAR LIGHTHOUSE
The Newburyport Range Lighthouses were established in 1873 and deactivated in 1961. The rear range light is privately owned. *Address:* Newburyport Harbor Rear Range Light *City:* Newburyport *State:* MA *Visitors welcome?* No *Operated by:* Private owner *NR?* Yes *NHL?* No *Year established/built:* 1873 *Latitude:* 42.8113 *Latitude:* -70.8661

NOBSKA POINT LIGHTHOUSE
The Nobska Point Lighthouse was established in 1829, and the current tower was built in 1876. Automated in 1985, the station is now the home for the regional U.S. Coast Guard commandant. *Address:* Nobska Point Light *City:* Woods Hole *State:* MA *Visitors welcome?* No *Operated by:* U.S. Coast Guard (District 1) *NR?* Yes *NHL?* No *Year established/built:* 1829 *Latitude:* 41.5158 *Latitude:* -70.6551

PALMER ISLAND LIGHTHOUSE
Established and built in 1849, the Palmer Island Lighthouse in New Bedford Harbor was automated in 1941 and deactivated in 1963. The Coast Guard relit the light in 1999. *Address:* Palmer Island *City:* New Bedford *State:* MA *Visitors welcome?* Yes *Hours:* Grounds only *Admission:* FREE *Operated by:* City of New Bedford *NR?* Yes *NHL?* No *Year established/built:* 1849 *Latitude:* 41.6251 *Latitude:* -70.9100

PLYMOUTH LIGHTHOUSE
Established in 1768, the current Plymouth Lighthouse, also known as the Gurnet Lighthouse, was constructed in 1843. Automated in 1986, the light is still an active aid to navigation. *Address:* Plymouth Light *City:* Duxbury *State:* MA *Zip:* 02331 *Web:* www.buglight.org *Email:* info@buglight.org *Visitors welcome?* Yes *Hours:* Grounds only *Admission:* Contact attraction directly *Operated by:* Project Gurnet & Bug Lights *NR?* Yes *NHL?* No *Year established/built:* 1768 *Latitude:* 42.0037 *Latitude:* -70.6006

POINT GAMMON LIGHTHOUSE
Established in 1816, the Point Gammon Lighthouse was built the same year. The lighthouse was discontinued in 1858, though it is maintained by the private owner. *Address:* Hyannis Harbor *City:* West Yarmouth *State:* MA *Visitors welcome?* No *Operated by:* Private owner *NR?* No *NHL?* No *Year established/built:* 1816 *Latitude:* 41.6479 *Latitude:* -70.2626

RACE POINT LIGHTHOUSE
Established in 1816, the current Race Point Lighthouse was built in 1876 and automated in 1872. The lighthouse is now cared for by a volunteer group. The nearby keeper's house is available for overnight stays. *Address:* Race Point Light *City:* Provincetown *State:* MA *Phone:* 508-487-9930 *Email:* racepointlighthouse@comcast.net *Visitors welcome?* Yes *Hours:* Some Saturdays, May to October *Admission:* Contact attraction directly *Operated by:* Cape Cod Chapter, ALF *NR?* Yes *NHL?* No *Year established/built:* 1816 *Latitude:* 42.0623 *Latitude:* -70.2430

SANDY NECK LIGHTHOUSE
Established in 1827, the current tower of Sandy Neck Lighthouse was rebuilt in 1857. The station was deactivated in 1931 and relit in 2007. It is privately owned. *Address:* Barnstable Harbor *City:* Cape Cod *State:* MA *Visitors welcome?* No *Operated by:* Private owner *NR?* Yes *NHL?* No *Year established/built:* 1827 *Latitude:* 41.7085 *Latitude:* -70.2926

SANKATY HEAD LIGHTHOUSE
Established and built in 1850, the current Sankaty Head Lighthouse was automated in 1965. In 2008, the lighthouse was moved to the west to avoid cliff erosion. *Address:* Sankaty Head Light *City:* Siasconset *State:*

MA *Visitors welcome?* Yes *Hours:* Grounds only *Admission:* FREE *Operated by:* Sconset Trust *NR?* Yes *NHL?* No *Year established/built:* 1850 *Latitude:* 41.2836 *Latitude:* -69.9652

SCITUATE LIGHTHOUSE
Established and built in 1811, the Scituate Lighthouse was deactivated in 1860 and relit in 1990 as a private aid to navigation. *Address:* Scituate Light *City:* Scituate *State:* MA *Visitors welcome?* Yes *Hours:* Grounds only daily, some tours *Admission:* Contact attraction directly *Operated by:* Scituate Historical Society *NR?* Yes *NHL?* No *Year established/built:* 1811 *Latitude:* 42.2032 *Latitude:* -70.7131

STAGE HARBOR LIGHTHOUSE
The Stage Harbor Lighthouse was established and constructed in 1880. Built of cast-iron, the tower was deactivated in 1933. It is now privately owned. *Address:* Stage Harbor *City:* Chatham *State:* MA *Visitors welcome?* No *Operated by:* Private owner *NR?* No *NHL?* No *Year established/built:* 1880 *Latitude:* 41.6604 *Latitude:* -69.9745

STRAITSMOUTH ISLAND LIGHTHOUSE
The lighthouse at Straitsmouth Island was established in 1835, and the current tower was constructed in 1896. The lighthouse was automated in 1967. *Address:* Straitsmouth Island Light *City:* Rockport *State:* MA *Visitors welcome?* No *Operated by:* U.S. Coast Guard (District 1) *NR?* Yes *NHL?* No *Year established/built:* 1835 *Latitude:* 42.6623 *Latitude:* -70.5881

TARPAULIN COVE LIGHTHOUSE
Established in 1759, the current structure of the Tarpaulin Cove Lighthouse was built in 1891, and it was automated in 1941. *Address:* Tarpaulin Cove Light *City:* Naushon Island *State:* MA *Visitors welcome?* No *Operated by:* Cuttyhunk Historical Society *NR?* Yes *NHL?* No *Year established/built:* 1759 *Latitude:* 41.4688 *Latitude:* -70.7575

TEN POUND ISLAND LIGHTHOUSE
The Ten Pound Island Lighthouse in Gloucester Harbor was established in 1821. The current structure was built in 1881. The light was deactivated by the U.S. Coast Guard in 1956 and relighted in 1989. *Address:* Ten Pound Island Light *City:* Gloucester *State:* MA *Visitors welcome?* Yes *Hours:* Grounds only *Admission:* FREE *Operated by:* City of Gloucester *NR?* Yes *NHL?* No *Year established/built:* 1821 *Latitude:* 42.6019 *Latitude:* -70.6656

THREE SISTERS OF NAUSET LIGHTHOUSE
Established in 1838 and originally the only light station in the U.S. with three towers, only one tower remains of the Three Sisters Lighthouse, sometimes called Twin Lights. Two of the towers were discontinued in 1911 and taken down. *Address:* Nauset Light *City:* Wellfleet *State:* MA *Visitors welcome?* Yes *Hours:* By appointment *Admission:* FREE *Operated by:* Cape Cod National Seashore *NR?* Yes *NHL?* No *Year established/built:* 1838 *Latitude:* 41.8600 *Latitude:* -69.9533

WEST CHOP LIGHTHOUSE
Established in 1818, the current West Chop Lighthouse was built in 1891, and it was automated in 1976. *City:* West Chop *State:* MA *Visitors welcome?* No *Operated by:* U.S. Coast Guard (District 1) *NR?* Yes *NHL?* No *Year established/built:* 1818 *Latitude:* 41.4801 *Latitude:* -70.6028

WINGS NECK LIGHTHOUSE
Wings Neck Light was established and built in 1849 because of heavy marine traffic traveling in Buzzards Bay to ports in Wareham and Sandwich. *Address:* Wings Neck Light *State:* MA *Phone:* 617-899-5063 *Email:*

admin@wingsnecklighthouse.com *Visitors welcome?* Yes *Hours:* Contact attraction directly *Admission:* Contact attraction directly *Operated by:* Wings Neck Lighthouse Trust *NR?* Yes *NHL?* No *Year established/built:* 1849 *Latitude:* 41.6822 *Latitude:* -70.6603

WOOD END LIGHTHOUSE

Established in 1864, the Wood End Lighthouse marks the entrance to Provincetown Harbor on Cape Cod. The current tower was built in 1872 and automated in 1961. The structure is located with the Cape Cod National Seashore. *Address:* Wood End Light *City:* Provincetown *State:* MA *Visitors welcome?* Yes *Hours:* Grounds only *Admission:* FREE *Operated by:* Cape Cod Chapter, ALF *NR?* Yes *NHL?* No *Year established/built:* 1864 *Latitude:* 42.0213 *Latitude:* -70.1935

NEW HAMPSHIRE

BURKEHAVEN LIGHTHOUSE

The Burkehaven Lighthouse on Lake Sunapee is a replica of a lighthouse built in 1989 and destroyed by ice in 1935. *Address:* Lake Sunapee *City:* Sunapee *State:* NH *Visitors welcome?* No *Operated by:* Lake Sunapee Protective Association *NR?* No *NHL?* No *Year established/built:* 1898 *Latitude:* 43.3802 *Latitude:* -72.0527

HERRICK COVE LIGHTHOUSE

Built in 1893, the Herrick Cove Lighthouse deteriorioated over the years until a local family sponsored a renovation in 2003. *Address:* Herrick Cove, Lake Sunapee *City:* Sunapee *State:* NH *Visitors welcome?* No *Operated by:* Lake Sunapee Protective Association *NR?* No *NHL?* No *Year established/built:* 1893 *Latitude:* 43.3802 *Latitude:* -72.0527

ISLE OF SHOALS LIGHTHOUSE

Established in 1822, the current Isle of Shoals Lighthouse, also called the White Island Lighthouse, was built in 1855. Still an active aid to navigation, the station is cared for by a local not-for-profit organization. *Address:* White Island Light *State:* NH *Visitors welcome?* Yes *Hours:* Grounds only *Admission:* FREE *Operated by:* Lighthouse Kids *NR?* No *NHL?* No *Year established/built:* 1822 *Latitude:* 42.9683 *Latitude:* -70.6258

LOON ISLAND LIGHTHOUSE

Constructed in 1893 by a steamship company, the Loon Island Lighthouse is still an active aid to navigation. *Address:* Loon Island, Lake Sunapee *City:* Sunapee *State:* NH *Visitors welcome?* No *Operated by:* Lake Sunapee Protective Association *NR?* No *NHL?* No *Year established/built:* 1893 *Latitude:* 43.3802 *Latitude:* -72.0527

PORTSMOUTH HARBOR LIGHTHOUSE

Established in 1771, the current Portsmouth Harbor Lighthouse was constructed in 1878. Still an active aid to navigation, the lighthouse is operated by a not-for-profit organization, which offers occasional guided tours. *Address:* Portsmouth Harbor Light *City:* New Castle *State:* NH *Web:* www.portsmouthharborlighthouse.org *Email:* info@portsmouthharborlighthouse.com *Visitors welcome?* Yes *Hours:* Contact attraction directly *Admission:* Contact attraction directly *Operated by:* Friends of Portsmouth Harbor Lighthouse *NR?* Yes *NHL?* No *Year established/built:* 1771 *Latitude:* 43.0710 *Latitude:* -70.7086

NEW JERSEY

ABSECON LIGHTHOUSE
Established and built in 1857, the Absecon Lighthouse is the tallest in New Jersey and the third tallest masonry lighthouse in the U.S. Decommissioned in 1933, the light is kept lit as a visitor attraction. The keepers house and light are also a museum. *Address:* 31 S. Rhode Island Ave. *City:* Atlantic City *State:* NJ *Zip:* 08401 *Phone:* 609-449-1360 *Web:* www.abseconlighthouse.org *Email:* jean@abseconlighthouse.org *Visitors welcome?* Yes *Hours:* September to June, Thursday to Monday, 11 a.m. to 4 p.m.; July and August, daily, 10 a.m. to 5 p.m. *Admission:* $7 adults, $5 seniors, $4 children 4-12, under four FREE *Operated by:* Absecon Lighthouse *NR?* Yes *NHL?* No *Year established/built:* 1857 *Latitude:* 39.3672 *Latitude:* -74.4155

BARNEGAT LIGHTHOUSE
Established in 1835, the current Barnegat Lighthouse tower was built in 1857. The lighthouse was run by the government until 1926, when the light was placed offshore on the Barnegat Lightship. The lighthouse was discontinued in 1944, and a public outcry led to restoration of the lighthouse. *Address:* Barnegat Lighthouse State Park *City:* Barnegat Light *State:* NJ *Zip:* 08006 *Phone:* 609-494-2016 *Web:* www.bl-hs.org *Visitors welcome?* Yes *Hours:* Daily, April 1 to Oct. 1, 9 a.m. to 4:30 p.m.; Wednesday to Sunday, Oct. 1 to April 1, 9 a.m. to 3:30 p.m. *Admission:* $1 all visitors *Operated by:* Barnegat Light Historical Society *NR?* Yes *NHL?* No *Year established/built:* 1835 *Latitude:* 39.7584 *Latitude:* -74.1012

BRANDYWINE SHOAL LIGHTHOUSE
Established in 1823, the Brandywine Shoal Lighthouse was first a lightship. The vessel was replaced in 1850 with the first screwpile lighthouse, in which the structure rests on pilings literally screwed into the bottom. *Address:* Brandywine Shoal Light *City:* Cape May *State:* NJ *Visitors welcome?* No *Operated by:* U.S. Coast Guard (District 5) *NR?* No *NHL?* No *Year established/built:* 1823 *Latitude:* 38.9864 *Latitude:* -75.1135

CAPE MAY LIGHTHOUSE
Established in 1823, the current Cape May Lighthouse was built in 1859, and it marks the northern entrance to Delaware Bay. The light was automated in 1933, and the property was turned over to the state of New Jersey, which sub-leases it to the Mid-Atlantic Center for the Arts and Humanities. *Address:* Cape May Light *City:* Cape May *State:* NJ *Zip:* 08204 *Phone:* 609-884-5404 *Web:* www.capemaymac.org *Email:* mac4arts@capemaymac.org *Visitors welcome?* Yes *Hours:* Contact attraction directly *Admission:* To climb the lighthouse: $7 adults, $3 children three to 12; Visitors center: FREE *Operated by:* Mid-Atlantic Center for the Arts and Humanities *NR?* Yes *NHL?* No *Year established/built:* 1823 *Latitude:* 38.9331 *Latitude:* -74.9603

CHAPEL HILL REAR RANGE LIGHTHOUSE
Established and built in 1856, the Chapel Hill Lighthouse served until 1957, when the light was moved to the south. The structure is now a private residence. *Address:* Chapel Hill Rear Range Light *City:* Leonardo *State:* NJ *Visitors welcome?* No *Operated by:* Private owner *NR?* No *NHL?* No *Year established/built:* 1856 *Latitude:* 40.3983 *Latitude:* -74.0587

CONOVER BEACON LIGHTHOUSE
Established in 1856, the current skeletal tower Conover Beacon Lighthouse was constructed in 1941. The beacon, also called Chapel Hill Front Range Lightouse, is no longer active. It was the companion to the Chapel Hill Rear Range Lighthouse. *Address:* Beach Avenue and North Leonard Avenue *City:* Leonardo *State:* NJ *Visitors welcome?* Yes *Hours:* Grounds only *Admission:* FREE *Operated by:* Monmouth County *NR?* No *NHL?* No *Year established/built:* 1856 *Latitude:* 40.4218 *Latitude:* -74.0564

CHAPTER 5 – LIGHTHOUSES & LIGHTSHIPS

CROSS LEDGE LIGHTHOUSE
Established and built in 1875, the Cross Ledge Lighthouse was discontinued in 1910, and only the foundation of the lighthouse remains. *City:* Fortescue *State:* NJ *Visitors welcome?* No *Operated by:* U.S. Coast Guard (District 5) *NR?* No *NHL?* No *Year established/built:* 1875 *Latitude:* 39.2376 *Latitude:* -75.1716

EAST POINT LIGHTHOUSE
Established and built in 1849, the East Point Lighthouse was first called the Maurice River Lighthouse for the river mouth it marks. It operated until 1941, when the U.S. Coast Guard discontinued it. It is now undergoing restoration by the Maurice River Historical Society. *Address:* East Point Light *City:* Heislerville *State:* NJ *Phone:* 856-785-1120 *Visitors welcome?* Yes *Hours:* Grounds open, tours by appointment *Admission:* Contact attraction directly *Operated by:* Maurice River Township *NR?* Yes *NHL?* No *Year established/built:* 1849 *Latitude:* 39.1958 *Latitude:* -75.0272

ELBOW OF CROSS LEDGE LIGHTHOUSE
Built in 1907 on an extension of Cross Ledge in Delaware Bay, the Elbow of Cross Ledge Lighthouse features a cast-iron design common around the turn of the 20th century. *Address:* Elbow of Cross Ledge Light *City:* Fortescue *State:* NJ *Visitors welcome?* No *Operated by:* U.S. Coast Guard (District 5) *NR?* No *NHL?* No *Year established/built:* 1907 *Latitude:* 39.1816 *Latitude:* -75.2683

FINNS POINT RANGE LIGHTHOUSE
Established and built in 1877, the Finns Point Range Light was one of a series of range lights that guided mariners up the Delaware River. The lights were closed down in 1950, though the wrought iron tower of the Finns Point light remains. *Address:* 197 Lighthouse Road *City:* Pennsville *State:* NJ *Zip:* 08070 *Phone:* 609-463-0994 *Visitors welcome?* Yes *Hours:* Grounds only *Admission:* FREE *Operated by:* Supawna Meadows Wildlife Refuge *NR?* Yes *NHL?* No *Year established/built:* 1877 *Latitude:* 39.6150 *Latitude:* -75.5285

GREAT BEDS LIGHTHOUSE
Established in 1880, the Great Beds Lighthouse marks an area known for its rich oyster beds. The lighthouse is still an active aid to navigation. *Address:* Great Beds Light *City:* South Amboy *State:* NJ *Visitors welcome?* No *Operated by:* U.S. Coast Guard (District 5) *NR?* No *NHL?* No *Year established/built:* 1880 *Latitude:* 40.4867 *Latitude:* -74.2533

HEREFORD INLET LIGHTHOUSE
Established and built in 1874, the Hereford Inlet Lighthouse was manned until 1964, when the light was automated. The buildings were taken over by the state of New Jersey and the City of North Wildwood and converted to a museum in 1988. *Address:* Central Avenue and East First Avenue *City:* Rio Grande *State:* NJ *Zip:* 08242 *Phone:* 609-522-4520 *Web:* www.herefordlighthouse.org *Visitors welcome?* Yes *Hours:* Mid-October to Mid-May, Wednesday to Sunday, 10 a.m. to 4 p.m.; Mid-May to Mid-October, daily, 9 a.m. to 4 p.m. *Admission:* $4 adults, $1 children *Operated by:* Friends of Hereford Lighthouse *NR?* Yes *NHL?* No *Year established/built:* 1874 *Latitude:* 40.8478 *Latitude:* -73.9968

LUDLUM BEACH LIGHTHOUSE
Established in 1885, the Ludlum Beach Lighthouse is now a summer rental house. *Address:* 3414 Landis Avenue *City:* Sea Isle City *State:* NJ *Visitors welcome?* No *Operated by:* Private owner *NR?* No *NHL?* No *Year established/built:* 1885 *Latitude:* 39.1598 *Latitude:* -74.6881

MIAH MAULL SHOAL LIGHTHOUSE
Built in 1913, the cast-iron Miah Maull Shoal Lighthouse is atop an underwater feature named for an 18th century citizen, Nehemiah Maull, who died in a shipwreck on the site. The lighthouse was auto-

mated in 1973. *Address:* Miah Maull Shoal Light *City:* Fortescue *State:* NJ *Visitors welcome?* No *Operated by:* U.S. Coast Guard (District 5) *NR?* Yes *NHL?* No *Year established/built:* 1913 *Latitude:* 39.1264 *Latitude:* -75.2097

NAVESINK LIGHTHOUSE

Established in 1828, the current brownstone Navesink Lighthouse with its twin light towers was constructed in 1862. The light was decommissioned in 1949 and turned over to the State of New Jersey. A not-for-profit operates a museum at the site. *Address:* Navesink Twin Lights *City:* Highlands *State:* NJ *Zip:* 07732 *Phone:* 732-872-1814 *Web:* twin-lights.org *Email:* info@twin-lights.org *Visitors welcome?* Yes *Hours:* Daily, Memorial Day to Labor, 10 a.m to 4:30 p.m.; Wednesday to Sunday, Labor Day to Memorial Day, 10 a.m. to 4:30 p.m. *Admission:* Donation *Operated by:* Twin Lights Historical Society *NR?* Yes *NHL?* Yes *Year established/built:* 1828 *Latitude:* 40.3962 *Latitude:* -73.9858

ROBBINS REEF LIGHTHOUSE

Established in 1839, the current coffee pot-style Robbins Reef Lighthouse was constructed in 1883. The light is still an active aid to navigation. *Address:* Robbins Reef Light *City:* Bayonne *State:* NJ *Visitors welcome?* No *Operated by:* U.S. Coast Guard (District 5) *NR?* Yes *NHL?* No *Year established/built:* 1839 *Latitude:* 40.6574 *Latitude:* -74.0656

ROMER SHOAL LIGHTHOUSE

Established by a daymark in 1838, the current Romer Shoal Lighthouse was constructed in 1898 using the coffee pot design. It is still an active aid to navigation. *Address:* Romer Shoal *City:* Keansburg *State:* NJ *Visitors welcome?* No *Operated by:* U.S. Coast Guard (District 5) *NR?* No *NHL?* No *Year established/built:* 1838 *Latitude:* 40.5068 *Latitude:* -74.0021

SANDY HOOK LIGHTHOUSE

Established in 1764, the original Sandy Hook Lighthouse was called the New York Lighthouse, because it marked the entrance to New York Harbor. The original tower still stands, though it was reinforced with brick in the 19th century, and it is no longer an active aid to navigation. *Address:* Sandy Hook *City:* Highlands *State:* NJ *Phone:* 732-872-5970 *Visitors welcome?* Yes *Hours:* Contact attraction directly *Admission:* Contact attraction directly *Operated by:* Gateway National Recreation Area *NR?* Yes *NHL?* Yes *Year established/built:* 1764 *Latitude:* 40.4432 *Latitude:* -73.9899

SEA GIRT LIGHTHOUSE

Established and built in 1896, the Sea Girt Lighthouse marks a harbor of refuge at the resort community of Sea Girt. The light fell into disuse during World War II, although it was revived in the 1990s by a local not-for-profit. *Address:* Sea Girt Light *City:* Sea Girt *State:* NJ *Zip:* 08750 *Phone:* 732-974-0514 *Web:* www.seagirtboro.com/lighthouse.html *Visitors welcome?* Yes *Hours:* Sunday, April to November, 2 p.m. to 4 p.m. *Admission:* Contact attraction directly *Operated by:* Sea Girt Lighthouse Citizens Committee *NR?* No *NHL?* No *Year established/built:* 1896 *Latitude:* 40.1367 *Latitude:* -74.0275

SHIP JOHN SHOAL LIGHTHOUSE

Established in 1854 and constructed in 1874, the Ship John Shoal Lighthouse was placed above an underwater feature named for a ship called John which had wrecked on the future in the 18th century. The light was automated in 1973 and it is still an active aid to navigation. *Address:* Ship John Shoal Light *City:* Woodland Beach *State:* NJ *Visitors welcome?* No *Operated by:* U.S. Coast Guard (District 5) *NR?* No *NHL?* No *Year established/built:* 1854 *Latitude:* 39.3053 *Latitude:* -75.3767

CHAPTER 5 – LIGHTHOUSES & LIGHTSHIPS

TINICUM ISLAND REAR RANGE LIGHTHOUSE
The Tinicum Island Rear Range Lighthouse is one of a series of four range lights built along the Delaware River in the late 19th century. Still in operation after a century and a quarter, the Tinicum light is now located within a baseball field complex. *Address:* Tinicum Island Rear Range Light *City:* Paulsboro *State:* NJ *Zip:* 08066 *Phone:* 856-423-1500 *Visitors welcome?* Yes *Hours:* Contact attraction directly *Admission:* Contact attraction directly *Operated by:* U.S. Coast Guard (District 5) *NR?* Yes *NHL?* No *Year established/built:* 1880 *Latitude:* 39.8475 *Latitude:* -75.2398

NEW YORK

BARBER'S POINT LIGHTHOUSE
Established and built in 1873, the Barber's Point Lighthouse was deactivated in 1935 and is now a private residence. *Address:* Barber Point Light *City:* Westport *State:* NY *Visitors welcome?* No *Operated by:* Private owner *NR?* Yes *NHL?* No *Year established/built:* 1873 *Latitude:* 44.1543 *Latitude:* -73.4045

BLACKWELL ISLAND LIGHTHOUSE
Built by the city of New York in 1872 at aid ships in the East River, the Blackwell Island Lighthouse stands in a park on what is today called Roosevelt Island. *Address:* Lighthouse Park *City:* New York *State:* NY *Zip:* 10038 *Visitors welcome?* Yes *Hours:* Daily *Admission:* FREE *Operated by:* New York City Department of Parks & Recreation *NR?* No *NHL?* No *Year established/built:* 1872 *Latitude:* 40.7715 *Latitude:* -73.9413

BLUFF POINT LIGHTHOUSE
Established and built in 1874, the Bluff Point Lighthouse was automated in 1930 and is still an active aid to navigation. *Address:* Bluff Point Light *City:* Valcour *State:* NY *Visitors welcome?* Yes *Hours:* Contact attraction directly *Admission:* Contact attraction directly *Operated by:* Clinton County Historical Association *NR?* Yes *NHL?* No *Year established/built:* 1874 *Latitude:* 44.6233 *Latitude:* -73.4319

BREWERTON RANGE REAR LIGHTHOUSE
The 85-foot Brewerton Range Rear Lighthouse marks the junction of the western end of Lake Oneida with the Oneida River, part of the New York State Barge Canal complex. *Address:* Oneida River *City:* Brewerton *State:* NY *Visitors welcome?* Yes *Hours:* Daily *Admission:* FREE *Operated by:* New York State Canals *NR?* No *NHL?* No *Year established/built:* 1916 *Latitude:* 43.2362 *Latitude:* -76.1174

CAYUGA INLET LIGHTHOUSE
The Cayuga Inlet Lighthouse was constructed in 1917 as part of a series of improvements to the Cayuga and Seneca Canal and other waterways. Now located at Alan Treman State Park, the lighthouse has a companion called the Cayuga Inlet Breakwater Lighthouse. *Address:* Cayuga Inlet *City:* Ithaca *State:* NY *Visitors welcome?* Yes *Hours:* No tower access *Admission:* FREE *Operated by:* New York State Office of Parks, Recreation and Historic Preservation *NR?* No *NHL?* No *Year established/built:* 1917 *Latitude:* 42.4595 *Latitude:* -76.5122

CEDAR ISLAND LIGHTHOUSE
Established in 1839, the current Cedar Island Lighthouse was constructed in 1868 and deactivated in 1934. The lighthouse is in the process of being preserved. *Address:* Cedar Point County Park *City:* Sag Harbor *State:* NY *Visitors welcome?* Yes *Hours:* Daily *Admission:* Grounds open, tower closed *Operated by:* Suffolk County, New York *NR?* Yes *NHL?* No *Year established/built:* 1839 *Latitude:* 40.9968 *Latitude:* -72.2615

CHAPTER 5 – LIGHTHOUSES & LIGHTSHIPS

COLD SPRING HARBOR
Address: Cold Spring Harbor Light *City:* Cold Spring Harbor *State:* NY *Visitors welcome?* No *Operated by:* Private owner *NR?* No *NHL?* No *Year established/built:* 1890 *Latitude:* 40.9061 *Latitude:* -73.4366

CONEY ISLAND LIGHTHOUSE
Established in 1890, the current Coney Island Lighthouse, also called the Nortons Point Lighthouse, was constructed in 1920. Still an active aid to navigation, the lighthouse is near one of the most famous resort areas in the country. *Address:* Coney Island Light *City:* Coney Island *State:* NY *Visitors welcome?* No *Operated by:* U.S. Coast Guard (District 1) *NR?* No *NHL?* No *Year established/built:* 1890 *Latitude:* 40.5767 *Latitude:* -74.0117

CUMBERLAND HEAD LIGHTHOUSE
Established in 1838, the current Cumberland Head Lighthouse was built in 1868 and deactivated in 1934. It is now a private residence. *Address:* Cumberland Head Light *City:* Plattsburgh *State:* NY *Visitors welcome?* No *Operated by:* U.S. Coast Guard (District 1) *NR?* No *NHL?* No *Year established/built:* 1838 *Latitude:* 44.6914 *Latitude:* -73.3853

DUNKIRK LIGHTHOUSE
Established in 1826, the current Dunkirk Lighthouse, also called the Point Gratiot Lighthouse, was constructed in 1875 and is still an active aid to navigation. It is operated by a local not-for-profit organization. *Address:* 1 Lighthouse Point Drive *City:* Dunkirk *State:* NY *Zip:* 14048 *Phone:* 716-366-5050 *Email:* LST551@juno.com *Visitors welcome?* Yes *Hours:* May to June, 10 a.m. to 2 p.m. (closed Wednesday and Sunday); July to August, 10 a.m. to 4 p.m. (closed Wednesday and Sunday); September to October, 10 a.m. to 2 p.m. (closed Wednesday and Sunday) *Admission:* $6 adults; $2.50 children 4 to 12; under 4, FREE *Operated by:* Dunkirk Lighthouse & Veterans Park Museum *NR?* Yes *NHL?* No *Year established/built:* 1826 *Latitude:* 42.4885 *Latitude:* -79.3514

> The Fyddeye Guide tries to be as accurate as possible. But we sometimes make mistakes. Email corrections to contact@fyddeye.com.

EATONS NECK LIGHTHOUSE
Established and built in 1799, the Eatons Neck Lighthouse is still an active aid to navigation. *Address:* Eatons Neck Light *City:* Asharoken *State:* NY *Visitors welcome?* No *Operated by:* U.S. Coast Guard (District 1) *NR?* Yes *NHL?* No *Year established/built:* 1799 *Latitude:* 40.9540 *Latitude:* -73.3951

ELM TREE BEACON LIGHTHOUSE
Elm Tree Lighthouse got its name from a large elm tree which once served as a beacon for early Dutch sailors. The lighthouse itself was built in 1856. It is located at Miller Field. *Address:* Elm Tree Beacon Light *City:* New Dorp *State:* NY *Visitors welcome?* Yes *Hours:* Grounds open *Admission:* FREE *Operated by:* Gateway National Recreation Area *NR?* No *NHL?* No *Year established/built:* 1856 *Latitude:* 40.5639 *Latitude:* -74.0953

ESOPUS MEADOWS LIGHTHOUSE
Established in 1839, the Esopus Meadows Lighthouse, also called the Middle Hudson Lighthouse, was automated in 1965 and is still an active aid to navigation. It is now operated by a local not-for-profit organization. *Address:* Esopus Meadows Light *City:* Esopus *State:* NY *Visitors welcome?* No *Operated by:* Save Esopus Lighthouse Commission *NR?* Yes *NHL?* No *Year established/built:* 1839 *Latitude:* 41.8686 *Latitude:* -73.9414

CHAPTER 5 – LIGHTHOUSES & LIGHTSHIPS

EXECUTION ROCKS LIGHTHOUSE
Established and built in 1850, the Execution Rocks Lighthouse was automated in 1979 and is still an active aid to navigation. *Address:* Execution Rocks Light *City:* Sands Point *State:* NY *Visitors welcome?* No *Operated by:* U.S. Coast Guard (District 1) *NR?* No *NHL?* No *Year established/built:* 1850 *Latitude:* 40.8783 *Latitude:* -73.7374

FIRE ISLAND LIGHTHOUSE
Established in 1827, the current Fire Island Lighthouse was built in 1858 and automated in 1986. Still an active aid to navigation, the lighthouse is operated by a local not-for-profit. *Address:* Fire Island Light *City:* Saltaire *State:* NY *Phone:* 631-661-4876 *Visitors welcome?* Yes *Hours:* Daily *Admission:* Contact attraction directly *Operated by:* Fire Island Lighthouse Preservation Society *NR?* Yes *NHL?* No *Year established/built:* 1827 *Latitude:* 40.6324 *Latitude:* -73.2186

FORT WADSWORTH LIGHTHOUSE
Established and built in 1903, the Fort Wadsworth Lighthouse was deactivated in 1963. It is now part of the Gateway National Recreation Area. *Address:* Fort Wadsworth Light *City:* Staten Island *State:* NY *Visitors welcome?* Yes *Hours:* Fort Wadsworth is open Wednesday through Sunday, 10 a.m. to 5 p.m. *Admission:* Free admission to Fort Wadsworth, tower closed *Operated by:* Gateway National Recreation Area *NR?* No *NHL?* No *Year established/built:* 1828 *Latitude:* 40.6058 *Latitude:* -74.0539

HORTON POINT LIGHTHOUSE
Established and built in 1857, the Horton Point Lighthouse was automated in 1933 and is still an active aid to navigation. *Address:* Horton Point Light *City:* Southold *State:* NY *Phone:* 631-765-5500 *Visitors welcome?* Yes *Hours:* Grounds open daily 8 a.m. to dusk Memorial Day to Columbus Day *Admission:* FREE *Operated by:* East End Lighthouses *NR?* Yes *NHL?* No *Year established/built:* 1857 *Latitude:* 41.0835 *Latitude:* -72.4466

HUDSON-ATHENS LIGHTHOUSE
Established and built in 1874, the Hudson-Athens Lighthouse, also called the Hudson City Lighthouse, was automated in 1949 and is still an active aid to navigation. It is operated by a local not-for-profit. *Address:* Hudson-Athens Light *City:* Athens *State:* NY *Phone:* 518-828-5294 *Web:* www.hudsonathenslighthouse.org *Visitors welcome?* Yes *Hours:* Contact attraction directly *Admission:* Contact attraction directly *Operated by:* Hudson-Athens Lighthouse Preservation Society *NR?* Yes *NHL?* No *Year established/built:* 1874 *Latitude:* 42.2625 *Latitude:* -73.8105

HUNTINGTON HARBOR LIGHTHOUSE
Established in 1857, the current Huntington Harbor Lighthouse, once known as the Lloyd Harbor Lighthouse, was automated in 1949 and is still an active aid to navigation. *Address:* Huntington Harbor Light *City:* Huntington Harbor *State:* NY *Visitors welcome?* Yes *Hours:* By appointment *Admission:* By appointment *Operated by:* Huntington Lighthouse Preservation Society *NR?* Yes *NHL?* No *Year established/built:* 1912 *Latitude:* 40.9108 *Latitude:* -73.4317

JEFFREYS HOOK LIGHTHOUSE
Jeffreys Hook Lighthouse is also known as the Little Red Lighthouse. *Address:* Riverside Drive & W 181st St *City:* New York *State:* NY *Phone:* 212-304-2365 *Visitors welcome?* Yes *Hours:* Dawn to dusk *Admission:* Tower closed *Operated by:* New York City Department of Parks & Recreation *NR?* Yes *NHL?* No *Year established/built:* 1921 *Latitude:* 40.8519 *Latitude:* -73.9419

CHAPTER 5 – LIGHTHOUSES & LIGHTSHIPS

LATIMER REEF LIGHTHOUSE
Established in 1804, the current Latimer Reef Lighthouse was constructed in 1884 and automated in 1974. It is currently an active aid to navigation. *City:* Fishers Island *State:* NY *Visitors welcome?* No *Operated by:* U.S. Coast Guard (District 1) *NR?* No *NHL?* No *Year established/built:* 1804 *Latitude:* 41.2570 *Latitude:* -72.0240

LITTLE GULL ISLAND LIGHTHOUSE
Established in 1806, the current Little Gull Island Lighthouse was built in 1869, and it is still an active aid to navigation. *Address:* Plum Island *State:* NY *Visitors welcome?* No *Operated by:* U.S. Coast Guard (District 1) *NR?* No *NHL?* No *Year established/built:* 1806 *Latitude:* 41.1792 *Latitude:* -72.2056

MONTAUK POINT LIGHTHOUSE
Authorized by President George Washington in 1796 and built the next year, the Montauk Point Lighthouse is an iconic American lighthouse. Automated in 1987, the lighthouse is now a museum. *Address:* Montauk Point Light *City:* Montauk *State:* NY *Zip:* 11954 *Phone:* 631-668-2544 *Web:* www.montauklighthouse.com *Email:* keeper@montauklighthouse.com *Visitors welcome?* Yes *Hours:* Daily during the summer, else weekends *Admission:* $8 adults, $6 seniors, $4 children *Operated by:* Montauk Historical Society *NR?* Yes *NHL?* No *Year established/built:* 1796 *Latitude:* 41.0710 *Latitude:* -71.8571

NEW DORP LIGHTHOUSE
Established and built in 1856, the New Dorp Lighthouse, also called the Swash Channel Rear Range Lighthouse, was deactivated in 1964 and is now a private residence. *Address:* New Dorp Light *City:* Staten Island *State:* NY *Visitors welcome?* No *Operated by:* Private owner *NR?* Yes *NHL?* No *Year established/built:* 1856 *Latitude:* 40.5808 *Latitude:* -74.1200

NORTH BROTHER ISLAND LIGHTHOUSE
Constructed in 1869, North Brother Island Lighthouse marks a treacherous area of the Narrows in Long Island Sound. The lighthouse has famous neighbors, including Riverside Hospital, home to Typhoid Mary and other quarantined patients, and Rikers Island. *Address:* North Brother Island Light *City:* New York *State:* NY *Visitors welcome?* No *Operated by:* City of New York *NR?* No *NHL?* No *Year established/built:* 1869 *Latitude:* 40.8012 *Latitude:* -73.8976

NORTH DUMPLING LIGHTHOUSE
Established in 1849, the current North Dumpling Lighthouse was constructed in 1871. Deactivated in 1959, it is now a private residence. *Address:* North Dumpling Island *City:* Fishers Island *State:* NY *Visitors welcome?* No *Operated by:* Private owner *NR?* No *NHL?* No *Year established/built:* 1849 *Latitude:* 41.2829 *Latitude:* -72.0162

OLD FIELD POINT LIGHTHOUSE
Established in 1823, the current Old Field Point Lighthouse was constructed in 1868 and automated in 1933. It is still an active aid to navigation and also serves as offices for the local municipality. *Address:* Old Field Point Light *City:* Village of Old Field *State:* NY *Zip:* 11733 *Phone:* 631-941-9412 *Email:* villageclerk@oldfieldny.org *Visitors welcome?* Yes *Hours:* Contact attraction directly *Admission:* Contact attraction directly *Operated by:* Village of Old Field *NR?* No *NHL?* No *Year established/built:* 1823 *Latitude:* 40.9770 *Latitude:* -73.1186

OLD ORCHARD SHOAL LIGHTHOUSE
Established and built in 1893, the Old Orchard Shoal Lighthouse is still an active aid to navigation. *Address:* Old Orchard Shoal Light *City:* Staten Island *State:* NY *Visitors welcome?* No *Operated by:* U.S. Coast Guard (District 1) *NR?* No *NHL?* No *Year established/built:* 1893 *Latitude:* 40.5122 *Latitude:* -74.0986

CHAPTER 5 – LIGHTHOUSES & LIGHTSHIPS

ORIENT LONG BEACH BAR LIGHTHOUSE
Known as Bug Light because of its perch on piles sunk into the sand, the Long Beach Bar Lighthouse was constructed in 1871 to mark the opening to Peconic Bay. Frequently damaged by ice during the winter, the station was taken out of service in 1948. *Address:* Orient Long Beach Bar Light *City:* Greenport *State:* NY *Zip:* 11944 *Phone:* 631-477-2100 *Email:* eseaport@verizon.net *Visitors welcome?* No *Operated by:* East End Seaport Museum & Marine Foundation *NR?* No *NHL?* No *Year established/built:* 1871 *Latitude:* 41.1089 *Latitude:* -72.3064

ORIENT POINT LIGHTHOUSE
Established and built in 1899, the Orient Point Lighthouse was automated in 1954 and is still an active aid to navigation. *Address:* Orient Point Light *City:* Orient Point *State:* NY *Visitors welcome?* No *Operated by:* U.S. Coast Guard (District 1) *NR?* No *NHL?* No *Year established/built:* 1899 *Latitude:* 41.1633 *Latitude:* -72.2233

PLUM ISLAND LIGHTHOUSE
Established in 1827, the current Plum Island Lighthouse, also called the Plum Gut Lighthouse, was built in 1870 and deactivated in 1978. The island is now the site of a USDA research facility. *Address:* Plum Island Light *City:* Plum Island *State:* NY *Visitors welcome?* No *Operated by:* U.S. Animal Disease Center *NR?* No *NHL?* No *Year established/built:* 1827 *Latitude:* 41.1737 *Latitude:* -72.2115

POINT AUX ROCHES LIGHTHOUSE
Established and built in 1858, the Point aux Roches Lighthouse was deactivated in 1989. *Address:* Point Au Roches Light *City:* Plattsburg *State:* NY *Visitors welcome?* No *Operated by:* Private owner *NR?* No *NHL?* No *Year established/built:* 1858 *Latitude:* 44.7994 *Latitude:* -73.3606

PRINCES BAY LIGHTHOUSE
Established and built in 1828, the Princes Bay Lighthouse was deactivated in 1922. *Address:* Mt. Loretto Unique Area *City:* Staten Island *State:* NY *Visitors welcome?* No *Operated by:* Mt. Loretto Unique Area *NR?* No *NHL?* No *Year established/built:* 1828 *Latitude:* 40.5834 *Latitude:* -74.1496

RACE ROCK LIGHTHOUSE
Established and built in 1828, the Race Rock Lighthouse was automated in 1978 and is still an active aid to navigation. *Address:* Race Rock Light *City:* Fishers Island *State:* NY *Visitors welcome?* No *Operated by:* U.S. Coast Guard (District 1) *NR?* Yes *NHL?* No *Year established/built:* 1878 *Latitude:* 41.2436 *Latitude:* -72.0469

RONDOUT CREEK LIGHTHOUSE
Established in 1838, the current Rondout Creek Lighthouse was built in 1915 and automated in 1954. Now owned by the local municipality, the lighthouse is still an active aid to navigation. *Address:* Rondout Light *City:* Kingston *State:* NY *Visitors welcome?* Yes *Hours:* Contact attraction directly *Admission:* Contact attraction directly *Operated by:* Hudson River Maritime Museum *NR?* Yes *NHL?* No *Year established/built:* 1838 *Latitude:* 41.9206 *Latitude:* -73.9622

SANDS POINT LIGHTHOUSE
Established and built in 1809, the Sands Point Lighthouse was deactivated in 1922. *Address:* Sands Point Light *City:* Sands Point *State:* NY *Visitors welcome?* No *Operated by:* Private owner *NR?* No *NHL?* No *Year established/built:* 1809 *Latitude:* 40.8659 *Latitude:* -73.7295

✦ SAUGERTIES LIGHTHOUSE
Established in 1836, the current Saugerties Lighthouse was built in 1869 and automated in 1954. It is still an active aid to navigation. *Address:* Saugerties Light *City:* Saugerties *State:* NY *Zip:* 12477 *Phone:*

845-247-0656 *Web:* www.saugertieslighthouse.com *Email:* info@saugertieslighthouse.com *Visitors welcome?* Yes *Hours:* Contact attraction directly *Admission:* Contact attraction directly *Operated by:* Saugerties Lighthouse Conservancy *NR?* Yes *NHL?* No *Year established/built:* 1836 *Latitude:* 42.0719 *Latitude:* -73.9303

SHINNECOCK LIGHTHOUSE
Constructed in 1858, Shinnecock Lighthouse, also called Great West Bay Lighthouse, was one of the tallest lights on the eastern seaboard at 150 feet. The U.S. Coast Guard replaced the brick tower with a steel skeleton tower in 1931. *City:* Shinnecock Bay *State:* NY *Visitors welcome?* No *Operated by:* U.S. Coast Guard (District 1) *NR?* No *NHL?* No *Year established/built:* 1858 *Latitude:* 40.8408 *Latitude:* -72.4741

SPLIT ROCK POINT LIGHTHOUSE
Established in 1838, the current Split Rock Point Lighthouse was built in 1867 and deactivated in 1928. It is now a private residence. *Address:* Split Rock Point, Adirondack Park Preserve *City:* Essex *State:* NY *Visitors welcome?* No *Operated by:* Private owner *NR?* No *NHL?* No *Year established/built:* 1838 *Latitude:* 44.3101 *Latitude:* -73.3526

STATEN ISLAND REAR RANGE LIGHTHOUSE
Established in 1909, the current Staten Island Rear Range Lighthouse was constructed in 1912 and is still an active aid to navigation. *Address:* Latourette Park *City:* Staten Island *State:* NY *Visitors welcome?* No *Operated by:* U.S. Coast Guard (District 1) *NR?* No *NHL?* No *Year established/built:* 1909 *Latitude:* 40.5659 *Latitude:* -74.1680

STATUE OF LIBERTY
Known as one of the greatest American icons, the Statue of Liberty was also a working lighthouse in the first few years of her operation after the statue was installed in 1886. It ceased being an official navigation aid in 1902. *Address:* Statue of Liberty *State:* NY *Zip:* 10004 *Phone:* 212-363-3200 *Web:* www.nps.gov/stli/ *Visitors welcome?* Yes *Hours:* Daily, 9 a.m. to 5 p.m. *Admission:* FREE *Operated by:* Statue of Liberty National Monument *NR?* Yes *NHL?* No *Year established/built:* 1886 *Latitude:* 40.6891 *Latitude:* -74.0446

STEPPING STONES LIGHTHOUSE
Established in 1866, the current Stepping Stones Lighthouse was constructed in 1877. Automated in 1967, it is still an active aid to navigation. *Address:* Stepping Stones Light *City:* Kings Point *State:* NY *Visitors welcome?* No *Operated by:* U.S. Coast Guard (District 1) *NR?* Yes *NHL?* No *Year established/built:* 1866 *Latitude:* 40.8244 *Latitude:* -73.7747

STONY POINT LIGHTHOUSE
Established in 1826, the current Stony Point Lighthouse, also known as the Henderson Lighthouse, was constructed in 1869 and deactivated in 1945. It is now in private hands. *Address:* Stony Point Light *City:* Henderson *State:* NY *Visitors welcome?* No *Operated by:* Private owner *NR?* No *NHL?* No *Year established/built:* 1826 *Latitude:* 43.8394 *Latitude:* -76.2983

STRATFORD SHOAL LIGHTHOUSE
Established in 1837, the current Stratford Shoal Lighthouse was constructed in 1877. Automated in 1970, the light is still an active aid to navigation. *Address:* Stratford Shoal Light *State:* NY *Visitors welcome?* No *Operated by:* U.S. Coast Guard (District 1) *NR?* Yes *NHL?* No *Year established/built:* 1837 *Latitude:* 41.0597 *Latitude:* -73.1014

TARRYTOWN LIGHTHOUSE
Established and built in 1883, the Tarrytown Lighthouse, also called the Kingsland Point Lighthouse, was deactivated in 1961. *Address:* Tarrytown Light *City:* Sleepy Hollow *State:* NY *Visitors welcome?* Yes *Hours:* Contact attraction directly *Admission:* Contact attraction directly *Operated by:* Westchester County Dept. of Parks *NR?* Yes *NHL?* No *Year established/built:* 1883 *Latitude:* 41.0842 *Latitude:* -73.8742

THROGS NECK LIGHTHOUSE
The State of New York decided in the 1820s that a lighthouse was needed at Throgs Neck, which juts out in the East River, and the structure was finished in 1827. The lighthouse was replaced in 1835 by temporary structures that lasted almost 50 years. *Address:* Throgs Neck Light *City:* Throggs Neck *State:* NY *Zip:* 10465 *Phone:* 718-409-7200 *Visitors welcome?* Yes *Hours:* Contact attraction directly *Admission:* Contact attraction directly *Operated by:* State University of New York Maritime College *NR?* No *NHL?* No *Year established/built:* 1827 *Latitude:* 40.8044 *Latitude:* -73.7906

VERONA BEACH LIGHTHOUSE
The Verona Beach Lighthouse was one of three constructed on Lake Oneida to mark the entrance to the Wood Creek Canal on the east end of the lake. The light was lit in 1917, and is now cared for by the not-for-profit Verona Beach Lighthouse Association. *Address:* Verona Beach State Park *City:* Verona Beach *State:* NY *Visitors welcome?* Yes *Hours:* Daily *Admission:* FREE *Operated by:* Verona Beach Lighthouse Association *NR?* No *NHL?* No *Year established/built:* 1917 *Latitude:* 43.1809 *Latitude:* -75.7168

WEST BANK LIGHTHOUSE
Established and constructed in 1901, the West Bank Lighthouse is the front range light for the Staten Island Lighthouse, both of which are still active aids to navigation. *Address:* West Bank Light *City:* Staten Island *State:* NY *Visitors welcome?* No *Operated by:* U.S. Coast Guard (District 1) *NR?* No *NHL?* No *Year established/built:* 1901 *Latitude:* 40.5381 *Latitude:* -74.0428

NORTH CAROLINA

BALD HEAD ISLAND LIGHTHOUSE
The Bald Head Island Lighthouse, often called Old Baldy Lighthouse, was built in 1817, making it North Carolina's oldest standing tower. This lighthouse replaced the first Bald Head Light (1795) that was destroyed due to beach erosion around 1813. *City:* Bald Head Island *State:* NC *Zip:* 28461 *Phone:* 910-457-7481 *Web:* www.oldbaldy.org *Email:* info@oldbaldy.org *Visitors welcome?* Yes *Hours:* Summer: Tuesday through Saturday, 10 a.m. to 4 p.m.; Winter (Dec. 1 to March 15): Friday to Saturday, 10 a.m. to 4 p.m.; Sunday, 11 a.m. to 4 p.m. *Admission:* $5 age 12 and up, $3 under 12, age 2 and under FREE *Operated by:* Old Baldy Foundation *NR?* Yes *NHL?* No *Year established/built:* 1795 *Latitude:* 33.9900 *Latitude:* -78.0424

BODIE ISLAND LIGHTHOUSE
Established in 1837, the current Bodie Island Lighthouse is the third on the island, built in 1872. Still an active aid to navigation, the light is now owned by the National Park Service, which operates a visitors center in the keepers house. *Address:* Bodie Island Light Station *City:* Whalebone *State:* NC *Phone:* 252-441-5711 *Web:* www.nps.gov/caha/ *Visitors welcome?* Yes *Hours:* Grounds only *Admission:* FREE *Operated by:* Cape Hatteras National Seashore *NR?* Yes *NHL?* No *Year established/built:* 1837 *Latitude:* 35.8185 *Latitude:* -75.5633

CAPE FEAR LIGHTHOUSE
Established in 1794 by the federal government, the Cape Fear Lighthouse was a series of three structures, the last of which was a skeletal tower that was torn down in 1958 in favor of the Oak Island Lighthouse. All that remains are the large concrete footings. *City:* Bald Head Island *State:* NC *Zip:* 28461 *Phone:* 910-457-0089 *Web:* www.bhic.org *Email:* email@bhic.org *Visitors welcome?* Yes *Hours:* Grounds only *Admission:* FREE *Operated by:* Bald Head Island Conservancy *NR?* Yes *NHL?* No *Year established/built:* 1794 *Latitude:* 33.9900 *Latitude:* -78.0424

CAPE HATTERAS LIGHTHOUSE
Established in 1803, the current Cape Hatteras Lighthouse, perhaps the most famous lighthouse in the United States, was constructed in 1870. Still an active aid to navigation, the lighthouse is near the site where the Wright Brothers first demonstrated powered flight. *Address:* Cape Hatteras Light *City:* Buxton *State:* NC *Zip:* 27959 *Phone:* 252-473-2111 *Web:* www.nps.gov/caha/ *Visitors welcome?* Yes *Hours:* Grounds only *Admission:* FREE *Operated by:* Cape Hatteras National Seashore *NR?* Yes *NHL?* Yes *Year established/built:* 1803 *Latitude:* 35.2506 *Latitude:* -75.5288

CAPE LOOKOUT LIGHTHOUSE
Established in 1812, the current Cape Lookout Lighthouse was constructed in 1859 and automated in 1950. Now owned by the National Park Service, the light is an active aid to navigation. *Address:* Cape Lookout Light *City:* Harkers Island *State:* NC *Zip:* 28531 *Phone:* 252-728-2250 *Web:* www.nps.gov/calo/ *Visitors welcome?* Yes *Hours:* Grounds only *Admission:* FREE *Operated by:* Cape Lookout National Seashore *NR?* Yes *NHL?* No *Year established/built:* 1812 *Latitude:* 34.6053 *Latitude:* -76.5361

CURRITUCK BEACH LIGHTHOUSE
Established in 1875, the Currituck Beach Lighthouse completed a string of lighthouses along the Outer Banks. It was automated in 1939, and in the 1970s, the grounds and light were taken over by a local group of preservationists, which have restored the preservation of the grounds and light. *Address:* 1101 Corolla Village Road *City:* Corolla *State:* NC *Zip:* 27927 *Phone:* 252-453-8152 *Web:* www.currituckbeachlight.com *Email:* info@currituckbeachlight.com *Visitors welcome?* Yes *Hours:* Daily, Easter through Thanksgiving, 9 a.m to 5 p.m.; until 8 p.m. Thursdays *Admission:* Parking and grounds free; $7 to climb the tower *Operated by:* Outer Banks Conservationists *NR?* Yes *NHL?* No *Year established/built:* 1875 *Latitude:* 36.3789 *Latitude:* -75.8322

OAK ISLAND LIGHTHOUSE
Established in 1849, the current Oak Island Lighthouse was constructed of concrete in 1958. The lighthouse is one of the few owned by the Coast Guard in which visitors are allowed to climb to the top. *Address:* Caswell Beach Road *City:* Caswell Beach *State:* NC *Zip:* 28465 *Web:* www.oakislandlighthouse.org *Email:* lighthouse@caswellbeach.org *Visitors welcome?* Yes *Hours:* Memorial Day to Labor Day, Wednesdays and Saturdays, 10 a.m. to 2 p.m. *Admission:* Contact attraction directly *Operated by:* Friends of Oak Island Lighthouse *NR?* Yes *NHL?* No *Year established/built:* 1849 *Latitude:* 33.8964 *Latitude:* -78.0494

OCRACOKE LIGHTHOUSE
Established in 1822 on a cove reportedly a favorite for the 18th-century pirate Blackbeard, the Ocracoke Lighthouse is still an active aid to navigation as the second oldest lighthouse in the U.S.. It is now owned by the National Park Service. *Address:* Lighthouse Road and Silverlark Drive *City:* Ocracoke *State:* NC *Phone:* 252-473-2111 *Web:* www.nps.gov/caha/ *Visitors welcome?* Yes *Hours:* Grounds only *Admission:* FREE *Operated by:* Cape Hatteras National Seashore *NR?* No *NHL?* No *Year established/built:* 1822 *Latitude:* 35.1146 *Latitude:* -75.9810

PRICE'S CREEK LIGHTHOUSE
The Price's Creek Lighthouse was one of a number of range lights along the Cape Fear River. *Address:* Price's Creek *City:* Southport *State:* NC *Visitors welcome?* No *Operated by:* Private owner *NR?* No *NHL?* No *Latitude:* 33.9355 *Latitude:* -78.0088

ROANOKE MARSHES LIGHTHOUSE
A replica of the last Roanake Marshes Lighthouse, which was lost in the 1950s, sits in the harbor at Manteo. It is operated by a local maritime museum. *Address:* Roanoke Marshes Light *City:* Manteo *State:* NC *Zip:* 27954 *Phone:* 252-475-1750 *Web:* www.obxmaritime.org *Visitors welcome?* Yes *Hours:* Contact attraction directly *Admission:* Contact attraction directly *Operated by:* North Carolina Maritime Museum on Roanoke Island *NR?* No *NHL?* No *Year established/built:* 1831 *Latitude:* 35.8111 *Latitude:* -75.7006

ROANOKE RIVER LIGHTHOUSE
Established by a lightship in 1832, the current Roanoke River Lighthouse was constructed on screwpiles in 1887. The U.S. Coast Guard deactivated the lighthouse in 1941. The lighthouse was eventually sold to the Edenton Historical Commission and moved to Colonial Park in Edenton. *Address:* Colonial Park *City:* Edenton *State:* NC *Zip:* 27932 *Phone:* 252-482-7800 *Web:* edentonhistoricalcommission.org *Email:* becky.winslow@edentonhistoricalcommission.org *Visitors welcome?* Yes *Hours:* Grounds only *Admission:* Contact attraction directly *Operated by:* Edenton Historical Commission *NR?* No *NHL?* No *Year established/built:* 1832 *Latitude:* 36.0579 *Latitude:* -76.6077

PENNSYLVANIA

TURTLE ROCK LIGHTHOUSE
The Turtle Rock Lighthouse is a private aid to navigation owned by a Philadelphia boat club. *Address:* 15 Kelly Drive *City:* Philadelphia *State:* PA *Visitors welcome?* Yes *Hours:* Grounds only *Admission:* FREE *Operated by:* Private owner *NR?* No *NHL?* No *Year established/built:* 1887 *Latitude:* 39.9694 *Latitude:* -75.1848

PUERTO RICO

ARECIBO LIGHTHOUSE
Established and built in 1898, the Arecibo Lighthouse, also called the Faro de Arecibo Lighthouse, was automated in 1964 and is still an active aid to navigation. It is now located with in a private park. *Address:* Carr #655 Bo. Islote, Sector El Muelle *City:* Arecibo *State:* PR *Phone:* 787-880-7540 *Web:* www.arecibolighthouse.com *Email:* mail@arecibolighthouse.com *Visitors welcome?* Yes *Hours:* Monday to Friday: 9 a.m. to 6 p.m.; Saturday and Sunday, 10 a.m. to 7 p.m. *Admission:* $10 adults, $8 children 2-12 and seniors *Operated by:* Arecibo Lighthouse & Historical Park *NR?* Yes *NHL?* No *Year established/built:* 1898 *Latitude:* 18.4724 *Latitude:* -66.7157

CABRAS ISLAND LIGHTHOUSE
Established in 1902, the original lighthouse structure was destroyed in 1965. The light is now on a skeletal metal tower. *Address:* Isla de Cabras National Park *City:* San Juan *State:* PR *Visitors welcome?* No *Operated by:*

CHAPTER 5 – LIGHTHOUSES & LIGHTSHIPS

U.S. Coast Guard (District 7) *NR?* No *NHL?* No *Year established/built:* 1902 *Latitude:* 18.4663 *Latitude:* -66.1057

CAPE ROJO LIGHTHOUSE
Established and built in 1882, the Cape Rojo Lighthouse was automated in 1967 and is still an active aid to navigation. *Address:* Cabo Rojo National Wildlife Refuge *City:* Cabo Rojo *State:* PR *Visitors welcome?* Yes *Hours:* Daily, Wednesday through Sunday *Admission:* FREE *Operated by:* City of Cabo Rojo *NR?* Yes *NHL?* No *Year established/built:* 1882 *Latitude:* 17.9747 *Latitude:* -67.1760

CAPE SAN JUAN LIGHTHOUSE
Established and constructed in 1880, the Cape San Juan Lighthouse was automated in 1975 and is still an active aid to navigation. *City:* Fajardo *State:* PR *Phone:* 787-722-5834 *Email:* fideicomiso@fideicomiso.org *Visitors welcome?* Yes *Hours:* By appointment *Admission:* Contact attraction directly *Operated by:* Conservation Trust of Puerto Rico *NR?* Yes *NHL?* No *Year established/built:* 1880 *Latitude:* 18.3258 *Latitude:* -65.6524

CARDONA ISLAND LIGHTHOUSE
Established and built in 1889, the Cardona Island Lighthouse was automated in 1962. It is still an active aid to navigation. *Address:* Cardono Island *City:* Ponce *State:* PR *Visitors welcome?* No *Operated by:* U.S. Coast Guard (District 7) *NR?* Yes *NHL?* No *Year established/built:* 1889 *Latitude:* 17.9572 *Latitude:* -66.6349

✛ CASTILLO SAN FELIPE DEL MORRO LIGHTHOUSE
Four lighthouses have stood on Castillo San Felipe del Morro 6th level in its long history. The first one was built in 1846. A second one replaced it in 1876 but took a direct hit during the 1898 bombardment of the Spanish-American War. However, its brick foundation was salvaged in 1899 to erect the first American lighthouse. The current lighthouse was built between 1908 and 1909. Restoration of the El Morro lighthouse was completed in August 2009. It has since been opened to visitors on a regular daily basis from 9 a.m. to 6 p.m. (weather allowing). *Address:* Castillo San Felipe del Morro *City:* San Juan *State:* PR *Phone:* 787-729-6754 *Web:* www.nps.gov/saju/ *Visitors welcome?* Yes *Hours:* 9 a.m. to 6 p.m. *Admission:* $3 adults, children 15 and under FREE *Operated by:* National Park Service, San Juan National Historic Site *NR?* Yes *NHL?* No *Year established/built:* 1846 *Latitude:* 18.4711 *Latitude:* -66.1242

CULEBRITA ISLAND LIGHTHOUSE
Established and built in 1886, the Culebrita Island Lighthouse was automated in 1964 and is still an active aid to navigation. *Address:* Culebrita Island *City:* Culebra *State:* PR *Visitors welcome?* No *Operated by:* City of Culebrita *NR?* Yes *NHL?* No *Year established/built:* 1886 *Latitude:* 18.3147 *Latitude:* -65.2288

GUANICA LIGHTHOUSE
Established and built in 1893, the Guanica Lighthouse was deactivated in 1950. *City:* Guanica *State:* PR *Visitors welcome?* Yes *Hours:* Grounds only *Admission:* FREE *Operated by:* Puerto Rico Dept. of Natural Resources *NR?* Yes *NHL?* No *Year established/built:* 1893 *Latitude:* 17.9750 *Latitude:* -66.9100

MONA ISLAND LIGHTHOUSE
Established and built in 1900, the Mona Island Lighthouse was deactivated in 1976. *Address:* Mona Island *City:* Mayaguez *State:* PR *Visitors welcome?* Yes *Hours:* Grounds only *Admission:* FREE *Operated by:* Puerto

Rico Dept. of Natural Resources *NR?* Yes *NHL?* No *Year established/built:* 1900 *Latitude:* 18.0897 *Latitude:* -67.8777

MUERTOS ISLAND LIGHTHOUSE

Established and built in 1887, the Muertos Island Lighthouse, or Isla Caja de Muertos Lighthouse, was automated in 1945 and is still an active aid to navigation. It is now within a wildlife refuge. *Address:* Muertos Island *City:* Ponce *State:* PR *Visitors welcome?* Yes *Hours:* Grounds only *Admission:* FREE *Operated by:* Puerto Rico Dept. of Natural Resources *NR?* Yes *NHL?* No *Year established/built:* 1887 *Latitude:* 17.8947 *Latitude:* -66.5199

NAVASSA ISLAND LIGHTHOUSE

Established and built in 1917, the Navassa Island Lighthouse off Jamaica was deactivated in 1996 and is now part of a wildlife refuge. *City:* Boqueron *State:* PR *Phone:* 787-851-7258 *Visitors welcome?* Yes *Hours:* Grounds only *Admission:* FREE *Operated by:* Navassa Island National Wildlife Refuge *NR?* No *NHL?* No *Year established/built:* 1917 *Latitude:* 18.0267 *Latitude:* -67.1733

NEW POINT BORINQUEN LIGHTHOUSE

Established in 1889, the New Point Borinquen Lighthouse was built in 1920 is now used for U.S. Coast Guard housing. *City:* Aquadilla *State:* PR *Visitors welcome?* No *Operated by:* U.S. Coast Guard (District 7) *NR?* Yes *NHL?* No *Year established/built:* 1889 *Latitude:* 18.4274 *Latitude:* -67.1541

OLD POINT BORINQUEN LIGHTHOUSE

Established in 1889, the Old Point Borinquen Lighthouse was nearly destroyed by a 1918 tsunami and is now in ruins. *City:* Aquadilla *State:* PR *Visitors welcome?* Yes *Hours:* Grounds only *Admission:* FREE *Operated by:* U.S. Coast Guard (District 7) *NR?* Yes *NHL?* No *Year established/built:* 1889 *Latitude:* 18.4274 *Latitude:* -67.1541

POINT FIGURAS LIGHTHOUSE

Established and built in 1893, the Point Figuras Lighthouse was deactivated in 1938. *City:* Guayama *State:* PR *Visitors welcome?* Yes *Hours:* Contact attraction directly *Admission:* Contact attraction directly *Operated by:* Puerto Rico Dept. of Natural Resources *NR?* Yes *NHL?* No *Year established/built:* 1893 *Latitude:* 17.9841 *Latitude:* -66.1138

POINT JIGUERO LIGHTHOUSE

Established in 1892, the current Point Jiguero Lighthouse, or Point Higuero Lighthouse, was constructed in 1922 and is still an active aid to navigation. *City:* Rincon *State:* PR *Visitors welcome?* Yes *Hours:* Grounds only *Admission:* FREE *Operated by:* City of Rincon *NR?* Yes *NHL?* No *Year established/built:* 1892 *Latitude:* 18.3410 *Latitude:* -67.2526

POINT MULAS LIGHTHOUSE

Established in 1885 and built the following year, the Point Mulas Lighthouse was automated in 1949, but is no longer an active aid to navigation. It is now home to a small marine museum. *City:* Vieques *State:* PR *Visitors welcome?* Yes *Hours:* Daily *Admission:* Contact attraction directly *Operated by:* City of Vieques *NR?* Yes *NHL?* No *Year established/built:* 1885 *Latitude:* 18.1475 *Latitude:* -65.4449

CHAPTER 5 – LIGHTHOUSES & LIGHTSHIPS

POINT TUNA LIGHTHOUSE
Established and built in 1892, the Point Tuna Lighthouse was automated in 1989. *City:* Maunabo *State:* PR *Visitors welcome?* No *Operated by:* U.S. Coast Guard (District 7) *NR?* Yes *NHL?* No *Year established/built:* 1892 *Latitude:* 18.0072 *Latitude:* -65.8993

PUERTO FERRO LIGHTHOUSE
Established and built in 1896, the Puerto Ferro Lighthouse was deactivated in 1926 and is now abandoned. *City:* Vieques *State:* PR *Visitors welcome?* Yes *Hours:* Grounds only *Admission:* FREE *Operated by:* U.S. Coast Guard (District 7) *NR?* No *NHL?* No *Year established/built:* 1896 *Latitude:* 18.1475 *Latitude:* -65.4449

RHODE ISLAND

 ## BEAVERTAIL LIGHTHOUSE
Established in 1749, the current Beavertail Lighthouse was constructed in 1856 and automated in 1972. Still an active aid to navigation, the lighthouse is now a museum. *Address:* Beavertail State Park *City:* Jamestown *State:* RI *Zip:* 02835 *Phone:* 401-423-3270 *Web:* www.beavertaillight.org *Email:* info@BeavertailLight.org *Visitors welcome?* Yes *Hours:* Memorial Day weekend to mid-June: Saturday and Sunday, noon to 3 p.m.; Mid-June to Labor Day, 10 a.m. to 4 p.m.; Labor Day to Columbus Day, noon to 3 p.m. *Admission:* Contact attraction directly *Operated by:* Beavertail Lighthouse Museum Association *NR?* Yes *NHL?* No *Year established/built:* 1749 *Latitude:* 41.4490 *Latitude:* -71.4000

BLOCK ISLAND NORTH LIGHTHOUSE
Established in 1829, the current Block Island North Lighthouse was built in 1867 and automated in 1955. It is still an active aid to navigation located within a wildlife refuge. *Address:* Block Island North Light *City:* Block Island *State:* RI *Visitors welcome?* Yes *Hours:* Grounds only *Admission:* FREE *Operated by:* Town of New Shoreham *NR?* Yes *NHL?* No *Year established/built:* 1829 *Latitude:* 41.2275 *Latitude:* -71.5761

BLOCK ISLAND SOUTHEAST LIGHTHOUSE
Established and built in 1875, the brick lighthouse was deactivated in 1990 and re-lighted in 1994. It is now operated by a local foundation. *Address:* Block Island Southeast Light *City:* Block Island *State:* RI *Zip:* 02807 *Phone:* 401-466-5009 *Email:* selight@verizon.net *Visitors welcome?* Yes *Hours:* Contact attraction directly *Admission:* Contact attraction directly *Operated by:* Block Island Southeast Lighthouse Foundation *NR?* Yes *NHL?* Yes *Year established/built:* 1875 *Latitude:* 41.1526 *Latitude:* -71.5553

BRISTOL FERRY LIGHTHOUSE
Established in 1846 and built in 1855, the Bristol Ferry Lighthouse operated until 1927 when the Mount Hope Bridge was under construction. It is now a private residence. *Address:* Bristol Ferry Light *City:* Bristol *State:* RI *Visitors welcome?* No *Operated by:* Private owner *NR?* Yes *NHL?* No *Year established/built:* 1846 *Latitude:* 41.6431 *Latitude:* -71.2603

CASTLE HILL LIGHTHOUSE
Established and built in 1890, the stone Castle Hill Lighthouse lights the entrance to Narrangansett Bay. The light was automated in 1957. *Address:* Castle Hill Light *City:* Newport *State:* RI *Visitors welcome?* Yes *Hours:* Grounds only *Admission:* FREE *Operated by:* U.S. Coast Guard (District 1) *NR?* Yes *NHL?* No *Year established/built:* 1890 *Latitude:* 41.4619 *Latitude:* -71.3633

CHAPTER 5 – LIGHTHOUSES & LIGHTSHIPS

CONANICUT ISLAND LIGHTHOUSE
Established and built in 1886, the Conanicut Lighthouse was discontinued in 1933. It is now a private residence. *Address:* Conanicut Island Light *City:* Jamestown *State:* RI *Visitors welcome?* No *Operated by:* Private owner *NR?* Yes *NHL?* No *Year established/built:* 1886 *Latitude:* 41.5733 *Latitude:* -71.3725

CONIMICUT SHOAL LIGHTHOUSE
Established on a shoal in 1868, the current Conimicut Shoal Lighthouse in the coffee pot style was built in 1883 and automated in 1960. *Address:* Providence River *City:* Warwick *State:* RI *Visitors welcome?* No *Operated by:* City of Warwick *NR?* Yes *NHL?* No *Year established/built:* 1868 *Latitude:* 41.7663 *Latitude:* -71.4038

DUTCH ISLAND LIGHTHOUSE
Dutch Island Lighthouse, in the west passage of Rhode Island's Narragansett Bay, is a 42-foot brick tower built in 1857. It was built to replace a lighthouse established in 1826. The lighthouse was restored in 2007 and is an active aid to navigation. *Address:* Dutch Island Light *City:* Saunderstown *State:* RI *Visitors welcome?* No *Operated by:* Dutch Island Lighthouse Society *NR?* Yes *NHL?* No *Year established/built:* 1826 *Latitude:* 41.4956 *Latitude:* -71.4044

HOG ISLAND SHOAL LIGHTHOUSE
Established in 1886 by a lightship, the current cast-iron coffee pot structure was built in 1901 and automated in 1964. It is now owned by a private party. *Address:* Hog Island *City:* Portsmouth *State:* RI *Visitors welcome?* No *Operated by:* Private owner *NR?* Yes *NHL?* No *Year established/built:* 1886 *Latitude:* 41.6440 *Latitude:* -71.2801

IDA LEWIS ROCK LIGHTHOUSE
Established and built in 1854 as Lime Rock Lighthouse, the station was renamed the Ida Lewis Rock Lighthouse in honor of a famous female lighthouse keeper who maintained the facility after her husband was incapacitated by a stroke. *Address:* Ida Lewis Rock Lighthouse *City:* Newport *State:* RI *Visitors welcome?* No *Operated by:* Private owner *NR?* Yes *NHL?* No *Year established/built:* 1854 *Latitude:* 41.4775 *Latitude:* -71.3260

NAYATT POINT LIGHTHOUSE
Established in 1828, the current Nayatt Point Lighthouse was constructed in 1856. The light was discontinued in 1868 and the facility is now a private residence. *Address:* Nayatt Point Light *City:* Barrington *State:* RI *Visitors welcome?* No *Operated by:* Private owner *NR?* Yes *NHL?* No *Year established/built:* 1828 *Latitude:* 41.7250 *Latitude:* -71.3397

NEWPORT HARBOR LIGHTHOUSE
Established in 1824, the current Newport Harbor Lighthouse was built in 1842 and automated in 1923. Still an active aid to navigation, a local not-for-profit raised money to fund restoration of the structure in 2006. *Address:* Newport Harbor Light *City:* Newport *State:* RI *Visitors welcome?* Yes *Hours:* Grounds only *Admission:* FREE *Operated by:* Friends of Newport Harbor Light *NR?* Yes *NHL?* No *Year established/built:* 1824 *Latitude:* 41.4933 *Latitude:* -71.3269

Do you have a lighthouse ghost story? Email it to contact@fyddeye.com.

PLUM BEACH LIGHTHOUSE
Established in 1897 and built in 1899 as a coffee pot lighthouse on a caisson, the Plum Beach Lighthouse was decommissioned in 1941 after the completion of the Jamestown Bridge. *Address:* Plum Beach Light *City:* North Kingstown *State:* RI *Visitors welcome?* No *Operated by:* Friends of Plum Beach Lighthouse *NR?* Yes *NHL?* No *Year established/built:* 1897 *Latitude:* 41.5300 *Latitude:* -71.4056

CHAPTER 5 – LIGHTHOUSES & LIGHTSHIPS

POINT JUDITH LIGHTHOUSE
Established in 1810, the current Point Judith Lighthouse was constructed of brownstone in 1857. It was automated in 1854 and is located on the grounds of the Point Judith Coast Guard Station. *Address:* Point Judith Light *City:* Point Judith *State:* RI *Visitors welcome?* Yes *Hours:* Grounds only *Admission:* FREE *Operated by:* U.S. Coast Guard (District 1) *NR?* Yes *NHL?* No *Year established/built:* 1810 *Latitude:* 41.3610 *Latitude:* -71.4814

POMHAM ROCKS LIGHTHOUSE
Established and built in 1871, the Pomham Rocks Lighthouse was deactivated in 1974 and re-lighted in 2006. *Address:* Pomham Rocks Light *City:* Kent Corner *State:* RI *Visitors welcome?* No *Operated by:* Friends of Pomham Rocks Lighthouse *NR?* Yes *NHL?* No *Year established/built:* 1871 *Latitude:* 41.7778 *Latitude:* -71.3703

POPLAR POINT LIGHTHOUSE
Established and constructed in 1831, the Poplar Point Lighthouse was active until 1882, when the light was moved to a new facility on Gay Rock. The Poplar Point Lighthouse is now a private residence. *Address:* Poplar Point Light *City:* North Kingston *State:* RI *Visitors welcome?* No *Operated by:* Private owner *NR?* Yes *NHL?* No *Year established/built:* 1831 *Latitude:* 41.5708 *Latitude:* -71.4397

PRUDENCE ISLAND LIGHTHOUSE
The Prudence Island Lighthouse was established in 1852, but the current structure was built in 1824 as the Goat Island Lighthouse. That building was dismantled and moved to Prudence Island in 1852. Prudence Island Light is the oldest lighthouse in Rhode Island. *Address:* Prudence Island Light *City:* Prudence Island *State:* RI *Visitors welcome?* Yes *Hours:* Grounds only *Admission:* FREE *Operated by:* Prudence Conservancy *NR?* Yes *NHL?* No *Year established/built:* 1852 *Latitude:* 41.6056 *Latitude:* -71.3031

ROSE ISLAND LIGHTHOUSE
Established and built in 1870, the Rose Island Lighthouse was deactivated in 1971 and re-lighted in 1993. The station accepts visitors and offers overnight stays in the restored keepers quarters. *Address:* Rose Island Light *City:* Newport *State:* RI *Zip:* 02840 *Phone:* 401-847-4242 *Web:* www.roseislandlighthouse.org *Email:* keeper@roseisland.org *Visitors welcome?* Yes *Hours:* April to October: daily, 10 a.m. to 4 p.m. *Admission:* Contact attraction directly *Operated by:* Rose Island Lighthouse Foundation *NR?* Yes *NHL?* No *Year established/built:* 1870 *Latitude:* 41.4956 *Latitude:* -71.3431

SAKONNET POINT LIGHTHOUSE
Established and built in 1884, the cast-iron Sakonnet Point Lighthouse was shut down in 1955. Relighted in 1997, it is now maintained by a local preservation group. *Address:* Sakonnet Light *City:* Little Compton *State:* RI *Visitors welcome?* No *Operated by:* Friends of Sakonnet Point Lighthouse *NR?* Yes *NHL?* No *Year established/built:* 1884 *Latitude:* 41.4531 *Latitude:* -71.2031

WARWICK LIGHTHOUSE
Established in 1827, the current Warwick Lighthouse was constructed in 1932 and now serves as U.S. Coast Guard housing. The light was automated in 1985. *Address:* Warwick Neck *City:* Warwick *State:* RI *Visitors welcome?* No *Operated by:* U.S. Coast Guard (District 1) *NR?* Yes *NHL?* No *Year established/built:* 1827 *Latitude:* 41.6804 *Latitude:* -71.3823

WATCH HILL LIGHTHOUSE
Established in 1808, the current Watch Hill Lighthouse was built in 1856 and automated in 1986. The grounds and a small museum in the oil house are open to the public. *Address:* Watch Hill Point *City:* Westerly *State:* RI *Visitors welcome?* Yes *Hours:* July to August: Tuesdays and Thursdays, 1 p.m. to 3 p.m. *Admission:*

Contact attraction directly *Operated by:* Watch Hill Lighthouse Keepers Association *NR?* Yes *NHL?* No *Year established/built:* 1808 *Latitude:* 41.3037 *Latitude:* -71.8584

SOUTH CAROLINA

BLOODY POINT BAR FRONT RANGE LIGHTHOUSE
Established in 1883, the Bloody Point Bar Front Range Lighthouse and its rear range partner light operated until 1921. The structure is now privately owned. *Address:* Dafuskie Island *City:* Forest Beach *State:* SC *Visitors welcome?* No *Operated by:* Private owner *NR?* No *NHL?* No *Year established/built:* 1883 *Latitude:* 32.1466 *Latitude:* -80.7437

CAPE ROMAIN LIGHTHOUSE
Established in 1827, the Cape Romain Lighthouse is one of the few stations with two towers, the latter built in 1858. The station was shut down in 1947 and later made part of a wildlife refuge. *Address:* Cape Romain National Wildlife Refuge *City:* McClellanville *State:* SC *Phone:* 843-928-3264 *Email:* caperomain@fws.gov *Visitors welcome?* Yes *Hours:* Grounds only *Admission:* FREE *Operated by:* Cape Romain National Wildlife Refuge *NR?* Yes *NHL?* No *Year established/built:* 1827 *Latitude:* 32.9930 *Latitude:* -79.6209

CHARLESTON LIGHTHOUSE
Established and built in 1962, the Charleston Lighthouse was the last major lighthouse built by the federal government. The point of its unique triangle shape points out to sea from Charleston Harbor. *Address:* Charleston Light *City:* Charleston *State:* SC *Visitors welcome?* Yes *Hours:* Grounds only *Admission:* FREE *Operated by:* U.S. Coast Guard (District 7) *NR?* No *NHL?* No *Year established/built:* 1962 *Latitude:* 32.7578 *Latitude:* -79.8431

GEORGETOWN LIGHTHOUSE
Established and built in 1812, the Georgetown Lighthouse was refurbished after damage during the Civil War. Automated in 1986, the lighthouse is now part of a nature preserve. *Address:* Georgetown Light *City:* Georgetown *State:* SC *Visitors welcome?* Yes *Hours:* Grounds only *Admission:* FREE *Operated by:* South Carolina Dept. of Natural Resources *NR?* Yes *NHL?* No *Year established/built:* 1812 *Latitude:* 33.2233 *Latitude:* -79.1850

HAIG POINT REAR RANGE LIGHTHOUSE
Established and built in 1872, the Haig Point Rear Range Lighthouse operated until 1934. It was re-lighted in 1987 as a private aid to navigation as part of the creation of the Daufuskie Island Historic District. *Address:* Daufuskie Island *City:* Hilton Head *State:* SC *Visitors welcome?* Yes *Hours:* Grounds only *Admission:* Contact attraction directly *Operated by:* Private owner *NR?* Yes *NHL?* No *Year established/built:* 1872 *Latitude:* 32.1160 *Latitude:* -80.8712

HARBOUR TOWN LIGHTHOUSE
The Harbour Town Lighthouse was built as a private aid to navigation in 1970. *Address:* 149 Lighthouse Road *City:* Hilton Head *State:* SC *Zip:* 29928 *Phone:* 866-561-8802 *Visitors welcome?* Yes *Hours:* Daily, 10 a.m. to 6 p.m. *Admission:* Contact attraction directly *Operated by:* Private owner *NR?* No *NHL?* No *Year established/built:* 1970 *Latitude:* 32.1396 *Latitude:* -80.8101

HILTON HEAD REAR RANGE LIGHTHOUSE
Established in 1877, the current Hilton Head Rear Range Lighthouse, also called the Leamington Lighthouse, and its companion light were completed in 1880. The lights were decommissioned in 1932 and the

front range light dismantled. The rear range light is still an active aid to navigation. *Address:* Hilton Head Rear Range Light *City:* Hilton Head *State:* SC *Phone:* 843-785-1106 *Visitors welcome?* Yes *Hours:* Grounds only *Admission:* Contact attraction directly *Operated by:* Palmetto Dunes Resort *NR?* Yes *NHL?* No *Year established/built:* 1877 *Latitude:* 32.1642 *Latitude:* -80.7400

HUNTING ISLAND LIGHTHOUSE
Established in 1859, the current Hunting Island Lighthouse constructed in 1875 to replaced the original tower destroyed during the Civil War. The light was deactivated in 1933, and the grounds became the most popular state park in South Carolina. *Address:* 2555 Sea Island Parkway *City:* Hunting Island *State:* SC *Zip:* 29920 *Phone:* 843-838-2011 *Email:* huntingisland@scprt.com *Visitors welcome?* Yes *Hours:* Monday through Sunday, 6 a.m. to 6 p.m. (9 p.m. during Daylight Savings Time) *Admission:* $4 adults, $2.50 seniors, $1.50 children six to 15, five and under FREE *Operated by:* South Carolina Dept. of Parks, Recreation and Tourism *NR?* Yes *NHL?* No *Year established/built:* 1859 *Latitude:* 32.3750 *Latitude:* -80.4383

MORRIS ISLAND LIGHTHOUSE
Established in 1673, the current Morris Island Lighthouse was constructed in 1876 to replace a light destroyed by Union troops in the Civil War. Erosion has slowly taken away the shoreline around the lighthouse, leaving the structure standing alone offshore. *Address:* Morris Island Light *City:* Charleston *State:* SC *Visitors welcome?* Yes *Hours:* Grounds only *Admission:* FREE *Operated by:* Save the Light *NR?* Yes *NHL?* No *Year established/built:* 1673 *Latitude:* 32.6953 *Latitude:* -79.8836

VERMONT

BURLINGTON BREAKWATER NORTH LIGHTHOUSE
Established in 1857 after the construction of a stone-crib breakwater, the current Burlington Breakwater North Lighthouse is a replica of the original wooden lighthouse. The replica was opened in 2004. *Address:* Burlington Harbor *City:* Burlington *State:* VT *Visitors welcome?* No *Operated by:* City of Burlington *NR?* No *NHL?* No *Year established/built:* 1857 *Latitude:* 44.4261 *Latitude:* -73.2517

BURLINGTON BREAKWATER SOUTH LIGHTHOUSE
Established in 1857 after the construction of a stone-crib breakwater, the current Burlington Breakwater South Lighthouse is a replica of the original wooden lighthouse. The replica was opened in 2004. *Address:* Burlington Harbor *City:* Burlington *State:* VT *Visitors welcome?* No *Operated by:* City of Burlington *NR?* No *NHL?* No *Year established/built:* 1857 *Latitude:* 44.4261 *Latitude:* -73.2517

COLCHESTER REEF LIGHTHOUSE
Established on a reef off Colchester Point in Lake Champlain, the Colchester Reef Lighthouse served until 1952, when it was purchased by the Shelburne Museum and moved to the museum site as one of several buildings in the museum's collection. *Address:* 5555 Shelburne Rd. *City:* Shelburne *State:* VT *Zip:* 05482 *Phone:* 802-985-3346 *Web:* www.shelburnemuseum.org *Email:* info@shelburnemuseum.org *Visitors welcome?* Yes *Hours:* Contact attraction directly *Admission:* Contact attraction directly *Operated by:* Shelburne Museum *NR?* No *NHL?* No *Year established/built:* 1871 *Latitude:* 44.3768 *Latitude:* -73.2285

ISLE LA MOTTE LIGHTHOUSE
Established in 1829, the current Isle La Motte Lighthouse is a cast-iron tower built in 1881 and decommissioned in 1933. The lighthouse was sold to a private party, although the tower is still an active aid to naviga-

CHAPTER 5 – LIGHTHOUSES & LIGHTSHIPS

tion. *Address:* Isle La Motte Light *City:* Isle La Motte *State:* VT *Visitors welcome?* No *Operated by:* Private owner *NR?* No *NHL?* No *Year established/built:* 1829 *Latitude:* 44.9065 *Latitude:* -73.3435

JUNIPER ISLAND LIGHTHOUSE
Established in 1826, the current Juniper Island Lighthouse was constructed in 1846 of cast-iron. In 1954, a skeletal tower replaced the cast-iron tower, and the lighthouse property was sold into private hands. *Address:* Juniper Island Light *City:* Burlington *State:* VT *Visitors welcome?* No *Operated by:* Private owner *NR?* No *NHL?* No *Year established/built:* 1826 *Latitude:* 44.4500 *Latitude:* -73.2763

WINDMILL POINT LIGHTHOUSE
Established as a private aid to navigation in 1830, the current stone Windmill Point Lighthouse was constructed in 1858. Replaced by a steel skeletal tower on the New York side of Lake Champlain, the Windmill Point Lighthouse was sold into private hands. *Address:* Windmill Point Light *City:* Alburg *State:* VT *Visitors welcome?* No *Operated by:* Private owner *NR?* No *NHL?* No *Year established/built:* 1830 *Latitude:* 44.9818 *Latitude:* -73.3418

VIRGIN ISLANDS

HAMS BLUFF LIGHTHOUSE
The Hams Bluff Lighthouse on St. Croix in the U.S. Virgin Islands is still an active aid to navigation. *Address:* Hams Bluff *City:* St. Croix *State:* VI *Visitors welcome?* Yes *Hours:* Grounds only *Admission:* FREE *Operated by:* U.S. Coast Guard (District 7) *NR?* No *NHL?* No *Year established/built:* 1915 *Latitude:* 17.7708 *Latitude:* -64.8726

VIRGINIA

ASSATEAGUE LIGHTHOUSE
Established in 1833, the current Assateague Lighthouse was constructed in 1967 and automated in 1965. The lighthouse is now within a wildlife refuge and the keepers house is used as ranger quarters. *Address:* Assateague Light *State:* VA *Phone:* 757-336-3696 *Web:* www.assateagueisland.com *Visitors welcome?* Yes *Hours:* Easter through Thanksgiving, Friday to Sunday, 9 a.m. to 3 p.m. *Admission:* $4 adults, $2 children aged two to 12 *Operated by:* Chincoteague Natural History Association *NR?* Yes *NHL?* No *Year established/built:* 1833 *Latitude:* 37.9111 *Latitude:* -75.3558

CAPE CHARLES LIGHTHOUSE
Established in 1828, the current 1895 skeletal tower lighthouse is the third lighthouse to stand on Smith Island. At 191 feet, the lighthouse is the tallest of its type in the U.S., and it is still an active aid to navigation. *Address:* Cape Charles Light *City:* Smith Island *State:* VA *Visitors welcome?* Yes *Hours:* Grounds only *Admission:* Grounds only *Operated by:* U.S. Coast Guard (District 5) *NR?* No *NHL?* No *Year established/built:* 1828 *Latitude:* 37.1198 *Latitude:* -75.9080

JONES POINT LIGHTHOUSE
Established and built in 1856, the Jones Point Lighthouse served until 1926, when the light was moved to a nearby steel skeletal tower. The obsolete structure was deeded to the Mount Vernon chapter of the Daughters of the American Revolution. The lighthouse is located in Jones Point Park. *Address:* Jones

Point Light *City:* Alexandria *State:* VA *Visitors welcome?* Yes *Hours:* Grounds only *Admission:* FREE *Operated by:* Daughters of the American Revolution *NR?* Yes *NHL?* No *Year established/built:* 1856 *Latitude:* 38.7904 *Latitude:* -77.0406

NEW CAPE HENRY LIGHTHOUSE
Built in 1881 to replace an older brick tower, the New Cape Henry Lighthouse is constructed of cast-iron and it is still an active aid to navigation. Because the light sits on a military reservation, visiting it is difficult because of tight security. *Address:* Cape Henry Light *City:* Virginia Beach *State:* VA *Visitors welcome?* No *Operated by:* U.S. Coast Guard (District 5) *NR?* Yes *NHL?* Yes *Year established/built:* 1881 *Latitude:* 36.9256 *Latitude:* -76.0083

NEW POINT COMFORT LIGHTHOUSE
Established in 1801, the current New Point Comfort Lighthouse was constructed in 1806, automated in 1930, and deactivated in 1963. The tower was renovated in 1989, although only the grounds are open to the public. *Address:* New Point Comfort Light *City:* Bavon *State:* VA *Visitors welcome?* Yes *Hours:* Grounds only *Admission:* FREE *Operated by:* New Point Comfort Lighthouse Preservation Task Forc *NR?* Yes *NHL?* No *Year established/built:* 1801 *Latitude:* 37.3006 *Latitude:* -76.2775

NEWPORT NEWS MIDDLE GROUND LIGHTHOUSE
Established in 1871, the current Newport News Middle Ground Lighthouse was constructed in the spark plug style in 1891. Automated in 1954, it is still an active aid to navigation, although it is now privately owned. *Address:* Newport News Middle Ground Light *City:* Newport News *State:* VA *Visitors welcome?* No *Operated by:* Private owner *NR?* Yes *NHL?* No *Year established/built:* 1871 *Latitude:* 36.9452 *Latitude:* -76.3915

OLD CAPE HENRY LIGHTHOUSE
Established in 1792, the original Cape Henry Lighthouse was deactivated in 1881 and the light moved to a new lighthouse a few hundred feet to the east. The older structure is still standing, though it is on a military reservation and security is tight. *Address:* Old Cape Henry Light *City:* Virginia Beach *State:* VA *Visitors welcome?* No *Operated by:* U.S. Coast Guard (District 5) *NR?* Yes *NHL?* Yes *Year established/built:* 1792 *Latitude:* 36.9256 *Latitude:* -76.0083

OLD POINT COMFORT LIGHTHOUSE
Established in 1774, the current Old Point Comfort Lighthouse was constructed in 1802. The lighthouse sits on one of the most historic military bases in the country, and due to security concerns, access to the lighthouse is limited. *Address:* Old Point Comfort Light *City:* Hampton *State:* VA *Phone:* 757-788-2000 *Visitors welcome?* Yes *Hours:* Contact attraction directly *Admission:* Contact attraction directly *Operated by:* U.S. Coast Guard (District 5) *NR?* Yes *NHL?* No *Year established/built:* 1774 *Latitude:* 37.0018 *Latitude:* -76.3064

SMITH POINT LIGHTHOUSE
Established in 1802 after the Civil War, the current Smith Point Lighthouse, built in 1897, replaced lightships and on-shore structures going back to the early 19th century. The current caisson-style structure is still an active aid to navigation. *Address:* Smith Point Light *City:* Sunnybank *State:* VA *Visitors welcome?* No *Operated by:* Private owner *NR?* Yes *NHL?* No *Year established/built:* 1802 *Latitude:* 37.8800 *Latitude:* -76.1839

THIMBLE SHOAL LIGHTHOUSE
Established in 1870, the current Thimble Shoal Lighthouse was built in 1914 with the so-called spark plug design. Automated in 1963 and still an active aid to navigation, the lighthouse is now privately owned. *Address:* Thimble Shoal Light *City:* Hampton *State:* VA *Visitors welcome?* No *Operated by:* Private owner *NR?* Yes *NHL?* No *Year established/built:* 1870 *Latitude:* 37.0146 *Latitude:* -76.2399

CHAPTER 5 – LIGHTHOUSES & LIGHTSHIPS

WOLF TRAP LIGHTHOUSE
Established in 1821 with lightships, the current Wolf Trap Lighthouse was constructed in the spark plug style in 1894. Automated in 1973 and still an active aid to navigation, the lighthouse is now privately owned. *Address:* Wolf Trap Light *City:* Mathews *State:* VA *Visitors welcome?* No *Operated by:* Private owner *NR?* Yes *NHL?* No *Year established/built:* 1821 *Latitude:* 37.3904 *Latitude:* -76.1897

GREAT LAKES LIGHTHOUSES

Marblehead Lighthouse (Marblehead, Ohio)

ILLINOIS

68TH ST. CRIB LIGHTHOUSE
Address: Yacht Harbor *City:* Chicago *State:* IL *Visitors welcome?* No *Operated by:* Chicago Dept. of Water Management *NR?* No *NHL?* No *Latitude:* 41.7768 *Latitude:* -87.5736

CHICAGO HARBOR LIGHTHOUSE
Established in 1832, the current Chicago Harbor Lighthouse was constructed in 1893. Automated in 1979, the lighthouse is still an active aid to navigation. *Address:* Chicago Harbor Light *City:* Chicago *State:* IL *Visitors welcome?* No *Operated by:* U.S. Coast Guard (District 9) *NR?* Yes *NHL?* No *Year established/built:* 1832 *Latitude:* 41.8894 *Latitude:* -87.5906

CHICAGO HARBOR SOUTHEAST GUIDEWALL LIGHTHOUSE
Address: Navy Pier *City:* Chicago *State:* IL *Visitors welcome?* No *Operated by:* U.S. Coast Guard (District 9) *NR?* No *NHL?* No *Latitude:* 41.8919 *Latitude:* -87.6041

FOUR MILE CRIB LIGHTHOUSE
Address: Navy Pier *City:* Chicago *State:* IL *Visitors welcome?* No *Operated by:* Chicago Dept. of Water Management *NR?* No *NHL?* No *Latitude:* 41.8919 *Latitude:* -87.6041

CHAPTER 5 – LIGHTHOUSES & LIGHTSHIPS

GROSSE POINT LIGHTHOUSE
Established and built in 1873, the Grosse Point Lighthouse was deactivated in 1935. Now a private aid to navigation, the lighthouse is now operated as a museum. *Address:* 2601 Sheridan Road *City:* Evanston *State:* IL *Zip:* 60201-1752 *Phone:* 847-328-6961 *Web:* www.grossepointlighthouse.net *Email:* lpdnhl@grossepoint-lighthouse.net *Visitors welcome?* Yes *Hours:* Contact attraction directly *Admission:* $6 adults; $3 children 8 to 12; under 8 FREE *Operated by:* Grosse Point Lighthouse Park District *NR?* No *NHL?* Yes *Year established/built:* 1873 *Latitude:* 42.0643 *Latitude:* -87.6771

WAUKEGAN HARBOR LIGHTHOUSE
Address: Waukegan Harbor *City:* Waukegan *State:* IL *Visitors welcome?* Yes *Hours:* Grounds only *Admission:* FREE *Operated by:* U.S. Coast Guard (District 9) *NR?* No *NHL?* No *Latitude:* 42.3624 *Latitude:* -87.8111

WILLIAM E. DEVER CRIB LIGHTHOUSE
Address: Milton Lee Olive Park *City:* Chicago *State:* IL *Visitors welcome?* No *Operated by:* Chicago Dept. of Water Management *NR?* No *NHL?* No *Latitude:* 41.8940 *Latitude:* -87.6109

WILSON AVENUE CRIB LIGHTHOUSE
City: Chicago *State:* IL *Visitors welcome?* No *Operated by:* Chicago Dept. of Water Management *NR?* No *NHL?* No *Latitude:* 41.8500 *Latitude:* -87.6501

INDIANA

BUFFINGTON HARBOR BREAKWATER LIGHTHOUSE
The Buffington Harbor Breakwater Lighthouse sits on the end of a private breakwater marking the entrance to Buffington Harbor and historically, the site of large cement plants. Today, the area is in transition from industrial to residential and retail. *Address:* Buffington Harbor *City:* Gary *State:* IN *Visitors welcome?* No *Operated by:* City of Gary *NR?* No *NHL?* No *Year established/built:* 1927 *Latitude:* 41.6439 *Latitude:* -87.4153

CALUMET HARBOR LIGHTHOUSE
First lit in 1853, the Calumet Harbor Lighthouse went through several transitions before its final configuration in 1995. It marks the mouth of the Calumet River, which lies to the west in Illinois, even though the lighthouse is in Indiana. *Address:* Calumet Harbor *State:* IN *Visitors welcome?* No *Operated by:* U.S. Coast Guard (District 9) *NR?* No *NHL?* No *Year established/built:* 1853 *Latitude:* 41.7339 *Latitude:* -87.5239

GARY HARBOR BREAKWATER LIGHTHOUSE
The Gary Harbor Breakwater Light marks the entrance to an artificial harbor built by U.S. Steel in the early 20th century. The light itself was established in 1911. *Address:* Gary Harbor *City:* Gary *State:* IN *Visitors welcome?* No *Operated by:* U.S. Steel *NR?* No *NHL?* No *Year established/built:* 1911 *Latitude:* 41.6311 *Latitude:* -87.3200

INDIANA HARBOR EAST BREAKWATER LIGHTHOUSE
The Indiana Harbor Breakwater Lighthouse was constructed approximately 1930 to mark the entrance to the Indiana Harbor Canal and the heavy industry that lined the canal and the shores of Lake Michigan. *Address:* Indiana Harbor East Breakwater Light *City:* East Chicago *State:* IN *Visitors welcome?* No *Operated by:* U.S. Coast Guard (District 9) *NR?* No *NHL?* No *Year established/built:* 1930 *Latitude:* 41.6808 *Latitude:* -87.4411

MICHIGAN CITY LIGHTHOUSES
Established in 1837, the Old Michigan City Lighthouse and the Michigan City East Pierhead Lighthouse were constructed in 1858 and 1904 respectively. The Old Michigan City Lighthouse is now a museum, while the pierhead light is still an active aid to navigation. *Address:* Michigan City East Light *City:* Michigan City *State:* IN *Visitors welcome?* No *Operated by:* U.S. Coast Guard (District 9) *NR?* Yes *NHL?* No *Year established/built:* 1837 *Latitude:* 41.7290 *Latitude:* -86.9117

MICHIGAN

ALPENA LIGHTHOUSE
Established in 1877, the original wooden tower was destroyed by fire and replaced with a cast-iron skeletal tower in 1914. The light is affectionately known as Sputnik after its resemblance to the first satellite to orbit the earth. *Address:* Alpena Light *City:* Alpena *State:* MI *Visitors welcome?* No *Operated by:* U.S. Coast Guard (District 9) *NR?* Yes *NHL?* No *Year established/built:* 1875 *Latitude:* 45.0604 *Latitude:* -83.4229

AU SABLE POINT LIGHTHOUSE
Established and built in 1874, the Au Sable Point Lighthouse was called Big Sable Lighthouse until 1910. Still a navigation aid, the lighthouse is now part of the Pictured Rocks National Lakeshore, and it is undergoing restoration by the National Park Service. *Address:* Au Sable Point *State:* MI *Phone:* 906-387-2607 *Web:* www.nps.gov/piro *Visitors welcome?* Yes *Hours:* Park Ranger-guided tours are available five days a week June, July, August and over the Labor Day weekend. *Admission:* FREE *Operated by:* Pictured Rocks National Lakeshore *NR?* Yes *NHL?* No *Year established/built:* 1874 *Latitude:* 46.6722 *Latitude:* -86.1418

BEAVER ISLAND HARBOR LIGHTHOUSE
The Beaver Island Harbor Lighthouse was established in 1856 and the original tower replaced in 1870. Automated in 1927, the tower is now owned by the local township. *Address:* Beaver Island Harbor Light *City:* Beaver Island *State:* MI *Zip:* 49782 *Visitors welcome?* No *Operated by:* St. James Township *NR?* No *NHL?* No *Year established/built:* 1856 *Latitude:* 45.7428 *Latitude:* -85.5086

BEAVER ISLAND LIGHTHOUSE
Established in 1851, the Beaver Island Lighthouse, also known as Beaver Head Lighthouse, was lit in 1858 and operated until 1962. It is now the site of an educational facility run by a local public school district. *Address:* Beaver Island Head Light *City:* Beaver Island *State:* MI *Phone:* 231-547-3200 *Visitors welcome?* Yes *Hours:* Contact attraction directly *Admission:* Contact attraction directly *Operated by:* Beaver Island Lighthouse School *NR?* Yes *NHL?* No *Year established/built:* 1851 *Latitude:* 45.5764 *Latitude:* -85.5725

CHAPTER 5 – LIGHTHOUSES & LIGHTSHIPS

Lighthouses of Michigan Tour Itinerary

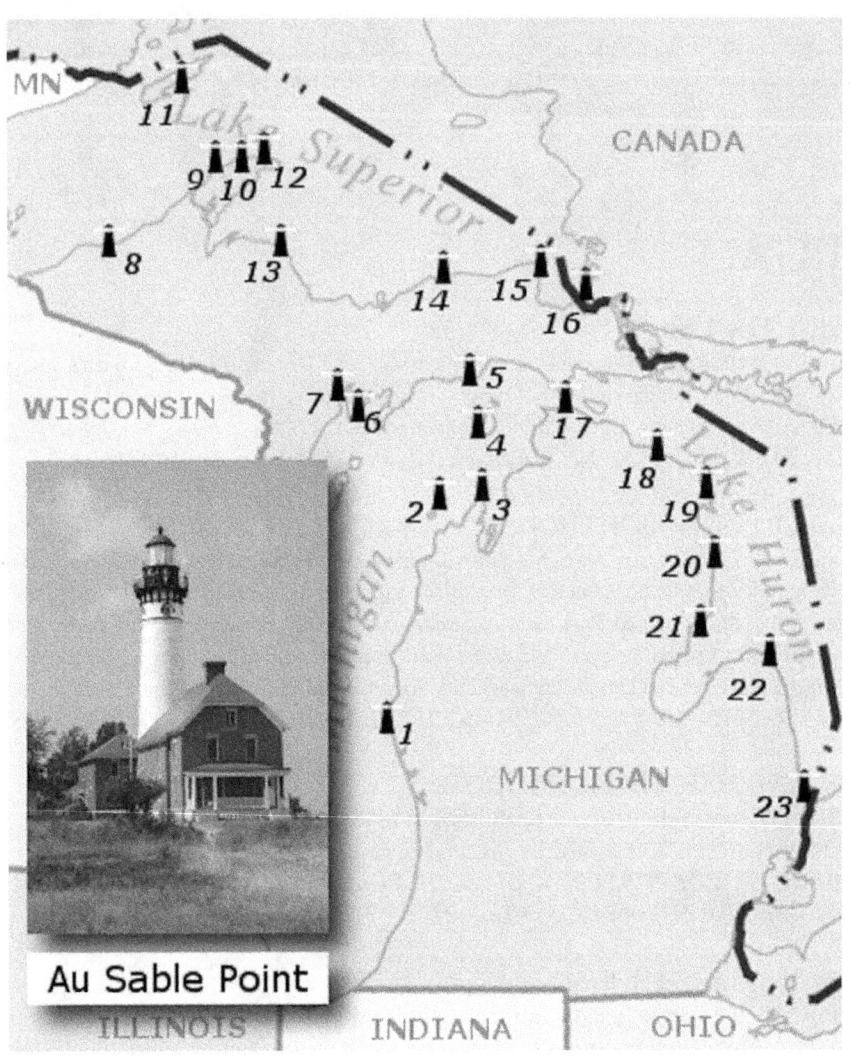

Au Sable Point

1. Big Sable Point (Ludington)
2. South Manitou Island
3. Grand Traverse (Northport)
4. Beaver Island
5. Seul Choix (Gulliver)
6. Peninsula Point (Rapid River)
7. Sand Point (Escanaba)
8. Ontonagon County (Ontonagon)
9. Sand Hill (Ahmeek)
10. Eagle Harbor (Eagle Harbor)
11. Rock Harbor (Isle Royale)
12. Copper Harbor (Copper Harbor)
13. Big Bay Point (Big Bay)

CHAPTER 5 – LIGHTHOUSES & LIGHTSHIPS

14. *Au Sable Point (Grand Marais)*
15. *Whitefish Point (Paradise)*
16. *Point Iroquois (Brimley)*
17. *Old Mackinac Point (Mackinaw City)*
18. *Forty Mile Point (Rogers City)*
19. *New/Old Presque Isle (Presque Isle)*
20. *Sturgeon Point (Harrisville)*
21. *Tawas Point (East Tawas)*
22. *Pointe Aux Barques (Port Hope)*
23. *Fort Gratiot (Port Huron)*

All the Great Lakes states are steeped in lighthouse history and lore, but Michigan features the most lighthouses of any state: 115. Begin a tour at Big Sable Point on Lake Michigan and follow U.S. Highway 31 north to Interstate 75. Cross the Mackinaw Bridge and head west on U.S. Highway 2 to Ontonagon. Backtrack to U.S. Highway 41 to Copper Harbor. Backtrack again on U.S. 41 and U.S. 2 and head south on I-75 across the Mackinaw Bridge. Find U.S. Highway 23 and head east, then south along with west shore of Lake Huron to Port Huron, almost the furthest point east of the Wolverine State.

BIG BAY POINT LIGHTHOUSE

Established and constructed in 1896, the Big Point Point Lighthouse was operational until 1961. In 1990, the facility was re-activated and is now operated as a bed and breakfast. *Address:* 3 Lighthouse Road *City:* Big Bay *State:* MI *Zip:* 49808 *Phone:* 906-345-9957 *Web:* www.bigbaylighthouse.com *Email:* keepers@BigBayLighthouse.com *Visitors welcome?* Yes *Hours:* Contact attraction directly *Admission:* Contact attraction directly *Operated by:* Big Bay Point Lighthouse Bed & Breakfast *NR?* Yes *NHL?* No *Year established/built:* 1896 *Latitude:* 46.8320 *Latitude:* -87.6851

BIG SABLE POINT LIGHTHOUSE

Completed in 1867, Big Sable Point Lighthouse was encased in steel in 1902 after the brick tower began to deteriorate. The station was automated in 1968. Some tours are available in the summer. *Address:* Big Sable Point Light *City:* Ludington *State:* MI *Phone:* 231-845-7343 *Web:* www.splka.org *Email:* bsplka@t-one.net *Visitors welcome?* Yes *Hours:* Grounds only *Admission:* FREE *Operated by:* Sable Point Lightkeepers Association *NR?* Yes *NHL?* No *Year established/built:* 1867 *Latitude:* 44.0577 *Latitude:* -86.5144

BOIS BLANC ISLAND LIGHTHOUSE

Established in 1829, the current Bois Blanc Island Lighthouse was constructed in 1867 and operated until 1924. It is now privately owned. *Address:* Bois Blanc Island Light *City:* Bois Blanc *State:* MI *Visitors welcome?* No *Operated by:* Private owner *NR?* No *NHL?* No *Year established/built:* 1829 *Latitude:* 45.7509 *Latitude:* -84.4594

CEDAR RIVER LIGHTHOUSE

The tower no longer exists, but the keeper's dwelling still stands, now used as a private residence. *Address:* Big Cedar River *City:* Cedar River *State:* MI *Visitors welcome?* No *Operated by:* Private owner *NR?* No *NHL?* No *Latitude:* 45.4111 *Latitude:* -87.3546

CHARITY ISLAND LIGHTHOUSE

Established and built in 1857, the Charity Island Lighthouse is now owned by a private party. *Address:* Charity Island Light *State:* MI *Visitors welcome?* No *Operated by:* Private owner *NR?* No *NHL?* No *Year established/built:* 1857 *Latitude:* 44.0314 *Latitude:* -83.4356

CHAPTER 5 – LIGHTHOUSES & LIGHTSHIPS

CHARLEVOIX SOUTH PIER LIGHTHOUSE
Originally a wooden structure built in 1885, the current steel tower Charlevoix South Pierhead Lighthouse was constructed in 1948. It is still an active aid to navigation. *Address:* Charlevoix South Pier Light Station *City:* Charlevoix *State:* MI *Visitors welcome?* Yes *Hours:* Grounds only *Admission:* FREE *Operated by:* U.S. Coast Guard (District 9) *NR?* Yes *NHL?* No *Year established/built:* 1885 *Latitude:* 45.3228 *Latitude:* -85.2697

CHEBOYGAN CRIB LIGHTHOUSE
Established in 1852 and originally built on a crib (artificial island) in the Cheboygan River, the Cheboygan Crib Lighthouse is now relocated to the mouth of the Cheboygan River. It is no longer an active aid to navigation. *Address:* Cheboygan Crib Light *City:* Cheboygan *State:* MI *Visitors welcome?* Yes *Hours:* Grounds only *Admission:* FREE *Operated by:* City of Cheboygan *NR?* No *NHL?* No *Year established/built:* 1852 *Latitude:* 45.6568 *Latitude:* -84.4650

CHEBOYGAN RIVER FRONT RANGE LIGHTHOUSE
The Cheboygan River Front Range Lighthouse was constructed in 1880, and it is still an active aid to navigation. The lighthouse is owned and operated by the Great Lakes Lighthouse Keepers Association. *Address:* Cheboygan River, Lake Huron *City:* Cheboygan *State:* MI *Phone:* 231-436-5580 *Web:* www.gllka.com *Email:* info@gllka.com *Visitors welcome?* Yes *Hours:* Saturdays, Sundays, and holidays from Memorial Day through the second weekend of October *Admission:* Contact attraction directly *Operated by:* Great Lakes Lighthouse Keepers Association *NR?* No *NHL?* No *Year established/built:* 1880 *Latitude:* 45.6470 *Latitude:* -84.4745

CHRISTMAS RANGE LIGHTHOUSE
The Christmas Range Lighthouses, also known as the End of the Road Lighthouses, mark the channel between Trout Bay and South Bay near Munising. *Address:* State Highway 28 *City:* Christmas *State:* MI *Visitors welcome?* Yes *Hours:* Grounds only *Admission:* FREE *Operated by:* Hiawatha National Forest *NR?* No *NHL?* No *Latitude:* 46.4369 *Latitude:* -86.7015

COPPER HARBOR LIGHTHOUSE
Established in 1849, the current tower of the Copper River Lighthouse was constructed in 1866. The light was automated in 1919 and deactivated in 1933. The site is now owned by the State of Michigan and managed as an historic site. *Address:* Copper Harbor Light *City:* Copper Harbor *State:* MI *Phone:* 906-289-4966 *Visitors welcome?* Yes *Hours:* Contact attraction directly *Admission:* Contact attraction directly *Operated by:* Michigan Historical Museum System *NR?* No *NHL?* No *Year established/built:* 1849 *Latitude:* 47.4743 *Latitude:* -87.8601

COPPER HARBOR RANGE LIGHTHOUSES
Established in 1849, the current tower of the Copper River Lighthouse was constructed in 1866. The light was automated in 1919 and deactivated in 1933. The site is now owned by the State of Michigan and managed as an historic site. *Address:* Copper Harbor Front Range Light *City:* Copper Harbor *State:* MI *Phone:* 906-289-4966 *Visitors welcome?* Yes *Hours:* Contact attraction directly *Admission:* Contact attraction directly *Operated by:* Michigan Historical Museum System *NR?* No *NHL?* No *Year established/built:* 1849 *Latitude:* 47.4811 *Latitude:* -87.8667

CRISP POINT LIGHTHOUSE
Established in built in 1904, the Crisp Point Lighthouse was deactivated in 1992. The station is maintained by a local not-for-profit. *Address:* Crisp Point Light *State:* MI *Phone:* 906-492-3206 *Web:* www.crisppointlighthouse.org *Visitors welcome?* Yes *Hours:* Daily, mid-June to September, noon to 5 p.m. *Admission:* Contact attraction directly *Operated by:* Crisp Point Light Historical Society *NR?* No *NHL?* No *Year established/built:* 1904 *Latitude:* 46.7529 *Latitude:* -85.2573

DETOUR REEF LIGHTHOUSE
The DeTour Reef Lighthouse was established in 1847, and the existing tower was constructed in 1931. The light is located one mile offshore in the St. Mary's River, the connection between Lakes Huron and Superior. The light was automated in 1974. *Address:* DeTour Reef Light *State:* MI *Phone:* 906-493-6609 *Email:* drlps@drlps.com *Visitors welcome?* Yes *Hours:* By appointment *Admission:* Contact attraction directly *Operated by:* DeTour Reef Light Preservation Society *NR?* Yes *NHL?* No *Year established/built:* 1847 *Latitude:* 45.9489 *Latitude:* -83.9031

DETROIT RIVER LIGHTHOUSE
Established in 1875, the current Detroit River Lighthouse, also called the Bar Point Shoal Lighthouse, was built in 1885 and automated in 1979. *Address:* Detroit River *City:* Detroit *State:* MI *Visitors welcome?* No *Operated by:* U.S. Coast Guard (District 9) *NR?* Yes *NHL?* No *Year established/built:* 1875 *Latitude:* 42.3525 *Latitude:* -82.8836

EAGLE HARBOR LIGHTHOUSE
Established in 1851, the current Eagle Harbor Lighthouse was constructed in 1871. Automated in 1980, the light is still an active aid to navigation. The lighthouse is now a museum operated by a local historical society. *Address:* Eagle Harbor Light *City:* Eagle Harbor *State:* MI *Visitors welcome?* Yes *Hours:* Mid-June to early October *Admission:* $4 adults, children FREE *Operated by:* Keweenaw County Historical Society *NR?* Yes *NHL?* No *Year established/built:* 1851 *Latitude:* 47.4596 *Latitude:* -88.1590

How do you include lighthouses in your travel plans? Tell us by emailing contact@fyddeye.com.

EAGLE HARBOR RANGE LIGHTHOUSE
Address: Highway 26 *City:* Eagle Harbor *State:* MI *Visitors welcome?* No *Operated by:* Private owner *NR?* No *NHL?* No *Latitude:* 47.4582 *Latitude:* -88.1623

EAGLE RIVER LIGHTHOUSE
Established in 1854, the current Eagle River Lighthouse was built in 1974 and deactivated in 1908. Located on West Main Street in Eagle River, the structure is now privately owned. *Address:* Eagle River Light *City:* Eagle River *State:* MI *Visitors welcome?* No *Operated by:* Private owner *NR?* Yes *NHL?* No *Year established/built:* 1854 *Latitude:* 47.4137 *Latitude:* -88.2983

FORT GRATIOT LIGHTHOUSE

The oldest light station in Michigan, the current tower was constructed in 1829 and extended in the 1860s. The lighthouse is now operated by the Port Huron Museum. *Address:* Fort Gratiot Light *City:* Port Huron *State:* MI *Zip:* 48060 *Phone:* 810-455-0214 *Web:* www.phmuseum.org *Visitors welcome?* Yes *Hours:* May to October, Friday, Saturday, Sunday, Monday, 11 a.m. to 5 p.m. *Admission:* Contact attraction directly *Operated by:* Port Huron Museum *NR?* No *NHL?* No *Year established/built:* 1814 *Latitude:* 43.0061 *Latitude:* -82.4222

FORTY MILE POINT LIGHTHOUSE
The Forty Mile Point Lighthouse was established and built in 1897 and automated in 1969. The site is now a museum. *Address:* Forty Mile Point Light *City:* Rogers City *State:* MI *Web:* www.40milepointlighthouse.org *Email:* webmaster@40milepointlighthouse.org *Visitors welcome?* Yes *Hours:* Memorial Day to mid-October; Saturdays and Sundays, noon to 4 p.m. *Admission:* Contact attraction directly *Operated by:* 40 Mile Point Lighthouse Society *NR?* Yes *NHL?* No *Year established/built:* 1897 *Latitude:* 45.4867 *Latitude:* -83.9133

CHAPTER 5 – LIGHTHOUSES & LIGHTSHIPS

FOURTEEN FOOT SHOAL LIGHTHOUSE
Established and constructed in 1930, the Fourteen Foot Shoal Lighthouse is still an active aid to navigation. *Address:* Fourteen Foot Shoal Light *City:* Cheboygan *State:* MI *Visitors welcome?* No *Operated by:* U.S. Coast Guard (District 9) *NR?* Yes *NHL?* No *Year established/built:* 1930 *Latitude:* 45.6798 *Latitude:* -84.4350

FOURTEEN MILE POINT LIGHTHOUSE
Established and constructed in 1894, the Fourteen Mile Point Lighthouse was deactivated in 1934. *Address:* Fourteen Mile Point *City:* Ontonagon *State:* MI *Visitors welcome?* No *Operated by:* Private owner *NR?* No *NHL?* No *Year established/built:* 1894 *Latitude:* 46.9916 *Latitude:* -89.1168

FRANKFORT NORTH BREAKWATER LIGHTHOUSE
Established in 1873, the existing cast-iron Frankfort North Breakwater Lighthouse has operated since 1932. *Address:* Frankfort North Breakwater Light *City:* Frankfort *State:* MI *Visitors welcome?* Yes *Hours:* Grounds only *Admission:* FREE *Operated by:* U.S. Coast Guard (District 9) *NR?* Yes *NHL?* No *Year established/built:* 1873 *Latitude:* 44.6306 *Latitude:* -86.2522

FRYING PAN ISLAND
Formerly located on Frying Pan Island in the St. Mary's River, the Frying Pan Island lighthouse is now on the grounds of the Sault Ste. Marie Coast Guard Station. *Address:* 337 Water Street *City:* Sault Ste. Marie *State:* MI *Visitors welcome?* Yes *Hours:* Grounds only *Admission:* FREE *Operated by:* U.S. Coast Guard (District 9) *NR?* No *NHL?* No *Latitude:* 46.4990 *Latitude:* -84.3383

GRAND HAVEN LIGHTHOUSE
Established in 1839, the Grand Haven Lighthouse is actually two lights placed on a pier extending into Lake Michigan. The current inner and outer pier lights were constructed in 1905 and automated in 1969. *Address:* Grand Haven Light *City:* Grand Haven *State:* MI *Visitors welcome?* Yes *Hours:* Grounds only *Admission:* FREE *Operated by:* U.S. Coast Guard (District 9) *NR?* No *NHL?* No *Year established/built:* 1839 *Latitude:* 43.0570 *Latitude:* -86.2539

GRAND ISLAND EAST CHANNEL
The wood-frame Grand Island East Channel lighthouse was established and built in 1870. It was deactivated in 1913. Recent work on the lighthouse was supported by the East Channel Lights Rescue Project. *Address:* Grand Island East Channel Light *City:* Munising *State:* MI *Visitors welcome?* No *Operated by:* Private owner *NR?* Yes *NHL?* No *Year established/built:* 1870 *Latitude:* 46.4502 *Latitude:* -86.6224

GRAND ISLAND NORTH LIGHTHOUSE
Established in 1854, the current Grand Island North Lighthouse, also called the Old North Lighthouse, was constructed in 1867 near the original site, which was high on a cliff. Automated in 1961, the property was sold to a private party in 1972. *Address:* Grand Island *City:* Munising *State:* MI *Visitors welcome?* No *Operated by:* Private owner *NR?* Yes *NHL?* No *Year established/built:* 1854 *Latitude:* 46.5255 *Latitude:* -86.6640

GRAND MARAIS RANGE LIGHTHOUSES
Established and built in 1908, the Grand Marais Range Lighthouses are still active aids to navigation. *Address:* Coast Guard Point *City:* Grand Marais *State:* MI *Zip:* 49839 *Visitors welcome?* Yes *Hours:* Grounds only *Admission:* FREE *Operated by:* U.S. Coast Guard (District 9) *NR?* No *NHL?* No *Year established/built:* 1908 *Latitude:* 46.6708 *Latitude:* -85.9852

CHAPTER 5 – LIGHTHOUSES & LIGHTSHIPS

GRAND TRAVERSE LIGHTHOUSE
Established by the government in 1852, the current Grand Traverse Lighthouse was built in 1858. The station was automated in 1972, and then opened as a museum in 1986 inside Leelanau State Park. *Address:* Grand Traverse Light *State:* MI *Phone:* 231-386-7195 *Web:* www.grandtraverselighthouse.com *Email:* gtlthse@triton.net *Visitors welcome?* Yes *Hours:* Daily: May, noon to 4 p.m.; June to Labor Day, 10 a.m. to 4 p.m.; Labor Day to 10/31, noon to 4 p.m. *Admission:* $4 adults, $2 children six to 12, under six FREE *Operated by:* Grand Traverse Lighthouse *NR?* Yes *NHL?* No *Year established/built:* 1852 *Latitude:* 45.2100 *Latitude:* -85.5500

GRANITE ISLAND LIGHTHOUSE
Established and constructed in 1868, the Granite Island Lighthouse was automated in 1939. The lighthouse, now restored, is in private hands. *Address:* Granite Island *State:* MI *Web:* www.graniteisland.com *Email:* sholman@graniteisland.com *Visitors welcome?* No *Operated by:* Private owner *NR?* Yes *NHL?* No *Year established/built:* 1868 *Latitude:* 46.7208 *Latitude:* -87.4115

GRAVELLY SHOAL LIGHTHOUSE
No description available. *Address:* Gravelly Shoal Light *State:* MI *Visitors welcome?* No *Operated by:* U.S. Coast Guard (District 9) *NR?* No *NHL?* No *Latitude:* 44.0183 *Latitude:* -83.5372

GRAYS REEF LIGHTHOUSE
The U.S. Lighthouse Service established the Grays Reef Lighthouse in 1891, and rebuilt the tower in 1936. The art-deco structure was automated in 1976. *Address:* Grays Reef *State:* MI *Visitors welcome?* No *Operated by:* U.S. Coast Guard (District 9) *NR?* Yes *NHL?* No *Year established/built:* 1891 *Latitude:* 45.7742 *Latitude:* -85.1753

GROSSE ILE NORTH CHANNEL RANGE LIGHTHOUSE
Established in 1894, the current Grosse Ile North Channel Range Front Lighthouse was constructed in 1906 and deactivated in 1963. *Address:* Grosse Ile Island *City:* Grosse Ile *State:* MI *Visitors welcome?* Yes *Hours:* Contact attraction directly *Admission:* Contact attraction directly *Operated by:* Grosse Ile Historical Society *NR?* Yes *NHL?* No *Year established/built:* 1894 *Latitude:* 42.1253 *Latitude:* -83.1583

GULL ROCK LIGHTHOUSE
Established and built in 1867, the light was later automated and the structures turned over to the Michigan Lighthouse Conservancy and the Gull Rock Lighthouse Keepers, which is working to restore the buildings. *Address:* Gull Rock Light *City:* Grant *State:* MI *Visitors welcome?* No *Operated by:* Gull Rock Lighthouse Keepers *NR?* Yes *NHL?* No *Year established/built:* 1867 *Latitude:* 47.4172 *Latitude:* -87.6636

HARBOR BEACH LIGHTHOUSE
Also known as Sand Beach Lighthouse, Harbor Beach Lighthouse was established in 1858, and the current cast-iron structure was completed in 1885. The tower was automated in 1968, and a local not-for-profit is working to restore the building and open it for tours. *Address:* Harbor Beach Light *City:* Harbor Beach *State:* MI *Visitors welcome?* No *Operated by:* Harbor Beach Lighthouse Preservation Society *NR?* Yes *NHL?* No *Year established/built:* 1858 *Latitude:* 43.8333 *Latitude:* -82.6167

HARSENS ISLAND REAR RANGE LIGHTHOUSE
No description available. *Address:* Harsens Island, St. Clair River *City:* Harsens Island *State:* MI *Visitors welcome?* No *Operated by:* Private owner *NR?* No *NHL?* No *Latitude:* 44.3148 *Latitude:* -85.6024

CHAPTER 5 – LIGHTHOUSES & LIGHTSHIPS

HOLLAND HARBOR LIGHTHOUSE
Established in 1872, the current 1936 Holland Harbor Lighthouse was constructed on a pier that extends into Lake Michigan. Automated in 1970, the lighthouse is now owned by the Holland Harbor Lighthouse Historical Commission. *Address:* Holland Harbor Light *City:* Macatawa *State:* MI *Visitors welcome?* Yes *Hours:* Grounds only *Admission:* FREE *Operated by:* Private owner *NR?* Yes *NHL?* No *Year established/built:* 1872 *Latitude:* 42.7727 *Latitude:* -86.2124

HURON ISLAND LIGHTHOUSE
Established in 1868, the Huron Island Lighthouse was first lit in 1871 and has been in continuous operation since, although it was automated in 1972. It is now located in a wildlife refuge in Lake Superior. *Address:* Lighthouse Island *State:* MI *Visitors welcome?* Yes *Hours:* Grounds only *Admission:* FREE *Operated by:* Huron National Wildlife Refuge *NR?* Yes *NHL?* No *Year established/built:* 1868 *Latitude:* 46.9624 *Latitude:* -87.9996

ISLE ROYALE LIGHTHOUSE
Established and built in 1875, the Isle Royale Lighthouse, formerly known as the Menagerie Island Lighthouse, was automated in 1913. It is now located within Isle Royale National Park. *Address:* Isle Royale Light *City:* Houghton *State:* MI *Visitors welcome?* Yes *Hours:* Grounds only *Admission:* FREE *Operated by:* U.S. Coast Guard (District 9) *NR?* Yes *NHL?* No *Year established/built:* 1875 *Latitude:* 47.9479 *Latitude:* -88.7612

JACOBSVILLE LIGHTHOUSE
Established in 1856, the current Jacobsville Lighthouse, also called the Portage River Lighthouse, was constructed in 1870. The station was deactivated in 1900 and is now operated as a bed and breakfast. *Address:* 38741 Jacobs St. *City:* Lake Linden *State:* MI *Phone:* 906-523-4137 *Web:* www.jacobsvillelighthouse.com *Email:* mditty23@netzero.com *Visitors welcome?* Yes *Hours:* Open year round *Admission:* Contact attraction directly *Operated by:* Jacobsville Lighthouse Inn *NR?* No *NHL?* No *Year established/built:* 1856 *Latitude:* 46.9795 *Latitude:* -88.4140

KEWEENAW WATERWAY LOWER ENTRANCE LIGHTHOUSE
Established in 1868, the current Keweenaw Waterway Lighthouse was constructed in 1920 and automated in 1973. The lighthouse is still an active aid to navigation. *Address:* Portage Lake *City:* Jacobsville *State:* MI *Visitors welcome?* No *Operated by:* U.S. Coast Guard (District 9) *NR?* No *NHL?* No *Year established/built:* 1868 *Latitude:* 46.9808 *Latitude:* -88.4101

KEWEENAW WATERWAY UPPER ENTRANCE LIGHTHOUSE
Address: Keweenaw Waterway *City:* Houghton *State:* MI *Visitors welcome?* No *Operated by:* U.S. Coast Guard (District 9) *NR?* No *NHL?* No *Latitude:* 47.1136 *Latitude:* -88.5217

LAKE ST. CLAIR LIGHTHOUSE
No description available. *Address:* Lake St. Clair *City:* St. Clair Shores *State:* MI *Visitors welcome?* No *Operated by:* U.S. Coast Guard (District 9) *NR?* No *NHL?* No *Latitude:* 42.4974 *Latitude:* -82.8964

LANSING SHOAL LIGHTHOUSE
Established in 1900, the current structure replaced a lightship in 1928. The lighthouse was automated in 1976. *Address:* Beaver Island *State:* MI *Visitors welcome?* No *Operated by:* U.S. Coast Guard (District 9) *NR?* Yes *NHL?* No *Year established/built:* 1900 *Latitude:* 45.7447 *Latitude:* -85.5213

LITTLE SABLE POINT LIGHTHOUSE
Established in 1874, the tower was once white-washed, then sandblasted clean after it was automated in 1955. *Address:* Little Sable Point Light *State:* MI *Phone:* 231-845-7343 *Web:* www.splka.org *Email:* bsplka@t-one.net

CHAPTER 5 – LIGHTHOUSES & LIGHTSHIPS

Visitors welcome? Yes *Hours:* Grounds only *Admission:* FREE *Operated by:* Sable Point Lightkeepers Association *NR?* Yes *NHL?* No *Year established/built:* 1874 *Latitude:* 43.6517 *Latitude:* -86.5389

LITTLE TRAVERSE LIGHTHOUSE
The Little Traverse Lighthouse is located in a gated community. *Address:* Little Traverse Light *City:* Harbor Springs *State:* MI *Visitors welcome?* No *Operated by:* Private owner *NR?* No *NHL?* No *Latitude:* 45.4189 *Latitude:* -84.9783

LUDINGTON NORTH BREAKWATER LIGHTHOUSE
Built of steel in 1924 to resemble the prow of a ship, the North Ludington Breakwater Lighthouse was established in 1871. The structure was renovated by the U.S. Coast Guard in 1993. *Address:* Ludington Light *City:* Ludington *State:* MI *Phone:* 231-845-7343 *Web:* www.splka.org *Email:* bsplka@t-one.net *Visitors welcome?* Yes *Hours:* Grounds only *Admission:* FREE *Operated by:* Sable Point Lightkeepers Association *NR?* Yes *NHL?* No *Year established/built:* 1924 *Latitude:* 43.9536 *Latitude:* -86.4694

MANISTEE LIGHTHOUSE
Established in 1875, the current Manistee North Pierhead Lighthouse was built in 1927 and automated the same year. The lighthouse is located on the end of a pier that marks the entrance to the Manistee River. *Address:* Manistee Pierhead Lights *City:* Manistee *State:* MI *Visitors welcome?* Yes *Hours:* Grounds only *Admission:* FREE *Operated by:* U.S. Coast Guard (District 9) *NR?* Yes *NHL?* No *Year established/built:* 1875 *Latitude:* 44.2517 *Latitude:* -86.3464

MANISTIQUE EAST BREAKWATER LIGHTHOUSE
Located on the end of a breakwater at the mouth of the Manistique River, the concrete Manistique Breakwater East Breakwater Lighthouse was constructed in 1915 and automated in 1969. *Address:* Manistique East Breakwater Light *City:* Manistique *State:* MI *Visitors welcome?* Yes *Hours:* Grounds only *Admission:* FREE *Operated by:* U.S. Coast Guard (District 9) *NR?* Yes *NHL?* No *Year established/built:* 1913 *Latitude:* 45.9446 *Latitude:* -86.2472

MANITOU ISLAND LIGHTHOUSE
Established in 1850, the current skeletal tower structure was built in 1861. The light was automated in 1978 and is now owned by a local land conservancy. *Address:* Manitou Island Light *City:* Hancock *State:* MI *Phone:* 906-482-0820 *Email:* evanmcdonald@keweenawlandtrust.org *Visitors welcome?* Yes *Hours:* Grounds only *Admission:* Contact attraction directly *Operated by:* Keweenaw Land Trust *NR?* Yes *NHL?* No *Year established/built:* 1850 *Latitude:* 45.0072 *Latitude:* -86.0939

MARQUETTE BREAKWATER LIGHTHOUSE
No description available. *City:* Marquette *State:* MI *Visitors welcome?* Yes *Hours:* Grounds only *Admission:* FREE *Operated by:* U.S. Coast Guard (District 9) *NR?* No *NHL?* No *Latitude:* 46.5336 *Latitude:* -87.3753

MARQUETTE HARBOR LIGHTHOUSE
Established in 1853, the current Marquette Harbor Lighthouse was constructed in 1866 with a second story added in 1909. Still an active aid to navigation, the lighthouse is now managed by the Marquette Maritime Museum. *Address:* Marquette Harbor Light *City:* Marquette *State:* MI *Zip:* 49855 *Phone:* 906-226-2006 *Web:* mqtmaritimemuseum.com *Email:* mqtmaritimemuseum@yahoo.com *Visitors welcome?* Yes *Hours:* Contact attraction directly *Admission:* Contact attraction directly *Operated by:* Marquette Maritime Museum *NR?* Yes *NHL?* No *Year established/built:* 1853 *Latitude:* 46.5468 *Latitude:* -87.3763

CHAPTER 5 – LIGHTHOUSES & LIGHTSHIPS

MARTIN REEF LIGHTHOUSE
The Martin Reef Lighthouse was established and built in 1927 and it is still an active aid to navigation. *City:* Port Dolomite *State:* MI *Visitors welcome?* No *Operated by:* U.S. Coast Guard (District 9) *NR?* Yes *NHL?* No *Year established/built:* 1927 *Latitude:* 45.9847 *Latitude:* -84.2750

MCGULPIN POINT LIGHTHOUSE
Established in 1869, the McGulpins Point Lighthouse was deactivated in 1906 after construction of the nearby Mackinac Point Lighthouse in 1892. *Address:* McGulpin Point Light *City:* Mackinaw City *State:* MI *Visitors welcome?* No *Operated by:* Private owner *NR?* No *NHL?* No *Year established/built:* 1869 *Latitude:* 45.7869 *Latitude:* -84.7722

MENDOTA LIGHTHOUSE
Established in 1870, the Mendota Lighthouse, also known as the Bete Grise Lighthouse, marks the Mendota Ship Channel from Bete Grise Bay to Lac La Belle. The current tower was constructed in 1895 and the light was deactivated in 1960. *City:* Lac La Belle *State:* MI *Visitors welcome?* No *Operated by:* Private owner *NR?* Yes *NHL?* No *Year established/built:* 1870 *Latitude:* 47.3746 *Latitude:* -87.9629

MENOMINEE NORTH PIER LIGHTHOUSE
Established in 1877, the current Menominee North Pier Lighthouse was constructed in 1927 and automated in 1972. *Address:* Menominee Pier Light *City:* Menominee *State:* MI *Visitors welcome?* Yes *Hours:* Grounds only *Admission:* FREE *Operated by:* U.S. Coast Guard (District 9) *NR?* No *NHL?* No *Year established/built:* 1877 *Latitude:* 45.1000 *Latitude:* -87.5833

MIDDLE ISLAND LIGHTHOUSE
Established and built in 1905, the Middle Island Lighthouse is still an operational aid to navigation. The tower is operated by the Friends of Middle Island Lighthouse, while the keeper's house is owned and operated by the Middle Island Lightkeepers Association. *Address:* Middle Island *City:* Alpena *State:* MI *Visitors welcome?* Yes *Hours:* Contact attraction directly *Admission:* Contact attraction directly *Operated by:* Friends of Middle Island Lighthouse *NR?* Yes *NHL?* No *Year established/built:* 1905 *Latitude:* 45.1925 *Latitude:* -83.3272

MIDDLE NEEBISH RANGE LIGHTHOUSE
Also called the Lower Nicolet Range Lighthouse, the Middle Neebish Lighthouse marks the entrance to the Middle Neebish Channel near Richards Landing. *Address:* Neebish Island *State:* MI *Visitors welcome?* No *Operated by:* U.S. Coast Guard (District 9) *NR?* No *NHL?* No *Latitude:* 46.3185 *Latitude:* -84.1707

MINNEAPOLIS SHOAL LIGHTHOUSE
Built in 1935, the concrete tower of Minneapolis Shoal Lighthouse was automated in 1979. *Address:* Minneapolis Shoal *City:* Delta *State:* MI *Visitors welcome?* No *Operated by:* U.S. Coast Guard (District 9) *NR?* Yes *NHL?* No *Year established/built:* 1935 *Latitude:* 45.5800 *Latitude:* -86.9987

MUNISING RANGE LIGHTHOUSE
Established in 1908, the Munising Range Lighthouse facility is now offices for the Pictured Rocks National Lakeshore. *Address:* State Highway 28 and West Munising Avenue *City:* Munising *State:* MI *Zip:* 49862-0040 *Phone:* 906-387-2607 *Visitors welcome?* Yes *Hours:* Grounds only *Admission:* FREE *Operated by:* Pictured Rocks National Lakeshore *NR?* No *NHL?* No *Year established/built:* 1908 *Latitude:* 46.4230 *Latitude:* -86.6641

MUSKEGON SOUTH BREAKWATER LIGHTHOUSE
Established in 1851, the current tower of the Muskegon South Breakwater Lighthouse was built in 1903. The tower is one of three lights that mark the channel from Lake Michigan to Lake Muskegon. *Address:* Muske-

gon Breakwater Light *City:* Muskegon *State:* MI *Visitors welcome?* Yes *Hours:* Grounds only *Admission:* FREE *Operated by:* U.S. Coast Guard (District 9) *NR?* Yes *NHL?* No *Year established/built:* 1851 *Latitude:* 43.2241 *Latitude:* -86.3471

NORTH MANITOU SHOAL LIGHTHOUSE
Constructed in 1935 to replace a series of lightships at its location, the North Manitou Shoal Lighthouse was automated in 1980. *Address:* Manitou Island *State:* MI *Visitors welcome?* No *Operated by:* U.S. Coast Guard (District 9) *NR?* Yes *NHL?* No *Year established/built:* 1935 *Latitude:* 47.4094 *Latitude:* -87.6059

OLD MACKINAC POINT LIGHTHOUSE
The castle-like structure, whose design is unique in the Great Lakes, has been restored to its 1910 appearance. *Address:* 526 North Huron Avenue *City:* Mackinaw City *State:* MI *Zip:* 49701 *Phone:* 231-436-4100 *Web:* www.mackinacparks.com *Email:* cottonl@michigan.gov *Visitors welcome?* Yes *Hours:* Daily, contact attraction directly for specifics *Admission:* $6 adults; $3.50 youths five to 17; children four and under FREE *Operated by:* Mackinac State Historic Parks *NR?* Yes *NHL?* No *Year established/built:* 1890 *Latitude:* 45.7780 *Latitude:* -84.7264

OLD MISSION POINT LIGHTHOUSE
Established and built in 1870, the Old Mission Point Lighthouse is no longer an active aid to navigation. Visitors are permitted to stay overnight with advance reservations. *Address:* Mission Point Light *State:* MI *Phone:* 231-223-7322 *Visitors welcome?* Yes *Hours:* Contact attraction directly *Admission:* Contact attraction directly *Operated by:* Peninsula Township *NR?* Yes *NHL?* No *Year established/built:* 1870 *Latitude:* 44.9913 *Latitude:* -85.4795

ONTONAGON LIGHTHOUSE
Established in 1852, the Ontonagon Lighthouse was active until 1964. It is now operated as an historic site by a local historical society. *Address:* 422 River Street *City:* Ontonagen *State:* MI *Zip:* 49953 *Phone:* 906-884-6165 *Visitors welcome?* Yes *Hours:* By appointment *Admission:* Contact attraction directly *Operated by:* Ontonagon County Historical Society *NR?* Yes *NHL?* No *Year established/built:* 1852 *Latitude:* 46.8719 *Latitude:* -89.3159

ONTONAGON PIERHEAD LIGHTHOUSE
Established in 1852, the Ontonagen Pierhead Lighthouse marks the entrance to the Ontonagon River. *Address:* Ontonagon River *City:* Ontonagen *State:* MI *Zip:* 49953 *Visitors welcome?* No *Operated by:* U.S. Coast Guard (District 9) *NR?* No *NHL?* No *Year established/built:* 1852 *Latitude:* 46.8760 *Latitude:* -89.3261

PASSAGE ISLAND LIGHTHOUSE
Established and constructed in 1882, the Passage Island Lighthouse was automated in 1978. The site is now part of Isle Royale National Park. *Address:* Passage Island *State:* MI *Visitors welcome?* Yes *Hours:* Grounds only *Admission:* FREE *Operated by:* U.S. Coast Guard (District 9) *NR?* Yes *NHL?* No *Year established/built:* 1885 *Latitude:* 48.2335 *Latitude:* -88.3509

PECHE ISLAND LIGHTHOUSE
Originally standing in Lake St. Clair, the Peche Island Lighthouse, also called the Peche Island Rear Range Light, is now in Marine City along the St. Clair riverfront. *Address:* Peche Island Light *City:* Marine City *State:* MI *Visitors welcome?* Yes *Hours:* Grounds only *Admission:* FREE *Operated by:* City of Marine City *NR?* No *NHL?* No *Year established/built:* 1908 *Latitude:* 42.7195 *Latitude:* -82.4921

CHAPTER 5 – LIGHTHOUSES & LIGHTSHIPS

PENINSULA POINT LIGHTHOUSE
Constructed in 1865, the Peninsula Point Lighthouse operated until 1936. It is now part of the Hiawatha National Forest. *Address:* Peninsula Point Light *State:* MI *Phone:* 906-786-4062 *Visitors welcome?* Yes *Hours:* Grounds only *Admission:* FREE *Operated by:* Hiawatha National Forest *NR?* Yes *NHL?* No *Year established/built:* 1865 *Latitude:* 45.6682 *Latitude:* -86.9666

PENTWATER/PORTAGE LAKE PIERHEAD LIGHTHOUSE
A pair of lights marks the entrance to a short channel leading to Pentwater Lake. *City:* Pentwater *State:* MI *Visitors welcome?* Yes *Hours:* Grounds only *Admission:* FREE *Operated by:* U.S. Coast Guard (District 9) *NR?* No *NHL?* No *Latitude:* 43.7822 *Latitude:* -86.4439

PETOSKEY PIERHEAD LIGHTHOUSE
The Petoskey Pierhead Light marks the breakwater at Petoskey, Mich. *City:* Petoskey *State:* MI *Visitors welcome?* Yes *Hours:* Grounds only *Admission:* FREE *Operated by:* U.S. Coast Guard (District 9) *NR?* No *NHL?* No *Latitude:* 45.3802 *Latitude:* -84.9617

PIPE ISLAND LIGHTHOUSE
Address: Pipe Island *State:* MI *Visitors welcome?* No *Operated by:* Private owner *NR?* No *NHL?* No *Latitude:* 46.0172 *Latitude:* -83.8989

POE REEF LIGHTHOUSE
Established in 1893, the current Poe Reef Lighthouse was constructed in 1929 on a site formerly marked by lightships. The lighthouse was automated in 1974. *Address:* Poe Reef Light *State:* MI *Visitors welcome?* No *Operated by:* U.S. Coast Guard (District 9) *NR?* Yes *NHL?* No *Year established/built:* 1893 *Latitude:* 45.6870 *Latitude:* -84.4437

POINT BETSIE LIGHTHOUSE
Established and built in 1858, the Point Betsie Lighthouse is still operational, though it was automated in 1983. The lighthouse is operated as a museum by a local not-for-profit organization. *Address:* Point Betsie Light *City:* Frankfort *State:* MI *Zip:* 49635-0601 *Phone:* 231-352-4915 *Email:* info@pointbetsie.org *Visitors welcome?* Yes *Hours:* Contact attraction directly *Admission:* $2 adults, $1 children under 12 *Operated by:* Friends of Point Betsie Lighthouse *NR?* Yes *NHL?* No *Year established/built:* 1858 *Latitude:* 44.6913 *Latitude:* -86.2552

POINT IROQUOIS LIGHTHOUSE
Established in 1855, the current tower of the Point Iroquois Lighthouse was built in 1871 and operated until 1971. The site is now within the Hiawatha National Forest. *Address:* 12942 West Lakeshore Drive *City:* Brimley *State:* MI *Phone:* 906-786-4062 *Visitors welcome?* Yes *Hours:* Grounds only *Admission:* FREE *Operated by:* Hiawatha National Forest *NR?* Yes *NHL?* No *Year established/built:* 1855 *Latitude:* 46.4816 *Latitude:* -84.6283

POINT SANILAC LIGHTHOUSE
Established and built in 1866, the Port Sanilac Lighthouse is still an operational aid to navigation. *Address:* Cherry Street and South Lake Street *City:* Port Sanilac *State:* MI *Visitors welcome?* No *Operated by:* Private owner *NR?* No *NHL?* No *Year established/built:* 1866 *Latitude:* 43.4287 *Latitude:* -82.5405

POINTE AUX BARQUES LIGHTHOUSE
Established in 1848, the current Pointe aux Barques Lighthouse was built in 1857 and automated in 1958. The facility is now a public park and museum, and it is operated by a local not-for-profit organization. *Address:*

Pointe aux Barques Light *City:* Port Hope *State:* MI *Email:* info@pointeauxbarqueslighthouse.org *Visitors welcome?* Yes *Hours:* Daily, Memorial Day weekend to Oct. 1 *Admission:* Contact attraction directly *Operated by:* Point aux Barques Lighthouse Society *NR?* Yes *NHL?* No *Year established/built:* 1848 *Latitude:* 44.0233 *Latitude:* -82.7933

PORT AUSTIN REEF LIGHTHOUSE
Established in 1878, the current Port Austin Reef Lighthouse was constructed the same year. The lighthouse is still an active aid to navigation. *Address:* Port Austin Light *City:* Port Austin *State:* MI *Visitors welcome?* No *Operated by:* U.S. Coast Guard (District 9) *NR?* No *NHL?* No *Year established/built:* 1878 *Latitude:* 44.0833 *Latitude:* -82.9833

POVERTY ISLAND LIGHTHOUSE
Established and built in 1874, the Poverty Island Lighthouse operated until 1976. It was reactivated in 1982 with an automated aid to navigation. *Address:* Poverty Island *State:* MI *Visitors welcome?* No *Operated by:* U.S. Coast Guard (District 9) *NR?* Yes *NHL?* No *Year established/built:* 1874 *Latitude:* 45.5275 *Latitude:* -86.6646

PRESQUE ISLE (NEW) LIGHTHOUSE
The Presque Isle (New) Lighthouse was established in 1840, with the newer of the peninsula's two lighthouses constructed in 1871. The station is now operated by a not-for-profit organization. *Address:* 4500 E. Grand Lake Road *City:* Presque Isle *State:* MI *Web:* www.keepershouse.org *Email:* neilsbungalow@yahoo.com *Visitors welcome?* Yes *Hours:* Contact attraction directly *Admission:* Contact attraction directly *Operated by:* Presque Isle Township Museum Society *NR?* Yes *NHL?* No *Year established/built:* 1840 *Latitude:* 45.3545 *Latitude:* -83.4902

PRESQUE ISLE (OLD) LIGHTHOUSE
The Presque Isle (Old) Lighthouse was established and built in 1840. It was deactivated in 1870 and a replacement built in 1871 a short distance north. The station is now operated by a not-for-profit organization. *Address:* 4500 E. Grand Lake Road *City:* Presque Isle *State:* MI *Web:* www.keepershouse.org *Email:* neilsbungalow@yahoo.com *Visitors welcome?* Yes *Hours:* Contact attraction directly *Admission:* Contact attraction directly *Operated by:* Presque Isle Township Museum Society *NR?* Yes *NHL?* No *Year established/built:* 1840 *Latitude:* 45.3545 *Latitude:* -83.4902

PRESQUE ISLE HARBOR BREAKWATER LIGHTHOUSE
No description available. *Address:* Presque Isle Harbor *City:* Marquette *State:* MI *Visitors welcome?* Yes *Hours:* Grounds only *Admission:* FREE *Operated by:* U.S. Coast Guard (District 9) *NR?* No *NHL?* No *Latitude:* 46.5740 *Latitude:* -87.3750

PRESQUE ISLE RANGE LIGHTHOUSES
The Presque Isle Front Range Lighthouse was restored by a private party and is now located in Presque Isle Range Light Park. The rear range light is at its original location off Grand Lake Road. *Address:* E. Grand Lake Road *City:* Presque Isle *State:* MI *Visitors welcome?* Yes *Hours:* Grounds only *Admission:* FREE *Operated by:* Private owner *NR?* No *NHL?* No *Latitude:* 45.2832 *Latitude:* -83.4619

ROCK HARBOR LIGHTHOUSE
Established in 1858, the Rock Harbor Lighthouse was deactivated in 1879 by the Lighthouse Service. The structure is now part of the Isle Royale National Park, and it is accessible only by boat. *Address:* Rock Harbor *City:* Isle Royale *State:* MI *Visitors welcome?* Yes *Hours:* Grounds only *Admission:* FREE *Operated by:* Isle Royale National Park *NR?* No *NHL?* No *Year established/built:* 1858 *Latitude:* 47.9959 *Latitude:* -88.9093

CHAPTER 5 – LIGHTHOUSES & LIGHTSHIPS

ROCK OF AGES LIGHTHOUSE
The Rock of Ages Lighthouse was established on an exposed rock in Lake Superior in 1908. It was automated in 1978 and its original fresnel lens is now on display at Windigo Information Station at Indigo National Park. *Address:* Rock of Ages Light *State:* MI *Visitors welcome?* No *Operated by:* U.S. Coast Guard (District 9) *NR?* Yes *NHL?* No *Year established/built:* 1908 *Latitude:* 47.8664 *Latitude:* -89.3146

ROUND ISLAND LIGHTHOUSE
Established and built in 1892, the Round Island Lighthouse is no longer operational, and it is now a private residence. *Address:* Round Island *City:* DeTour *State:* MI *Visitors welcome?* No *Operated by:* Private owner *NR?* Yes *NHL?* No *Year established/built:* 1892 *Latitude:* 45.9953 *Latitude:* -84.0146

ROUND ISLAND LIGHTHOUSE
Established and built in 1895, the Round Island Lighthouse operated until 1947, and it was relit in 1996. *Address:* Round Island Light *City:* Mackinac Island *State:* MI *Visitors welcome?* Yes *Hours:* Grounds only *Admission:* FREE *Operated by:* U.S. Coast Guard (District 9) *NR?* No *NHL?* No *Year established/built:* 1895 *Latitude:* 45.8372 *Latitude:* -84.6166

ROUND ISLAND PASSAGE LIGHTHOUSE
One of the newer lighthouses in the nation's inventory, Round Island Passage lighthouse was established and constructed in 1948 and automated in 1973. *Address:* Mackinac Island *City:* Mackinac Island *State:* MI *Visitors welcome?* No *Operated by:* U.S. Coast Guard (District 9) *NR?* No *NHL?* No *Year established/built:* 1948 *Latitude:* 45.8492 *Latitude:* -84.6189

SAGINAW RIVER REAR RANGE LIGHTHOUSE
Established and constructed in 1876, the Saginaw River Rear Range Lighthouse and its companion front range light replaced an earlier light station built in 1841. The deactivated range lighthouses are now owned by the Dow Chemical Company. *Address:* Saginaw River Rear Range Light *City:* Bay City *State:* MI *Visitors welcome?* No *Operated by:* Saginaw River Marine Historical Society *NR?* Yes *NHL?* No *Year established/built:* 1876 *Latitude:* 43.6355 *Latitude:* -83.8506

SAND HILLS LIGHTHOUSE
Established and built in 1919, the yellow brick Sand Hills Lighthouse was deactivated in 1954. It is now operated as a bed and breakfast. *Address:* Sand Hills Light *State:* MI *Zip:* 49901 *Phone:* 906-337-1744 *Web:* www.sandhillslighthouseinn.com *Visitors welcome?* Yes *Hours:* Contact attraction directly *Admission:* Contact attraction directly *Operated by:* Sand Hills Lighthouse Inn *NR?* Yes *NHL?* No *Year established/built:* 1919 *Latitude:* 47.3919 *Latitude:* -88.3704

SAND POINT (BARAGA) LIGHTHOUSE
Established in 1878, the Sand Point Lighthouse, also known as the Baraga Lighthouse, was constructed the same year. The light is now deactivated. *Address:* Sand Point *City:* Baraga *State:* MI *Visitors welcome?* Yes *Hours:* Grounds only *Admission:* FREE *Operated by:* Keweenaw Bay Indian Community *NR?* Yes *NHL?* No *Year established/built:* 1878 *Latitude:* 46.7816 *Latitude:* -88.4710

SAND POINT (ESCANABA) LIGHTHOUSE
Established and built in 1867, the Sand Point (Escanaba) Lighthouse was deactivated in 1939. It is now operated as a museum. *Address:* Sand Point *City:* Escanaba *State:* MI *Phone:* 906-789-6790 *Web:* www.deltahistorical.org/lighthouse.htm *Email:* deltacountyhistsoc@sbcglobal.net *Visitors welcome?* Yes *Hours:* June, July, and August: 9 a.m. to 5 p.m.; September: 1 p.m. to 5 p.m. *Admission:* Contact attraction directly *Operated by:*

Delta County Historical Society *NR?* Yes *NHL?* No *Year established/built:* 1867 *Latitude:* 45.7436 *Latitude:* -87.0415

SEUL CHOIX POINTE LIGHTHOUSE
Established in 1892, the Seul Choix Pointe Lighthouse was constructed three years later. The light is still an active aid to navigation, and the facility is operated as a museum by a local historical society. *Address:* Seul Choix Point *City:* Gulliver *State:* MI *Phone:* 906-283-3183 *Web:* www.greatlakelighthouse.com *Email:* seulchoix@reiters.net *Visitors welcome?* Yes *Hours:* Daily, Memorial Day to mid-October, 10 a.m to 6 p.m. *Admission:* Contact attraction directly *Operated by:* Gulliver Historical Society *NR?* Yes *NHL?* No *Year established/built:* 1892 *Latitude:* 45.9216 *Latitude:* -85.9109

SKILLAGALEE ISLAND LIGHTHOUSE
Established in 1850, the Skillagelee Lighthouse, also known as the Ile Aux Galets Lighthouse, was constructed in 1888. *Address:* Skillagallee Island Light Station *State:* MI *Visitors welcome?* No *Operated by:* U.S. Coast Guard (District 9) *NR?* No *NHL?* No *Year established/built:* 1850 *Latitude:* 45.6764 *Latitude:* -85.1731

SOUTH FOX ISLAND LIGHTHOUSES
Established in 1867, two lighthouses sit on the southern tip of South Fox Island, one a brick structure, the other a skeletal metal tower. The lights were deactivated in 1934. *Address:* South Fox Island *State:* MI *Visitors welcome?* Yes *Hours:* Grounds only *Admission:* FREE *Operated by:* Michigan Dept. of Natural Resources *NR?* No *NHL?* No *Year established/built:* 1867 *Latitude:* 45.3992 *Latitude:* -85.8301

SOUTH HAVEN SOUTH PIER LIGHTHOUSE
Established in 1872, the current South Haven Lighthouse was constructed on the end of a pier in 1903. *Address:* South Haven Light *City:* South Haven *State:* MI *Visitors welcome?* No *Operated by:* U.S. Coast Guard (District 9) *NR?* No *NHL?* No *Year established/built:* 1872 *Latitude:* 42.4022 *Latitude:* -86.2844

SOUTH MANITOU ISLAND LIGHTHOUSE
Established in 1839, the current lighthouse tower was constructed in 1872. The lighthouse was discontinued in 1958 and incorporated in the Sleeping Bear Dunes National Lakeshore. *Address:* South Manitou Island Light *State:* MI *Phone:* 231-326-5134 *Visitors welcome?* Yes *Hours:* Grounds only *Admission:* FREE *Operated by:* Sleeping Bear Dunes National Lakeshore *NR?* Yes *NHL?* No *Year established/built:* 1839 *Latitude:* 45.0072 *Latitude:* -86.0939

SPECTACLE REEF LIGHTHOUSE
Established and built in 1867, the Spectacle Reef Lighthouse is described as the best specimen of monolithic stone masonry in the U.S. Still an active aid to navigation, the light was automated in 1972. *Address:* Spectacle Reef Light *State:* MI *Visitors welcome?* No *Operated by:* U.S. Coast Guard (District 9) *NR?* Yes *NHL?* No *Year established/built:* 1870 *Latitude:* 45.7732 *Latitude:* -84.1367

SQUAW ISLAND LIGHTHOUSE
Established and constructed in 1892, the Squaw Island Lighthouse is no longer operational and is now a private residence. *Address:* Squaw Island *State:* MI *Visitors welcome?* No *Operated by:* Private owner *NR?* No *NHL?* No *Year established/built:* 1892 *Latitude:* 46.0395 *Latitude:* -83.9042

ST. CLAIR FLATS OLD CHANNEL RANGE LIGHTHOUSE
Established in 1859, the two range lights were automated in 1970 and transferred to a not-for-profit, which is attempting to restore them. *City:* St. Clair Flats *State:* MI *Visitors welcome?* Yes *Hours:* By appointment

CHAPTER 5 – LIGHTHOUSES & LIGHTSHIPS

Admission: Contact attraction directly *Operated by:* Save Our South Channel Lights *NR?* Yes *NHL?* No *Year established/built:* 1859 *Latitude:* 42.5959 *Latitude:* -82.6327

ST. HELENA ISLAND LIGHTHOUSE
Established and built in 1873, the St. Helena Lighthouse was automated in 1922. It is now owned and operated by the Great Lakes Lighthouse Keepers Association as an educational facility. Visitors are welcome to visit the lighthouse at any time by boat. *Address:* St. Helena Island Light *City:* St. Ignace *State:* MI *Phone:* 231-436-5580 *Email:* info@gllka.com *Visitors welcome?* Yes *Hours:* By appointment *Admission:* Contact attraction directly *Operated by:* Great Lakes Lighthouse Keepers Association *NR?* Yes *NHL?* No *Year established/built:* 1873 *Latitude:* 45.8583 *Latitude:* -84.8708

ST. JOSEPH NORTH PIER LIGHTS
Established in 1832, the St. Joseph North Pier Lighthouses are today a pair of range rights built in 1906 and 1907. They are still active aids to navigation. *Address:* St. Joseph River *City:* St. Joseph *State:* MI *Visitors welcome?* Yes *Hours:* Grounds only *Admission:* FREE *Operated by:* U.S. Coast Guard (District 9) *NR?* No *NHL?* No *Year established/built:* 1832 *Latitude:* 42.1158 *Latitude:* -86.4936

ST. MARTIN ISLAND LIGHTHOUSE
Constructed in 1905 with a unique hexagonal shape, the St. Martin Island Lighthouse has since been deactivated and is now owned by a Native American tribe. *Address:* St. Martin Island *State:* MI *Visitors welcome?* No *Operated by:* Little Traverse Bay Band of Odawa Indians *NR?* Yes *NHL?* No *Year established/built:* 1905 *Latitude:* 45.5042 *Latitude:* -86.7590

STANNARD ROCK LIGHTHOUSE
Stannard Rock Lighthouse was constructed in 1882, 34 years after it was discovered by a ship that wrecked on it. The station was automated by the U.S. Coast Guard after a gas explosion killed one Coast Guardsman and hurt two others. The lighthouse is still an active aid to navigation. *Address:* Stannard Rock Light *State:* MI *Zip:* 49855 *Phone:* 906-226-2006 *Web:* mqtmaritimemuseum.com *Email:* mqtmaritimemuseum@yahoo.com *Visitors welcome?* No *Operated by:* Marquette Maritime Museum *NR?* Yes *NHL?* No *Year established/built:* 1882 *Latitude:* 47.1835 *Latitude:* -87.2251

STURGEON POINT LIGHTHOUSE
Established and constructed in 1869, the Sturgeon Point Lighthouse is still an active aid to navigation and is now operated by a local historical society. *Address:* Sturgeon Point Light *City:* Harrisville *State:* MI *Phone:* 989-724-6297 *Web:* theenchantedforest.com/AlconaHistoricalSociety/ *Visitors welcome?* Yes *Hours:* Memorial Day through September, Monday to Thursday, 12 p.m. to 3 p.m., Saturday and Sunday, 11 a.m. to 4 p.m.; Tower open 12 p.m to 3 p.m. Friday, Saturday and Sunday *Admission:* Contact attraction directly *Operated by:* Alcona Historical Society *NR?* Yes *NHL?* No *Year established/built:* 1869 *Latitude:* 44.7127 *Latitude:* -83.2727

TAWAS POINT LIGHTHOUSE
Established in 1853, the current Tawas Point Lighthouse was constructed in 1876. Tawas Point has been called the Cape Cod of the West, and the tower was an important part of the development of transportation on Lake Huron. *Address:* Tawas Point Light *City:* East Tawas *State:* MI *Zip:* 48730 *Phone:* 989-362-5041 *Visitors welcome?* Yes *Hours:* Grounds only, tower in season *Admission:* FREE *Operated by:* Michigan Dept. of Natural Resources *NR?* Yes *NHL?* No *Year established/built:* 1853 *Latitude:* 44.2540 *Latitude:* -83.4490

THUNDER BAY ISLAND LIGHTHOUSE
Established and built in 1832, the Thunder Bay Island Lighthouse was automated in 1980. In 1997, a local not-for-profit leased the property from the U.S. Coast Guard, and it is now in the process of restoring the

structures. *Address:* Thunder Bay Island *City:* Alpena *State:* MI *Visitors welcome?* Yes *Hours:* By appointment *Admission:* Contact attraction directly *Operated by:* Thunder Bay Island Lighthouse Preservation Society *NR?* Yes *NHL?* No *Year established/built:* 1832 *Latitude:* 45.0417 *Latitude:* -83.2000

Which Michigan lighthouse stands out for you. Wisconsin? Ohio? Log on to Fyddeye at www.fyddeye.com and tell us!

WAUGOSHANCE LIGHTHOUSE
Established in 1832, the current tower was built in 1851. The lighthouse is no longer operational, though a local historical society is working to restore it. *Address:* Waugoshance Light *City:* Mackinaw City *State:* MI *Web:* www.waugoshance.org *Email:* info@waugoshance.org *Visitors welcome?* No *Operated by:* Waugoshance Lighthouse Preservation Society *NR?* Yes *NHL?* No *Year established/built:* 1832 *Latitude:* 45.7862 *Latitude:* -85.0912

WHITE RIVER LIGHTHOUSE
Established and built in 1875, the White River Lighthouse was automated in 1945 and deactivated in 1960. It is now managed by a not-for-profit as a museum. *Address:* 6199 Murray Road *City:* Whitehall *State:* MI *Zip:* 49461 *Phone:* 231-894-8265 *Web:* www.whiteriverlightstation.org *Visitors welcome?* Yes *Hours:* Grounds only, tower in season *Admission:* Contact attraction directly *Operated by:* White River Light Station Museum *NR?* No *NHL?* No *Year established/built:* 1875 *Latitude:* 43.3728 *Latitude:* -86.4226

WHITE SHOAL LIGHTHOUSE
Established in 1891, the current White Shoal Lighthouse tower was first lit in 1910. The light is still an active aid to navigation. *Address:* White Shoal Light *State:* MI *Visitors welcome?* No *Operated by:* U.S. Coast Guard (District 9) *NR?* Yes *NHL?* No *Year established/built:* 1891 *Latitude:* 45.8417 *Latitude:* -85.1349

WHITEFISH POINT LIGHTHOUSE
Established in 1848, the current skeletal metal tower was constructed in 1861. The lighthouse was automated in 1870 and operations turned over to the Great Lakes Shipwreck Historical Society, which invites guests for overnight stays in the keepers quarter *Address:* Whitefish Point Light *City:* Paradise *State:* MI *Zip:* 49768 *Phone:* 888-492-3747 *Web:* www.shipwreckmuseum.com *Visitors welcome?* Yes *Hours:* Contact attraction directly *Admission:* Contact attraction directly *Operated by:* Great Lakes Shipwreck Historical Society *NR?* Yes *NHL?* No *Year established/built:* 1848 *Latitude:* 46.7706 *Latitude:* -84.9567

WINDMILL POINT LIGHTHOUSE
The Windmill Point Lighthouse marks the entrance to the Detroit River from Lake St. Clair. *Address:* Windmill Point *City:* Detroit *State:* MI *Visitors welcome?* Yes *Hours:* Grounds only *Admission:* FREE *Operated by:* U.S. Coast Guard (District 9) *NR?* No *NHL?* No *Latitude:* 42.3578 *Latitude:* -82.9299

MINNESOTA

DULUTH HARBOR NORTH BREAKWATER LIGHTHOUSE
Established in 1908, the cast-iron tower of the Duluth Harbor North Breakwater Lighthouse was finished in 1910. The light remains an active aid to navigation. *Address:* Duluth Harbor *City:* Duluth *State:* MN *Visitors welcome?* Yes *Hours:* Grounds only *Admission:* FREE *Operated by:* U.S. Coast Guard (District 9) *NR?* No *NHL?* No *Year established/built:* 1908 *Latitude:* 46.7219 *Latitude:* -92.0433

CHAPTER 5 – LIGHTHOUSES & LIGHTSHIPS

DULUTH HARBOR SOUTH BREAKWATER INNER LIGHTHOUSE
Established in 1889, the current skeletal tower of the Duluth Harbor South Breakwater Inner Lighthouse was completed in 1901. The light is still an active aid to navigation. *Address:* South Lake Avenue *City:* Duluth *State:* MN *Visitors welcome?* Yes *Hours:* Grounds only *Admission:* FREE *Operated by:* U.S. Coast Guard (District 9) *NR?* No *NHL?* No *Year established/built:* 1889 *Latitude:* 46.7778 *Latitude:* -92.0924

DULUTH HARBOR SOUTH BREAKWATER OUTER LIGHTHOUSE
Established in 1874 on a new breakwater for the port of Duluth, the Duluth Harbor South Breakwater Outer Lighthouse guides mariners through some of the thickest and most persistent fogs in the world. The current tower was completed in 1901. *Address:* South Lake Avenue *City:* Duluth *State:* MN *Visitors welcome?* Yes *Hours:* Grounds only *Admission:* FREE *Operated by:* U.S. Coast Guard (District 9) *NR?* No *NHL?* No *Year established/built:* 1874 *Latitude:* 46.7775 *Latitude:* -92.0917

GRAND MARAIS LIGHTHOUSE
Established in 1885, the Grand Marais Lighthouse marks the entrance to the small Grand Marais harbor on the north shore of Lake Superior. *Address:* Grand Marais Harbor *City:* Grand Marais *State:* MN *Visitors welcome?* Yes *Hours:* Grounds only *Admission:* FREE *Operated by:* U.S. Coast Guard (District 9) *NR?* No *NHL?* No *Year established/built:* 1885 *Latitude:* 47.7504 *Latitude:* -90.3343

MINNESOTA POINT LIGHTHOUSE
Established in 1858, the Minnesota Point Lighthouse was abandoned in 1885. Only a portion of the tower remains. *Address:* Minnesota Point *City:* Duluth *State:* MN *Visitors welcome?* Yes *Hours:* Grounds only *Admission:* FREE *Operated by:* U.S. Army Corps of Engineers (Duluth) *NR?* No *NHL?* No *Year established/built:* 1858 *Latitude:* 46.7307 *Latitude:* -92.0522

SPLIT ROCK LIGHTHOUSE
Completed by the U.S. Lighthouse Service in 1910, Split Rock Lighthouse was soon one of Minnesota's best known landmarks. Restored to its 1920s appearance, the lighthouse offers a glimpse of lighthouse life in this remote and spectacular setting. *Address:* 3713 Split Rock Lighthouse Rd *City:* Two Harbors *State:* MN *Zip:* 55616 *Phone:* 218-226-6372 *Web:* www.mnhs.org/places/sites/srl/ *Email:* splitrock@mnhs.org *Visitors welcome?* Yes *Hours:* Daily, May 15 to October 15, 10 a.m. to 6 p.m.; Thursdays to Mondays, 11 a.m. to 4 p.m. (Visitor Center only) *Admission:* Contact attraction directly *Operated by:* Minnesota Historical Society *NR?* Yes *NHL?* No *Year established/built:* 1910 *Latitude:* 47.0227 *Latitude:* -91.6707

TWO HARBORS BREAKWATER LIGHTHOUSE
City: Two Harbors *State:* MN *Visitors welcome?* Yes *Hours:* Grounds only *Admission:* FREE *Operated by:* U.S. Coast Guard (District 9) *NR?* No *NHL?* No *Latitude:* 47.0106 *Latitude:* -91.6696

TWO HARBORS LIGHTHOUSE
Constructed in 1892, the Two Harbors Lighthouse is now operated as a bed and breakfast by the Lake County Historical Society. The light is still an active aid to navigation. *Address:* Two Harbors Light *City:* Two Harbors *State:* MN *Zip:* 55616 *Phone:* 218-834-4814 *Web:* www.lighthousebb.org *Email:* lakehist@lakenet.com *Visitors welcome?* Yes *Hours:* Contact attraction directly *Admission:* Contact attraction directly *Operated by:* Lighthouse Bed & Breakfast *NR?* Yes *NHL?* No *Year established/built:* 1892 *Latitude:* 47.0140 *Latitude:* -91.6636

NEW YORK

BARCELONA LIGHTHOUSE
Also called the Portland Harbor Lighthouse, the Barcelona Lighthouse was built in 1829 to serve cargo and passenger vessels traveling between Erie, Penn. and Buffalo. The tower was constructed of fieldstone around a wooden framework. *Address:* State Highway 5 *City:* Barcelona *State:* NY *Visitors welcome?* No *Operated by:* Private owner *NR?* Yes *NHL?* No *Year established/built:* 1829 *Latitude:* 42.3408 *Latitude:* -79.5950

BRADDOCK POINT LIGHTHOUSE
Established and built in 1896, the Braddock Point Lighthouse was deactivated in 1954 and is now a private residence. *Address:* Braddock Point Light *City:* Davison Beach *State:* NY *Visitors welcome?* No *Operated by:* Private owner *NR?* No *NHL?* No *Year established/built:* 1896 *Latitude:* 43.3411 *Latitude:* -77.7625

BUFFALO INTAKE CRIB LIGHTHOUSE
Mariners in Lake Erie needed better markers of the treacherous shoals and reefs near Buffalo. Engineers determined that the area around Horseshoe Reef was a good location, but it was on the Canadian side of the international border. After years of diplomacy, the lighthouse was located at its current location. *Address:* Buffalo Harbor *City:* Buffalo *State:* NY *Visitors welcome?* No *Operated by:* City of Buffalo *NR?* No *NHL?* No *Year established/built:* 1856 *Latitude:* 42.8967 *Latitude:* -78.8937

BUFFALO MAIN LIGHTHOUSE
Established in 1818, the current Buffalo Lighthouse was constructed in 1833 and deactivated in 1914. It is now managed by a local not-for-profit organization. *Address:* Buffalo Harbor *City:* Buffalo *State:* NY *Visitors welcome?* No *Operated by:* U.S. Coast Guard (District 9) *NR?* Yes *NHL?* No *Year established/built:* 1818 *Latitude:* 42.8967 *Latitude:* -78.8937

BUFFALO SOUTH ENTRANCE NORTH SIDE LIGHTHOUSE
The Buffalo South Entrance North Side lighthouse and its companion South Side lighthouse were constructed in 1903, and they guided grain and lumber ships into the bustling Buffalo harbor. The North Side Lighthouse was decommissioned in 1988. *Address:* Point Gratiot *City:* Dunkirk *State:* NY *Zip:* 14048 *Phone:* 716-366-5050 *Email:* LST551@juno.com *Visitors welcome?* Yes *Hours:* Contact attraction directly *Admission:* Contact attraction directly *Operated by:* Dunkirk Lighthouse & Veterans Park Museum *NR?* No *NHL?* No *Year established/built:* 1903 *Latitude:* 42.4937 *Latitude:* -79.3542

BUFFALO SOUTH ENTRANCE SOUTH SIDE LIGHTHOUSE
Completed in 1903, the Buffalo South Entrance South Side Lighthouse guards the shoreline near the Lackawanna Steel Plant, one of the largest and most historic steel facilities in the country. The U.S. Coast Guard deactivated the lighthouse in 1935. *City:* Buffalo *State:* NY *Visitors welcome?* Yes *Hours:* By appointment *Admission:* Grounds open, tower closed *Operated by:* U.S. Coast Guard (District 9) *NR?* No *NHL?* No *Year established/built:* 1903 *Latitude:* 42.8864 *Latitude:* -78.8784

CAPE VINCENT BREAKWATER LIGHTHOUSE
Built in 1907 to replace a pair of post lights, the Cape Vincent Breakwater Lighthouse was constructed on the end of a breakwater that the keeper could reach by holding on to a lifeline during stormy periods. *Address:* Market Street *City:* Cape Vincent *State:* NY *Visitors welcome?* Yes *Hours:* Daily *Admission:* FREE *Operated by:* Village of Cape Vincent *NR?* No *NHL?* No *Year established/built:* 1907 *Latitude:* 44.1244 *Latitude:* -76.3355

CHAPTER 5 – LIGHTHOUSES & LIGHTSHIPS

CROSSOVER ISLAND LIGHTHOUSE
Established in 1842, the current Crossover Island Lighthouse was built in 1882 and deactivated in 1941. *Address:* Crossover Island *City:* Oak Point *State:* NY *Visitors welcome?* No *Operated by:* Private owner *NR?* No *NHL?* No *Year established/built:* 1848 *Latitude:* 44.4961 *Latitude:* -75.7781

EAST CHARITY SHOAL LIGHTHOUSE
Established in 1929, the East Charity Shoal Lighthouse structure was built in 1877, and originally served as the Vermillion Lighthouse. The East Charity station is still an active aid to navigation. *Address:* East Charity Shoal Light *City:* Cape Vincent *State:* NY *Visitors welcome?* No *Operated by:* U.S. Coast Guard (District 9) *NR?* No *NHL?* No *Year established/built:* 1929 *Latitude:* 44.0481 *Latitude:* -76.4758

FORT NIAGARA LIGHTHOUSE
Established in 1782, the current Fort Niagara Lighthouse was built in 1872 and deactivated in 1993. It is now part of Fort Niagara National Historic Landmark. *Address:* Fort Niagara Light *City:* Youngstown *State:* NY *Phone:* 716-745-7611 *Visitors welcome?* Yes *Hours:* Daily, 9 a.m. to 5 p.m. *Admission:* $10 adults; $6 children 6 to 12; Under six, FREE *Operated by:* Old Fort Niagara Association *NR?* Yes *NHL?* No *Year established/built:* 1782 *Latitude:* 43.2617 *Latitude:* -79.0633

GALLOO ISLAND LIGHTHOUSE
Established in 1820, the current Galloo Island Lighthouse was constructed in 1867 and automated in 1963. It is no longer an active aid to navigation. *Address:* Galloo Island Light *City:* Galloo Island *State:* NY *Visitors welcome?* No *Operated by:* Private owner *NR?* Yes *NHL?* No *Year established/built:* 1820 *Latitude:* 43.8883 *Latitude:* -76.4450

GRAND ISLAND FRONT RANGE LIGHTHOUSE
First used by the Seneca tribe for hunting and fishing, Grand Island became a getaway for the wealthy in the late 19th century. *Address:* 503 East River Road *City:* Grand Island *State:* NY *Zip:* 14072 *Phone:* 716-773-7629 *Email:* jim@buffalolaunchclub.com *Visitors welcome?* Yes *Hours:* By appointment *Admission:* FREE with permission *Operated by:* Buffalo Launch Club *NR?* No *NHL?* No *Year established/built:* 1917 *Latitude:* 42.9756 *Latitude:* -78.9466

HORSE ISLAND LIGHTHOUSE
Established in 1831, the current Horse Island Lighthouse, also called the Sacketts Harbor Lighthouse, was constructed in 1870 and deactivated in 1957. It is now privately owned. *Address:* Horse Island Light *City:* Sackets Harbor *State:* NY *Visitors welcome?* No *Operated by:* Private owner *NR?* No *NHL?* No *Year established/built:* 1831 *Latitude:* 43.9431 *Latitude:* -76.1444

HORSESHOE REEF LIGHTHOUSE
Growing commerce in the eastern end of Lake Erie led to needs for a more extensive set of navigation aids, including a lighthouse on Horseshoe Reef, built in 1856. Horseshoe Reef was abandoned in 1930 and is now in ruins. *Address:* Lake Erie *City:* Buffalo *State:* NY *Visitors welcome?* No *Operated by:* U.S. Coast Guard (District 9) *NR?* No *NHL?* No *Year established/built:* 1856 *Latitude:* 42.0669 *Latitude:* -81.3399

OAK ORCHARD HARBOR LIGHTHOUSE
The Oak Orchard Harbor Lighthouse, sometimes called the Point Breeze Lighthouse, is a replica of an 1871 lighthouse that stood on a pier in the Oak Orchard River. The replica is next to the river in Point Breeze. *City:* Point Breeze *State:* NY *Visitors welcome?* Yes *Operated by:* Oak Orchard Lighthouse Museum *NR?* No *NHL?* No *Year established/built:* 2010 *Latitude:* 43.377105 *Latitude:* -78.190298

CHAPTER 5 – LIGHTHOUSES & LIGHTSHIPS

OGDENSBURG HARBOR LIGHTHOUSE
Established and built in 1834, the Ogdensburg Harbor Lighthouse is no longer an active aid to navigation and privately owned. *Address:* Ogdensburg Harbor Light *City:* Ogdensburg *State:* NY *Visitors welcome?* No *Operated by:* Private owner *NR?* No *NHL?* No *Year established/built:* 1834 *Latitude:* 44.6978 *Latitude:* -75.5033

OLCOTT LIGHTHOUSE
The Olcott Lighthouse is a 2003 replica of an historic lighthouse that guided ships into Olcott Harbor starting in 1873. *Address:* Lockport-Olcott Road *City:* Newfane *State:* NY *Phone:* 716-778-8531 *Visitors welcome?* Yes *Hours:* Daily *Admission:* FREE *Operated by:* Town of Newfane *NR?* No *NHL?* No *Year established/built:* 1873 *Latitude:* 43.2802 *Latitude:* -78.7069

OSWEGO HARBOR WEST PIERHEAD LIGHTHOUSE
Established in 1822, the current Oswego Harbor West Pierhead Lighthouse was built in 1924. Automated in 1968, it is still an active aid to navigation. *Address:* Oswego Harbor West Pierhead Light *City:* Oswego *State:* NY *Visitors welcome?* No *Operated by:* U.S. Coast Guard (District 9) *NR?* Yes *NHL?* No *Year established/built:* 1934 *Latitude:* 43.4733 *Latitude:* -76.5168

PORT OF GENESSEE LIGHTHOUSE
Established and built in 1822, the Port of Genessee Lighthouse, also called the Charlotte-Genessee Lighthouse, was deactivated in 1881 and relighted in 1992. *Address:* 70 Lighthouse St. *City:* Rochester *State:* NY *Zip:* 14612 *Phone:* 585-621-6179 *Visitors welcome?* Yes *Hours:* May to October, Saturday and Sunday, 1 p.m. to 5 p.m. *Admission:* Donation requested *Operated by:* Charlotte-Genesee Lighthouse Historical Society *NR?* Yes *NHL?* No *Year established/built:* 1822 *Latitude:* 43.2529 *Latitude:* -77.6109

ROCHESTER HARBOR LIGHTHOUSE
First constructed in 1822 on a bluff overlooking Rochester Harbor on Lake Ontario, the lighthouse was moved to a pier extending into the lake in 1838, although the lighthouse on the bluff operated until 1881. The modern tower was on the pier in 1995. *Address:* Charlotte Genesee Lighthouse *City:* Rochester *State:* NY *Web:* www.geneseelighthouse.org *Visitors welcome?* Yes *Hours:* Daily *Admission:* FREE *Operated by:* U.S. Coast Guard (District 9) *NR?* No *NHL?* No *Year established/built:* 1822 *Latitude:* 43.2529 *Latitude:* -77.6109

ROCK ISLAND LIGHTHOUSE
Established in 1848, the current Rock Island Lighthouse was built in 1882 and deactivated in the 1930s and is now within a state park. *City:* Fishers Landing *State:* NY *Visitors welcome?* Yes *Hours:* Tower closed *Admission:* Tower closed *Operated by:* New York State Office of Parks, Recreation and Historic Preservation *NR?* Yes *NHL?* No *Year established/built:* 1848 *Latitude:* 44.2764 *Latitude:* -76.0080

SELKIRK LIGHTHOUSE
Established and built in 1838, the Selkirk Lighthouse, also called the Salmon River Lighthouse, was automated in 1989 and is a private aid to navigation. *Address:* 6 Lake Road Ext *City:* Richland *State:* NY *Zip:* 13114 *Phone:* 315-298-6688 *Web:* www.salmonriverlighthousemarina.com *Visitors welcome?* Yes *Hours:* Contact attraction directly *Admission:* Contact attraction directly *Operated by:* Salmon River Lighthouse Marina *NR?* Yes *NHL?* No *Year established/built:* 1838 *Latitude:* 43.5763 *Latitude:* -76.2024

SODUS OUTER LIGHTHOUSE
First settled by Europeans in 1792, Sodus Bay is a the largest natural harbor on Lake Ontario. By 1824, a lighthouse was established on the bay to guide growing maritime traffic. A new structure was built in 1871. *Address:* Sodus Outer Light *City:* Sodus Point *State:* NY *Visitors welcome?* Yes *Hours:* No public access to struc-

CHAPTER 5 – LIGHTHOUSES & LIGHTSHIPS

ture, pier open *Admission:* No public access to structure, pier open *Operated by:* Sodus Bay Historical Society *NR?* No *NHL?* No *Year established/built:* 1901 *Latitude:* 43.2767 *Latitude:* -76.9750

SODUS POINT LIGHTHOUSE
First settled by Europeans in 1792, Sodus Bay is a the largest natural harbor on Lake Ontario. By 1824, a lighthouse was established on the bay to guide growing maritime traffic. *Address:* 7606 N. Ontario St. *City:* Sodus Point *State:* NY *Zip:* 14555 *Phone:* 315-483-4936 *Web:* www.soduspointlighthouse.org *Email:* bmccreary@soduspointlighthouse.org *Visitors welcome?* Yes *Hours:* May through October, Tuesday to Sunday, 10 a.m. to 5 p.m. *Admission:* $3 adults; $1 children 11 to 17 *Operated by:* Sodus Bay Historical Society *NR?* Yes *NHL?* No *Year established/built:* 1824 *Latitude:* 43.2738 *Latitude:* -76.9865

STONY POINT LIGHTHOUSE
Established and built in 1826, the Stony Point Lighthouse on the Hudson River is now a private aid to navigation. *Address:* Stony Point Light *City:* Stony Point *State:* NY *Visitors welcome?* Yes *Hours:* Daily *Admission:* FREE *Operated by:* Palisades Interstate Parks Commission *NR?* Yes *NHL?* No *Year established/built:* 1826 *Latitude:* 41.2414 *Latitude:* -73.9722

SUNKEN ROCK LIGHTHOUSE
Established in 1847, the current Sunken Rock Lighthouse was constructed in 1884 and continues as a private aid to navigation. *Address:* Sunken Rock Light *City:* Alexandria Bay *State:* NY *Visitors welcome?* No *Operated by:* St. Lawrence Seaway Development Corp. *NR?* No *NHL?* No *Year established/built:* 1847 *Latitude:* 44.3456 *Latitude:* -75.9153

THIRTY MILE POINT LIGHTHOUSE
Established and built in 1876, the Thirty Mile Point Lighthouse was automated in 1959 and is now a private aid to navigation within a state park. *Address:* Thirty Mile Point Light *City:* Lyndonville *State:* NY *Visitors welcome?* Yes *Hours:* Daily *Admission:* FREE *Operated by:* New York State Office of Parks, Recreation and Historic Preservation *NR?* Yes *NHL?* No *Year established/built:* 1876 *Latitude:* 43.3750 *Latitude:* -78.4864

THREE SISTERS ISLAND LIGHTHOUSE
Established and built in 1870, the Three Sisters Island Lighthouse was deactivated in the 1950s and is now privately owned. *Address:* Three Sisters Island *City:* Alexandria *State:* NY *Visitors welcome?* No *Operated by:* Private owner *NR?* No *NHL?* No *Year established/built:* 1870 *Latitude:* 44.3676 *Latitude:* -75.8594

TIBBETTS POINT LIGHTHOUSE
Established in 1827, the current Tibbetts Point Lighthouse was constructed in 1854. Automated in 1981, it is still an active aid to navigation. The keepers house is used as a youth hostel. *Address:* Tibbetts Point Light *City:* Cape Vincent *State:* NY *Phone:* 315-654-2700 *Web:* www.capevincent.org/lighthouse/lighthouse_001.htm *Visitors welcome?* Yes *Hours:* Late May to early June: Friday to Monday, 10 a.m. to 7 p.m.; Late June through early September: Daily, 10 a.m. to 7 p.m. ; Early September to early October: Friday to Monday, 10 a.m. to 7 p.m. *Admission:* Contact attraction directly *Operated by:* Tibbetts Point Lighthouse Society *NR?* Yes *NHL?* No *Year established/built:* 1827 *Latitude:* 44.1000 *Latitude:* -76.3700

OHIO

ASHTABULA LIGHTHOUSE
Established in 1836, the current Ashtabula Lighthouse was constructed in 1905 and automated in 1973. The lighthouse is still an active aid to navigation. The keepers quarters are now a maritime museum.

CHAPTER 5 – LIGHTHOUSES & LIGHTSHIPS

Address: Ashtabula Light *City:* Ashtabula *State:* OH *Visitors welcome?* Yes *Hours:* Grounds only *Admission:* FREE *Operated by:* Ashtabula Lighthouse Restoration and Preservation Society *NR?* Yes *NHL?* No *Year established/built:* 1836 *Latitude:* 41.9186 *Latitude:* -80.7959

CEDAR POINT LIGHTHOUSE
Established in 1839, the current Cedar Point Lighthouse was constructed in 1862. The lighthouse is now within a resort that's part of an amusement park. *Address:* Cedar Point Amusement Park *City:* Sandusky *State:* OH *Zip:* 44870 *Phone:* 419-627-2350 *Visitors welcome?* Yes *Hours:* Contact attraction directly *Admission:* Contact attraction directly *Operated by:* Private owner *NR?* No *NHL?* No *Year established/built:* 1839 *Latitude:* 41.4861 *Latitude:* -82.6888

CELINA LIGHTHOUSE
The Celina Lighthouse is a private aid to navigation on Grand Lake St. Marys. *Address:* South Main Street and Lakeshore Drive *City:* Celina *State:* OH *Zip:* 45822 *Visitors welcome?* Yes *Hours:* Grounds only *Admission:* FREE *Operated by:* City of Celina *NR?* No *NHL?* No *Year established/built:* 1986 *Latitude:* 40.5489 *Latitude:* -84.5702

CLEVELAND EAST ENTRANCE LIGHTHOUSE
Established in 1915, the current Cleveland East Entrance light is a steel tower that guides vessels into Cleveland Harbor. *Address:* Cleveland Harbor *City:* Cleveland *State:* OH *Visitors welcome?* No *Operated by:* U.S. Coast Guard (District 9) *NR?* No *NHL?* No *Year established/built:* 1915 *Latitude:* 41.5195 *Latitude:* -81.6887

CLEVELAND HARBOR EAST PIERHEAD LIGHTHOUSE
Established in 1831, the current east and west pierhead lights that make up the Cleveland Harbor lighthouses were first lit in 1911. These lights are still active aids to navigation. *Address:* Cuyahoga River *City:* Cleveland *State:* OH *Visitors welcome?* No *Operated by:* U.S. Coast Guard (District 9) *NR?* No *NHL?* No *Year established/built:* 1831 *Latitude:* 41.5037 *Latitude:* -81.7124

CLEVELAND HARBOR WEST PIERHEAD LIGHTHOUSE
Established in 1831, the current east and west pierhead lights that make up the Cleveland Harbor lighthouses were first lit in 1911. These lights are still active aids to navigation. *Address:* Cuyahoga River *City:* Cleveland *State:* OH *Visitors welcome?* No *Operated by:* U.S. Coast Guard (District 9) *NR?* Yes *NHL?* No *Year established/built:* 1831 *Latitude:* 41.5037 *Latitude:* -81.7124

CONNEAUT HARBOR WEST BREAKWATER LIGHTHOUSE
Established in 1835, the current Art-Deco style Conneaut Lighthouse was constructed in 1936. Previous lighthouses were constructed of brick and steel in the coffee pot style. *Address:* Conneaut Harbor *City:* Conneaut *State:* OH *Visitors welcome?* Yes *Hours:* Grounds only *Admission:* FREE *Operated by:* U.S. Coast Guard (District 9) *NR?* Yes *NHL?* No *Year established/built:* 1835 *Latitude:* 41.9739 *Latitude:* -80.5536

FAIRPORT HARBOR WEST BREAKWATER LIGHTHOUSE
Established and built in 1925, the Fairport Harbor West Breakwater guards the entrance to the Grand River on Lake Erie. The lighthouse is still an active aid to navigation. *Address:* Fairport Harbor West Breakwater Light *City:* Fairport Harbor *State:* OH *Zip:* 44077 *Visitors welcome?* Yes *Hours:* Grounds only *Admission:* FREE *Operated by:* U.S. Coast Guard (District 9) *NR?* Yes *NHL?* No *Year established/built:* 1925 *Latitude:* 41.7679 *Latitude:* -81.2812

CHAPTER 5 – LIGHTHOUSES & LIGHTSHIPS

GRAND RIVER LIGHTHOUSE
Established in 1825, the current Grand River Lighthouse, also called the Fairport Harbor Lighthouse, was constructed in 1871 and deactivated in 1925. It is now a maritime museum. *Address:* 129 Second Street *City:* Painsville *State:* OH *Zip:* 44077 *Phone:* 440-354-4825 *Web:* www.ncweb.com/org/fhlh/ *Email:* fhhs@ncweb.com *Visitors welcome?* Yes *Hours:* Memorial Day through September: Wednesdays, Saturdays, Sundays: 1 p.m. to 6 p.m. *Admission:* $3 adults, $2 seniors, $1 ages 6-12, under six FREE *Operated by:* Fairport Harbor Marine Museum *NR?* No *NHL?* No *Year established/built:* 1825 *Latitude:* 41.7571 *Latitude:* -81.2777

GREEN ISLAND LIGHTHOUSE
Established in 1851, the current light on Green Island is a skeletal tower. But the stone lighthouse built in 1864 is still on the island, though it's in ruinous condition. The island is now a wildlife refuge. *Address:* Green Island *City:* Put-in-Bay *State:* OH *Visitors welcome?* No *Operated by:* Ohio Dept. of Natural Resources *NR?* No *NHL?* No *Year established/built:* 1851 *Latitude:* 41.6459 *Latitude:* -82.8666

HURON HARBOR LIGHTHOUSE
Established in 1835, the current Art Moderne Huron Harbor Lighthouse was constructed in 1936. It is still an active aid to navigation. *Address:* Huron Harbor *City:* Huron *State:* OH *Visitors welcome?* Yes *Hours:* Grounds only *Admission:* FREE *Operated by:* U.S. Coast Guard (District 9) *NR?* Yes *NHL?* No *Year established/built:* 1835 *Latitude:* 41.4045 *Latitude:* -82.5442

LORAIN LIGHTHOUSE
Established in 1837, the current Lorain Lighthouse was constructed in 1917. The lighthouse was deactivated in 1966, but its exterior was restored in the 1990s. *Address:* Black River *City:* Lorain *State:* OH *Visitors welcome?* No *Operated by:* U.S. Coast Guard (District 9) *NR?* Yes *NHL?* No *Year established/built:* 1837 *Latitude:* 41.4728 *Latitude:* -82.1840

MANHATTAN FRONT AND REAR RANGE LIGHTHOUSES
The Manhattan Rear and Front Range Lighthouses guide ships up the Maumee River into the Port of Toledo. *Address:* North Summit Street and Troy Street *City:* Toledo *State:* OH *Visitors welcome?* No *Operated by:* Private owner *NR?* No *NHL?* No *Year established/built:* 1895 *Latitude:* 41.6772 *Latitude:* -83.4984

✣ MARBLEHEAD LIGHTHOUSE
Established in 1821, making it the oldest lighthouse in Ohio, the Marblehead Lighthouse, formerly the Sandusky Bay Lighthouse, is now within Marblehead Lighthouse State Park in Sandusky. The current structure was constructed in 1821 and is open for tours. *Address:* 110 Lighthouse Drive *City:* Marblehead *State:* OH *Zip:* 43440 *Phone:* 419-734-4424 *Web:* ohiodnr.com/?TabId=763 *Visitors welcome?* Yes *Hours:* Daily *Admission:* FREE *Operated by:* Ohio Dept. of Natural Resources *NR?* Yes *NHL?* No *Year established/built:* 1821 *Latitude:* 41.5367 *Latitude:* -82.7133

NORTHWOOD LIGHTHOUSE
Built in 1923, the Northwood Lighthouse is an inactive private aid to navigation. It was built to resemble the Eddystone Lighthouse in Cornwall, England. *Address:* State Highway 703 *City:* Northwood *State:* OH *Visitors welcome?* No *Operated by:* Private owner *NR?* No *NHL?* No *Year established/built:* 1923 *Latitude:* 40.4932 *Latitude:* -83.7108

PORT CLINTON LIGHTHOUSE
Established in 1832, the Port Clinton Lighthouse originally stood on a pier in the Port Clinton harbor. The 1896 structure was later moved to the entrance to Brands' Marina, where it sits today, still an active aid to navigation. *Address:* 451 W. Lakeshore Dr. *City:* Port Clinton *State:* OH *Zip:* 43452 *Phone:* 419-734-4212

Visitors welcome? Yes *Hours:* Grounds only *Admission:* FREE *Operated by:* Brands' Marina *NR?* No *NHL?* No *Year established/built:* 1832 *Latitude:* 41.5170 *Latitude:* -82.9485

SANDUSKY HARBOR BREAKWATER LIGHTHOUSE
The Sandusky Harbor Breakwater Lighthouse marks the entrance to Sandusky Bay. It was originally a range light. It's companion was discontinued in 1904. *Address:* Cedar Point *City:* Sandusky *State:* OH *Visitors welcome?* No *Operated by:* U.S. Coast Guard (District 9) *NR?* No *NHL?* No *Latitude:* 41.4942 *Latitude:* -82.6817

SOUTH BASS ISLAND LIGHTHOUSE
Established and built in 1897, the South Bass Island Lighthouse operated as an aid to navigation until it was deactivated in 1962. It is now a field research station operated by Ohio State University. *Address:* South Bass Island Light *City:* Put-in-Bay *State:* OH *Zip:* 43456 *Phone:* 419-285-2341 *Email:* southbasslighthouse@osu.edu *Visitors welcome?* Yes *Hours:* By appointment *Admission:* Contact attraction directly *Operated by:* Stone Laboratory, Ohio State University *NR?* Yes *NHL?* No *Year established/built:* 1897 *Latitude:* 41.6290 *Latitude:* -82.8415

TOLEDO HARBOR LIGHTHOUSE
Established and constructed in 1904 to guide ships into Toledo from Lake Erie, the Toledo Harbor Lighthouse was automated in 1966. Still an active aid to navigation, the lighthouse is now owned by a Toledo not-for-profit. *Address:* Toledo Harbor *City:* Toledo *State:* OH *Visitors welcome?* No *Operated by:* Toledo Harbor Lighthouse Preservation Society *NR?* Yes *NHL?* No *Year established/built:* 1904 *Latitude:* 41.7175 *Latitude:* -83.4315

TURTLE ISLAND LIGHTHOUSE
Established in 1831, the current Turtle Island Lighthouse structure, a remnant of the operating facility, was constructed in 1866. The light was decommissioned in 1904 and is no longer active. *Address:* Turtle Island *State:* OH *Visitors welcome?* No *Operated by:* Private owner *NR?* No *NHL?* No *Year established/built:* 1831 *Latitude:* 41.7525 *Latitude:* -83.3908

VERMILLION LIGHTHOUSE
Established in 1847, the Vermillion Lighthouse on the grounds of the Inland Seas Museum is a replica of the 1877 lighthouse that stood on a pier in Vermillion Harbor. *Address:* 480 Main Street *City:* Vermilion *State:* OH *Zip:* 44089 *Phone:* 440-967-3467 *Email:* glhs1@inlandseas.org *Visitors welcome?* Yes *Hours:* Grounds only *Admission:* FREE *Operated by:* Great Lakes Historical Society *NR?* No *NHL?* No *Year established/built:* 1847 *Latitude:* 41.4249 *Latitude:* -82.3668

WEST SISTER ISLAND LIGHTHOUSE
Established in 1821, the current West Sister Lighthouse was constructed in 1848, though the lantern is now missing. Still an active aid to navigation, the light is now in a wildlife refuge. *Address:* West Sister Island *City:* Jerusalem *State:* OH *Visitors welcome?* No *Operated by:* U.S. Coast Guard (District 9) *NR?* Yes *NHL?* No *Year established/built:* 1821 *Latitude:* 41.7392 *Latitude:* -83.1049

PENNSYLVANIA

ERIE LAND LIGHTHOUSE
Established in 1818, the current Erie Land Lighthouse, also called the Old Presque Isle Lighthouse, was constructed in 1867. The light was deactivated when the Presque Island Lighthouse went into service. *Address:* 2

CHAPTER 5 – LIGHTHOUSES & LIGHTSHIPS

Lighthouse Street *City:* Erie *State:* PA *Visitors welcome?* Yes *Hours:* Grounds only *Admission:* FREE *Operated by:* City of Erie *NR?* Yes *NHL?* No *Year established/built:* 1818 *Latitude:* 42.1443 *Latitude:* -80.0617

PRESQUE ISLE LIGHTHOUSE
Established in 1872 and lit a year later, the Presque Isle Lighthouse replaced the Erie Land Lighthouse on the mainland. Still an active aid to navigation, the lighthouse is now quarters for Presque Island State Park personnel. *Address:* Presque Isle Light *City:* Erie *State:* PA *Phone:* 814-833-0176 *Visitors welcome?* Yes *Hours:* Grounds only *Admission:* FREE *Operated by:* Pennsylvania Dept. of Conservation and Natural Resources *NR?* Yes *NHL?* No *Year established/built:* 1872 *Latitude:* 42.1634 *Latitude:* -80.1155

PRESQUE ISLE NORTH PIERHEAD LIGHTHOUSE
Established in 1857, the Presque Island North Pierhead Lighthouse, also known as the Erie Harbor Pierhead Lighthouse, is still an active aid to navigation. *Address:* Presque Isle Peninsula *City:* Erie *State:* PA *Visitors welcome?* Yes *Hours:* Grounds only *Admission:* FREE *Operated by:* U.S. Coast Guard (District 9) *NR?* No *NHL?* No *Year established/built:* 1857 *Latitude:* 42.1481 *Latitude:* -80.0807

WISCONSIN

ALGOMA PIERHEAD LIGHTHOUSE
Established in 1893, the current Algoma Pierhead Lighthouse was constructed in 1932 and automated in 1973. *Address:* Algoma Pierhead Light *City:* Algoma *State:* WI *Visitors welcome?* Yes *Hours:* Grounds only *Admission:* FREE *Operated by:* U.S. Coast Guard (District 9) *NR?* No *NHL?* No *Year established/built:* 1893 *Latitude:* 44.6069 *Latitude:* -87.4294

ASHLAND BREAKWATER LIGHTHOUSE
Established in 1911 and first lit in 1915, the Ashland Breakwater Lighthouse is still an active aid to navigation. *Address:* Ashland Harbor Breakwater Light *City:* Ashland *State:* WI *Visitors welcome?* No *Operated by:* U.S. Coast Guard (District 9) *NR?* No *NHL?* No *Year established/built:* 1911 *Latitude:* 46.6283 *Latitude:* -90.8700

ASYLUM LIGHTHOUSE
Though never lit, the Asylum Point Lighthouse is a prominent landmark in the Oshkosh area. Located on the grounds of the Winnebago Mental Health Institute, the project was built by the Works Progress Administration in 1937. *Address:* Asylum Light *City:* Oshkosh *State:* WI *Visitors welcome?* Yes *Hours:* Grounds only *Admission:* FREE *Operated by:* Winnebago County *NR?* No *NHL?* No *Year established/built:* 1937 *Latitude:* 44.0624 *Latitude:* -88.5146

BAILEYS HARBOR LIGHTHOUSE
Established in 1853, the current skeletal tower Baileys Harbor Lighthouse was built in 1869 and deactivated in the 1960s. It is now privately owned. *Address:* Baileys Harbor Light *City:* Baileys Harbor *State:* WI *Visitors welcome?* No *Operated by:* Private owner *NR?* No *NHL?* No *Year established/built:* 1853 *Latitude:* 45.0558 *Latitude:* -87.0969

BAILEY'S HARBOR RANGE LIGHTHOUSE
Established in 1853, the historic Baileys Harbor Range Lighthouses are now within a state park. The range lights themselves were moved to a different location in 1969. *Address:* Baileys Harbor Range Lights *City:*

Baileys Harbor *State:* WI *Visitors welcome?* Yes *Hours:* Grounds only *Admission:* FREE *Operated by:* Door County Maritime Museum & Lighthouse Preservation Society *NR?* Yes *NHL?* No *Year established/built:* 1853 *Latitude:* 45.0700 *Latitude:* -87.1200

BOYER BLUFF LIGHTHOUSE
The Boyer Bluff Lighthouse is a steel skeletal tower on Washington Island. *Address:* Washington Island *City:* Detroit Harbor *State:* WI *Visitors welcome?* No *Operated by:* U.S. Coast Guard (District 9) *NR?* No *NHL?* No *Latitude:* 45.3567 *Latitude:* -86.9307

BRAY'S POINT LIGHTHOUSE
The Bray's Point Lighthouse is a private aid to navigation built in 1909. The grounds and tower are closed to visitors, but the site can be see clearly from a street. *Address:* Bay Shore Drive and Lake Street *City:* Oshkosh *State:* WI *Visitors welcome?* Yes *Operated by:* Private owner *NR?* No *NHL?* No *Year established/built:* 1909 *Latitude:* 44.0076 *Latitude:* -88.5199

CALUMET HARBOR LIGHTHOUSE
Originally built as a water tower, the Calumet Lighthouse was first lit in 1936 and deactivated in the 1980s. It is now used as a public observation tower. *Address:* Calumet Light *City:* Pipe *State:* WI *Visitors welcome?* Yes *Hours:* Daily *Admission:* FREE *Operated by:* Fond du Lac County *NR?* No *NHL?* No *Year established/built:* 1936 *Latitude:* 43.9150 *Latitude:* -88.3324

CANA ISLAND LIGHTHOUSE
Established and built in 1870, the Cana Island Lighthouse was automated in 1945, and it is still an active aid to navigation. Now managed by the Door County Museum, visitors are allowed to climb the historic tower. *Address:* Cana Island Light *City:* Baileys Harbor *State:* WI *Phone:* 920-743-5958 *Web:* www.dcmm.org *Email:* info@dcmm.org *Visitors welcome?* Yes *Hours:* May to October, daily, 10 a.m. to 5 p.m. *Admission:* $4 adults, $2 children, additional $2 to climb the tower *Operated by:* Door County Maritime Museum & Lighthouse Preservation Society *NR?* Yes *NHL?* No *Year established/built:* 1870 *Latitude:* 45.0883 *Latitude:* -87.0467

CHAMBERS ISLAND LIGHTHOUSE
Established and built in 1868, the Chambers Island Lighthouse was deactivated in 1961. *Address:* Chambers Island Light *State:* WI *Visitors welcome?* Yes *Hours:* Grounds only *Admission:* FREE *Operated by:* Town of Gibralter *NR?* Yes *NHL?* No *Year established/built:* 1868 *Latitude:* 45.2025 *Latitude:* -87.3647

CHEQUAMEGON POINT LIGHTHOUSE
Established in 1858, the Chequamegon Lighthouse skeletal tower was constructed in 1896 and supplemeted by a nearby modern tower in 1987. *Address:* Chequamegon Point Light *City:* Ashland *State:* WI *Phone:* 715-779-3397 *Web:* www.nps.gov/apis/historyculture/lighthouses.htm *Visitors welcome?* Yes *Hours:* Grounds only *Admission:* FREE *Operated by:* Apostle Islands National Lakeshore *NR?* Yes *NHL?* No *Year established/built:* 1858 *Latitude:* 46.7283 *Latitude:* -90.8094

DEVILS ISLAND LIGHTHOUSE
Established in 1891, the current Devils Island Lighthouse was constructed in 1898 with extra reinforcing added in 1914. The lighthouse is now part of the Apostle Islands National Lakeshore. *Address:* Devils Island Light *City:* Ashland *State:* WI *Phone:* 715-779-3397 *Web:* www.nps.gov/apis/historyculture/lighthouses.htm *Visitors welcome?* Yes *Hours:* Grounds only *Admission:* FREE *Operated by:* Apostle Islands National Lakeshore *NR?* Yes *NHL?* No *Year established/built:* 1891 *Latitude:* 47.0800 *Latitude:* -90.7283

CHAPTER 5 – LIGHTHOUSES & LIGHTSHIPS

EAGLE BLUFF LIGHTHOUSE
Established and built in 1868, the Eagle Bluff Lighthouse was automated in 1926. Still an active aid to navigation, the lighthouse is now within a state park. *Address:* Eagle Bluff Light *State:* WI *Phone:* 920-868-3258 *Visitors welcome?* Yes *Hours:* Contact attraction directly *Admission:* Contact attraction directly *Operated by:* Wisconsin Dept. of Natural Resources *NR?* Yes *NHL?* No *Year established/built:* 1868 *Latitude:* 45.1683 *Latitude:* -87.2367

GRASSY ISLAND RANGE LIGHTHOUSES
The Grassy Island Range Lighthouses once stood on an island in Green Bay, Lake Michigan. *Address:* Grassy Island Range Lights *City:* Green Bay *State:* WI *Phone:* 920-432-0168 *Visitors welcome?* No *Operated by:* Green Bay Yacht Club *NR?* No *NHL?* No *Year established/built:* 1872 *Latitude:* 44.5361 *Latitude:* -88.0051

GREEN BAY HARBOR ENTRANCE LIGHTHOUSE
Built in 1935, the Green Bay Harbor Lighthouse is nine miles north of Green Bay in the middle of Green Bay itself. *Address:* Green Bay Harbor *City:* Green Bay *State:* WI *Visitors welcome?* No *Operated by:* U.S. Coast Guard (District 9) *NR?* No *NHL?* No *Year established/built:* 1935 *Latitude:* 44.6628 *Latitude:* -87.9126

> Fyddeye welcomes news releases from Navy and Coast Guard veterans groups. Please put contact@fyddeye.com on your email distribution list.

GREEN ISLAND LIGHTHOUSE
Established in 1863, the original Green Island Lighthouse is now a ruin, although the light is still operational atop a skeletal tower. *Address:* Green Island *City:* Marinette *State:* WI *Visitors welcome?* No *Operated by:* Private owner *NR?* No *NHL?* No *Year established/built:* 1863 *Latitude:* 45.0594 *Latitude:* -87.5009

GULL ISLAND LIGHTHOUSE
Established and built in 1928, the skeletal steel tower of the Gull Island Lighthouse is off Michigan Island, which is part of the Apostle Islands National Lakeshore. *Address:* Gull Island Light *City:* Bayfield *State:* WI *Visitors welcome?* No *Operated by:* U.S. Coast Guard (District 9) *NR?* No *NHL?* No *Year established/built:* 1928 *Latitude:* 46.9069 *Latitude:* -90.4422

KENOSHA NORTH PIER LIGHTHOUSE
Address: Kenosha North Pier Light *City:* Kenosha *State:* WI *Visitors welcome?* Yes *Hours:* Grounds only *Admission:* FREE *Operated by:* U.S. Coast Guard (District 9) *NR?* No *NHL?* No *Latitude:* 42.5888 *Latitude:* -87.8086

KENOSHA-SOUTHPORT LIGHTHOUSE
Established in 1848, the current Kenosha Lighthouse, also called the Southport Lighthouse, was constructed in 1866 and automated in 1996 after it was re-lighted. It is now part of a museum. *Address:* 220 51st Place *City:* Kenosha *State:* WI *Zip:* 53140 *Phone:* 262-654-5770 *Email:* kchs@kenoshahistorycenter.org *Visitors welcome?* Yes *Hours:* Tuesday to Friday, 10 a.m. to 4:30 p.m.; Saturday, 10 a.m. to 4 p.m.; Sunday, noon to 4 p.m. *Admission:* $10 adults, $5 children *Operated by:* Kenosha History Center *NR?* Yes *NHL?* No *Year established/built:* 1848 *Latitude:* 42.588160 *Latitude:* -87.813701

KEVICH LIGHTHOUSE
Built as a private aid to navigation, Kevich Lighthouse sits on a bluff overlooking Lake Michigan. *Address:* Kevich Light *City:* Grafton *State:* WI *Visitors welcome?* No *Operated by:* Private owner *NR?* No *NHL?* No *Year established/built:* 1981 *Latitude:* 43.3240 *Latitude:* -87.8889

CHAPTER 5 – LIGHTHOUSES & LIGHTSHIPS

KEWAUNEE PIERHEAD LIGHTHOUSE
Established in 1891, the current Kewaunee Pierhead Lighthouse was constructed in 1931 and is still an active aid to navigation. *Address:* Kewaunee Pierhead Light *City:* Kewaunee *State:* WI *Visitors welcome?* Yes *Hours:* Grounds only *Admission:* FREE *Operated by:* U.S. Coast Guard (District 9) *NR?* No *NHL?* No *Year established/built:* 1891 *Latitude:* 44.4572 *Latitude:* -87.4931

LA POINT LIGHTHOUSE
Established in 1858, the current skeletal tower was built in 1896 and automated in 1964. Still an active aid to navigation, the lighthouse is one of the oldest skeletal lighthouses in the Great Lakes. *Address:* Chequamegon Bay *State:* WI *Phone:* 715-779-3397 *Visitors welcome?* Yes *Hours:* Grounds only *Admission:* FREE *Operated by:* Apostle Islands National Lakeshore *NR?* Yes *NHL?* No *Year established/built:* 1858 *Latitude:* 46.7290 *Latitude:* -90.7852

LONG TAIL POINT LIGHTHOUSE
Now in ruins, the Long Tail Point Lighthouse is within a state wildlife refuge. *Address:* Long Tail Point *City:* Suamico *State:* WI *Visitors welcome?* Yes *Hours:* Grounds only *Admission:* FREE *Operated by:* Wisconsin Dept. of Natural Resources *NR?* No *NHL?* No *Latitude:* 44.5867 *Latitude:* -87.9804

MANITOWOC BREAKWATER LIGHTHOUSE
Established in 1895, the current Manitowoc Breakwater Lighthouse was constructed in 1918. Automated in 1971, it is still an active aid to navigation. *Address:* Manitowoc Breakwater Light *City:* Manitowoc *State:* WI *Visitors welcome?* Yes *Hours:* Grounds only *Admission:* FREE *Operated by:* U.S. Coast Guard (District 9) *NR?* No *NHL?* No *Year established/built:* 1895 *Latitude:* 44.0928 *Latitude:* -87.6436

MICHIGAN ISLAND (NEW)
Established in 1856, the current skeletal tower of the Michigan Island Lighthouse was built in 1880 where it guided mariners in the Delaware River before it was taken down and reassembled at Michigan Island in 1929. The light is still an active aid to navigation. *Address:* Michigan Island Light *State:* WI *Phone:* 715-779-3397 *Web:* www.nps.gov/apis/historyculture/lighthouses.htm *Visitors welcome?* Yes *Hours:* Grounds only *Admission:* FREE *Operated by:* Apostle Islands National Lakeshore *NR?* Yes *NHL?* No *Year established/built:* 1856 *Latitude:* 46.8717 *Latitude:* -90.4967

MICHIGAN ISLAND (OLD)
Established in 1856, the first Michigan Island lighthouse was built in error; the contractors picked the wrong island and the lighthouse was closed a year later. Restarted in 1869, it was again closed down in favor of a replacement skeletal tower. *Address:* Michigan Island Light *State:* WI *Phone:* 715-779-3397 *Web:* www.nps.gov/apis/historyculture/lighthouses.htm *Visitors welcome?* Yes *Hours:* Grounds only *Admission:* FREE *Operated by:* Apostle Islands National Lakeshore *NR?* Yes *NHL?* No *Year established/built:* 1856 *Latitude:* 46.8717 *Latitude:* -90.4967

MILWAUKEE BREAKWATER LIGHTHOUSE
Established and buit in 1926, the Milwaukee Breakwater Lighthouse is still an active aid to navigation. *Address:* Milwaukee Breakwater Light *City:* Milwaukee *State:* WI *Visitors welcome?* No *Operated by:* U.S. Coast Guard (District 9) *NR?* No *NHL?* No *Year established/built:* 1926 *Latitude:* 43.0270 *Latitude:* -87.8820

MILWAUKEE PIERHEAD LIGHTHOUSE
Established in 1872, the current Milwaukee Pierhead Lighthouse was constructed in 1906 and is still an active aid to navigation. *Address:* Milwaukee Pierhead Light *City:* Milwaukee *State:* WI *Visitors welcome?* Yes

Hours: Grounds only *Admission:* FREE *Operated by:* U.S. Coast Guard (District 9) *NR?* No *NHL?* No *Year established/built:* 1872 *Latitude:* 43.0260 *Latitude:* -87.8953

NEENAH LIGHTHOUSE
The Neenah Lighthouse at Kimberly Point on the shore of Lake Winnebago in Neenah, Wisconsin has stood for the last 50 years in a place where Indian Tribesman met for pow-wows 150 years ago at the mouth of the Fox River. *Address:* Neenah Light *City:* Neenah *State:* WI *Zip:* 54956 *Visitors welcome?* Yes *Hours:* Grounds only *Admission:* FREE *Operated by:* City of Neenah *NR?* No *NHL?* No *Year established/built:* 1947 *Latitude:* 44.1855 *Latitude:* -88.4414

NORTH POINT LIGHTHOUSE
Established in 1855, the current North Point Lighthouse, also known as the Milwaukee Lighthouse, was constructed in 1888 and deactivated in 1994. In 2007, local residents completed a restoration of the lighthouse, which is now in a public park. *Address:* 2650 N. Wahl Ave. *City:* Milwaukee *State:* WI *Zip:* 53211 *Phone:* 414-332-6754 *Web:* www.northpointlighthouse.org *Email:* keeper@northpointlighthouse.org *Visitors welcome?* Yes *Hours:* May to October, Saturdays, 1 p.m. to 4 p.m.; November to April, first Saturday of the month, 1 p.m. to 4 p.m. *Admission:* $5 adults, $3 children, under five FREE *Operated by:* North Point Lighthouse Friends *NR?* Yes *NHL?* No *Year established/built:* 1855 *Latitude:* 43.0656 *Latitude:* -87.8700

OUTER ISLAND LIGHTHOUSE
Established and built in 1874, the Outer Island Lighthouse is within the Apostle Islands National Lakeshore and is still an active aid to navigation. *Address:* Outer Island Light *City:* Bayfield *State:* WI *Phone:* 715-779-3397 *Web:* www.nps.gov/apis/historyculture/lighthouses.htm *Visitors welcome?* Yes *Hours:* Contact attraction directly *Admission:* FREE *Operated by:* Apostle Islands National Lakeshore *NR?* Yes *NHL?* No *Year established/built:* 1874 *Latitude:* 47.0767 *Latitude:* -90.4167

PESHTIGO REEF LIGHTHOUSE
Built in 1934 to replace a lightship, the Peshtigo Reef Lighthouse is still an active aid to navigation. *Address:* Peshtigo Harbor *City:* Peshtigo *State:* WI *Visitors welcome?* No *Operated by:* U.S. Coast Guard (District 9) *NR?* No *NHL?* No *Year established/built:* 1934 *Latitude:* 44.9724 *Latitude:* -87.6495

PILOT ISLAND LIGHTHOUSE
Established and built in 1858, the Pilot Island Lighthouse is within a wildlife refuge. Automated in 1962, it is still an active aid to navigation. *Address:* Pilot Island Light *State:* WI *Visitors welcome?* No *Operated by:* U.S. Coast Guard (District 9) *NR?* Yes *NHL?* No *Year established/built:* 1858 *Latitude:* 45.2844 *Latitude:* -86.9193

PLUM ISLAND REAR RANGE LIGHTHOUSE
Established and built in 1897, the skeletal tower of the Plum Island Rear Range Lighthouse was automated in 1969 and it is still an active aide to navigation. *Address:* Plum Island Range Rear Light *State:* WI *Visitors welcome?* No *Operated by:* U.S. Coast Guard (District 9) *NR?* Yes *NHL?* No *Year established/built:* 1897 *Latitude:* 45.3078 *Latitude:* -86.9581

PORT WASHINGTON BREAKWATER LIGHTHOUSE
Established in 1889 to supplement and then replace the on-shore Port Washington Lighthouse, the current Port Washington Breakwater Lighthouse was built in the 1935 and is still an active aid to navigation. *Address:* Port Washington Harbor *City:* Port Washington *State:* WI *Zip:* 53074 *Visitors welcome?* Yes *Hours:* Grounds only *Admission:* FREE *Operated by:* U.S. Coast Guard (District 9) *NR?* No *NHL?* No *Year established/built:* 1889 *Latitude:* 43.3853 *Latitude:* -87.8601

CHAPTER 5 – LIGHTHOUSES & LIGHTSHIPS

PORT WASHINGTON LIGHTHOUSE
Established in 1848, the current Port Washington Lighthouse was constructed in 1860 and deactivated in 1903. *Address:* 311 Johnson St. *City:* Port Washington *State:* WI *Zip:* 53074 *Phone:* 262-284-7240 *Web:* www.portlightstation.org *Email:* 1860lightstation@sbcglobal.net *Visitors welcome?* Yes *Hours:* Summer: Saturdays, 11 a.m. to 4 p.m., Sunday, noon to 4 p.m. *Admission:* Contact attraction directly *Operated by:* Port Washington Historical Society *NR?* Yes *NHL?* No *Year established/built:* 1849 *Latitude:* 43.3912 *Latitude:* -87.8684

POTTAWATOMIE LIGHTHOUSE
Established in 1837, the current Pottawatomie Lighthouse, also called the Rock Island Lighthouse, was constructed in 1858 and automated in 1966. *Address:* Pottawatomie Light *State:* WI *Email:* kirby.foss@wisconsin.gov *Visitors welcome?* Yes *Hours:* Contact attraction directly *Admission:* Contact attraction directly *Operated by:* Friends of Rock Island State Park *NR?* Yes *NHL?* No *Year established/built:* 1837 *Latitude:* 45.4275 *Latitude:* -86.8281

RACINE BREAKWATER LIGHTHOUSE
Established in 1872 shortly after the construction of a breakwater, the current Racine Breakwater Lighthouse is inactive, although it is beloved by the community as a marker of its maritime heritage. *City:* Racine *State:* WI *Visitors welcome?* No *Operated by:* City of Racine *NR?* No *NHL?* No *Year established/built:* 1872 *Latitude:* 42.7261 *Latitude:* -87.7829

RASPBERRY ISLAND LIGHTHOUSE
Established and built in 1863, the Raspberry Island Lighthouse was deactivated in 1957. The light station is now part of the Apostle Islands National Lakeshore. *Address:* Raspberry Island Light *City:* Bayfield *State:* WI *Phone:* 715-779-3397 *Web:* www.nps.gov/apis/historyculture/lighthouses.htm *Visitors welcome?* Yes *Hours:* Contact attraction directly *Admission:* Contact attraction directly *Operated by:* Apostle Islands National Lakeshore *NR?* Yes *NHL?* No *Year established/built:* 1863 *Latitude:* 46.9706 *Latitude:* -90.8050

RAWLEY POINT LIGHTHOUSE
Established in 1853, the current cast-iron skeletal tower of the Rawley Point Lighthouse, also called the Twin River Lighthouse, was constructed in 1894. Automated in 1979, the light is still an active aid to navigation. *Address:* Rawley Point *City:* Two Rivers *State:* WI *Visitors welcome?* Yes *Hours:* Grounds only *Admission:* FREE *Operated by:* U.S. Coast Guard (District 9) *NR?* Yes *NHL?* No *Year established/built:* 1853 *Latitude:* 44.2125 *Latitude:* -87.5079

SAND ISLAND LIGHTHOUSE
Established and built in 1881, the Sand Point Lighthouse is an active aid to navigation within the Apostle Islands National Lakeshore. *Address:* Sand Island Light *City:* Bayfield *State:* WI *Phone:* 715-779-3397 *Web:* www.nps.gov/apis/historyculture/lighthouses.htm *Visitors welcome?* Yes *Hours:* Grounds only *Admission:* FREE *Operated by:* Apostle Islands National Lakeshore *NR?* Yes *NHL?* No *Year established/built:* 1881 *Latitude:* 47.0033 *Latitude:* -90.9367

SHEBOYGAN BREAKWATER LIGHTHOUSE
Established in 1905, the current Sheboygan Breakwater Lighthouse was installed in 1915 and is still an active aid to navigation. *Address:* Sheboygan Harbor *City:* Sheboygan *State:* WI *Visitors welcome?* Yes *Hours:* Grounds only *Admission:* FREE *Operated by:* U.S. Coast Guard (District 9) *NR?* No *NHL?* No *Year established/built:* 1905 *Latitude:* 43.7496 *Latitude:* -87.6930

SHERWOOD POINT LIGHTHOUSE
Established and built in 1883, the Sherwood Point Lighthouse is used as recreational facilities for U.S. Coast Guard personnel. The light is still an active aid to navigation. *Address:* Sherwood Point Light *City:* Idlewild

State: WI *Visitors welcome?* No *Operated by:* U.S. Coast Guard (District 9) *NR?* Yes *NHL?* No *Year established/built:* 1883 *Latitude:* 44.8933 *Latitude:* -87.4333

STURGEON BAY SHIP CANAL LIGHTHOUSE
Established and built in 1899, the Sturgeon Bay Ship Canal Lighthouse is still an active aid to navigation. *Address:* Sturgeon Bay Canal Light *City:* Sturgeon Bay *State:* WI *Visitors welcome?* Yes *Hours:* Grounds only *Admission:* FREE *Operated by:* U.S. Coast Guard (District 9) *NR?* Yes *NHL?* No *Year established/built:* 1899 *Latitude:* 44.7950 *Latitude:* -87.3133

STURGEON BAY SHIP CANAL PIERHEAD LIGHTHOUSE
Established in 1882, the current Sturgeon Bay Ship Canal North Pierhead Lighthouse was constructed in 1903 and is still an active aid to navigation. *Address:* Sturgeon Bay Ship Canal *City:* Sturgeon Bay *State:* WI *Visitors welcome?* Yes *Hours:* Grounds only *Admission:* FREE *Operated by:* U.S. Coast Guard (District 9) *NR?* No *NHL?* No *Year established/built:* 1882 *Latitude:* 44.7920 *Latitude:* -87.3094

TWO RIVERS LIGHTHOUSE
The Two Rivers Lighthouse, now on the site of the Rogers Street Fishing Village, once sat on a breakwater guiding mariners into Two Rivers Harbor. *Address:* 2010 Rogers St. *City:* Two Rivers *State:* WI *Zip:* 54241 *Phone:* 920-793-5905 *Web:* www.rogersstreet.com *Email:* szipperer@rogersstreet.com *Visitors welcome?* Yes *Hours:* May to October: Daily, 10 a.m. to 4 p.m. *Admission:* $4 adults, $2 children under 16 *Operated by:* Rogers Street Fishing Village & Great Lakes Coast Guard Museum *NR?* No *NHL?* No *Year established/built:* 1886 *Latitude:* 44.1518 *Latitude:* -87.5626

WIND POINT LIGHTHOUSE
Established and built in 1880, the Wind Point Lighthouse was automated in 1964 and is still an active aid to navigation. It is now cared for by the City of Wind Point and a local not-for-profit organization. *Address:* Wind Point Light *City:* Wind Point *State:* WI *Phone:* 262-639-2026 *Visitors welcome?* Yes *Hours:* July to October, First Sunday *Admission:* Contact attraction directly *Operated by:* Friends of Wind Point Lighthouse *NR?* Yes *NHL?* No *Year established/built:* 1880 *Latitude:* 42.7811 *Latitude:* -87.7583

WISCONSIN POINT LIGHTHOUSE
Established and built in 1913, the Wisconsin Point Lighthouse is still an active aid to navigation. *Address:* Wisconsin Point Light *City:* Superior *State:* WI *Visitors welcome?* Yes *Hours:* Grounds only *Admission:* FREE *Operated by:* U.S. Coast Guard (District 9) *NR?* No *NHL?* No *Year established/built:* 1913 *Latitude:* 46.7101 *Latitude:* -92.0064

GULF COAST LIGHTHOUSES

ALABAMA

MOBILE BAY LIGHTHOUSE
Established and built in 1885, the Mobile Bay Lighthouse is an example of a screw-pile lighthouse, in which pilings with screw-like head are driven into the sand. Deactivated in 1967, the lighthouse is now under the

care of a not-for-profit organization. *Address:* Mobile Bay Light   *City:* Mobile *State:* AL *Visitors welcome?* No *Operated by:* Alabama Lighthouse Association *NR?* Yes *NHL?* No *Year established/built:* 1885 *Latitude:* 30.4375 *Latitude:* -88.0114

MOBILE POINT LIGHTHOUSE
Established and built in 1822, the remains of the Mobile Point Lighthouse are at Fort Morgan, a memorial to the Civil War Battle of Mobile Bay. *Address:* Mobile Point Lighthouse *State:* AL *Zip:* 36542 *Visitors welcome?* Yes *Hours:* Daily *Admission:* FREE *Operated by:* Alabama Lighthouse Association *NR?* No *NHL?* No *Year established/built:* 1822 *Latitude:* 30.2278 *Latitude:* -88.0239

SAND ISLAND LIGHTHOUSE
Established in 1837, the current Sand Island Lighthouse was constructed in 1873, replaced an 1859 tower destroyed during the Civil War. Residents of nearby Dauphin Island are leading a project to restore the now automated lighthouse. *Address:* Dauphin Island *City:* Mobile *State:* AL *Visitors welcome?* No *Operated by:* Alabama Lighthouse Association *NR?* Yes *NHL?* No *Year established/built:* 1837 *Latitude:* 30.2555 *Latitude:* -88.1097

FLORIDA

ALLIGATOR REEF LIGHTHOUSE
Established and built in 1873, the cast-iron Alligator Reef Lighthouse was automated in 1963 and is still an active aid to navigation. *Address:* Alligator Reef Light   *State:* FL *Visitors welcome?* No *Operated by:* U.S. Coast Guard (District 7) *NR?* No *NHL?* No *Year established/built:* 1873 *Latitude:* 24.8517 *Latitude:* -80.6183

AMERICAN SHOAL LIGHTHOUSE
Established and built in 1880, the American Shoal Lighthouse was automated in 1963 and is still an active aid to navigation. *Address:* American Shoal Light   *State:* FL *Visitors welcome?* No *Operated by:* U.S. Coast Guard (District 7) *NR?* No *NHL?* No *Year established/built:* 1880 *Latitude:* 24.5250 *Latitude:* -81.5200

ANCLOTE KEY LIGHTHOUSE
Established and built in 1887, the Anclote Key Lighthouse was deactivated in 1985 and is now within a wildlife refuge. *Address:* Anclote Key Preserve State Park *State:* FL *Visitors welcome?* Yes *Hours:* Grounds only *Admission:* FREE *Operated by:* Florida Division of Recreation and Parks *NR?* Yes *NHL?* No *Year established/built:* 1887 *Latitude:* 28.1726 *Latitude:* -82.8466

CAPE SAN BLAS LIGHTHOUSE
Established in 1848, the current Cape San Blas Lighthouse was constructed in 1885 and deactivated in 1996. *Address:* Cape San Blas Light   *City:* Port St. Joe *State:* FL *Visitors welcome?* Yes *Hours:* Daily, grounds only *Admission:* FREE *Operated by:* Gulf County *NR?* No *NHL?* No *Year established/built:* 1848 *Latitude:* 29.6712 *Latitude:* -85.3563

CAPE ST. GEORGE LIGHTHOUSE
Established in 1833, the current Cape St. George Lighthouse was constructed in 1852. Deactivated in 1994, the lighthouse is now a museum. *Address:* Franklin Boulevard and West Gulf Beach Drive *City:* St. George Island *State:* FL *Phone:* 850-927-7744 *Web:* www.stgeorgelight.org *Visitors welcome?* Yes *Hours:* Monday, Tuesday, Wednesday: 9 a.m. to noon and 1 p.m. to 3 p.m.; Saturday: 9 a.m. to 1 p.m.; Sunday: 1 p.m. to 3 p.m.

CHAPTER 5 – LIGHTHOUSES & LIGHTSHIPS

Admission: $5 adults, $3 six to 16, under six FREE *Operated by:* St. George Lighthouse Association *NR?* Yes *NHL?* No *Year established/built:* 1833 *Latitude:* 29.6408 *Latitude:* -84.9124

CEDAR KEYS LIGHTHOUSE
Established and built in 1854, the Cedar Keys Lighthouse was deactivated in 1915. Also known as Seahorse Key Lighthouse, the site is now used by the University of Florida. *Address:* Seahorse Key *City:* Cedar Key *State:* FL *Phone:* 352-392-1101 *Web:* www.zoology.ufl.edu *Email:* hbl@zoology.ufl.edu *Visitors welcome?* Yes *Hours:* Contact attraction directly *Admission:* Contact attraction directly *Operated by:* Seahorse Key Marine Laboratory (University of Florida) *NR?* Yes *NHL?* No *Year established/built:* 1854 *Latitude:* 29.0972 *Latitude:* -83.0660

CROOKED RIVER LIGHTHOUSE
Established and built in 1895, the Crooked River Lighthouse, also known as Carrabelle Lighthouse, was deactivated in 1995 and is now in a public park. *Address:* Crooked River Light *City:* Franklin *State:* FL *Visitors welcome?* Yes *Hours:* Daily *Admission:* FREE *Operated by:* Carrabelle Lighthouse Association *NR?* Yes *NHL?* No *Year established/built:* 1895 *Latitude:* 29.8275 *Latitude:* -84.7011

EGMONT KEY LIGHTHOUSE
Established in 1848, the current Egmont Key Lighthouse was constructed in 1858. Automated in 1989, the lighthouse is still an active aid to navigation within a wildlife refuge. *Address:* Egmont Key Light *City:* Anna Maria *State:* FL *Visitors welcome?* Yes *Hours:* Daily, grounds only *Admission:* FREE *Operated by:* Florida Division of Recreation and Parks *NR?* Yes *NHL?* No *Year established/built:* 1848 *Latitude:* 27.6008 *Latitude:* -82.7608

GASPARILLA ISLAND RANGE LIGHTHOUSE
Established in 1890, the front range Gasparilla Island Lighthouse was constructed in 1890, and the rear range tower was built in 1932. Both lights, as known as the Boca Grande Range Lighthouses, are still active aids to navigation. *Address:* Gasparilla Island Lights *City:* Boca Grande *State:* FL *Visitors welcome?* No *Operated by:* Florida Division of Recreation and Parks *NR?* Yes *NHL?* No *Year established/built:* 1890 *Latitude:* 26.7419 *Latitude:* -82.2633

KEY LARGO LIGHTHOUSE
The lighthouse is privately owned. *Address:* Oleander Circle *City:* Key Largo *State:* FL *Visitors welcome?* No *Operated by:* Private owner *NR?* No *NHL?* No *Year established/built:* 1953 *Latitude:* 25.0921 *Latitude:* -80.4346

KEY WEST LIGHTHOUSE
Established in 1825, the current Key West Lighthouse was constructed in 1847. Deactivated in 1969, the lighthouse is within the Key West National Historic District. *Address:* 938 Whitehead Street *City:* Key West *State:* FL *Zip:* 33040 *Phone:* 305-294-0012 *Web:* www.kwahs.com *Email:* cpennington@kwahs.org *Visitors welcome?* Yes *Hours:* Daily, 9:30 a.m. to 4:30 p.m. *Admission:* Contact attraction directly *Operated by:* Key West Art & Historical Society *NR?* Yes *NHL?* No *Year established/built:* 1825 *Latitude:* 24.5505 *Latitude:* -81.8008

PENSACOLA LIGHTHOUSE
Established in 1825, the current Pensacola Lighthouse was constructed in 1859 and is still an active aid to navigation within the Pensacola Naval Air Station. *Address:* Pensacola Light *City:* Pensacola *State:* FL *Visitors welcome?* Yes *Hours:* By appointment *Admission:* By appointment *Operated by:* Pensacola Naval Air Station *NR?* Yes *NHL?* No *Year established/built:* 1825 *Latitude:* 30.3464 *Latitude:* -87.3081

PORT BOCA GRANDE LIGHTHOUSE
Built in 1890 by the U.S. Lighthouse Service to mark the entrance into Charlotte Harbor from the Gulf of Mexico, the Boca Grande Lighthouse is the oldest building on Gasparilla Island and its most recognized landmark. *Address:* Port Boca Grande Light *City:* Boca Grande *State:* FL *Phone:* 941-964-0060 *Web:* www.barrierislandparkssociety.org *Email:* barrierislandparkssociety@yahoo.com *Visitors welcome?* Yes *Hours:* Contact attraction directly *Admission:* Contact attraction directly *Operated by:* Barrier Islands Park Society *NR?* Yes *NHL?* No *Year established/built:* 1890 *Latitude:* 26.7419 *Latitude:* -82.2633

SAND KEY LIGHTHOUSE
Established in 1826, the Sand Key Lighthouse was constructed in 1853. Automated in 1938, the lighthouse is still an active aid to navigation. *Address:* Sand Key *State:* FL *Visitors welcome?* No *Operated by:* U.S. Coast Guard (District 7) *NR?* Yes *NHL?* No *Year established/built:* 1826 *Latitude:* 27.9591 *Latitude:* -82.8277

SANIBEL ISLAND LIGHTHOUSE
Established and built in 1884, the Sanibel Island Lighthouse was automated in 1949 and is still an active aid to navigation. *Address:* Sanibel Light *City:* Sanibel Island *State:* FL *Visitors welcome?* Yes *Hours:* Daily, grounds only *Admission:* FREE *Operated by:* U.S. Coast Guard (District 7) *NR?* Yes *NHL?* No *Year established/built:* 1884 *Latitude:* 26.4540 *Latitude:* -82.0137

SOMBRERO KEY LIGHTHOUSE
Established and built in 1858, the Sombrero Key Lighthouse was automated in 1960 and is still an active aid to navigation. *Address:* Sombrero Key Light *City:* Marathon *State:* FL *Visitors welcome?* No *Operated by:* U.S. Coast Guard (District 7) *NR?* No *NHL?* No *Year established/built:* 1858 *Latitude:* 24.6279 *Latitude:* -81.1116

ST. MARKS REAR RANGE LIGHTHOUSE
Established in 1831, the current St. Marks Rear Range Lighthouse was constructed in 1842. Automated in 1960, the lighthouse is still an active aid to navigation in a national wildlife refuge. *Address:* St. Marks National Wildlife Refuge *City:* St. Marks *State:* FL *Visitors welcome?* Yes *Hours:* Grounds only *Admission:* Refuge entrance fee *Operated by:* U.S. Coast Guard (District 7) *NR?* Yes *NHL?* No *Year established/built:* 1831 *Latitude:* 30.1610 *Latitude:* -84.2063

TORTUGAS HARBOR LIGHTHOUSE
Established in 1825, the current Tortugas Harbor Lighthouse, also known as the Fort Jefferson Lighthouse or Garden Key Lighthouse, was deactivated in 1921. It is now part of Fort Jefferson National Monument. *Address:* Garden Key Light   *State:* FL *Phone:* 305-242-7700 *Visitors welcome?* Yes *Hours:* Contact attraction directly *Admission:* Contact attraction directly *Operated by:* Dry Tortugas National Park *NR?* Yes *NHL?* No *Year established/built:* 1825 *Latitude:* 24.6281 *Latitude:* -82.8722

LOUISIANA

CHANDELEUR ISLAND LIGHTHOUSE
Established and built in 1896, the Chandeleur Island Lighthouse was destroyed by Hurricane Katrina in 2005. *Address:* Chandeleur Islands *City:* New Orleans *State:* LA *Visitors welcome?* No *Operated by:* Breton National Wildlife Refuge *NR?* No *NHL?* No *Year established/built:* 1896 *Latitude:* 29.8362 *Latitude:* -88.8387

CHAPTER 5 – LIGHTHOUSES & LIGHTSHIPS

NEW CANAL LIGHTHOUSE
Established in 1838, the current 1890 New Canal Lighthouse is undergoing reconstruction after it was destroyed by Hurricane Katrina in 2005. It will be used as an environmental education center. *Address:* Lakeshore Drive *City:* Metairie *State:* LA *Phone:* 504-836-2215 *Visitors welcome?* No *Operated by:* Lake Pontchartrain Basin Foundation *NR?* Yes *NHL?* No *Year established/built:* 1838 *Latitude:* 30.0206 *Latitude:* -90.1705

PASS A L'OUTRE LIGHTHOUSE
Established and built in 1855, the Pass a l'Outre Lighthouse was decommissioned in 1930 and is now in a decaying condition. *Address:* Pass A Loutre Wildlife Management Area *City:* New Iberia *State:* LA *Visitors welcome?* Yes *Hours:* Grounds only *Admission:* FREE *Operated by:* Pass A Loutre Wildlife Management Area *NR?* No *NHL?* No *Year established/built:* 1855 *Latitude:* 30.0035 *Latitude:* -91.8187

PASS MANCHAC LIGHTHOUSE
Established in 1839, the current Pass Manchac Lighthouse was deactivated in 1987. *Address:* Lake Ponchartrain *City:* New Orleans *State:* LA *Visitors welcome?* Yes *Hours:* Grounds only *Admission:* Grounds only *Operated by:* Lake Maurepas Society *NR?* Yes *NHL?* No *Year established/built:* 1839 *Latitude:* 30.2051 *Latitude:* -90.1121

POINT AU FER REEF LIGHTHOUSE
Established and built in 1916, the Point Au Fer Reef Lighthouse was automated in 1975. *Address:* Eugene Island, Atchafalaya Bay *City:* Berwick *State:* LA *Visitors welcome?* No *Operated by:* U.S. Coast Guard (District 8) *NR?* No *NHL?* No *Year established/built:* 1916 *Latitude:* 29.6947 *Latitude:* -91.2190

PORT PONTCHARTRAIN LIGHTHOUSE
Established in 1832, the current Port Pontchartrain Lighthouse was constructed in 1855 and deactivated in 1929. *Address:* Lakeshore Drive *City:* New Orleans *State:* LA *Visitors welcome?* Yes *Hours:* Grounds only *Admission:* FREE *Operated by:* University of New Orleans *NR?* Yes *NHL?* No *Year established/built:* 1832 *Latitude:* 30.0307 *Latitude:* -90.0602

SABINE PASS LIGHTHOUSE
Established and built in 1856, the Sabine Pass Lighthouse was deactivated in 1952. *City:* Sabine Pass *State:* LA *Visitors welcome?* Yes *Hours:* Grounds only *Admission:* FREE *Operated by:* Cameron Preservation Alliance - Sabine Pass Lighthouse *NR?* Yes *NHL?* No *Year established/built:* 1856 *Latitude:* 29.7331 *Latitude:* -93.8944

SHIP SHOAL LIGHTHOUSE
Established and built in 1858, the Ship Shaol Lighthouse was deactivated in 1965. The Town of Berwich hopes to bring the structure ashore to a city park. *City:* Cocodrie *State:* LA *Visitors welcome?* No *Operated by:* U.S. Coast Guard (District 8) *NR?* No *NHL?* No *Year established/built:* 1858 *Latitude:* 29.2469 *Latitude:* -90.6615

SOUTH PASS RANGE LIGHTHOUSES
Also called the Port Eads Lighthouse, the South Pass Rear Range Lighthouse was built in 1881 and is still an active aid to navigation. The companion front range light was constructed in 1947. *Address:* South Pass *State:* LA *Visitors welcome?* Yes *Hours:* Grounds only *Admission:* FREE *Operated by:* U.S. Coast Guard (District 8) *NR?* Yes *NHL?* No *Year established/built:* 1832 *Latitude:* 28.9947 *Latitude:* -89.1428

SOUTHWEST PASS LIGHTHOUSE 1
Several lighthouses have marked Southwest Pass, the major shipping entrance to the Mississippi River, including one built in 1871. The first lighthouse to mark the entrance was constructed in 1832, and the

last one built in 1953 on the end of a jetty at t *Address:* Southwest Pass *City:* New Orleans *State:* LA *Visitors welcome?* No *Operated by:* Private owner *NR?* No *NHL?* No *Year established/built:* 1839 *Latitude:* 29.0141 *Latitude:* -89.3442

SOUTHWEST PASS LIGHTHOUSE 2
Several lighthouses have marked Southwest Pass, the major shipping entrance to the Mississippi River, including one built in 1871. The first lighthouse to mark the entrance was constructed in 1832, and the last one built in 1953 on the end of a jetty at t *Address:* Southwest Pass, Mississippi River *City:* New Orleans *State:* LA *Visitors welcome?* No *Operated by:* U.S. Coast Guard (District 8) *NR?* No *NHL?* No *Year established/built:* 1871 *Latitude:* 30.1144 *Latitude:* -89.7039

SOUTHWEST PASS LIGHTHOUSE 3
Several lighthouses have marked Southwest Pass, the major shipping entrance to the Mississippi River, including one built in 1871. The first lighthouse to mark the entrance was constructed in 1832, and the last one built in 1953 on the end of a jetty at t *Address:* Southwest Pass *City:* New Orleans *State:* LA *Visitors welcome?* No *Operated by:* U.S. Coast Guard (District 8) *NR?* No *NHL?* No *Year established/built:* 1871 *Latitude:* 29.0141 *Latitude:* -89.3442

SOUTHWEST REEF LIGHTHOUSE
Established and built in 1858, the Southwest Reef Lighthouse was deactivated in 1916. It is now located in a city park in the Town of Berwick. *Address:* Atchafalaya River *City:* Berwick *State:* LA *Zip:* 70342 *Phone:* 985-384-8858 *Visitors welcome?* Yes *Hours:* Grounds only *Admission:* FREE *Operated by:* Town of Berwick *NR?* Yes *NHL?* No *Year established/built:* 1858 *Latitude:* 29.6947 *Latitude:* -91.2190

TCHEFUNCTE RIVER LIGHTHOUSE
Established in 1838, the current Tchefuncte River Lighthouse was constructed in 1868 and is still an active aid to navigation. It is operated as a museum by a local historical society. *Address:* Tchefuncte River *City:* Madisonville *State:* LA *Zip:* 70447 *Phone:* 985-845-9200 *Web:* www.lpbmaritimemuseum.org *Visitors welcome?* Yes *Hours:* Contact attraction directly *Admission:* Contact attraction directly *Operated by:* Lake Pontchartrain Basin Maritime Museum *NR?* Yes *NHL?* No *Year established/built:* 1838 *Latitude:* 30.3776 *Latitude:* -90.1634

WEST RIGOLETS LIGHTHOUSE
Established and built in 1855, the West Rigolets Lighthouse was destroyed by Hurricane Katrina in 2005. *Address:* Fort Pike Historic Site *City:* New Orleans *State:* LA *Zip:* 70129 *Phone:* 504-255-9171 *Toll-free:* 888-662-5703 *Visitors welcome?* No *Operated by:* Fort Pike Historic Site *NR?* No *NHL?* No *Year established/built:* 1855 *Latitude:* 30.1662 *Latitude:* -89.7371

MISSISSIPPI

BILOXI LIGHTHOUSE
Built in 1848, the Biloxi Lighthouse was one of the original cast-iron lighthouses constructed in the U.S. It is believed to be the only remaining lighthouse marking the Mississippi shore. *Address:* State Highway 90 *City:* Biloxi *State:* MS *Zip:* 39533 *Phone:* 228-435-6305 *Visitors welcome?* Yes *Hours:* Grounds only *Admission:* FREE *Operated by:* City of Biloxi *NR?* No *NHL?* No *Year established/built:* 1848 *Latitude:* 30.3944 *Latitude:* -88.9214

CHAPTER 5 – LIGHTHOUSES & LIGHTSHIPS

ROUND ISLAND LIGHTHOUSE
Established in 1833, the current Round Island Lighthouse was constructed in 1859. Decommissioned in the 1940s, the lighthouse was toppled by a hurricane in 1998. *Address:* Round Island *State:* MS *Phone:* 228-938-2356 *Visitors welcome?* Yes *Hours:* Grounds only *Admission:* FREE *Operated by:* City of Pascagoula *NR?* Yes *NHL?* No *Year established/built:* 1833 *Latitude:* 30.2949 *Latitude:* -88.5867

SHIP ISLAND LIGHTHOUSE
Established in 1853, the original Ship Island Lighthouse tower was destroyed by Confederate troops during the Civil War. It was rebuilt by Union troops in 1862. *Address:* Ship Island *State:* MS *Visitors welcome?* Yes *Hours:* Grounds only *Admission:* FREE *Operated by:* U.S. Coast Guard (District 8) *NR?* No *NHL?* No *Year established/built:* 1853 *Latitude:* 30.2082 *Latitude:* -88.9569

TEXAS

GALVESTON JETTY LIGHTHOUSE
Established and built in 1918, the Galveston Jetty Lighthouse was deactivated in 1972 and collapsed in 2000. The lantern room, rescued before the collapse, is now on display at Galveston College. *Address:* Galveston College *City:* Galveston *State:* TX *Visitors welcome?* Yes *Hours:* Grounds only *Admission:* FREE *Operated by:* Private owner *NR?* No *NHL?* No *Year established/built:* 1904 *Latitude:* 29.2841 *Latitude:* -94.8083

HALF MOON REEF LIGHTHOUSE
Established in 1858, the Half Moon Reef Lighthouse originally guided mariners through Matagorda Bay. The lighthouse survived several hurricanes, only to be threatened by bombing practice in 1942. The now deactivated lighthouse was moved ashore in 1978. *Address:* 301 South Ann Street *City:* Port Lavaca *State:* TX *Phone:* 361-552-9793 *Visitors welcome?* Yes *Hours:* Contact attraction directly *Admission:* Contact attraction directly *Operated by:* City of Port Lavaca *NR?* No *NHL?* No *Year established/built:* 1858 *Latitude:* 28.6128 *Latitude:* -96.6255

LYDIA ANN LIGHTHOUSE
Established in 1855 and built in 1857, the Lydia Ann Lighthouse, originally called the Aransas Pass Lighthouse, was destroyed by Confederate soldiers during the Civil War. The second, current structure was built in 1867, was deactivated in 1952. *Address:* Lydia Ann Channel *City:* Port Aransas *State:* TX *Visitors welcome?* No *Operated by:* Private owner *NR?* Yes *NHL?* No *Year established/built:* 1855 *Latitude:* 27.7151 *Latitude:* -97.1425

MATAGORDA ISLAND LIGHTHOUSE
Established and built in 1852, the cast-iron Matagorda Island Lighthouse was damaged during the Civil War. After the war, it was moved to avoid encroachment by the Gulf of Mexico. The lighthouse is now within a state park. *Address:* Matagorda Island State Park *State:* TX *Phone:* 979-244-7697 *Visitors welcome?* Yes *Hours:* Grounds only *Admission:* FREE *Operated by:* Matagorda Island Foundation *NR?* Yes *NHL?* No *Year established/built:* 1852 *Latitude:* 28.1689 *Latitude:* -96.7387

POINT BOLIVAR LIGHTHOUSE
Established in 1852, the cast-iron Point Bolivar Lighthouse was dismantled at the beginning of the Civil War so that its plating could be used for armaments. A new iron tower was lit in 1872 and remained active until

1933. The lighthouse is now in private *City:* Port Bolivar *State:* TX *Visitors welcome?* No *Operated by:* Private owner *NR?* Yes *NHL?* No *Year established/built:* 1852 *Latitude:* 29.3808 *Latitude:* -94.7644

PORT ISABEL LIGHTHOUSE
The Port Isabel Lighthouse, also called the Point Isabel Lighthouse, was built in 1852 in response to requests from sea captains for help in navigating around the low-lying Texas coast. *Address:* 421 East Queen Isabella Blvd *City:* Port Isabel *State:* TX *Zip:* 78578 *Phone:* 956-943-2262 *Visitors welcome?* Yes *Hours:* Sunday to Thursday, 10 a.m. to 6 p.m.; Friday and Saturday, 11 a.m. to 8 p.m. *Admission:* Contact attraction directly *Operated by:* Museums of Port Isabel *NR?* Yes *NHL?* No *Year established/built:* 1852 *Latitude:* 26.0774 *Latitude:* -97.2076

SABINE PASS LIGHTHOUSE
Established in 1906, the coffee pot-style Sabine Pass Lighthouse is located 15 miles from the mouth of the Sabine River in the Gulf of Mexico. The lighthouse's lantern was removed in 2002 and placed on shore as an exhibit. *Address:* Lions Park *City:* Sabine *State:* TX *Visitors welcome?* Yes *Hours:* Grounds only *Admission:* FREE *Operated by:* Private owner *NR?* No *NHL?* No *Year established/built:* 1906 *Latitude:* 29.8764 *Latitude:* -93.9276

Did Fyddeye goof? Email your correction to contact@fyddeye.com.

Best West Coast Lighthouse Books
by
Steven Wells

Ever since Congress established the first lighthouses on the west coast in 1848 at Cape Disappointment and New Dungeness, American authors and photographers have tried to capture their lonely and noble beauty. Today, each of Washington, Oregon, California, and Alaska's 95 beacons seemed to have inspired a picture book of their own. Canadian writers and photographers have added their volumes to the mix as well, creating a whole library of books on British Columbia's 49 coastal lights, which share towering seas, devilish fogs, and treacherous shoals similar to their Lower 48 and Alaska cousins.

A reader new to the subject can feel overwhelmed by the amount of available material. But the compelling prose and striking photographs of just a few books published in the last two decades stand out as perfect places to start. Donald Graham's early book *Lights of the Inside Passage* is an excellent way to begin. It's a passionate retelling of the history of lighthouse development in British Columbia motivated by his own firsthand experience as a keeper.

Two books cover B.C.'s lighthouses in detail
First published in 1986, before automation had completely taken day-to-day management of lighthouses from human hands, *Lights of the Inside Passage* paints a detailed account of the lives of the keepers, their isolated existence and sometimes fatal efforts to keep the beacons burning at night. In the early days, keepers were tasked with winding turning mechanisms, replenishing whale oil and wicks, cleaning soot off glass, and making repairs after violent storms, all while living without electricity, medical help, or regular access to food and supplies. Graham carefully researched the early history of 21 lighthouses. He has written a vivid narrative strengthened by historical black and white photographs and numerous government, newspaper and personal accounts. The most recent edition was published in 1992.

CHAPTER 5 – LIGHTHOUSES & LIGHTSHIPS

> *...then the dam burst, flooding sea water and debris into the kitchen, pantry, basement, living room and cistern. Neither keeper was injured by flying glass even though I had bare feet and fled the room while it was still awash. There was no warning a moment later from the wave that gained the sea wall and flooded the station.*
>
> *--Lights of the Inside Passage*

In a second book, inspired by the historical accounts of Graham's books, authors Chris Jaksa and Lynn Tanod traveled by boat and helicopter to many lighthouses, organizing their research into four geographical regions for *Guiding Lights: British Columbia's Lighthouses and Their Keepers*. Each lighthouse is described with several pages of text, beautiful color photographs, maps, and informational sidebars. Chris Jaksa is an experienced photographer and his pictures in this 1998 volume feature lighthouses, outbuildings, local seascapes, and many human subjects, which capture the natural splendor and rugged isolation of lighthouse locations.

Cape Blanco Lighthouse, Oregon's southernmost lighthouse

CHAPTER 5 – LIGHTHOUSES & LIGHTSHIPS

A tragedy and turning point for lighthouses

Pacific Northwest Lighthouses by Bruce Roberts and Ray Jones opens with a detailed account of the shipwreck of the steamship *S.S. Valencia* off the coast of Vancouver Island in 1906. Captain O.M. Johnson, who knew the route from San Francisco to Victoria well, faced several days of blinding fog after departing San Francisco and traveling up the Washington State coast. Navigating by means of dead reckoning—essentially estimating his location by carefully noting his course and speed—he began his turn east from the Pacific Ocean into the Strait of Juan de Fuca too late.

Instead, he sailed well to the north of the strait and blundered onto the jagged rocks near Pachena Point on Vancouver Island. His nightmare had only begun. Each launch of a lifeboat ended in tragedy as it overturned and dumped terrified passengers into the raging surf to drown or be dashed on the rocks. The remaining passengers could only climb to the upper decks and watch with horror as the ship was pounded by powerful waves. By the end of the two-day ordeal, only thirty-seven of the 154 passengers survived.

But this horrible tragedy signaled a turning point for lighthouses. Until the loss of the *Valencia*, demand for lighthouses came mostly from commercial interests. Now the government of Canada increased funding for lighthouses in the Pacific Northwest as the general public demanded stronger safety measures for passenger vessels.

The "worst lighthouse duty in America"

The U.S. Congress did little to provide for safe navigation in Alaskan waters after the Alaska Purchase of 1867 added 6,740 miles of remote and rugged coastline to the country. And just as the steamship *Valencia* accident prompted the Canadian government to take action, it took tragedy in Alaskan waters to prompt lawmakers to act. In 1898, on a typically cold February afternoon, the steamship *Clara Nevada*, carrying gold from the Klondike mines, departed Skagway with as many as 150 passengers. During the night, northerly winds up to eighty miles per hour pushed the southbound steamer wildly down Lynn Canal. The vessel struck an uncharted submerged obstacle near Eldred Rock. No one survived the icy and snowy waters that night. Three years later, the ship *Islander*, laden with gold and forty-two passengers and crew, struck an iceberg off Douglass Island and sank. Again, there were no survivors.

Faced with demands from an outraged public, Congress finally approved funds for development of two of Alaska's first lighthouses, Five Fingers Island and Sentinel Island, established in 1902. These two lighthouses and five others in Alaska are profiled in Roberts and Jones' book. Accompanying photographs bring to life the degree of isolation at these locations through images of snowy islands, jagged rocks, and raging seas.

> *Some keepers considered this the 'worst lighthouse duty station in America', and it is easy to see why. Fresh meat and vegetables were rarely seen on the dinner table at this lighthouse. Keepers sometimes found themselves vying with the gulls for fish that had been marooned by the tides on the rocks below the lighthouse.*
>
> *-- Pacific Northwest Lighthouses*

Roberts and Jones' 1997 book focuses on a total of forty-four lighthouses in Oregon, Washington, British Columbia, and Alaska. Each review is accompanied by recent color photos highlighting the site, existing structures, and features such as Fresnel lenses. Maps are conveniently included to help readers locate the lighthouses. The authors have contributed to several lifestyle magazines and their work is easy to read and wonderful to look at.

A full-bodied coffee table book

What sets *Lighthouses of the Pacific Coast* by Randy Leffingwell and Pamela Welty apart from other books is a combination of well-written history with brilliant photos printed on high quality stock. In his role of author and photographer, Leffingwell's talent is amply displayed. The book's prologue recounts the efforts of a commercial restoration crew flown by helicopter to the lighthouse on Cape Flattery. An accompanying photograph is a bird's eye view over the shoulder of a U.S. Coast Guard flight chief lying on his stomach on the floor of the helicopter. He leans out an open door and guides the pilot closer to the lighthouse to drop a load of supplies. Looking out the door and down to the lighthouse buildings with the coastline in the distance and surrounding dark blue sea is enough to give anyone with vertigo pause.

Suitable for any coffee table, the engaging text of the book is organized in chronological chapters beginning with the formation of the U.S. Light House Establishment in 1848 and ending with efforts to automate lighthouses and other coastal navigation aids. By the time, the Coast Guard merged with the Lighthouse Bureau in 1939, there were 4,100 lighthouse keepers and 400 lighthouses across the country. The Lighthouse Bureau pioneered the modern principle of "equal pay for equal work" as one of the first government organizations that recognized the skills and dedication of women by establishing equal pay and benefits for positions identical to men's. By the early 1970s, the last keepers were replaced by automated batteries, sensors and remote controls.

Each of these four books provides a wonderful starting point for those who want learn about the early development of aids to navigation throughout the Pacific coasts of the United States and British Columbia. They describe the dedication of civil servants who built and operated these facilities in some of the most inhospitable conditions imaginable. And they remind us of the many personal sacrifices these men and women made to help develop our great countries. As time and technology march on, it's hard not to feel a mixture of sadness and nostalgia as the human component of these lighthouses, unlike their lights, is extinguished. But these books are outstanding records of their legacy.

Steve Wells is a Seattle winemaker and writer.

Lights of the Inside Passage: A History of British Columbia's Lighthouse and Their Keepers by Donald Graham
Harbour Publishing, 269 pages, paperback 1992
Guiding Lights: British Columbia's Lighthouses and Their Keepers
Text by Lynn Tanod, photography by Chris Jaksa
Harbour Publishing, 112 pages, 1998
Pacific Northwest Lighthouses: Oregon, Washington, Alaska, and British Columbia by Bruce Roberts, and Ray Jones
The Globe Pequot Press, 88 pages, paperback 1997
Lighthouses of the Pacific Coast: Your Guide to the Lighthouses of California, Oregon, and Washington
Text by Randy Leffingwell and Pamela Welty, photography by Randy Leffingewell
Voyager Press, 176 pages, 2000

WEST COAST, ALASKA, AND HAWAII LIGHTHOUSES

Heceta Head Lighthouse (Florence, Ore.)

ALASKA

CAPE DECISION LIGHTHOUSE
Established and built in 1932, the Cape Decision Lighthouse was the last constructed in Alaskan waters. Still an active aid to navigation, it is now managed by a not-for-profit. *Address:* Cape Decision *State:* AK *Visitors welcome?* Yes *Hours:* By appointment *Admission:* Contact attraction directly *Operated by:* Cape Decision Lighthouse Society *NR?* Yes *NHL?* No *Year established/built:* 1932 *Latitude:* 56.0056 *Latitude:* -134.1330

CAPE HINCHINBROOK LIGHTHOUSE
Established in 1910, the current Cape Hinchinbrook Lighthouse was constructed in 1934. The light was automated in 1974 and is still an active aid to navigation at the entrance to Prince William Sound. *Address:* Cape Hinchinbrook Light *City:* Cordova *State:* AK *Visitors welcome?* No *Operated by:* U.S. Coast Guard (District 17) *NR?* No *NHL?* No *Year established/built:* 1910 *Latitude:* 60.2375 *Latitude:* -146.6470

CAPE SPENCER LIGHTHOUSE
Established in 1913, the current Cape Spencer Lighthouse was constructed in 1925 and automated in 1974. The light is still an active aid to navigation. *Address:* Cape Spencer Light *State:* AK *Visitors welcome?* No

CHAPTER 5 – LIGHTHOUSES & LIGHTSHIPS

Operated by: U.S. Coast Guard (District 17) *NR?* Yes *NHL?* No *Year established/built:* 1913 *Latitude:* 58.1989 *Latitude:* -136.6440

CAPE ST. ELIAS LIGHTHOUSE
Established and built in 1916, the Cape St. Elias lighthouse is at the south end of Kodiak Island and is still an active aid to navigation. *Address:* Cape St. Elias Light *City:* Cordova *State:* AK *Visitors welcome?* Yes *Hours:* Contact attraction directly *Admission:* Contact attraction directly *Operated by:* Cape Saint Elias Lighthouse Keepers Association *NR?* Yes *NHL?* No *Year established/built:* 1916 *Latitude:* 59.7983 *Latitude:* -144.5990

ELDRED ROCK LIGHTHOUSE
Established and built in 1905, the Eldred Rock Lighthouse was renovated in 1996 and leased to a local museum. It is still an active aid to naviation. *Address:* Eldred Rock Light *City:* Haines *State:* AK *Visitors welcome?* No *Operated by:* U.S. Coast Guard (District 17) *NR?* Yes *NHL?* No *Year established/built:* 1905 *Latitude:* 58.9717 *Latitude:* -135.2210

FIVE FINGERS ISLAND LIGHTHOUSE
Established in 1902, the Five Fingers Island Lighthouse is the first Alaskan lighthouse. The current structure was built in 1935 and is now managed by a not-for-profit organization. *Address:* Five Finger Islands Light *State:* AK *Visitors welcome?* Yes *Hours:* Contact attraction directly *Admission:* Contact attraction directly *Operated by:* Juneau Lighthouse Association *NR?* Yes *NHL?* No *Year established/built:* 1902 *Latitude:* 57.2703 *Latitude:* -133.6310

GUARD ISLAND LIGHTHOUSE
Established in 1904, the current Guard Island Lighthouse was built in 1924 and automated in 1969. It is still an active aid to navigation. *Address:* Guard Island Light *State:* AK *Visitors welcome?* No *Operated by:* U.S. Coast Guard (District 17) *NR?* Yes *NHL?* No *Year established/built:* 1905 *Latitude:* 55.4458 *Latitude:* -131.8810

MARY ISLAND LIGHTHOUSE
Established in 1903, the current Mary Island Lighthouse was constructed in 1937 and is still an active aid to navigation. *Address:* Mary Island *City:* Ketchikan *State:* AK *Visitors welcome?* No *Operated by:* U.S. Coast Guard (District 17) *NR?* No *NHL?* No *Year established/built:* 1903 *Latitude:* 55.0985 *Latitude:* -131.1840

ODIAK PHAROS
The Odiak Pharos is a small, privately owned navigation aid. *Address:* 1315 Whitshed Rd. *City:* Cordova *State:* AK *Visitors welcome?* Yes *Hours:* Daily *Admission:* FREE *Operated by:* Cordova Rose Lodge *NR?* No *NHL?* No *Year established/built:* 1992 *Latitude:* 60.5391 *Latitude:* -145.7530

POINT RETREAT LIGHTHOUSE
Established in 1903, the current Point Retreat Lighthouse was constructed in 1924 and is still an active aid to navigation. It is now managed by a not-for-profit. *Address:* Admirality Island *City:* Douglas *State:* AK *Visitors welcome?* Yes *Hours:* By appointment *Admission:* Contact attraction directly *Operated by:* Alaska Lighthouse Association *NR?* Yes *NHL?* No *Year established/built:* 1903 *Latitude:* 57.6269 *Latitude:* -134.3630

POINT SHERMAN LIGHTHOUSE
Established in 1904, the Point Sherman Lighthouse was downgraded to a minor light by World War I. Today, only a dayboard and a light mark the location of the original structures. *Address:* Point Sherman Light *City:* Juneau *State:* AK *Visitors welcome?* No *Operated by:* U.S. Coast Guard (District 17) *NR?* No *NHL?* No *Year established/built:* 1904 *Latitude:* 58.8550 *Latitude:* -135.1520

CHAPTER 5 – LIGHTHOUSES & LIGHTSHIPS

SENTINEL ISLAND LIGHTHOUSE
Established in 1902. the current Sentinel Island Lighthouse was constructed in 1935 and automated in 1966. It is still an active aid to navigation and managed by a local historical society. *Address:* Sentinel Island Light *State:* AK *Phone:* 907-586-5338 *Visitors welcome?* Yes *Hours:* Contact attraction directly *Admission:* Contact attraction directly *Operated by:* Gastineau Channel Historical Society *NR?* Yes *NHL?* No *Year established/built:* 1902 *Latitude:* 58.5461 *Latitude:* -134.9230

TREE POINT LIGHTHOUSE
Established in 1903, the current Tree Point Lighthouse was constructed in 1935 and automated in 1969. It is still an active aid to navigation. *Address:* Misty Fjords National Monument *City:* Ketchikan *State:* AK *Visitors welcome?* No *Operated by:* U.S. Coast Guard (District 17) *NR?* No *NHL?* No *Year established/built:* 1903 *Latitude:* 55.6217 *Latitude:* -130.6070

CALIFORNIA

ALCATRAZ ISLAND LIGHTHOUSE
Established in 1853, the original tower of the Alcatraz Lighthouse was destroyed by the 1906 San Francisco Earthquake. The replacement tower was constructed shortly afterward, and it is now part of the Alcatraz Island National Historic Landmark. *Address:* Alcatraz Island Light *City:* San Francisco *State:* CA *Visitors welcome?* Yes *Hours:* By appointment *Admission:* FREE *Operated by:* Golden Gate National Parks *NR?* Yes *NHL?* No *Year established/built:* 1853 *Latitude:* 37.8262 *Latitude:* -122.4220

ANACAPA ISLAND LIGHTHOUSE
Established in 1930 and built in 1932, the Anacapa Island Lighthouse is now part of Channels Islands National Park. *Address:* Anacapa Island Light *State:* CA *Zip:* 93001 *Visitors welcome?* Yes *Hours:* Grounds open, tower closed *Admission:* FREE *Operated by:* Channel Islands National Park *NR?* Yes *NHL?* No *Year established/built:* 1930 *Latitude:* 34.0156 *Latitude:* -119.3580

ANO NUEVO LIGHTHOUSE
Established in 1872, the tower for Ano Nuevo Lighthouse off Pigeon Point near Santa Cruz was first lit in 1890, but the Coast Guard shut it down in 1948. The ruins are now in the Ano Nuevo State Reserve. *Address:* New Years Creek Road *City:* Pescadero *State:* CA *Visitors welcome?* No *Operated by:* California Dept. of Parks and Recreation *NR?* No *NHL?* No *Year established/built:* 1872 *Latitude:* 37.1082 *Latitude:* -122.3370

BATTERY POINT LIGHTHOUSE
Established and built in 1855, the Battery Point Lighthouse was named for cannon salvaged from a nearby wreck. Automated in 1953, the lighthouse, known officially as the Crescent City Lighthouse, is now operated by the Del Norte Historical Society as a museum. *Address:* Battery Point Light *City:* Crescent City *State:* CA *Visitors welcome?* Yes *Hours:* 10 a.m. to 4 p.m., Wednesday through Sunday, April through September *Admission:* Contact attraction directly *Operated by:* Del Norte County Historical Society *NR?* Yes *NHL?* No *Year established/built:* 1855 *Latitude:* 41.7440 *Latitude:* -124.2030

CHAPTER 5 – LIGHTHOUSES & LIGHTSHIPS

California Coastal Lighthouse Tour Itinerary

1. *St. George Reef*
2. *Battery Point (Crescent City)*
3. *Trinidad Head (Trinidad)*
4. *Old Table Bluff (Eureka)*
5. *Punta Gorda*
6. *Cape Mendocino*
7. *Point Cabrillo (Mendocino)*
8. *Point Reyes (Point Reyes Station)*

CHAPTER 5 – LIGHTHOUSES & LIGHTSHIPS

9. *Farallon Islands*
10. *Alcatraz Island (San Francisco Bay)*
11. *Point Montara (Moss Beach)*
12. *Pigeon Point (Pescadero)*
13. *Walton (Santa Cruz)*
14. *Point Pinos (Pacific Grove)*
15. *Point Sur (Carmel)*
16. *Piedras Blancas*
17. *Port Hartford (San Luis Obispo)*
18. *Point Conception (Concepcion)*
19. *Santa Barbara*
20. *Port Hueneme*
21. *Anacapa Island*
22. *Point Vicente (Rancho Palos Verdes)*
23. *Point Fermin (San Pedro)*
24. *Old Point Loma (San Diego)*

California lighthouses mark some of the most spectacular maritime scenery in the country. Begin with Battery Point in Crescent City and follow U.S. Highway 101 to the California Highway 1 cutoff. Then follow Highway 1 all the way to where it joins Interstate 5 near Dana Point. Then make your way to San Diego and Old Point Loma at the Cabrillo National Monument. It's a five to ten day trip--and unforgettable.

CAPE MENDOCINO LIGHTHOUSE
Constructed in 1867 and 1868 on the westernmost tip of California, Cape Mendocino Lighthouse warned mariners away from one of the most dangerous shorelines in the state. *Address:* Cape Medocino *State:* CA *Visitors welcome?* Yes *Hours:* Grounds open, tower closed *Admission:* FREE *Operated by:* Cape Mendocino Lighthouse Preservation Society - Shelter Cove *NR?* No *NHL?* No *Year established/built:* 1867 *Latitude:* 40.4401 *Latitude:* -124.4100

CARQUINEZ STRAIT LIGHTHOUSE
Built in 1910, the lighthouse was one of seventeen stations in the San Francisco Bay Area, In 1955, the U.S. Coast Guard automated the light and fog horn, and the light station residence was sold to a private owner who moved the building to its present position. *Address:* 2000 Glen Cove Marina Rd *City:* Vallejo *State:* CA *Zip:* 94591 *Phone:* 707-552-3236 *Web:* www.glencovemarina.net *Email:* glencovemarina@gmail.com *Visitors welcome?* Yes *Hours:* Contact attraction directly *Admission:* Contact attraction directly *Operated by:* Glen Cove Marina *NR?* No *NHL?* No *Year established/built:* 1910 *Latitude:* 38.0693 *Latitude:* -122.2130

EAST BROTHER ISLAND LIGHTHOUSE
Built on San Pablo Strait in 1874 at the request of ship captains, East Brother Island Lighthouse is at the point where the San Francisco and San Pablo bays meet. It is now a bed & breakfast. *Address:* East Brother Island Light *City:* North Richmond *State:* CA *Visitors welcome?* Yes *Hours:* By appointment *Admission:* Contact attraction directly *Operated by:* East Brother Light Station, Inc. *NR?* Yes *NHL?* No *Year established/built:* 1874 *Latitude:* 37.9633 *Latitude:* -122.4330

FARALLON ISLAND LIGHTHOUSE
Established and built in 1855, the Farallon Islands Lighthouse was constructed on the tallest point of the rocky, lonely Farallon Islands. The station was automated in 1972, and the islands are now part of the Farallon Islands National Wildlife Refuge. *Address:* Farallon Islands *City:* San Francisco *State:* CA *Zip:* 94560 *Visitors*

CHAPTER 5 – LIGHTHOUSES & LIGHTSHIPS

welcome? No *Operated by:* U.S. Coast Guard (District 11) *NR?* No *NHL?* No *Year established/built:* 1855 *Latitude:* 37.6993 *Latitude:* -123.0040

FORT POINT LIGHTHOUSE
Established in 1853, the current Fort Point Lighthouse was built two years later and served until 1934, when navigational aids on the Golden Gate Bridge replaced it. The lighthouse is now part of Fort Point National Historic Site. *Address:* Fort Point Light *City:* San Francisco *State:* CA *Visitors welcome?* Yes *Hours:* Thursday through Monday, 10 a.m. to 5 p.m. *Admission:* FREE *Operated by:* Golden Gate National Parks *NR?* Yes *NHL?* No *Year established/built:* 1853 *Latitude:* 37.8110 *Latitude:* -122.4770

HUMBOLDT HARBOR LIGHTHOUSE
Established and built in 1856, the Humboldt Harbor Lighthouse served until 1896, when the site was abandoned by the Coast Guard. Only the ruins of the lighthouse remains, although the original Fresnel lens is at the nearby Humboldt Bay Maritime Museum. *City:* Samoa *State:* CA *Visitors welcome?* Yes *Hours:* Dawn to dusk *Admission:* FREE *Operated by:* Samoa Dunes Recreation Area *NR?* No *NHL?* No *Year established/built:* 1856 *Latitude:* 40.8187 *Latitude:* -124.1860

LIME POINT LIGHTHOUSE
Established in 1833, the original tower, now gone, was built in 1900. Only the fog signal building remains of the automated station. *Address:* Lime Point Light *City:* Sausalito *State:* CA *Visitors welcome?* No *Operated by:* Golden Gate National Parks *NR?* No *NHL?* No *Year established/built:* 1833 *Latitude:* 37.8255 *Latitude:* -122.4780

LONG BEACH HARBOR LIGHTHOUSE
Completed in 1949, the Long Beach Harbor Lighthouse guides container ships into one of the busiest container shipping facilities in the world. *Address:* Long Beach Light *City:* Long Beach *State:* CA *Visitors welcome?* No *Operated by:* U.S. Coast Guard (District 11) *NR?* No *NHL?* No *Year established/built:* 1949 *Latitude:* 33.7231 *Latitude:* -118.1870

LOS ANGELES HARBOR LIGHTHOUSE
Address: Los Angeles Harbor Light *City:* San Pedro *State:* CA *Visitors welcome?* Yes *Hours:* Dawn to dusk *Admission:* FREE *Operated by:* U.S. Coast Guard (District 11) *NR?* No *NHL?* No *Year established/built:* 1913 *Latitude:* 33.7083 *Latitude:* -118.2510

MILE ROCK LIGHTHOUSE
Established and built in 1906, the Mile Rock Lighthouse was automated in 1966 and a helicopter pad added by the Coast Guard. *Address:* Mile Rock *City:* San Francisco *State:* CA *Visitors welcome?* No *Operated by:* U.S. Coast Guard (District 11) *NR?* No *NHL?* No *Year established/built:* 1906 *Latitude:* 37.7928 *Latitude:* -122.5100

NEW POINT LOMA LIGHTHOUSE
Built in 1889 to replace the Old Point Loma Lighthouse, the New Point Loma Lighthouse on Pigeon Point is used today as Coast Guard quarters. *Address:* Cabrillo National Monument *City:* San Diego *State:* CA *Visitors welcome?* No *Operated by:* U.S. Coast Guard (District 11) *NR?* No *NHL?* No *Year established/built:* 1889 *Latitude:* 37.1819 *Latitude:* -122.3950

OAKLAND HARBOR LIGHTHOUSE
Established and built in 1890, the 1903 Oakland Harbor Lighthouse building was moved in the 1960s to its current location at Embarcadero Cove Marina. It is now a restaurant. *Address:* 1951 Embarcadero East *City:* Oakland *State:* CA *Zip:* 94606 *Phone:* 510-536-2050 *Web:* www.quinnslighthouse.com *Email:* quinnslighthouse@aol.com *Visitors welcome?* Yes *Hours:* Contact attraction directly *Admission:* FREE *Operated by:* Quinn's

CHAPTER 5 – LIGHTHOUSES & LIGHTSHIPS

Lighthouse Restaurant & Pub *NR?* No *NHL?* No *Year established/built:* 1890 *Latitude:* 37.7817 *Latitude:* -122.2430

OLD POINT LOMA LIGHTHOUSE
One of the first set of eight lighthouses on the California coast, Old Point Loma stands near the place where the first European set foot on California in 1542. Completed in 1854, the station was the highest in the nation for many years, at 462 feet above sea level. *Address:* Point Loma Light *City:* San Diego *State:* CA *Zip:* 92106-3601 *Phone:* 619-557-5450 *Visitors welcome?* Yes *Hours:* Daily, 9 a.m. to 5 p.m. *Admission:* FREE *Operated by:* Cabrillo National Monument *NR?* Yes *NHL?* No *Year established/built:* 1854 *Latitude:* 32.6717 *Latitude:* -117.2410

PIEDRAS BLANCAS LIGHTHOUSE
Named for a white rock outcrop near the point itself, Piedras Blancas Lighthouse was built in 1875. A two-story Victorian-style dwelling was added later that year, though it was later torn down. *Address:* Piedras Blancas Light Station *State:* CA *Visitors welcome?* Yes *Hours:* By appointment *Admission:* Donation requested for tours. *Operated by:* Piedras Blancas Light Station Association *NR?* Yes *NHL?* No *Year established/built:* 1875 *Latitude:* 35.6653 *Latitude:* -121.2840

PIGEON POINT LIGHTHOUSE
Built in 1872, the Pigeon Point Lighthouse south of San Francisco is one of the tallest in the U.S. at 115 feet. It is still an active aid to navigation. *Address:* 210 Pigeon Point Road *City:* Pescadero *State:* CA *Zip:* 94060 *Phone:* 650-879-2120 *Web:* www.parks.ca.gov/default.asp?page_id=533 *Visitors welcome?* Yes *Hours:* 8 a.m. to sunset *Admission:* Contact attraction directly *Operated by:* California Dept. of Parks and Recreation *NR?* Yes *NHL?* No *Year established/built:* 1872 *Latitude:* 37.1821 *Latitude:* -122.3940

POINT ARENA LIGHTHOUSE
Established in 1870, the current Point Arena Lighthouse was constructed in 1908, and it is still an active aid to navigation. The lighthouse was automated in 1977, and the keepers quarters are rented out to visitors. *Address:* Point Arena Light *City:* Point Arena *State:* CA *Zip:* 95468 *Phone:* 877-725-4448 *Web:* www.pointarenalighthouse.com *Email:* palight@mcn.org *Visitors welcome?* Yes *Hours:* Daily, 10 a.m. to 3:30 p.m. *Admission:* $5 adults; $1 children under 12 *Operated by:* Point Arena Lighthouse Keepers *NR?* No *NHL?* No *Year established/built:* 1870 *Latitude:* 38.9547 *Latitude:* -123.7410

POINT ARGUELLO LIGHTHOUSE
First lit in 1901, the Point Arguello Lighthouse looked over one of the most treacherous areas of California coastline, famed for taking dozens of ships and many lives, before and after it began operations. *Address:* Point Arguello Light *State:* CA *Visitors welcome?* No *Operated by:* U.S. Coast Guard (District 11) *NR?* No *NHL?* No *Year established/built:* 1901 *Latitude:* 34.5769 *Latitude:* -120.6470

POINT BLUNT LIGHTHOUSE
Point Blunt Lighthouse, really a large shed on a prominent point on Angel Island, helped marked the entrance to San Francisco Bay beginning in 1915. The lighthouse was torn down in the 1960s when the Coast Guard automated the station. *Address:* Point Blunt Light *City:* San Francisco *State:* CA *Visitors welcome?* No *Operated by:* U.S. Coast Guard (District 11) *NR?* No *NHL?* No *Year established/built:* 1915 *Latitude:* 37.8531 *Latitude:* -122.4190

POINT BONITA LIGHTHOUSE
Established in 1855, the current Point Bonita Lighthouse was constructed in 1877 and automated in 1980. It is still an active aid to navigation. *Address:* Point Bonita Lighthouse *City:* Sausalito *State:* CA *Visitors welcome?*

No *Operated by:* Golden Gate National Parks *NR?* Yes *NHL?* No *Year established/built:* 1855 *Latitude:* 37.8159 *Latitude:* -122.5290

POINT CABRILLO LIGHTHOUSE
Established and built in 1909, the Point Cabrillo Lighthouse was automated in 1973 and is still an active aid to navigation. *Address:* Point Cabrillo Light *City:* Mendocino *State:* CA *Visitors welcome?* Yes *Hours:* Daily, 9 a.m. to dusk *Admission:* FREE *Operated by:* Point Cabrillo Lightkeepers Association *NR?* Yes *NHL?* No *Year established/built:* 1909 *Latitude:* 39.3483 *Latitude:* -123.8260

POINT CONCEPTION LIGHTHOUSE
Established in 1854, the current Point Conception Lighthouse was constructed in 1882 and automated in 1973. It is still an active aid to navigation. *Address:* Point Conception Lighthouse *City:* Concepcion *State:* CA *Visitors welcome?* No *Operated by:* U.S. Coast Guard (District 11) *NR?* Yes *NHL?* No *Year established/built:* 1856 *Latitude:* 34.4485 *Latitude:* -120.4710

POINT DIABLO LIGHTHOUSE
Established and built in 1923, the Point Diablo Lighthouse is now an automated aid to navigation. *Address:* Point Diablo Light *City:* Sausalito *State:* CA *Visitors welcome?* No *Operated by:* Golden Gate National Parks *NR?* No *NHL?* No *Year established/built:* 1923 *Latitude:* 37.8200 *Latitude:* -122.5000

 ## POINT FERMIN LIGHTHOUSE
Established and buit in 1874, the Point Fermin Lighthouse was deactivated in 1942, and it is now owned by the City of Los Angeles as a public facility. *Address:* 807 W. Paseo Del Mar *City:* San Pedro *State:* CA *Zip:* 90731 *Phone:* 310-241-0684 *Web:* www.pointferminlighthouse.org *Visitors welcome?* Yes *Hours:* Tuesday through Sunday, 1 p.m. to 4 p.m. *Admission:* Donation requested *Operated by:* Point Fermin Lighthouse Historic Site and Museum *NR?* Yes *NHL?* No *Year established/built:* 1874 *Latitude:* 33.7122 *Latitude:* -118.3040

POINT HUENEME LIGHTHOUSE
Established in 1874, the current Point Hueneme Lighthouse was constructed in 1941, and it is still an active aid to navigation. *Address:* Point Hueneme Light *City:* Port Hueneme *State:* CA *Zip:* 93041 *Phone:* 310-541-0334 *Web:* huenemelight.org *Visitors welcome?* Yes *Hours:* Contact attraction directly *Admission:* Contact attraction directly *Operated by:* U.S. Coast Guard (District 11) *NR?* No *NHL?* No *Year established/built:* 1874 *Latitude:* 34.1450 *Latitude:* -119.2100

POINT KNOX LIGHTHOUSE
Established in 1885, the Point Knox Lighthouse is located on the southwest corner of Angel Island in San Francisco Bay. *Address:* Point Knox *State:* CA *Visitors welcome?* No *Operated by:* California Dept. of Parks and Recreation *NR?* No *NHL?* No *Year established/built:* 1885 *Latitude:* 37.8564 *Latitude:* -122.4420

POINT MONTARA LIGHTHOUSE
Established in 1875, the current Point Montara Lighthouse was constructed in 1928. Automated in 1970, the lighthouse is still an active aid to navigation. *Address:* Point Montara Light *City:* Moss Beach *State:* CA *Visitors welcome?* Yes *Hours:* Grounds open, tower closed. *Admission:* FREE *Operated by:* California Dept. of Parks and Recreation *NR?* Yes *NHL?* No *Year established/built:* 1875 *Latitude:* 37.5363 *Latitude:* -122.5190

POINT PINOS LIGHTHOUSE
Established and built in 1855, the Point Pinos Lighthouse was automated in 1975. The lighthouse was decommissioned in 1993, but it is still operated as a private aid to navigation. *Address:* 165 Forest Avenue *City:* Pacific Grove *State:* CA *Zip:* 93950 *Phone:* 831-648-5716 *Web:* www.pgmuseum.org *Visitors wel-

come? Yes *Hours:* 1 p.m. to 4 p.m., Thursday through Monday *Admission:* $1 youths; $2 adults *Operated by:* Pacific Grove Museum of Natural History *NR?* Yes *NHL?* No *Year established/built:* 1855 *Latitude:* 36.6219 *Latitude:* -121.9170

POINT REYES LIGHTHOUSE
Established and built in 1870, the Point Reyes Lighthouse was deactivated in 1975. It is part of the Point Reyes National Seashore. *Address:* Point Reyes National Seashore *City:* Point Reyes Station *State:* CA *Zip:* 94956 *Phone:* 415-464-5100 *Visitors welcome?* Yes *Hours:* 10 a.m. to 4:30 p.m., Thursday through Monday *Admission:* FREE *Operated by:* Point Reyes National Seashore *NR?* Yes *NHL?* No *Year established/built:* 1870 *Latitude:* 38.0670 *Latitude:* -122.8760

POINT SUR LIGHTHOUSE
Established and buit in 1889, the sandstone Point Sur Lighthouse was automated in 1972 and is still an active aid to navigation. *Address:* Point Sur Lighthouse Reservation *City:* Carmel *State:* CA *Zip:* 93923 *Phone:* 831-625-4419 *Web:* www.pointsur.org *Email:* info@pointsur.org *Visitors welcome?* Yes *Hours:* Daily *Admission:* $8 adults; children six to 17, $4; under six FREE. *Operated by:* Point Sur State Historic Park and Lighthouse *NR?* Yes *NHL?* No *Year established/built:* 1889 *Latitude:* 36.3064 *Latitude:* -121.9020

POINT VICENTE LIGHTHOUSE
Established and buit in 1926, the Point Vicente Lighthouse was automated in 1973 and is still an active aid to navigation. *Address:* Point Vicente Light *City:* Rancho Palos Verdes *State:* CA *Zip:* 90275 *Phone:* 310-541-0334 *Visitors welcome?* Yes *Hours:* Some tours *Admission:* Contact attraction directly *Operated by:* U.S. Coast Guard (District 11) *NR?* Yes *NHL?* No *Year established/built:* 1926 *Latitude:* 33.7419 *Latitude:* -118.4110

PUNTA GORDA LIGHTHOUSE
Established in 1911 and built the following year, the Punta Gorda Lighthouse was deactivated in 1951. *Address:* Punta Gorda Light *State:* CA *Visitors welcome?* Yes *Hours:* Daily *Admission:* FREE *Operated by:* King Range National Conservation Area *NR?* Yes *NHL?* No *Year established/built:* 1911 *Latitude:* 40.2493 *Latitude:* -124.3500

SAN LUIS OBISPO LIGHTHOUSE
Established and built in 1890, the San Luis Obispo Lighthouse is also known as the Port Harford Lighthouse. Deactivated in 1975, the station was recently restored by a local not-for-profit organization. *Address:* San Luis Light *City:* San Luis Obispo *State:* CA *Visitors welcome?* Yes *Hours:* Contact attraction directly *Admission:* Contact attraction directly *Operated by:* Point San Luis Lighthouse Keepers *NR?* Yes *NHL?* No *Year established/built:* 1890 *Latitude:* 35.1601 *Latitude:* -120.7600

SANTA BARBARA LIGHTHOUSE
Established in 1856, the original lighthouse was lost in a 1925 earthquake and is now a skeletal metal tower. *Address:* Santa Barbara Light *City:* Santa Barbara *State:* CA *Visitors welcome?* No *Operated by:* U.S. Coast Guard (District 11) *NR?* No *NHL?* No *Year established/built:* 1856 *Latitude:* 34.3958 *Latitude:* -119.7230

SANTA CRUZ BREAKWATER LIGHTHOUSE
Constructed in 2001, the Santa Cruz breakwater has shown a beacon since the 1960s. The local community wanted a more traditional-looking lighthouse, and money was raised to build the current structure. *Address:* Santa Cruz Breakwater Light *City:* Santa Cruz *State:* CA *Visitors welcome?* Yes *Hours:* Grounds open, tower closed *Admission:* FREE *Operated by:* U.S. Coast Guard (District 11) *NR?* No *NHL?* No *Year established/built:* 2001 *Latitude:* 36.9604 *Latitude:* -122.0020

CHAPTER 5 – LIGHTHOUSES & LIGHTSHIPS

SANTA CRUZ LIGHTHOUSE

Established in 1869, the current Santa Cruz Lighthouse is a reconstruction of a lighthouse that was demolished in 1948. The structure is now home to the Santa Cruz Surfing Museum. *Address:* 701 West Cliff Drive *City:* Santa Cruz *State:* CA *Zip:* 95060 *Phone:* 831-420-6289 *Web:* www.santacruzsurfingmuseum.org *Visitors welcome?* Yes *Hours:* Winter: Thursday through Monday, noon to 4 p.m.; Summer: Summer hours (July 4th through Labor Day): Wednesday through Monday, 10 a.m. to 5 p.m. *Admission:* FREE *Operated by:* Santa Cruz Surfing Museum *NR?* No *NHL?* No *Year established/built:* 1869 *Latitude:* 36.9687 *Latitude:* -122.0160

SOUTHAMPTON SHOALS LIGHTHOUSE

Built in 1905, the Southampton Shoal lighthouse stood on navigational hazard along the eastern side of the shipping channel that runs between Angel Island and the Tiburon Peninsula near Berkeley. *Address:* Tinsley Island *City:* Stockton *State:* CA *Phone:* 209-607-3199 *Visitors welcome?* Yes *Hours:* Members only *Admission:* Members only *Operated by:* St. Francis Yacht Club *NR?* No *NHL?* No *Year established/built:* 1905 *Latitude:* 38.0377 *Latitude:* -121.4960

ST. GEORGE REEF LIGHTHOUSE

Established in 1867, the current St. George Reef Lighthouse was deactivated from 1975 to 2002, when it was returned to active service. It is often known as the most expensive lighthouse in America, taking ten years to construct. *Address:* St. George Reef Light *State:* CA *Visitors welcome?* No *Operated by:* St. George Reef Lighthouse Preservation Society *NR?* Yes *NHL?* No *Year established/built:* 1867 *Latitude:* 41.8363 *Latitude:* -124.3760

TABLE BLUFF LIGHTHOUSE

Established and built in 1892, the Table Bluff Lighthouse was moved to its current location in 1987. *Address:* Table Bluff Light *City:* Eureka *State:* CA *Zip:* 95502 *Visitors welcome?* Yes *Hours:* Grounds only; tower is closed *Admission:* FREE *Operated by:* Humboldt Bay Harbor Recreation & Conservation District *NR?* No *NHL?* No *Year established/built:* 1890 *Latitude:* 40.6958 *Latitude:* -124.2740

TRINIDAD HEAD LIGHTHOUSE

Established in 1866, the current Trinidad Head Lighthouse was buit in 1871 and automated in 1974. It is still an active aid to navigation. *Address:* Trinidad Head Light *City:* Trinidad *State:* CA *Visitors welcome?* No *Operated by:* U.S. Coast Guard (District 11) *NR?* Yes *NHL?* No *Year established/built:* 1866 *Latitude:* 41.0518 *Latitude:* -124.1510

TRINIDAD MEMORIAL LIGHTHOUSE

The Trinidad Memorial Lighthouse was constructed in 1949 as a memorial to local residents lost at sea. The bell is rung daily at noon. The structure was improved with new windows and a new dome in 1998. The actual Trinidad Head Lighthouse is located nearby. *Address:* Edwards Street *City:* Trinidad *State:* CA *Zip:* 95570 *Visitors welcome?* Yes *Hours:* Grounds open, tower closed *Admission:* FREE *Operated by:* City of Trinidad *NR?* No *NHL?* No *Year established/built:* 1949 *Latitude:* 41.0585 *Latitude:* -124.1450

YERBA BUENA LIGHTHOUSE

Established and built in 1875, the Yerba Buena Lighthouse, also known as the Goat Island Lighthouse, was automated in 1958 and is still an active aid to navigation. The keepers quarters, built in 1873, is home to the local U.S. Coast Guard district commandant. *Address:* Yerba Buena Light *City:* San Francisco *State:* CA *Visitors welcome?* No *Operated by:* U.S. Coast Guard (District 11) *NR?* Yes *NHL?* No *Year established/built:* 1873 *Latitude:* 37.8073 *Latitude:* -122.3630

HAWAII

BARBERS POINT LIGHTHOUSE
Established in 1888, the current Barbers Point Lighthouse was constructed in 1933. Automated since 1964, the lighthouse is still an active aid to navigation. *Address:* Barbers Point Light *City:* Honolulu *State:* HI *Visitors welcome?* Yes *Hours:* Grounds only *Admission:* FREE *Operated by:* U.S. Coast Guard (District 14) *NR?* No *NHL?* No *Year established/built:* 1888 *Latitude:* 21.2964 *Latitude:* -158.1060

CAPE KUMUKAHI LIGHTHOUSE
Established in 1929, the current skeletal metal tower of the Cape Kumukahi Lighthouse was constructed in 1934. Automated in 1960, the lighthouse is still an active aid to navigation. *Address:* Cape Kumukahi Light *City:* Hilo *State:* HI *Visitors welcome?* Yes *Hours:* Grounds only *Admission:* FREE *Operated by:* U.S. Coast Guard (District 14) *NR?* No *NHL?* No *Year established/built:* 1929 *Latitude:* 19.5160 *Latitude:* -154.8110

DIAMOND HEAD LIGHTHOUSE
Established in 1899, the current Diamond Head Lighthouse was constructed in 1918. Automated in 1924, the light is still an active aid to navigation. It is now housing for Coast Guard personnel. *Address:* Below Diamond Head State Monument *City:* Honolulu *State:* HI *Visitors welcome?* No *Operated by:* U.S. Coast Guard (District 14) *NR?* Yes *NHL?* No *Year established/built:* 1899 *Latitude:* 21.2593 *Latitude:* -157.8110

KAUHOLA POINT LIGHTHOUSE
Established in 1897, the current Kauhola Point Lighthouse was constructed in the 1930s. Automated in 1951, the lighthouse is still an active aid to navigation. *Address:* Kauhola Point Light *State:* HI *Visitors welcome?* Yes *Hours:* Grounds only *Admission:* FREE *Operated by:* U.S. Coast Guard (District 14) *NR?* No *NHL?* No *Year established/built:* 1897 *Latitude:* 20.2453 *Latitude:* -155.7720

KILAUEA POINT LIGHTHOUSE
Established and built in 1913, the Kilauea Point Lighthouse was deactivated in 1976. The lighthouse is now within a national wildlife refuge. *Address:* Kilauea Point Light *City:* Kilauea *State:* HI *Zip:* 96754 *Phone:* 808-828-1413 *Visitors welcome?* Yes *Hours:* Grounds only *Admission:* FREE *Operated by:* Kilauea Point National Wildlife Refuge *NR?* Yes *NHL?* No *Year established/built:* 1913 *Latitude:* 22.2316 *Latitude:* -159.4020

LAHAINA LIGHTHOUSE
Ordered constructed by King Kamehameha in 1840, the first Lahaina Lighthouse was a wooden structure to guide ships into Lahaina Harbor. A second lighthouse was constructed, replacing the old wooden tower, sometime before 1860. *Address:* Lahiana Harbor *City:* Lahaina *State:* HI *Zip:* 96761 *Phone:* 808-661-3262 *Visitors welcome?* Yes *Hours:* Grounds only *Admission:* FREE *Operated by:* Lahaina Restoration Foundation *NR?* No *NHL?* No *Year established/built:* 1840 *Latitude:* 20.8739 *Latitude:* -156.6810

MAKAPUU LIGHTHOUSE
Established and built in 1909, the Makapu'u Lighthouse was automated in 1974 and is still an active aid to navigation. *Address:* Makapuu Light *City:* Waimanalo Beach *State:* HI *Visitors welcome?* Yes *Hours:* Grounds only *Admission:* FREE *Operated by:* U.S. Coast Guard (District 14) *NR?* Yes *NHL?* No *Year established/built:* 1909 *Latitude:* 21.3099 *Latitude:* -157.6500

MOLOKAI LIGHTHOUSE
Established and constructed in 1909, the Molokai Lighthouse, also called the Kalaupapa Lighthouse, was automated in 1970 and is still an active aid to navigation. It is now part of the Kalaupapa National Historical

CHAPTER 5 – LIGHTHOUSES & LIGHTSHIPS

Park. *Address:* Kalaupapa National Historical Park *City:* Kalaupapa *State:* HI *Zip:* 96742 *Phone:* 808-567-6802 *Visitors welcome?* No *Operated by:* Kalaupapa National Historic Park *NR?* Yes *NHL?* No *Year established/built:* 1909 *Latitude:* 21.1925 *Latitude:* -156.9860

NAWILIWILI LIGHTHOUSE
Established in 1906, the current Nawiliwili Lighthouse was constructed in 1933. Automated in 1953, the lighthouse is still an active aid to navigation. *Address:* Ninini Point *City:* Lihue *State:* HI *Visitors welcome?* Yes *Hours:* Grounds only *Admission:* FREE *Operated by:* U.S. Coast Guard (District 14) *NR?* No *NHL?* No *Year established/built:* 1906 *Latitude:* 21.9548 *Latitude:* -159.3360

OREGON

CAPE ARAGO LIGHTHOUSE
Established in 1866, the current Cape Arago Lighthouse, also called the Cape Gregory Lighthouse, was constructed in 1934 and automated in 1966. Now deactivated, the lighthouse is served by an 1889 iron bridge. *Address:* Cape Arago Light *City:* Coos Bay *State:* OR *Visitors welcome?* No *Operated by:* U.S. Coast Guard (District 13) *NR?* Yes *NHL?* No *Year established/built:* 1866 *Latitude:* 43.3436 *Latitude:* -124.3750

Got a prize-winning photo of a West Coast lighthouse? Post it at www.fyddeye.com.

CAPE BLANCO LIGHTHOUSE
Established and built in 1870, the Cape Blanco Lighthouse is the oldest and southernmost of Oregon's Lighthouses. It is now within a state park, although the lighthouse itself is managed by the federal Bureau of Land Management. *Address:* Cape Blanco Light *City:* Port Orford *State:* OR *Zip:* 97465 *Phone:* 541-332-0248 *Web:* www.oregonstateparks.org/park_62.php *Visitors welcome?* Yes *Hours:* Daily, April to October *Admission:* $2 adults, $1 children under 12, $5 family *Operated by:* Friends of Cape Blanco *NR?* Yes *NHL?* No *Year established/built:* 1870 *Latitude:* 42.8358 *Latitude:* -124.5610

CAPE MEARES LIGHTHOUSE
Established and built in 1890, the Cape Meares Lighthouse marks the entrance to Tillamook Bay. The lighthouse, replaced by a nearby tower in 1963, is now a local attraction. *Address:* Cape Meares Light *City:* Tillamook *State:* OR *Phone:* 503-842-3182 *Web:* www.capemeareslighthouse.org *Email:* capemeareslighthouse@earthlink.net *Visitors welcome?* Yes *Hours:* Daily, April to October, 11 a.m. to 4 p.m. *Admission:* FREE *Operated by:* Friends of Cape Meares Lighthouse *NR?* Yes *NHL?* No *Year established/built:* 1890 *Latitude:* 45.4866 *Latitude:* -123.9780

CLEFT-OF-THE-ROCK LIGHTHOUSE
Built by maritime historian Jim Gibbs, the Clef-of-the-Rock Lighthouse, also called the Cape Perpetua Lighthouse, was added to the official list of navigation aids in 1979. *Address:* Cleft-of-the-Rock Light *City:* Yachats *State:* OR *Visitors welcome?* No *Operated by:* Private owner *NR?* No *NHL?* No *Year established/built:* 1976 *Latitude:* 44.2905 *Latitude:* -124.1110

COQUILLE RIVER LIGHTHOUSE
Established and built in 1896, the Coquille River Lighthouse, also called the Bandon Lighthouse, was constructed to guide lumber ships into the Coquille River and its sawmills. The lighthouse is now within a state park. *Address:* Coquille River Light *City:* Bandon *State:* OR *Zip:* 97411 *Phone:* 541-347-3501 *Visitors*

welcome? Yes *Hours:* Daily, May to October, 10 a.m. to 4 p.m.; Daily, June to September, Monday and Tuesday, 10 a.m. to 4 p.m., Wednesday to Sunday, 9 a.m. to 6 p.m. *Admission:* Contact attraction directly *Operated by:* Oregon Parks and Recreation Dept. *NR?* Yes *NHL?* No *Year established/built:* 1896 *Latitude:* 43.1239 *Latitude:* -124.4240

HECETA HEAD LIGHTHOUSE

Established and built in 1894, Heceta Head Lighthouse sits on a high bluff, making it one of the most photographed lighthouses in Oregon. Now part of a state park, the grounds include the keepers dwelling, which operates as a bed and breakfast. *Address:* Heceta Head Light *City:* Florence *State:* OR *Phone:* 541-547-3416 *Web:* www.oregonstateparks.org/park_124.php *Visitors welcome?* Yes *Hours:* May to September: Daily, 11 a.m. to 5 p.m.; March, April, October: daily, 11 a.m. to 3 p.m. *Admission:* FREE *Operated by:* Oregon Parks and Recreation Dept. *NR?* Yes *NHL?* No *Year established/built:* 1894 *Latitude:* 44.1374 *Latitude:* -124.1280

TILLAMOOK ROCK LIGHTHOUSE

Established and built in 1881, the Tillamook Rock Lighthouse, known affectionately at Terrible Tilly, was decommissioned by the U.S. Coast Guard in 1957. *Address:* Tillamook Rock Light *State:* OR *Visitors welcome?* No *Operated by:* Private owner *NR?* Yes *NHL?* No *Year established/built:* 1881 *Latitude:* 45.9375 *Latitude:* -124.0190

UMPQUA RIVER LIGHTHOUSE

Established in 1856, the current Umpqua River Lighthouse was constructed in 1894 to aid ships entering the Umpqua River. The light was automated in 1966, and it's now within a state park. *Address:* Umpqua River Light *State:* OR *Phone:* 541-957-7007 *Visitors welcome?* Yes *Hours:* May to October, daily, 10 a.m. to 4 p.m. *Admission:* Contact attraction directly *Operated by:* Douglas County Museum *NR?* Yes *NHL?* No *Year established/built:* 1856 *Latitude:* 43.6618 *Latitude:* -124.1980

WARRIOR ROCK LIGHT

Established in 1889, the current concrete Warrior Rock Lighthouse was constructed in the 1930s. It is still an active aid to navigation. *Address:* Warrior Rock Light *City:* St. Helens *State:* OR *Visitors welcome?* Yes *Hours:* Grounds only *Admission:* FREE *Operated by:* U.S. Coast Guard (District 13) *NR?* No *NHL?* No *Year established/built:* 1889 *Latitude:* 45.8486 *Latitude:* -122.7880

YAQUINA BAY LIGHTHOUSE

Established and built in 1871 and decommissioned just three years later, the Yaquina Bay Lighthouse is now a private aid to navigation and a museum. *Address:* Yaquina Bay Light *City:* Newport *State:* OR *Zip:* 97365 *Phone:* 541-265-5679 *Web:* www.yaquinalights.org *Visitors welcome?* Yes *Hours:* Daily, Memorial Day to September, 11 a.m. to 5 p.m.; October to Memorial Day, noon to 4 p.m. *Admission:* FREE *Operated by:* Friends of Yaquina Lighthouses *NR?* Yes *NHL?* No *Year established/built:* 1871 *Latitude:* 44.6241 *Latitude:* -124.0630

YAQUINA HEAD LIGHTHOUSE

Established and built in 1873, Yaquina Head Lighthouse on Cape Foulweather replaced the Yaquina Bay Lighthouse as an aid to navigation. Rehabilitated in 1992, the lighthouse is now a museum and local attraction. *Address:* Yaquina Head Light *City:* Agate Beach *State:* OR *Phone:* 541-574-3100 *Web:* www.yaquinalights.org *Visitors welcome?* Yes *Hours:* Summer, daily, 9 a.m to 5 p.m.; Winter, daily, 10 a.m. to 4 p.m. *Admission:* Contact attraction directly *Operated by:* Friends of Yaquina Lighthouses *NR?* Yes *NHL?* No *Year established/built:* 1873 *Latitude:* 44.6768 *Latitude:* -124.0790

CHAPTER 5 – LIGHTHOUSES & LIGHTSHIPS

WASHINGTON

ADMIRALTY HEAD LIGHTHOUSE
Established in 1860, the current Admiralty Head Lighthouse was constructed in 1903 and deactivated in 1922. It is now within a state park. *Address:* Admiralty Head Light *City:* Coupeville *State:* WA *Visitors welcome?* Yes *Hours:* June to August: Daily, 11 a.m. to 5 p.m; Other times, contact owner *Admission:* FREE *Operated by:* Keepers of Admiralty Head Lighthouse *NR?* Yes *NHL?* No *Year established/built:* 1860 *Latitude:* 48.1608 *Latitude:* -122.6810

ALKI POINT LIGHTHOUSE
Established in 1887, the current Alki Point Lighthouse was constructed in 1913. Automated in 1984, the light is still an active aid to navigation. *Address:* Alki Point Light *City:* Seattle *State:* WA *Visitors welcome?* Yes *Hours:* Contact attraction directly *Admission:* Contact attraction directly *Operated by:* U.S. Coast Guard (District 13) *NR?* No *NHL?* No *Year established/built:* 1913 *Latitude:* 47.5764 *Latitude:* -122.4210

BROWNS POINT LIGHTHOUSE
Established in 1887, the current Browns Point Lighthouse was constructed in 1933. Automated in 1963, the lighthouse is still an active aid to navigation. *Address:* 201 Tulalip Street NE *City:* Tacoma *State:* WA *Visitors welcome?* Yes *Hours:* Daily *Admission:* FREE *Operated by:* Points Northeast Historical Society *NR?* Yes *NHL?* No *Year established/built:* 1887 *Latitude:* 47.3054 *Latitude:* -122.4410

BURROWS ISLAND LIGHTHOUSE
Established and built in 1906, the Burrows Island Lighthouse is still an active aid to navigation. *Address:* Burrows Island Light *City:* Anacortes *State:* WA *Visitors welcome?* Yes *Hours:* Contact attraction directly *Admission:* FREE *Operated by:* Washington State Parks *NR?* No *NHL?* No *Year established/built:* 1906 *Latitude:* 48.4781 *Latitude:* -122.7140

BUSH POINT LIGHTHOUSE
The Bush Point Lighthouse was built in 1933 to guide mariners through the middle reaches of Admiralty Inlet into Puget Sound. *Address:* Bush Point *City:* Freeland *State:* WA *Visitors welcome?* Yes *Hours:* Daily *Admission:* FREE *Operated by:* U.S. Coast Guard (District 13) *NR?* No *NHL?* No *Year established/built:* 1933 *Latitude:* 48.0309 *Latitude:* -122.6070

CAPE DISAPPOINTMENT LIGHTHOUSE
Established and built in 1856, the Cape Disappointment Lighthouse is located within a state park and it is still an active aid to navigation. *Address:* Cape Disappointment Light *City:* Ilwaco *State:* WA *Visitors welcome?* Yes *Hours:* Call 360-642-3078 *Admission:* Call 360-642-3078 *Operated by:* U.S. Coast Guard (District 13) *NR?* Yes *NHL?* No *Year established/built:* 1856 *Latitude:* 46.2756 *Latitude:* -124.0520

CAPE FLATTERY LIGHTHOUSE
Established and built in 1857, the Cape Flattery Lighthouse was automated in 1977 and is still an active aid to navigation. *Address:* Cape Flattery Light *City:* Neah Bay *State:* WA *Visitors welcome?* Yes *Hours:* Contact attraction directly *Admission:* Contact attraction directly *Operated by:* U.S. Coast Guard (District 13) *NR?* Yes *NHL?* No *Year established/built:* 1857 *Latitude:* 48.3917 *Latitude:* -124.7370

CATTLE POINT LIGHTHOUSE
Built in 1935, the Cattle Point Lighthouse is near the San Juan Islands National Historical Park. *Address:* Cattle Point Light *City:* Friday Harbor *State:* WA *Visitors welcome?* Yes *Hours:* Contact attraction directly

Admission: Contact attraction directly *Operated by:* San Juan National Historical Park *NR?* No *NHL?* No *Year established/built:* 1935 *Latitude:* 48.4560 *Latitude:* -122.9620

DESTRUCTION ISLAND LIGHTHOUSE
Established and built in 1891, the Destruction Island Lighthouse was automated in 1968 and is still an active aid to navigation. *Address:* Destruction Island Light *State:* WA *Visitors welcome?* Yes *Operated by:* U.S. Coast Guard (District 13) *NR?* No *NHL?* No *Year established/built:* 1891 *Latitude:* 47.6752 *Latitude:* -124.4870

DOFFLEMYER POINT LIGHTHOUSE
The Dofflemyer Point Lighthouse was built in 1934 to guard the entrance to Budd Inlet, the location of the Port of Olympia and the state capital. *Address:* Dofflemyer Point Light *City:* Olympia *State:* WA *Visitors welcome?* No *Operated by:* U.S. Coast Guard (District 13) *NR?* No *NHL?* No *Year established/built:* 1934 *Latitude:* 47.1404 *Latitude:* -122.9070

EDIZ HOOK LIGHTHOUSE
Established by Abraham Lincoln in 1862, the Ediz Hook Lighthouse was first lit in 1865. The keepers residence is now a private home in Port Angeles. *Address:* Marine Dr. and W. Hill St. *City:* Port Angeles *State:* WA *Visitors welcome?* No *Operated by:* U.S. Coast Guard (District 13) *NR?* No *NHL?* No *Year established/built:* 1862 *Latitude:* 48.1287 *Latitude:* -123.4630

GIG HARBOR LIGHTHOUSE
Built in 1988, the Gig Harbor Lighthouse marks the entrance to Gig Harbor, a small inlet northwest of Tacoma. *Address:* Goodman Dr. NW and 26th Ave. NW *City:* Gig Harbor *State:* WA *Visitors welcome?* Yes *Hours:* Contact attraction directly *Admission:* Contact attraction directly *Operated by:* Gig Harbor Lighthouse Association *NR?* No *NHL?* No *Year established/built:* 1988 *Latitude:* 47.3293 *Latitude:* -122.5730

GRAYS HARBOR LIGHTHOUSE
Established and built in 1898, the Grays Harbor Lighthouse, also called the Westport Lighthouse, is still an active aid to navigation cared for a local maritime museum. *Address:* 1020 West Ocean Avenue *City:* Westport *State:* WA *Visitors welcome?* Yes *Hours:* Contact attraction directly *Admission:* Contact attraction directly *Operated by:* Westport South Beach Historical Society *NR?* Yes *NHL?* No *Year established/built:* 1898 *Latitude:* 46.8877 *Latitude:* -124.1170

LIME KILN LIGHTHOUSE
Established in 1914 and built in 1919, the Lime Kiln Lighthouse was automated in 1962 and is still an active aid to navigation. *Address:* Lime Kiln Point *City:* Friday Harbor *State:* WA *Visitors welcome?* Yes *Hours:* Daily, dawn to dusk *Admission:* FREE *Operated by:* Washington State Parks *NR?* Yes *NHL?* No *Year established/built:* 1914 *Latitude:* 48.5161 *Latitude:* -123.1520

MARROWSTONE POINT LIGHTHOUSE
Established in 1882, the current Marrowstone Point Lighthouse was built in 1912 and automated in 1962. It is still an active aid to navigation. *Address:* Marrowstone Light *City:* Port Townsend *State:* WA *Visitors welcome?* Yes *Hours:* Site open daily *Admission:* FREE *Operated by:* Washington State Parks *NR?* Yes *NHL?* No *Year established/built:* 1882 *Latitude:* 48.1018 *Latitude:* -122.6880

MUKILTEO LIGHTHOUSE
Established and built in 1906, the Mukilteo Lighthouse is still an active aid to navigation. It is now operated by a local not-for-profit organization. *Address:* Mukilteo Light *City:* Mukilteo *State:* WA *Visitors welcome?* Yes

CHAPTER 5 – LIGHTHOUSES & LIGHTSHIPS

Hours: April to September, weekends and holidays, noon to 5 p.m. *Admission:* FREE *Operated by:* Mukilteo Historical Society *NR?* Yes *NHL?* No *Year established/built:* 1906 *Latitude:* 47.9487 *Latitude:* -122.3060

NEW DUNGENESS LIGHTHOUSE
Established and built in 1857, the New Dungeness Lighthouse was automated in 1976 and is now operated by a local not-for-profit which allows guest lightkeepers. *Address:* Marine Dr. and Cays Rd. *City:* Sequim *State:* WA *Visitors welcome?* Yes *Hours:* Contact attraction directly *Admission:* Contact attraction directly *Operated by:* New Dungeness Light Station Association *NR?* Yes *NHL?* No *Year established/built:* 1857 *Latitude:* 48.1486 *Latitude:* -123.1670

NORTH HEAD LIGHTHOUSE
Established and built in 1889, the North Head Lighthouse is still an active aid to navigation within a state park. *Address:* North Head Light *City:* Ilwaco *State:* WA *Visitors welcome?* Yes *Hours:* Call 360-642-3078 *Admission:* Call 360-642-3078 *Operated by:* Keepers of the North Head Lighthouse *NR?* Yes *NHL?* No *Year established/built:* 1898 *Latitude:* 46.2989 *Latitude:* -124.0780

PATOS ISLAND LIGHTHOUSE
Established in 1893, the current Patos Island Lighthouse was built in 1908. Automated in 1974, the lighthouse is now within a state park. *Address:* Patos Island Light *State:* WA *Visitors welcome?* No *Hours:* Daily *Admission:* FREE *Operated by:* Washington State Parks *NR?* Yes *NHL?* No *Year established/built:* 1893 *Latitude:* 48.7890 *Latitude:* -122.9710

POINT NO POINT (WASHINGTON) LIGHTHOUSE
Established and built in 1879, the Point No Point Lighthouse gain earlier prominence as the site of a critical treaty between the U.S. and local Indian tribes giving the Americans control of most of Puget Sound. *Address:* Point No Point Light *City:* Hansville *State:* WA *Visitors welcome?* Yes *Hours:* Dawn to dusk *Admission:* FREE *Operated by:* Kitsap County Parks & Recreation *NR?* Yes *NHL?* No *Year established/built:* 1879 *Latitude:* 47.9119 *Latitude:* -122.5260

POINT ROBINSON LIGHTHOUSE
Established in 1885, the current Point Robinson Lighthouse was constructed in 1915. Automated in 1978, the light is still an active aid to navigation and operated by a local not-for-profit. *Address:* Point Robinson Light *City:* Vashon Island *State:* WA *Visitors welcome?* Yes *Hours:* Dawn to dusk *Admission:* FREE *Operated by:* Keepers of Point Robinson *NR?* No *NHL?* No *Year established/built:* 1885 *Latitude:* 47.3881 *Latitude:* -122.3750

POINT WILSON LIGHTHOUSE
Established in 1879, the Point Wilson Lighthouse marks the entrance to Admiralty Inlet, the main route to Puget Sound in the 19th and early 20th centuries. *Address:* Point Wilson Light *City:* Port Townsend *State:* WA *Visitors welcome?* Yes *Hours:* Contact attraction directly *Admission:* Contact attraction directly *Operated by:* U.S. Coast Guard (District 13) *NR?* No *NHL?* No *Year established/built:* 1914 *Latitude:* 48.1442 *Latitude:* -122.7550

SKUNK BAY LIGHTHOUSE
Built in 1965, the Skunk Bay Lighthouse near the northern tip of Bainbridge Island is a fully operational lighthouse owned and operated by a private association. *Address:* Skunk Bay Light *City:* Hansville *State:* WA *Visitors welcome?* No *Operated by:* Skunk Bay Lighthouse Association *NR?* No *NHL?* No *Year established/built:* 1965 *Latitude:* 47.9187 *Latitude:* -122.5540

CHAPTER 5 – LIGHTHOUSES & LIGHTSHIPS

SLIP POINT LIGHTHOUSE
Located at Slip Point on the east end of Clallam Bay, overlooking the Strait of Juan de Fuca, the Slip Point Lighthouse faded into local memory after the lighthouse and the structures were demolished in the mid-20th century. However, the original two-story lighthouse keepers residence is now the home of the Clallam County Sheriff's Department. *Address:* Slip Point Light *State:* WA *Visitors welcome?* Yes *Hours:* Contact attraction directly *Admission:* Contact attraction directly *Operated by:* Clallam County *NR?* No *NHL?* No *Year established/built:* 1905 *Latitude:* 48.2645 *Latitude:* -124.2510

TURN POINT LIGHTHOUSE
Established in 1893, the current Turn Point Lighthouse was constructed in 1936. Automated in 1974, the lighthouse is still an active aid to navigation. A local not-for-profit operates the lighthouse as a museum. *Address:* Turn Point *City:* Friday Harbor *State:* WA *Visitors welcome?* Yes *Hours:* Tuesday, Wednesday, Friday, Saturday, Sunday; Noon to 4 p.m. *Admission:* Donation *Operated by:* Turn Point Lighthouse Preservation Society *NR?* No *NHL?* No *Year established/built:* 1893 *Latitude:* 48.6884 *Latitude:* -123.2370

WEST POINT LIGHT STATION
Established and built in 1881, the West Point Lighthouse was automated in 1984. Still an active aid to navigation, the lighthouse is within a city park. *Address:* West Point Light *City:* Seattle *State:* WA *Visitors welcome?* Yes *Hours:* Dawn to dusk *Admission:* FREE *Operated by:* Seattle Parks and Recreation *NR?* Yes *NHL?* No *Year established/built:* 1881 *Latitude:* 47.6619 *Latitude:* -122.4360

LIGHTSHIPS

LIGHTSHIP AMBROSE (WLV-613)
A lightship designated Ambrose has served as the main beacon marking Ambrose Channel, the main shipping channel for New York Harbor from 1823 to 1967. Several ships served as the lightship, and the last, WLV 613, was commissioned in 1952. *Address:* 12 Fulton St. *City:* New York *State:* NY *Zip:* 10038 *Phone:* 212-748-8600 *Web:* www.southstreetseaportmuseum.org *Email:* info@southstseaport.org *Visitors welcome?* Yes *Hours:* November-March: Friday to Sunday, 10 a.m. to 5 p.m.; Monday 10am-5pm: Schermerhorn Row galleries only. Tuesday to Sunday 10 a.m. to 6 p.m: All galleries and ships open *Admission:* $10 adults, $8 students/seniors, $5 children 5-12, under 5 FREE *Operated by:* South Street Seaport Museum *NR?* Yes *NHL?* Yes *Year established/built:* 1907 *Latitude:* 40.7066 *Latitude:* -74.0034

LIGHTSHIP BARNEGAT (LV 79/WAL 506)
Commissioned in 1904, the Lightship Barnegat (LV 79/WAL 506)'s station was off the Barnegat Lighthouse. The ship was decommissioned in 1967, and it has passed through the hands of several owners. It is now awaiting restoration. *Address:* Foot of North Seventh Street *City:* Camden *State:* NJ *Visitors welcome?* Yes *Hours:* Grounds only *Admission:* Contact attraction directly *Operated by:* Private owner *NR?* No *NHL?* No *Year established/built:* 1904 *Latitude:* 39.9259 *Latitude:* -75.1196

LIGHTSHIP CHESAPEAKE (LV 116)
U.S. Lightship 116 "Chesapeake" marked the mouth of the Chesapeake Bay for over 29 years. Lightship 116 was initially assigned to Fenwick Island, Delaware in 1930. In 1933, Lightship 116 was transferred to the approaches of the Chesapeake Bay where her bright red hull, masthead lamp, and loud foghorn guided mariners to safe harbor for 29 years. From 1965-1970, Lightship 116 finished her career marking the Delaware Bay approaches.

(Photo courtesy Historic Ships in Baltimore) *Address:* Pier 3, Baltimore Inner Harbor (301 E. Pratt St.) *City:* Baltimore *State:* MD *Zip:* 21202 *Phone:* 410-539-1797 *Web:* www.historicships.org *Email:* administration@historicships.org *Visitors welcome?* Yes *Hours:* Contact attraction directly *Admission:* Contact attraction directly *Operated by:* Historic Ships in Baltimore *NR?* Yes *NHL?* Yes *Year established/built:* 1930 *Latitude:* 39.2866 *Latitude:* -76.6087

 LIGHTSHIP COLUMBIA (WLV 604)
Built in 1950 in Boothbay, Maine, Lightship Columbia (WLV 604) served as the lightship marking the entrance to the Columbia River and its treacherous bar. Decommissioned in 1979, the lightship now welcomes visitors at the Columbia River Maritime Museum. *Address:* 1792 Marine Drive *City:* Astoria *State:* OR *Zip:* 97103 *Phone:* 503-325-2323 *Web:* www.crmm.org *Email:* admin@crmm.org *Visitors welcome?* Yes *Hours:* Daily, 9:30 a.m. to 5:00 p.m. *Admission:* Children under 6, FREE; Children 6-17, $4; Seniors, $7; Adults, $8; Families, $24 *Operated by:* Columbia River Maritime Museum *NR?* Yes *NHL?* Yes *Year established/built:* 1950 *Latitude:* 46.1893 *Latitude:* -123.8230

LIGHTSHIP FRYING PAN SHOALS (LV-115)
Built in 1929, Lightship Frying Pan Shoals (LV-115) guarded Frying Pan Shoals, 30 miles off of Cape Fear, North Carolina, from 1930 to 1965. She is 133 feet and 3 inches in length with a 30 foot beam and she is 632 gross tons. *Address:* Pier 63, Chelsea Waterside Park *City:* New York *State:* NY *Phone:* 212-989-6363 *Web:* www.fryingpan.com *Email:* info@fryingpan.com *Visitors welcome?* Yes *Hours:* Contact attraction directly *Admission:* Contact attraction directly *Operated by:* Lightship Frying Pan *NR?* Yes *NHL?* No *Year established/built:* 1929 *Latitude:* 40.7143 *Latitude:* -74.0060

LIGHTSHIP HURON (LV 103)
Built in 1920, Lightship Huron (LV 103) is now a museum ship in Port Huron, Mich. *Address:* Pine Grove Park *City:* Port Huron *State:* MI *Zip:* 48060 *Phone:* 810-982-0891 *Web:* www.phmuseum.org *Email:* lightship@phmuseum.org *Visitors welcome?* Yes *Hours:* Daily, Memorial Day to Labor Day, 11 a.m. to 5 p.m.; Sept. to Dec., Thursday to Monday; April to May, Thursday to Monday; Jan. to March, closed *Admission:* Contact attraction directly *Operated by:* Port Huron Museum *NR?* Yes *NHL?* Yes *Year established/built:* 1921 *Latitude:* 42.9882 *Latitude:* -82.4275

LIGHTSHIP LIBERTY (LV 107)
Built in 1923 at the Bath Iron Works in Bath, Maine, Lightship Libery (LV 107) first served at Cape Lookout Shoals, North Carolina, from 1924 to 1933. Its next station was Winter Quarter Shoals on Chesapeake Bay, where it marked the entrance until 1960, e *Address:* 80 Audrey Zapp Drive *City:* Jersey City *State:* NJ *Zip:* 7304 *Phone:* 201-985-8000 *Email:* info@libertylandingmarina.com *Visitors welcome?* Yes *Hours:* Contact attraction directly *Admission:* Contact attraction directly *Operated by:* Liberty Landing Marina *NR?* No *NHL?* No *Year established/built:* 1923 *Latitude:* 40.7094 *Latitude:* -74.0478

LIGHTSHIP NANTUCKET (LV-112)
Built in 1936, Lightship Nantucket (LV-112) was powered by a 600 IEP steam engine driven by two oil-fired Babcock-Wilcox boilers. In 1960, the ship was re-powered with a Cooper-Bessemer 900 HP diesel and the tall smoke stack was replaced with a smaller on *Address:* Town Pier *City:* Long Island *State:* NY *Visitors welcome?* No *Operated by:* National Lighthouse Museum *NR?* No *NHL?* No *Year established/built:* 1936 *Latitude:* 40.8168 *Latitude:* -73.0662

LIGHTSHIP NANTUCKET (WLV-612)
Built in Curtis Bay, Maryland, Lightship Nantucket (WLV-612) was the last lightship built by the Coast Guard. It is now a private vessel available for charter. *Address:* Nantucket Harbor *City:* Nantucket *State:*

MA *Zip:* 2554 *Phone:* 617-821-6771 *Web:* www.nantucketlightship.com *Email:* info@nantucketlightship.com *Visitors welcome?* Yes *Hours:* Contact attraction directly *Admission:* Contact attraction directly *Operated by:* Nantucket Lightship WLV-612 *NR?* No *NHL?* No *Year established/built:* 1950 *Latitude:* 41.3043 *Latitude:* -70.0453

LIGHTSHIP NANTUCKET II (WLV-613)
The Lightship Nantucket II (WLV-613) was built in 1952 and originally stationed at Ambrose Channel in New York until 1967. In 1979, it was stationed off Nantucket Island. It alternated duty with WLV-612, also known as Lightship Nantucket I. One ship would *Address:* Agawam River *City:* Wareham *State:* MA *Visitors welcome?* No *Operated by:* Private owner *NR?* No *NHL?* No *Year established/built:* 1952 *Latitude:* 41.7626 *Latitude:* -70.6762

LIGHTSHIP NO. 114
Launched in 1930, Lightship No. 114 is now a floating exhibit in New Bedford. *Address:* Commonwealth Electric Pier *City:* New Bedford *State:* MA *Visitors welcome?* Yes *Hours:* Contact attraction directly *Admission:* Contact attraction directly *Operated by:* City of New Bedford *NR?* No *NHL?* No *Year established/built:* 1930 *Latitude:* 41.6362 *Latitude:* -70.9342

LIGHTSHIP OVERFALLS (LV 118)
The Lightship Overfalls (LV 118) was the last lightship built by the U.S. government. Commissioned in 1938, LV 118 served off Connecticut and Massachusetts between 1938 and 1972. *Address:* Pilottown Road *City:* Lewes *State:* DE *Phone:* 302-645-7377 *Web:* www.overfalls.org *Email:* bernheisel@juno.com *Visitors welcome?* Yes *Hours:* Contact attraction directly *Admission:* $2 adults; $1 children under 12 *Operated by:* Overfalls Maritime Museum Foundation *NR?* Yes *NHL?* No *Year established/built:* 1938 *Latitude:* 38.7823 *Latitude:* -75.1550

LIGHTSHIP PORTSMOUTH (LV-101)
Built in 1915, the Plymouth Lightship, also known as the Cape Charles Lightship, served at several stations until she was retired in 1964. The ship is now a land-based museum. *Address:* 2 High Street *City:* Portsmouth *State:* VA *Zip:* 23704 *Phone:* 757-393-8591 *Web:* www.portsnavalmuseums.com *Email:* navalmuseums@portsmouthva.gov *Visitors welcome?* Yes *Hours:* Memorial Day to Labor Day: Monday to Saturday, 10 a.m. to 5 p.m., Sunday, 1 p.m. to 5 p.m.; September to November, March to May: Saturday, 10 a.m. to 5 p.m., Sunday 1 p.m. to 5 p.m. *Admission:* Memorial Day to Labor Day: $3; September to May: $1.50 adults, $.50 students two to 18, under two FREE *Operated by:* Portsmouth Naval Shipyard Museum *NR?* Yes *NHL?* Yes *Year established/built:* 1915 *Latitude:* 36.8355 *Latitude:* -76.2969

LIGHTSHIP RELIEF (WLV-605)
Lightship Relief (WLV-605), one of six lightships constructed for the Coast Guard, was built by Rice Brothers Shipyard in Boothbay, Maine, in 1950. She saw service off Delaware *Address:* Jack London Square *City:* Oakland *State:* CA *Zip:* 94607 *Phone:* 510-272-0544 *Visitors welcome?* Yes *Hours:* Friday, Saturday and Sunday, 11 a.m. to 4 p.m. *Admission:* Contact attraction directly *Operated by:* United States Lighthouse Society *NR?* Yes *NHL?* Yes *Year established/built:* 1950 *Latitude:* 37.7942 *Latitude:* -122.2760

LIGHTSHIP SWIFTSURE (LV-83)
Launched in 1904, the lightship Swiftsure (LV-83) is a floating exhibit in Seattle. *Address:* 860 Terry Ave. N. *City:* Seattle *State:* WA *Zip:* 0 *Phone:* 206-447-9800 *Web:* www.nwseaport.org *Email:* seaport@oz.net *Visitors welcome?* Yes *Hours:* Contact attraction directly *Admission:* Donation *Operated by:* Northwest Seaport Maritime Heritage Ctr *NR?* No *NHL?* Yes *Year established/built:* 1904 *Latitude:* 47.6276 *Latitude:* -122.3370

LIGHTSHIP UMATILLA (LV 196)
The Lightship Umatilla (LV 196) was the fourth vessel to mark Umatilla Reef off Washington State's coast. Retired in 1971, the Coast Guard decommissioned her, and it is now owned by a Ketchikan businessman. *Address:* Lewis Reef *City:* Ketchikan *State:* AK *Visitors welcome?* No *Operated by:* Southeast Stevedoring *NR?* No *NHL?* No *Latitude:* 55.3750 *Latitude:* -131.7380

LILAC
Launched in 1933, the lighthouse tender Lilac is a floating exhibit on New York's waterfront. *Address:* Pier 40 *City:* New York *State:* NY *Zip:* 10013 *Phone:* 845-612-1950 *Web:* lilacpreservationproject.org *Email:* charlie@lilacpreservationproject.org *Visitors welcome?* Yes *Hours:* Contact attraction directly *Admission:* Contact attraction directly *Operated by:* Lilac Preservation Project *NR?* No *NHL?* No *Year established/built:* 1933 *Latitude:* 40.7295 *Latitude:* -74.0127

CHAPTER 6 – LIFE-SAVING STATIONS

Coastal stations dedicated to preserving the lives of seamen and women in distress

Pamet River Lifeboat Station (Truro, Mass.)

Many of the modern shore-based rescue facilities operated by the U.S. Coast Guard trace their roots to the life-saving station, where highly trained men waited for a call of distress from the sea. The first stations were established in New England and the mid-Atlantic states in the mid-nineteenth century and manned by volunteers who braved the surf and rocky coasts in open boats. As shipping grew and accidents increased, the loosely organized stations were brought under a newly created U.S. Life-Saving Service in 1878, which was later merged into the modern Coast Guard. This chapter lists life-saving stations preserved as museums dedicated to the volunteers and professionals who risked their lives to bring safely home seamen in peril.

EAST COAST

ASSATEAGUE LIFEBOAT STATION
Established in 1875, the current Assateague Lifeboat Station was constructed in 1922 and is now part of the Assateague Island National Seashore. *Address:* 726 National Seashore Lane *City:* Berlin *State:* MD *Zip:* 21811 *Phone:* 410-641-1441 *Visitors welcome?* Yes *Hours:* Daylight hours *Admission:* FREE *Operated by:* Assateague Island National Seashore *NR?* No *NHL?* No *Year established/built:* 1875 *Latitude:* 38.2499 *Latitude:* -75.1559

CHAPTER 6 – LIFE-SAVING STATIONS

CAFFEY'S INLET LIFE-SAVING STATION
Established and built in 1874, the Caffeys Inlet Life-Saving Station is now a resort. *Address:* 1461 Duck Road *City:* Kitty Hawk *State:* NC *Zip:* 27949 *Phone:* 252-261-8419 *Web:* www.thesanderling.com *Visitors welcome?* Yes *Hours:* Contact attraction directly *Admission:* Contact attraction directly *Operated by:* Sanderling Inn Resort *NR?* No *NHL?* No *Year established/built:* 1874 *Latitude:* 36.2234 *Latitude:* -75.7709

CAHOONS HOLLOW LIFE-SAVING STATION
Established in 1897, the Cahoons Hollow Life-Saving Station was decommissioned and sold to a local businessman in 1853. It is now the Beachcomber Restaurant. *Address:* 1120 Cahoon Hollow Rd. *City:* Wellfleet *State:* MA *Zip:* 02667 *Phone:* 508-349-6055 *Web:* www.thebeachcomber.com *Email:* dan@thebeachcomber.com *Visitors welcome?* Yes *Hours:* Contact attraction directly *Admission:* Contact attraction directly *Operated by:* Private owner *NR?* No *NHL?* No *Year established/built:* 1897 *Latitude:* 41.9437 *Latitude:* -69.9856

CHICAMACOMICO LIFE-SAVING STATION
Established and built in 1874 as one of North Carolina's original group of life-saving stations, the Chicamacomico Life-Saving Station was decommissioned in 1954 and is now a museum. *Address:* 23645 N.C. Highway 12 *City:* Rodanthe *State:* NC *Zip:* 27968 *Phone:* 252-987-1552 *Web:* www.chicamacomico.net *Email:* clss@embarqmail.com *Visitors welcome?* Yes *Hours:* Mid-April to November, Monday to Friday, noon to 5 p.m. *Admission:* $6 adults, $4 seniors and students *Operated by:* Chicamacomico Historical Association *NR?* Yes *NHL?* No *Year established/built:* 1874 *Latitude:* 35.6898 *Latitude:* -75.4898

CROSS ISLAND LIFE-SAVING STATION
The Cross Island Life-Saving Station is now owned by an Outward Bound facility. *Address:* Cross Island Life-Saving Station *City:* Machiasport *State:* ME *Phone:* 207-594-5548 *Email:* info@hurricaneisland.org *Visitors welcome?* Yes *Hours:* Contact attraction directly *Admission:* Contact attraction directly *Operated by:* Hurricane Island Outward Bound School *NR?* No *NHL?* No *Latitude:* 44.6987 *Latitude:* -67.3947

FORGE RIVER LIFEBOAT STATION
The Forge River Lifeboat Station is now a restaurant in Ocean Bay Park. *Address:* 1 Cayuga St. *City:* Ocean Bay Park *State:* NY *Zip:* 11770 *Phone:* 631-583-5000 *Visitors welcome?* Yes *Hours:* Contact attraction directly *Admission:* Contact attraction directly *Operated by:* Private owner *NR?* No *NHL?* No *Latitude:* 40.6513 *Latitude:* -73.1369

GURNET POINT LIFE-SAVING STATION
The former Gurnet Point Life-Saving Station is now a private residence. *Address:* Gurnet Point Life-Saving Station *City:* Duxbury *State:* MA *Visitors welcome?* No *Operated by:* Private owner *NR?* No *NHL?* No *Latitude:* 42.0418 *Latitude:* -70.6723

HORSENECK POINT LIFE-SAVING STATION
Established in 1888, the Horseneck Point Life-Saving Station is now being restored. *Address:* Horseneck Point *City:* Westport *State:* MA *Web:* westportriver.org/life-saving-station.html *Email:* wfa@westportriver.org *Visitors welcome?* Yes *Hours:* Contact attraction directly *Admission:* Contact attraction directly *Operated by:* Westport Fisherman's Association *NR?* No *NHL?* No *Year established/built:* 1888 *Latitude:* 41.5112 *Latitude:* -71.0884

HOUSE OF REFUGE MUSEUM AT GILBERT'S BAR
The House of Refuge Museum at Gilbert Bar is the oldest structure on the Treasure Coast. *.Address:* 301 SE MacArthur Boulevard *City:* Stuart *State:* FL *Zip:* 34996 *Phone:* 772-225-1875 *Web:* elliottmuseumfl.org/pages/house_refuge.php *Email:* info@elliottmuseumfl.org *Visitors welcome?* Yes *Hours:* Monday to Saturday, 10 a.m. to 4 p.m.; Sunday, 1 p.m. to 5 p.m. *Admission:* $5 adults, $2 children six to 12, under six

FREE *Operated by:* Historical Society of Martin County *NR?* Yes *NHL?* No *Year established/built:* 1876 *Latitude:* 27.1992 *Latitude:* -80.1654

INDIAN RIVER LIFE-SAVING STATION
Established in 1876, the current Indian River Life-Saving Station was built in 1905 and recently restored. It is now a state park. *Address:* 725039 Coastal Highway *City:* Rehoboth Beach *State:* DE *Zip:* 19971 *Phone:* 302-227-6991 *Web:* www.destateparks.com/attractions/life-saving-station/ *Email:* Cassandra.Petersen@state.de.us *Visitors welcome?* Yes *Hours:* Contact attraction directly *Admission:* Contact attraction directly *Operated by:* Indian River Life-Saving Station: Delaware Seashore State Park *NR?* Yes *NHL?* No *Year established/built:* 1876 *Latitude:* 38.7062 *Latitude:* -75.0880

KITTY HAWK LIFE-SAVING STATION
Established and built in 1874 as one of North Carolina's orginal group of life-saving stations, the Kitty Hawk Life-Saving Station is now a restaurant. *Address:* MP 4 Oceanfront *City:* Kitty Hawk *State:* NC *Zip:* 27949 *Phone:* 252-261-3171 *Web:* www.blackpelican.com *Email:* events@blackpelican.com *Visitors welcome?* Yes *Hours:* Contact attraction directly *Admission:* Contact attraction directly *Operated by:* Black Pelican Restaurant *NR?* Yes *NHL?* No *Year established/built:* 1874 *Latitude:* 36.0646 *Latitude:* -75.7057

MONMOUTH BEACH LIFE-SAVING STATION
Established in 1849, the current Monmouth Beach Life-Saving Station was constructed in 1895. Deactivated by the Coast Guard in the late 1950s, the building is now home to a local cultural center. *Address:* 128 Ocean Avenue *City:* Monmouth Beach *State:* NJ *Zip:* 07750 *Phone:* 732-229-4527 *Web:* www.surfmen.com *Email:* mbculturalcenter@comcast.net *Visitors welcome?* Yes *Hours:* Wednesday to Saturday, 10 a.m. to 2 p.m. *Admission:* Contact attraction directly *Operated by:* Monmouth Beach Cultural Center *NR?* No *NHL?* No *Year established/built:* 1849 *Latitude:* 40.3424 *Latitude:* -73.9740

 ## NANTUCKET SHIPWRECK & LIFESAVING MUSEUM
Located next to important shipping lanes running along the East Coast when maritime travel was in its heyday, Nantucket Island saw hundreds of vessels passing by each day. *Address:* 158 Polpis Road *City:* Nantucket *State:* MA *Zip:* 02554 *Phone:* 508-228-1885 *Web:* www.nantucketlifesavingmuseum.com *Visitors welcome?* Yes *Hours:* July 1 to October 13, daily, 10 a.m. to 4 p.m. *Admission:* Contact attraction directly *Operated by:* Nantucket Shipwreck & Lifesaving Museum *NR?* No *NHL?* No *Year established/built:* 1968 *Latitude:* 41.2912 *Latitude:* -70.0449

Fyddeye wants to hear about your family shipwreck story. Go to www.fyddeye.com and share!

NARRAGANSETT PIER LIFE-SAVING STATION
Constructed in 1888, the Narrangansett Pier Life-Saving Station is now a restaurant. *Address:* 40 Ocean Road *City:* Narragansett *State:* RI *Zip:* 02882 *Phone:* 401-789-0700 *Web:* www.thecoastguardhouse.com *Email:* office@thecoastguardhouse.com *Visitors welcome?* Yes *Hours:* Contact attraction directly *Admission:* FREE *Operated by:* Coast Guard House *NR?* Yes *NHL?* No *Year established/built:* 1885 *Latitude:* 41.4302 *Latitude:* -71.4554

NEW SHOREHAM LIFESAVING STATION
The New Shoreham Lifesaving Station once stood at Block Island, and it is now part of the Mystic Seaport collection. *Address:* 75 Greenmanville Avenue *City:* Mystic *State:* CT *Zip:* 06355 *Phone:* 860-572-5315 *Web:* www.mysticseaport.org *Visitors welcome?* Yes *Hours:* Daily, April to October, 9 a.m. to 5 p.m.; November to March, 10 a.m. to 4 p.m. *Admission:* Adults, $18.50; Seniors, $16.50; Children 6-17, $13; Under six, FREE *Operated by:* Mystic Seaport: The Museum of America and the Sea *NR?* No *NHL?* No *Latitude:* 41.3617 *Latitude:* -71.9634

CHAPTER 6 – LIFE-SAVING STATIONS

OAK ISLAND BEACH LIFE-SAVING STATION

Established and built in 1861, the Oak Island Beach Life-Saving Station is now a community center. *City:* Babylon *State:* NY *Zip:* 11757 *Phone:* 631-957-3000 *Visitors welcome?* Yes *Hours:* Contact attraction directly *Admission:* Contact attraction directly *Operated by:* Town of Babylon *NR?* No *NHL?* No *Year established/built:* 1861 *Latitude:* 40.6920 *Latitude:* -73.3768

OCEAN CITY LIFE-SAVING STATION MUSEUM

Established about 1874, the current Ocean City Life-Saving Station was constructed in 1901. In 1977, the building was moved to its present location, where it is used as a museum and local attraction. *Address:* 813 S Boardwalk *City:* Ocean City *State:* MD *Zip:* 21843 *Phone:* 410-289-4991 *Web:* www.ocmuseum.org *Email:* curator@ocmuseum.org *Visitors welcome?* Yes *Hours:* June to Sept., daily, 10 a.m. to 10 p.m.; May and October, daily, 10 a.m. to 4 p.m. *Admission:* $3 adults, $1 children six to 12, under six FREE *Operated by:* Ocean City Museum Society *NR?* No *NHL?* No *Year established/built:* 1874 *Latitude:* 38.3387 *Latitude:* -75.0810

OCRACOKE LIFEBOAT STATION

The Ocracoke Lifeboat Station is a subunit of U.S. Coast Guard Station Hatteras Inlet. *Address:* Ocracoke Island *City:* Ocracoke *State:* NC *Visitors welcome?* Yes *Hours:* Contact attraction directly *Admission:* Contact attraction directly *Operated by:* U.S. Coast Guard (District 5) *NR?* No *NHL?* No *Year established/built:* 1883 *Latitude:* 35.1049 *Latitude:* -75.9615

OLD HARBOR LIFE-SAVING STATION

Established and built in 1897, the Old Harbor Life-Saving Station was deactivated in 1944. In 1977, the building was moved from Nauset Beach to Race Point Beach when the structure was threatened by erosion. It is now within the Cape Cod National Seashore. *Address:* Race Point Beach *City:* Provincetown *State:* MA *Phone:* 508-771 - 2144 *Web:* www.nps.gov/caco/historyculture/old-harbor-life-saving-station.htm *Visitors welcome?* Yes *Hours:* Daily *Admission:* FREE *Operated by:* Cape Cod National Seashore *NR?* Yes *NHL?* No *Year established/built:* 1897 *Latitude:* 42.0812 *Latitude:* -70.2161

PAMET RIVER LIFEBOAT STATION

The Pamet River Lifeboat Station is now a youth hostel. *Address:* North Pamet Road *City:* Truro *State:* MA *Zip:* 02666 *Phone:* 508-349-3889 *Web:* www.usahostels.org/cape/hitr/index.shtml *Visitors welcome?* Yes *Hours:* Contact attraction directly *Admission:* Contact attraction directly *Operated by:* Hostelling International-New England *NR?* No *NHL?* No *Latitude:* 42.0010 *Latitude:* -70.0373

POINT ALLERTON LIFE-SAVING STATION

The Hull Lifesaving Museum, the museum of Boston Harbor heritage, preserves the region's lifesaving tradition and maritime culture through collections, exhibits, experiential and interpretive education, research and service to others. *Address:* 1117 Nantasket Ave. *City:* Hull *State:* MA *Zip:* 02045 *Phone:* 781-925-5433 *Web:* www.lifesavingmuseum.org *Email:* lifesavingmuseum@comcast.net *Visitors welcome?* Yes *Hours:* Daily *Admission:* $5 adults, $3 seniors, children under 18 FREE *Operated by:* Hull Lifesaving Museum *NR?* No *NHL?* No *Latitude:* 42.3055 *Latitude:* -70.8974

POINT JUDITH LIFE-SAVING STATION

The Point Judith Life-Saving Station is adjacent to the Point Judith Lighthouse. *Address:* Point Judith Coast Guard Station *City:* Point Judith *State:* RI *Visitors welcome?* Yes *Hours:* Grounds only *Admission:* FREE *Operated by:* U.S. Coast Guard (District 1) *NR?* Yes *NHL?* No *Year established/built:* 1810 *Latitude:* 41.3654 *Latitude:* -71.4867

POPHAM BEACH LIFE-SAVING STATION
Established and built in 1883, the Popham Beach Life-Saving Station, also known as the Hunniwells Beach Life-Saving Station, was decommissioned in 1971 and is now a bed and breakfast. *Address:* 4 Riverview Avenue *City:* Phippsburg *State:* ME *Zip:* 04562 *Phone:* 207-389-2409 *Web:* www.pophambeachbandb.com *Email:* stay@pophambeachbandb.com *Visitors welcome?* Yes *Hours:* Contact attraction directly *Admission:* Contact attraction directly *Operated by:* Popham Beach Bed & Breakfast *NR?* No *NHL?* No *Year established/built:* 1883 *Latitude:* 43.7499 *Latitude:* -69.7823

PORTSMOUTH HARBOR LIFE-SAVING STATION
Portsmouth Harbor Life-Saving Station, also called Wood Island Life-Saving Station, is accessed through Fort Foster State Park. *Address:* Fort Foster State Park *City:* Kittery Point *State:* ME *Visitors welcome?* Yes *Hours:* Contact attraction directly *Admission:* Contact attraction directly *Operated by:* Wood Island Preservation Group *NR?* No *NHL?* No *Latitude:* 43.0691 *Latitude:* -70.6864

SPERMACETI COVE LIFE-SAVING STATION
Established in 1849, the Spermaceti Cove Life-Saving Station was deactivated in 1946. It is now a visitors center for the Sandy Hook unit of the Gateway National Recreation Area. *Address:* Rt. 36 at Hartshorne Dr. *City:* Fort Hancock *State:* NJ *Zip:* 07732 *Phone:* 732-872-5970 *Visitors welcome?* Yes *Hours:* Daily, 10 a.m. to 5 p.m. *Admission:* FREE *Operated by:* Gateway National Recreation Area *NR?* Yes *NHL?* Yes *Year established/built:* 1849 *Latitude:* 40.4262 *Latitude:* -73.9856

SURFSIDE LIFE-SAVING STATION
Established in 1873, the Surfside Life-Saving Station is now a youth hostel. *Address:* 31 Western Ave. *City:* Nantucket *State:* MA *Zip:* 02554 *Phone:* 508-228-0433 *Web:* www.usahostels.org/cape/hint/index.shtml *Visitors welcome?* Yes *Hours:* Contact attraction directly *Admission:* Contact attraction directly *Operated by:* Hostelling International-New England *NR?* Yes *NHL?* No *Year established/built:* 1873 *Latitude:* 41.2443 *Latitude:* -70.0980

VIRGINIA BEACH LIFE-SAVING STATION
Established and built in 1903, the Virginia Beach Life-Saving Station, also called the Seatack Life-Saving Station, is now operated as the Old Coast Guard Museum. *Address:* 2400 Atlantic Ave. *City:* Virginia Beach *State:* VA *Zip:* 23451 *Phone:* 757-422-1587 *Web:* www.oldcoastguardstation.com *Email:* info@oldcoastguardstation.com *Visitors welcome?* Yes *Hours:* Monday through Saturday, 10 a.m. to 5 p.m.; Sunday, noon to 5 p.m. *Admission:* $4 adults, $3 seniors/military, $2 children six to 18, under six FREE *Operated by:* Old Coast Guard Station *NR?* No *NHL?* No *Year established/built:* 1903 *Latitude:* 36.8525 *Latitude:* -75.9766

WHITEHEAD LIFE-SAVING STATION
Address: Spruce Head *City:* St. George *State:* ME *Visitors welcome?* No *Operated by:* Private owner *NR?* No *NHL?* No *Latitude:* 44.0115 *Latitude:* -69.1328

GREAT LAKES

CALUMET HARBOR LIFEBOAT STATION
The Calumet Life-Saving Station, also called the South Chicago Life-Saving Station, is part of U.S. Coast Guard Station Calumet Harbor. *Address:* 4001 E. 98th Street *City:* South Chicago *State:* IL *Zip:* 60617 *Phone:*

CHAPTER 6 – LIFE-SAVING STATIONS

773-768-4093 *Visitors welcome?* Yes *Hours:* By appointment *Admission:* FREE *Operated by:* U.S. Coast Guard (District 9) *NR?* No *NHL?* No *Latitude:* 41.7176 *Latitude:* -87.5268

GRAND MARAIS HARBOR OF REFUGE
The Harbor of Refuge house was built in 1908 by the U.S. Life Saving Service as the Lightkeeper's dwelling. It was constructed at a cost of $5,000, and is a duplicate to the station at the Munising Range Lights. U.S. Coast Guard families lived in the home. *Address:* Coast Guard Point Road *City:* Grand Marais *State:* MI *Phone:* 906-387-2607 *Web:* www.nps.gov/piro/ *Visitors welcome?* Yes *Hours:* Contact attraction directly *Admission:* FREE *Operated by:* Pictured Rocks National Lakeshore *NR?* No *NHL?* No *Year established/built:* 1908 *Latitude:* 46.6708 *Latitude:* -85.9852

GRAND MARAIS LIFEBOAT STATION
Established in 1899, the current Grand Marais Life-Saving Station was constructed in 1938 and deactivated in 1981. The station is now within the Pictured Rocks National Lakeshore. *Address:* Coast Guard Point Road *City:* Grand Marais *State:* MI *Phone:* 906-387-2607 *Web:* www.nps.gov/piro/ *Visitors welcome?* Yes *Hours:* Contact attraction directly *Admission:* FREE *Operated by:* Pictured Rocks National Lakeshore *NR?* No *NHL?* No *Year established/built:* 1899 *Latitude:* 46.6708 *Latitude:* -85.9852

MUNISING LIFEBOAT STATION
Established in 1932, the Munising Life-Saving Station, also known as the Sand Point Life-Saving Station, was operated by the U.S. Coast Guard until 1960. It is now the headquarters for the Pictured Rocks National Lakeshore. *Address:* Sand Point Road *City:* Munising *State:* MI *Phone:* 906-387-2607 *Web:* www.nps.gov/piro/ *Visitors welcome?* Yes *Hours:* Contact attraction directly *Admission:* FREE *Operated by:* Pictured Rocks National Lakeshore *NR?* No *NHL?* No *Year established/built:* 1932 *Latitude:* 46.4369 *Latitude:* -86.6128

NORTH MANITOU ISLAND LIFE-SAVING STATION
Established and built in 1854, the North Manitou Island Life-Saving Station was deactivated in 1939. It is now within the Sleeping Bear Dunes National Lakeshore. *Address:* Manitou Passage, Lake Michigan *City:* Leland *State:* MI *Phone:* 231-326-5134 *Visitors welcome?* Yes *Hours:* Grounds only *Admission:* FREE *Operated by:* Sleeping Bear Dunes National Lakeshore *NR?* Yes *NHL?* Yes *Year established/built:* 1854 *Latitude:* 45.0231 *Latitude:* -85.7598

POINTE AUX BARQUES LIFE-SAVING STATION
Established in 1876, the Pointe aux Barques Life-Saving Station is now deactivated. The building was moved to Huron City Museum in 1964. *Address:* 7995 Pioneer Drive *City:* Port Austin *State:* MI *Phone:* 989-428-4123 *Email:* info@huroncitymuseums.com *Visitors welcome?* Yes *Hours:* Daily, Memorial Day through Sept. 30, Monday through Saturday, 10 a.m. to 6 p.m., Sunday, 11 a.m. to 6 p.m. *Admission:* Contact attraction directly *Operated by:* Point aux Barques Lighthouse Society *NR?* No *NHL?* No *Year established/built:* 1876 *Latitude:* 44.0294 *Latitude:* -82.8362

RACINE HARBOR LIGHTHOUSE & LIFE-SAVING STATION
Established and built in 1866, the Racine Harbor Lighthouse & Life-Saving Station, located at the mouth of the Root River, was deactivated in 1903. The light is atop a skeletal steel tower, and the site is now on private property. *Address:* Entrance to Racine Harbor at Pugh Marina *City:* Racine *State:* WI *Zip:* 53402 *Phone:* 262-632-8515 *Visitors welcome?* Yes *Hours:* Grounds only *Admission:* Contact attraction directly *Operated by:* Private owner *NR?* No *NHL?* No *Year established/built:* 1866 *Latitude:* 42.7261 *Latitude:* -87.7829

SLEEPING BEAR POINT LIFE-SAVING STATION
Established in 1902, the Sleeping Bear Point Life-Saving Station was deactivated in 1942 and is now part of the Sleeping Bear Dunes National Lakeshore. *Address:* Michigan State Route 209 *City:* Glen Arbor *State:* MI *Phone:* 616-326-5134 *Visitors welcome?* Yes *Hours:* Daily *Admission:* FREE *Operated by:* Sleeping Bear Dunes National Lakeshore *NR?* Yes *NHL?* No *Year established/built:* 1902 *Latitude:* 44.8960 *Latitude:* -85.9873

SOUTH MANITOU ISLAND LIFE-SAVING STATION
Established in 1901, the South Manitou Island Life-Saving Station was deactivated in 1958. It is now part of the Sleeping Bear Dunes National Lakeshore. *Address:* South Manitou Island, Lake Michigan *City:* Leland *State:* MI *Phone:* 231-326-5134 *Visitors welcome?* Yes *Hours:* Grounds only *Admission:* FREE *Operated by:* Sleeping Bear Dunes National Lakeshore *NR?* Yes *NHL?* No *Year established/built:* 1901 *Latitude:* 45.0231 *Latitude:* -85.7598

ST. JOSEPH LIFE-SAVING STATION
Established in 1874, the St. Joseph Life-Saving Station is now Station St. Joseph of the U.S. Coast Guard. *Address:* 127 North Pier Street *City:* St. Joseph *State:* MI *Zip:* 49085 *Phone:* 269-983-6114 *Visitors welcome?* Yes *Hours:* Contact attraction directly *Admission:* FREE *Operated by:* U.S. Coast Guard (District 9) *NR?* No *NHL?* No *Year established/built:* 1874 *Latitude:* 42.1140 *Latitude:* -86.4856

TWO RIVERS LIFEBOAT STATION
Believed established in the Civil War era, the current Two Rivers Lifeboat Station was constructed in 1909. It is still an active Coast Guard unit, known as Station Two Rivers. *Address:* 13 East Street *City:* Two Rivers *State:* WI *Zip:* 54241 *Phone:* 920-793-1304 *Visitors welcome?* Yes *Hours:* Contact attraction directly *Admission:* Contact attraction directly *Operated by:* U.S. Coast Guard (District 9) *NR?* No *NHL?* No *Year established/built:* 1865 *Latitude:* 44.1487 *Latitude:* -87.5630

TWO RIVERS LIFE-SAVING STATION
The Two Rivers Life-Saving Station is part of the Rogers Street Fishing Village museum. *Address:* 2010 Rogers St. *City:* Two Rivers *State:* WI *Zip:* 54241 *Phone:* 920-793-5905 *Web:* www.rogersstreet.com *Email:* szipperer@rogersstreet.com *Visitors welcome?* Yes *Hours:* May to October: Daily, 10 a.m. to 4 p.m. *Admission:* $4 adults, $2 children under 16 *Operated by:* Rogers Street Fishing Village & Great Lakes Coast Guard Museum *NR?* No *NHL?* No *Year established/built:* 1877 *Latitude:* 44.1518 *Latitude:* -87.5626

 ## WHITEFISH POINT LIFE-SAVING STATION
Established in 1923 on the grounds of the Whitefish Point Lighthouse, the Whitefish Point Lifeboat Station is now owned by a local museum. The building is available for overnight stays. *Address:* Whitefish Point Light *City:* Paradise *State:* MI *Zip:* 49768 *Phone:* 888-492-3747 *Web:* www.shipwreckmuseum.com *Visitors welcome?* Yes *Hours:* Contact attraction directly *Admission:* Contact attraction directly *Operated by:* Great Lakes Shipwreck Historical Society *NR?* Yes *NHL?* No *Year established/built:* 1923 *Latitude:* 46.7706 *Latitude:* -84.9567

GULF COAST

MAYOR ANDREW BROADDUS
Launched in 1929, the floating lifesaving station Mayor Andrew Broaddus is now floating offices for the Belle of Louisiana Operating Board. *Address:* 401 W. River Road *City:* Louisville *State:* KY *Zip:* 40202 *Phone:* 502-

574-2992 *Web:* belleoflouisville.org *Visitors welcome?* Yes *Hours:* Contact attraction directly *Admission:* Contact attraction directly *Operated by:* Belle of Louisville & Spirit of Jefferson Cruises *NR?* Yes *NHL?* Yes *Year established/built:* 1929 *Latitude:* 38.2589 *Latitude:* -85.7523

SANTA ROSA LIFE-SAVING STATION
Established in 1885, the Santa Rosa Life-Saving Station was deactivated in 1986. The current structure, which serves as a ranger station and office for a campground about one mile away, was built circa 1908. It is now a campground within the Gulf Islands National Seashore, which is operated by the National Park Service. *Address:* Santa Rosa Island, Gulf Islands National Seashore *City:* Gulf Breeze *State:* FL *Phone:* 850-934-2600 *Web:* www.nps.gov/guis/ *Visitors welcome?* Yes *Hours:* Daily, 8 a.m. to 5 p.m. *Admission:* Contact attraction directly *Operated by:* Gulf Islands National Seashore *NR?* No *NHL?* No *Year established/built:* 1908 *Latitude:* 30.3478 *Latitude:* -87.0449

WEST COAST

ARENA COVE LIFESAVING STATION
Established and built in 1901, the Arena Cove Lifesaving Station (#314) is now a bed & breakfast. *Address:* 695 Arena Cove *City:* Point Arena *State:* CA *Zip:* 95468 *Phone:* 707-882-2442 *Web:* www.coastguardhouse.com *Email:* coast@mcn.org *Visitors welcome?* Yes *Hours:* Contact attraction directly *Admission:* Contact attraction directly *Operated by:* Coast Guard House Historic Inn *NR?* Yes *NHL?* No *Year established/built:* 1901 *Latitude:* 38.9141 *Latitude:* -123.7090

COOS BAY LIFEBOAT STATION
In 1878, the first life-saving station, later to become a Coast Guard station, was located at Cape Arago below the lighthouse on a small sandy beach. *Address:* Coos Bay Lifeboat Station *City:* Charleston *State:* OR *Zip:* 97420 *Phone:* 541-888-3267 *Visitors welcome?* Yes *Hours:* Contact attraction directly *Admission:* Contact attraction directly *Operated by:* U.S. Coast Guard (District 13) *NR?* No *NHL?* No *Year established/built:* 1874 *Latitude:* 43.3532 *Latitude:* -124.0780

COQUILLE RIVER LIFEBOAT STATION
Located on the south bank of the Coquille River, the Coquille River Lifeboat Station is now a multipurpose structure. *Address:* 390 SW First St. *City:* Bandon *State:* OR *Zip:* 97411 *Visitors welcome?* Yes *Hours:* Contact attraction directly *Admission:* Contact attraction directly *Operated by:* Port of Bandon *NR?* No *NHL?* No *Latitude:* 43.1205 *Latitude:* -124.4180

 ### GRAYS HARBOR LIFEBOAT STATION
Established in 1939, the Grays Harbor Lifeboat Station is now operated as the Westport Maritime Museum. The historic lifeboat Grays Harbor is located at the U.S. Coast Guard station 1/2 mile south of the museum. *Address:* 2201 Westhaven Dr. *City:* Westport *State:* WA *Zip:* 98595 *Phone:* 360-268-0078 *Web:* www.westportwa.com/museum/ *Email:* westport.maritime@comcast.net *Visitors welcome?* Yes *Hours:* Daily, April to Sept., 10 a.m. to 4 p.m.; Oct. to March, Friday to Monday, 12 p.m. to 4 p.m. *Admission:* Contact attraction directly *Operated by:* Westport South Beach Historical Society *NR?* No *NHL?* No *Year established/built:* 1939 *Latitude:* 46.9077 *Latitude:* -124.1120

CHAPTER 6 – LIFE-SAVING STATIONS

HUMBOLDT BAY (SAMOA) LIFEBOAT STATION
The Humboldt Bay Lifeboat Station is still an active service operated by the U.S. Coast Guard. *Address:* Samoa Peninsula *City:* Samoa *State:* CA *Phone:* 707-443-2213 *Visitors welcome?* Yes *Hours:* Contact attraction directly *Admission:* Contact attraction directly *Operated by:* U.S. Coast Guard (District 11) *NR?* No *NHL?* No *Latitude:* 40.8226 *Latitude:* -124.1850

POINT REYES LIFEBOAT STATION
Established in 1890, the Point Reyes Lifeboat Station, now known as the Historic Lifeboat Station at Point Reyes National Seashore, is used an educational facility. *Address:* Point Reyes Lifeboat Station *City:* Point Reyes *State:* CA *Phone:* 415-663-8522 *Visitors welcome?* Yes *Hours:* Contact attraction directly *Admission:* Contact attraction directly *Operated by:* Point Reyes National Seashore *NR?* No *NHL?* No *Year established/built:* 1890 *Latitude:* 37.9939 *Latitude:* -122.9740

PORT ORFORD LIFEBOAT STATION
Established and built in 1934, the Port Orford Lifeboat Station is now a museum. *Address:* Port Orford Head State Park *City:* Port Orford *State:* OR *Zip:* 97465 *Phone:* 541-332-0521 *Web:* www.portorfordlifeboatstation.org *Email:* info@portorfordlifeboatstation.org *Visitors welcome?* Yes *Hours:* April to October, Monday to Thursday, 10 a.m. to 3:30 p.m. *Admission:* FREE *Operated by:* Port Orford Heritage Society *NR?* Yes *NHL?* No *Year established/built:* 1934 *Latitude:* 42.7457 *Latitude:* -124.4970

YAQUINA BAY LIFEBOAT STATION
The Yaquina Bay Lifeboat Station is an active U.S. Coast Guard facility. *Address:* 925 SW Naterlin Dr. *City:* Newport *State:* OR *Zip:* 97365 *Phone:* 541-265-5381 *Visitors welcome?* Yes *Hours:* By appointment *Admission:* FREE *Operated by:* U.S. Coast Guard (District 13) *NR?* No *NHL?* No *Latitude:* 44.6265 *Latitude:* -124.0570

CHAPTER 7 – EDUCATION

FOUR-YEAR, TWO-YEAR, AND SPECIALTY SCHOOLS FOCUSING ON MARITIME KNOWLEDGE AND SKILLS

Training vessel USCG Eagle (New London, Conn.)

In recent years, a new industry has grown up around maritime heritage: specialty schools and institutes that teach traditional crafts related to boatbuilding. Examples include the Northwest School of Wooden Boatbuilding in Port Hadlock, Wash., and the International Yacht Restoration School in Newport, R.I. These institutions join traditional four-year and two-year degree programs that pass on the ancient skills of navigation and seamanship while preparing young people for 21st-century high-tech jobs aboard the newest cargo and support vessels. This chapter lists some of the most-respected maritime education schools and programs in the country.

HIGHER EDUCATION

COLLEGE OF THE ATLANTIC
College of the Atlantic is a small school where all students major in Human Ecology. One of its properties is Mount Desert Lighthouse off Bar Harbor, Maine. *Address:* 105 Eden Street *City:* Bar Harbor *State:* ME *Zip:* 04609 *Phone:* 207-288-5015 *Fax:* 207-288-4126 *Web:* www.coa.edu *Email:* inquiry@coa.edu *Latitude:* 44.3923 *Latitude:* -68.2195

DENBIGH PROJECT
The Denbigh Project is an effort by the Institute of Nautical Archaeology at Texas A&M University to identify, document and preserve the wreck of Denbigh (41GV143), one of the most successful blockade runners of the American Civil War. *Address:* Institute of Nautical Archaeology *City:* College Station *State:* TX *Zip:* 77843 *Phone:* 979-458-0919 *Web:* nautarch.tamu.edu/PROJECTS/denbigh/denbigh.html *Email:* barnold@tamu.edu *Latitude:* 30.6079 *Latitude:* -96.3538

MASSACHUSETTS MARITIME ACADEMY
For over 100 years, Massachusetts Maritime Academy has been preparing women and men for exciting and rewarding careers on land and sea. As the nation's oldest and finest co-ed maritime college, MMA challenges students to succeed by balancing a unique regimented lifestyle with a typical four-year college environment. *Address:* 101 Academy Drive *City:* Buzzards Bay *State:* MA *Zip:* 02532 *Phone:* 508-830-5000 *Web:* www.maritime.edu *Email:* comments@maritime.edu *Visitors welcome?* Yes *Hours:* Contact owner *Admission:* Contact owner *Operated by:* Massachusetts Maritime Academy *NR?* No *NHL?* No *Year established/built:* 1891 *Latitude:* 41.7403 *Latitude:* -70.6215

STATE UNIVERSITY OF NEW YORK MARITIME COLLEGE
Founded in 1874, the State University of New York Maritime College is an undergraduate and graduate institution focused on engineering, business, science, and maritime transportation. *Address:* 6 Pennyfield Avenue *City:* Throggs Neck *State:* NY *Zip:* 10465 *Phone:* 718-409-7200 *Web:* www.sunymaritime.edu *Latitude:* 40.8093 *Latitude:* -73.8019

U.S. COAST GUARD ACADEMY
Address: 15 Mohegan Ave *City:* New London *State:* CT *Zip:* 06320 *Phone:* 860-444-8444 *Web:* www.cga.edu *Latitude:* 41.3702 *Latitude:* -72.1060

SCHOOLS

COHASSET MARITIME INSTITUTE
Cohasset Maritime Institute is a non-profit organization which offers recreational and competitive ocean rowing instruction for both students and adults and maritime education, including small boat building. Located on Cohasset Harbor, it offers an ideal setting for a safe, scenic and enjoyable rowing experience. We welcome people of all ability to join. *Address:* 40 Parker Avenue *City:* Cohasset *State:* MA *Zip:* 02025 *Web:* www.rowcmi.com *Email:* info@rowcmi.com *Visitors welcome?* Yes *Operated by:* Cohasset Maritime Institute *NR?* No *NHL?* No *Latitude:* 42.2388 *Latitude:* -70.7874

DISCOVERY MODELERS EDUCATION CENTER
The Discovery Modelers Education Center carries on the traditions and skills of ship modeling. The organization does this through hands-on education, including classes, seminars and workshops for people of all ages and abilities, through model exhibits, and other activities. *Address:* 860 Terry Ave. N. *City:* Seattle *State:* WA *Zip:* 98109 *Phone:* 206-282-0985 *Email:* discoverymodelers@yahoo.com *Latitude:* 47.6276 *Latitude:* -122.3370

DUXBURY BAY MARITIME SCHOOL
The mission of the Duxbury Bay Maritime School is to connect people of all ages, abilities and means to Duxbury Bay through educational and recreational programs that stimulate individual growth and an enduring love and appreciation of the sea. *Address:* 457 Washington St. *City:* Duxbury *State:* MA *Zip:* 02332 *Phone:* 781-934-7555 *Web:* www.dbms.org

ECHO HILL OUTDOOR SCHOOL
Echo Hill's outdoor classes and residential programs are grounded in a desire to have students live and learn closely with nature. The school's historic craft includes the skipjack Elsworth, the buyboat Annie D., and the deadrise workboat Spirit. *Address:* 13655 Bloomingneck Road *City:* Worton *State:* MD *Zip:* 21678 *Phone:* 410-348-5880 *Web:* www.ehos.org *Email:* john@ehos.org *Latitude:* 39.3554 *Latitude:* -76.1130

INSTITUTE OF MARITIME HISTORY
The Institute of Maritime History (IMH) is a non-profit 501(c)3 corporation dedicated to research, preservation, and education in nautical archaeology and maritime history. *Address:* PO Box 29 *City:* Kensington *State:* MD *Zip:* 20895 *Phone:* 301-949-7545 *Web:* www.maritimehistory.org *Email:* David.Howe@MaritimeHistory.org *Latitude:* 39.0257 *Latitude:* -77.0764

INTERNATIONAL YACHT RESTORATION SCHOOL
The International Yacht Restoration School is a non-profit institution dedicated to education and maritime preservation. The school teaches the skills, history, art and science of building, restoring and maintaining boats and their systems. *Address:* 449 Thames St. *City:* Newport *State:* RI *Zip:* 02840 *Phone:* 401-848-5777 *Fax:* 401-842-0669 *Web:* www.iyrs.org *Email:* info@iyrs.org *Latitude:* 41.4810 *Latitude:* -71.3147

LOS ANGELES MARITIME INSTITUTE
Since its founding in 1992, the mission of The Los Angeles Maritime Institute's TopSail Youth Program has been to use sail training to provide youth with real-life challenges that develop knowledge, skills and attitudes needed to live healthy, productive lives. *Address:* Berth 84 *City:* San Pedro *State:* CA *Zip:* 90731 *Phone:* 310-833-6055 *Fax:* 310-548-2055 *Web:* www.lamitopsail.org *Email:* stephanie@lamitopsail.org *Latitude:* 33.7595 *Latitude:* -118.2620

MAINE MARITIME ACADEMY
Maine Maritime Academy (MMA), a small, co-educational, public college on the coast of Maine, offers you a world of opportunities. *Address:* PO Box C-3 *City:* Castine *State:* ME *Zip:* 04420 *Phone:* 800-227-8465 *Web:* www.mainemaritime.edu *Latitude:* 44.3850 *Latitude:* -68.8096

NORTHEAST MARITIME INSTITUTE
Northeast Maritime offers a wide range of U.S. Coast Guard and Commonwealth of Dominica Maritime Administration approved and STCW compliant courses and a variety of courses for professional development

and licensing upgrades. *Address:* 32 Washington St. *City:* Fairhaven *State:* MA *Zip:* 02719 *Phone:* 508-992-4025 *Fax:* 508-992-9184 *Web:* www.northeastmaritime.com *Email:* registration@northeastmaritime.com *Latitude:* 41.6374 *Latitude:* -70.9034

PAUL HALL CENTER FOR MARITIME TRAINING AND EDUCATION
Founded in 1967, the Paul Hall Center for Maritime Training and Education offers the most U.S. Coast Guard-approved courses of any maritime school in the nation. *Address:* PO Box 75 *City:* Piney Point *State:* MD *Zip:* 20674 *Phone:* 301-994-0010 *Web:* www.seafarers.org/phc/ *Latitude:* 38.1476 *Latitude:* -76.5080

PITCAIRN ISLANDS STUDY CENTER
The Pitcairn Island Study Center preserves archives and records related to the 18th century mutiny on HMS Bounty. *Address:* Pacific Union College *City:* Angwin *State:* CA *Zip:* 94508 *Phone:* 707-965-6625 *Web:* library.puc.edu/pitcairn/studycenter/index.shtml *Email:* hford@puc.edu *Latitude:* 38.5693 *Latitude:* -122.4400

SCHOOL OF OCEAN SAILING
Address: TLC 1, 5600 Royal Dane Mall - Suite 12 *City:* St. Thomas *State:* VI *Zip:* 00802 *Phone:* 207-321-9249 *Web:* www.sailingschool.com *Email:* svsamana@sailingschool.com *Latitude:* 18.3436 *Latitude:* -64.9322

SEATTLE MARITIME ACADEMY
The Seattle Maritime Academy is a unit of Seattle Central Community College. *Address:* 1701 Broadway *City:* Seattle *State:* WA *Zip:* 98122 *Phone:* 206-587-3800 *Web:* www.seattlecentral.edu *Latitude:* 47.6164 *Latitude:* -122.3210

TABOR ACADEMY
Address: 66 Spring Street *City:* Marion *State:* MA *Zip:* 02738 *Phone:* 508-748-2000 *Web:* www.taboracademy.org *Email:* communications@taboracademy.org *Latitude:* 41.7067 *Latitude:* -70.7682

U.S. MERCHANT MARINE ACADEMY
Address: 300 Steamboat Road *City:* Kings Point *State:* NY *Zip:* 11024 *Phone:* 516-773-5000 *Web:* www.usmma.edu *Latitude:* 40.8131 *Latitude:* -73.7610

Fyddeye is expanding its educational listings. Send your information to contact@fyddeye.com.

CHAPTER 8 – DISTRICTS
LIVING HISTORIC MARITIME ENVIRONMENTS WHERE YOU CAN STEP BACK IN TIME

Howard Steamboat Museum (Jeffersonville, Indiana)

Virtually every major and minor port has a waterfront that was often the first neighborhood settled by immigrants. Over the decades, the docks, wharves and piers expanded to include offices, warehouses, and industrial sites that served the thriving maritime industry. Everyone from laborers to ship owners lived nearby. As local economies changed, the dockyards and surrounding business districts and residential neighborhoods sometimes fell into decay. But farsighted residents in a few cities preserved neighborhoods as a way to honor and teach the past, as well as provide a livelihood for many local people. This chapter lists historic districts with a maritime flavor enjoyed by visitors and residents alike.

ALASKA

 GOLDSTREAM DREDGE NO. 8
The Goldstream Dredge No. 8 National Historic District preserves the history of gold mining in Fairbanks. *Address:* 1755 Old Steese Hwy N. *City:* Fairbanks *State:* AK *Zip:* 99712 *Phone:* 907-457-6058 *Web:* www.golddredgeno8.com *Email:* info@golddredgeno8.com *Visitors welcome?* Yes *Hours:* Daily *Admission:* Contact attraction directly *Operated by:* Gold Dredge No. 8 *NR?* No *NHL?* No *Latitude:* 64.9417 *Latitude:* -147.6560

CALIFORNIA

ARENA COVE HISTORIC DISTRICT
The Arena Cove Historic District cover 10 buildings and three structures on 200 acres in Point Arena. *Address:* Point Arena *City:* Point Arena *State:* CA *Visitors welcome?* Yes *Hours:* Daily *Admission:* FREE *Operated by:* Private owner *NR?* Yes *NHL?* No *Year established/built:* 1990 *Latitude:* 38.9088 *Latitude:* -123.6930

MARE ISLAND HISTORIC PARK
The Mare Island Historic District features a museum preserving the story of the west coast's first naval base and shipyard, established in 1854. *Address:* Building 46, Mare Island *City:* Vallejo *State:* CA *Zip:* 94592 *Phone:* 707-557-1538 *Web:* www.mareislandhpf.org *Visitors welcome?* Yes *Hours:* Weekdays, 10 a.m. to 2 p.m.; 1st and 3rd weekends, 10 a.m. to 4 p.m. *Admission:* Contact attraction directly *Operated by:* Mare Island Historic Park Foundation *NR?* No *NHL?* No *Latitude:* 38.0949 *Latitude:* -122.2750

OLD SACRAMENTO RIVERFRONT
The Old Sacramento riverfront district features living history exhibits and the sternwheeler Delta King. *Address:* Old Sacramento *City:* Sacramento *State:* CA *Zip:* 95814 *Phone:* 916-808-4980 *Web:* www.oldsacramento.com *Email:* jwest@cityofsacramento.org *Visitors welcome?* Yes *Hours:* Daily *Admission:* FREE *Operated by:* Old Sacramento *NR?* No *NHL?* No *Latitude:* 38.5734 *Latitude:* -121.5110

HAWAII

LAHAINA HISTORIC DISTRICT
The Lahaina Historic District, which covers the old harbor area, includes the Baldwin Home Museum. *Address:* Lahaina Historic District *City:* Lahaina *State:* HI *Zip:* 96761 *Phone:* 808-661-3262 *Web:* www.lahainarestoration.org *Email:* lrf@hawaii.rr.com *Visitors welcome?* Yes *Hours:* Daily *Admission:* FREE *Operated by:* Lahaina Restoration Foundation *NR?* No *NHL?* No *Latitude:* 20.8759 *Latitude:* -156.6760

LOUISIANA

PLAQUEMINE HISTORIC DISTRICT
The Plaquemine Historic District features Greek Revival structures that survived the decline of this key Mississippi River-side community. *Address:* Plaquemine Historic District *City:* Plaquemine *State:* LA *Phone:* 225-687-5190 *Visitors welcome?* Yes *Hours:* Daily *Admission:* FREE *Operated by:* Private owner *NR?* No *NHL?* No *Year established/built:* 1838 *Latitude:* 30.2880 *Latitude:* -91.2343

MAINE

PENOBSCOT MARINE MUSEUM SEACOAST VILLAGE
Eight buildings listed on National Register of Historic Places grace the grounds at the Penobscot Maritime Museum. *Address:* 5 Church Street *City:* Searsport *State:* ME *Zip:* 04974 *Phone:* 207-548-2529 *Web:* www.

penobscotmarinemuseum.org *Email:* museumoffices@pmm-maine.org *Visitors welcome?* Yes *Hours:* Monday to Saturday, 10 a.m. to 5 p.m.; Sunday, Noon to 5 p.m. (May to October) *Admission:* $8 adults; $3 children seven to 12; children six and under, FREE *Operated by:* Penobscot Marine Museum *NR?* Yes *NHL?* No *Year established/built:* 1810 *Latitude:* 44.4209 *Latitude:* -69.0006

MASSACHUSETTS

BRADFORD FAMILY HOUSES
The Capt. Gamaliel Bradford House, the Capt. Gershom Bradford House, the Capt. Daniel Bradford House and the King Caesar House in Duxbury, Mass. exemplify two-story, wood-frame, Federal style residences. *Address:* Tremont Street *City:* Duxbury *State:* MA *Zip:* 02331 *Phone:* 781-934-6106 *Web:* www.duxburyhistory.org *Email:* aarnold@duxburyhistory.org *Visitors welcome?* Yes *Hours:* Contact attraction directly *Admission:* Contact attraction directly *Operated by:* Duxbury Rural and Historical Society *NR?* No *NHL?* No *Latitude:* 42.0437 *Latitude:* -70.6902

BRADFORD-UNION STREET HISTORIC DISTRICT
The Bradford-Union Street Historic District, consisting of approximately 6 acres of land and more than 30 buildings, was once an active commercial harbor area dominated by industrial buildings. *City:* Plymouth *State:* MA *Visitors welcome?* Yes *Hours:* Daily *Admission:* FREE *Operated by:* Private owner *NR?* No *NHL?* No *Latitude:* 41.9584 *Latitude:* -70.6673

CORAM SHIPYARD HISTORIC DISTRICT
The Coram Shipyard Historic District was the site of Dighton's earliest 18th-century shipbuilding industry and continued to play a significant role in the town's commerce and maritime industries throughout the 18th and into the mid-19th centuries. *Address:* 2125 Water St. *City:* Dighton *State:* MA *Visitors welcome?* Yes *Hours:* Daily *Admission:* FREE *Operated by:* Private owner *NR?* No *NHL?* No *Year established/built:* 1698 *Latitude:* 41.8123 *Latitude:* -71.1174

CUSTOM HOUSE DISTRICT
Consisting of 70 buildings and sites on 15.9 acres in downtown Boston, the Custom House District is a collection of 19th-century mercantile buildings in addition to many well-preserved skyscrapers dating from the first half of the 20th century. *City:* Boston *State:* MA *Visitors welcome?* Yes *Hours:* Daily *Admission:* FREE *Operated by:* Private owner *NR?* No *NHL?* No *Latitude:* 42.3584 *Latitude:* -71.0598

DERBY WATERFRONT DISTRICT
The Derby Waterfront District in Salem includes the famed House of the Seven Gables, the centerpiece of the Nathaniel Hawthorne novel. *Address:* 115 Derby St. *City:* Salem *State:* MA *Phone:* 978-744-0991 *Web:* www.7gables.org *Email:* info@7gables.org *Visitors welcome?* Yes *Hours:* Daily *Admission:* FREE *Operated by:* House of the Seven Gables *NR?* No *NHL?* No *Latitude:* 42.5226 *Latitude:* -70.8844

DIGHTON WHARVES HISTORIC DISTRICT
The Dighton Wharves Historic district played a significant role in the late 18th and early-to-mid 19th century development of Dighton's maritime trade industry. *Address:* 2298 Pleasant St. *City:* Dighton *State:* MA *Visitors welcome?* Yes *Hours:* Daily *Admission:* FREE *Operated by:* Private owner *NR?* No *NHL?* No *Year established/built:* 1770 *Latitude:* 41.8091 *Latitude:* -71.1198

EAST GLOUCESTER SQUARE HISTORIC DISTRICT
Located on the Cape Ann peninsula, the East Gloucester Square Historic District is a well-preserved fishing village on the sheltered waters of Gloucester's Inner Harbor. *Address:* East Main St. and Mount Pleasant Ave. *City:* Gloucester *State:* MA *Phone:* 978-281-8865 *Toll-free:* 800-649-6839 *Visitors welcome?* Yes *Hours:* Daily *Admission:* FREE *Operated by:* Private owner *NR?* No *NHL?* No *Latitude:* 42.6044 *Latitude:* -70.6538

EDGARTOWN VILLAGE HISTORIC DISTRICT
Located on the island of Martha's Vineyard, the Edgartown Harbor Village Historic District covers an area of about 150 acres and contains approximately 500 buildings, exhibiting a mix of commercial, residential and industrial land uses. *City:* Edgartown *State:* MA *Zip:* 02539 *Phone:* 508-627-6110 *Visitors welcome?* Yes *Hours:* Daily *Admission:* FREE *Operated by:* City of Edgartown *NR?* No *NHL?* No *Latitude:* 41.3714 *Latitude:* -70.5384

ESSEX NATIONAL HERITAGE AREA
Designated in 1996 by the U.S. Congress, the Essex National Heritage Area covers the 500 square miles of eastern Massachusetts that lies north of Boston. It's not one location, but thousands of historical sites. *Address:* Essex County *City:* Salem *State:* MA *Zip:* 01970 *Phone:* 978-740-0444 *Web:* www.essexheritage.org *Visitors welcome?* Yes *Hours:* Contact attraction directly *Admission:* Contact attraction directly *Operated by:* Essex National Heritage Commission *NR?* No *NHL?* No *Year established/built:* 1996 *Latitude:* 42.5124 *Latitude:* -70.9131

FISH FLAKE HILL HISTORIC DISTRICT
Situated on a ridge overlooking Beverly Harbor, the Fish Flake Hill Historic District is the oldest neighborhood in Beverly, Mass. The first colonial settlers, led by Roger Conant, came to the area from Salem, Mass., in 1626. *Address:* Bartlett Street and Water Street *City:* Beverly *State:* MA *Phone:* 978-740-0444 *Web:* www.essexheritage.org *Visitors welcome?* Yes *Hours:* Daily *Admission:* FREE *Operated by:* Essex National Heritage Commission *NR?* No *NHL?* No *Year established/built:* 1626 *Latitude:* 42.5413 *Latitude:* -70.8818

MARKET SQUARE HISTORIC DISTRICT
The Market Square Historic District in Newburyport is is one of the last seaport business districts remaining from the golden days of New England shipping. *City:* Newburyport *State:* MA *Phone:* 978-462-8681 *Web:* www.essexheritage.org *Visitors welcome?* Yes *Hours:* Daily *Admission:* FREE *Operated by:* Essex National Heritage Commission *NR?* No *NHL?* No *Latitude:* 42.8126 *Latitude:* -70.8773

MERRILL'S WHARF HISTORIC DISTRICT
The Merrill's Wharf Historic District comprises less than one acre along the New Bedford waterfront and includes the Steamship Authority Pier, the Coal Pocket Pier and the unaltered portion of Merrill's Wharf and the Merrill's Wharf Building. *Address:* MacArthur Drive *City:* New Bedford *State:* MA *Visitors welcome?* Yes *Hours:* Daily *Admission:* FREE *Operated by:* City of New Bedford *NR?* No *NHL?* No *Latitude:* 41.6314 *Latitude:* -70.9222

NANTUCKET HISTORIC DISTRICT
Nantucket Historic District is the finest surviving architectural and environmental example of a late 18th- and early 19th-century New England seaport town. *Address:* 25 Federal St. *City:* Nantucket *State:* MA *Zip:* 02554 *Phone:* 508-228-1387 *Visitors welcome?* Yes *Hours:* Daily *Admission:* FREE *Operated by:* Nantucket Preservation Trust *NR?* No *NHL?* Yes *Latitude:* 41.2843 *Latitude:* -70.0991

NEW BEDFORD HISTORIC DISTRICT
Comprised of approximately 20 historic buildings situated within 12 city blocks and totaling approximately 20 acres, the New Bedford Historic District is a good example of the commercial district of a major New England seaport between 1810 and 1855. *Address:* New Bedford Historic District *City:* New Bedford *State:*

MA *Visitors welcome?* Yes *Hours:* Daily *Admission:* FREE *Operated by:* City of New Bedford *NR?* No *NHL?* No *Latitude:* 41.6353 *Latitude:* -70.9242

 ### NEW BEDFORD WHALING NATIONAL HISTORICAL PARK
New Bedford was the mid-19th century center for the New England whaling industry. *Address:* 33 William St. *City:* New Bedford *State:* MA *Zip:* 02740 *Phone:* 508-996-4095 *Web:* www.nps.gov/nebe/ *Visitors welcome?* Yes *Hours:* Daily *Admission:* FREE *Operated by:* New Bedford Whaling National Historical Park *NR?* No *NHL?* No *Latitude:* 41.6358 *Latitude:* -70.9240

OLD SHIPBUILDER'S HISTORIC DISTRICT
Located along the shore of Duxbury Bay and the mouth of the Bluefish River in Duxbury, the Old Shipbuilder's Historic District is dominated by Federal period dwellings built between 1780 and 1840. *Address:* 479 Washington St. *City:* Duxbury *State:* MA *Zip:* 02331 *Phone:* 781-934-6106 *Web:* www.duxburyhistory.org *Email:* aarnold@duxburyhistory.org *Visitors welcome?* Yes *Hours:* Daily *Admission:* FREE *Operated by:* Duxbury Rural and Historical Society *NR?* No *NHL?* No *Latitude:* 42.0392 *Latitude:* -70.6717

RUSSIA WHARF BUILDINGS
The Russia Wharf Buildings form a commercial block on the edge of downtown Boston. *Address:* Congress Street *City:* Boston *State:* MA *Zip:* 02210 *Visitors welcome?* Yes *Hours:* Daily *Admission:* FREE *Operated by:* Private owner *NR?* No *NHL?* No *Year established/built:* 1897 *Latitude:* 42.3494 *Latitude:* -71.0464

 ### SALEM NATIONAL MARITIME HISTORIC SITE
Salem, Massachusetts has looked to the sea since the community was founded in 1626. *Address:* 2 New Liberty Street *City:* Salem *State:* MA *Zip:* 01970 *Phone:* 978-740-1650 *Web:* www.nps.gov/sama/ *Visitors welcome?* Yes *Hours:* Daily, 9 a.m. to 5 p.m. *Admission:* $5 adults, $3 children and seniors, children under six FREE *Operated by:* Salem National Maritime Historic Site *NR?* No *NHL?* No *Latitude:* 42.5227 *Latitude:* -70.8920

TWIN LIGHTS HISTORIC DISTRICT
Established in 1771, two lighthouse were built together on Thacher Island, also known as Cape Ann. Two new towers were constructed of granite in 1961. The light on the northeast tower was shut down in 1932. The lighthouse is now owned by the City of Rockport. *Address:* Twin Lights Historic District *City:* Rockport *State:* MA *Zip:* 01966 *Phone:* 617-599-2590 *Web:* www.thacherisland.org *Email:* info@thacherisland.org *Visitors welcome?* Yes *Hours:* Contact attraction directly *Admission:* Contact attraction directly *Operated by:* Thacher Island Association *NR?* Yes *NHL?* No *Year established/built:* 1771 *Latitude:* 42.6557 *Latitude:* -70.6203

 ### WELLFLEET CENTER HISTORIC DISTRICT
The Wellfleet Center Historic District is a well-preserved group of residential, commercial and institutional buildings associated with the growth of Wellfleet from a small harbor village in the late 18th century to a flourishing maritime community in the 20th century. *Address:* 266 Main St. *City:* Wellfleet *State:* MA *Zip:* 02667 *Phone:* 508-349-9157 *Web:* www.wellfleethistoricalsociety.com *Email:* museum@wellfleethistoricalsociety.com *Visitors welcome?* Yes *Hours:* Daily *Admission:* FREE *Operated by:* Wellfleet Historical Society *NR?* No *NHL?* No *Latitude:* 41.9385 *Latitude:* -70.0304

OHIO

CANAL FULTON'S CANALWAY CENTER
Address: 125 Tuscarawas St. W. *City:* Canal Fulton *State:* OH *Zip:* 44614 *Phone:* 330-854-6835 *Toll-free:* 888-281-6650 *Web:* www.discovercanalfulton.com/canalway_center.html *Email:* canalway@cityofcanalfulton-oh.

gov *Visitors welcome?* Yes *Hours:* April and October: Saturday and Sunday, 10 a.m. to 4 p.m.; May to September: Daily, 10 a.m. to 6 p.m. *Admission:* Contact attraction directly *Operated by:* Canal Fulton Heritage Society *NR?* No *NHL?* No *Year established/built:* 2006 *Latitude:* 40.8892 *Latitude:* -81.5985

PENNSYLVANIA

PENN'S LANDING
Penn's Landing is a Delaware River waterfront district featuring several maritime attractions. *Address:* 301 S. Columbus Blvd. *City:* Philadelphia *State:* PA *Zip:* 19106 *Phone:* 215-928-8801 *Visitors welcome?* Yes *Hours:* Daily *Admission:* FREE *Operated by:* Delaware River Waterfront Corp. *NR?* No *NHL?* No *Latitude:* 39.9441 *Latitude:* -75.1422

WASHINGTON

MARINE RESERVATION HISTORIC DISTRICT
Address: Decatur Avenue and Doyen Street *City:* Bremerton *State:* WA *Visitors welcome?* Yes *NR?* Yes *NHL?* No *Year established/built:* 1911 *Latitude:* 47.5591 *Latitude:* -122.6470

OFFICERS' ROW HISTORIC DISTRICT
Address: 602 Pacific Avenue *City:* Bremerton *State:* WA *Visitors welcome?* Yes *NR?* Yes *NHL?* No *Year established/built:* 1937 *Latitude:* 47.5678 *Latitude:* -122.6260

OYSTERVILLE NATIONAL HISTORIC DISTRICT
The California Gold Rush of 1849 drew the first significant numbers of Anglo-European settlers to Willapa Bay, which native peoples had exploited for centuries as a food source. The settlers created the town of Oysterville, where they harvested wild oysters. The tiny community is now preserved as a national historic district. *Address:* Oysterville Road and Territory Road *City:* Oysterville *State:* WA *Visitors welcome?* Yes *Hours:* Daily *Admission:* FREE *Operated by:* Pacific County *NR?* Yes *NHL?* No *Year established/built:* 1976 *Latitude:* 46.5491 *Latitude:* -124.0290

PIER 54-59, SEATTLE
Piers 54-59 on Seattle's Central Waterfront was once the heart of the city's thriving industrial waterfront. Today, it's the site of family activities, such as the Seattle Aquarium, shopping, and fine restaurants. *Address:* 1400 Alaskan Way *City:* Seattle *State:* WA *Visitors welcome?* Yes *Hours:* Daily *Admission:* FREE *NR?* No *NHL?* No *Latitude:* 47.6074 *Latitude:* -122.3410

PORT GAMBLE HISTORIC DISTRICT
Founded in 1853 on the northern tip of the Kitsap Peninsula, Port Gamble was one of the earliest and most important lumber-producing centers on the Pacific Coast. It is now an historic district. *Address:* State Highway 104 and NE Rainier Ave. *City:* Port Gamble *State:* WA *Visitors welcome?* Yes *Hours:* Contact attraction directly *Admission:* FREE *Operated by:* Port Gamble *NR?* No *NHL?* Yes *Year established/built:* 1853 *Latitude:* 47.8543 *Latitude:* -122.5840

PORT TOWNSEND HISTORIC DISTRICT
Port Townsend Historic District covers most of downtown Port Townsend, the first U.S. port-of-entry on Puget Sound. The city is now the home of the nationally recognized Port Townsend Wooden Boat Festival. *Address:* Water St. and Polk St. *City:* Port Townsend *State:* WA *Visitors welcome?* Yes *Hours:* Daily *Admission:* FREE *Operated by:* City of Port Townsend *NR?* No *NHL?* Yes *Latitude:* 48.1136 *Latitude:* -122.7590

PUGET SOUND NAVAL SHIPYARD
Puget Sound Naval Shipyard was originally established at Bremerton in 1891 as a naval station and was designated as a U.S. Navy shipyard in 1901. PSNS was the principal repair establishment for the Navy's battle-damaged battleships and aircraft carriers. *Address:* Gregory Way and Naval Ave. *City:* Bremerton *State:* WA *Visitors welcome?* Yes *Hours:* Contact attraction directly *Admission:* Contact attraction directly *Operated by:* Puget Sound Naval Shipyard *NR?* No *NHL?* Yes *Year established/built:* 1891 *Latitude:* 47.5642 *Latitude:* -122.6460

PUGET SOUND RADIO STATION HISTORIC DISTRICT
Address: 285 Fifth Street *City:* Bremerton *State:* WA *Visitors welcome?* Yes *NR?* Yes *NHL?* No *Year established/built:* 1920 *Latitude:* 47.5663 *Latitude:* -122.6260

CHAPTER 8 – DISTRICTS

Maritime Festivals Celebrate Culinary and Cultural Heritage
by
Joe Follansbee

Most community festivals focus on a central theme: music, the arts, food, local history. The community maritime festival often brings all these themes together under an umbrella of life in, on, and around the water. Some celebrate the hard work of maritime industry, such as the Seattle Maritime Festival in early May, which features tugboat races that draw working and historic tugs from as far away as Canada. Other festivals revolve around folk traditions, particularly music, such as September's Portsmouth Maritime Folk Festival in Portsmouth, N.H. Seafood is a major element of most maritime festivals, and sometimes the main element, as in the Florida Seafood Festival in Apalachicola, Fla. in November. And though most festivals happen in the warmer months of the year, especially spring and early summer, you can find a maritime festival somewhere in the U.S. almost any month of the year.

Here's a list of the most popular maritime-themed festival from around the nation.

February
Chicago Maritime Festival
Chicago, IL
Chicago Maritime Festival
chriskastle@yahoo.com
www.chicagomaritimefestival.org

Fisher Poets Gathering
Astoria, OR
Clatsop Community College
503-325-4972
www.clatsopcollege.com/fisherpoets/
fsage@clatsopcc.edu

Great Lakes Shipwreck Festival
Ann Arbor, MI
Dossin Great Lakes Museum
www.shipwreckfestival.org

March
Ghost Ships Festival
Milwaukee, WI
Great Lakes Shipwreck Research Foundation
info@ghost-ships.org
www.ghost-ships.org

Gulf Maritime Festival
Tarpon Springs, FL

City of Tarpon Springs
floridamaritimeheritage.org

St. Augustine Lighthouse Festival
St. Augustine, FL
St. Augustine Lighthouse & Museum
904-829-0745
www.staugustinelighthouse.com
info@staugustinelighthouse.com

April
Astoria Warrenton Crab, Seafood & Festival
Astoria, OR
Astoria & Warrenton Area Chamber of Commerce
800-875-6807
www.oldoregon.com/events/entry/astoria-warrenton-crab-seafood-wine-festival/
info@oldoregon.com

Blessing of the Fleet
Darien, GA
Darien-McIntosh County Chamber of Commerce
www.blessingofthefleet.com

Crystal River Boat Bash
Crystal River, FL
Crystal River Reserve State Park
850-245-2157
www.floridastateparks.org/crystalriverpreserve/

May
Cape Cod Maritime Days
Hyannis, MA
Cape Cod Chamber of Commerce
508-362-3225
www.ecapechamber.com/MaritimeDays/
info@capecodchamber.org

Hudson River Shad Festival
Kingston, NY
Hudson River Maritime Museum
845-338-0071
www.hrmm.org
hrmm@hvc.rr.com

Juneau Maritime Festival
Juneau, AK
Juneau Maritime Festival
907-523-2330
juneaumaritimefestival.org

jrintala@jedc.org

Mackinaw Maritime Festival
Mackinaw City, MI
Great Lakes Lighthouse Keepers Association
231-436-5580
www.mackinawmaritimefestival.com
info@gllka.com

Maryland Maritime Heritage Festival
Annapolis, MD
Maryland Maritime Heritage Festival
410-693-8394
davehanson1011@gmail.com

Passaic River Maritime Festival
Newark, NJ
Passaic River Maritime Festival
www.passaicrivermaritimefestival.com
info@passaicrivermaritimefestival.com

Penn Cove Water Festival
Coupeville, WA
Penn Cove Water Festival
www.penncovewaterfestival.com
RoseAnn@IslandCountyTourism.com

Sea Festival
Santa Barbara, CA
Santa Barbara Maritime Museum
805-962-8404
www.sbmm.org/Featured-Events/seafestival.html

Seattle Maritime Festival
Seattle, WA
Seattle Propeller Club
206-282-6858
www.seattlepropellerclub.org/maritimefestival.html
Ken@HamiltonSaunderson.com

Solomons Maritime Festival
Solomons, MD
Calvert Marine Museum
410-326-2042
www.calvertmarinemuseum.com

June
James River Batteau Festival
Lynchburg, VA

Virginia Canals & Navigations Society
www.batteau.org

Northport Lighthouse and Maritime Festival
Northport, MI
Grand Traverse Lighthouse Museum
231-386-7195
www.grandtraverselighthouse.com
gtlthse@triton.net

Windjammer Days Festival
Boothbay Harbor, ME
Maine Windjammer Association
207-374-2993
www.sailmainecoast.com/about_mwa/fleetevents.htm

Wooden Boat Show
Mystic, CT
Wooden Boat Magazine
800-273-7447
www.thewoodenboatshow.com
michele@woodenboat.com

July
Ballard SeafoodFest
Seattle, WA
Ballard Chamber of Commerce
206-784-9705
www.seafoodfest.org
seafoodfest@ballardchamber.com

Beaufort Water Festival
Beaufort, SC
Beaufort Water Festival
843-524-0600
www.bftwaterfestival.com
info@bftwaterfestival.com

Mandeville Seafood Festival
Mandeville, LA
Greater Mandeville Seafood Association
985-624-9762
www.seafoodfest.com

Merrimack River Maritime Festival
Salisbury Beach, MA
Salisbury Beach State Reservation
978-462-7874
www.beachfests.org

CHAPTER 8 – DISTRICTS

Oswego Harborfest
Oswego, NY
Oswego Harbor Festivals
315-343-6858
www.oswegoharborfest.com

Thunder Bay Maritime Festival
Alpena, MI
Thunder Bay National Marine Sanctuary
989-356-8805
thunderbay.noaa.gov/

August
Commencement Bay Maritime Festival
Tacoma, WA
Commencement Bay Maritime Fest
253-318-2210
www.maritimefest.org
maritime_fest@yahoo.com

Family Maritime Festival
Essex, CT
Connecticut River Museum
860-767-8269
www.ctrivermuseum.org

Lake Champlain Maritime Festival
Burlington, VT
Lake Champlain Maritime Festival
802-482-3313
www.lcmfestival.com
bigredpenproductions@hotmail.com

Rogers City Nautical Festival
Rogers City, WI
Nautical City Festival
nautical@charterinternet.com
www.nauticalfestival.org

September
Dana Point Tall Ships Festival
Dana Point, CA
Ocean Institute
949-496-2274
www.ocean-institute.org

Greenport Maritime Festival
Greenport, NY
East End Seaport Museum and Marine Foundation

631-477-2100
eseaport@verizon.net

Hampton Beach Seafood Festival
Hampton, NH
Hampton Area Chamber of Commerce
603-926-8718
www.hamptonbeachseafoodfestival.com
info@hamptonchamber.com

Michigan Schooner Festival
Traverse City, MI
Maritime Heritage Alliance
231-946-2647
www.michiganschoonerfestival.org
Mark@MaritimeHeritageAlliance.org

Ohio River Sternwheel Festival
Marietta, OH
Washington County Convention and Visitors Bureau
800-288-2577
www.ohioriversternwheelfestival.org

Olympia Harbor Days
Olympia, WA
Olympia Harbor Days
harbordays@comcast.net
www.harbordays.com

Pittsburg Seafood Festival
Pittsburg, PA
Pittsburg Chamber of Commerce
925-432-7301
www.pittsburgchamber.org

Port Townsend Wooden Boat Festival
Port Townsend, WA
Wooden Boat Foundation
360-385-3628
www.woodenboat.org/festival/
ask@woodenboat.org

Portsmouth Maritime Folk Festival
Portsmouth, NH
New England Folk Network
pmff@comcast.net
www.newenglandfolknetwork.org/pmff/

Redondo Beach Lobster Festival
Redondo Beach, CA

Redondo Beach Chamber of Commerce & Visitors Bureau
310-376-6911
www.lobsterfestival.com
info@redondochamber.org

October
Boast the Coast Maritime Festival
Lewes, DE
Lewes Chamber of Commerce
877-465-3937
www.leweschamber.com

Classic & Wooden Boat Festival
Sturgeon Bay, WI
Door County Maritime Museum
920-743-5958
www.dcmm.org
info@dcmm.org

North Carolina Seafood Festival
Morehead City, NC
North Carolina Seafood Festival
252-726-NCSF
www.ncseafoodfestival.org
fun@ncseafoodfestival.org

North Coast Seafood Festival
Tillamook, OR
North Coast Seafood Festival
503-398-5223
www.northcoastseafoodfestival.com
seafoodfestival@oregoncoast.com

November
Florida Seafood Festival
Apalachicola, FL
Florida Seafood Festival
888-653-8011
www.floridaseafoodfestival.com
information@floridaseafoodfestival.com

Fyddeye is expanding its maritime festival calendar. Submit your annual event at www.fyddeye.com.

CHAPTER 9 – STRUCTURES & SITES
STAND-ALONE BUILDINGS, STRUCTURES AND MARITIME HISTORY SITES

Naval gun firing at the National Civil War Naval Museum (Columbus, Ga.)

In most port cities, even in those that haven't preserved older neighborhoods or didn't have a large waterfront, a few buildings or structures remain that are tied to the community's maritime past. They're re-used as office buildings, community gathering places, natural areas, or museums, often with a maritime theme. Some are the preserved homes of individuals, literally "captains" of industry. In some places, a specific geographic site, such as a falls or stretch of riverbank or beach, holds significance in the maritime past, though there's nothing beyond a signpost to remind the visitor of the local event. This chapter includes stand-alone structures or sites not generally part of a district or other maritime history attraction.

CALIFORNIA

 CABRILLO NATIONAL MONUMENT

Climbing out of his boat and onto shore in 1542, Juan Rodriguez Cabrillo stepped into history as the first European to set foot on what is now the West Coast of the United States. In addition to telling the story of 16th century exploration, the park is home to two historic lighthouses. *Address:* 1800 Cabrillo Memorial

Drive *City:* San Diego *State:* CA *Zip:* 92106 *Phone:* 619-557-5450 *Web:* www.nps.gov/cabr/ *Visitors welcome?* Yes *Hours:* Daily, 9 a.m. to 5 p.m. *Admission:* FREE *Operated by:* Cabrillo National Monument *NR?* No *NHL?* No *Latitude:* 32.7015 *Latitude:* -117.2490

CHINA CABIN
The China Cabin is the preserved saloon from the steamship China, now on a pier in Belvedere and used as a meeting facility. *Address:* 54 Beach Road *City:* Belvedere *State:* CA *Zip:* 94920 *Phone:* 415-435-1853 *Web:* www.landmarks-society.org *Visitors welcome?* Yes *Hours:* Contact attraction directly *Admission:* Contact attraction directly *Operated by:* Belvedere-Tiburon Landmarks Society *NR?* No *NHL?* No *Year established/built:* 1866 *Latitude:* 37.8733 *Latitude:* -122.4630

MUNICIPAL FERRY TERMINAL
The Municipal Ferry Terminal in San Pedro is now the home to the Los Angeles Maritime Museum. *Address:* Berth 84, Foot of 6th St. *City:* San Pedro *State:* CA *Zip:* 90731 *Phone:* 310-548-7618 *Web:* www.lamaritimemuseum.org *Visitors welcome?* Yes *Hours:* Tuesday to Saturday, 10 a.m. to 5 p.m.; Sunday, noon to 5 p.m. *Admission:* $3 adults, $1 seniors/youths, children FREE *Operated by:* Los Angeles Maritime Museum *NR?* Yes *NHL?* No *Year established/built:* 1941 *Latitude:* 33.7387 *Latitude:* -118.2790

FLORIDA

BARNACLE HISTORIC STATE PARK
The Barnacle Historic State Park offers a lovely ever-changing view of Biscayne Bay and a steady gaze back in time into Old Florida. *Address:* 3485 Main Highway *City:* Coconut Grove *State:* FL *Zip:* 33133 *Phone:* 305-442-6866 *Web:* www.floridastateparks.org/thebarnacle/ *Visitors welcome?* Yes *Hours:* Wednesday to Monday, 9 a.m. to 5 p.m. *Admission:* $1 adults, six and under FREE *Operated by:* Florida Division of Recreation and Parks *NR?* No *NHL?* No *Latitude:* 25.7253 *Latitude:* -80.2425

VINCE J. WHIBBS SR COMMUNITY MARITIME PARK
The Vince J. Whibbs Sr Community Maritime Park is a waterfront development in Pensacola, Florida that converts a former refinery site to public use with shopping, dining, residential development, and a new maritime museum. *City:* Pensacola *State:* FL *Web:* maritimetimepark.us *Email:* info@maritimepark.us *Visitors welcome?* No *Hours:* Contact owner *Admission:* Contact owner *Operated by:* City of Pensacola *NR?* No *NHL?* No *Year established/built:* 2004

ILLINOIS

GAYLORD BUILDING
The Gaylord Building played a major role in creation of the Illinois & Michigan Canal, the final link in America *Address:* 200 W. Eighth St. *City:* Lockport *State:* IL *Zip:* 60441 *Phone:* 815-838-9400 *Web:* 128.121.65.131/gaylord/ *Email:* gaylord@canalcor.org *Visitors welcome?* Yes *Hours:* Tuesday to Saturday, 11 am. to 5 p.m.; Sunday, noon to 5 p.m. *Admission:* Contact attraction directly *Operated by:* Canal Corridor Association *NR?* No *NHL?* No *Latitude:* 41.5906 *Latitude:* -88.0580

ILLINOIS & MICHIGAN CANAL NATIONAL HERITAGE CORRIDOR

The Illinois & Michigan Canal National Heritage Corridor is a group of heritage sites, including maritime heritage sites, along the historic I&M Canal. *City:* Joliet *State:* IL *Phone:* 800-926-2262 *Toll-free:* 800-926-2262 *Web:* www.heritagecorridorcvb.com *Email:* info@heritagecorridorcvb.com *Visitors welcome?* Yes *Hours:* Contact attraction directly *Admission:* Contact attraction directly *Operated by:* Illinois & Michigan Canal National Heritage Corridor *NR?* No *NHL?* No *Latitude:* 41.5250 *Latitude:* -88.0817

MISSISSIPPI RIVER VISITOR CENTER

The Mississippi River Visitors Center welcomes over 60,000 people annually and is handicapped accessible. In addition to providing lock and dam tours during the summer months, rangers also offer a wide range of programs to the local community. *Address:* Bldg 382, Rock Island Arsenal *City:* Rock Island *State:* IL *Zip:* 61201 *Phone:* 309-794-5338 *Web:* www.mvr.usace.army.mil/missriver/VC%20Page/Mississippi%20River%20Vistor.htm *Visitors welcome?* Yes *Hours:* Daily, 9 a.m. to 5 p.m. *Admission:* FREE *Operated by:* U.S. Army Corps of Engineers (Rock Island District) *NR?* No *NHL?* No *Latitude:* 41.5180 *Latitude:* -90.5370

INDIANA

FALLS OF THE OHIO STATE PARK

The Interpretive Center at Falls of the Ohio State Park includes reproduction pilot houses from a steamboat and a modern towboat. *Address:* 201 West Riverside Dr. *City:* Clarksville *State:* IN *Zip:* 47129 *Phone:* 812-280-9970 *Web:* www.fallsoftheohio.org *Email:* park@fallsoftheohio.org *Visitors welcome?* Yes *Hours:* Daily, 7 a.m. to 11 p.m. *Admission:* Contact attraction directly *Operated by:* Falls of the Ohio State Park *NR?* No *NHL?* No *Latitude:* 38.2766 *Latitude:* -85.7630

WABASH & ERIE CANAL PARK

Founded in 1972, the Carroll County Wabash & Erie Canal is dedicated to the preservation of the stretch of the Wabash & Erie Canal located in Delphi, Indiana. *Address:* 3198 N 700 W. *City:* Delphi *State:* IN *Zip:* 46923 *Phone:* 765-564-6572 *Web:* www.wabashanderiecanal.org *Email:* mccain@carlnet.org *Visitors welcome?* Yes *Hours:* Daily *Admission:* FREE *Operated by:* Carroll County Wabash and Erie Canal *NR?* No *NHL?* No *Year established/built:* 1972 *Latitude:* 40.5974 *Latitude:* -86.6602

WHITEWATER CANAL STATE HISTORIC SITE

A 14-mile stretch of the Whitewater Canal, an important navigation project for the region, is open to visitors, and include canal boat rides. *Address:* 19083 Clayborn St. *City:* Metamora *State:* IN *Zip:* 47030 *Phone:* 765-647-6512 *Web:* www.in.gov/ism/StateHistoricSites/WhitewaterCanal/ *Email:* whitewatercanalshs@dnr.in.gov *Visitors welcome?* Yes *Hours:* Wednesday to Sunday, 9 a.m. to 5 p.m. *Admission:* $4 adults, $3.50 seniors, $2 children four to 11, three and under FREE *Operated by:* Whitewater Canal State Historic Site *NR?* No *NHL?* No *Year established/built:* 1836 *Latitude:* 39.4161 *Latitude:* -85.1376

MAINE

JOHN HANCOCK WHARF
The John Hancock Warehouse is the only remaining commercial building from the Colonial period in York, which was an important town on the York River. *City:* York *State:* ME *Phone:* 207-363-4974 *Web:* www.oldyork.org *Email:* oyhs@oldyork.org *Visitors welcome?* Yes *Hours:* Contact attraction directly *Admission:* Contact attraction directly *Operated by:* Old York Historical Society *NR?* No *NHL?* No *Latitude:* 43.1546 *Latitude:* -70.6589

MASSACHUSETTS

 ### BOSTON NAVAL SHIPYARD (CHARLESTOWN NAVY YARD)
The Boston Naval Shipyard, also called the Charlestown Navy Yard, is part of the Boston National Historical Park. *Address:* Boston National Historic Park, Charlestown Navy Yard *City:* Boston *State:* MA *Zip:* 02129 *Phone:* 617-242-5601 *Web:* www.nps.gov/bost/historyculture/usscassinyoung.htm *Visitors welcome?* Yes *Hours:* Daily, 9 a.m. to 5 p.m. *Admission:* FREE *Operated by:* Boston National Historical Park *NR?* No *NHL?* No *Year established/built:* 1800 *Latitude:* 42.3722 *Latitude:* -71.0546

CAPT. JOHN WILSON HOUSE
The Captain John Wilson House is the last relatively unaltered building remaining from the early years of the commercial maritime era of the town of Cohasset. *Address:* 4 Elm St. *City:* Cohasset *State:* MA *Zip:* 02025 *Phone:* 781-383-1434 *Web:* www.cohassethistoricalsociety.org *Email:* cohassethistory@yahoo.com *Visitors welcome?* Yes *Hours:* Contact attraction directly *Admission:* Contact attraction directly *Operated by:* Cohasset Historical Society *NR?* No *NHL?* No *Year established/built:* 1810 *Latitude:* 42.2408 *Latitude:* -70.8016

EDWARD PENNIMAN HOUSE
Sitting atop Fort Hill in Eastham is the Second Empire style home of Captain Edward Penniman. *Address:* Fort Hill Rd. and Governor Prence Rd. *City:* Eastham *State:* MA *Zip:* 02642 *Phone:* 508-487-1256 *Web:* www.nps.gov/caco/ *Visitors welcome?* Yes *Hours:* Summers. Contact attraction directly. *Admission:* FREE *Operated by:* Cape Cod National Seashore *NR?* Yes *NHL?* No *Year established/built:* 1868 *Latitude:* 41.8186 *Latitude:* -69.9666

GLOUCESTER NET AND TWINE COMPANY
Incorporated in 1884, the Gloucester Net and Twine Company is associated with the intense development of fisheries in the late 19th and early 20th centuries in Gloucester. *Address:* Maplewood Ave. and Grove St. *City:* Gloucester *State:* MA *Visitors welcome?* No *Operated by:* Private owner *NR?* No *NHL?* No *Year established/built:* 1884 *Latitude:* 42.6215 *Latitude:* -70.6687

LONG WHARF AND CUSTOM HOUSE BLOCK
Established in 1710, the Long Wharf and Custom House Block are privately owned, though visitors can access the site. *Address:* Foot of State Street *City:* Boston *State:* MA *Zip:* 02110 *Visitors welcome?* Yes *Hours:* Daily *Admission:* FREE *Operated by:* Private owner *NR?* No *NHL?* Yes *Year established/built:* 1710 *Latitude:* 42.6479 *Latitude:* -71.3066

MARINER'S HOUSE
Constructed in 1847 as a temperance boardinghouse for seamen, the Mariner's House is significant as one of the oldest continuously operating sailors' boardinghouses in the United States and for its association with Father Edward Thompson Taylor. *Address:* 11 North Square *City:* Boston *State:* MA *Zip:* 02113 *Phone:* 617-227-3979 *Toll-free:* 877-732-9494 *Web:* www.marinershouse.org *Email:* inn@marinershouse.org *Visitors welcome?* Yes *Hours:* Contact attraction directly *Admission:* Contact attraction directly *Operated by:* Boston Port and Seaman's Aid Society *NR?* No *NHL?* No *Year established/built:* 1847 *Latitude:* 42.3639 *Latitude:* -71.0531

NATHANIAL BOWDITCH HOUSE
The Nathaniel Bowditch House was occupied by Nathaniel Bowditch and his family in the early 19th century. *Address:* 9 North St. *City:* Salem *State:* MA *Phone:* 978-745-0799 *Web:* www.historicsalem.org *Email:* info@historicsalem.org *Visitors welcome?* Yes *Hours:* Contact attraction directly *Admission:* Contact attraction directly *Operated by:* Historic Salem *NR?* No *NHL?* Yes *Latitude:* 42.5216 *Latitude:* -70.8987

NAVAL HOSPITAL BOSTON HISTORIC DISTRICT
Established in 1857, the Chelsea Naval Hospital is now privately owned within the Naval Hospital Boston Historic District. Structures are viewable from the street. *Address:* Mystic River *City:* Chelsea *State:* MA *Visitors welcome?* Yes *Hours:* Daily *Admission:* FREE *Operated by:* Private owner *NR?* No *NHL?* No *Year established/built:* 1857 *Latitude:* 42.3930 *Latitude:* -71.0810

OUR LADY OF GOOD VOYAGE CHURCH
Originally dedicated in 1893, Our Lady of Good Voyage was built for the Portuguese community in Gloucester, after they petitioned the Roman Catholic Church for the establishment of a place to worship dedicated to the Madonna. *Address:* 142 Prospect St. *City:* Gloucester *State:* MA *Phone:* 978-283-1490 *Visitors welcome?* Yes *Hours:* Contact attraction directly *Admission:* Contact attraction directly *Operated by:* Private owner *NR?* No *NHL?* No *Year established/built:* 1914 *Latitude:* 42.6172 *Latitude:* -70.6573

UNION OYSTER HOUSE
Established in 1826, the Union Oyster House is the oldest continuously operating restaurant in the U.S. *Address:* 41 Union St. *City:* Boston *State:* MA *Zip:* 02135 *Phone:* 617-227-2750 *Web:* www.unionoysterhouse.com *Email:* info@unionoysterhouse.com *Visitors welcome?* Yes *Hours:* Contact attraction directly *Admission:* Contact attraction directly *Operated by:* Union Oyster House *NR?* No *NHL?* Yes *Year established/built:* 1826 *Latitude:* 42.3454 *Latitude:* -71.1494

UNION WHARF
Established in 1845, Union Wharf is now privately owned. *Address:* Commercial Street *City:* Boston *State:* MA *Visitors welcome?* No *Operated by:* Private owner *NR?* No *NHL?* No *Year established/built:* 1845 *Latitude:* 42.3630 *Latitude:* -71.0517

U.S. CUSTOM HOUSE (NEW BEDFORD)
Completed in 1836, the U.S. Custom House in New Bedford is the oldest continuously operating Custom House in the nation. *Address:* 37 N. Second St. *City:* New Bedford *State:* MA *Zip:* 02740 *Phone:* 508-996-4095 *Web:* www.nps.gov/nebe/ *Visitors welcome?* Yes *Hours:* Monday through Friday, 9 a.m. to 5 p.m. *Admission:* FREE *Operated by:* New Bedford Whaling National Historical Park *NR?* No *NHL?* No *Year established/built:* 1836 *Latitude:* 41.6354 *Latitude:* -70.9245

MARYLAND

CHESAPEAKE & OHIO NATIONAL HISTORICAL PARK
In the 19th century the C&O Canal provided jobs and opportunities for people throughout the Potomac River Valley. Today the canal's remains provide a place to recreate and enjoy nature, but most importantly they tell the story of the canal's important role in economic history. *Address:* 11710 MacArthur Blvd. *City:* Potomac *State:* MD *Zip:* 20854 *Phone:* 301-767-3714 *Web:* www.nps.gov/choh/index.htm *Visitors welcome?* Yes *Hours:* Daily *Admission:* FREE *Operated by:* Chesapeake & Ohio National Historical Park *NR?* No *NHL?* No *Latitude:* 39.0014 *Latitude:* -77.2465

MICHIGAN

SOO LOCKS VISITORS CENTER
Located within the Soo Locks on Portage Avenue, this park and information center offers visitors to the Sault a tremendous opportunity to experience the engineering marvel that is the Soo Locks. *Address:* 536 Ashmun St. *City:* Sault St. Marie *State:* MI *Zip:* 49783 *Phone:* 906-253-9101 *Web:* www.soolocksvisitorscenter.com *Email:* info@saultstemarie.com *Visitors welcome?* Yes *Hours:* Mother's Day weekend through mid-October: Daily, 9 a.m. to 9 p.m. *Admission:* FREE *Operated by:* Soo Locks Visitors Center Association *NR?* No *NHL?* No *Latitude:* 46.3931 *Latitude:* -84.2887

ST. JOSEPH LIGHTHOUSE DEPOT
The St. Joseph Lighthouse Depot is now the home to the St. Joseph River Yacht Club. *Address:* St. Joseph River *City:* St. Joseph *State:* MI *Visitors welcome?* No *Operated by:* Private owner *NR?* No *NHL?* No *Latitude:* 42.1142 *Latitude:* -86.4884

THUNDER BAY NATIONAL MARINE SANCTUARY
The Thunder Bay National Marine Sanctuary includes information on shipwrecks, which attract recreational divers from around the world. *Address:* 500 W Fletcher St. *City:* Alpena *State:* MI *Zip:* 49707 *Phone:* 989-356-8805 *Web:* www.thunderbay.noaa.gov *Email:* thunderbay@noaa.gov *Visitors welcome?* Yes *Hours:* Contact attraction directly *Admission:* Contact attraction directly *Operated by:* Thunder Bay National Marine Sanctuary *NR?* No *NHL?* No *Latitude:* 45.0673 *Latitude:* -83.4330

MINNESOTA

SANDY LAKE AND DAM
The Big Sandy Lake Lock and Dam was originally built of wood in 1895 and is now a major recreation area. *City:* McGregor *State:* MN *Zip:* 55760 *Phone:* 218-426-3482 *Web:* www.mvp.usace.army.mil/navigation/default.asp?pageid=148 *Email:* lake.sandy@usace.army.mil *Visitors welcome?* Yes *Hours:* Contact attraction directly *Admission:* Contact attraction directly *Operated by:* U.S. Army Corps of Engineers (St. Paul District) *NR?* No *NHL?* No *Latitude:* 46.6067 *Latitude:* -93.3128

NEW HAMPSHIRE

JOHN PAUL JONES HOUSE
Address: 43 Middle St. *City:* Portsmouth *State:* NH *Zip:* 03802 *Phone:* 603-436-8420 *Web:* www.portsmouth-history.org *Visitors welcome?* Yes *Hours:* Memorial Day through October: Daily, 11 a.m. to 5 p.m. *Admission:* $6 adults, $5 Portsmouth residents, 12 and under FREE *Operated by:* Portsmouth Historical Society *NR?* No *NHL?* No *Year established/built:* 1781 *Latitude:* 43.0645 *Latitude:* -70.7679

NEW YORK

CADDEL DRY DOCK
The vintage dry dock is used by the North River Tugboat Museum for vessel maintenance. *Address:* 300 Greenkill Ave. *City:* Kingston *State:* NY *Zip:* 12401 *Phone:* 845-340-0506 *Web:* www.tugmuseum.com *Email:* steve@tugmuseum.com *Visitors welcome?* No *Hours:* Contact attraction directly *Admission:* Contact attraction directly *Operated by:* North River Tugboat Museum *NR?* No *NHL?* No *Year established/built:* 1916 *Latitude:* 41.9230 *Latitude:* -74.0155

GUY PARK STATE HISTORIC SITE
Guy Park State Historic Site is near an operating barge canal lock on the Erie Canal. *Address:* 366 W. Main St. *City:* Amsterdam *State:* NY *Zip:* 12012 *Phone:* 518-842-7150 *Visitors welcome?* Yes *Hours:* Contact attraction directly *Admission:* Contact attraction directly *Operated by:* New York State Office of Parks, Recreation and Historic Preservation *NR?* No *NHL?* No *Year established/built:* 1773 *Latitude:* 42.9463 *Latitude:* -74.2086

NEW YORK STATE CANAL SYSTEM
The New York State Canal System--made up of the Erie, Champlain, Oswego, and Cayuga Seneca Canals--is a navigable 524-mile inland waterway that crosses upstate New York. It forms an extensive transportation network providing intermodal linkages within and outside the state. *Address:* 200 Southern Blvd. *City:* Albany *State:* NY *Zip:* 12201 *Phone:* 518-436-2700 *Toll-free:* 800-422-6254 *Web:* www.nyscanals.gov *Visitors welcome?* Yes *Hours:* Contact attraction directly *Admission:* Contact attraction directly *Operated by:* New York State Canals *NR?* No *NHL?* No *Latitude:* 42.6298 *Latitude:* -73.7765

OLD ERIE CANAL STATE HISTORIC PARK
Old Erie Canal State Historic Park is a 36-mile stretch of the 363-mile Old Erie Canal, which has been designated a National Recreational Trail by the National Parks Service. *Address:* 8729 Andrus Rd. *City:* Kirkville *State:* NY *Zip:* 13082 *Phone:* 315-687-7821 *Web:* nysparks.state.ny.us/sites/info.asp?siteID=31 *Visitors welcome?* Yes *Hours:* Daily *Admission:* FREE *Operated by:* New York State Office of Parks, Recreation and Historic Preservation *NR?* No *NHL?* No *Latitude:* 43.0713 *Latitude:* -75.9249

PENNSYLVANIA RAILROAD BARGE
No information available. *Address:* 300 Greenkill Ave. *City:* Kingston *State:* NY *Zip:* 12401 *Phone:* 845-340-0506 *Web:* www.tugmuseum.com *Email:* steve@tugmuseum.com *Visitors welcome?* No *Hours:* Contact attraction directly *Admission:* Contact attraction directly *Operated by:* North River Tugboat Museum *NR?* No *NHL?* No *Year established/built:* 1930 *Latitude:* 41.9230 *Latitude:* -74.0155

CHAPTER 9 – STRUCTURES & SITES

PIER 66 MARITIME
Pier 66 Maritime is a barge moored at Pier 66 on New York Harbor. It is home to several activities and organizations, including the fireboat John J. Harvey and the lightship Frying Pan. *Address:* Pier 66 *City:* New York *State:* NY *Zip:* 10011 *Phone:* 212-989-6363 *Web:* www.pier66maritime.com *Email:* info@pier-66maritime.com *Visitors welcome?* Yes *Hours:* Contact attraction directly *Admission:* Contact attraction directly *Operated by:* Pier 66 Maritime *NR?* No *NHL?* No *Latitude:* 40.9233 *Latitude:* -73.9047

SCHOHARIE CROSSING STATE HISTORIC SITE
Schoharie Crossing State Historic Site is dedicated to the preservation and interpretation of the Erie Canal as one of the 19th century's greatest commercial and engineering projects. The Visitor Center exhibit traces the history of the Erie Canal and its *Address:* 129 Schoharie St. *City:* Fort Hunger *State:* NY *Zip:* 12069 *Phone:* 518-829-7516 *Web:* nysparks.state.ny.us/sites/info.asp?siteID=26 *Visitors welcome?* Yes *Hours:* May: Wednesday to Saturday, 10 a.m. to 5 p.m.; Sunday, 1 p.m. to 5 p.m.; June to October: Wednesday to Monday: 10 a.m. to 5 p.m. *Admission:* FREE *Operated by:* New York State Office of Parks, Recreation and Historic Preservation *NR?* No *NHL?* No *Latitude:* 42.9412 *Latitude:* -74.2821

OHIO

ROSCOE VILLAGE
Once a bustling port on the Ohio & Erie Canal, Historic Roscoe Village now mixes the charm and history of the 1800s with plenty of fun and adventure for today. *Address:* 600 N. Whitewoman St. *City:* Coshocton *State:* OH *Zip:* 43812 *Phone:* 740-622-9310 *Toll-free:* 800-877-1830 *Web:* www.roscoevillage.com *Visitors welcome?* Yes *Hours:* Daily *Admission:* Contact attraction directly *Operated by:* Roscoe Village Foundation *NR?* No *NHL?* No *Latitude:* 40.2816 *Latitude:* -81.8766

OKLAHOMA

JON R. STUART MARITIME PARK
The Jon R. Stuart Maritime Park features the historic towboat Charley Border and the Oklahoma Maritime Education Center. *Address:* 5350 Cimarron Road *City:* Catoosa *State:* OK *Zip:* 74015 *Phone:* 918-266-2291 *Web:* www.tulsaweb.com *Email:* museum@tulsaport.com *Visitors welcome?* Yes *Hours:* Contact attraction directly *Admission:* Contact attraction directly *Operated by:* Arkansas River Historical Society *NR?* No *NHL?* No *Latitude:* 36.2312 *Latitude:* -95.7417

PENNSYLVANIA

ERIE EXTENSION CANAL LOCKTENDER'S HOUSE
The Erie Extension Canal's Locktender House is an exhibit of the National Canal Museum. *Address:* 30 Centre Square *City:* Easton *State:* PA *Zip:* 18042 *Phone:* 610-559-6613 *Web:* canals.org *Email:* toms@canals.org *Visitors welcome?* Yes *Hours:* Contact attraction directly *Admission:* Contact attraction directly *Operated by:* National Canal Museum *NR?* No *NHL?* No *Latitude:* 40.6912 *Latitude:* -75.2099

SCHUYKILL CANAL PARK
Schuykill Canal Park includes a 2.5-mile waterway and some five miles of towpath and trails in the undeveloped greenway between the canal and the Schuykill River, all totaling about 60 linear acres. *City:* Phoenixville *State:* PA *Zip:* 19460 *Phone:* 610-917-0021 *Web:* www.schuylkillcanal.com *Email:* programs@schuylkillcanal.com *Visitors welcome?* Yes *Hours:* Daily *Admission:* FREE *Operated by:* Schuykill Canal Association *NR?* No *NHL?* No *Latitude:* 40.1304 *Latitude:* -75.5149

RHODE ISLAND

JOHN H. CHAFEE BLACKSTONE RIVER VALLEY NATIONAL HERITAGE CORRIDOR
The John H. Chafee Blackstone River Valley National Heritage Corridor is a virtual park featuring 24 communities that stretch from the headwaters of the Blackstone River in Worcester, Mass. to Narragansett Bay. *Address:* One Depot Square *City:* Woonsocket *State:* RI *Zip:* 02895 *Phone:* 401-762-0250 *Web:* www.nps.gov/archive/blac/home.htm *Email:* Barbara_Dixon@nps.gov *Visitors welcome?* Yes *Hours:* Daily *Admission:* FREE *Operated by:* John H. Chafee Blackstone River Valley Commission *NR?* No *NHL?* No *Latitude:* 42.0037 *Latitude:* -71.5132

SOUTH CAROLINA

LANDSFORD CANAL STATE PARK
Stretched along the Catawba River along the South Carolina fall line, the park is home to the well-preserved remains of the canal system that made the river commercially navigable from 1820 to 1835. *Address:* 2051 Park Dr. *City:* Catawba *State:* SC *Zip:* 29704 *Phone:* 803-789-5800 *Web:* www.southcarolinaparks.com/parkfinder/state-park/916.aspx *Email:* landsfordcanal@scprt.com *Visitors welcome?* Yes *Hours:* Daily, 9 a.m. to 6 p.m. *Admission:* $2 adults, $1.25 seniors, 15 and under FREE *Operated by:* South Carolina Dept. of Parks, Recreation and Tourism *NR?* No *NHL?* No *Latitude:* 34.6993 *Latitude:* -80.8946

OLD SANTEE CANAL PARK
Old Santee Canal Park commemorates South Carolina's beautiful natural resources and emphasizes the tremendous historical significance of the Santee Canal. *Address:* 900 Stony Landing Road *City:* Moncks Corner *State:* SC *Zip:* 29461 *Phone:* 843-899-5200 *Web:* www.oldsanteecanalpark.org *Email:* parkinfo@santeecooper.com *Visitors welcome?* Yes *Hours:* Daily, 9 a.m. to 5 p.m. *Admission:* $3 adults, $2 seniors, children six and under FREE *Operated by:* Old Santee Canal Park *NR?* No *NHL?* No *Latitude:* 33.1960 *Latitude:* -80.0131

WASHINGTON

BELL STREET TERMINAL, PIER 66
Address: Pier 66 *City:* Seattle *State:* WA *Visitors welcome?* Yes *Hours:* Daily *Admission:* FREE *Operated by:* Propeller Club *NR?* No *NHL?* No *Latitude:* 47.6062 *Latitude:* -122.3320

CHAPTER 9 – STRUCTURES & SITES

BUILDING 50, PSNS
City: Bremerton *State:* WA *Visitors welcome?* Yes *Operated by:* Puget Sound Naval Shipyard *NR?* Yes *NHL?* No *Year established/built:* 1896 *Latitude:* 47.5673 *Latitude:* -122.6330

CAPT. THOMAS W. PHILLIPS HOUSE
Captain Thomas W. Phillips played an important role in the history of Puget Sound. *Address:* 11312 SW 232nd Street *City:* Vashon Island *State:* WA *Visitors welcome?* Yes *Hours:* Contact attraction directly *Admission:* Contact attraction directly *NR?* No *NHL?* No *Year established/built:* 1925 *Latitude:* 47.3983 *Latitude:* -122.4800

CHITTENDEN LOCKS / LAKE WASH. SHIP CANAL
Opened in 1917, the Hiram M. Chittenden Locks are the gateway from Lake Union and Lake Washington to Puget Sound. *Address:* 3015 NW 54th St *City:* Seattle *State:* WA *Visitors welcome?* Yes *Hours:* Visitor center: Winter (October 1 to April 30): 10 a.m. to 4 p.m., closed on Tuesdays and Wednesdays; Summer: (May 1 to September 30): daily, 10 a.m. to 6 p.m. *Admission:* FREE *Operated by:* U.S. Army Corps of Engineers (Seattle District) *NR?* Yes *NHL?* No *Year established/built:* 1906 *Latitude:* 47.6675 *Latitude:* -122.3980

DOCKTON
Address: 99th Ave. SW and SW Windmill St. *City:* Vashon Island *State:* WA *Visitors welcome?* Yes *Hours:* Daily *Admission:* FREE *NR?* No *NHL?* No *Year established/built:* 1908 *Latitude:* 47.3719 *Latitude:* -122.4610

What is your favorite historic district to take visitors? Email your suggestion to contact@fyddeye.com.

FISHERMAN'S TERMINAL
Fisherman's Terminal in Seattle is the home port for much of the Alaska fishing fleet and a popular tourist attraction. *Address:* 3919 18TH Ave W. *City:* Seattle *State:* WA *Visitors welcome?* Yes *Hours:* Daily *Admission:* FREE *Operated by:* Port of Seattle *NR?* No *NHL?* No *Year established/built:* 1917 *Latitude:* 47.6552 *Latitude:* -122.3800

FORT WORDEN STATE PARK
Address: 200 Battery Way *City:* Port Townsend *State:* WA *Visitors welcome?* Yes *Hours:* Daily *Admission:* FREE *Operated by:* Fort Worden State Park *NR?* No *NHL?* Yes *Latitude:* 48.1358 *Latitude:* -122.7670

GRAVEYARD OF THE PACIFIC
The mouth of the Columbia River, one of the longest rivers in North America, has claimed nearly 2,000 lives and hundreds of ships since explorers Meriwether Lewis and William Clark first saw the area in 1805. The bar *Address:* 2nd Ave. SW and Spruce St. E. *City:* Ilwaco *State:* WA *Visitors welcome?* Yes *Hours:* Summer: 6:30 a.m. to 10 p.m; Winter: 6:30 a.m. to 4 p.m. *Admission:* FREE *Operated by:* Lewis & Clark Interpretive Center *NR?* No *NHL?* No *Latitude:* 46.3088 *Latitude:* -124.0450

HISTORIC WHALING BUILDING, MEYDENBAUER BAY MARINA
Address: 2 - 99th Avenue NE *City:* Bellevue *State:* WA *Visitors welcome?* Yes *Operated by:* Bellevue Parks & Community Services *NR?* No *NHL?* No *Latitude:* 47.6101 *Latitude:* -122.2090

INDIANOLA PIER
In the years before an extensive network of paved roads criss-crossed the area, a fleet of small passenger steamers cruised the waters of Puget Sound. The mosquito fleet stopped at nearly every small town and large city on the Sound, including the community of Indianola. *Address:* Indianola Rd. NE and NE Shore Dr. *City:*

Indianola *State:* WA *Visitors welcome?* Yes *Hours:* Dawn to dusk *Admission:* FREE *NR?* No *NHL?* No *Latitude:* 47.7476 *Latitude:* -122.5260

JACK BLOCK PARK
Jack Block Park is one of several waterfront parks in the Seattle area offering a close-up view of waterfront activities. *Address:* Harbor Ave. SW and Lotus Ave. SW *City:* Seattle *State:* WA *Visitors welcome?* Yes *Hours:* Seven days, 6 a.m. to 9 p.m. *Admission:* FREE *Operated by:* Port of Seattle *NR?* No *NHL?* No *Year established/built:* 2001 *Latitude:* 47.5827 *Latitude:* -122.3740

LAKE UNION PARK
Lake Union Park features several outdoor maritime history exhibits, including Heritage Wharf, the berth for several historic vessels, including Virginia V, Duwamish, and Arthur Foss. *Address:* 860 Terry Ave. N. *City:* Seattle *State:* WA *Visitors welcome?* Yes *Hours:* Daily *Admission:* FREE *Operated by:* Seattle Parks and Recreation *NR?* No *NHL?* No *Year established/built:* 1999 *Latitude:* 47.6276 *Latitude:* -122.3370

MARITIME EVENT CENTER
The Maritime Event Center, formerly known at the Odyssey Maritime Discover Center, supports the maritime industry of Puget Sound with a premier meeting and educational facility. *Address:* 2205 Alaskan Way *City:* Seattle *State:* WA *Zip:* 98121 *Phone:* 206-269-4108 *Web:* www.ody.org *Email:* csandkam@MaritimeEventCenter.com *Visitors welcome?* Yes *Hours:* Contact attraction directly *Admission:* Contact attraction directly *Operated by:* Maritime Event Center *NR?* No *NHL?* No *Latitude:* 47.6115 *Latitude:* -122.3490

MODELS OF HISTORIC PUGET SOUND SHIPS
Nearly all of the actual vessels that plied the waters of Puget Sound are gone, but the Discovery Modelers Education Center of Seattle has recreated them with detailed scale models available to the public. Located at Lake Union Park, models include Capt. George Vancouver's Discovery and the first steamer on Puget Sound, the S.S. Beaver. *Address:* 860 Terry Ave. N. *City:* Seattle *State:* WA *Visitors welcome?* Yes *Hours:* Daily *Admission:* FREE *Operated by:* Discovery Modelers Education Center *NR?* No *NHL?* No *Latitude:* 47.6276 *Latitude:* -122.3370

NAVAL RESERVE BUILDING
Lake Union Park in Seattle is a focal point for maritime heritage, with the Naval Reserve Building its most prominent feature. Built in 1941, the blue, white and gold structure was the local headquarters for the U.S. Naval Reserve before it was purchased the City of Seattle. It will soon become the home of the Museum of History & Industry. *Address:* 860 Terry Ave. N. *City:* Seattle *State:* WA *Visitors welcome?* Yes *Hours:* Contact attraction directly *Admission:* Contact attraction directly *Operated by:* Seattle Parks and Recreation *NR?* No *NHL?* No *Year established/built:* 1941 *Latitude:* 47.6276 *Latitude:* -122.3370

NORTH WIND'S FISH WEIR
North Wind's Fish Weir is a traditional landmark and fishing spot for the Duwamish, Muckleshoot and other native tribes that live in the Puget Sound area. *Address:* Tukwila International blvd and E. Marginal Way S. *City:* Tukwila *State:* WA *Visitors welcome?* Yes *Hours:* Daily *Admission:* FREE *NR?* No *NHL?* No *Latitude:* 47.5098 *Latitude:* -122.2920

SEAPORT LEARNING CENTER
The Seaport Learning Center is the Grays Harbor Historical Seaport Authority's facility designed for hands-on learning of maritime skills and other activities. *Address:* 712 Hagara St. *City:* Aberdeen *State:* WA *Zip:* 98520 *Phone:* 369-532-8611 *Web:* www.historicalseaport.org *Email:* ghhsa_admin@historicalseaport.org *Visitors welcome?* Yes *Hours:* Contact attraction directly *Admission:* Contact attraction directly *Operated by:*

Grays Harbor Historical Seaport Authority *NR?* No *NHL?* No *Year established/built:* 1985 *Latitude:* 46.9685 *Latitude:* -123.7730

STAN SAYRES MEMORIAL PITS
Stan Sayres Memorial Pits is the launching point for hydroplanes during the annual Seafair Hydroplane Regatta in Seattle. *Address:* 3808 Lake Washington Blvd S *City:* Seattle *State:* WA *Visitors welcome?* Yes *Hours:* 4 a.m. to 11:30 p.m. *Admission:* FREE *Operated by:* Seattle Parks and Recreation *NR?* No *NHL?* No *Year established/built:* 1957 *Latitude:* 47.5700 *Latitude:* -122.2770

SKANSIE BROTHERS NET SHED
The Skansie Brothers Net Shed on the Gig Harbor waterfront is one of the last commercial buildings from the city's heyday as a fishing village. *Address:* 3155 Harborview Dr. *City:* Gig Harbor *State:* WA *Visitors welcome?* No

UNIVERSITY SHELL HOUSE
University Shell House is the home of the University of Washington's crew team and their shells. *Address:* Montlake Blvd NE and NE Pacific St. *City:* Seattle *State:* WA *Visitors welcome?* Yes *Hours:* Contact attraction directly *Admission:* Contact attraction directly *Operated by:* University of Washington Facilities *NR?* No *NHL?* No *Year established/built:* 1900 *Latitude:* 47.6490 *Latitude:* -122.3050

WASHINGTON STREET PUBLIC BOAT LANDING
Address: 1 Yesler Way *City:* Seattle *State:* WA *Visitors welcome?* Yes *Hours:* Daily *Admission:* FREE *Operated by:* Seattle Parks and Recreation *NR?* Yes *NHL?* No *Year established/built:* 1920 *Latitude:* 47.6015 *Latitude:* -122.3360

WISCONSIN

HOKENSON BROTHERS FISHERY
The Hokenson Brothers operated a fishing outfit at what is now the site of a visitors center for the Apostle Islands National Lakeshore. *Address:* Little Sand Bay Road *City:* Bayfield *State:* WI *Phone:* 715-779-7007 *Web:* www.nps.gov/apis/ *Visitors welcome?* Yes *Hours:* Contact attraction directly *Admission:* FREE *Operated by:* Apostle Islands National Lakeshore *NR?* No *NHL?* No *Latitude:* 46.9329 *Latitude:* -90.8730

PORTAGE CANAL
Constructed in 1849, the Portage Canal became an important waterway in late 19th century Wisconsin. It is now undergoing restoration. *City:* Portage *State:* WI *Zip:* 53901 *Web:* www.portagecanalsociety.com *Email:* dollar1@charter.net *Visitors welcome?* Yes *Hours:* Daily *Admission:* FREE *Operated by:* Portage Canal Society *NR?* No *NHL?* No *Year established/built:* 1849 *Latitude:* 43.5392 *Latitude:* -89.4626

CHAPTER 10 – MARKERS & MONUMENTS

STRUCTURES AND ARTWORK INTENDED TO REMIND VIEWERS OF IMPORTANT EVENTS OR LOCAL FACTS

USS Arizona Memorial (Honolulu, Hawaii)

When events and places carry far more long-term emotional importance than their immediate impact, people often mark the area with a monument or an object intended to convey the meaning. The best known of these in the maritime world are memorials to fishermen who lost their lives pursuing their livelihood. Many of these memorials become sacred places where the faithful and families gather with a religious leader to remember the dead. Other structures are memorials to sailors and marines lost in war; often these memorials are warships that participated in the conflict. World War II is especially well-marked in this way. A few monuments recall ordinary people, such as passengers, caught up in a great disaster. This chapter lists some of these memorials and markers.

ARKANSAS

USS SNOOK MEMORIAL
The USS Snook Memorial recalls the loss of the submarine USS Snook in 1945 in the Pacific. *Address:* 120 Riverfront Park Dr. *City:* North Little Rock *State:* AR *Zip:* 72114 *Phone:* 501-371-8320 *Web:* www.aimm.museum *Email:* info@aimm.museum *Visitors welcome?* Yes *Hours:* Friday, 10 a.m. to 6 p.m.; Saturday, 10 a.m. to 6 p.m.; Sunday, 1 p.m. to 6 p.m. *Admission:* Contact attraction directly *Operated by:* Arkansas Inland Maritime Museum *NR?* No *NHL?* No *Latitude:* 34.7541 *Latitude:* -92.2681

HAWAII

BATTLESHIP MISSOURI MEMORIAL
Launched in 1944, the battleship USS Missouri was the site where the Imperial Japanese surrendered at the end of World War II. The ship is now a floating exhibit and war memorial. *Address:* 1 Arizona Memorial Road *City:* Honolulu *State:* HI *Zip:* 96818 *Phone:* 808-455-1600 *Toll-free:* 877-644-4896 *Web:* www.ussmissouri.com *Email:* MightyMo@ussmissouri.org *Visitors welcome?* Yes *Hours:* Daily, 9 a.m. to 5 p.m. *Admission:* $16 adults, $8 children *Operated by:* USS Missouri Memorial Association *NR?* Yes *NHL?* No *Year established/built:* 1944 *Latitude:* 21.3643 *Latitude:* -157.9370

USS ARIZONA MEMORIAL
The USS Arizona Memorial marks the place where the battleship Arizona sank during the Imperial Japanese attack on Pearl Harbor. The USS Arizona serves as the final resting place for many of the battleship's 1,177 crew members who lost their lives on December 7, 1941. *Address:* 1 Arizona Memorial Place *City:* Honolulu *State:* HI *Zip:* 96818 *Phone:* 808-422-0561 *Web:* www.nps.gov/usar *Visitors welcome?* Yes *Hours:* Daily, 7:30 a.m. to 5 p.m. *Admission:* FREE *Operated by:* USS Arizona *NR?* Yes *NHL?* Yes *Year established/built:* 1941 *Latitude:* 21.3643 *Latitude:* -157.9370

USS UTAH MEMORIAL
The USS Utah Memorial marks the place where the battleship Utah sank during the Imperial Japanese attack on Pearl Harbor. The USS Utah serves as the final resting place for many of the battleship's crew members who lost their lives on December 7, 1941. *Address:* 1 Arizona Memorial Place *City:* Honolulu *State:* HI *Zip:* 96818 *Phone:* 808-422-0561 *Web:* www.nps.gov/usar *Visitors welcome?* Yes *Hours:* Daily, 7:30 a.m. to 5 p.m. *Admission:* FREE *Operated by:* USS Arizona *NR?* Yes *NHL?* Yes *Year established/built:* 1909 *Latitude:* 21.3643 *Latitude:* -157.9370

IOWA

NATIONAL RIVERS HALL OF FAME
The National Rivers Hall of Fame is part of the National Mississippi River Museum & Aquarium campus on the Dubuque riverfront. *Address:* 350 East Third St. *City:* Dubuque *State:* IA *Zip:* 52001 *Phone:* 563-557-9545 *Toll-free:* 800-226-3369 *Web:* www.rivermuseum.com *Email:* info@rivermuseum.com *Visitors welcome?* Yes *Hours:* Memorial Day weekend through Labor Day: Daily, 9 a.m. – 6 p.m.; Labor Day through October 31st: Daily, 9 a.m. – 5 p.m.; November through Memorial Day Weekend: Daily, 10 a.m. – 5 p.m.; Holiday Hours: Closed Thanksgiving and Christmas Day. Open Christmas Eve, 10 a.m. to 2 p.m. *Admission:* $10.50 adults, $9.50 seniors, $8 youth seven to 17, $4.50 children three to six, under three FREE *Operated by:* Dubuque County Historical Society *NR?* No *NHL?* No *Latitude:* 42.4963 *Latitude:* -90.6591

MASSACHUSETTS

CHILDREN'S MEMORIAL AT THE EDGARTOWN LIGHTHOUSE
The Edgartown Harbor Lighthouse, a symbol of safety and guidance for mariners, is also the home for a memorial for children who have died. *Address:* Chappaquidick Ferry *City:* Edgartown *State:* MA *Phone:* 508-627-4441 *Email:* KGorman@mvmuseum.org *Visitors welcome?* Yes *Hours:* Grounds only *Admission:* FREE

Operated by: Martha's Vineyard Historical Society *NR?* No *NHL?* No *Year established/built:* 1828 *Latitude:* 41.3890 *Latitude:* -70.5134

GLOUCESTER FISHERMAN'S MEMORIAL
Resting on a granite base in the center of Gloucester's long, narrow Stacy Esplanade is the Gloucester Fisherman's Memorial. *Address:* Stacey Boulevard *City:* Gloucester *State:* MA *Visitors welcome?* Yes *Hours:* Daily *Admission:* FREE *Operated by:* City of Gloucester *NR?* No *NHL?* No *Year established/built:* 1923 *Latitude:* 42.6159 *Latitude:* -70.6620

MICHIGAN

ROBERT H. MANNING MEMORIAL LIGHTHOUSE
The Robert H. Manning Memorial Lighthouse was built to honor a life-long resident of Empire. *Address:* Village Park *City:* Empire *State:* MI *Visitors welcome?* Yes *Hours:* Grounds only *Admission:* FREE *Operated by:* Town of Empire *NR?* No *NHL?* No *Year established/built:* 1991 *Latitude:* 44.8137 *Latitude:* -86.0673

SILENT SERVICE MEMORIAL
The Silent Service Memorial and the McClintock Annex to the Marquette Maritime Museum were begun to recognize the accomplishments of a Marquette native son in the largest naval battle in history: the Battle for Leyte Gulf, Phillipines, October 1944. Capta *Address:* Elwood Mattson Lower Harbor Park *City:* Marquette *State:* MI *Zip:* 49855 *Phone:* 906-226-2006 *Web:* mqtmaritimemuseum.com *Email:* mqtmaritimemuseum@yahoo.com *Visitors welcome?* Yes *Hours:* Daily *Admission:* FREE *Operated by:* Marquette Maritime Museum *NR?* No *NHL?* No *Year established/built:* 2008 *Latitude:* 46.5435 *Latitude:* -87.3954

WILLIAM LIVINGSTONE MEMORIAL
The William Livingstone Memorial Lighthouse was built in 1929 to mark the contributions of a prominent Detroit citizen who oversaw transportation improvements in the early 20th century. *Address:* Belle Isle Island Municipal Golf Course *City:* Detroit *State:* MI *Visitors welcome?* Yes *Hours:* Grounds only *Admission:* FREE *Operated by:* City of Detroit Dept. of Recreation *NR?* Yes *NHL?* No *Year established/built:* 1929 *Latitude:* 42.3314 *Latitude:* -83.0458

NEW YORK

CROWN POINT LIGHTHOUSE
The Crown Point Lighthouse, first lit in 1859, was transformed in 1909 into a memorial to the discovery, exploration, and deep history of Lake Champlain. The site itself was the scene of battles between the French and English, and later the English and Am *Address:* Crown Point State Historic Site *City:* Crown Point *State:* NY *Visitors welcome?* Yes *Hours:* Daily *Admission:* FREE *Operated by:* New York State Dept. of Environmental Conservation *NR?* No *NHL?* No *Year established/built:* 1859 *Latitude:* 43.9503 *Latitude:* -73.4371

TITANIC MEMORIAL LIGHTHOUSE AND TIME BALL
Address: Pearl and Fulton Streets *City:* New York *State:* NY *Visitors welcome?* Yes *Hours:* Daily *Admission:* FREE *Operated by:* South Street Seaport Museum *NR?* No *NHL?* No *Year established/built:* 1913 *Latitude:* 40.7074 *Latitude:* -74.0041

OHIO

GRIMM MEMORIAL
The Grimm Memorial is a marker to the life of a local resident, Stanley Mike Grimm, who enjoyed lighthouses. *Address:* 5490 Behm Road *City:* St. Marys *State:* OH *Visitors welcome?* No *Operated by:* Private owner *NR?* No *NHL?* No *Year established/built:* 2003 *Latitude:* 40.5092 *Latitude:* -84.4731

✦ PERRY'S VICTORY AND INTERNATIONAL PEACE MEMORIAL
Established to honor those who fought in the Battle of Lake Erie, during the war of 1812, but in equal part it is here to celebrate the long-lasting peace between Britain, Canada and the U.S. *Address:* South Bass Island, Lake Erie *City:* Put-in-Bay *State:* OH *Zip:* 42907 *Phone:* 419-285-2184 *Visitors welcome?* Yes *Hours:* April to mid-October, 10 a.m . To 5 p.m. *Admission:* FREE *Operated by:* National Park Service -- Perry Memorial *NR?* No *NHL?* No *Year established/built:* 1915

SOUTH CAROLINA

COLD WAR SUBMARINE MEMORIAL
Located in the heart of the Charleston Harbor, the Cold War Submarine Memorial is an enduring tribute to the dedicated men who served in our naval submarines during the Cold War from 1947-1989. *Address:* 40 Patriots Point Road *City:* Mount Pleasant *State:* SC *Zip:* 29464 *Phone:* 843-884-2727 *Toll-free:* 866-831-1720 *Web:* www.patriotspoint.org *Visitors welcome?* Yes *Hours:* Contact attraction directly *Admission:* Contact attraction directly *Operated by:* Patriots Point Naval & Maritime Museum *NR?* No *NHL?* No *Latitude:* 32.7940 *Latitude:* -79.9051

TEXAS

SEAWOLF PARK
Seawolf Park is a memorial to the lost crew of the submarine USS Seawolf, lost during World War II. *Address:* Seawolf Park *City:* Galveston *State:* TX *Zip:* 77550 *Phone:* 409-797-5114 *Web:* www.galveston.com/seawolfpark/ *Email:* macm@galvestonparkboard.org *Visitors welcome?* Yes *Hours:* Daily, 8 a.m. to dusk *Admission:* FREE *Operated by:* Seawolf Park *NR?* No *NHL?* No *Latitude:* 29.3349 *Latitude:* -94.7791

WASHINGTON

BALLAST ISLAND
Address: Foot of Washington Street *City:* Seattle *State:* WA *Visitors welcome?* Yes *Operated by:* Propeller Club *NR?* No *NHL?* No *Latitude:* 47.6008 *Latitude:* -122.3130

ELLIOTT BAY
Address: Pier 55 *City:* Seattle *State:* WA *Visitors welcome?* Yes *Operated by:* Propeller Club *NR?* No *NHL?* No *Year established/built:* 1982 *Latitude:* 47.6012 *Latitude:* -122.3390

CHAPTER 10 – MARKERS & MONUMENTS

GOLDEN GARDENS PARK -- INDIAN CANOE CONSTRUCTION
Address: Golden Gardens Park *City:* Seattle *State:* WA *Visitors welcome?* Yes *Hours:* 6 a.m. to 11:30 p.m. *Admission:* FREE *Operated by:* Seattle Parks and Recreation *NR?* No *NHL?* No *Latitude:* 47.6902 *Latitude:* -122.4010

GREAT WHITE FLEET DISEMBARKATION SITE
Address: Pier 64 *City:* Seattle *State:* WA *Visitors welcome?* Yes *Operated by:* Propeller Club *NR?* No *NHL?* No *Year established/built:* 1908 *Latitude:* 47.6062 *Latitude:* -122.3320

HOSPITAL SHIP IDAHO
Address: Foot of S. Washington St. *City:* Seattle *State:* WA *Visitors welcome?* Yes *NR?* No *NHL?* No *Latitude:* 47.6008 *Latitude:* -122.3130

INDIANS ATTACK SEATTLE! (USS DECATUR ANCHORAGE)
Address: Pier 50 *City:* Seattle *State:* WA *Visitors welcome?* Yes *Operated by:* Propeller Club *NR?* No *NHL?* No *Year established/built:* 1959 *Latitude:* 47.6017 *Latitude:* -122.3370

LAKE WASHINGTON SHIPYARD/CARILLON POINT
Address: 3240 Carillon Point *City:* Kirkland *State:* WA *Visitors welcome?* Yes *Hours:* Contact attraction directly *Admission:* FREE *NR?* No *NHL?* No *Year established/built:* 1923 *Latitude:* 47.6564 *Latitude:* -122.2060

MIIKE MARU ARRIVAL SITE
Address: Alaskan Way and Union Street *City:* Seattle *State:* WA *Visitors welcome?* Yes *Operated by:* Propeller Club *NR?* No *NHL?* No *Year established/built:* 1896 *Latitude:* 47.6069 *Latitude:* -122.3410

MOSQUITO FLEET TRAIL
The Mosquito Fleet Trail is approximately 100 miles of roadside hiking and biking along the shores of the Kitsap Peninsula on Puget Sound. *City:* Bremerton *State:* WA *Visitors welcome?* Yes *Operated by:* Kitsap County Public Works Dept. *NR?* No *NHL?* No *Year established/built:* 2005 *Latitude:* 47.5673 *Latitude:* -122.6330

PACIFIC STEAMSHIP CO. BUILDING
Address: Alaskan Way *City:* Seattle *State:* WA *Visitors welcome?* Yes *Operated by:* Propeller Club *NR?* No *NHL?* No *Latitude:* 47.6091 *Latitude:* -122.3450

SEATTLE FISHERMANS MEMORIAL
Address: Fishermans Terminal *City:* Seattle *State:* WA *Visitors welcome?* Yes *Hours:* Daily *Admission:* FREE *Operated by:* Port of Seattle *NR?* No *NHL?* No *Year established/built:* 1988 *Latitude:* 47.6062 *Latitude:* -122.3320

SEATTLE'S FIRST PIER (YESLER'S WHARF)
Address: Pier 50 *City:* Seattle *State:* WA *Visitors welcome?* Yes *Operated by:* Propeller Club *NR?* No *NHL?* No *Year established/built:* 1964 *Latitude:* 47.6017 *Latitude:* -122.3370

SHIPMATES LIGHT
Shipmates Light is a small structure with a ship's light installed in memory of sailors lost at sea. Located on the edge of Elliott Bay at Myrtle Edwards Park near the Central Waterfront, the marker was sponsored by Seattle area maritime unions, the Port of Seattle, the U.S. Coast Guard, and others. *Address:* 3130 Alaskan Way W *City:* Seattle *State:* WA *Visitors welcome?* Yes *Hours:* Daily *Admission:* FREE *Operated by:* Port of Seattle *NR?* No *NHL?* No *Year established/built:* 1977 *Latitude:* 47.6256 *Latitude:* -122.3710

CHAPTER 10 – MARKERS & MONUMENTS

SKINNER & EDDY SHIPYARD
Address: Terminal 46 *City:* Seattle *State:* WA *Visitors welcome?* Yes *Operated by:* Propeller Club *NR?* No *NHL?* No *Latitude:* 47.5943 *Latitude:* -122.3400

SMITH COVE/NORTHERN PACIFIC COAL PIER
Address: Smith Cove Park *City:* Seattle *State:* WA *Visitors welcome?* Yes *Operated by:* Propeller Club *NR?* No *NHL?* No *Year established/built:* 1978 *Latitude:* 47.6324 *Latitude:* -122.3880

STEAMER DIX SINKING
Address: Duwamish Head *City:* Seattle *State:* WA *Visitors welcome?* Yes *Operated by:* Propeller Club *NR?* No *NHL?* No *Latitude:* 47.5954 *Latitude:* -122.3870

TON OF GOLD AND SAILING OF WILLAPA SITE
Address: Foot Of Pike Street *City:* Seattle *State:* WA *Visitors welcome?* Yes *Operated by:* Propeller Club *NR?* No *NHL?* No *Year established/built:* 1895 *Latitude:* 47.6107 *Latitude:* -122.3360

USCG CUTTER BEAR STATION
Address: Pier 55 *City:* Seattle *State:* WA *Visitors welcome?* Yes *Operated by:* Propeller Club *NR?* No *NHL?* No *Year established/built:* 1963 *Latitude:* 47.6012 *Latitude:* -122.3390

USS NEBRASKA LAUNCH SITE
Address: Terminal 46 *City:* Seattle *State:* WA *Visitors welcome?* Yes *Operated by:* Propeller Club *NR?* No *NHL?* No *Latitude:* 47.5943 *Latitude:* -122.3400

WELCOMING FIGURE, RICHMOND BEACH PARK
Native peoples lived and traveled on Puget Sound waterways in canoes thousands of years before the arrival of European explorers and traders. In 1998, artists Steve Brown, Joe Gobin, and Andy Wilbur created Welcoming Figure, a ten-foot high bronze sculpture. *Address:* 22nd Ave. NW and NW 190th St. *City:* Shoreline *State:* WA *Visitors welcome?* Yes *Hours:* Daily, dawn to dusk *Admission:* FREE *Operated by:* Shoreline Parks & Recreation *NR?* No *NHL?* No *Year established/built:* 1998 *Latitude:* 47.7670 *Latitude:* -122.3850

WESTPORT FISHERMANS MEMORIAL
The Westport Fishermans Memorial at the Westport Marina honors fisherman who have lost their lives at sea. *Address:* 871 Neddie Rose Dr *City:* Westport *State:* WA *Zip:* 98595 *Visitors welcome?* Yes *Hours:* Daily *Admission:* FREE *NR?* No *NHL?* No *Year established/built:* 1960 *Latitude:* 46.9117 *Latitude:* -124.1160

WISCONSIN

FOND DU LAC LIGHTHOUSE
The Fond du Lac Lighthouse was a gift to the city in 1932 by lumberman W. J. Nuss. *Address:* Lakeside Park *City:* Fond du Lac *State:* WI *Visitors welcome?* Yes *Hours:* Daily *Admission:* FREE *Operated by:* City of Fond du Lac *NR?* No *NHL?* No *Year established/built:* 1932 *Latitude:* 43.7958 *Latitude:* -88.4440

CHAPTER 11 – ORGANIZATIONS

ASSOCIATIONS, FOUNDATIONS, AND OTHER GROUPS ORGANIZED TO PRESERVE AND INTERPRET MARITIME HISTORY

Mayflower II (Plymouth, Mass.)

Behind the vast majority of tall ships, museums, historic lighthouses, and other historic attractions is an organization with a mission. Men and women who value history have created associations, foundations, and historical societies to provide a legal structure to support their activities, primarily for fundraising, and often with an educational core. Most are not-for-profits under internal revenue laws, which lets them apply for grants-in-aid from governments and other NPOs. In addition, donors receive tax advantages when they give money to these groups. Virtually all are cash-strapped; so as you study this list, please consider making a donation to an organization that interests you.

ALASKA

ALASKA LIGHTHOUSE ASSOCIATION
The Alaska Lighthouse Association is dedicated to the preservation of Alaska's maritime heritage, including the preservation and restoration of Alaska's lighthouses and maritime artifacts, promoting public access

to and education about Alaska's lighthouse heritage. *Address:* 2116 Second St. *City:* Douglas *State:* AK *Zip:* 99824 *Web:* www.aklighthouse.org *Email:* info@aklighthouse.org

CAPE DECISION LIGHTHOUSE SOCIETY
The Cape Decision Lighthouse Society is dedicated to the preservation of the Cape Decision Lighthouse and surrounding wilderness areas for public recreation. *Address:* 224 Katlian Dr. *City:* Sikta *State:* AK *Zip:* 99835 *Web:* www.capedecision.org *Email:* capedecisionlighthouse@yahoo.com

CAPE SAINT ELIAS LIGHTHOUSE KEEPERS ASSOCIATION
Organized in 1997, the association is dedicated to restoring and preserving the complex of buildings at Cape Elias. *Address:* PO Box 1023 *City:* Cordova *State:* AK *Zip:* 99574 *Phone:* 907-424-5182 *Web:* www.kayakisland.org *Email:* info@kayakisland.org

FAIRBANKS HISTORICAL PRESERVATION FOUNDATION
Address: PO Box 70552 *City:* Fairbanks *State:* AK *Zip:* 99707 *Phone:* 907-456-8848

GASTINEAU CHANNEL HISTORICAL SOCIETY
The Gastineau Channel Historical Society owns and operates the Sentinel Island Lighthouse. *Address:* PO Box 21264 *City:* Juneau *State:* AK *Zip:* 99802 *Phone:* 907-586-5338

JUNEAU LIGHTHOUSE ASSOCIATION
The Five Finger Lighthouse is owned and managed by the Juneau Lighthouse Association, a 501(c)(3) non-profit dedicated to the restoration, preservation and future public accessibility to the lighthouse. *Address:* PO Box 22163 *City:* Juneau *State:* AK *Zip:* 99802 *Web:* www.5fingerlighthouse.com *Email:* info@5fingerlighthouse.com

> Did we miss your historical society or heritage organization? Please submit corrections or additions to contact@fyddeye.com.

U.S. COAST GUARD (DISTRICT 17)
U.S. Coast Guard District 17 is reponsible for health and safety of maritime commerce and recreation in the waters of Alaska. *Address:* 709 W 9th St. *City:* Juneau *State:* AK *Zip:* 99801 *Phone:* 907-463-2000 *Web:* www.uscg.mil/d17/

ALABAMA

ALABAMA LIGHTHOUSE ASSOCIATION
The Alabama Lighthouse Association supports and promotes efforts that preserve Alabama lighthouses through educational programs, newsletters, literature, films, publicity, and tours. *Address:* PO Box 250 *City:* Mobile *State:* AL *Zip:* 36601 *Phone:* 251-626-4743 *Web:* alabamalighthouses.com *Email:* CaptHal1@aol.com

USS ALABAMA
Address: PO Box 65 *City:* Mobile *State:* AL *Zip:* 36601 *Phone:* 251-433-2703 *Fax:* 251-433-2777 *Web:* www.ussalabama.com *Email:* btunnell@ussalabama.com

ARKANSAS

JACKSONPORT STATE PARK
Address: 205 Avenue St. *City:* Newport *State:* AR *Zip:* 72112 *Phone:* 870-523-2143 *Web:* www.arkansasstateparks.com/jacksonport/ *Email:* jacksonport@arkansas.com

CALIFORNIA

AIRCRAFT CARRIER HORNET FOUNDATION
The mission of the Aircraft Carrier Hornet Foundation is to preserve and honor the legacy of the Hornet name and the role of this national historic landmark in World War II and Apollo Space Vehicle Recovery operations in order to educate the public. *Address:* PO Box 460 *City:* Alameda *State:* CA *Zip:* 94501 *Phone:* 510-521-8448 *Fax:* 510-521-8327 *Web:* www.uss-hornet.org *Email:* info@uss-hornet.org

BELVEDERE-TIBURON LANDMARKS SOCIETY
Address: 1550 Tiburon Blvd, Suite M *City:* Tiburon *State:* CA *Zip:* 94920 *Phone:* 415-435-1853 *Fax:* 360-242-2654 *Web:* www.landmarks-society.org

CALL OF THE SEA
Address: #278, 3020 Bridgeway *City:* Sausalito *State:* CA *Zip:* 94965 *Phone:* 415-331-3214 *Fax:* 415-331-1412 *Web:* www.callofthesea.org *Email:* info@callofthesea.org

CAPE MENDOCINO LIGHTHOUSE PRESERVATION SOCIETY - SHELTER COVE
The Society maintains the Cape Mendocino Lighthouse. *Address:* PO Box 454 *City:* Whitehorn *State:* CA *Zip:* 95589

CHILDREN'S MARITIME FOUNDATION
Address: 4676 Lakeview Ave 109E *City:* Yorba Linda *State:* CA *Zip:* 92886 *Phone:* 714-970-8800 *Fax:* 714-970-8474 *Web:* www.americanpride.org *Email:* theamericanpride@aol.com

CHINA LAKE MUSEUM FOUNDATION
The China Lake Museum Foundation supports the U.S. Naval Museum of Armament and Technology. *Address:* PO Box 217 *City:* Ridgecrest *State:* CA *Zip:* 93556 *Phone:* 760-939-3530 *Fax:* 760-939-0564 *Web:* www.chinalakemuseum.org *Email:* clmf1@ridgenet.net

DEL NORTE COUNTY HISTORICAL SOCIETY
Del Norte County is in the extreme northwest corner of California. *Address:* 577 H Street *City:* Crescent City *State:* CA *Zip:* 95531 *Phone:* 707-464-3922 *Web:* www.delnortehistory.org

FRIENDS OF BANNING MUSEUM
Address: 401 East M Street *City:* Wilmington *State:* CA *Zip:* 90748 *Phone:* 310-548-2005 *Web:* www.banningmuseum.org

CHAPTER 11 – ORGANIZATIONS

GOLDEN GATE NATIONAL PARKS
Golden Gate National Parks chronicle two hundred years of history, from the Native American culture, the Spanish Empire frontier and the Mexican Republic, to maritime history, the California Gold Rush, the evolution of American coastal fortifications. *Address:* Building 201, Fort Mason *City:* San Francisco *State:* CA *Zip:* 94123 *Phone:* 415-561-4700 *Web:* www.nps.gov/goga/

HISTORIC SHIPS MEMORIAL AT PACIFIC SQUARE
The Historic Ships Memorial at Pacific Square is the foundation established in 1996 to acquire the USS Iowa (BB-61), passionately dedicated to preserving USS Iowa at the west coast's first naval Installation, Mare Island, Vallejo, as a premier naval memorial. *Address:* PO Box 361 *City:* Vallejo *State:* CA *Zip:* 94590 *Phone:* 415-905-5700 *Web:* www.battleshipiowa.org *Email:* info@battleshipiowa.org

HISTORIC TUGBOAT RESTORATION AND EDUCATION SOCIETY
We are a group of volunteers who banded together in 2002 to create the nonprofit Historic Tugboat Education and Restoration Society. *City:* San Francisco *State:* CA *Web:* www.hters.org *Email:* info@hters.org

LUCID MSO-458 FOUNDATION
Address: PO Box 1058 *City:* Rio Vista *State:* CA *Zip:* 94571 *Phone:* 877-285-8243 *Web:* www.usslucid.org *Email:* usslucid@usslucid.org

LYNX EDUCATIONAL FOUNDATION
The Lynx Educational Foundation is a non-profit, non-partisan, educational organization, dedicated to hands-on educational programs that teach the history of America's struggle to preserve its independence. *Address:* 509 29th St. *City:* Newport Beach *State:* CA *Zip:* 92663 *Phone:* 866-446-5969 *Fax:* 949-723-1958 *Web:* www.privateerlynx.org *Email:* privateerlynx1812@verizon.net

MARE ISLAND HISTORIC PARK FOUNDATION
Address: Railroad Avenue and 8th Street *City:* Vallejo *State:* CA *Zip:* 94592 *Phone:* 707-557-1538 *Web:* www.mareislandhpf.org

MARITIME HERITAGE PROJECT
The Maritime Heritage Project is a U.S. registered 501(c)(3) tax exempt charitable corporation established in San Francisco, California, U.S.A. by D.A. Blethen Levy in 1998 to preserve San Francisco's shipping history from the mid-1800s to the turn of the 20th century. *Address:* PO Box 2878 *City:* Sausalito *State:* CA *Zip:* 94966 *Web:* www.maritimeheritage.org *Email:* DALevy@maritimeheritage.org

MARITIME MUSEUM ASSOCIATION OF SAN DIEGO
The Maritime Museum Association of San Diego is a not-for-profit organization that owns and operates the Maritime Museum of San Diego and its collections. *Address:* 1306 N. Harbor Dr. *City:* San Diego *State:* CA *Zip:* 92101 *Phone:* 619-234-9153 *Web:* www.sdmaritime.com *Email:* info@sdmaritime.org

MONTEREY HISTORY & ART ASSOCIATION
Address: The Stanton Center *City:* Monterey *State:* CA *Zip:* 93940 *Phone:* 831-372-2608 *Fax:* 831-655-3054 *Web:* www.montereyhistory.org *Email:* AlexDVance@MontereyHistory.org

NATIONAL LIBERTY SHIP MEMORIAL, SS JEREMIAH O'BRIEN
The National Liberty Ship Memorial organizatoin operates the SS Jeremiah O'Brien, the last fully functional Liberty Ship of World War II. *Address:* 1275 Columbus Ave., Suite 300 *City:* San Francisco *State:* CA *Zip:*

94133 *Phone:* 415-544-0100 *Fax:* 415-544-9890 *Web:* www.ssjeremiahobrien.org *Email:* liberty@ssjeremiahobrien.org

OLD SACRAMENTO
Address: 1101 Second St. *City:* Sacramento *State:* CA *Zip:* 95814 *Phone:* 916-808-4980 *Web:* www.oldsacramento.com *Email:* jwest@cityofsacramento.org

ORANGE COUNTY BSA -- NEWPORT SEA BASE
The Newport Sea Base has a history of providing quality maritime programs for youth since 1937. *Address:* 1211 E. Dyer Rd. *City:* Santa Ana *State:* CA *Zip:* 92705 *Phone:* 714-546-4990 *Fax:* 714-546-0415 *Web:* www.ocbsa.org/site/c.khKQIWPBIoE/b.3841869/

PIEDRAS BLANCAS LIGHT STATION ASSOCIATION
The not-for-profit Piedras Blancas Light Station Association was founded to provide the public with a chance to discover this historic site and its structures, one of eight of the largest lighthouse installations on the California Coast. *Address:* PO Box 127 *City:* San Simeon *State:* CA *Zip:* 93452 *Phone:* 805-927-3719 *Fax:* 805-924-1114 *Web:* www.piedrasblancas.org *Email:* membership@piedrasblancas.org

POINT ARENA LIGHTHOUSE KEEPERS
In 1984, the not-for-profit Point Arena Lighthouse Keepers acquired the light station as part of a 25-year land lease from the Coast Guard and the Department of Transportation. In November of 2000, the group became the official owners of the property. *Address:* PO Box 11 *City:* Point Arena *State:* CA *Zip:* 95468 *Phone:* 877-725-4448 *Fax:* 707-882-2111 *Web:* www.pointarenalighthouse.com *Email:* palight@mcn.org

POINT CABRILLO LIGHTKEEPERS ASSOCIATION
The not-for-profit Point Cabrillo Lightkeepers Association manages the Point Cabrillo State Park, a California historical park. *Address:* PO Box 641 *City:* Mendocino *State:* CA *Zip:* 95460 *Web:* www.pointcabrillo.org *Email:* info@pointcabrillo.org

POINT LOBOS ASSOCIATION
Point Lobos Association is a charitable non-profit association formed in 1978 to support interpretive and educational programs at Point Lobos Reserve and to assist California State Parks in preserving Point Lobos. *Address:* Route 1, Box 62 *City:* Carmel *State:* CA *Zip:* 93923 *Phone:* 831-624-4909 *Web:* pt-lobos.parks.state.ca.us *Email:* pointlobos@parks.ca.gov

POINT RICHMOND HISTORY ASSOCIATION
The Point Richmond History Association owns and operates the World War II-era Victory Ship Red Oak Victory. *Address:* PO Box 1267 *City:* Richmond *State:* CA *Zip:* 94802 *Phone:* 510-235-7387 *Web:* www.richmondmuseumofhistory.org

POINT SAN LUIS LIGHTHOUSE KEEPERS
The Point San Luis Lighthouse Keepers is a not-for-profit organization established in 1995 to provide the leadership, talent and organization to restore and maintain the lightstation. *Address:* PO Box 13556 *City:* San Luis Obispo *State:* CA *Zip:* 93406 *Phone:* 805-546-4904 *Web:* www.sanluislighthouse.org *Email:* info@sanluislighthouse.org

SAN FRANCISCO MARITIME NATIONAL HISTORICAL PARK
Stand on the stern of Balclutha, face west to feel the fresh wind blowing in from the Pacific Ocean. Located in the Fisherman's Wharf neighborhood, San Francisco Maritime National Historical Park offers the sights, sounds,

smells and stories of Pacific Coast maritime history. *Address:* Lower Fort Mason, Building E, Room 265 *City:* San Francisco *State:* CA *Zip:* 94123 *Phone:* 415-561-7000 *Fax:* 415-556-1624 *Web:* www.nps.gov/safr/

SAN FRANCISCO MARITIME NATIONAL PARK ASSOCIATION
The San Francisco National Maritime Park Association supports the work of the San Francisco National Maritime Historical Park and the submarine USS Pampanito. *Address:* PO Box 470310 *City:* San Francisco *State:* CA *Zip:* 94147 *Phone:* 415-561-6662 *Fax:* 415-561-6660 *Web:* www.maritime.org

SCHOONER PILOT TRUST
Address: 1220 Roseevans St., Suite 308 *City:* San Diego *State:* CA *Zip:* 92106 *Phone:* 805-686-4484

ST. GEORGE REEF LIGHTHOUSE PRESERVATION SOCIETY
The SGRLPS is a not-for-profit organization formed in 1988, whose goals were to first acquire and then preserve the St. George Reef Lighthouse. *Address:* PO Box 577 *City:* Crescent City *State:* CA *Zip:* 95531 *Phone:* 707-464-8299 *Web:* www.stgeorgereeflighthouse.us *Email:* SGRLPS@stgeorgereeflighthouse.us

U.S. COAST GUARD (DISTRICT 11)
District 11 of the U.S. Coast Guard covers the states of California, Utah, and Arizona. *Address:* Building 42, Coast Guard Island *City:* Alameda *State:* CA *Zip:* 94501 *Phone:* 510-437-2904 *Web:* www.uscgsanfrancisco.com/go/site/823/

USS POTOMAC ASSOCIATION
Address: PO Box 2064 *City:* Oakland *State:* CA *Zip:* 94604 *Phone:* 510-627-1215 *Web:* www.usspotomac.org

CONNECTICUT

AMISTAD AMERICA
Address: 746 Chapel Street, Suite 300 *City:* New Haven *State:* CT *Zip:* 06510 *Phone:* 203-495-1839 *Fax:* 203-495-8647 *Web:* www.amistadamerica.org *Email:* operations@amistadamerica.org

AVERY POINT LIGHTHOUSE SOCIETY
The Avery Point Lighthouse Society was formed to raise funds and oversee the restoration of the Avery Point Lighthouse at the University of Connecticut campus at Avery Point near Groton. *City:* Groton *State:* CT *Phone:* 860-445-5417 *Web:* www.averypointlight.com *Email:* JimStreetr@aol.com

BEACON PRESERVATION
Beacon Preservation, Inc. is a 501(c)(3) not-for-profit organization dedicated to the preservation of lighthouses and their environments for educational, cultural, recreational, and historical preservation purposes. *Address:* 117 Main Street *City:* Ansonia *State:* CT *Zip:* 06401 *Phone:* 203-736-9300 *Fax:* 203-736-2900 *Web:* www.beaconpreservation.org *Email:* info@beaconpreservation.org

COAST GUARD FOUNDATION/NATIONAL COAST GUARD MUSEUM ASSOCIATION
The Coast Guard Foundation is a 501(c)(3) non-profit organization founded in 1969. *Address:* 394 Taugwonk Rd. *City:* Stonington *State:* CT *Zip:* 06378 *Phone:* 860-535-0786 *Fax:* 860-535-0944 *Web:* www.cgfdn.org *Email:* info@cgfdn.org

CHAPTER 11 – ORGANIZATIONS

FAULKNER'S LIGHT BRIGADE
The Faulkner's Light Brigade was formed as a commission of the Guilford Preservation Alliance in 1991. Its fundamental mission was to investigate the ways and means of saving the historic Faulkner's Island Lighthouse. *Address:* PO Box 444 *City:* Guilford *State:* CT *Zip:* 06437 *Phone:* 203-453-8400 *Web:* www.lighthouse.cc/FLB/ *Email:* faulknerslightbrigade@gmail.com

GLACIER SOCIETY
The Glacier Society is a non-profit 501-(c)3 educational foundation dedicated to the restoration and operation of the USS/USCGC Glacier in honor of all who served in the exploration of the North and South Poles. *Address:* 905 Honeyspot Road *City:* Stratford *State:* CT *Zip:* 06615 *Phone:* 203-375-6638 *Web:* www.glaciersociety.org *Email:* glockett@glaciersociety.org

NEW LONDON LEDGE LIGHTHOUSE FOUNDATION
The New London Ledge Lighthouse Foundation cares for the New London Ledge Lighthouse near New London. *Address:* PO Box 855 *City:* New London *State:* CT *Zip:* 06320 *Phone:* 860-442-2222

NEW LONDON MARITIME SOCIETY
The mission of the New London Maritime Society is to preserve New London's U.S. Custom House and New London Harbor Light, and to promote and interpret the maritime history of the port of New London and the surrounding region through museum exhibitions and educational programs. *Address:* 150 Bank St *City:* New London *State:* CT *Zip:* 06320 *Phone:* 860-447-2501 *Web:* www.nlmaritimesociety.org

NORWALK SEAPORT ASSOCIATION
Operating since 1979, the Norwalk Seaport Association is a not-for-profit environmental, preservation and maritime educational organization offering a wide array of special events and community projects. *Address:* 132 Water Street *City:* South Norwalk *State:* CT *Zip:* 06854 *Phone:* 203-838-9444 *Fax:* 203-855-1017 *Web:* www.seaport.org *Email:* info@seaport.org

SCHOONER, INC
Schooner Inc is a nonprofit 501(c)(3) organization dedicated to protecting Long Island Sound through environmental education and sailing. *Address:* 60 South Water St. *City:* New Haven *State:* CT *Zip:* 06519 *Phone:* 203-865-1737 *Fax:* 203-624-8816 *Web:* www.schoonerinc.org *Email:* director@schoonerinc.org

STONINGTON HISTORICAL SOCIETY
The Stonington Historical Society is dedicated to illuminating the more than 350 years of history of the Town of Stonington, located in the southeastern corner of Connecticut. *Address:* PO Box 103 *City:* Stonington *State:* CT *Zip:* 06378 *Phone:* 860-535-8445 *Web:* www.stoningtonhistory.org

SUBMARINE FORCE LIBRARY & MUSEUM ASSOCIATION
Address: PO Box 501 *City:* Groton *State:* CT *Zip:* 06349 *Phone:* 860-448-0893 *Fax:* 860-405-0568 *Web:* www.submarinemuseum.org *Email:* director@submarinemuseum.org

DELAWARE

DELAWARE RIVER & BAY LIGHTHOUSE FOUNDATION
The Delaware River & Bay Lighthouse Foundation is dedicated to fostering, advocating and participating in the preservation of historic Delaware River and Bay lighthouses. *Address:* PO Box 708 *City:* Lewes *State:* DE *Zip:* 19958 *Fax:* 302-644-7046 *Web:* www.delawarebaylights.org

INDIAN RIVER LIFE-SAVING STATION: DELAWARE SEASHORE STATE PARK
The Indian River Life-Saving Station has been meticulously restored to its 1905 appearance, complete with diamond-shaped trim. *Address:* 725039 Coastal Highway *City:* Rehoboth Beach *State:* DE *Zip:* 19971 *Phone:* 302-227-6991 *Fax:* 302-227-6438 *Web:* www.destateparks.com/attractions/life-saving-station/ *Email:* Cassandra.Petersen@state.de.us

KALMAR NYCKEL FOUNDATION
Address: 1124 East 7th St. *City:* Wilmington *State:* DE *Zip:* 19801 *Phone:* 302-429-7447 *Fax:* 302-429-0350 *Web:* www.kalmarnyckel.org *Email:* info@kalmarnyckel.org

LEWES HISTORICAL SOCIETY
Address: 110 Shipcarpenter St. *City:* Lewes *State:* DE *Zip:* 19958 *Phone:* 302-645-7670 *Fax:* 302-645-2375 *Web:* www.historiclewes.org *Email:* info@historiclewes.org

OVERFALLS MARITIME MUSEUM FOUNDATION
The mission of the Overfalls Maritime Museum Foundation is to collect, preserve, honor and teach the maritime history of Lewes, Delaware Bay and the coastal region. Additionally, the Foundation plans to preserve, maintain and display the Lightship Overfalls. *City:* Lewes *State:* DE *Phone:* 302-645-7377 *Web:* www.overfalls.org *Email:* bernheisel@juno.com

DISTRICT OF COLUMBIA

DAUGHTERS OF THE AMERICAN REVOLUTION
Address: 1776 D St. NW *City:* Washington *State:* DC *Zip:* 20006 *Phone:* 202-628-1776 *Web:* www.dar.org

EARTH CONSERVATION CORPS
Address: 2000 Half Street SW *City:* Washington *State:* DC *Zip:* 20024 *Phone:* 202-554-1960 *Web:* www.ecc1.org

MARITIME HERITAGE PROGRAM, NATIONAL PARK SERVICE
The National Park Service Maritime Heritage Program works to advance awareness and understanding of the role of maritime affairs in the history of the United States. *Address:* 1849 C Street NW *City:* Washington *State:* DC *Zip:* 20240 *Phone:* 202-354-2260 *Fax:* 202-371-5180 *Web:* www.nps.gov/history/maritime/ *Email:* kevin_foster@nps.gov

NATIONAL MARITIME HERITAGE FOUNDATION
The National Maritime Heritage Foundation is dedicated to inspiring young people and enhancing lives through maritime adventures. NMHF accomplishes this mission by motivating young people to achieve through the sport of sailing, by increasing community awareness of maritime history, and by enhancing the local waterfront. *Address:* 236 Massachusetts Ave NE, Suite 410 *City:* Washington *State:* DC *Zip:* 20002 *Phone:* 202-547-1250 *Fax:* 202-547-0250 *Web:* www.nmhf.org *Email:* ktraver@nmhf.org

NAVAL HISTORY & HERITAGE COMMAND
As the official history program of the United States Navy, the Naval Historical Center manages the Navy Department Library, twelve Navy museums, art collections, archives, and an underwater archaeology program. *Address:*

Washington Navy Yard *City:* Washington *State:* DC *Zip:* 20374 *Phone:* 202-433-4882 *Fax:* 202-433-8200 *Web:* www.history.navy.mil

USCG HISTORIAN'S OFFICE
Address: 2100 Second St. SW *City:* Washington *State:* DC *Zip:* 20593 *Web:* www.uscg.mil/history/

FLORIDA

CAPE CANAVERAL LIGHTHOUSE FOUNDATION
The Cape Canaveral Lighthouse Foundation supports the maintenance of Cape Canaveral Lighthouse, located on the grounds of Patrick Air Force Base. *Address:* PO Box 1978 *City:* Cape Canaveral *State:* FL *Zip:* 32920 *Web:* www.capecanaverallighthousefoundation.com

FLORIDA MARITIME HERITAGE ASSOCIATION
The mission of the Florida Maritime Heritage Association is to increase public awareness and accessibility of Florida's maritime heritage through a cooperative network of professionals and organizations active in the research, preservation, documentation, and interpretation of the state's unique maritime history and cultures. *City:* Key Largo *State:* FL *Zip:* 33037 *Web:* flmha.org

FRIENDS OF THE GOVERNOR STONE
The Friends of the Governor Stone is a not-for-profit organization dedicated to the preservation and maintenance of the schooner Governor Stone. *Address:* PO Box 2435 *City:* Fort Walton Beach *State:* FL *Zip:* 32549 *Web:* govstone.com *Email:* govstone@cox.net

FRIENDS OF THE VINCE WHIBBS SR. COMMUNITY MARITIME PARK
Address: P.O. Box 12910 *City:* Pensacola *State:* FL *Zip:* 32521 *Phone:* 850-436-5655 *Fax:* 850-595-1143 *Web:* www.communitymaritimepark.com *Email:* ESpears@ci.pensacola.fl.us

GULF ISLANDS NATIONAL SEASHORE
Address: 1801 Gulf Breeze Parkway *City:* Gulf Breeze *State:* FL *Zip:* 32563 *Phone:* 850-934-2600 *Fax:* 850-932-9654 *Web:* www.nps.gov/guis/

HILLSBORO LIGHTHOUSE PRESERVATION SOCIETY
The mission of the Hillsboro Lighthouse Preservation Society is to promote the history of the Hillsboro Lighthouse Station and the Hillsboro Inlet area through preservation of structures and artifacts, education and public access tours. *Address:* PO Box 610326 *City:* Pompano Beach *State:* FL *Zip:* 33061 *Phone:* 954-942-2102 *Web:* www.hillsborolighthouse.org *Email:* info@hillsborolighthouse.org

HISTORICAL SOCIETY OF MARTIN COUNTY
Address: 825 NE Ocean Boulevard *City:* Stuart *State:* FL *Zip:* 34996 *Phone:* 772-225-1961 *Web:* elliottmuseumfl.org *Email:* info@elliottmuseumfl.org

KEY WEST ART & HISTORICAL SOCIETY
The Key West Art & Historical Society manages Key West Lighthouse among other institutions in Key West. *Address:* 938 Whitehead St. *City:* Key West *State:* FL *Zip:* 33040 *Phone:* 306-294-0012 *Web:* www.kwahs.com *Email:* cpennington@kwahs.org

MEL FISHER MARITIME HERITAGE SOCIETY
The Mel Fisher Maritime Heritage Society is a 501 (c)(3) accredited, not-for-profit organization existing for the purpose of accumulating and disseminating information; providing educational services to the public on maritime and colonial activity in the Florida Keys. *Address:* 200 Greene Street *City:* Key West *State:* FL *Zip:* 33040 *Phone:* 305-294-2633 *Web:* www.melfisher.org *Email:* office@melfisher.org

NAVAL AVIATION MUSEUM FOUNDATION
The Naval Aviation Museum Association supports the operations of the National Naval Aviation Museum in Pensacola, Fla. *Address:* 1750 Radford Blvd., Suite B *City:* Pensacola *State:* FL *Zip:* 32508 *Phone:* 850-453-2389 *Fax:* 850-457-3032 *Web:* www.navalaviationmuseum.org *Email:* namfoffice@navalaviationmuseum.org

OLD ISLAND RESTORATION FOUNDATION
Address: PO Box 689 *City:* Key West *State:* FL *Zip:* 33041 *Phone:* 305-294-9501 *Fax:* 305-294-4509 *Web:* www.oirf.org/museums/oldesthouse.htm *Email:* oldisland@comcast.net

PTF 3 RESTORATION PROJECT
Address: PO Box 740789 *City:* Orange City *State:* FL *Zip:* 32774 *Phone:* 800-694-7161 *Web:* www.ptf3restoration.org *Email:* redbarn2@embarqmail.com

ST. AUGUSTINE LIGHTHOUSE
The St. Augustine Lighthouse is dedicated to discovering, preserving, presenting and keeping alive the story of nation's oldest port. *Address:* 81 Lighthouse Avenue *City:* St. Augustine *State:* FL *Zip:* 32080 *Phone:* 904-829-0745 *Web:* www.staugustinelighthouse.com *Email:* info@staugustinelighthouse.com

ST. GEORGE LIGHTHOUSE ASSOCIATION
Address: 201 Bradford St. *City:* St. George Island *State:* FL *Zip:* 32328 *Phone:* 850-927-2972 *Web:* www.stgeorgelight.org

U.S. COAST GUARD (DISTRICT 7)
The Seventh U.S. Coast Guard District oversees safety and navigation in U.S. waters off Florida, Georgia, South Carolina, and Puerto Rico. *Address:* 909 SE 1st Avenue *City:* Miami *State:* FL *Zip:* 33131 *Web:* www.uscg.mil/d7/

GEORGIA

COASTAL GEORGIA HISTORICAL SOCIETY
The purpose of the Coastal Georgia Historical Society is to aid in the administration, restoration, and maintenance of those historic facilities and resources entrusted to its care. *Address:* PO Box 21136 *City:* St. Simons Island *State:* GA *Zip:* 31522 *Phone:* 912-638-4666 *Fax:* 912-638-6609 *Web:* www.saintsimonslighthouse.org *Email:* ssi1872@comcast.net

PEACEMAKER MARINE
Peacemaker Marine is a not-for-profit organization that owns and operates the barkentine Peacemaker. *City:* Brunswick *State:* GA *Phone:* 912-399-6946 *Web:* www.peacemakermarine.com *Email:* lee@peacemakermarine.com

TYBEE ISLAND LIGHT STATION
The Tybee Island Light Station cares for the Tybee Island Lighthouse and its grounds. *Address:* PO Box 366 *City:* Tybee Island *State:* GA *Zip:* 31328 *Phone:* 912-786-5801 *Fax:* 912-786-6538 *Web:* www.tybeelighthouse.org

HAWAII

LAHAINA RESTORATION FOUNDATION
The Lahaina Restoration Foundation is a 501(c)(3) Hawaii nonprofit organization chartered in 1962. Its purpose is to cooperate with all community-oriented interests in an effort to restore, maintain and preserve the physical and cultural legacies and history of Lahaina. *Address:* 120 Dickenson St. *City:* Lahaina *State:* HI *Zip:* 96761 *Phone:* 808-661-3262 *Fax:* 808-661-9309 *Web:* www.lahainarestoration.org *Email:* lrf@hawaii.rr.com

MARIMED FOUNDATION
Address: 45-021 Likeke Place *City:* Kaneohe *State:* HI *Zip:* 96744 *Phone:* 808-236-2288 *Fax:* 808-235-1074 *Web:* www.marimed.org *Email:* info@marimed.org

PACIFIC FLEET SUBMARINE MEMORIAL ASSOCIATION
The Pacific Fleet Submarine Memorial Association owns and operates the USS Bowfin Submarine Museum & Park. The organization's mission is to restore and preserve the World War II submarine USS Bowfin (SS-287), and submarine-related artifacts on our grounds. *Address:* 11 Arizona Memorial Drive *City:* Honolulu *State:* HI *Zip:* 96818 *Phone:* 808-423-1341 *Fax:* 808-422-5201 *Web:* www.bowfin.org *Email:* info@bowfin.org

U.S. COAST GUARD (DISTRICT 14)
The 14th District of the U.S. Coast Guard oversees the Hawaiian Islands. *Address:* 300 Ala Moana Blvd, Room 9-204 *City:* Honolulu *State:* HI *Zip:* 96850 *Phone:* 800-818-8724 *Web:* www.uscg.mil/d14/

USS MISSOURI MEMORIAL ASSOCIATION
Address: PO Box 879 *City:* Alea *State:* HI *Zip:* 96701 *Phone:* 808-455-1600 *Web:* www.ussmissouri.com *Email:* execoffices@ussmissouri.org

IDAHO

YANKEE FORK GOLD DREDGE ASSOCIATION
Address: PO Box 136 *City:* Clayton *State:* ID *Zip:* 83227 *Phone:* 208-838-2529

ILLINOIS

CANAL CORRIDOR ASSOCIATION
The Canal Corridor Association preserves history, protects nature and open space, and creates destinations where people can learn and have fun in the I&M Canal National Heritage Corridor. *Address:* 754 First St. *City:* La Salle *State:* IL *Zip:* 61301 *Phone:* 818-220-1848 *Web:* www.canalcor.org

CHAPTER 11 – ORGANIZATIONS

CHICAGO MARITIME SOCIETY
The Chicago Maritime Society was founded in 1982 to research, educate and celebrate Chicago's maritime heritage. *Address:* 310 S. Racine Ave. *City:* Chicago *State:* IL *Zip:* 60607 *Phone:* 312-421-9096 *Web:* www.chicagomaritimesociety.org *Email:* geraldhthomas@cs.com

GREAT LAKES NAVAL MUSEUM ASSOCIATION
Address: PO Box 886307 *City:* Great Lakes *State:* IL *Zip:* 60088 *Phone:* 847-688-3154 *Web:* www.greatlakesnavalmuseum.org *Email:* therese.gonzales@cnet.navy.mil

GROSSE POINT LIGHTHOUSE PARK DISTRICT
The Lighthouse Park District has its roots in the Northeast Park District that was established in 1929 as an independent governmental unit within the State of Illinois. *Address:* 2601 Sheridan Road *City:* Evanston *State:* IL *Zip:* 60201 *Phone:* 847-328-6961 *Web:* www.grossepointlighthouse.net *Email:* lpdnhl@grossepointlighthouse.net

ILLINOIS & MICHIGAN CANAL NATIONAL HERITAGE CORRIDOR
Address: 339 W. Jefferson St. *City:* Joliet *State:* IL *Zip:* 60435 *Phone:* 800-926-2262 *Web:* www.heritagecorridorcvb.com *Email:* info@heritagecorridorcvb.com

WILL COUNTY HISTORICAL SOCIETY
Address: 803 South State St. *City:* Lockport *State:* IL *Zip:* 60441 *Phone:* 815-838-5080 *Fax:* 815-838-4547 *Web:* www.willcountyhistory.org *Email:* info@willcountyhistory.org

INDIANA

CARROLL COUNTY WABASH AND ERIE CANAL
Founded in 1972, the Carroll County Wabash & Erie Canal is dedicated to the preservation of the stretch of the Wabash & Erie Canal located in Delphi, Indiana. *Address:* 1030 N. Washington St. *City:* Delphi *State:* IN *Zip:* 46923 *Phone:* 765-564-6572 *Web:* www.wabashanderiecanal.org *Email:* mccain@carlnet.org

HISTORIC STERNWHEELER PRESERVATION SOCIETY
Address: 11 Ashland Cove Road *City:* Vevay *State:* IN *Zip:* 47043 *Phone:* 812-427-9480 *Fax:* 812-427-2483 *Web:* www.hspsi.org *Email:* info@hspsi.org

MICHIGAN CITY HISTORICAL SOCIETY
The Michigan City Historical Society operates the Old Lighthouse Museum. *Address:* PO Box 512 *City:* Michigan City *State:* IN *Zip:* 46361 *Phone:* 219-872-6133 *Web:* www.michigancity.com/MCHistorical/

USS LST SHIP MEMORIAL
Address: 840 LST Drive *City:* Evansville *State:* IN *Zip:* 47713 *Phone:* 812-435-8678 *Web:* www.lstmemorial.com *Email:* webskipper@LSTMemorial.Org

WHITEWATER CANAL STATE HISTORIC SITE
Address: PO Box 88 *City:* Metamora *State:* IN *Zip:* 47030 *Phone:* 765-647-6512 *Fax:* 765-647-2734 *Web:* www.in.gov/ism/StateHistoricSites/WhitewaterCanal/ *Email:* whitewatercanalshs@dnr.in.gov

LOUISIANA

CAMERON PRESERVATION ALLIANCE - SABINE PASS LIGHTHOUSE
The Cameron Preservation Alliance works to preserve the history of Cameron Parish, including the lighthouse at Sabine Pass. *Address:* PO Box 590 *City:* Cameron Parish *State:* LA *Zip:* 70631

LAKE PONTCHARTRAIN BASIN MARITIME MUSEUM
The mission of the Lake Pontchartrain Basin Maritime Museum is to bring Louisiana 's unique maritime history to life. *Address:* 133 Mabel Dr. *City:* Madisonville *State:* LA *Zip:* 70447 *Phone:* 905-845-9200 *Web:* www.lpbmaritimemuseum.org

LOUISIANA NAVAL WAR MEMORIAL COMMISSION
The Louisiana Naval War Memorial Commission cares for the World War II-era destroyer USS Kidd. *Address:* 306 S. River Rd. *City:* Baton Rouge *State:* LA *Zip:* 70802 *Phone:* 504-342-1942 *Fax:* 225-342-2039 *Web:* www.usskidd.com *Email:* info@usskidd.com

U.S. COAST GUARD (DISTRICT 8)
The U.S. Coast Guard's Eighth District covers most of the Mississippi River basin and the western Gulf of Mexico. *Address:* Hale Boggs Federal Building *City:* New Orleans *State:* LA *Zip:* 70130 *Web:* www.uscg.mil/d8/

MAINE

ACADIA NATIONAL PARK
Address: PO Box 177 *City:* Bar Harbor *State:* ME *Zip:* 04609 *Phone:* 207-288-3338 *Fax:* 207-288-8813 *Web:* www.nps.gov/acad

AMERICAN LIGHTHOUSE FOUNDATION
The mission of the American Lighthouse Foundation is to save and preserve our nation's historic light stations and their rich heritage. This will be accomplished through the restoration, promotion and adaptive re-use of America's historic light stations, as well as educational initiatives that foster the sustainable preservation of lighthouses and perpetuate the legacy of the men and women who have tended them. *Address:* PO Box 565 *City:* Rockland *State:* ME *Zip:* 04841 *Phone:* 207-594-4174 *Fax:* 207-596-1091 *Web:* www.lighthousefoundation.org *Email:* info@lighthousefoundation.org

ASSOCIATION FOR MARITIME PRESERVATION
Based in Rockland, Maine, the Association for Maritime Preservation is a non-profit actively engaged in preserving significant historic sailing vessels and their maritime history through education and preservation projects. AMP was created out of the passion for touching, feeling, seeing and experiencing history and is committed to historic and environmental stewardship. *Address:* PO Box 1541 *City:* Rockland *State:* ME *Zip:* 04841 *Phone:* 207-226-3878 *Fax:* 207-594-1875 *Web:* www.maritimepreservation.org *Email:* amp@maritimepreservation.org

BOOTHBAY REGION HISTORICAL SOCIETY
Address: PO Box 272 *City:* Boothbay Harbor *State:* ME *Zip:* 04538 *Phone:* 207-633-0820 *Web:* www.boothbayhistorical.org *Email:* brhs@gwi.net

BORDER HISTORICAL SOCIETY
The Border Historical Society is an organization of Eastport area residents committed to preserving local history and operating the Barracks Museum, Quoddy Dam Model Museum, Quoddy Craft Shop and the site at Fort Sullivan and Powder House. *Address:* PO Box 95 *City:* Eastport *State:* ME *Zip:* 04631 *Web:* www.borderhistoricalsociety.com *Email:* borderhistoricalsociety@yahoo.com

FRANKLIN LIGHT PRESERVATION INC.
Address: PO Box 481 *City:* New Harbor *State:* ME *Zip:* 04554

FRIENDS OF LITTLE RIVER LIGHTHOUSE
Friends of Little River Lighthouse is a chapter of the American Lighthouse Foundation. *Address:* PO Box 671 *City:* East Machias *State:* ME *Zip:* 04630 *Web:* www.littleriverlight.org

FRIENDS OF SEGUIN ISLAND LIGHTHOUSE
The foremost purpose of our organization is the preservation, restoration, and maintenance of Seguin's buildings and grounds, to keep the Seguin's buildings and grounds open for public use, and carry out programs of education and research. *Address:* 72 Front Street, Suite 3 *City:* Bath *State:* ME *Zip:* 04530 *Phone:* 207-443-4808 *Web:* www.seguinisland.org *Email:* keeper@seguinisland.org

HURRICANE ISLAND OUTWARD BOUND SCHOOL
Address: 75 Mechanic Street *City:* Rockland *State:* ME *Zip:* 04841 *Phone:* 207-594-5548 *Fax:* 207-594-9425 *Email:* info@hurricaneisland.org

KENNEBUNKPORT CONSERVATION TRUST
The Kennebunkport Conservation Trust is a community organization dedicated to preserving the natural beauty of our town. *Address:* PO Box 7004 *City:* Cape Porpoise *State:* ME *Zip:* 04014 *Web:* www.thekennebunkportconservationtrust.org

KITTERY HISTORICAL & NAVAL SOCIETY
Address: 200 Rogers Road Extension *City:* Kittery *State:* ME *Zip:* 03904 *Phone:* 207-439-3080 *Web:* www.kitterymuseum.com *Email:* kitterymuseum@netzero.net

Is your local maritime heritage threatened by financial problems or even demolition? Email your story with photos to contact@fyddeye.com.

MAINE WINDJAMMER ASSOCIATION
Founded in 1977, the Maine Windjammer Association represents the largest fleet of traditional sailing schooners in North America. All 12 Maine windjammers are individually owned and operated by U.S. Coast Guard-licensed captains. *State:* ME *Phone:* 207-374-2993 *Web:* www.sailmainecoast.com

MARITIME MAINE HERITAGE TRAIL
The Maritime Maine Heritage Trail is a non-profit organization interested in the preservation and sharing of Maine's nautical heritage. *State:* ME *Phone:* 207-641-0985 *Web:* www.maritimemaine.org *Email:* sail@maritimemaine.com

OCEAN CLASSROOM FOUNDATION
The Ocean Classroom Foundation is committed to sending students and their teachers to sea, on voyages in which the traditions, values and adventure of maritime life provide a unique context for education. *Address:*

29 McKown St. *City:* Boothbay Harbor *State:* ME *Zip:* 04538 *Phone:* 207-633-2750 *Fax:* 207-633-4337 *Web:* www.oceanclassroom.org *Email:* mail@oceanclassroom.org

OLD BERWICK HISTORICAL SOCIETY
The Old Berwick Historical Society promotes public awareness of and appreciation for local and regional history through a variety of activities that explore, preserve, interpret, and celebrate the past. *Address:* PO Box 296 *City:* South Berwick *State:* ME *Zip:* 03908 *Phone:* 207-384-0000 *Web:* www.obhs.net *Email:* info@obhs.net

OLD YORK HISTORICAL SOCIETY
Address: PO Box 312 *City:* York *State:* ME *Zip:* 03909 *Phone:* 207-363-4974 *Fax:* 207-363-4021 *Web:* www.oldyork.org *Email:* oyhs@oldyork.org

RANGE LIGHT KEEPERS
The Kennebec Ranger Keepers maintain the Kennebec River Range Lights and the Fiddlers Reach Fog Bell Tower. *Address:* 58 Iron Mine Road *City:* Arrowsic *State:* ME *Zip:* 04530 *Phone:* 207-442-7443 *Web:* www.rlk.org *Email:* fogdog@rlk.org

SPRING POINT LEDGE LIGHT TRUST
The Spring Point Ledge Light Trust was formed by the Portland Harbor Museum in early 1998 to acquire ownership of the Spring Point Ledge Lighthouse. *Address:* PO Box 2311 *City:* South Portland *State:* ME *Zip:* 04106 *Phone:* 207-699-2676 *Web:* www.springpointlight.org *Email:* info@springpointlight.org

ST. CROIX HISTORICAL SOCIETY
The St. Croix Historical Society supports historic preservation in Calais and in the St. Croix Valley it shares with our Canadian neighbors across the St. Croix River. *Address:* PO Box 242 *City:* Calais *State:* ME *Zip:* 04619 *Web:* www.stcroixhistorical.org *Email:* schs@stcroixhistorical.org

SWAN'S ISLAND LIGHTHOUSE COMMITTEE
Address: Town of Swan's Island *City:* Swan's Island *State:* ME *Zip:* 04685 *Web:* www.swansisland.org *Email:* swanisle@tdstelme.net

WHITEHEAD LIGHT STATION
At Whitehead Light Station, we seek to give participants an unparalleled opportunity to enjoy the dramatic coast of Maine in an atmosphere that will broaden knowledge, strengthen skills, and promote renewal. *Address:* PO Box 242 *City:* Brunswick *State:* ME *Zip:* 04011 *Phone:* 207-729-7714 *Web:* www.whiteheadlightstation.org *Email:* info@whiteheadlightstation.org

WOOD ISLAND PRESERVATION GROUP
Address: 5 Goodwin Rd. *City:* Kittery Point *State:* ME *Zip:* 03905 *Phone:* 207-439-2603

MARYLAND

AMERICAN ACADEMY OF INDUSTRY
Address: 1195 Generals Highway *City:* Crownsville *State:* MD *Zip:* 21032 *Web:* www.aai-acacia.org *Email:* overnights@uscgcacacia.org

CHAPTER 11 – ORGANIZATIONS

ASSATEAGUE ISLAND NATIONAL SEASHORE
Address: 7206 National Seashore Lane *City:* Berlin *State:* MD *Zip:* 21811 *Phone:* 410-641-1441 *Web:* www.nps.gov/asis/

BALTIMORE AND CHESAPEAKE STEAMBOAT COMPANY
The mission of the Baltimore and Chesapeake Steamboat Company is to maintain the steam tug Baltimore and operate it as an educational museum highlighting the tug's unique place in American history. *Address:* 1415 Key Highway *City:* Baltimore *State:* MD *Zip:* 21230 *Phone:* 410-727-4818 *Fax:* 410-727-4869 *Web:* www.steamtug.org *Email:* Sgheaver@aol.com

CHESAPEAKE & OHIO NATIONAL HISTORICAL PARK
Address: 1850 Dual Highway, Suite 100 *City:* Hagerstown *State:* MD *Zip:* 21740 *Phone:* 301-739-4200 *Web:* www.nps.gov

CHESAPEAKE BAY FOUNDATION
Address: 6 Herndon Avenue *City:* Annapolis *State:* MD *Zip:* 21403 *Phone:* 410-268-8816 *Fax:* 410-268-6687 *Web:* www.cbf.org *Email:* educationcoordinator@cbf.org

CHESAPEAKE HERITAGE CONSERVANCY
The Chesapeake Heritage Conservancy owns the skipjack Martha Lewis. *Address:* 121 North Union Ave, Suite C *City:* Havre de Grace *State:* MD *Zip:* 21078 *Phone:* 410-939-4078 *Fax:* 410-939-4121 *Web:* www.skipjackmarthalewis.org *Email:* director@skipjackmarthalewis.org

COASTAL HERITAGE ALLIANCE
Coastal Heritage Alliance is a not-for-profit educational organization dedicated to the preservation and advancement of commercial fishing family cultural heritage as it still exists in the persons, vessels, skills and stories of a rapidly vanishing industry. *Address:* PO Box 313 *City:* St. Michaels *State:* MD *Zip:* 21663 *Web:* www.coastalheritage.org *Email:* mikev@coastalheritage.org

CRISFIELD HERITAGE FOUNDATION
Address: PO Box 253 *City:* Crisfield *State:* MD *Zip:* 21817 *Phone:* 410-968-2501 *Fax:* 410-968-0350 *Web:* www.crisfieldheritagefoundation.org *Email:* contactus@crisfieldheritagefoundation.org

DORCHESTER SKIPJACK COMMITTEE
Address: PO Box 1224 *City:* Cambridge *State:* MD *Zip:* 21613 *Web:* www.skipjack-nathan.org *Email:* info@skipjack-nathan.org

FRIENDS OF CONCORD POINT LIGHTHOUSE
Friends of Concord Point Lighthouse is a not-for-profit group that supports lighthouse and a small museum. *Address:* PO Box 212 *City:* Havre de Grace *State:* MD *Zip:* 21078 *Phone:* 410-939-3213 *Email:* directorcpt@verizon.net

JAMES B. RICHARDSON FOUNDATION
The James B. Richardson Foundation operates three facilities in Cambridge, Md: the Richardson Maritime Museum, the Ruark Boatworks, and the Brannock Center, which is scheduled to open to public soon. *Address:* 401 High St. *City:* Cambridge *State:* MD *Zip:* 21613 *Phone:* 401-221-8844 *Web:* www.richardsonmuseum.org *Email:* info@richardsonmuseum.org

LIVING CLASSROOMS FOUNDATION
Living Classrooms Foundation is a non-profit organization, operated for the benefit of the community at large, providing hands-on education and job skills training for students from diverse backgrounds, with a special emphasis on serving at-risk youth. *Address:* 802 S. Caroline St. *City:* Baltimore *State:* MD *Zip:* 21231 *Phone:* 410-685-0295 *Web:* www.livingclassrooms.org *Email:* web@livingclassrooms.org

OCEAN CITY MUSEUM SOCIETY
The Ocean City Museum Society is a non-profit organization dedicated to preserving and interpreting the rich natural and cultural history of this coastal community through memorabilia collections, rotating exhibits, educational programs and area research. *Address:* PO Box 603 *City:* Ocean City *State:* MD *Zip:* 21843 *Phone:* 410-289-4991 *Web:* www.ocmuseum.org *Email:* curator@ocmuseum.org

PATUXENT RIVER NAVAL AIR MUSEUM ASSOCIATION
The Patuxent River Naval Air Museum Association supports the growth and development of the Patuxent River Naval Air Museum. *Address:* 22156 Three Notch Road *City:* Lexington Park *State:* MD *Zip:* 20653 *Phone:* 301-863-7418 *Fax:* 301-342-7947 *Web:* www.paxmuseum.com *Email:* director@paxmuseum.com

POINT LOOKOUT LIGHTHOUSE PRESERVATION SOCIETY
The Point Lookout Lighthouse Preservation Society was formed to restore the Point Lookout Lighthouse buildings to the 1927 time period and to educate the public on the rich history of the lighthouse. *Address:* PO Box 135 *City:* St. Leonard *State:* MD *Zip:* 20685 *Web:* www.pllps.org *Email:* volunteer@PLLPS.org

PROJECT LIBERTY SHIP
The primary mission of Project Liberty Ship is to preserve, maintain and operate the World War II Liberty Ship S.S. John W. Brown to serve as an operating vessel and living museum in paying tribute to the shipbuilders who built the Liberty Ships, the merc *Address:* PO Box 25846 *City:* Baltimore *State:* MD *Zip:* 21224 *Phone:* 410-558-0646 *Fax:* 410-558-1737 *Web:* www.liberty-ship.com *Email:* john.w.brown@usa.net

ST. MARY'S COUNTY MUSEUM DIVISION
Address: 23115 Leonard Hall Dr. *City:* Leonardtown *State:* MD *Zip:* 20650 *Phone:* 301-475-4200 *Fax:* 301-475-4935 *Web:* www.co.saint-marys.md.us *Email:* john.savich@co.saint-marys.md.us

SULTANA PROJECTS
A grass-roots, private non-profit, Sultana Projects is dedicated to a mission of providing unique, hands-on educational opportunities that promote stewardship of the Chesapeake's historic, cultural and environmental legacies. *Address:* PO Box 524 *City:* Chestertown *State:* MD *Zip:* 21620 *Phone:* 410-778-5954 *Fax:* 410-778-4531 *Web:* www.sultanaprojects.org *Email:* dmcmullen@sultanaprojects.org

MASSACHUSETTS

BOSTON MARINE SOCIETY
Founded in 1754, the Boston Marine Society, an organization of sea captains, is the oldest society of its kind in the world. *Address:* National Historical Park, Bldg 32 *City:* Boston *State:* MA *Zip:* 02129 *Phone:* 617-242-0522 *Fax:* 617-241-0505 *Web:* www.bostonmarinesociety.org *Email:* info@bostonmarinesociety.org

CHAPTER 11 – ORGANIZATIONS

BOSTON NATIONAL HISTORICAL PARK
Boston National Historical Park visitor centers can be found at two convenient location along the Freedom Trail. The downtown visitor center is located at 15 State Street, next to the Old State House. *Address:* Building 5, Charlestown Navy Yard *City:* Boston *State:* MA *Zip:* 02129 *Phone:* 617-242-5601 *Fax:* 617-242-6006 *Web:* www.nps.gov/bost/

BOSTON PORT AND SEAMAN'S AID SOCIETY
The Boston Port and Seamen's Aid Society was founded in 1829 under the guidance of Father Edward Thompson Taylor, known as the Sailor Preacher in Boston's historic North Square. *Address:* 11 North Square *City:* Boston *State:* MA *Zip:* 02113 *Phone:* 617-227-3979 *Fax:* 617-227-4005 *Web:* www.marinershouse.org *Email:* inn@marinershouse.org

CAPE COD CHAPTER, ALF
The Cape Cod Chapter of the American Lighthouse Foundation is a non-profit organization made up of volunteer members whose mission is the restoration and preservation of Race Point Lighthouse. *Address:* PO Box 570 *City:* Truro *State:* MA *Zip:* 02652 *Phone:* 508-487-9930 *Web:* www.racepointlighthouse.net *Email:* racepointlighthouse@comcast.net

CAPE COD NATIONAL SEASHORE
The great Outer Beach described by Thoreau in the 1800s is protected within the national seashore. Forty miles of pristine sandy beach, marshes, ponds, and uplands support diverse species. Lighthouses, cultural landscapes, and wild cranberry bogs offer a *Address:* 99 Marconi Site Road *City:* Wellfleet *State:* MA *Zip:* 02667 *Phone:* 508-349-3785 *Fax:* 508-349-9052 *Web:* www.nps.gov/caco/

COHASSET HISTORICAL SOCIETY
Address: PO Box 627 *City:* Cohasset *State:* MA *Zip:* 02025 *Phone:* 781-383-1434 *Web:* www.cohassethistoricalsociety.org *Email:* cohassethistory@yahoo.com

CUTTYHUNK HISTORICAL SOCIETY
The purpose of the Cuttyhunk Historical Society is to preserve the traditions, records and history of the Elizabeth Islands for the benefit of present and future generations. *Address:* 23 Tower Hill Rd *City:* Cuttyhunk *State:* MA *Zip:* 02713 *Phone:* 508-984-4611 *Web:* www.cuttyhunkhistoricalsociety.org

DUXBURY RURAL AND HISTORICAL SOCIETY
The Duxbury Rural and Historical Society is a non-profit organization seeking to foster a better understanding of the heritage and rural environment of Duxbury, Mass. *Address:* PO Box 2865 *City:* Duxbury *State:* MA *Zip:* 02331 *Phone:* 781-934-6106 *Fax:* 781-934-5730 *Web:* www.duxburyhistory.org *Email:* aarnold@duxburyhistory.org

EGAN MARITIME INSTITUTE
Address: 4 Winter St. *City:* Nantucket *State:* MA *Zip:* 02554 *Phone:* 508-228-2505 *Web:* www.eganmaritime.org *Email:* egan@eganmaritime.org

ESSEX HISTORICAL SOCIETY & SHIPBUILDING MUSEUM
The mission of the Essex Historical Society and Shipbuilding Museum is to preserve the history of Essex, Massachusetts, with particular emphasis on the town's shipbuilding industry and the role it played in the development of the American fishing schooner. *Address:* 66 Main Street *City:* Essex *State:* MA *Zip:* 01929 *Phone:* 978-768-7541 *Fax:* 978-768-2541 *Web:* www.essexshipbuildingmuseum.org *Email:* info@essexshipbuildingmuseum.org

CHAPTER 11 – ORGANIZATIONS

FRIENDS OF PLUM ISLAND LIGHT
Address: PO Box 381 *City:* Newburyport *State:* MA *Zip:* 01950

HISTORIC SALEM
Address: 9 North St. *City:* Salem *State:* MA *Phone:* 978-745-0799 *Web:* www.historicsalem.org *Email:* info@historicsalem.org

LUNA PRESERVATION SOCIETY
The Luna Preservation Society is a not-for-profit organization dedicated to the restoration and preservation of the tugboat Luna, a National Historic Landmark moored in Boston, Mass. *Address:* PO Box 1866 *City:* Brookline *State:* MA *Zip:* 02446 *Phone:* 617-282-1941 *Web:* www.tugboatluna.org *Email:* info@tugboatluna.org

MARTHA'S VINEYARD HISTORICAL SOCIETY
The Martha *Address:* PO Box 1310 *City:* Edgartown *State:* MA *Zip:* 02539 *Phone:* 508-627-4441 *Fax:* 508-627-4436 *Web:* www.mvmuseum.org *Email:* KGorman@mvmuseum.org

MIDDLESEX CANAL ASSOCIATION
Address: 71 Faulkner St. *City:* North Billerica *State:* MA *Zip:* 01862 *Phone:* 978-670-2740 *Web:* www.middlesexcanal.org *Email:* middlesexcanalcomm.jreardon@juno.com

NANTUCKET HISTORICAL ASSOCIATION
The Nantucket Historical Association preserves and interprets the history of Nantucket Island and fosters an appreciation of its historic significance. *Address:* PO Box 1016 *City:* Nantucket *State:* MA *Zip:* 02554 *Phone:* 508-228-1894 *Fax:* 508-228-5618 *Web:* www.nha.org

NANTUCKET PRESERVATION TRUST
The Nantucket Preservation Trust serves as an advocate for Nantucket Island. *Address:* 2 Union St. *City:* Nantucket *State:* MA *Zip:* 02554 *Phone:* 508-228-1387 *Fax:* 508-228-1371 *Web:* www.nantucketpreservation.org *Email:* info@nantucketpreservation.org

NAUSET LIGHT PRESERVATION SOCIETY
A group of citizens in Eastham formed the Nauset Light Preservation Society, a non-profit volunteer organization whose original mission was to rescue the lighthouse. This was accomplished in November 1996. The mission now is the preservation and restoration of the structure and grounds. *Address:* PO Box 941 *City:* Eastham *State:* MA *Zip:* 02642 *Phone:* 508-240-2612 *Web:* www.nausetlight.org *Email:* nausetlight@capecod.net

ORLEANS HISTORICAL SOCIETY
The Orleans Historical Society, a non-profit organization founded under the laws of the Commonwealth of Massachusetts in 1958, was organized to collect and preserve the history of the Town of Orleans. *Address:* PO Box 353 *City:* Orleans *State:* MA *Zip:* 02653 *Phone:* 508-240-1329 *Web:* www.orleanshistoricalsociety.org *Email:* orleanshs@verizon.net

OSTERVILLE HISTORICAL SOCIETY
Address: 155 West Bay Road *City:* Osterville *State:* MA *Zip:* 02655 *Phone:* 508-428-5861 *Web:* www.osterville.org/OHSindex.htm *Email:* welcome@osterville.org

SCITUATE HISTORICAL SOCIETY
The mission of the Scituate Historical Society is to promote the study of local history and to preserve the antiquities of Scituate and those municipalities that were anciently a part of our town. Our membership is open to all. *Address:* PO Box 276 *City:* Scituate *State:* MA *Zip:* 02066 *Phone:* 781-545-1083 *Web:* www.scituatehistoricalsociety.org *Email:* director@scituatehistoricalsociety.org

SCONSET TRUST
Address: PO Box 821 *City:* Siasconset *State:* MA *Zip:* 02564 *Phone:* 508-228-9917 *Fax:* 508-228-0810 *Web:* www.sconsettrust.org *Email:* info@sconsettrust.org

SEA EDUCATION ASSOCIATION
Address: PO Box 6 *City:* Woods Hole *State:* MA *Zip:* 02543 *Phone:* 508-540-3954 *Web:* www.sea.edu *Email:* admission@sea.edu

SHENANDOAH FOUNDATION
Address: PO Box 429 *City:* Vineyard Haven *State:* MA *Zip:* 02568 *Phone:* 508-693-1699 *Fax:* 508-693-1881 *Web:* www.shenandoahfoundation.org *Email:* morgan@shenandoahfoundation.org

TRURO HISTORICAL SOCIETY
Address: PO Box 486 *City:* Truro *State:* MA *Zip:* 02666 *Phone:* 508-487-3397 *Web:* trurohistorical.org

U.S. LIFE-SAVING SERVICE HERITAGE ASSOCIATION
The goal of the U.S. Life-Saving Service Heritage Association is to preserve the stations, history, boats, and equipment of the U.S. Life-Saving Service and the U.S. Coast Guard. *Address:* 158 Polpis Road *City:* Nantucket *State:* MA *Zip:* 02554 *Web:* www.uslife-savingservice.org *Email:* mo72506@nantucket.net

U.S. COAST GUARD (DISTRICT 1)
District 1 of the U.S. Coast Guard serves the states of Maine, Vermont, Massachusetts, New Hampshire, Connecticute, Rhode Island, and portions of New York. *Address:* 408 Atlantic Avenue *City:* Boston *State:* MA *Zip:* 02110 *Web:* www.uscg.mil/d1/

USCG LIGHTSHIP SAILORS ASSOCIATION
Address: 7 Ridge Road *City:* Palmer *State:* MA *Zip:* 01069 *Web:* www.uscglightshipsailors.org *Email:* webmaster@gryder.com

WELLFLEET HISTORICAL SOCIETY
The Wellfleet Historical Society was organized in 1951 to foster an interest in the town and its history. *Address:* 266 Main St. *City:* Wellfleet *State:* MA *Zip:* 02667 *Phone:* 508-349-9157 *Web:* www.wellfleethistoricalsociety.com *Email:* museum@wellfleethistoricalsociety.com

WESTPORT FISHERMAN'S ASSOCIATION
The Westport Fisherman's Association is restoring the Horseneck Point Life-Saving Station. *Address:* PO Box 83 *City:* Westport *State:* MA *Zip:* 02791 *Web:* westportriver.org *Email:* wfa@westportriver.org

MICHIGAN

40 MILE POINT LIGHTHOUSE SOCIETY
Address: PO Box 205 *City:* Rogers City *State:* MI *Zip:* 49779 *Web:* www.40milepointlighthouse.org *Email:* webmaster@40milepointlighthouse.org

ALCONA HISTORICAL SOCIETY
The Alcona Historical Society was formed to preserve the rich history of the Alcona County area. The society realizes the value of the past and its importance to future generations. *Address:* PO Box 174 *City:* Hansville *State:* MI *Zip:* 48740 *Phone:* 989-724-6297 *Web:* theenchantedforest.com/AlconaHistoricalSociety/

BAY COUNTY HISTORICAL SOCIETY
Address: 321 Washington Ave. *City:* Bay City *State:* MI *Zip:* 48708 *Phone:* 989-893-5733 *Web:* www.bchs-museum.org

BAYSAIL
Address: 107 Fifth Street *City:* Bay City *State:* MI *Zip:* 48708 *Phone:* 989-895-5193 *Fax:* 989-460-1472 *Web:* www.baysailbaycity.org *Email:* info@baysailbaycity.org

BEAVER ISLAND HISTORICAL SOCIETY
Address: 38105 Michigan Ave. *City:* Beaver Island *State:* MI *Zip:* 49782 *Phone:* 231-448-2479 *Web:* beaverisland.net/history/

BEAVER ISLAND LIGHTHOUSE SCHOOL
Address: Charlevoix Public Schools *City:* Charlevoix *State:* MI *Zip:* 49720 *Phone:* 213-547-3200 *Fax:* 231-547-0556 *Web:* www.rayder.net *Email:* cpsinfo@rayder.net

CRISP POINT LIGHT HISTORICAL SOCIETY
Address: PO Box 229 *City:* Paradise *State:* MI *Zip:* 49768 *Phone:* 906-492-3206 *Web:* www.crisppointlighthouse.org *Email:* donross@jamadots.com

DELTA COUNTY HISTORICAL SOCIETY
The Delta County Historical Society was founded in 1948. The primary objective of this newly formed non-profit organization was to collect local historical materials, preserve them, and present this information to the citizens of Delta County. *Address:* 16 Water Plant Road *City:* Escanaba *State:* MI *Zip:* 49829 *Phone:* 906-789-6790 *Web:* www.deltahistorical.org *Email:* deltacountyhistsoc@sbcglobal.net

DETOUR REEF LIGHT PRESERVATION SOCIETY
In January 1998, civic leaders from DeTour Village and Drummond Island, Michigan, met to form the DeTour Reef Light Preservation Society, a nonprofit 501c3 organization. *Address:* PO Box 307 *City:* Drummond Island *State:* MI *Zip:* 49726 *Phone:* 906-493-6609 *Web:* www.drlps.com *Email:* drlps@drlps.com

GRAND MARAIS HISTORICAL SOCIETY
Address: PO Box 179 *City:* Grand Marais *State:* MI *Zip:* 49839 *Phone:* 906-494-2404 *Web:* historicalsociety.grandmaraismichigan.com

CHAPTER 11 – ORGANIZATIONS

GREAT LAKES MARITIME INSTITUTE
The Great Lakes Maritime Institute promotes interest in the Great Lakes; preserves items related to their history; encourages building of scale models of lake ships, small craft and racing boats and furthers programs of the Dossin Great Lakes Museum. *Address:* 100 Strand on Belle Isle *City:* Detroit *State:* MI *Zip:* 48207 *Phone:* 313-852-4051 *Web:* www.glmi.org *Email:* web@glmi.org

GREAT LAKES SHIPWRECK HISTORICAL SOCIETY
Address: 111 Ashmun Street *City:* Sault Ste. Marie *State:* MI *Zip:* 49783 *Phone:* 800-635-1742 *Web:* www.shipwreckmuseum.com

GROSSE ILE HISTORICAL SOCIETY
The Grosse Ile Historical Society was organized in 1959 and has, since 1967, operated a museum in the old Michigan Central Railroad depot at the corner of East River Road and Grosse Ile Parkway. *Address:* PO Box 131 *City:* Grosse Ile *State:* MI *Zip:* 48138

GULLIVER HISTORICAL SOCIETY
The Gulliver Historical Society manages the Seal Choix Lighthouse Park and Museums. *Address:* 672N West Gulliver Lk. Rd. *City:* Gulliver *State:* MI *Zip:* 49840 *Phone:* 906-283-3183 *Web:* www.greatlakelighthouse.com *Email:* seulchoix@reiters.net

INLAND SEAS EDUCATION ASSOCIATION
The Inland Seas Education Association is a non-profit organization whose mission is to help people of all ages experience the science and spirit of the Great Lakes through shipboard and on-shore programs. *Address:* PO Box 218 *City:* Suttons Bay *State:* MI *Zip:* 49682 *Phone:* 231-271-3077 *Fax:* 231-271-3088 *Web:* www.schoolship.org *Email:* isea@schoolship.org

KEWEENAW BAY INDIAN COMMUNITY
Address: 16429 Beartown Rd. *City:* Baraga *State:* MI *Zip:* 49908 *Phone:* 906-353-6623 *Web:* www.kbic-nsn.gov

KEWEENAW COUNTY HISTORICAL SOCIETY
The Keweenaw County Historical Society, a not-for-profit 501(c)(3) organization, was established in 1981 to preserve and share the history of the county. It has over 960 members, many of whom are life members. *Address:* 670 Lighthouse Road *City:* Eagle Harbor *State:* MI *Zip:* 49950 *Web:* www.keweenawhistory.org

KEWEENAW LAND TRUST
The mission of the Keweenaw Land Trust is as a community partner protecting land, water, and quality of life through conservation, stewardship and education. *Address:* 801 North Lincoln Drive *City:* Hancock *State:* MI *Zip:* 49930 *Phone:* 906-482-0820 *Web:* www.keweenawlandtrust.org *Email:* evanmcdonald@keweenawlandtrust.org

LES CHENEAUX HISTORICAL ASSOCIATION
Formed in 1967, the Les Cheneaux Historical Association encourages the appreciation of social and historical heritage and natural history of the Les Cheneaux Islands and their vicinity. *Address:* PO Box 301 *City:* Cedarville *State:* MI *Zip:* 49719 *Phone:* 906-484-2821 *Web:* www.lchistorical.org *Email:* lcha@lchistorical.org

LITTLE TRAVERSE BAY BAND OF ODAWA INDIANS
Address: 7500 Odawa Circle *City:* Harbor Springs *State:* MI *Zip:* 49740 *Phone:* 231-242-1400 *Web:* www.ltbbodawa-nsn.gov

CHAPTER 11 – ORGANIZATIONS

MACKINAC STATE HISTORIC PARKS
At Mackinac State Historic Parks, we protect, preserve and present Mackinac's rich historical and natural resources to provide outstanding educational and recreational experiences for the public. *Address:* PO Box 873 *City:* Mackinaw City *State:* MI *Zip:* 49701 *Phone:* 231-436-4100 *Web:* www.mackinacparks.com *Email:* cottonl@michigan.gov

MARITIME HERITAGE ALLIANCE
The Maritime Heritage Alliance is a 501(c)3 non-profit organization dedicated to preserving interpreting, and promoting an appreciation of the maritime heritage of the Great Lakes. *Address:* 322 Sixth St. *City:* Traverse City *State:* MI *Zip:* 49684 *Phone:* 231-946-2647 *Web:* www.maritimeheritagealliance.org *Email:* kelly@maritimeheritagealliance.org

MICHIGAN HISTORICAL MUSEUM SYSTEM
Address: PO Box 30738 *City:* Lansing *State:* MI *Zip:* 48909 *Phone:* 517-241-2236 *Fax:* 517-241-2930 *Web:* www.michigan.gov/hal

MICHIGAN LIGHTHOUSE CONSERVANCY
The Michigan Lighthouse Conservancy web site contains information about lighthouses and life saving stations located in Michigan. Links to other related sites outside of Michigan are also presented where they are appropriate. *Address:* PO Box 973 *City:* Fenton *State:* MI *Zip:* 48430 *Phone:* 810-750-9236 *Web:* www.michiganlights.com *Email:* rescuetwo@aol.com

ONTONAGON COUNTY HISTORICAL SOCIETY
The Ontonagon County Historical Society was founded in 1957 to collect and preserve the artifacts of the county's history and to educate the public about that history and related topics. *Address:* 422 River Street *City:* Ontonagon *State:* MI *Zip:* 49953 *Phone:* 906-884-6165 *Web:* www.ontonagonmuseum.org *Email:* ochs@jamadots.com

POINT AUX BARQUES LIGHTHOUSE SOCIETY
The Pointe aux Barques Lighthouse Society was formed for the purpose of preserving the history of the Pointe aux Barques Lighthouse and surrounding waters of Lake Huron and to assist Huron County with the maintenance and preservation of Lighthouse buildings. *Address:* PO Box 97 *City:* Port Hope *State:* MI *Zip:* 48468 *Web:* www.pointeauxbarqueslighthouse.org *Email:* info@pointeauxbarqueslighthouse.org

PRESQUE ISLE TOWNSHIP MUSEUM SOCIETY
The Presque Isle Township Museum Society operates the Keepers House, New Presque Isle Lighthouse and Old Presque Isle Lighthouse. *Address:* PO Box 208 *City:* Presque Isle *State:* MI *Zip:* 49777 *Web:* www.keepershouse.org *Email:* neilsbungalow@yahoo.com

S.S. MILWAUKEE CLIPPER PRESERVATION
Address: PO Box 1370 *City:* Muskegon *State:* MI *Zip:* 49443 *Phone:* 231-755-0990 *Web:* www.milwaukeeclipper.com *Email:* RES035d8@gte.net

SABLE POINT LIGHTKEEPERS ASSOCIATION
The Sable Point Lighthouse Keepers Association maintains the Little Sable Point, Big Sable Point, and Ludington North Breakwater lighthouses. *Address:* PO Box 673 *City:* Ludington *State:* MI *Zip:* 49431 *Phone:* 231-845-7343 *Web:* www.splka.org *Email:* bsplka@t-one.net

SAGINAW RIVER MARINE HISTORICAL SOCIETY
The Saginaw River Marine Historical Society is a non-profit organization dedicated to the preservation and appreciation of the history of the Saginaw River and connecting waters. The Society was founded in 1989. *Address:* Dept. SRL *City:* Bay City *State:* MI *Zip:* 48707 *Web:* www.boatnerd.com/museums/srmhs/

SLEEPING BEAR DUNES NATIONAL LAKESHORE
Sleeping Bear Dunes National Lakeshore is one of the most beautiful natural areas in Michigan *Address:* 9922 Front Street *City:* Empire *State:* MI *Zip:* 49630 *Phone:* 231-326-5134 *Web:* www.nps.gov/slbe/

SOO LOCKS VISITORS CENTER ASSOCIATION
The Soo Locks Visitors Center Association's mission is to convey the past, showcase the present, and enlighten the future of the Soo Locks. *Address:* PO Box 666 *City:* Sault Ste Marie *State:* MI *Zip:* 49783 *Phone:* 800-657-2858 *Web:* www.sooslocksvisitorscenter.com *Email:* info@saultstemarie.com

THUNDER BAY ISLAND LIGHTHOUSE PRESERVATION SOCIETY
The Thunder Bay Island Lighthouse Preservation Society is an IRS 501(c)(3) not-for-profit corporation, and it is licensed to solicit by the State of Michigan. We are dedicated to the education, preservation and restoration of Thunder Bay Island and its history. *Address:* PO Box 212 *City:* Alpena *State:* MI *Zip:* 49797 *Web:* www.thunderbayislandsociety.org *Email:* info@thunderbayislandsociety.org

U.S. COAST GUARD (DISTRICT 9)
The Ninth Coast Guard District, Guardians of the Great Lakes, provides safety and security for the more than 30 million people in the Great Lakes region. *City:* Sault St. Marie *State:* MI *Phone:* 906-635-2440 *Web:* www.uscg.mil/d9/

WAUGOSHANCE LIGHTHOUSE PRESERVATION SOCIETY
We at the Waugoshance Lighthouse Preservation Society believes this castle of the lake needs to be preserved for future generations to be able to share in the history of the Great Lakes. *Address:* PO Box 1601 *City:* Mackinaw City *State:* MI *Zip:* 49701 *Web:* www.waugoshance.org *Email:* info@waugoshance.org

MINNESOTA

HISTORICAL AND CULTURAL SOCIETY OF CLAY COUNTY
Address: PO Box 157 *City:* Moorhead *State:* MN *Zip:* 56561 *Phone:* 218-299-5511 *Fax:* 218-299-5510 *Web:* www.hjemkomst-center.com *Email:* maureen.jonason@ci.moorhead.mn.us

MINNESOTA HISTORICAL SOCIETY
The Minnesota Historical Society is chief caretaker of Minnesota's story. *Address:* 345 W. Kellogg Blvd. *City:* St. Paul *State:* MN *Zip:* 55102 *Phone:* 651-259-3000 *Web:* www.mnhs.org

NORTHEASTERN MARITIME HISTORICAL FOUNDATION
The goal of the Northeastern Maritime Historical Foundation is to assemble a first-rate collection of historically significant commercial vessels for preservation and display on the Great Lakes. *Address:* PO Box 16687 *City:* Duluth *State:* MN *Zip:* 55816 *Web:* www.northeasternmaritime.org *Email:* contact@northeasternmaritime.org

CHAPTER 11 – ORGANIZATIONS

U.S. ARMY CORPS OF ENGINEERS (DULUTH)
Address: 901 Minnesota Ave *City:* Duluth *State:* MN *Zip:* 55802 *Phone:* 218-720-5269

U.S. ARMY CORPS OF ENGINEERS (ST. PAUL DISTRICT)
Address: Sibley Square at Mears Park *City:* St. Paul *State:* MN *Zip:* 55101 *Phone:* 651-290-5201 *Web:* www.mvp.usace.army.mil

MISSISSIPPI

CEC/SEABEE HISTORICAL FOUNDATION
The CEC/Seabee Historical Foundation is currently developing a new museum for the preservation of the history of the U.S. Navy Seabees. *Address:* PO Box 657 *City:* Gulfport *State:* MS *Zip:* 39502 *Phone:* 228-865-0480 *Web:* www.seabeehf.org *Email:* info@seabeehf.org

MISSISSIPPI MARITIME HERITAGE FOUNDATION
The Mississippi Maritime Heritage Foundation is a non-profit organization dedicated to the preservation and interpretation of the maritime heritage of the Gulf Coast and Mississippi River. *City:* Ocean Springs *State:* MS *Phone:* 228-282-5298 *Web:* www.myspace.com/thepirateproject

NEBRASKA

CAPTAIN MERIWETHER LEWIS FOUNDATION
Address: PO Box 145 *City:* Brownville *State:* NE *Zip:* 68321 *Phone:* 401-825-4131 *Web:* www.meriwetherlewisfoundation.org *Email:* jm62006@navix.net

NEW HAMPSHIRE

FRIENDS OF PORTSMOUTH HARBOR LIGHTHOUSE
Friends of Portsmouth Harbor Lighthouse was founded in 2001 as a chapter of the American Lighthouse Foundation. Our mission is to work for the preservation of Portsmouth Harbor Lighthouse and associated structures, as well as to gather and preserve the history of this important historic site and to share these resources with the public. *Address:* PO Box 8232 *City:* Portsmouth *State:* NH *Zip:* 03802 *Web:* www.portsmouthharborlighthouse.org *Email:* info@portsmouthharborlighthouse.org

GUNDALOW COMPANY
The Gundalow Company promotes awareness of the maritime heritage and the contemporary coastal environment in the Piscataqua Region using a replica gundalow in collaboration with other nonprofit organizations. *Address:* PO Box 425 *City:* Portsmouth *State:* NH *Zip:* 03802 *Phone:* 603-433-9505 *Fax:* 603-433-6403 *Web:* www.gundalow.org *Email:* info@gundalow.org

LIGHTHOUSE PRESERVATION SOCIETY
Address: 11 Seaborne Dr. *City:* Dover *State:* NH *Zip:* 03820 *Web:* www.lighthousepreservation.org *Email:* lps@naisp.net

PISCATAQUA MARITIME COMMISSION
Address: PO Box 545 *City:* Portsmouth *State:* NH *Zip:* 03802 *Web:* www.pmcportsmouth.org *Email:* lrjob@comcast.net

PORTSMOUTH HISTORICAL SOCIETY
The Portsmouth Historical Society is dedicated to increasing public understanding and enthusiasm for local history. *Address:* PO Box 728 *City:* Portsmouth *State:* NH *Zip:* 03802 *Phone:* 603-436-8420 *Web:* www.portsmouthhistory.org

NEW JERSEY

BARNEGAT LIGHT HISTORICAL SOCIETY
The Barnegat Light Historical Society is a not-for-profit corporation organized under the laws of New Jersey whose purposes are exclusively charitable and educational. Our main objective is to keep the history of Barnegat Light alive and available to the public. *Address:* PO Box 386 *City:* Barnegat Light *State:* NJ *Zip:* 08006 *Phone:* 609-494-8578 *Web:* www.bl-hs.org *Email:* klarson767@aol.com

BAYSHORE DISCOVERY PROJECT
The Bayshore Discovery Project's mission is to motivate people to take care of the environment, the history, and the culture of New Jersey's Bayshore Region through education, preservation, and example. *Address:* 2800 High St., Bivalve *City:* Port Norris *State:* NJ *Zip:* 08349 *Phone:* 856-785-2060 *Fax:* 856-785-2893 *Web:* www.ajmeerwald.org *Email:* info@bayshorediscoveryproject.org

> Fyddeye wants to hear how you saved your maritime heritage for future generations. Become a member at www.fyddeye.com and post your story!

CANAL SOCIETY OF NEW JERSEY
Address: PO Box 737 *City:* Morristown *State:* NJ *Zip:* 07963 *Phone:* 908-722-9556 *Web:* www.canalsocietynj.org *Email:* nj-cnal@googlegroups.com

CUMBERLAND COUNTY HISTORICAL SOCIETY
Organized in 1905, the Cumberland County Historical Society maintains and preserves records and artifacts related to Cumberland County, New Jersey and the surrounding area. *Address:* PO Box 16 *City:* Greenwich *State:* NJ *Zip:* 08323 *Phone:* 856-455-4055 *Web:* www.cchistsoc.org

SEA GIRT LIGHTHOUSE CITIZENS COMMITTEE
Address: PO Box 83 *City:* Sea Girt *State:* NJ *Zip:* 08750 *Phone:* 732-974-0514 *Web:* www.seagirtboro.com/sglighthouse.html

SUBMARINE MEMORIAL ASSOCIATION
The Submarine Memorial Association owns and operates the New Jersey Naval Museum and the submarine USS Ling as a floating exhibit. *Address:* PO Box 395 *City:* Hackensack *State:* NJ *Zip:* 07602 *Phone:* 201-342-3268 *Web:* www.njnm.com

TOMS RIVER SEAPORT SOCIETY
The Toms River Seaport Society is a non-profit organization dedicated to the preservation of the rich maritime heritage of the Barnegat Bay in New Jersey. *Address:* PO Box 1111 *City:* Toms River *State:* NJ *Zip:* 08754 *Phone:* 732-349-9209 *Fax:* 732-349-2498 *Web:* www.tomsriverseaport.org *Email:* tomsriverssmm@yahoo.com

TWIN LIGHTS HISTORICAL SOCIETY
The Twin Lights Historical Society was formed in 1956 by a group of citizens concerned by the decaying condition of the once famous Navesink Lightstation. The Society adopted as its purpose the preservation and restoration of the Twin Lights of Navesink. *Address:* Lighthouse Road *City:* Highlands *State:* NJ *Zip:* 07732 *Phone:* 732-872-1814 *Web:* twin-lights.org *Email:* info@twin-lights.org

NEW YORK

BUFFALO LIGHTHOUSE ASSOCIATION
The Buffalo Lighthouse Association is working to restore Buffalo Main Lighthouse and interpret its history for future generations. *Address:* U.S. Coast Guard Base *City:* Buffalo *State:* NY *Zip:* 14203

BUFFALO MARITIME CENTER
Located on the Lake Erie shore, the Buffalo Maritime Center includes the Historic Boat Museum, featuring more than 100 small craft, and the Boat-Building Center, a hands-on learning environment. *Address:* 901 Fuhrmann Blvd. *City:* Buffalo *State:* NY *Zip:* 14203 *Phone:* 716-878-6532 *Web:* www.buffalomaritimecenter.org *Email:* info@buffalomaritimecenter.org

CANAL SOCIETY OF NEW YORK STATE
The Canal Society of New York State brings together canal enthusiasts from across the state, to learn about the history, development and on-going activities associated with the numerous canal systems found throughout the state. *Address:* 2527 Cherry Valley Turnpike *City:* Marcellus *State:* NY *Zip:* 13108 *Phone:* 315-730-4495 *Fax:* 315-673-1864 *Web:* www.canalsnys.org *Email:* mbeilman@twcny.rr.com

CHARLOTTE-GENESEE LIGHTHOUSE HISTORICAL SOCIETY
The Charlotte-Genesee Lighthouse Historical Society is entrusted to maintain the lighthouse property including the keeper's house and tower for Monroe County, which owns the property and buildings on it. *Address:* 70 Lighthouse St. *City:* Rochester *State:* NY *Zip:* 14612 *Phone:* 585-621-6179 *Web:* www.geneseelighthouse.org

CITY ISLAND HISTORICAL SOCIETY AND NAUTICAL MUSEUM
Address: PO Box 82 *City:* City Island *State:* NY *Zip:* 10464 *Phone:* 718-885-0008 *Web:* www.cityislandmuseum.org *Email:* CIHS@cityislandmuseum.org

CHAPTER 11 – ORGANIZATIONS

CLINTON COUNTY HISTORICAL ASSOCIATION
The Clinton County Historical Association is dedicated to preserving Clinton County's heritage. With its museum, historic sites and period houses the association reveals the way the county's inhabitants lived and worked for over three hundred years. *Address:* 98 Ohio Avenue *City:* Plattsburgh *State:* NY *Zip:* 12903 *Phone:* 518-561-0340 *Web:* clintoncountyhistorical.org *Email:* director@clintoncountyhistorical.org

D & H CANAL HISTORICAL SOCIETY
The purpose of the D & H Canal Historical Society is to preserve, protect and perpetuate the unique history of the Delaware and Hudson Canal, particularly in Ulster County. *Address:* PO Box 23 *City:* High Falls *State:* NY *Zip:* 12440 *Phone:* 845-687-9311 *Web:* www.canalmuseum.org *Email:* info@canalmuseum.org

DESTROYER HISTORY FOUNDATION
The purposes of the Destroyer History Foundation are to perpetuate interest in U.S. Navy destroyer history by preserving and making accessible records, accounts, images and other artifacts that might otherwise be lost when U.S. Navy destroyer veterans pass on. *Address:* PO Box 1695 *City:* Bolton Landing *State:* NY *Zip:* 12814 *Web:* www.destroyerhistory.org *Email:* destroyers@domeisland.com

DUNKIRK LIGHTHOUSE & VETERANS PARK MUSEUM
The Dunkirk Lighthouse and Veterans Park Museum cares for the historic Dunkirk Lighthouse. *Address:* 1 Lighthouse Point Drive *City:* Dunkirk *State:* NY *Zip:* 14048 *Phone:* 716-366-5050 *Web:* www.dunkirklighthouse.com *Email:* LST551@juno.com

EAST END LIGHTHOUSES
East End Lighthouses is a not-for-profit organization dedicated to the preservation, restoration, and where applicable, acquisition of the offshore lighthouses of eastern Long Island. East End Lighthouses is an all-volunteer organization with no paid staff. *Address:* P.O. Box 21 *City:* Greenport *State:* NY *Zip:* 11944 *Phone:* 631-477-4121 *Fax:* 631-477-0198 *Web:* www.eastendlighthouses.org *Email:* eastlite@optonline.net

EAST HAMPTON HISTORICAL SOCIETY
Address: 101 Main St. *City:* East Hampton *State:* NY *Zip:* 11937 *Phone:* 631-324-6850 *Web:* easthampton-history.org

FIRE ISLAND LIGHTHOUSE PRESERVATION SOCIETY
The not-for-profit Fire Island Lighthouse Preservation Society actively supports the Fire Island Lighthouse and its grounds. *State:* NY *Phone:* 631-321-7028 *Web:* www.fireislandlighthouse.com *Email:* programs@fireislandlighthouse.com

FRIENDS OF THE EDWARD M. COTTER
Address: 726 Exchange St. *City:* Buffalo *State:* NY *Zip:* 14210 *Phone:* 716-846-4265 *Web:* www.emcotter.com *Email:* neotechnics@adelphia.net

HISTORICAL SOCIETY OF GREATER PORT JEFFERSON
Address: 115 Prospect St. *City:* Port Jefferson *State:* NY *Zip:* 11777 *Phone:* 631-473-2665 *Web:* www.portjeffhistorical.org

HUDSON RIVER SLOOP CLEARWATER
The Hudson River Sloop Clearwater conducts environmental education, advocacy programs and celebrations. The nucleus of the activities is to protect the Hudson River, its tributaries and related water bodies, and to

create public awareness of the estuary. *Address:* 112 Little Market St. *City:* Poughkeepsie *State:* NY *Zip:* 12601 *Phone:* 845-454-7673 *Fax:* 845-454-7953 *Web:* www.clearwater.org *Email:* office@clearwater.org

HUDSON-ATHENS LIGHTHOUSE PRESERVATION SOCIETY
The Hudson-Athens Lighthouse Preservation Society is a not-for-profit organization established to maintain, preserve and restore the historic Hudson-Athens Lighthouse. The society is responsible for the restoration, preservation and operation of the light. *Address:* PO Box 145 *City:* Athens *State:* NY *Zip:* 12015 *Phone:* 518-828-5294 *Fax:* 518-828-5294 *Web:* www.hudsonathenslighthouse.org *Email:* lighthouse@hudsonathenslighthouse.org

HUNTINGTON LIGHTHOUSE PRESERVATION SOCIETY
The Huntington Lighthouse Preservation Society preserves the Huntington Lighthouse as a part of local history. *Address:* PO Box 2454 *City:* Halesite *State:* NY *Zip:* 11743 *Phone:* 631-421-1985 *Fax:* 631-423-0965 *Web:* www.huntingtonlighthouse.org

LILAC PRESERVATION PROJECT
The mission of the Lilac Preservation Project is to preserve, restore and renew the Lilac to its original condition and purpose as a steaming vessel; to serve as an educational aide and service vessel to the community. *Address:* 80 White Street *City:* New York *State:* NY *Zip:* 10013 *Phone:* 845-612-1950 *Web:* lilacpreservationproject.org *Email:* charlie@lilacpreservationproject.org

MONTAUK HISTORICAL SOCIETY
The Montauk Historical Society is a privately funded, not-for-profit organization dedicated to preserving the history of Montauk. The Montauk Historical Society also operates the Second House Museum in Montauk, which is the site of two art and crafts fairs. *Address:* 2000 Montauk Highway *City:* Montauk *State:* NY *Zip:* 11954 *Phone:* 631-668-2544 *Fax:* 631-668-2546 *Web:* www.montauklighthouse.com *Email:* keeper@montauklighthouse.com

NATIONAL MARITIME HISTORICAL SOCIETY
The National Maritime Historical Society's mission is to preserve and perpetuate the maritime history of the United States and to invite all Americans to share in the challenging heritage of seafaring. *Address:* PO Box 68 *City:* Peekskill *State:* NY *Zip:* 10566 *Phone:* 914-737-7878 *Fax:* 914-737-7816 *Web:* www.seahistory.org *Email:* juliachurch@seahistory.org

NEW YORK STATE CANALS
The New York State Canal System is a navigable 524-mile inland waterway that crosses upstate New York. It forms an extensive transportation network providing intermodal linkages within and beyond the state's borders. *Address:* 200 Southern Blvd. *City:* Albany *State:* NY *Zip:* 12201 *Phone:* 518-436-2700 *Web:* www.nyscanals.gov

NEW YORK STATE OFFICE OF PARKS, RECREATION AND HISTORIC PRESERVATION
The New York State Office of Parks, Recreation and Historic Preservation manages the state's parks and historic sites. *Address:* Empire State Plaza *City:* Albany *State:* NY *Zip:* 12238 *Phone:* 518-474-0456 *Web:* www.nysparks.state.ny.us

NORTHPORT HISTORICAL SOCIETY
The purposes of the Northport Historical Society are: To discover, procure, interpret and preserve historical material pertaining to Northport and its environs, including East Northport, Fort Salonga, Asharoken

and Eaton's Neck; To promote interest in history of the area. *Address:* PO Box 545 *City:* Northport *State:* NY *Zip:* 11768 *Phone:* 631-757-9859 *Fax:* 631-757-9398 *Web:* www.northporthistorical.org *Email:* info@northporthistorical.org

OLD FORT NIAGARA ASSOCIATION
Old Fort Niagara is operated by the Old Fort Niagara Association, Inc., in cooperation with the New York State Office of Parks, Recreations and Historic Preservation. *Address:* PO Box 169 *City:* Youngstown *State:* NY *Zip:* 14174 *Phone:* 716-745-7611 *Web:* oldfortniagara.org

S.S. COLUMBIA PROJECT
Address: 232 E. 11th Street *City:* New York *State:* NY *Zip:* 10003 *Phone:* 212-228-3128 *Fax:* 212-471-9987 *Web:* www.sscolumbia.org *Email:* contact@sscolumbia.org

SAUGERTIES LIGHTHOUSE CONSERVANCY
The lighthouse is owned by the Saugerties Lighthouse Consevancy, a not-for-profit organization. The purpose of the Conservancy is to maintain and operate the lighthouse for the benefit of the public as well as to educate visitors of the value and heritage of the area. *Address:* 168 Lighthouse Drive *City:* Saugerties *State:* NY *Zip:* 12477 *Phone:* 845-247-0656 *Web:* www.saugertieslighthouse.com *Email:* info@saugertieslighthouse.com

SAVE ESOPUS LIGHTHOUSE COMMISSION
The Save Esopus Lighthouse Commission is a group of dedicated people who are in the process of restoring the only remaining wooden lighthouse on the Hudson River. *Address:* PO Box 1290 *City:* Port Ewen *State:* NY *Zip:* 12466 *Phone:* 845-331-1478 *Web:* esopuslighthouse.org *Email:* info@esopuslighthouse.org

SODUS BAY HISTORICAL SOCIETY
The mission of the Sodus Bay Historical Society is to collect, preserve and exhibit records, writings, historical items and artifacts; to preserve and disseminate information in the field of history connected with the Sodus Bay area; to serve the educational needs of the area. *Address:* 7606 N. Ontario St. *City:* Sodus Point *State:* NY *Zip:* 14555 *Phone:* 315-483-4936 *Web:* www.soduspointlighthouse.org *Email:* bmccreary@soduspointlighthouse.org

SOUTHAMPTON HISTORICAL MUSEUMS AND RESEARCH CENTER
Address: PO Box 303 *City:* Southampton *State:* NY *Zip:* 11969 *Phone:* 631-283-2494 *Fax:* 631-283-4540 *Web:* www.southamptonhistoricalmuseum.org *Email:* info@southamptonhistoricalmuseum.org

SOUTHOLD HISTORICAL SOCIETY
The Southold Historical Society was founded in 1960 to promote interest in and education about the history of Southold. *Address:* 54325 Main Road *City:* Southold *State:* NY *Zip:* 11971 *Phone:* 631-765-5500 *Fax:* 631-765-8510 *Web:* www.southoldhistoricalsociety.org *Email:* sohissoc@optonline.net

SSS LOTUS
The Lotus is a Sea Scout ship. *Address:* 4045 Cuyler Drive *City:* Williamson *State:* NY *Zip:* 14589 *Phone:* 315-589-6781 *Web:* ithilien.anitrasmith.net/lotus/ *Email:* bellis10@rochester.rr.com

TIBBETTS POINT LIGHTHOUSE SOCIETY
City: Cape Vincent *State:* NY *Phone:* 315-654-2700 *Web:* www.capevincent.org/lighthouse/lighthouse_001.htm

CHAPTER 11 – ORGANIZATIONS

TUG PEGASUS PRESERVATION PROJECT
The mission of the Tug Pegasus Preservation Project is restore and preserve of the 1907-built tug Pegasus, a maritime icon whose very existence tells an important story about the history of the Port of New York/New Jersey. *Address:* 83 Murray Street, No. 4 *City:* New York *State:* NY *Zip:* 10007 *Web:* www.tugpegasus.org *Email:* info@tugpegasus.org

VERONA BEACH LIGHTHOUSE ASSOCIATION
The Verona Beach Lighthouse Association is a not-for-profit organization dedicated to the restoration and preservation of the Verona Beach Lighthouse. *Address:* PO Box 202 *City:* Verona Beach *State:* NY *Zip:* 13162 *Email:* babbitt153@gmail.com

WATERFORD MARITIME HISTORICAL SOCIETY
The Waterford Maritime Historical Society *Address:* PO Box 476 *City:* Waterford *State:* NY *Zip:* 12188 *Web:* www.waterfordmaritime.org *Email:* info@waterfordmaritime.org

NORTH CAROLINA

BALD HEAD ISLAND CONSERVANCY
Address: PO Box 3109 *City:* Bald Head Island *State:* NC *Zip:* 28461 *Phone:* 910-457-0089 *Fax:* 910-457-9824 *Web:* www.bhic.org *Email:* email@bhic.org

CAPE HATTERAS NATIONAL SEASHORE
A haven for recreation and reflection, the islands of Cape Hatteras National Seashore are constantly changing by tide, storm, current, and wind. The plants, wildlife and people who live here adapt continually. *Address:* 1401 National Park Drive *City:* Manteo *State:* NC *Zip:* 27954 *Phone:* 252-473-2111 *Fax:* 252-473-2595 *Web:* www.nps.gov/caha/

CAPE LOOKOUT NATIONAL SEASHORE
Take a boat trip three miles off-shore to the islands of Cape Lookout National Seashore. Here you can enjoy remote beaches, watch wild horses and other wildlife, or visit one of the historic districts. *Address:* 131 Charles St. *City:* Harkers Island *State:* NC *Zip:* 28531 *Phone:* 252-728-2250 *Fax:* 252-728-2160 *Web:* www.nps.gov/calo/

CHICAMACOMICO HISTORICAL ASSOCIATION
The Chicamacomico Historical Association is a private, 501(c)(3) non-profit organization that is working to restore, preserve and interpret the buildings and history of Chicamacomico Life-saving Station, as well as the U.S. Life-Saving Service and its succesors. *Address:* PO Box 5 *City:* Rodanthe *State:* NC *Zip:* 27968 *Phone:* 252-987-1552 *Fax:* 252-987-1559 *Web:* www.chicamacomico.net *Email:* clss@embarqmail.com

EDENTON HISTORICAL COMMISSION
The commission arranges public-private partnerships that drive historic preservation efforts. We undertake projects that would be too complex for the local government and too small for the state government. *Address:* 505 South Broad Street *City:* Edenton *State:* NC *Zip:* 27932 *Phone:* 252-482-7800 *Fax:* 252-482-2065 *Web:* edentonhistoricalcommission.org *Email:* becky.winslow@edentonhistoricalcommission.org

CHAPTER 11 – ORGANIZATIONS

FRIENDS OF OAK ISLAND LIGHTHOUSE
Friends of Oak Island Lighthouse is a not-for-profit organization dedicated to the protection, preservation, maintenance and development of the Oak Island Lighthouse, lighthouse site and related oceanfront property for the public good. *Address:* 1100 Caswell Beach Road *City:* Caswell Beach *State:* NC *Zip:* 28465 *Web:* www.oakislandlighthouse.org *Email:* lighthouse@caswellbeach.org

OLD BALDY FOUNDATION
The Old Baldy Foundation owns and operates the Bald Island Lighthouse and the Smith Island Museum. *Address:* PO Box 3007 *City:* Bald Head Island *State:* NC *Zip:* 28461 *Phone:* 910-457-7481 *Web:* www.oldbaldy.org *Email:* info@oldbaldy.org

OUTER BANKS CONSERVATIONISTS
The mission of Outer Banks Conservationists is to protect natural, cultural, and historic resources through preservation and conservation of a sense of place, and through public education, interpretation, and outreach, and to instill these values in others. *Address:* PO Box 58 *City:* Corolla *State:* NC *Zip:* 27927 *Phone:* 252-453-8152 *Web:* www.currituckbeachlight.com *Email:* info@currituckbeachlight.com

OUTER BANKS LIGHTHOUSE SOCIETY
The Outer Banks Lighthouse Society was organized in 1994 to aid in the preservation of the lighthouses in the area and work with the National Park Service and other agencies and non-profit groups to achieve the safe-keeping of the buildings, artifacts and sites. *Address:* PO Box 1005 *City:* Moorhead City *State:* NC *Zip:* 28557 *Web:* www.outer-banks.com/lighthouse-society/ *Email:* lhsociety2@outer-banks.com

SS UNITED STATES CONSERVANCY
The SS United States Conservancy, an initiative of the SS United States Preservation Society, seeks to preserve and revitalize the SS United States, the largest and fastest ocean liner ever built in her namesake's country. *Address:* PO Box 90482 *City:* Raleigh *State:* NC *Zip:* 27675 *Phone:* 617-320-8459 *Web:* www.ssunitedstatesconservancy.org *Email:* info@ssunitedstatesconservancy.org

WASHINGTON COUNTY WATERWAYS COMMISSION
The mission of the Washington County Waterways Commission is to collect, preserve, interpret and present the maritime history of Washington County and eastern North Carolina through education and tourism. The commission operates the Roanoke River Lighthouse. *Address:* West Water Street *City:* Plymouth *State:* NC *Zip:* 27962 *Phone:* 252-217-2204 *Web:* www.roanokeriverlighthouse.org *Email:* info@roanokeriverlighthouse.org

OHIO

ASHTABULA LIGHTHOUSE RESTORATION AND PRESERVATION SOCIETY
Address: PO Box 221 *City:* North Kingsville *State:* OH *Zip:* 44068 *Web:* www.ashtabulalighthouse.com *Email:* straitliner@windstream.net

ASSOCIATION FOR GREAT LAKES MARITIME HISTORY
The Association for Great Lakes Maritime History is an international organization of museums, historical societies, libraries, archives, and individuals interested in preserving Great Lakes maritime history. *Address:* PO Box 484 *City:* Bowling Green *State:* OH *Zip:* 43402 *Web:* www.aglmh.org *Email:* svh@coslink.net

GREAT LAKES HISTORICAL SOCIETY
The Great Lakes Historical Society is a 501 (c)(3) nonprofit organization dedicated to the preservation of Great Lakes history. *Address:* 480 Main St. *City:* Vermilion *State:* OH *Zip:* 44089 *Phone:* 440-967-3467 *Web:* www.inlandseas.org *Email:* glhs1@inlandseas.org

LAKE ERIE ISLANDS HISTORICAL SOCIETY
Address: PO Box 25 *City:* Put-in-Bay *State:* OH *Zip:* 43456 *Phone:* 419-285-2804 *Web:* www.leihs.org *Email:* themuseum@leihs.org

MARINE HISTORICAL SOCIETY OF DETROIT
The Marine Historical Society of Detroit, a non-profit organization founded in 1944, provides a focal point for individuals and organizations interested in and concerned with the history of the Great Lakes and its maritime heritage. *Address:* Department W *City:* Port Clinton *State:* OH *Zip:* 43452

MIAMI & ERIE CANAL CORRIDOR ASSOCIATION
The Miami & Erie Canal Corridor Association works to preserve and enhance the Miami & Erie Canal Corridor as a viable resource; advancing the cultural, historical, natural, commerical, and recreational opportunities that exist along the corridor. *Address:* 130 S. Washington St. *City:* New Bremen *State:* OH *Zip:* 45869 *Phone:* 419-733-6451 *Web:* www.meccainc.org *Email:* meccadirector@nktelco.net

OHIO HISTORICAL SOCIETY
Address: 1982 Velma Avenue *City:* Columbus *State:* OH *Zip:* 43211 *Phone:* 614-297-2300 *Web:* www.ohiohistory.org *Email:* webmaster@ohiohistory.org

OHIO SHOWBOAT DRAMA
Address: PO Box 572 *City:* Marietta *State:* OH *Zip:* 45750 *Phone:* 614-373-6033

ROSCOE VILLAGE FOUNDATION
Address: 600 N. Whitewoman Street *City:* Coshocton *State:* OH *Zip:* 43812 *Phone:* 740-622-9310 *Web:* www.roscoevillage.com

TOLEDO HARBOR LIGHTHOUSE PRESERVATION SOCIETY
The Toledo Harbor Lighthouse Preservation Society is an all-volunteer non-profit organization that seeks to preserve, restore and provide public outreach and access to the lighthouse. *Address:* 1750 Park Rd. #2 *City:* Oregon *State:* OH *Zip:* 43618 *Phone:* 419-691-3788 *Web:* www.toledoharborlighthouse.org *Email:* sandylakeerie@aol.com

USS RADFORD ASSOCIATION
Address: 132 West Canal St. *City:* Newcomerstown *State:* OH *Zip:* 43832 *Phone:* 740-498-4446 *Web:* www.ussradford446.org *Email:* vanescott@sbcglobal.net

OKLAHOMA

ARKANSAS RIVER HISTORICAL SOCIETY
The Arkansas River Historical Society, established in 1981, seeks to preserve the history and increase public awareness of the Arkansas River and the development of its basin. Through the acquisition, research, interpreta-

tion and display or artifacts, and *Address:* 5350 Cimarron Road *City:* Catoosa *State:* OK *Zip:* 74015 *Phone:* 918-266-7678 *Fax:* 918-266-2291 *Web:* www.tulsaweb.com/port/ *Email:* museum@tulsaport.com

OREGON

COOS COUNTY HISTORICAL SOCIETY
Address: 1220 Sherman Ave. *City:* North Bend *State:* OR *Zip:* 97459 *Phone:* 541-756-6320 *Web:* www.cooshistory.org *Email:* info@cooshistory.org

FRIENDS OF CAPE BLANCO
The Friends of Cape Blanco is a group of volunteers providing educational and interpretive visitor services for this rugged and beautiful area. We care about the rich heritage of Oregon's south coast and seek to preserve historical reminders. *Address:* PO Box 1178 *City:* Port Orford *State:* OR *Zip:* 97465 *Phone:* 541-332-0248 *Web:* www.portorfordoregon.com/Friends/

FRIENDS OF CAPE MEARES LIGHTHOUSE
Address: PO Box 262 *City:* Netarts *State:* OR *Zip:* 97143 *Web:* www.capemeareslighthouse.org *Email:* capemeareslighthouse@earthlink.net

FRIENDS OF SUMPTER VALLEY DREDGE
The mission of the Friends of Sumpter Valley Dredge is the establishment, promotion and improvement of the historical interpretive opportunities in the Pacific Northwest that had an influence on the development and history of the region. *Address:* PO Box 291 *City:* Sumpter *State:* OR *Zip:* 97877 *Phone:* 541-894-2472 *Web:* www.friendsofthedredge.com *Email:* info@friendsofthedredge.com

FRIENDS OF YAQUINA LIGHTHOUSES
Friends of Yaquina Lighthouses' goal is to maintain and preserve Yaquina Bay and Yaquina Head lighthouses. We also aid the educational, interpretive, maintenance and operations programs. *Address:* PO Box 410 *City:* Newport *State:* OR *Zip:* 97365 *Web:* www.yaquinalights.org

LINCOLN COUNTY HISTORICAL SOCIETY
The Lincoln County Historical Society operates the Oregon Coast History Museum. *Address:* 545 SW Ninth Street *City:* Newport *State:* OR *Zip:* 97365 *Phone:* 541-265-7509 *Web:* www.oregoncoast.history.museum

PORT ORFORD HERITAGE SOCIETY
The Point Orford Heritage Society is a community-based non-profit 501(c)(3) organization in the town of Port Orford. *Address:* PO Box 1132 *City:* Port Orford *State:* OR *Zip:* 97465 *Phone:* 541-332-0521 *Web:* www.portorfordlifeboatstation.org *Email:* info@portorfordlifeboatstation.org

SAVE THE BETTY CHARITABLE FOUNDATION
The mission of the Save the Betty Charitable Foundation is to educate the public on preservation and restoration of maritime sailing vessels. *Address:* PO Box 6051 *City:* Brookings *State:* OR *Zip:* 97415 *Phone:* 541-469-3970 *Web:* www.savethebetty.org *Email:* elloboarts@charter.net

SAVE THE PT BOAT, INC.
Save the PT Boat, Inc. was formed by a group of gray-haired ex-PT boaters to take custody of an historic relic, PT-658, a Navy-owned World-War II motor torpedo boat, and restore it to original operating condition. *Address:* PO Box 13422 *City:* Portland *State:* OR *Zip:* 97213 *Web:* www.savetheptboatinc.com *Email:* nissenk@spessart.com

PENNSYLVANIA

AMERICAN CANAL SOCIETY
The American Canal Society is dedicated to historic canal research, preservation, restoration, and parks. The society was formed in 1972 to promote the wise use of America's many historic canal resources through research, preservation, and restoration. *Address:* 117 Main St. *City:* Freemansburg *State:* PA *Zip:* 18017 *Web:* www.americancanals.org

BERKS COUNTY HERITAGE CENTER
Address: 2201 Tulpehocken Road *City:* Wyomissing *State:* PA *Zip:* 19610 *Phone:* 610-374-8839 *Web:* www.co.berks.pa.us/parks/cwp/view.asp?a=1229&q=447562

FLAGSHIP NIAGARA LEAGUE
The Flagship Niagara League is a locally operated, 501(c) 3 non-profit educational associate organization of the Pennsylvania Historical and Museum Commission, chartered to facilitate citizen participation and operation of the U.S. Brig Niagara and its home port.*Address:* 150 East Front Street *City:* Erie *State:* PA *Zip:* 16507 *Phone:* 814-452-2744 *Web:* www.brigniagara.org *Email:* bjohnson@brigniagara.org

GREENVILLE HISTORICAL SOCIETY
Address: PO Box 25 *City:* Greenville *State:* PA *Zip:* 16125 *Phone:* 724-588-3230 *Web:* www.greenvillehistoricalsociety.org *Email:* mariejulian@pathway.net

PENNSYLVANIA CANAL SOCIETY
The aim of the Pennsylvania Canal Society is to preserve the rich heritage of canaling in Pennsylvania. *Address:* National Canal Museum *City:* Easton *State:* PA *Zip:* 18042 *Phone:* 610-559-6613 *Web:* www.pacanalsociety.org *Email:* administrator@pacanalsociety.org

SCHUYKILL CANAL ASSOCIATION
The Schuykill Canal Association's mission is to preserve, maintain and appropriately restore the Schuylkill Canal and its surrounding lands and man-made structures. *Address:* PO Box 966 *City:* Oaks *State:* PA *Zip:* 19456 *Phone:* 610-917-0021 *Web:* www.schuylkillcanal.com *Email:* programs@schuylkillcanal.com

U.S. ARMY CORPS OF ENGINEERS (PHILADELPHIA DISTRICT)
Address: 100 Penn Square East, Suite 600 *City:* Philadelphia *State:* PA *Zip:* 19107 *Phone:* 215-656-6515 *Fax:* 215-656-6820 *Web:* www.nap.usace.army.mil *Email:* edward.c.voigt@usace.army.mil

CHAPTER 11 – ORGANIZATIONS

PUERTO RICO

CONSERVATION TRUST OF PUERTO RICO
Address: PO Box 9023554 *City:* San Juan *State:* PR *Zip:* 00902 *Phone:* 787-722-5834 *Fax:* 787-722-5872 *Web:* www.fideicomiso.org *Email:* fideicomiso@fideicomiso.org

RHODE ISLAND

AMERICAN SAIL TRAINING ASSOCIATION
The American Sail Training Association is a 501(c)(3) nonprofit organization focused on youth education, leadership development and the preservation of the maritime heritage of North America. In addition to organizing the TALL SHIPS CHALLENGE® Series, ASTA manages scholarship programs to make sail training experiences more affordable for young people, grant programs to assist crew of ASTA member vessels with the costs of professional development courses and licensing requirements and publishes SAIL TALL SHIPS! A Directory of Sail Training and Adventure at Sea. *Address:* 240 Thames Street *City:* Newport *State:* RI *Zip:* 02840 *Phone:* 401-846-1775 *Fax:* 401-849-5400 *Web:* www.sailtraining.org *Email:* asta@sailtraining.org

BEAVERTAIL LIGHTHOUSE MUSEUM ASSOCIATION
Address: PO Box 83 *City:* Jamestown *State:* RI *Zip:* 02835 *Phone:* 401-423-3270 *Web:* www.beavertaillight.org *Email:* info@BeavertailLight.org

BLOCK ISLAND SOUTHEAST LIGHTHOUSE FOUNDATION
Address: Box 949 *City:* Block Island *State:* RI *Zip:* 02807 *Phone:* 401-466-5009 *Email:* selight@verizon.net

DUTCH ISLAND LIGHTHOUSE SOCIETY
The Dutch Island Lighthouse Society (DILS) was formed as a chapter of the American Lighthouse Foundation. DILS is working for the complete restoration of this historic 1857 lighthouse, which is on the National Register of Historic Places. *Address:* PO Box 435 *City:* Saunderstown *State:* RI *Zip:* 02874 *Web:* www.lighthouse.cc/DILS/ *Email:* Scott.Chapin@Thermofisher.com

FRIENDS OF NEWPORT HARBOR LIGHT
Friends of Newport Harbor Light is a chapter of the American Lighthouse Foundation. *Address:* PO Box 714 *City:* Newport *State:* RI *Zip:* 02840 *Email:* thinwatersailor@verizon.net

FRIENDS OF PLUM BEACH LIGHTHOUSE
Friends of Plum Beach Lighthouse is a private, non profit 501(c)(3) group whose mission is to protect, preserve and promote the Plum Beach Lighthouse located in the waters of Narragansett Bay in North Kingstown, Rhode Island. *Address:* PO Box 1041 *City:* North Kingstown *State:* RI *Zip:* 02852 *Web:* www.plumbeachlighthouse.org *Email:* dazapper316@hotmail.com

FRIENDS OF POMHAM ROCKS LIGHTHOUSE
Friends of Pomham Rocks Lighthouse is a chapter of the American Lighthouse Foundation. *Address:* PO Box 15121 *City:* Riverside *State:* RI *Zip:* 02915 *Phone:* 401-438-1212 *Email:* pomhamrockslighthouse@yahoo.com

FRIENDS OF SAKONNET POINT LIGHTHOUSE
Address: PO Box 154 *City:* Little Compton *State:* RI *Zip:* 02837

PROVIDENCE MARITIME HERITAGE FOUNDATION
Address: PO Box 1261 *City:* Providence *State:* RI *Zip:* 02901 *Phone:* 401-274-7447 *Web:* www.sloopprovidenceonline.org *Email:* inf_sloopprovidenceri@cox.net

PRUDENCE CONSERVANCY
Prudence Conservancy is a charitable land trust established in 1987 with the specific goal of preserving the unique character and protecting the natural diversity and beauty of Prudence Island. *Address:* PO Box 115 *City:* Prudence Island *State:* RI *Zip:* 02872 *Web:* www.prudenceconservancy.org *Email:* webmaster@prudenceconservancy.org

ROSE ISLAND LIGHTHOUSE FOUNDATION
Address: PO Box 1419 *City:* Newport *State:* RI *Zip:* 02840 *Phone:* 401-847-4242 *Fax:* 401-847-7262 *Web:* www.roseislandlighthouse.org *Email:* keeper@roseisland.org

STEAMSHIP HISTORICAL SOCIETY OF AMERICA
The Steamship Historical Society of America is dedicated to recording, preserving, and distributing information of and about the history of engine powered vessels. *Address:* 1029 Waterman Ave. *City:* East Providence *State:* RI *Zip:* 02914 *Phone:* 401-274-0805 *Fax:* 401-274-0836 *Web:* www.sshsa.org *Email:* info@sshsa.org

USS SARATOGA MUSEUM FOUNDATION
The USS Saratoga Museum Foundation was founded to lead the development of a museum and exhibit for the aircraft carrier USS Saratoga. *Address:* PO Box 845 *City:* North Kingstown *State:* RI *Zip:* 02852 *Phone:* 401-398-1000 *Fax:* 401-885-1290 *Web:* www.saratogamuseum.org *Email:* saratogamuseum@aol.com

WATCH HILL LIGHTHOUSE KEEPERS ASSOCIATION
Address: 14 Lighthouse Road *City:* Watch Hill *State:* RI *Zip:* 02891

SOUTH CAROLINA

CAPE ROMAIN NATIONAL WILDLIFE REFUGE
Address: 5801 Highway 17 N. *City:* Awendaw *State:* SC *Zip:* 29429 *Phone:* 843-928-3264 *Fax:* 843-928-3803 *Web:* www.fws.gov/caperomain *Email:* caperomain@fws.gov

FRIENDS OF CHARLES TOWNE LANDING
Address: PO Box 31731 *City:* Charleston *State:* SC *Zip:* 29417 *Phone:* 843-852-4200 *Web:* www.charlestowne.org *Email:* FriendsofCTL@netscape.net

FRIENDS OF THE HUNLEY
Address: Warren Lasch Conservation Center *City:* North Charleston *State:* SC *Zip:* 29405 *Phone:* 843-743-4865 *Fax:* 843-744-1480 *Web:* www.hunley.org *Email:* info@hunley.org

OLD SANTEE CANAL PARK
Old Santee Canal Park commemorates South Carolina's beautiful natural resources and emphasizes the tremendous historical significance of the Santee Canal. *Address:* 900 Stony Landing Road *City:* Moncks Corner *State:* SC *Zip:* 29461 *Phone:* 843-899-5200 *Fax:* 843-761-7032 *Web:* www.oldsanteecanalpark.org *Email:* parkinfo@santeecooper.com

SAVE THE LIGHT
Save the Light is a grass roots non-profit organization that was formed to save the Morris Island Lighthouse from being lost to the sea. *Address:* PO Box 12490 *City:* Charleston *State:* SC *Zip:* 29422 *Phone:* 843-633-0099 *Web:* www.savethelight.org *Email:* info@savethelight.org

SOUTH CAROLINA MARITIME HERITAGE FOUNDATION
The mission of the South Carolina Maritime Heritage Foundation is to offer effective, unique educational opportunities for the students of South Carolina, focusing on the history, math, science and literature of South Carolina's water resources and encouraging their preservation. *Address:* PO Box 22405 *City:* Charleston *State:* SC *Zip:* 29413 *Phone:* 843-722-1030 *Fax:* 843-722-2243 *Web:* www.scmaritime.org *Email:* info@scmaritime.org

TENNESSEE

MUD ISLAND RIVER PARK
The mission of Mud Island River Park is to preserve and promote the natural and cultural history of the Lower Mississippi River Valley through excellence in education, interpretation and exhibits. *Address:* 125 North Front St. *City:* Memphis *State:* TN *Zip:* 38103 *Phone:* 901-576-7241 *Fax:* 901-576-6666 *Web:* www.mudisland.com

> Without your hard work preservation our maritime past, our nation would be the poorer. Thank you from Fyddeye for your contribution!

PT BOATS, INC.
P.T. Boats, Inc., is a 501(c)(3) historical nonprofit organization established by veterans of World War II PT service to preserve the history of Patrol Torpedo Boats, their shore bases and tenders, ships, and the men who manned them. *Address:* PO Box 38070 *City:* Germantown *State:* TN *Zip:* 38183 *Phone:* 901-755-8440 *Fax:* 901-751-0522 *Web:* www.ptboats.org

TEXAS

ADMIRAL NIMITZ FOUNDATION
The Admiral Nimitz Foundation, a 501 (c)(3) non *Address:* 340 East Main St. *City:* Fredericksburg *State:* TX *Zip:* 78624 *Phone:* 830-997-4379 *Fax:* 830-997-8220 *Web:* www.nimitz-museum.org *Email:* info@nimitz-foundation.org

BATTLESHIP TEXAS FOUNDATION
The Battleship Texas Foundation supports the preservation of the USS Texas in La Porte, Texas. *Address:* 908 Town & Country Blvd., Suite 120 *City:* Houston *State:* TX *Zip:* 77024 *Phone:* 713-827-9620 *Fax:* 713-827-9621 *Web:* www.battleshiptexas.org *Email:* bb35foundation@sbcglobal.net

CAVALLA HISTORICAL FOUNDATION
Address: 2504 Church St. *City:* Galveston *State:* TX *Zip:* 77550 *Phone:* 409-744-7854 *Web:* www.cavalla.org *Email:* macm@airmail.net

CHAPTER 11 – ORGANIZATIONS

GALVESTON HISTORICAL FOUNDATION
Galveston Historical Foundation is one of the largest not-for-profit historic preservation organizations working at the local level in the country. *Address:* 1861 Custom House *City:* Galveston *State:* TX *Zip:* 77550 *Phone:* 409-765-7834 *Fax:* 409-765-7851 *Web:* www.galvestonhistory.org *Email:* foundation@galvestonhistory.org

MATAGORDA ISLAND FOUNDATION
The Foundation, a non-profit organization, is dedicated to the public enjoyment and preservation of history, environment, and wildlife of Matagorda Island and its adjacent waters. The foundation is in the process of raising funds for restoration of the Matagorda Island Lighthouse. *Address:* 5858 Westheimer, Suite 400 *City:* Houston *State:* TX *Zip:* 77057 *Phone:* 713-974-5550 *Web:* www.matagordalighthouse.com

SEAWOLF PARK
Seawolf Park is home to the submarine USS Cavalla and the destroyer escort USS Stewart. *Address:* PO Box 3306 *City:* Galveston *State:* TX *Zip:* 77550 *Phone:* 409-797-5114 *Web:* www.galveston.com/seawolfpark/ *Email:* macm@galvestonparkboard.org

SOUTHEAST TEXAS WAR MEMORIAL AND HERITAGE FOUNDATION
Address: PO Box 3005 *City:* Orange *State:* TX *Zip:* 77631 *Phone:* 409-882-9191 *Fax:* 409-883-7795 *Web:* www.ussorleck.org *Email:* info@ussorleck.org

VERMONT

HARBOR BEACH LIGHTHOUSE PRESERVATION SOCIETY
Address: 330 Brooklake Road *City:* Colchester *State:* VT *Zip:* 05446 *Phone:* 802-863-2486 *Email:* hoerrfam@msn.com

VIRGIN ISLANDS

COLUMBUS FOUNDATION
The Columbus Foundation operates the replicas Nina and Santa Clara. *Address:* Box 305179 *City:* St. Thomas *State:* VI *Zip:* 00803 *Phone:* 284-495-4618 *Fax:* 284-495-9935 *Web:* www.thenina.com *Email:* columfnd@surfbvi.com

WORLD OCEAN SCHOOL
Address: PO Box 25034 *City:* Christiansted *State:* VI *Zip:* 00824 *Phone:* 340-626-7877 *Web:* www.worldoceanschool.org *Email:* wos@worldoceanschool.org

VIRGINIA

ALEXANDRIA SEAPORT FOUNDATION
Through the building and use of wooden boats, the Alexandria Seaport Foundation helps young people turn their lives around and provides families, community groups, and schools with meaningful educational,

social, and recreational experiences. *Address:* PO Box 25036 *City:* Alexandria *State:* VA *Zip:* 22313 *Phone:* 703-549-7078 *Fax:* 703-549-6715 *Web:* www.alexandriaseaport.org *Email:* ASFOffice@alexandriaseaport.org

CHINCOTEAGUE NATURAL HISTORY ASSOCIATION
Address: PO Box 917 *City:* Chincoteague *State:* VA *Zip:* 23336 *Web:* www.assateague.org/plover/ *Email:* cnha@verizon.net

COLONIAL NATIONAL HISTORICAL PARK
Address: PO Box 210 *City:* Yorktown *State:* VA *Zip:* 23690 *Phone:* 757-898-2410 *Fax:* 757-898-6346 *Web:* www.nps.gov/york/

HISTORIC NAVAL SHIPS ASSOCIATION
The mission of the Association is to assist its Fleet Members in the acquisition, restoration, and display of their museums and memorials. *Address:* PO Box 401 *City:* Smithfield *State:* VA *Zip:* 23431 *Phone:* 757-356-9422 *Fax:* 757-356-9433 *Web:* www.hnsa.org

HISTORICAL PLACE PRESERVATION
Historical Place Preservation is a not-for-profit organization working to preserve the Craighill Range Lights of Chesapeake Bay. *Address:* 1069 W. Broad, #217 *City:* Falls Church *State:* VA *Zip:* 22046 *Phone:* 703-967-8118 *Web:* www.craighillrange.org

JAMESTOWN-YORKTOWN FOUNDATION
The Jamestown-Yorktown Foundation, an agency of the Commonweath of Virginia, operates the Jamestown Settlement and the Yorktown Victory Center, two living-history museums that explore America. *Address:* PO Box 1607 *City:* Williamsburg *State:* VA *Zip:* 23187 *Phone:* 757-253-4838 *Fax:* 757-253-5299 *Web:* www.jamestown-yorktown.state.va.us

U.S. COAST GUARD (DISTRICT 5)
The Fifth Coast Guard District ensures the safety and security of the oceans, coastal areas, and marine transportation system within America. *Address:* 431 Crawford St. *City:* Portsmouth *State:* VA *Zip:* 23704 *Phone:* 757-398-6272 *Web:* www.uscg.mil/d5/

VIRGINIA CANALS AND NAVIGATION SOCIETY
The Virginia Canals & Navigation Society helps preserve Virginia's historic waterways and organizes the annual James River Batteau Festival. *Address:* General Delivery *City:* Valentine *State:* VA *Zip:* 23887 *Phone:* 434-577-2427 *Web:* www.vacanals.org

VIRGINIA MARITIME HERITAGE FOUNDATION
Address: 500 E. Main Street, Suite 600 *City:* Norfolk *State:* VA *Zip:* 23510 *Phone:* 757-627-7400 *Fax:* 757-627-8300 *Web:* www.schoonervirginia.org *Email:* jon@schoonervirginia.org

ZUNI MARITIME FOUNDATION
The mission of the Zuni Maritime Foundation is to restore and preserve the USS Zuni/USCGC Tamaroa and to provide an operational maritime educational platform. *Address:* PO Box 28042 *City:* Richmond *State:* VA *Zip:* 23228 *Phone:* 804-273-0247 *Web:* zunitamaroa.org *Email:* snafu.manor@verizon.net

WASHINGTON

ANCIENT BOAT SOCIETY
The Ancient Boat Society is a not-for-profit organization that preserves maritime heritage through several programs, including restoration of the 1928 Lake Union Dreamboat Barbalee, and support for the restoration of the art deco ferry Kalakala. *Address:* 13601-C Highway 99 *City:* Everett *State:* WA *Zip:* 98204 *Phone:* 206-234-1351 *Email:* planetchris777@hotmail.com

ANTIQUE AND CLASSIC BOAT SOCIETY
The Pacific Northwest Chapter of the Antique and Classic Boat Society, founded in 1980, is one of the largest and most active in the ACBS. *Address:* 24115 SR 530 NE *City:* Arlington *State:* WA *Zip:* 98223 *Phone:* 360-385-5038 *Web:* www.acbs-pnw.org *Email:* marty@islandboatshop.com

BAINBRIDGE ISLAND HISTORICAL SOCIETY
The Bainbridge Island Historical Society collects, preserves, and interprets the the colorful history of Bainbridge Island in Puget Sound. *Address:* 215 Ericksen Avenue NE *City:* Bainbridge Island *State:* WA *Zip:* 98110 *Phone:* 206-842-2773 *Fax:* 206-842-0914 *Web:* www.bainbridgehistory.org *Email:* info@bainbridgehistory.org

CLALLAM COUNTY HISTORICAL SOCIETY
Since 1948, the Clallam County Historical Society has been dedicated to keeping the story of the north Olympic Peninsula alive. *Address:* PO Box 1327 *City:* Port Angeles *State:* WA *Zip:* 98362 *Phone:* 360-452-2662 *Web:* www.clallamhistoricalsociety.com *Email:* artifact@olypen.com

COMANCHE 202 FOUNDATION
The Comanche 202 Foundation is a not-for-profit organization formed in 2007 to ensure the restoration, preservation and operation of the historic U.S. Navy tug and Coast Guard vessel Comanche. *Address:* 403 Garfield St. S. *City:* Tacoma *State:* WA *Zip:* 98444 *Phone:* 253-536-9080 *Email:* comanche_202@hotmail.com

COMBATANT CRAFT OF AMERICA
Combatant Craft of America is a non-profit corporation with the mission of recognizing and honoring the history, vessel type (Wheeler patrol boat), and veterans who served aboard these and similar Coast Guard vessels. *Address:* 1400 E. Ludlow Ridge Rd. *City:* Port Ludlow *State:* WA *Zip:* 98365 *Phone:* 360-437-0125 *Web:* www.cg83527.org *Email:* 83527@warboats.org

DRAYTON HARBOR MARITIME
Drayton Harbor Maritime is a not-for-profit, volunteer-run organization that operates Semiahmoo Park Maritime Museum on the Semiahmoo spit near Blaine, Wash. DHM operates and maintains the historic passenger ferry Plover, which is listed on the National Reigster of Historic Places. *Address:* 1218 Fourth St. *City:* Blaine *State:* WA *Zip:* 98230 *Phone:* 360-332-4544 *Web:* www.draytonharbormaritime.org *Email:* rcs3-dhm@comcast.net

FORT WORDEN STATE PARK
Address: 200 Battery Way *City:* Port Townsend *State:* WA *Zip:* 98368 *Phone:* 360-344-4400 *Web:* fortworden.org *Email:* kate.burke@parks.wa.gov

FRIENDS OF POINT NO POINT LIGHTHOUSE
Friends of Point No Point Lighthouse manage tours of the Point No Point Lighthouse on Puget Sound. *Address:* PO Box 223 *City:* Hansville *State:* WA *Zip:* 98340 *Web:* pointnopointlighthouse.com

GRAYS HARBOR HISTORICAL SEAPORT AUTHORITY
The Grays Harbor Historical Seaport Authority is a not-for-profit, 501(c)(3) public development authority based in Aberdeen, Wash. that owns and operates the tall ships Hawaiian Chieftain and Lady Washington, launched March 7, 1989, now the Official Ship of the State of Washington. GHHSA's mission is to provide educational, vocational, recreational and ambassadorial activities and experiences that promote and preserve the maritime history of Grays Harbor, the Pacific Northwest, and our nation while serving the needs of the community. *Address:* 712 Hagara St. *City:* Aberdeen *State:* WA *Zip:* 98520 *Phone:* 360-532-8611 *Toll-free:* 800-200-5239 *Fax:* 360-533-9384 *Web:* www.historicalseaport.org *Email:* ghhsa_admin@historicalseaport.org

ISLAND COUNTY HISTORICAL SOCIETY
The Island County Historical Society began in 1949 as an effort to save a historic home and expanded to include the history of Island County, which is primarily Whidbey Island, the largest island in Puget Sound. *Address:* PO Box 305 *City:* Coupeville *State:* WA *Zip:* 98239 *Phone:* 360-378-3110 *Web:* www.islandhistory.org *Email:* ichscpvl@whidbey.net

JEFFERSON COUNTY HISTORICAL SOCIETY
The Jefferson County Historical Society is a non-profit organization located in the 1890s downtown historic district of Port Townsend, located on the northeastern tip of the Olympic Peninsula. *Address:* 210 Polk St., #11 *City:* Port Townsend *State:* WA *Zip:* 98368 *Phone:* 360-385-1003 *Web:* www.jchsmuseum.org *Email:* jchsmuseum@olympus.net

KALAKALA ALLIANCE FOUNDATION
The Kalakala Alliance Foundation is dedicated to assisting with environmental education programs throughout Puget Sound and regional waterways. The foundation is currently restoring the 1935 art deco ferry Kalakala. *Address:* PO Box 1475 *City:* Tacoma *State:* WA *Zip:* 98402 *Phone:* 253-277-0518 *Web:* www.kalakala.org *Email:* kalakala.info@comcast.net

KEEPERS OF POINT ROBINSON
The Keepers of Point Robinson is a not-for-profit volunteer organization devoted to the preservation of Point Robinson Light Station on Maury Island in Puget Sound. The organization is working closely with the local agencies to develop educational prog *Address:* PO Box 13234 *City:* Burton *State:* WA *Zip:* 98103 *Phone:* 206-567-0033

KEEPERS OF THE NORTH HEAD LIGHTHOUSE
Keepers of the North Head Lighthouse support the North Head Lighthouse at Cape Disappointment State Park near Ilwaco, WA. KNHL is a sub-group of non-profit Friends of the Columbia River Gateway. *Address:* PO Box K *City:* Ilwaco *State:* WA *Zip:* 98624

KEEPERS OF THE PATOS LIGHT
Keepers of the Patos Light maintains the Patos Island Lighthouse in Washington State. *State:* WA *Web:* patoslightkeepers.org *Email:* patoslightkeepers@hotmail.com

MARITIME LEADERSHIP
Address: 9017 North Harborview Drive *City:* Gig Harbor *State:* WA *Zip:* 98332 *Phone:* 253-851-0737 *Web:* maritimeleadership.org *Email:* info@maritimeleadership.org

MUKILTEO HISTORICAL SOCIETY
The Mukilteo Historical Society cares for the historic Mukilteo Lighthouse in the city of Mukilteo, just south of Everett. The lighthouse was built in 1906, and now houses the society *Address:* 304 Lincoln Ave. #101 *City:* Mukilteo *State:* WA *Zip:* 98275 *Phone:* 425-513-9602 *Fax:* 425-353-8662 *Web:* www.mukilteohistorical.org *Email:* kmhirte@msn.com

MV LOTUS HERITAGE FOUNDATION
The MV Lotus Heritage Foundation is dedicated to the restoration, preservation and maintenance of the historic 1909 houseboat cruiser Lotus. The foundation took over the vessel in September 2004. The vessel is maintained by the foundation *Address:* 313 Jackson St. *City:* Port Townsend *State:* WA *Zip:* 98368 *Phone:* 360-643-3302 *Fax:* 360-385-4538 *Web:* www.mvlotus.org *Email:* info@mvlotus.org

NORTHWEST SCHOONER SOCIETY
The Northwest Schooner Society is dedicated to the restoration and preservation of the nation's maritime heritage. *Address:* PO Box 9504 *City:* Seattle *State:* WA *Zip:* 98109 *Phone:* 800-551-6977 *Web:* www.nwschooner.org *Email:* joannpoconnor@yahoo.com

NORTHWEST SEAPORT MARITIME HERITAGE CENTER
Northwest Seaport owns and operates the historic vessels Swiftsure, Twilight, and Arthur Foss. It is also managing conservation of artifacts from the schooner Wawona. *Address:* PO Box 9744 *City:* Seattle *State:* WA *Zip:* 98109 *Phone:* 206-447-9800 *Fax:* 206-447-0598 *Web:* www.nwseaport.org *Email:* info@nwseaport.org

NORTHWEST STEAM SOCIETY
The Northwest Steam Society, a not-for-profit volunteer organization, was formed in 1973 for the mutual benefit of steam enthusiasts in the Pacific Northwest and beyond. *Address:* 3618 Seeley Street *City:* Bellingham *State:* WA *Zip:* 98226 *Phone:* 360-647-5112 *Web:* www.pcez.com/~artemis/NWSShome.htm *Email:* nw-steamboats@comcast.net

OLYMPIA WOODEN BOAT ASSOCIATION
The not-for-profit Olympia Wooden Boat Association helps its members and the public keep the rich history and traditions of wooden boats in the South Puget Sound area alive. *Address:* PO Box 2035 *City:* Olympia *State:* WA *Zip:* 98507 *Phone:* 360-491-1817 *Web:* www.olywoodenboat.org *Email:* association@olywoodenboat.org

PACIFIC COUNTY HISTORICAL SOCIETY
The Pacific County Historical Society is a not-for-profit organization devoted to preserving and presenting the history of Pacific County, located in coastal southwestern Washington State. *Address:* PO Box P *City:* South Bend *State:* WA *Zip:* 98586 *Phone:* 360-875-5224 *Web:* www.pacificcohistory.org *Email:* museum@willapabay.org

PACIFIC NORTHWEST SCHOONER ASSOCIATION
Composed of the largest fleet of associated sailing schooners in the United States, the Pacific Northwest Schooner Association include a wide variety of ship sizes, designs and histories. *City:* Tacoma *State:* WA *Web:* www.nwwindjammers.com

CHAPTER 11 – ORGANIZATIONS

POINTS NORTHEAST HISTORICAL SOCIETY
Points Northeast Historical Society studies and preserves the history of Browns Point, located across Commencement Bay from downtown Tacoma. *Address:* 6622 Eastside Dr. NE, PMB 135 *City:* Browns Point *State:* WA *Zip:* 98422 *Phone:* 253-927-2536 *Web:* www.pointsnortheast.org *Email:* lighthouse@southsound.com

PUGET SOUND FIREBOAT FOUNDATION
The Puget Sound Fireboat Foundation is a volunteer-based not-for-profit organization that owns and operates the Duwamish, an historic fireboat built in 1909. *Address:* 13407 Greenwood Ave N. Suite 202 *City:* Seattle *State:* WA *Zip:* 98133 *Phone:* 206-579-6207 *Web:* www.fireboatduwamish.org *Email:* davidhmorse@comcast.net

PUGET SOUND MARITIME HISTORICAL SOCIETY
The Puget Sound Maritime Historical Society was founded in 1948 to help residents and visitors learn about the maritime heritage of the Pacific Northwest. *Address:* PO Box 9731 *City:* Seattle *State:* WA *Zip:* 98109 *Phone:* 206-624-3028 *Web:* www.pugetmaritime.org *Email:* ewlindgren@hotmail.com

RESOLUTE SAILING FOUNDATION
Address: PO Box 88834 *City:* Steilacoom *State:* WA *Zip:* 98388 *Phone:* 253-588-3066 *Web:* www.resolutesailing.org *Email:* resolute@telisphere.com

SAND MAN FOUNDATION
The Sand Man Foundation is a not-for-profit, volunteer-run organization dedicated to the restoration and maintenance of the historic 1910 tug Sand Man, which is listed on the National Register of Historic Places. *Address:* 4312 Cleveland Ave. *City:* Tumwater *State:* WA *Zip:* 98501 *Phone:* 360-786-9474 *Web:* www.tugsandman.org *Email:* pderanleau@msn.com

SCHOONER MARTHA FOUNDATION
The not-for-profit Schooner Martha Foundation owns and operates the 1907 schooner yacht Martha. The Foundation *Address:* PO Box 1811 *City:* Port Townsend *State:* WA *Zip:* 98368 *Phone:* 206-310-8573 *Web:* www.schoonermartha.org *Email:* rob@nwmaritime.org

SOUTH SOUND MARITIME HERITAGE ASSOCIATION
The South Sound Maritime Heritage Association is a not-profit volunteer organization that welcomes members from all walks of life to share our mission of celebrating and preserving maritime history in the South Puget Sound region. *Address:* PO Box 2351 *City:* Olympia *State:* WA *Zip:* 98507 *Phone:* 360-556-0498 *Web:* www.harbordays.com *Email:* harbordays@comcast.net

STEAMER VIRGINIA V FOUNDATION
The mission of the Steamer Virginia V Foundation is to promote the Puget Sound's maritime heritage through the restoration, preservation, operation, and interpretation of the National Historic Landmark vessel Virginia V. *Address:* PO Box 9566 *City:* Seattle *State:* WA *Zip:* 98109 *Phone:* 206-624-9119 *Fax:* 206-381-3715 *Web:* www.virginiav.org *Email:* info@virginiav.org

TACOMA WOODEN BOAT SOCIETY
City: Tacoma *State:* WA *Email:* west1943@earthlink.net

UNITED STATES LIGHTHOUSE SOCIETY
The United States Lighthouse Society is a not-for-profit historical and educational organization incorporated to educate, inform, and entertain those who are interested in lighthouses, past and present. *Address:* 9005 Point No Point Rd. NE *City:* Hansville *State:* WA *Zip:* 98340 *Phone:* 415-362-7255 *Web:* uslhs.org *Email:* info@uslhs.org

CHAPTER 11 – ORGANIZATIONS

U.S. ARMY CORPS OF ENGINEERS (SEATTLE DISTRICT)
The Seattle District of the U.S. Army Corp of Engineers manages its historic properties through its office of Expertise Preservation of Historic Buildings and Structures (CX). *Address:* 3105 Northwest 54th St. *City:* Seattle *State:* WA *Zip:* 98107 *Phone:* 206-783-7059 *Web:* www.nws.usace.army.mil/PublicMenu/Menu.cfm?sitename=lwsc&pagename=mainpage

U.S. COAST GUARD (DISTRICT 13)
District 13 of the U.S. Coast Guard covers the states of Washington, Oregon, Idaho and Montana, and the Pier 36 facility in Seattle hosts Coast Guard Museum Northwest. Click the link below to learn more about the museum. *Address:* 1519 Alaskan Way S. *City:* Seattle *State:* WA *Zip:* 98134 *Phone:* 206-903-0245 *Web:* www.uscg.mil/d13/default.htm

U.S. COAST GUARD AUXILIARY
The Seattle chapter of the U.S. Coast Guard Auxiliary conducts tours of the Alki Point Lighthouse and helps maintain the structure and the grounds. *Address:* 4725 Shilshole Ave NW #3 *City:* Seattle *State:* WA *Zip:* 98107 *Phone:* 425-653-2704 *Web:* www.uscgaux.org/~130/ *Email:* pdfco@aol.com

VIETNAM WOODEN BOAT FOUNDATION
The Vietnam Wooden Boat Foundation is a not-for-profit organization with a near-term goal of producing a documentary film and pictorial/written record of traditional Vietnamese boat building. *Address:* 425 Washington St. *City:* Port Townsend *State:* WA *Zip:* 98368 *Web:* www.vietnamboats.org

WESTPORT SOUTH BEACH HISTORICAL SOCIETY
The mission of the Westport South Beach Historical Society is to interpret and preserve the history of the South Beach area of Grays Harbor County in Washington State, with an emphasis on the impact of local natural resources on the regional growth and development. *Address:* PO Box 1074 *City:* Westport *State:* WA *Zip:* 98595 *Phone:* 360-268-0078 *Fax:* 360-268-0078 *Web:* westportwa.com/museum/ *Email:* westport.maritime@comcast.net

WHATCOM MARITIME ASSOCIATION
The Whatcom Maritime Association is a not-for-profit organization dedicated to cataloging, recording, preserving and restoring the past and present elements of Whatcom County's maritime heritage. *Address:* 121 Prospect St. *City:* Bellingham *State:* WA *Zip:* 98225 *Phone:* 800-426-8860 *Email:* s.ayers@lfsinc.com

WOODEN BOAT FOUNDATION
The not-for-profit Wooden Boat Foundation recently merged with the Northwest Maritime Center. *Address:* 380 Jefferson Street *City:* Port Townsend *State:* WA *Zip:* 98368 *Phone:* 360-385-3628 *Web:* www.woodenboat.org *Email:* info@woodenboat.org

YANKEE CLIPPER FOUNDATION
Address: 2226 Eastlake Ave. E., #97 *City:* Seattle *State:* WA *Zip:* 98102 *Phone:* 206-947-6199 *Web:* www.tallshiptraining.org *Email:* info@tallshiptraining.org

YOUTH MARINE FOUNDATION
The Youth Marine Foundation is a not-for-proft organization sponsoring the Tacoma chapter of the Sea Scouts and the annual Commencement Bay Maritime Fest. *Address:* 5308 Norpoint Way NE *City:* Tacoma *State:* WA *Zip:* 98422 *Phone:* 253-952-6282 *Web:* www.maritimefest.org *Email:* maritime_fest@yahoo.com

YOUTH MARITIME TRAINING ASSOCIATION
The Youth Maritime Training Association is a not-for-profit organization that serves students in Washington State public schools. *Address:* PO Box 70425 *City:* Seattle *State:* WA *Zip:* 98127 *Phone:* 206-300-5559 *Web:* www.ymta.net *Email:* garystauffer47@msn.com

WISCONSIN

APOSTLE ISLANDS NATIONAL LAKESHORE
Along windswept beaches and cliffs, visitors experience where water meets land and sky, culture meets culture, and past meets present. The 21 islands and 12 miles of mainland host a unique blend of cultural and natural resources. *Address:* 415 Washington Ave. *City:* Bayfield *State:* WI *Zip:* 54814 *Phone:* 715-779-3397 *Web:* www.nps.gov/apis/

FRIENDS OF ROCK ISLAND STATE PARK
State: WI *Web:* www.fori.us

FRIENDS OF WIND POINT LIGHTHOUSE
Address: 5110 Wind Point Road *City:* Racine *State:* WI *Zip:* 53402 *Phone:* 262-639-2026

PORT WASHINGTON HISTORICAL SOCIETY
Address: PO Box 491 *City:* Port Washington *State:* WI *Zip:* 53074 *Phone:* 262-268-9150 *Web:* www.portwashingtonhistoricalsociety.org *Email:* portwashhistsoc@att.net

PORTAGE CANAL SOCIETY
City: Portage *State:* WI *Zip:* 53901 *Web:* www.portagecanalsociety.com *Email:* dollar1@charter.net

NATIONAL

AMERICAN LIGHTHOUSE COORDINATING COMMITTEE
The American Lighthouse Coordinating Committee (ALCC) is a non-profit corporation composed of a consortium of organizations and individuals dedicated to the preservation, restoration, and interpretation of American lighthouses. *Web:* amlhcc.org *Email:* info@amlhcc.org

COUNCIL OF AMERICAN MARITIME MUSEUMS
The Council of American Maritime Museums (CAMM) is an organization dedicated to preserving North America's maritime history. Our 80+ Members include museums, museum professionals and scholars from United States, Mexico, Bermuda, Australia and Canada. *Web:* www.councilofamericanmaritimemuseums.org *Email:* president@CouncilofAmericanMaritimeMuseums.org

CHAPTER 12 – OTHER
ORGANIZATIONS, ATTRACTIONS, AND OTHER UNCATEGORIZED LISTINGS

Whitefish Point Lighthouse (Paradise, Mich.)

ANACORTES COMMUNITY MARITIME CENTER
The Anacortes Community Maritime Center is a not-for-profit organizations that offers classes and activities to help Anacortes-area residents and visitors learn more North Puget Sound's maritime heritage and environmental stewardship. *Address:* 1905 - 10th Street *City:* Anacortes *State:* WA *Zip:* 98221 *Phone:* 360-299-9075 *Web:* www.anacortescommunitymaritimecenter.org *Email:* anacomaritimectr@msn.com *Latitude:* 48.5141 *Latitude:* -122.6270

CARVING CULTURAL CONNECTIONS
Carving Cultural Connections is operated by Haida canoe carver Robert Peele, also called Saaduuts. *Address:* PO Box 77381 *City:* Seattle *State:* WA *Zip:* 98177 *Phone:* 206-524-3546 *Fax:* 206-524-3546 *Email:* melibeekoch@hotmail.com *Latitude:* 47.7429 *Latitude:* -122.3670

SEA SCOUTS
The Sea Scout program is an international component of the Boy Scouts of America Venturing program for young men and women aged 14 to 21. Sea Scouting is organized to promote better citizenship and to improve members' boating skills and knowledge through hands-on learning. *Address:* 3120 Rainier Ave. S.

City: Seattle *State:* WA *Zip:* 98144 *Phone:* 206-725-5200 *Web:* www.seattleseascouts.org *Latitude:* 47.5750 *Latitude:* -122.2950

SOUND EXPERIENCE
Sound Experience is a not-for-profit environmental education organization that sails the historic schooner Adventuress on Puget Sound and uses the ship as a metaphor for the planet; a closed system that requires understanding and care and sails best when all work together. *Address:* PO Box 1390 *City:* Port Townsend *State:* WA *Zip:* 98368 *Phone:* 360-379-0438 *Web:* www.soundexp.org *Email:* mail@soundexp.org *Latitude:* 48.0665 *Latitude:* -122.8170

TACOMA TALL SHIPS ORGANIZATION
Tall Ships Tacoma is a not-for-profit organization that produces tall ship events in the Tacoma area. *Address:* 535 Dock Street, Suite 210 *City:* Tacoma *State:* WA *Zip:* 98402 *Phone:* 253-272-5650 *Web:* www.tallshipstacoma.com *Email:* info@tallshipstacoma.com *Latitude:* 47.2605 *Latitude:* -122.4390

THE HARRY BRIDGES PROJECT
The Harry Bridges Project was created to promote the legacy of labor leader Harry Bridges and to aid in the public's understanding of his importance to history. A live performance of "From Wharf Rats to Lords of the Docks" is an entertaining way to enjoy a fascinating slice of American history and be inspired. Harry's story does just that – it inspires people to discover their own history and stand up for what's right in today's world. *Address:* PO Box 662018 *City:* Los Angeles *State:* CA *Zip:* 90066 *Web:* theharrybridgesproject.org *Email:* ianruskin@theharrybridgesproject.org *Hours:* Contact owner *Admission:* Contact owner *Operated by:* The Harry Bridges Project *Latitude:* 34.0050 *Latitude:* -118.4340

CITY INDEX

The following index contains all cities in the *Fyddeye Guide to America's Maritime History*. Some cities appear more than once on a directory page. However, their pages are listed only once in the index.

Aberdeen, MD, 174
Aberdeen, WA, 19, 22, 144, 307, 356
Addison, ME, 168
Agate Beach, OR, 261
Ahmeek, MI, 208
Airdele, MD, 174
Alameda, CA, 43, 73, 317, 320
Albany, NY, 46, 60, 78, 119, 303, 343
Alburg, VT, 203
Alea, HI, 325
Alexandria Bay, NY, 228
Alexandria, MN, 114
Alexandria, NY, 228
Alexandria, VA, 131, 354
Algoma, WI, 232
Alpena, MI, 112, 207, 216, 223, 294, 302, 338
Amagansett, NY, 119
Amesbury, MA, 109
Amsterdam, NY, 303
Anacortes, WA, 54, 262, 361
Angwin, CA, 150, 282
Ann Arbor, MI, 290
Anna Maria, FL, 240
Annapolis, MD, 32, 37, 104, 106, 29, 330
Annisquam, MA, 175
Ansonia, CT, 320
Apalachicola, FL, 97, 296
Aquadilla, PR, 197
Arecibo, PR, 195
Arlington, WA, 355
Arnolds Park, IA, 101
Arrowsic, ME, 164, 166, 170, 329

Asharoken, NY, 188
Ashland, WI, 232, 233
Ashtabula, OH, 124, 229
Astoria, OR, 126, 266, 290, 291
Athens, GA, 99
Athens, NY, 189, 343
Atlantic City, NJ, 156, 184
Avalon, CA, 138
Awendaw, SC, 351
Babylon, NY, 272
Baileys Harbor, WI, 232, 233
Bainbridge Island, WA, 144, 355
Bald Head Island, NC, 193, 194, 345, 346
Bald Island, NC, 143
Baltimore, MD, 22, 25, 28, 31, 38, 68, 76, 80, 85, 106, 156, 174, 266, 330, 331
Bandon, OR, 260, 276
Bar Harbor, ME, 165, 280, 327
Baraga, MI, 220, 336
Barcelona, NY, 225
Barnegat Light, NJ, 184, 340
Barrington, RI, 199
Bass Harbor, ME, 162
Bath, ME, 31, 103, 328
Baton Rouge, LA, 77, 327
Bavon, VA, 204
Bay City, MI, 10, 70, 113, 141, 151, 220, 335, 338
Bayfield, WI, 54, 79, 234, 236, 237, 308, 360
Bayonne, NJ, 186
Beach Haven, NJ, 116
Beaufort, NC, 123
Beaufort, SC, 293

CITY INDEX

Beaver Island, MI, 111, 207, 214, 335
Belevedere, CA, 298
Bellevue, WA, 306
Bellingham, WA, 70, 71, 133, 146, 357
Berlin, MD, 269, 330
Berwick, LA, 242, 243
Beverly, MA, 179, 286
Biddeford, ME, 171
Biddle's Corner, DE, 159
Big Bay, MI, 208, 209
Biloxi, MS, 17, 25, 114, 243
Bivalve, NJ, 116
Blaine, WA, 136, 355
Block Island, RI, 198, 350
Blue Mountain Lake, NY, 62, 142
Boca Grande, FL, 240, 241
Bois Blanc, MI, 209
Bolton Landing, NY, 342
Boothbay Harbor, ME, 18, 32, 36, 139, 163, 164, 293, 327, 329
Boothbay, ME, 169
Boqueron, PR, 197
Boston, MA, 11, 22, 43, 68, 77, 107, 110, 147, 156, 176, 177, 178, 179, 285, 287, 300, 301, 331, 332, 334
Bowers Beach, DE, 158
Bowling Green, OH, 151, 346
Bradford Island, CA, 70
Bremerton, WA, 48, 73, 134, 135, 288, 289, 306, 313
Brewerton, NY, 187
Bridgeport, CT, 154, 157
Brimley, MI, 209, 218
Brinnon, WA, 25
Bristol, RI, 128, 198
Bronx, NY, 121
Brookings, OR, 348
Brookline, MA, 333
Brooklyn, NY, 51, 61, 122
Browns Point, Wa, 358
Brownville, NE, 47, 115, 339
Brunswick, GA, 27, 324
Brunswick, ME, 329
Brunswick, MO, 69
Buffalo, NY, 7, 70, 72, 76, 77, 83, 117, 118, 225, 226, 341, 342
Burlingame, CA, 49
Burlington, VT, 5, 202, 203, 294
Burton, WA, 356
Buxton, NC, 194
Buzzards Bay, MA, 177, 280
Cabo Rojo, PR, 196
Cairo, IL, 100
Calais, ME, 329
Calumet Harbor, IN, 206

Cambridge, MA, 108, 148
Cambridge, MD, 21, 26, 105, 106, 330
Camden, ME, 9, 18, 22, 24, 25, 27, 33, 164
Camden, NJ, 74, 115, 265
Cameron Parish, LA, 327
Canal Fulton, OH, 45, 287
Canastoga, NY, 118
Canton, NJ, 34
Cape Canaveral, FL, 159, 323
Cape Charles, VA, 8
Cape Cod, MA, 181
Cape Elizabeth, ME, 163, 169
Cape May, NJ, 9, 156, 184
Cape Porpoise, ME, 165, 328
Cape St. Clair, MD, 174
Cape Vincent, NY, 225, 226, 228, 344
Carmel, CA, 92, 253, 257, 319
Carrollton, AL, 51
Cascade Locks, OR, 55, 126
Castine, ME, 11, 164, 281
Caswell Beach, NC, 194, 346
Catawba, SC, 305
Catoosa, OK, 39, 125, 304, 348
Cedar Key, FL, 240
Cedar River, MI, 209
Cedarville, MI, 112, 336
Celina, OH, 229
Charity Island, MI, 209
Charleston, OR, 276
Charleston, SC, 8, 32, 45, 144, 201, 202, 351, 352
Charlevoix, MI, 210, 335
Chatham, MA, 177, 182
Cheboygan, MI, 210, 212
Chelsea, MA, 301
Chesapeake City, MD, 105, 172
Chestertown, MD, 33, 331
Chicago, IL, 29, 36, 85, 148, 205, 206, 290, 326
China Lake, CA, 91
Chincoteague, VA, 131, 254
Chittenango, NY, 118
Christiansted, VI, 30, 353
Christmas, MI, 210
Cincinnati, OH, 51, 149
City Island, NY, 118, 341
Clarksville, IN, 299
Clayton, ID, 325
Clayton, NY, 51, 117
Cleveland, OH, 64, 83, 229
Clinton, IA, 55
Cocodrie, LA, 242
Coconut Grove, FL, 19, 36, 298
Cohasset, MA, 107, 280, 300, 332
Colchester, VT, 353
Cold Spring Harbor, NY, 119, 188

College Station, TX, 280
Colton's Point, MD, 88, 140
Columbus, GA, 67, 68, 99
Columbus, OH, 347
Concepcion, CA, 253, 256
Coney Island, NY, 188
Conneaut, OH, 229
Coos Bay, OR, 260
Copper Harbor, MI, 208, 210
Cordova, AK, 249, 250, 316
Corolla, NC, 194, 346
Corpus Christi, TX, 130
Coshocton, NY, 304
Coshocton, OH, 347
Coupeville, WA, 145, 262, 292, 356
Cove Point, MD, 172
Covington, KY, 43, 54
Creola, AL, 32
Crescent City, CA, 251, 252, 317, 320
Crisfield, MD, 140, 330
Croton-on-Hudson, NY, 18, 121
Crown Point, NY, 311
Crownsville, MD, 329
Crystal River, FL, 291
Cuddebackville, NY, 142
Culebra, PR, 196
Culver, IN, 29
Cumberland Island, GA, 161
Cuttyhunk, MA, 177, 332
Dana Point, CA, 28, 32, 294
Darien, GA, 291
Davison Beach, NY, 225
De Tour Village, MI, 111
Deal Island, MD, 13, 16, 20, 23, 30, 31
Deland, FL, 72
Delaware City, DE, 96
Delphi, IN, 299, 326
Delta, MI, 216
Depoe Bay, OR, 63
DeTour, MI, 220
Detroit Harbor, WI, 233
Detroit, MI, 59, 60, 111, 211, 223, 311, 336
Dighton, MA, 285
Dolomite, MI, 216
Douglas, AK, 250, 316
Dover, NH, 340
Drummond Island, MI, 335
Dubuque, IA, 42, 43, 46, 47, 55, 101, 102, 147, 310
Duluth, MN, 44, 45, 50, 54, 64, 114, 223, 224, 338, 339
Dunkirk, NY, 188, 225, 342
Duxbury, MA, 178, 181, 270, 281, 285, 287, 332
Eagle Harbor, MI, 208, 211, 336
Eagle Island, ME, 164

Eagle River, MI, 211
East Chicago, IN, 206
East Hampton, NY, 342
East Machias, ME, 167, 328
East Mayport, FL, 161
East Northport, NY, 24
East Providence, RI, 351
East Tawas, MI, 209, 222
Eastham, MA, 141, 180, 300, 333
Easton, PA, 42, 127, 304
Eastport, ME, 18, 54, 103, 328
Edenton, NC, 195, 345
Edgartown, MA, 156, 286, 310, 33
Edgemoor, DE, 158, 159
Edgewater, NJ, 5
Elizabeth City, NC, 143
Empire, MI, 47, 311, 338
Erie, PA, 27, 232, 127, 349
Escanaba, MI, 208, 220, 335
Esopus, NY, 188
Essex, CT, 95, 294
Essex, MA, 15, 108, 332
Essex, NY, 192
Eureka, CA, 61, 78, 252, 248
Evanston, IL, 206, 326
Evansville, IN, 79, 326
Everett, WA, 15, 71, 355
Excelsior, MN, 51
Fairbank, MD, 174
Fairbanks, AK, 49, 56, 283, 316
Fairfield, CT, 157
Fairhaven, MA, 17
Fairport Harbor, OH, 229
Fajardo, PR, 196
Fall River, MA, 70, 74, 76, 77, 78, 84, 107, 109, 110, 150, 176
Falls Church, VA, 354
Fenton, MI, 337
Fenwick Island, DE, 96, 158
Fenwick, CT, 157
Fernandina Beach, FL, 159
Fishers Island, NY, 190, 191
Fishers Landing, NY, 227
Florence, OR, 261
Fond du Lac, WI, 315
Forest Beach, SC, 201
Fort Eustis, VA, 60, 69
Fort Hancock, NJ, 273
Fort Howard, MD, 172
Fort Hunger, NY, 304
Fort Pierce, FL, 98
Fort Walton Beach, FL, 323
Fort Walton, FL, 18
Fort Washington, MD, 173

CITY INDEX

Fort Worth, TX, 70
Fortescue, NJ, 185
Frankfort, MI, 212, 218
Franklin, FL, 240
Frederica, DE, 96
Fredericksburg, TX, 81, 83, 129, 352
Freeland, WA, 262
Freemansburg, PA, 349
Frenchboro, ME, 165
Friday Harbor, WA, 31, 59, 135, 146, 262, 263, 265
Galloo Island, NY, 226
Galveston, TX, 14, 52, 53, 78, 82, 130, 244, 312, 352, 353
Garibaldi, OR, 126
Gary, IN, 206
Georgetown, DE, 96
Georgetown, ME, 168
Georgetown, SC, 201
Germantown, TN, 352
Gig Harbor, WA, 9, 53, 134, 263, 308, 357
Gills Rock, WI, 41, 136
Glen Arbor, MI, 275
Glen Haven, MI, 113
Gloucester, MA, 7, 34, 108, 178, 182, 286, 300, 301, 311
Gorton, CT, 66
Grafton, WI, 234
Grand Bay, AL, 137
Grand Haven, MI, 212
Grand Marais, MI, 53, 113, 209, 212, 274, 335
Grand Marais, MN, 224
Grant, MI, 213
Great Lakes, IL, 326
Green Bay, WI, 234
Greenport, NY, 119, 291, 294, 342
Greenville, ME, 60, 104
Greenville, PA, 127, 249
Greenwich, NJ, 116, 340
Grosse Ile, MI, 213, 336
Groton, CT, 67, 83, 85, 95, 150, 320, 321
Guanica, PR, 196
Guayama, PR, 197
Guilford, CT, 321
Gulf Breeze, FL, 276, 323
Gulfport, MS, 339
Gulliver, MI, 208, 271
Hackensack, NJ, 71, 84, 85, 117, 341
Hagerstown, MD, 330
Haines, AK, 250
Halesite, NY, 343
Hampton, NH, 295
Hampton, VA, 204
Hancock, MI, 215, 336
Hansville, MI, 335

Hansville, WA, 264, 356, 358
Harbor Beach, MI, 213
Harbor Springs, MI, 215, 336
Harbor, OR, 47
Harkers Island, NC, 194, 345
Harrisville, MI, 209, 22
Harsens Island, MI, 213
Hatteras, NC, 123
Haverstraw, NY, 5
Havre de Grace, MD, 24, 106, 172, 330
Heislerville, NJ, 185
Henderson, NY, 192
Hendricks Harbor, ME, 166
High Falls, NY, 119, 342
Highland Beach, MD, 175
Highlands, NJ, 156, 186, 341
Hilo, HI, 259
Hilton Head, SC, 201, 202
Homewood, CA, 91
Honolulu, HI, 16, 16, 74, 82, 84, 259, 310, 325
Hoopersville, MD, 173
Houghton, MI, 214
Houston, TX, 129, 352, 353
Hull, MA, 108, 272
Hunting Island, SC, 202
Huntington Harbor, NY, 189
Huron, OH, 230
Hyannis, MA, 107, 179, 291
Idlewild, WI, 237
Ilwaco, WA, 134, 262, 264, 306, 356
Indianola, WA, 307
Irvington, VA, 61
Isle au Haut, ME, 166
Isle La Motte, VT, 203
Isle Royale, MI, 208, 219
Islesboro, ME, 11, 105, 165
Ithaca, NY, 187
Jacksonville, FL, 97
Jacksonville, NC, 79
Jacobsville, MI, 214
Jamestown, MA, 156
Jamestown, RI, 198, 199, 350
Jeffersonville, IN, 100
Jensen Beach, FL, 97
Jersey City, NJ, 22, 266
Jerusalem, OH, 231
Joliet, IL, 299, 326
Jonesport, ME, 155, 167
Juneau, AK, 250, 291, 316
Jupiter, FL, 160
Kalaupapa, HI, 260
Kaneohe, HI, 23, 325
Kansas City, MO, 87
Keansburg, NJ, 186

CITY INDEX

Kemah, TX, 82
Kennebunkport, ME, 103, 140
Kenosha, WI, 137, 234
Kensington, MD, 281
Kent Corner, RI, 200
Kent, WA, 134
Keokuk, IA, 40, 101
Ketchikan, AK, 250, 251, 268
Kewaunee, WI, 43, 137, 235
Key Biscayne, FL, 160
Key Largo, FL, 98, 160, 240, 323
Key West, FL, 36, 75, 76, 98, 138, 160, 240, 323, 324
Keyport, NJ, 116
Kilauea, HI, 259
Kings Point, NY, 117, 192, 282
Kingston, NY, 38, 39, 40, 42, 43, 45, 120, 122, 191, 291, 303
Kinsale, VA, 35, 36
Kinston, NC, 123
Kirkland, WA, 6, 313
Kirkville, NY, 303
Kittery Point, ME, 273, 329
Kittery, ME, 171, 238
Kitty Hawk, NC, 270, 271
Kodiak, AK, 89
La Claire, IA, 42
La Porte, TX, 69
La Salle, IL, 325
Lac La Belle, MI, 216
Lahaina, HI, 99, 259, 284, 325
Lake Linden, MI, 214
Lamb, IN, 38, 43
Langley, WA, 33
Lansing, MI, 141, 337
Leland, MI, 111, 274, 275
Leonardo, NJ, 184
Leonardstown, MD, 331
Lewes, DE, 96, 156, 158, 267, 296, 321, 322
Lexington Park, MD, 331
Lexington, MD, 106
Lihue, HI, 260
Linwood, NJ, 116
Little Compton, RI, 200, 350
Little Cranberry Island, ME, 140
Little Deer Isle, ME, 169
Little Torch Key, FL, 14
Lockport, IL, 100, 298, 326
Lockport, NY, 120
Long Beach, CA, 9, 34, 67, 254
Long Island, NY, 156, 266
Lorain, OH, 230
Los Angeles, CA, 362
Louisville, KY, 55, 55, 56, 139, 275
Lubec, ME, 104, 155, 167, 170

Ludington, MI, 5, 208, 209, 215, 337
Lycoming, NY, 56
Lynchburg, VA, 292
Lyndonville, NY, 228
Macaraw, MI, 214
Machiasport, ME, 166, 270
Mackinac Island, MI, 220
Mackinaw City, MI, 75, 112, 209, 216, 217, 223, 292, 337, 338
Madisonville, LA, 103, 243, 327
Manchester, ME, 166
Mandeville, LA, 293
Manistee, MI, 5, 46, 141, 215
Manistique, MI, 215
Manitowoc, WI, 83, 137, 235
Manteo, NC, 15, 123, 195, 345
Marblehead, MA, 179
Marblehead, OH, 230
Marcellus, NY, 341
Marietta, OH, 39, 46, 125, 295, 347
Marine City, MI, 217
Marinette, WI, 234
Marion, MA, 34, 175
Marquette, MI, 113, 215, 219, 311
Martha's Vineyard, MA, 177, 178
Matagorda Bay, TX, 88
Mathews, VA, 205
Matinicus, ME, 167
Mattpoisett, MA, 180
Maunabo, PR, 198
Mayaguez, PR, 196
Mayport, FL, 161
Mayville, NY, 55
McClellanville, SC, 201
McGregor, MN, 302
Memphis, TN, 129, 352
Mendocino, CA, 252, 256, 319
Menominee, MI, 216
Metairie, LA, 242
Metamora, IN, 299, 326
Miami, FL, 324
Michigan City, IN, 101, 207, 326
Milbridge, ME, 168
Milton, MA, 141
Milwaukee, WI, 14, 41, 148, 235, 236, 290
Missouri Valley, IA, 88
Mobile, AL, 71, 74, 83, 90, 239, 316
Moncks Corner, SC, 305, 351
Monmouth Beach, NJ, 271
Montauk, NY, 190, 343
Monterey, CA, 91, 318
Moorhead City, NC, 346
Moorhead, MN, 50, 338
Morehead City, NC, 296

CITY INDEX

Morgan City, LA, 52
Morristown, NJ, 340
Moss Beach, CA, 253, 256
Mount Pleasant, SC, 71, 74, 77, 82, 128, 312
Mukegon, MI, 112
Mukilteo, WA, 263, 357
Munising, MI, 212, 216, 274
Muskegon, MI, 61, 75, 79, 85, 217, 337
Muskogee, OK, 82
Mystic, CT, 10, 12, 15, 17, 20, 21, 26, 29, 42, 62, 95, 149, 271, 293
Nahcotta, WA, 136
Nantucket, MA, 108, 109, 176, 179, 180, 267, 271, 273, 286, 332, 333, 334
Narragansett, RI, 271
Naushon Island, MA, 182
Neah Bay, WA, 145, 262
Necomerstown, OH, 125
Neenah, WI, 236
Netarts, OR, 348
New Bedford, MA, 15, 156, 176, 177, 181, 267, 286, 287, 301
New Bremen, OH, 347
New Castle, DE, 159
New Castle, NH, 183
New Dorp, NY, 188
New Harbor, ME, 328
New Haven, CT, 9, 29, 154, 156, 320, 321
New Iberia, LA, 242
New London, CT, 14, 26, 95, 156, 280, 321
New Orleans, LA, 56, 241, 242, 243, 327
New York, NY, 6, 22, 27, 28, 35, 40, 44, 46, 61, 65, 73, 120, 122, 156, 187, 189, 190, 265, 266, 268, 304, 311, 343, 344, 345
Newark, NJ, 292
Newburyport, MA, 108, 181, 286, 333
Newcomerstown, OH, 347
Newfane, NY, 227
Newfield, ME, 139
Newport Beach, CA, 10, 23, 91, 318
Newport News, VA, 68, 131, 132, 149
Newport, AR, 56, 138, 317
Newport, OR, 143, 151, 261, 277, 348
Newport, RI, 10, 31, 34, 128, 198, 199, 200, 281, 350, 351
Noank, CT, 155
Norfolk, VA, 13, 35, 41, 75, 132, 354
North Bend, OR, 63, 126, 348
North Billerica, MA, 109, 333
North Charleston, SC, 66, 351
North Chicago, IL, 100
North East, MD, 141
North Haven, MA, 156
North Haven, ME, 165

North Kingston, RI, 11, 351
North Kingstown, RI, 199, 200, 350
North Kingsville, OH, 346
North Little Rock, AR, 41, 84, 90, 309
North Myrtle Beach, SC, 11
North Richmond, CA, 253
Northeast Harbor, ME, 103, 163
Northport, MI, 208, 293
Northport, NY, 122
Northwood, OH, 230
Norwalk, CT, 19, 156
Oak Point, NY, 226
Oakington, MD, 173
Oakland, CA, 62, 254, 267, 320
Oakley, MD, 50, 53
Oaks, PA, 349
Ocean Bay Park, NY, 270
Ocean City, MD, 272, 331
Ocean Springs, MS, 339
Ocracoke, NC, 194, 272
Ogdensburg, NY, 227
Olympia, WA, 45, 263, 295, 357, 358
Omaha, NE, 66, 79, 81
Ontonagon, MI, 208, 212, 217, 337
Orange City, FL, 324
Orange, TX, 130, 353
Oregon, OH, 347
Orient Point, NY, 191
Orlando, FL, 71
Orleans, MA, 48, 333
Oshkosh, WI, 232
Osterville, MA, 109, 333
Oswego, NY, 48, 51, 60, 86, 120, 227, 294
Owls Head, ME, 168, 169
Oyster Bay, NY, 12, 122
Oysterville, WA, 288
Pacific Grove, CA, 253, 256
Paducah, KY, 101
Painsville, OH, 124, 230
Palm Beach, FL, 98
Palmer, MA, 334
Panama City Beach, FL, 97
Paradise, MI, 112, 209, 223, 275, 335
Pascagoula, MS, 53
Paterson, NJ, 65, 66, 142
Paulsboro, NJ, 187
Peekskill, NY, 343
Pennsville, NJ, 185
Pensacola, FL, 98, 139, 148, 240, 298, 323, 324
Pentwater, MI, 218
Permaquid, ME, 168
Pescadero, CA, 251, 253, 255
Peshtigo, WI, 236
Petersburg, AK, 48

CITY INDEX

Petoskey, MI, 218
Philadelphia, PA, 17, 26, 42, 63, 68, 82, 127, 195, 288, 349
Phippsburg, ME, 168, 273
Phoenixville, PA, 305
Piedras Blancas, CA, 255
Piney Point, MD, 13, 20, 48, 282
Pipe, WI, 233
Piqua, OH, 49, 143
Pittsburg, PA, 84, 295
Plaquemine, LA, 284
Plattsburgh, NY, 188, 191, 342
Plum Island, NY, 190, 191
Plymouth, MA, 25, 88, 285
Plymouth, NC, 346
Point Arena, CA, 255, 276, 284, 319
Point Breeze, NY, 226
Point Judith, RI, 200, 272
Point Reyes Station, CA, 252, 257
Point Reyes, CA, 277
Polson, MT, 44
Pompano Beach, FL, 160, 323
Ponce Inlet, FL, 40, 160
Ponce, PR, 196, 197
Port Angeles, WA, 145, 263, 355
Port Aransas, TX, 244
Port Austin, MI, 219, 274
Port Bolivar, TX, 245
Port Clinton, OH, 230, 247
Port Clyde, ME, 167
Port Ewen, NY, 40, 344
Port Gamble, WA, 288
Port Hope, MI, 209, 219
Port Hueneme, CA, 256
Port Huron, MI, 19, 69, 111, 209, 211, 266
Port Isabel, TX, 130, 245
Port Jefferson, NY, 121, 342
Port Lavaca, TX, 244
Port Ludlow, WA, 75, 355
Port Norris, NJ, 7, 340
Port Orford, OR, 260, 277, 348
Port Penn, DE, 158
Port Sanilac, MI, 218
Port St. Joe, FL, 239
Port Townsend, WA, 8, 24, 51, 136, 145, 263, 289, 295, 306, 355, 357, 358, 359, 362
Port Washington, WI, 236, 237, 360
Portage, WI, 308, 360
Portland, ME, 10, 36, 156, 166, 169, 170
Portland, OR, 44, 72, 126, 349
Portsmouth, NH, 12, 65, 115, 150, 156, 295, 303, 339, 340
Portsmouth, RI, 199
Portsmouth, VA, 132, 267, 354
Potomac, MD, 302
Poughkeepsie, NY, 13, 343
Presque Isle, MI, 209, 219, 337
Prospect Harbor, ME, 169
Providence, RI, 28, 66, 149, 351
Provincetown, MA, 110, 156, 179, 181, 183, 272
Prudence Island, RI, 200, 351
Put-in-Bay, OH, 125, 230, 231, 312, 347
Queenstown, MD, 19
Quincy, MA, 72, 85, 110
Racine, WI, 237, 274, 360
Raleigh, NC, 346
Ramona Beach, MD, 172
Rancho Palos Verdes, CA, 253, 257
Rapid River, MI, 208
Raymond, WA, 136
Redondo Beach, CA, 295
Reedsport, OR, 144
Reedville, VA, 13, 15, 31, 49, 132
Rehoboth Beach, DE, 271, 322
Richland, NY, 227
Richmond, CA, 81, 138, 319
Richmond, VA, 65, 76, 354
Ridgecrest, CA, 317
Rincon, PR, 197
Rio Vista, CA, 318
River Rouge, MI, 62
Riverside, RI, 350
Roanoke Rapids, NC, 124
Rochester, NY, 227, 341
Rock Hall, MD, 7
Rock Island, IL, 299
Rockland, ME, 9, 19, 20, 26, 33, 35, 103, 169, 327, 328
Rockport, MA, 176, 182, 287
Rockport, ME, 34, 156, 166
Rockport, TX, 130
Rodanthe, NC, 270, 345
Rogers City, MI, 111, 209, 211, 294, 335
Romancoke, MD, 172
Rome, NY, 120
Sabine Pass, LA, 242
Sabine, TX, 245
Sackets Harbor, NY, 226
Sacramento, CA, 55, 72, 284, 319
Sadorus, IL, 100
Sag Harbor, NY, 122, 187
Salem, MA, 16, 17, 109, 110, 117, 178, 285, 286, 287, 301, 333
Salisbury Beach, MA, 293
Saltaire, NY, 189
Samoa, CA, 254, 277
San Diego, CA, 5, 12, 32, 33, 61, 65, 73, 91, 92, 254, 255, 298, 318, 320

CITY INDEX

San Francisco, CA, 6, 8, 11, 12, 39, 40, 41, 46, 47, 80, 84, 251, 253, 254, 255, 258, 318, 320
San Juan, PR, 195, 196, 350
San Luis Obispo, CA, 253, 257, 319
San Pedro, CA, 7, 11, 16, 30, 34, 62, 80, 86, 90, 151, 254, 256, 281, 298
San Rafael, CA, 60, 86
San Simeon, CA, 319
Sands Point, NY, 189, 191
Sandusky, OH, 125, 229, 231
Sanibel Island, FL, 241
Santa Ana, CA, 319
Santa Barbara, CA, 91, 257, 292
Santa Cruz, CA, 253, 257
Santa Cruz, CA, 258
Sapelo Island, GA, 162
Saugatuck, MI, 44, 45, 60, 112
Saugerties, NY, 191, 344
Sault Ste. Marie, MI, 302, 63, 142, 212, 302, 336, 338
Saunderstown, RI, 199, 350
Sausalito, CA, 30, 149, 254, 255, 256, 317, 318
Savannah, GA, 99, 161, 162
Scituate, MA, 88, 109, 182, 334
Scott Cove, CT, 154
Sea Girt, NJ, 66, 186, 340
Sea Isle City, NJ, 185
Seal Harbor, ME, 162
Searsport, ME, 50, 104, 150, 284
Seattle, WA, 6, 22, 28, 37, 39, 50, 52, 54, 62, 63, 133, 135, 144, 145, 146, 262, 265, 268, 281, 292, 293, 305, 306, 307, 308, 312, 313, 314, 357, 358, 359, 360, 361, 362
Sequim, WA, 264
Sequin Island, ME, 170
Sheboygan, WI, 237
Shelburne, VT, 63, 202
Shinnecock, NY, 192
Shoreline, WA, 314
Siasconset, MA, 156, 181, 334
Silverdale, WA, 65, 135
Simmons Bayou, FL, 161
Sioux City, IA, 45, 102
Sioux Falls, SD, 129
Sitka, AK, 316
Sleepy Hollow, NY, 193
Smith Island, MD, 175
Smith Island, VA, 203
Smithfield, VA, 354
Sodus Point, NY, 227, 228, 344
Solomons, MD, 36, 52, 105, 173, 292
Somers Point, NJ, 115
South Amboy, NJ, 185
South Bend, WA, 60, 146, 357
South Berwick, ME, 140, 329

South Chicago, IL, 273
South Haven, MI, 17, 49, 113, 149, 221
South Norwalk, CT, 157, 321
South Portland, ME, 168, 329
Southampton, NY, 118, 344
Southold, NY, 189, 344
Southport, NC, 123, 195
Southwest Harbor, ME, 8
Sparrows Point, MD, 173
St. Augustine, FL, 161, 291, 342
St. Charles, MO, 56
St. Clair Flats, MI, 221
St. Clair Shores, MI, 214
St. Croix, VI, 203
St. George Island, FL, 239, 324
St. George, ME, 273
St. Helens, OR, 261
St. Ignace, MI, 222
St. Joseph, MI, 302
St. Leonard, MD, 174, 331
St. Louis, MO, 47, 56, 148, 151
St. Marks, FL, 241
St. Mary's City, MD, 24
St. Marys, GA, 99
St. Marys, OH, 312
St. Michaels, MD, 12, 14, 18, 30, 40, 52, 105, 173, 330
St. Paul, MN, 338, 339
St. Simons Island, GA, 99, 162, 324
St. Thomas, VI, 27, 30, 282, 353
St. Louis, MO, 114
Stamford, CT, 157
Stanhope, NJ, 116
Staten Island, NY, 44, 21, 189, 190, 191, 192, 193
Statue of Liberty, NY, 192
Steilacoom, WA, 29, 358
Steuben, ME, 168
Stockton, CA, 258
Stockton, ME, 165
Stonington, CT, 94, 95, 152, 320, 321
Stonington, ME, 164
Stony Point, NY, 228
Stow, NY, 5
Stratford, CT, 321
Stuart, FL, 270, 323
Sturgeon Bay, WI, 41, 146, 238, 296
Suamico, WI, 235
Sumpter, OR, 54, 348
Sunapee, NH, 183
Sunbeam, ID, 55
Sunnybank, VA, 204
Superior, WI, 61, 238
Suquamish, WA, 146
Suttons Bay, MI, 20, 336
Swan's Island, ME, 163, 329

CITY INDEX

Swarthmore, PA, 52
Syracuse, NY, 120
Tacoma, WA, 6, 7, 134, 262, 294, 355, 356, 357, 359, 362
Tallahasee, FL, 139
Tampa, FL, 80
Tarpon Springs, FL, 290
Taylor's Bridge, DE, 159
Tenants Harbor, ME, 170
Thomaston, ME, 104
Throggs Neck, NY, 193, 280
Tiburon, CA, 317
Tilghman Island, MD, 19, 27, 34
Tilghman, MD, 21, 29
Tillamook, OR, 260, 296
Toledo, OH, 64, 230, 231
Toms River, NJ, 117, 341
Traverse City, MI, 23, 24, 35, 50, 295, 337
Triangle, VA, 132
Trinidad, CA, 252, 258
Truro, MA, 176, 272, 332, 334
Tuckerton, NJ, 117
Tukwila, WA, 307
Tumwater, WA, 358
Two Harbors, MN, 40, 224
Two Rivers, WI, 38, 137, 237, 238, 275
Tybee Island, GA, 162, 325
Valcour, NY, 187
Valentine, VA, 354
Vallejo, CA, 72, 74, 79, 92, 150, 253, 284, 318
Vancouver, WA, 78
Vashon Island, WA, 264, 306
Ventura, CA, 92
Vergennes, VT, 23, 27, 38, 48, 53, 133
Vermilion, OH, 124, 148, 149, 231, 347
Verona Beach, NY, 193, 345
Vevay, IN, 326
Vicksburg, MS, 67
Vieques, PR, 197, 198
Village of Old Field, NY, 190
Vinalhaven, ME, 163, 166, 170
Vineyard Haven, MA, 8, 31, 334
Virginia Beach, VA, 204, 273
Waimanalo Beach, HI, 259
Wareham, MA, 107, 267
Warwick, RI, 199, 200

Washington, DC, 50, 67, 68, 69, 72, 79, 96, 322, 323
Watch Hill, RI, 351
Waterford, NY, 38, 345
Waukegan, IL, 206
Webster, NY, 23
Wellfleet, MA, 179, 182, 270, 287, 332, 334
Wenona, MD, 13, 20, 33
West Chop, MA, 182
West Dennis, MA, 175
West Denton, MD, 105
West Denton, MI, 16, 3
West Mystic, CT, 26
West Sayville, NY, 26, 28, 35, 29, 121
West Yarmouth, MA, 181
Westbrook, CT, 47, 49
Westerly, RI, 200
Westfield, NY, 30
Westport, MA, 270, 334
Westport, NY, 187
Westport, WA, 136, 263, 276, 315, 359
Whalebone, NC, 193
Whitehall, MI, 223
Whitehall, NY, 142
Whitehorn, CA, 317
Whitlocks Mill, ME, 171
Williamsburg, VA, 14, 18, 33, 133, 354
Williamson, NY, 344
Wilmington, CA, 138, 317
Wilmington, DE, 21, 96, 158, 322
Wilmington, NC, 75, 123
Wind Point, WI, 238
Winona, MN, 114
Winter Harbor, ME, 171
Woodland Beach, NJ, 186
Woods Hole, MA, 29, 110, 151, 181, 334
Woonsocket, RI, 305
Worton, MD, 15, 281
Wyomissing, PA, 127, 349
Yachats, OR, 260
Yarmouth, MA, 176
Yarmouth, ME, 140, 167
Yorba Linda, CA, 317
York, ME, 163, 164, 300, 329
Yorktown, VA, 132, 133, 354
Youngstown, NY, 226, 344

PHOTO CREDITS

MAP INSERTS
Historic Battleships and Aircraft Carrier in the United States: Photos of Hornet, Lexington, Missouri, Intrepid, Midway, Yorktown, Iowa, Alabama, Wisconsin, New Jersey, North Carolina, Texas courtesy U.S. Navy and/or Wikimedia Commons; Photo of Massachusetts courtesy Battleship Cove; California Lighthouses Itinerary: Photos of Point Cabrillo and Port Hartford lighthouses courtesy Wikimedia Commons; Michigan Lighthouses Itinerary: Photo of Au Sable Point Lighthouse courtesy National Park Service; New England Lighthouses Itinerary: Photo of Portsmouth Harbor Lighthouse by Photos Jeremy D'Entremont; Photo of Cape May Lighthouse by Craig Terry.

OTHER PHOTOS
Pilgrim, courtesy of the Ocean Institute / Cliff Wassmann; Lady Washington, Ron Arel; Adventuress, courtesy Sound Experience; Sand Man, Tim Robinson; Steamer Okanogan and "u-bolt", Okanogan County Historical Society; Blueback, Oregon Museum of Science and Industry; Lane Victory, courtesy SS Lane Victory; H.L. Hunley, courtesy Friends of the Hunley; Nauticus with USS Wisconsin, courtesy Nauticus; Crew scrambles…, Joe Follansbee; Sergeant Floyd, ©2003 Bob Rasmus. Used by permission; Submarine Force Museum, courtesy Submarine Force Museum & Library; Cove Point Lighthouse, courtesy Calvert Marine Museum; Marblehead Lighthouse (Ohio), courtesy Ohio State Parks; Heceta Head Lighthouse and Cape Blanco Lighthouse, courtesy Oregon Parks and Recreation; Pamet River Lifeboat Station, courtesy Hosteling International; Eagle, courtesy U.S. Coast Guard; Howard Steamboat Museum, courtesy Howard Steamboat Museum; Naval gun firing…, courtesy National Civil War Naval Museum; USS Arizona Memorial, USS Arizona Memorial Photo Collection; Mayflower II, courtesy Plimoth Plantation; Whitefish Point Lighthouse, courtesy Great Lakes Shipwreck Historical Society.

ACKNOWLEDGEMENTS

The Fyddeye Guide to America's Maritime History builds on the work of thousands of people, ranging from *Guide* contributors to the individuals and not-for-profit organizations in small and large communities fighting to preserve our maritime heritage. First, I'm grateful to my wife Edith and daughters Emily and Abbey for their constant support. I would like to thank Hans Detliv Bendixsen, the builder of the 1897 schooner *Wawona*. Without his extraordinary vessel, now lost to history, I would not have started on this journey into maritime heritage. A key arts and heritage organization in Seattle, 4Culture, provided funding for Maritime Heritage Network, which opened my mind to the potential of a similar website with a national footprint. The open-source software community, especially the creators of Linux, Apache, MySQL, PHP, and Joomla! provided the tools for making my dream of a publicly available online directory for maritime heritage possible. Many websites provided key information to help me on my path, especially Lighthouse Friends (www.lighthousefriends.com), the National Park Service (www.nps.gov), and individual sites for many organizations, many of which graciously provided photos. Finally, without the hard work of volunteers and staff at heritage organizations across the country—Northwest Seaport and the Center for Wooden Boats in Seattle are just two examples—a directory such as the *Fyddeye Guide* would not have been possible, because so much of our heritage would otherwise have been lost. They are the unsung heroes in this story.

-- Joe Follansbee, Spring 2010

www.ingramcontent.com/pod-product-compliance
Lightning Source LLC
Chambersburg PA
CBHW080528170426
43195CB00016B/2502